ADDISON-WESLEY
SECONDARY MATH

Focus on
Algebra

AN INTEGRATED APPROACH

RANDALL I. CHARLES
ALBA GONZÁLEZ THOMPSON
Trudi Hammel Garland • Stephen E. Moresh • Kathy A. Ross

PROGRAM CONCEPTUALIZERS

Barbara Alcala

Randall I. Charles

John A. Dossey

Betty M. Foxx

Alan R. Hoffer

Roberta Koss

Sid Rachlin

Freddie L. Renfro

Cathy L. Seeley

Charles B. Vonder Embse

Scott Foresman
Addison Wesley

Editorial Offices: Menlo Park, California • Glenview, Illinois
Sales Offices: Reading, Massachusetts • Atlanta, Georgia •
Glenview, Illinois • Carrollton, Texas • Menlo Park, California

http://www.sf.aw.com

Cover Images

Front:

Left: Kachina Song Poetry, 1985, by Michael Kabotie (Hopi). Acrylic on canvas. Photo by Jerry Jacka Photography. *Right:* Circuit board by Jon Feingersh/Tom Stack & Associates.

Back:

Top left: Photo of financial district, Toronto, Ontario by Thomas Kitchin/Tom Stack & Associates. *Top center left: Castle and Sun,* 1928, by Paul Klee. Private Collection, London, Great Britain. Photo by Giraudon/Art Resource, NY. *Top center right: Kachina Song Poetry,* 1985, by Michael Kabotie (Hopi). Acrylic on canvas. Photo by Jerry Jacka Photography. *Top right:* Circuit board by Jon Feingersh/Tom Stack & Associates. *Bottom left:* Armillary (predecessor to the astrolabe) from the Vatican. Photo by Art Resource, NY. *Bottom center left: Wedding Basket,* 1989, by Mary Black (Navajo/Paiute). Courtesy of the Museum of Northern Arizona, Flagstaff. Photo by Jerry Jacka Photography. *Bottom center right:* Italian ceramic tile by Cheryl Fenton*. *Bottom right:* Fractal from the Mandelbrot Set by Antonio M. Rosario/The Image Bank.

Copyright © 1998 by Addison Wesley Longman, Inc.

Printed in the United States of America.

ISBN 0-201-86950-0

3 4 5 6 7 8 9 10-VH-02 01 00 99 98

PROGRAM CONCEPTUALIZERS

Barbara Alcala
Whittier High School
Whittier, California

Randall I. Charles
San Jose State University
San Jose, California

John A. Dossey
Illinois State University
Normal, Illinois

Betty M. Foxx
Chicago Public Schools
Chicago, Illinois

Alan R. Hoffer
University of California
Irvine, California

Roberta Koss
Redwood High School
Larkspur, California

Sid Rachlin
East Carolina University
Greenville, North Carolina

Freddie L. Renfro
Fort Bend Independent
School District
Houston, Texas

Cathy L. Seeley
Texas Statewide
Systemic Initiative
Austin, Texas

Charles B. Vonder Embse
Central Michigan University
Mt. Pleasant, Michigan

FOCUS ON ALGEBRA AUTHORS

Randall I. Charles
Lead author
San Jose State University
San Jose, California

Alba González Thompson
Associate lead author
(In Memorium)

Trudi Hammel Garland
The Head-Royce School
Oakland, California

Stephen E. Moresh
Seward Park
High School and
City College of New York
New York, New York

Kathy A. Ross
(Formerly) Jefferson Parish
Public School System
Harvey, Louisiana

OTHER SERIES AUTHORS

Barbara Alcala
Whittier High School
Whittier, California

Jerry D. Beckmann
East High School
Lincoln, Nebraska

Penelope P. Booth
Baltimore County Public Schools
Towson, Maryland

James R. Choike
Oklahoma State University
Stillwater, Oklahoma

David S. Daniels
Longmeadow High School
Longmeadow, Massachusetts

John A. Dossey
Illinois State University
Normal, Illinois

Phillip E. Duren
California State University
Hayward, California

Pamela Patton Giles
Jordan School District
Sandy, Utah

Virginia Gray
Columbia College
Sonora, California
(Formerly) South Medford
High School

Julia L. Hernandez
Rosemead High School
Rosemead, California

Alan R. Hoffer
University of California
Irvine, California

Howard C. Johnson
Syracuse University
Syracuse, New York

Roberta Koss
Redwood High School
Larkspur, California

J. Irene Murphy
Ilisagvik College
(Formerly) North Slope Borough
School District
Barrow, Alaska

Andy Reeves
(Formerly) Florida Department
of Education
Tallahassee, Florida

Beth M. Schlesinger
San Diego High School
San Diego, California

Cathy L. Seeley
Texas Statewide
Systemic Initiative
Austin, Texas

Charles B. Vonder Embse
Central Michigan University
Mt. Pleasant, Michigan

Catherine Wiehe
San Jose High Academy
San Jose, California

Sheryl M. Yamada
Beverly Hills High School
Beverly Hills, California

CONSULTANTS AND REVIEWERS

CONTENT REVIEWERS

Velna Allen
Conway High School
Conway, South Carolina

Martin J. Badoian
Canton High School
Canton, Massachusetts

Ernestina E. Cano
Edinburg High School
Edinburg, Texas

Donna Carlyle
Warren East High School
Bowling Green, Kentucky

Diane Dauer
Clear Creek High School
League City, Texas

Kristin Gilliam
Elsik Alief High School
Houston, Texas

David Hammett
South Cobb High School
Austell, Georgia

Lorraine Largmann
Jamaica High School
Jamaica, New York

Roger A. Larson
Champlin Park High School
Champlin, Minnesota

Arne Lim
Palo Alto High School
Palo Alto, California

Vena M. Long
University of Missouri
Kansas City, Missouri

Beverly W. Nichols
Shawnee Mission Public Schools
Overland Park, Kansas

Duane Olson
North Thurston High School
Lacey, Washington

Charlyn Shepherd
Alan C. Pope High School
Marietta, Georgia

Regeta Slaughter
Lane Technical High School
Chicago, Illinois

MULTICULTURAL REVIEWERS

Claudette Bradley
University of Alaska
Fairbanks, Alaska

Yolanda De La Cruz
Arizona State University West
Phoenix, Arizona

Genevieve Lau
Skyline College
San Bruno, California

William Tate
University of Wisconsin
Madison, Wisconsin

INDUSTRY CONSULTANTS

Joseph M. Cahalen
Xerox Corporation
Stamford, Connecticut

Clare DeYonker
AMATECH
Bingham Farms, Michigan

Harry Garland
Canon Research Center
America, Inc.
Palo Alto, California

Timothy M. Schwalm, Sr.
Eastman Kodak Company
Rochester, New York

Diane Sotos
Maxim Integrated Products
Sunnyvale, California

Earl R. Westerlund
Eastman Kodak Company
Rochester, New York

Charles Young
General Electric Research and
Development Center
Schenectady, New York

John Zils
Skidmore, Owings & Merrill
Chicago, Illinois

Table of Contents

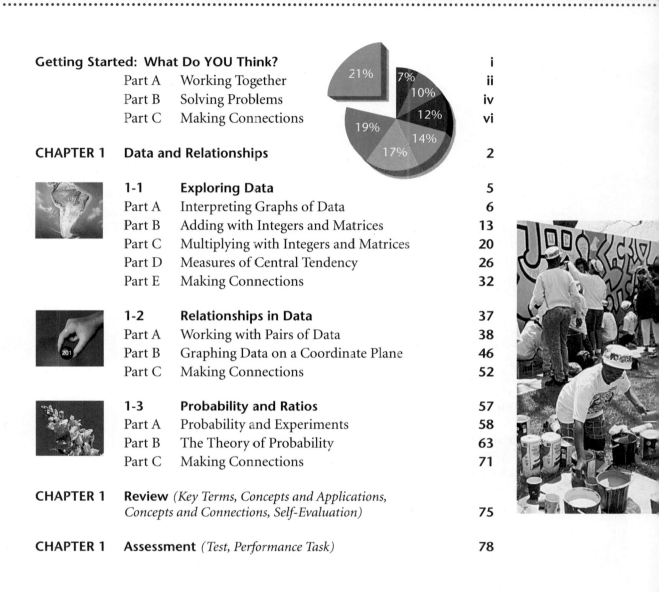

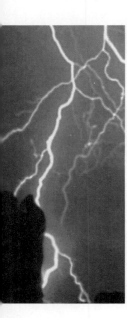

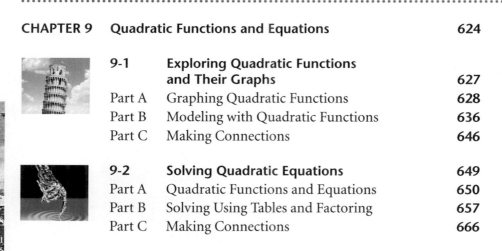

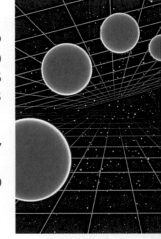

REFERENCE CENTER

Getting Started

What Do YOU Think

In the twenty-first century, computers will do a lot of the work that people used to do. Even in today's workplace, there is little need for someone to add up daily invoices or compute sales tax. Engineers and scientists already use computer programs to do calculations and solve equations. By the twenty-first century, a whole new set of skills will be needed by almost everyone in the work force.

Some important skills for the twenty-first century will be the ability to think creatively about mathematics and to reason logically. It will also be important to work as a team member and to be able to explain your thinking. Although it will still be necessary to be able to do computations, it will become increasingly necessary to analyze problems and determine the most appropriate way to solve them. After all, what good is it to solve an equation if it is the wrong equation?

This course will help you to develop many of the skills you will need for the future. On the way, you will see the value of creative thinking. The students shown here will be sharing their ideas throughout this book. But the key question will always be "What do YOU think?"

1. In your last math class, what was the most interesting or useful thing you learned?
2. Why do you think teamwork is becoming more and more important in the workplace today? What are some advantages to working as a team?
3. Why is it important to be able to analyze and solve problems, even if a computer is available to help you do calculations?

i

PART A Working Together

← C O N N E C T → *There are times when working together can be more productive and motivating than working alone. If you've had experience working in groups, you are aware that it takes skill and planning to work together effectively. We will look at some of the ways to make working together effective.*

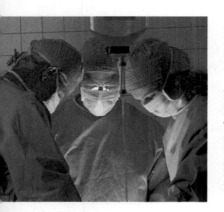

No man is an island, entire of itself; every man is a piece of the continent, a part of the main.

—John Donne

Working effectively as a team is an important skill in today's workplace, just as important as teamwork is in sports.

In order to work effectively together, you must be able to communicate clearly with others. Communicating your ideas in a convincing way can help you to clarify your own thoughts.

CONSIDER

?

1. **What happens to a team when members don't communicate clearly or work together cooperatively?**

Here are some suggestions to consider when you are working in a group.

- Let everyone have a chance to participate.
- Everyone has a responsibility to participate. Don't be a *hitchhiker*.
- Each group member should be willing to help any other member of the group.
- Ask your teacher for help *only* if every member of your group has had a chance to resolve the issue.
- Talk only to members of your own group.
- Always be open-minded and show respect for one another. Work to problem solve rather than criticize.

1. Form a group of two. Take turns interviewing each other. Include the following questions in your interview. Be sure to take notes.
   a. What is your name?
   b. Where did you go to school last year?
   c. What city have you lived in or visited that is the farthest from here?
   d. What was the last math course you took?
2. Form a group of four by joining another pair of students. Tell the new pair about your partner.
3. Develop a plan for organizing cooperative groups for your class. The plan should be designed for groups of two or four students, and every student must work with every other student in the class at least once during the course.

Working cooperatively in groups can be an exciting and effective way to learn math. You will have many opportunities for teamwork in this course.

REFLECT

1. Does working cooperatively mean sitting in groups while you work?
2. Describe a situation, other than learning mathematics, in which teamwork plays an important role.
3. Are there situations where working individually is preferable to working in a group? Explain.

Exercises

1. In general, do you prefer to work alone or in groups? What do you like about working in groups? What do you dislike about working in groups?

2. Describe a situation in which you worked in a group. How did teamwork help your group accomplish more than they might have if they had worked individually?

3. How do you think teamwork played a role in NASA landing astronauts on the moon? What teams do you think were involved?

4. Describe a problem you learned to solve in your previous mathematics course and solve the problem.

5. Which two expressions have the same value?
   (a) $168 \div 3$　　　　　　　　(b) 14×4　　　　　　　　(c) 75% of 80

← C O N N E C T → *You have solved many problems before taking this class, and you have probably used some type of problem-solving guidelines and strategies. All of these strategies and techniques can be used in this class.*

Problem solving means more than just finding the answer to a math problem. It means solving all types of problems, including everyday problems. You may have trouble working a problem, or you may have a problem simply doing your homework. In either case, there is a problem to solve.

CONSIDER

?

1. What are some strategies you have used to solve problems?

Whenever the solution to a problem is not immediately apparent, it may be helpful to ask yourself some of the questions listed below.

PROBLEM-SOLVING GUIDELINES	
Understand the Problem What is the situation all about? What are you trying to find out? What are the key data/conditions? What are the assumptions?	**Develop a Plan** Have you ever worked a similar problem before? Will you estimate or calculate? What strategies can you use?
Implement the Plan What is the solution? Did you interpret correctly? Did you calculate correctly? Did you answer the question?	**Look Back** Could you work the problem another way? Is there another solution? Is the answer reasonable?

MATERIALS

Scissors, String

1. Measure the arm span (from fingertip to fingertip) of each person in your group using only string. Cut a piece of string that best represents the typical or average arm span of the members of your group.
2. Measure the height of each person in your group using only string. Cut a piece of string that best represents the typical or average height of the members of your group.
3. How does the typical arm span compare to the typical height for members of your group? If a classmate is 5 feet 4 inches tall, what do you think her arm span might be? How did you decide?

REFLECT

1. Describe any strategies or guidelines that helped you in the Explore.
2. Describe a helpful question or strategy you would add to the list of Problem-Solving Guidelines.

Exercises

Use the Problem-Solving Guidelines to help you with each exercise.

1. Find the next number in the sequence: 1, 2, 4, 8, _____.
2. Find the next number in the sequence: 1, 3, 6, 10, _____.
3. Find the answer to this well known riddle.

As I was going to St. Ives,
I met a Man with seven Wives.
Every wife had seven Sacks,
Every sack had seven Cats.
Every cat had seven Kits,
Kits, Cats, Sacks, and Wives,
How many were going to St. Ives?

PART C Making Connections

You have worked in groups and used problem-solving guidelines and strategies to help you solve problems. There is often more than one approach to solving a problem. The features in this book can help you to develop your mathematical skills and choose problem-solving methods wisely.

You will have many opportunities throughout this book to work in groups (in Explore activities) and to practice what you have learned (in Try It activities). You will also see a feature called What Do YOU Think?, in which you can share and compare the thinking of other students as they solve problems.

WHAT DO **YOU** THINK?

Which two figures at the right have the same area? Explain how you decided.

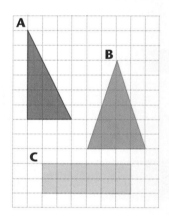

Elizabeth thinks...

I'll add up the areas of the squares and pieces of squares within each figure.

Triangle A: Triangle A contains 6 whole squares and 6 pieces that add up to about 3 whole squares. So the area is 6 + 3, or 9.

Triangle B: Triangle B contains 6 whole squares and 12 pieces that add up to about 6 whole squares. So the area is 6 + 6, or 12.

Rectangle C: Rectangle C contains 12 whole squares, so its area is 12.

Triangle B and Rectangle C have the same area.

Taktuk thinks...

The area of a rectangle is the base times the height, and the area of a triangle is half the base times the height.

Triangle A: The area of Triangle A is $\frac{1}{2}(3 \cdot 6) = \frac{1}{2}(18) = 9$.

Triangle B: The area of Triangle B is $\frac{1}{2}(4 \cdot 6) = \frac{1}{2}(24) = 12$.

Rectangle C: The area of Rectangle C is $6 \cdot 2 = 12$.

Triangle B and Rectangle C have the same area.

1. Do you think problem-solving strategies are only useful for mathematics problems? Explain.
2. Why do you think it is important to understand the connections between mathematics and other disciplines?

Exercises

1. Find the area and the perimeter of the rectangle below.

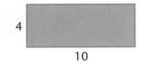

4

10

2. Find the area and the perimeter of the triangle below.

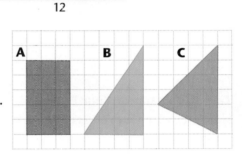

13

5

12

3. Which two figures at the right have the same area? Explain how you decided.

4. If a triangle and a rectangle have the same base and the same area, how do their heights compare? Explain.

A   B   C

Problem-Solving Tip

Draw a diagram.

5. How do you think teamwork plays a role in conserving natural resources? What teams do you think are involved?

6. Find the next number in the sequence: 1, 5, 7, 11, _____.

7. How many phone lines are needed to connect eight households? A separate line must be used to connect each pair of houses.

LOOK AHEAD

Simplify.

8. 0×17

9. $0 \div 8$

10. $\frac{4}{5} + \frac{3}{5}$

11. $1.7 + 3.3$

12. $12.4 - 9.5$

13. $\frac{3}{10} - \frac{1}{20}$

14. $22 \times \frac{3}{2}$

15. $\frac{21}{5} \div 3$

16. $\frac{3}{4} \times \frac{4}{9}$

Chapter 1

Data and Relationships

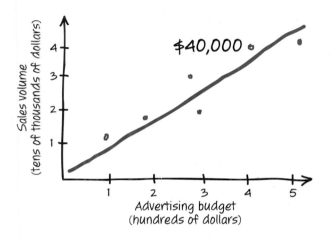

$40,000

Sales volume (tens of thousands of dollars)

Advertising budget (hundreds of dollars)

Project B
Jump on the Bandwagon
How do political candidates use statistics to influence voters?

Project A
Take Command of Your Data
How much data do you need to make a good prediction?

Project C
It's Dinner Time in Tokyo
Is it tomorrow in Australia yet?
What time is it? Are you sure?

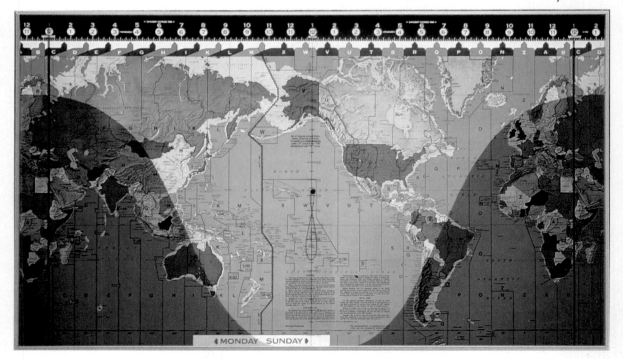

DAN McINTYRE

I loved geometry in high school but I suffered through my other math courses, thinking I was a mathematical simpleton. I did it because I wanted to be a merchant mariner.

Now I use math to illuminate economic facts and circumstances that have an impact on health care. I study data on people and their needs to compare the health care systems of industrialized countries. I study the economic relationships between diseases and their treatments. It's hard to appreciate this fact in high school, but math will be a foundation of job security in the next century.

Dan McIntyre
Director of Policy and
 Public Affairs
*Miles Inc. Pharmaceutical
 Division*
West Haven, Connecticut

**1-1
Exploring
Data**

In 1-1 you will organize, interpret, and summarize data to find patterns and make predictions. You will need to round numbers and find percentages.

Round the following numbers to the nearest thousand. [Previous course]

1. 56,478   **2.** 3,286,470   **3.** 879   **4.** 342,521

Find each percentage. [Pages 750–751]

5. 8% of 30   **6.** 95% of 650   **7.** 10% of 200   **8.** 6% of 30

9. What percent of 52 is 26?   **10.** What percent of 76 is 1.9?

**1-2
Relationships
in Data**

In 1-2 you will graph pairs of data to find relationships and make predictions. You will need to know how to use number lines and recognize patterns.

11. Plot and label each point on a number line. [1-1]

    a. $A(-3)$ **b.** $B(0)$ **c.** $C\left(1\frac{1}{2}\right)$ **d.** $D(-4.2)$ **e.** $E(0.8)$

Predict the next number in the pattern. [Previous course]

12. IN: _4_ , OUT: _8_   IN: _2.3_ , OUT: _4.6_   IN: _31_ , OUT: _?_

13. IN: _7_ , OUT: _6.6_   IN: _3.8_ , OUT: _3.4_   IN: _0.6_ , OUT: _?_

14. IN: _3_ , OUT: _5_   IN: _7_ , OUT: _13_   IN: _6_ , OUT: _?_

**1-3
Probability
and Ratios**

In 1-3 you will learn about probability—a measure of the chance something will occur in the long run—to make predictions. You will be using fractions and percentages.

Simplify each expression. [Page 744]

15. $1 - \dfrac{83}{100}$ **16.** $1 - 0.34$ **17.** $\dfrac{2}{5} + \dfrac{40}{100}$ **18.** $\dfrac{50}{100} - \dfrac{1}{4}$

Write each number as a fraction, percent, or decimal. [Page 746]

19. decimal and percent   **a.** $\dfrac{29}{100}$ **b.** $\dfrac{3}{50}$ **c.** $\dfrac{3}{8}$ **d.** $\dfrac{4}{5}$

20. fraction and decimal   **a.** 68%   **b.** 134%   **c.** 10%   **d.** 7%

21. fraction and percent   **a.** 0.65   **b.** 7.34   **c.** 0.15   **d.** 0.09

1-1 Exploring Data

¿CUAL ES EL IDIOMA?
WHAT IS THE LANGUAGE?
QUAL É O IDIOMA?

The popular TV quiz program *Jeopardy* has a unique gimmick. Contestants are given an answer, and they have to respond with a matching question. On one "Final Jeopardy" segment, the contestants were told, "It is the most widely spoken language in South America." They each responded, "What is Spanish?" But each contestant was wrong!

The players knew that Spanish is the official language of most South American countries. What they overlooked is that Brazil is the largest country in South America, with close to half of the land area and 56.9% of the population of the continent. Brazil's official language is Portuguese, and the correct response to "Final Jeopardy" was, "What is Portuguese?"

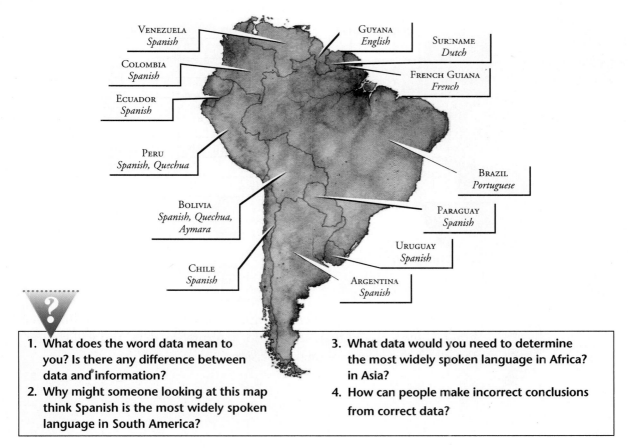

VENEZUELA
Spanish

COLOMBIA
Spanish

ECUADOR
Spanish

PERU
Spanish, Quechua

BOLIVIA
Spanish, Quechua, Aymara

CHILE
Spanish

GUYANA
English

SURINAME
Dutch

FRENCH GUIANA
French

BRAZIL
Portuguese

PARAGUAY
Spanish

URUGUAY
Spanish

ARGENTINA
Spanish

1. What does the word data mean to you? Is there any difference between data and information?
2. Why might someone looking at this map think Spanish is the most widely spoken language in South America?
3. What data would you need to determine the most widely spoken language in Africa? in Asia?
4. How can people make incorrect conclusions from correct data?

Interpreting Graphs of Data

← C O N N E C T →

You've seen graphs of data before and will find them to be important again in algebra. You'll now examine some graphs of numerical data and make interpretations based on those graphs.

How many schools should be built in the next decade? how many roads? Making decisions like these can require vast amounts of data about people and their needs. In the United States, a census is taken every 10 years to gather these kinds of data. Graphing data often makes it easier to interpret them and make decisions.

The table of data below shows the distribution of land area within South America. The graphs in the following Explore were generated from these data by a computer **spreadsheet** program. **Bar graphs** and **circle graphs,** also called **pie charts,** are two of the most common and useful types of graphs.

South American Land Areas (in square miles)	
Country	**Area**
Brazil	3,286,470
Argentina	1,065,189
Peru	496,222
Colombia	439,735
Bolivia	424,165
Venezuela	352,141
Chile	292,257
Other	517,556

You will investigate six different graphs of the same data. Sometimes one graph is more useful than another for interpreting data. You will choose the graph that helps you make decisions.

Use these six graphs of land areas within South America to answer the questions. Land area is given in thousands (,000) of square miles.

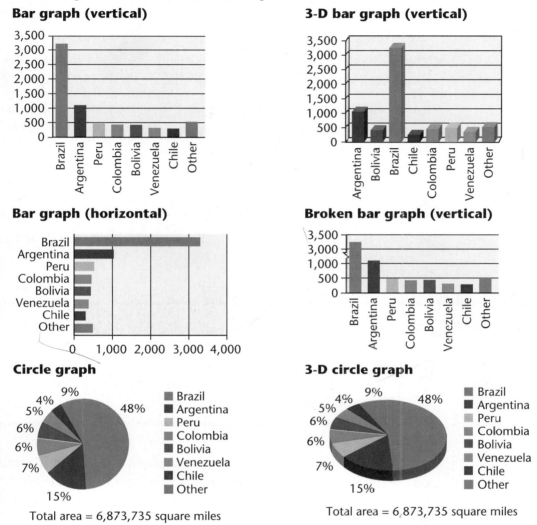

Bar graph (vertical)

3-D bar graph (vertical)

Bar graph (horizontal)

Broken bar graph (vertical)

Circle graph

Total area = 6,873,735 square miles

3-D circle graph

Total area = 6,873,735 square miles

1. Which country has approximately 500,000 square miles of land area? Which graph did you use to decide?
2. Which country has about twice the land area of another country? Which graph did you use to decide?
3. Which graphs show the portion of South American land area within each country best? Which show the actual areas best?
4. Could any of the graphs mislead someone about the data? Explain.
5. Write a statement based on these graphs comparing the uses of graphs in different situations.

You can estimate the value represented by a sector of a circle graph by using information from the graph.

EXAMPLE

Use the circle graph of South American land areas to find the area of Argentina.

The circle graph shows that Argentina's land area is about 15% of the total. Below the graph, we see that the total area is 6,873,735 square miles.

$0.15 \times 6,873,735 = 1,031,060.25$ sq mi   Note: 15% in decimal form is 0.15.

The land area of Argentina is about 1,031,060 square miles.

TRY IT

a. If a circle graph represents 536 votes, how many votes does a sector labeled 36% represent?

b. If a circle graph represents 2.4 million people, how many people are represented by a sector labeled 17%?

CONSIDER

Explain which type of graph you would find most useful to show the following.
1. How does a family spend its monthly income?
2. How many cars were sold for each of the years 1985 through 1994?

You've seen that the most useful way to display data in graphs depends on the situation and the decisions you have to make. With bar graphs, you can compare two values of data easily. With circle graphs, you can see each value as a percentage of the whole.

REFLECT

1. Why do you think several categories are combined in some graphs?
2. Describe a situation where a circle graph is more useful than a bar graph.
3. Describe a situation where a bar graph is more useful than a circle graph.
4. The actual land area of Argentina is 1,065,189 square miles. Why is this different from the area found in the example?
5. What is the sum of the percentages in a circle graph?

Exercises

CORE

1. **Getting Started** A **circle graph** shows different parts of the data in relation to all of the data. Each sector of the circle represents a different portion of the data, and the entire circle represents *all* of the data.
   a. Which sector of the circle represents approximately 25%?
   b. What common fraction can you use to approximate sector B?
   c. What sector or sectors of the circle represent 100%?
   d. If the whole circle represents 1200 people, approximately how many people are represented by sector C?
   e. If sector B represents 90 dogs, how many dogs does the whole circle represent?

2. What is 11% of 425?

3. What percent of 80 is 60?

4. 29% of a number is 580. What is the number?

5. Write the letter of the second pair that best matches the first pair.
   sector: circle graph as (a) bar: bar graph, (b) data: table, (c) Argentina: languages, (d) whole: part

6. Use the circle graph of South American land areas to find Bolivia's area.

7. The first bar in this graph represents a minority enrollment of 552 students at Cleveland High. Estimate the minority enrollments for the other schools and the total minority enrollment for all of the Tyne County schools. Explain how you estimated the results.

Minority Enrollment, Tyne County Schools

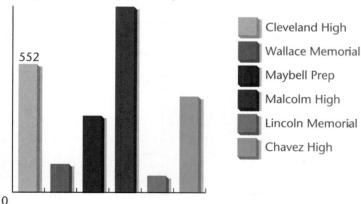

Cleveland High
Wallace Memorial
Maybell Prep
Malcolm High
Lincoln Memorial
Chavez High

8. For what kinds of data is a circle graph more appropriate than a bar graph? For what kinds of data is a bar graph more appropriate than a circle graph?

9. Truckin' This graph might have appeared in an advertisement.

a. Whose advertisement could this have been? Why? Why didn't they draw the scale to show percentages from 0% to 100%?

b. What other considerations besides truck quality might explain the graph?

10. Smoke Rises What impressions do the following graphs of the data on smoke-free communities give? Explain the differences between them.

a.

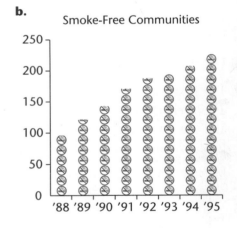

b.

Smoke-Free Communities

11. Chopped Wheat This chart shows the percentage of grains in a popular cereal. Explain what happens when you chop off the bottom of a bar graph to create a new graph.

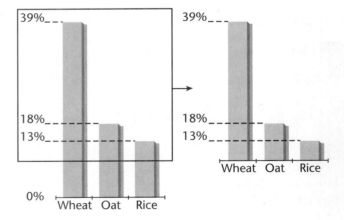

12. Silly Sector A sector of a circle graph may be separated to show that it is a sector of particular interest. Is the graph shown a fair representation of the data? Why or why not?

13. How can an accurate circle graph have percentages that have a sum of 99% or 101%?

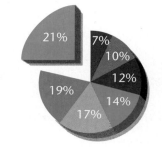

LOOK BACK

Simplify. [Previous course]

14. $\dfrac{3}{5} + \dfrac{2}{5}$

15. $\dfrac{5}{8} - \dfrac{1}{3}$

16. $0.75 - 0.18$

17. $2.86 + 8.6$

18. $\dfrac{7}{9} - \dfrac{4}{9}$

19. $\dfrac{11}{20} + 1\dfrac{7}{10}$

20. $\dfrac{3}{8} \times 56$

21. 0.0125×80

22. $\dfrac{3}{40} \times \dfrac{80}{3}$

23. $2\dfrac{5}{6} \times \dfrac{1}{3}$

24. $\dfrac{2}{5} \times 5\dfrac{1}{2}$

25. $\dfrac{8}{7} \times \dfrac{4}{4}$

26. $\dfrac{1}{7} \div \dfrac{2}{7}$

27. $\dfrac{24}{17} \div 3$

28. $\dfrac{50}{15} \div 1$

29. $9 \div \dfrac{1}{6}$

30. $1\dfrac{3}{4} \div \dfrac{1}{4}$

31. $\dfrac{1}{5} \div \dfrac{2}{9}$

MORE PRACTICE

Find each percentage.

32. 70% of 400

33. 19% of 250

34. 0.5% of 1000

35. 10% of 89

36. 1% of 89

37. 0.1% of 89

38. 50% of 67

39. 25% of 72

40. 72% of 25

41. 36% of 410

42. 33.3% of 90

43. 12.5% of 200

44. 9% of 21

45. 96% of 4

46. 75% of 78

47. What percent of 50 is 32?

48. Twelve is what percent of 45?

49. Eight is what percent of 64?

50. What percent of 200 is 98?

51. A circle graph represents 180 kittens. What does $\dfrac{1}{4}$ of the circle represent?

52. A circle graph represents 270 million people. What does 3% of the circle represent?

53. If a sector of a circle graph marked 14% represents 714 bicycles, what does the entire circle graph represent?

54. If a sector of a circle graph marked 25% represents 321 gallons of fuel, what does a sector marked 5% represent?

Match the correct sector to each percentage.

55.

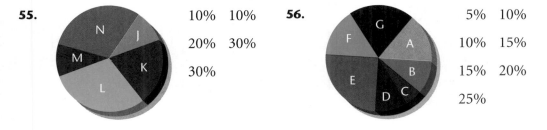

10%	10%
20%	30%
30%	

56.

5%	10%
10%	15%
15%	20%
25%	

MORE MATH REASONING

Social Science

57. African Facts The population of Nigeria is approximately 90 million. The following table shows the top six ethnic groups, by population. Match the groups with the sectors on the graph. (One sector represents all other ethnic groups.)

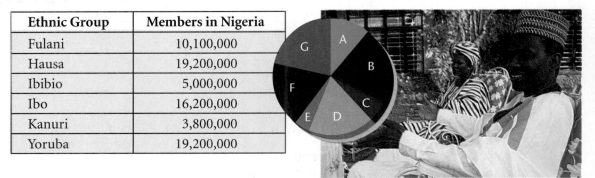

Ethnic Group	Members in Nigeria
Fulani	10,100,000
Hausa	19,200,000
Ibibio	5,000,000
Ibo	16,200,000
Kanuri	3,800,000
Yoruba	19,200,000

58. Picturing Test Results Ms. Chen gave her algebra class a test. The following is a *histogram* of the test scores. A histogram is a bar graph that combines data into equal intervals. Each bar is a bar graph that shows how many students had scores in that interval of scores.

a. Use the histogram to find how many students scored between 95 and 100.

b. What interval had the most scores?

c. What interval had the fewest scores?

d. How many students took the test?

e. Is it possible to determine the average test score from the graph? Explain why or why not.

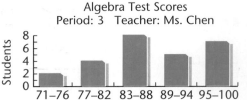

Algebra Test Scores
Period: 3 Teacher: Ms. Chen

(histogram: Students (0–8) vs. Test scores; intervals 71–76, 77–82, 83–88, 89–94, 95–100)

1-1
PART B — Adding with Integers and Matrices

← **CONNECT** → *You've interpreted graphs of data. Now you will explore how numerical data can be organized in a matrix for efficient storage and use. You will also review how to work with positive and negative integers.*

You can use a **matrix** to organize numerical data. A matrix is especially helpful when working with a large amount of data. The numbers at the heart of a table or spreadsheet, after you remove the labels, are an example of a matrix.

Supermarket Comparison	SuperSav	Jumboshop	Value Foods	Kenesha's
Beef, chopped (3 lb)	$2.37	$3.27	$2.97	$2.34
Chicken, cut-up fryer (3 lb)	1.77	2.37	2.25	1.47
Milk, 1% fat (1/2 gal)	1.39	1.15	1.09	1.24
G'Rain bread (24 oz)	1.99	1.99	1.89	2.09
Greenpaper towels	1.65	0.99	1.35	1.57
Krakkers	2.39	2.45	1.98	2.19
Big Dog dog food (4 cans)	3.56	3.00	3.92	3.40

The numerical data within the preceding table can be written as the following *matrix*, denoted by *A*.

Matrix *A* has 7 **rows** and 4 **columns**. The **dimension** of *A* is 7 × 4, read "7 by 4."

$$A = \begin{bmatrix} 2.37 & 3.27 & 2.97 & 2.34 \\ 1.77 & 2.37 & 2.25 & 1.47 \\ 1.39 & 1.15 & 1.09 & 1.24 \\ 1.99 & 1.99 & 1.89 & 2.09 \\ 1.65 & 0.99 & 1.35 & 1.57 \\ 2.39 & 2.45 & 1.98 & 2.19 \\ 3.56 & 3.00 & 3.92 & 3.40 \end{bmatrix}$$

A **matrix** is a rectangular arrangement of numbers written between brackets. (The plural of matrix is **matrices.**) The numbers in a matrix are called **entries.**

Give the dimension of each matrix.

a. $\begin{bmatrix} 2 & 4 & -1 \\ 3.5 & 2 & 0 \\ 0 & 2 & 1 \end{bmatrix}$ **b.** $\begin{bmatrix} 5 \\ 0 \end{bmatrix}$ **c.** $[2 \quad 4 \quad 6 \quad 8]$ **d.** $\begin{bmatrix} 1 & 2 & 3 \\ 4 & 5 & 6 \\ 7 & 8 & 9 \\ 10 & 9 & 8 \\ 7 & 6 & 5 \end{bmatrix}$

EXPLORE: BRRR!

Weather bureaus throughout the world record temperatures and other data on an hourly basis. Here are the high and low temperatures in Detroit, Michigan, and Oslo, Norway, for one winter week.

Detroit Temperature							
	Mon	Tues	Wed	Thur	Fri	Sat	Sun
High in °C	−1	0	2	8	6	8	10
Low in °C	−8	−6	−4	1	−3	−4	0
Oslo Temperature							
	Mon	Tues	Wed	Thur	Fri	Sat	Sun
High in °C	0	−2	2	−1	6	9	6
Low in °C	−9	−11	−6	−8	0	1	−2

1. Find the difference between the temperatures in Detroit and Oslo for both the high and low for each day. The thermometer at the right may be helpful. Copy and complete the table that follows.

Difference in Temperatures (Detroit and Oslo)							
	Mon	Tues	Wed	Thur	Fri	Sat	Sun
High in °C	−1						
Low in °C	1						

2. What does a *positive* number in your table mean? What does a *negative* number mean? (Recall that positive numbers are usually written without the + sign.)

3. Was it generally colder or warmer in Detroit than in Oslo that week? Explain how you used your table to decide.

4. Write the data in each table as a matrix. What do you think it means to subtract two matrices? See if you agree with classmates.

Recall that the **whole numbers** are 0, 1, 2, 3, ... The **integers** are the whole numbers and their **opposites,** −1, −2, −3, . . . , where 0 is its own opposite. We represent these numbers as **sets** and show them on the **number line,** which consists of all of the **real numbers.**

$$\text{Whole numbers} = \{0, 1, 2, 3, \ldots\}$$

$$\text{Integers} = \{\ldots, -3, -2, -1, 0, 1, 2, 3, \ldots\}$$

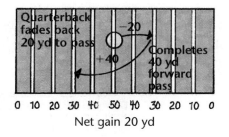

Recall that when you add two positive numbers, the sum is positive, and when you add two negative numbers, the sum is negative.

EXAMPLES

Add the numbers.

1. $8 + 12$

$8 + 12 = 20$ positive + positive = positive

2. $-3 + (-5)$

$-3 + (-5) = -8$ negative + negative = negative

To add a positive number and a negative number, it may help to think of running on a football field.

Quarterback fades back 20 yd to pass

−20

+40

Completes 40 yd forward pass

0 10 20 30 40 50 40 30 20 10 0

Net gain 20 yd

EXAMPLES

Add the numbers.

3. $-10 + 15$

$-10 + 15 = 5$ A loss of 10 and a gain of 15 give a net gain of 5.

4. $8 + (-19)$

$8 + (-19) = -11$ A gain of 8 and a loss of 19 give a net loss of 11.

5. $4 + (-4)$

$4 + (-4) = 0$ A gain of 4 and a loss of 4 give a net result of 0.

Subtraction gives the *difference* between two numbers, as in the preceding Explore. Subtracting a number is the same as *adding its opposite.*

EXAMPLES

6. $6 - (-2) =$

To subtract –2,

$$6 - (-2) = 6 + 2 = 8$$

add the opposite, 2.

7. $-12 - 4 =$

To subtract 4,

$$-12 - 4 = -12 + (-4) = -16$$

add the opposite, –4.

TRY IT

Add or subtract the numbers.

e. $-7 + 11$ **f.** $18 + (-8)$ **g.** $13 - (-3)$ **h.** $-6 - 14$

You can also add and subtract two *matrices* if they have the same dimension. To add them, add the corresponding entries. To subtract them, subtract the corresponding entries.

EXAMPLE

8. $A = \begin{bmatrix} 2 & 1 & 6 \\ 1 & 2 & 4 \end{bmatrix}$ and $B = \begin{bmatrix} -5 & 3 & 6 \\ 4 & -1 & 3 \end{bmatrix}$. Find $A + B$.

$$A + B = \begin{bmatrix} 2 + (-5) & 1 + 3 & 6 + 6 \\ 1 + 4 & 2 + (-1) & 4 + 3 \end{bmatrix} = \begin{bmatrix} -3 & 4 & 12 \\ 5 & 1 & 7 \end{bmatrix}$$

Graphing calculators will add and subtract matrices of the same dimension, as illustrated below. The screens may look different on your graphing calculator.

TRY IT

i. Find $A - B$.   **j.** Find $B - A$.

CONSIDER

?

1. Can two matrices with different dimensions be added and subtracted? Explain.

REFLECT

1. How is a matrix different from a table?
2. Why do you think matrices make it easier to handle large tables of data?
3. Describe another way to think about adding integers, besides the image of running on a football field.
4. If you add two matrices, how is the dimension of the sum related to the dimension of each original matrix?

Exercises

CORE

1. **Getting Started** Complete each pattern.

   a. $4 - 4 = 0$
   $4 - 3 = 1$
   $4 - 2 = 2$
   $4 - 1 = 3$
   $4 - 0 = 4$
   $4 - (-1) = ?$
   $4 - (-2) = ?$

   b. $-2 + 4 = 2$
   $-2 + 3 = 1$
   $-2 + 2 = 0$
   $-2 + 1 = ?$
   $-2 + 0 = ?$
   $-2 + (-1) = ?$
   $-2 + (-2) = ?$

   c. $-1 - 2 = -3$
   $-1 - 1 = -2$
   $-1 - 0 = -1$
   $-1 - (-1) = ?$
   $-1 - (-2) = ?$
   $-1 - (-3) = ?$
   $-1 - (-4) = ?$

2. Add 6 and -9. Explain your method.

3. Add -6 and 9. Explain your method.

4. Which of the following sums are positive? How do you know?
   a. $3 + (-5)$ **b.** $17 + (-12)$ **c.** $-5 + 7$ **d.** $10 + (-10)$

5. Match the phrase with the word it describes.
   a. a computer display of data
   b. a whole number or its opposite
   c. an arrangement of numbers in which each row has the same number of entries
   d. the number of rows and columns in an arrangement of numbers

   i. dimension
   ii. matrix
   iii. integer
   iv. spreadsheet

6. What is the dimension of matrix A, where $A = \begin{bmatrix} 1 & 6 & -2 & 4 & 6 \\ 0 & 3 & 4 & -9 & 7 \end{bmatrix}$?

7. Sequels Opinions about movies can be put into a table.

Film	Super	Good	Fair	Poor
Triassica: The Reopening	52	21	17	2
Galaxy XXIII	37	45	12	5
Return of Percy	0	1	14	35

a. Write the data in matrix form.
b. What is the dimension of the matrix?
c. Who might use this information? Explain.

Find the sum or the difference of the two matrices, if possible. If impossible, explain why.

$$A = \begin{bmatrix} 1 & 4 & 2 \\ 3 & 6 & 8 \end{bmatrix} \quad B = \begin{bmatrix} 3 & 2 \\ 9 & 8 \\ 4 & 7 \end{bmatrix} \quad C = \begin{bmatrix} -1 & -7 & 2 \\ 5 & 3 & -2 \\ -4 & 0 & 7 \end{bmatrix} \quad D = \begin{bmatrix} -3 & -4 & -2 \\ 0 & 8 & 8 \\ -4 & 4 & 2 \end{bmatrix}$$

8. $C + D$ **9.** $A - A$ **10.** $B - A$ **11.** $C - D$

12. What are all the possible dimensions for a matrix with 10 entries? Justify your answer.

13. What could be meant by a *square* matrix?

14. Heart and Soul Patients recovering from heart surgery can control their weight better by joining a support group. Matrix W shows the weights of five patients the first week in the program. Matrix C represents the change in weights the following week.

$W = \begin{bmatrix} 177 & 185 & 140 & 117 & 210 \end{bmatrix}$
$C = \begin{bmatrix} -4 & -5 & +2 & 0 & -3 \end{bmatrix}$

a. What is the dimension of W? of C?
b. How do these matrices differ from most of those you have seen previously in this part?
c. Find the matrix $W + C$. Explain what it represents.

Health

LOOK AHEAD

Write each as a percentage and as a decimal.

15. $\dfrac{3}{8}$ **16.** 12 out of 27 **17.** 10 of the original U.S. colonies

MORE PRACTICE

Add or subtract.

18. $-6 + 4$ **19.** $-4 + 6$ **20.** $3 + (-5)$ **21.** $-7 + (-4)$

22. $-6 - 4$ **23.** $-4 - 6$ **24.** $3 - (-5)$ **25.** $-7 - (-4)$

26. $-\frac{1}{4} + \left(-\frac{1}{4}\right)$ **27.** $\frac{3}{8} + \left(-\frac{1}{2}\right)$ **28.** $-1 + \left(-\frac{1}{3}\right)$ **29.** $-\frac{1}{4} - \left(-\frac{1}{6}\right)$

30. The high temperature one day in New Jersey was 10°F. On the same day, the low temperature was -3°F. What was the difference in temperature on this day?

Use the matrices to find each of the sums or differences.

$$A = \begin{bmatrix} 2 & -3 & 1 & 4 \\ 0 & 1 & 1 & 2 \\ 5 & -1 & 2 & 0 \end{bmatrix} \qquad B = \begin{bmatrix} -2 & 3 & 3 & -1 \\ 1 & 1 & 2 & 3 \\ 0 & 2 & -1 & 1 \end{bmatrix} \qquad C = \begin{bmatrix} -1 & 1 & -1 & 0 \\ 0 & -1 & 1 & 4 \\ 1 & 0 & 2 & 1 \end{bmatrix}$$

31. $A + B$ **32.** $A - B$ **33.** $B - A$ **34.** $A + C$

35. $C - B$ **36.** $B + C$ **37.** $A + C - B$

MORE MATH REASONING

38. Suppose that data are given in a 4×5 matrix. Explain how the data can be rearranged to form a 5×4 matrix.

39. Cell Structure A computer *spreadsheet* can help you do matrix arithmetic. A spreadsheet is made up of *cells*, designated by column and row. The number -7 in the spreadsheet that follows is located in cell A3. This section of the spreadsheet shows how an office worker adds two matrices,

$$\begin{bmatrix} 6 & 3 \\ -7 & -5 \end{bmatrix} \text{ and } \begin{bmatrix} 4 & -3 \\ 5 & -4 \end{bmatrix}$$

Calculate the matrix sum by evaluating the formulas. If you have access to a spreadsheet, test the formulas by changing the numbers in either matrix.

	A	B	C	D	E	F	G	H
1								
2	6	3		4	-3		=A2+D2	=B2+E2
3	-7	-5		5	-4		=A3+D3	=B3+E3

← CONNECT → *You've explored addition and subtraction with integers and matrices. Now you will review multiplication of integers. This will enable you to perform scalar multiplication.*

EXPLORE: LIGHTS, CAMERA, ACTION!

Think about someone skiing forward or backward. If you have a VCR tape of the skier, you can play the tape forward or in reverse. How will this affect the way the skier appears to move?

The skier

Filmed moving forward

Filmed moving backward

The VCR

Playing forward

Playing in reverse

If the skier is moving forward (to the right) and the VCR is playing forward, the screen will show the skier moving forward. Use similar reasoning to copy and complete the following table. Briefly describe your reasoning in each case.

VCR's Direction	Skier's Direction	Direction of Skier on Screen
Forward	Forward	Forward
Forward	Backward	
Reverse	Forward	
Reverse	Backward	

If you think of *forward* as positive and *backward* or *reverse* as negative, then the preceding Explore illustrates how to determine the sign of a product or quotient of numbers.

> The product or quotient of two numbers with the *same sign* is *positive*.
> The product or quotient of two numbers with *opposite signs* is *negative*.

For example, $-5 \times 4 = -20$. This also shows that $\frac{-20}{-5} = 4$, and $\frac{-20}{4} = -5$.

TRY IT

Multiply or divide the numbers.

a. $-3 \times (-5)$ **b.** $-8 \cdot (-0.2)$ **c.** $\frac{30}{-5}$

CONSIDER

1. What is the sign of the product of three negative numbers? two positive numbers and one negative number? Explain.

2. What is the value of $\frac{3}{0}$? $\frac{-3}{0}$? Explain your answers.

You can also multiply matrices by numbers.

Matrix *J* represents the prices, in yen, of three models of CD players at two Japanese electronics stores. The rows represent the stores, and the columns represent the models.

$$J = \begin{bmatrix} 15{,}000 & 18{,}000 & 22{,}000 \\ 13{,}000 & 18{,}000 & 23{,}000 \end{bmatrix}$$

At the current *exchange rate*, 1 yen is worth about $0.009. Multiply each entry by 0.009 to find the equivalent prices in dollars at each store.

$$\begin{bmatrix} 0.009 \times 15{,}000 & 0.009 \times 18{,}000 & 0.009 \times 22{,}000 \\ 0.009 \times 13{,}000 & 0.009 \times 18{,}000 & 0.009 \times 23{,}000 \end{bmatrix} = \begin{bmatrix} 135 & 162 & 198 \\ 117 & 162 & 207 \end{bmatrix}$$

When you multiply each entry of a matrix by a single number, you are performing **scalar multiplication**. The new matrix in the example is the **scalar product** of 0.009 and *J*.

$$0.009J = \begin{bmatrix} 135 & 162 & 198 \\ 117 & 162 & 207 \end{bmatrix}$$

Find each scalar product, using the following matrix.

d. $5A$ **e.** $-2A$

f. $\dfrac{1}{2}A$ **g.** $0.5A$ $A = \begin{bmatrix} -3 & 4 & -5 & 0 \\ 2 & -1 & 0 & 1 \\ -8 & 2 & 7 & -3 \end{bmatrix}$

The ancient Babylonians recorded tables of mathematical and astrological data on clay tablets. Today, industries such as air transportation and communications rely on matrices to deal with the large amount of data they use every day.

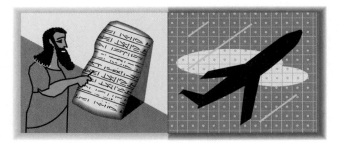

REFLECT

1. Decide if the number described is positive or negative.
   a. the product of an even number of negative numbers
   b. the product of an odd number of negative numbers
2. If the product of three numbers is positive and two of the numbers are negative, what is the sign of the third number?
3. Explain how scalar multiplication is different from the multiplication of two numbers. How is it similar?

Exercises

CORE

1. Getting Started Complete each pattern.

   a. $4 \times 4 = 16$ **b.** $-2 \times 4 = -8$
        $4 \times 3 = 12$ $-2 \times 3 = -6$
        $4 \times 2 = 8$ $-2 \times 2 = -4$
        $4 \times 1 = 4$ $-2 \times 1 = -2$
        $4 \times 0 = 0$ $-2 \times 0 = 0$
        $4 \times (-1) = ?$ $-2 \times (-1) = ?$
        $4 \times (-2) = ?$ $-2 \times (-2) = ?$
                                           $-2 \times (-3) = ?$

Find the products.

2. $-4 \cdot (-6)$

3. $7 \cdot (-21) \cdot (-2)$

4. $0.01 \cdot (-5)$

5. $-231 \cdot (-17) \cdot (-1)$

6. $-0.01 \cdot 5$

7. $1\frac{1}{2} \cdot 3$

8. Choose the correct definition of *scalar product*.
(a) the product of two matrices
(b) the sum of a number and a matrix
(c) a matrix that can be multiplied by a number
(d) the product of a number and a matrix
(e) the product of a matrix and its dimension

Divide.

9. $\dfrac{-81}{3}$

10. $\dfrac{-120}{-8}$

11. $\dfrac{12}{-8}$

Use the following matrices for Exercises 12–19.

$$A = \begin{bmatrix} -3 & 2 \\ -2 & -1 \end{bmatrix} \quad B = [1 \quad -3] \quad C = \begin{bmatrix} -4 & 3 \\ 0 & 9 \end{bmatrix}$$

12. Find $3B$.

13. Find $-7A$.

14. Find $-0.5C$.

15. Find $A - C$.

16. Find $\frac{1}{3}B$.

17. Find $2A + C$.

18. Could you multiply A by a scalar to obtain $\begin{bmatrix} 6 & -4 \\ 4 & 2 \end{bmatrix}$? If so, what is the scalar?

19. Could you multiply C by a scalar to obtain $\begin{bmatrix} 12 & 9 \\ 0 & -27 \end{bmatrix}$? If so, what is the scalar?

20. To increase each number of a matrix by 25%, use 1.25 as your scalar multiplier. Write a matrix, R. Then create matrix K, where K is $1.25R$.

21. Wheeling Country Ms. Simon wants the best deal on a bicycle. She investigated four different models at three different stores and summarized the prices in matrix B. Her city charges 9% sales tax. Use matrix B to find the final price of each bike in each store *including tax*. Write your answers in a new matrix, D.

$$B = \begin{bmatrix} 450 & 500 & 450 & 400 \\ 350 & 300 & 300 & 350 \\ 500 & 500 & 400 & 450 \end{bmatrix}$$

22. Write a matrix, D. How do $2D$ and $D + D$ compare? Explain.

Industry

23. Boarding House Boarding House manufactures three models of skateboards using two different materials. A sporting goods store pays the following prices for the skateboards.

	Fireball	Cyclo	Wild Ride
Viberglass	\$14.35	\$16.75	\$19.55
Flexboard	\$22.60	\$26.40	\$30.80

a. Let matrix M represent the data in the table. What is the dimension of M?

b. The sporting goods store will sell the skateboards for 2.75 times the price it pays for the skateboards. Write a matrix representing the selling price, with each entry rounded to the nearest nickel.

Fine Arts

24. The baseball season is 162 games long for each team. The players listed in the following table are on a team that has played 72 games. Write the data in a matrix. Use scalar multiplication to project each player's year-end totals, each rounded to the nearest whole number.

Problem-Solving Tip

Set up a proportion first.

Ralph Fasanella, *Night Game-Yankee Stadium,* 1981. Oil on canvas.

Player	Hits	Doubles	Triples	Home Runs	RBI
Malzone	83	17	1	10	37
Uhlander	79	11	3	2	29
Barlow	68	9	0	24	50
Harmon	65	12	2	12	44
Jefferson	59	15	6	18	54

LOOK AHEAD

Use the numbers 2, −3, 0, −1, 4, −6, and −2.

25. Arrange these numbers in order from least to greatest.

26. Which number is greatest?

27. Which number is least?

28. Plot these points on a number line.

    a. 4   **b.** 0   **c.** -2.5 **d.** $\dfrac{1}{3}$ **e.** $\dfrac{-10}{4}$

MORE PRACTICE

Find the products.

29. $5 \cdot (-20)$ **30.** $0 \cdot (-21)$ **31.** $-6 \cdot (-4) \cdot 3$

32. $-517 \cdot (-32)$ **33.** $1\dfrac{1}{3} \cdot 1\dfrac{1}{3}$ **34.** $-0.05 \cdot 20 \cdot (-4)$

35. $\dfrac{1}{6} \cdot (-42)$ **36.** $\dfrac{2}{3} \cdot \dfrac{3}{2}$ **37.** $-0.707 \cdot (-0.707) \cdot (-1)$

Divide.

38. $\dfrac{-105}{35}$ **39.** $\dfrac{2}{-6}$ **40.** $\dfrac{-100}{-1}$

41. $\dfrac{0}{-4}$ **42.** $\dfrac{-3}{0}$ **43.** $\dfrac{-8}{-0.5}$

Use the following matrices for Exercises 44–49. Find each scalar product.

$$A = \begin{bmatrix} 4 & 0 \\ -7 & 6 \end{bmatrix} \qquad B = \begin{bmatrix} 10 & 5 & -3 \\ -2 & 4 & 0 \end{bmatrix} \qquad C = \begin{bmatrix} 6 & 7 \\ -3 & -2 \end{bmatrix}$$

44. $4C$ **45.** $1.5B$ **46.** $\dfrac{1}{2}A$

47. $-B$ **48.** $-0.25B$ **49.** $-3A$

MORE MATH REASONING

50. When matrix A is multiplied by $\dfrac{1}{5}$, the resulting matrix has whole-number entries. Describe the entries in matrix A.

Describe the entries in matrix A.

51. Is the following statement always true? Explain your answer.

    Multiplying a matrix by a negative number changes the sign of every entry of the matrix.

52. An **identity matrix** is a square matrix (same number of rows and columns) that has 1 as an entry when the row and column number of the entry are the same, and 0 as an entry when the row and column number are different.

    a. Find the 3 × 3 identity matrix.

    b. Find the 4 × 4 identity matrix.

    c. Find the matrix that, when multiplied by $\dfrac{1}{3}$, gives the 3 × 3 identity matrix.

Measures of Central Tendency

←CONNECT→ *You've seen ways of representing, organizing, and visualizing data. Now you'll investigate ways to summarize numerical data with a single, convenient number.*

Averages are often used to summarize sets of numerical data.

The *average* daily temperature in February in Barrow, Alaska, is −20°F.

The *average* number of words in a president's inaugural address is 2,399.

Barry Bonds has a batting *average* of .324.

The average, or **mean,** is a *measure of central tendency*—a single, central value that summarizes a set of numerical data. Other common measures of central tendency include the **mode** and the **median.**

The **mean** is the sum of the data divided by the number of data.

The **mode** is the most frequently occurring value from the data.

When the data are arranged in numerical order, the **median** is the value of the middle item of data or the average of the middle two items of data.

Data: 5, 1, 4, 0, 1, 5, 5.

$$\text{Mean} = \frac{5 + 1 + 4 + 0 + 1 + 5 + 5}{7} = 3$$

The value 5 occurs most often.
Mode = 5

Arranged in numerical order, the data are

$$0, 1, 1, 4, 5, 5, 5$$

Median = 4

CONSIDER
?

1. When would a set of data have one middle item of data? two middle items?

The following is *Article 1* of the United Nations' *Universal Declaration of Human Rights* in three different languages.

[English] Article 1

All human beings are born free and equal in dignity and rights. They are endowed with reason and conscience and should act towards one another in a spirit of brotherhood.

[French] Article premier

Tous les êtres humains naissent libres et égaux en dignité et en droits. Ils sont doués de raison et conscience et doivent agir les uns envers les autres dans un espirit de fraternité.

[Spanish] Articulo 1

Todos los seres humanos nacen libres e iguales en dignidad y derechos y; dotados como están de razón y conciencia, deben comportarse fraternalmente los unos con los otros.

1. Find the *mean* word length in *Article 1* for each language.

2. Find the *mode* word length in *Article 1* for each language.

3. Find the *median* word length in *Article 1* for each language.

4. Which language has the largest mean? mode? median? Which of these measures of central tendency do you think best describes the typical word length in *Article 1* for each language? Why?

Sometimes the data have negative values. The mean, mode, and median are found in the same way as when the data have positive values.

EXAMPLE

One number used to evaluate a hockey player is called the *plus/minus*. A player's plus/minus is the difference between his team's goals and the goals of opposing teams *while he was on the ice* that season. Here are the plus/minus data for the top 10 scorers for the 1985 Buffalo Sabres.

1985 Buffalo Sabres—Top Ten Scorers			
Player	**Plus/Minus**	**Player**	**Plus/Minus**
Dave Andreychuk	3	Paul Cyr	4
Mike Foligno	25	Gilles Hamel	−27
John Tucker	0	Doug Smith	−27
Phil Housley	−9	Lindy Ruff	8
Gil Perrault	−10	Mike Ramsay	1

Find the mean, median, and mode of these data.

Arranged in numerical order, the data are
−27, −27, −10, −9, 0, 1, 3, 4, 8, 25.

$$\left.\begin{array}{r}-27\\-27\\-10\\-9\\0\end{array}\right\} = -73 \qquad \left.\begin{array}{r}1\\3\\4\\8\\25\end{array}\right\} = 41$$

> **Problem-Solving Tip**
>
> Make an organized list of the data.

The sum of the 10 data items is $-73 + 41 = -32$, so the mean is $\frac{-32}{10} = -3.2$.

The median is the average of the middle two data, $\frac{0+1}{2} = 0.5$.

The mode is -27, because no other value occurs more than once.

TRY IT

a. Find the mean, median, and mode of the average monthly temperatures (°F) in Barrow, Alaska.

Month	Temp.	Month	Temp.	Month	Temp.
January	−14	May	19	September	31
February	−20	June	33	October	14
March	−16	July	39	November	−1
April	−2	August	38	December	−13

The mean, median, and mode allow you to summarize data by using an average, the middle value, or the most common value. Each of these measures of central tendency tells a different story about data in a single, convenient number.

1. If a data set contains 12 positive numbers and their opposites, what measures of central tendency do you know? Why?
2. Which measure of central tendency
   a. tells the value that occurs most often in a set of data?
   b. is the average of the data?
   c. has just as many data less than its value as greater than its value?
   d. takes into account every item in a set of data?
3. What are some advantages and disadvantages of summarizing data with a single number?

Exercises

CORE

1. **Getting Started** Use the data −4, 8, −6, 0, 11, −14, 20, 3, −5, −7.
   Sort the data from least to greatest.
   a. Add only the positive numbers.
   b. Add only the negative numbers.
   c. What is the sum?
   d. How many data values are given? What is their sum divided by the number of data values?
   e. Is the number of data values odd or even?
   f. What are the two middle values? What is their average? What is the median?

2. Match the phrase with the word it describes.
   a. the middle data item   **i.** mean
   b. the data item that occurs most often   **ii.** median
   c. the quotient of the sum of the data   **iii.** mode
      and the number of data items

3. What is the mean of the counting numbers from 1 through 10?

4. What is the median of the counting numbers from 1 through 10?

Which measure of central tendency is described?

Fine Arts

5. The average number of dancers in dance companies is 12.

6. Half of all figure skaters can do more than 30 push-ups.

7. The most common amount inserted in the jukebox was 50¢.

Alvin Ailey American Dance Theater

8. Find the mean, median, and mode of each data set. Give examples for **g** and **h.**

   a. 3, 4.5, 1, 0, 2, 3, 6, 1, 1, 2.5   **b.** −45, −12, −62, −50, −33, −29, −33, 0

   c. 7, 0, −12, 2.25, −10, 6.75, 7, −11, 7   **d.** 100, 76, 99, 85, 59, 88, 64, 99

   e. 9, 8, 15, 11, 16, 20, 13, 5, 13   **f.** −6, 14, 18, −8, 14, −21, −13, 5

   g. Can a set of data have identical values for mean, median, and mode?

   h. Can two different sets of data have identical medians but different means?

9. a. If five data values are arranged in numerical order, will one of the values be the median? Explain.

   b. If eight data values are arranged in numerical order, will one of the values be the median? Explain.

   c. If one of the data points is not the median, explain how to find the median.

10. Create a data set of six different values that has a mean of 7.

11. Half the class scored higher than 78 on the test, and half scored lower. What else can you conclude?

12. The Count The following is an excerpt from *The Man Who Counted.* The counting man told this story:

> *We traveled together for eight days exactly. During that time, clarifying points and mulling over things that interest me, I have spoken exactly 414,720 words. Since in eight days there are 11,520 minutes, one can deduce that during the journey I uttered an average of 36 words per minute—that is 2,160 per hour. These numbers show that I spoke little, that I was discreet and did not waste your time with pointless discourses.*

Cover art by: Patricia Reid Baquero, *The Man Who Counted,* 1972. W.W. Norton & Company, Inc.

   a. What measure of central tendency was he using? Could a different measure have been used?

   b. Assuming that the man had to sleep, how would you counter his argument numerically?

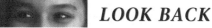 **LOOK BACK**

Simplify. [1-1]

13. −17 + 6 + (−3)   **14.** $\dfrac{-2}{3} \cdot \dfrac{-3}{2}$ **15.** 15.8(−10)

Find the greatest common factor for each set of numbers. [Previous course]

16. 10, 15   **17.** 48, 36   **18.** 33, 9

MORE PRACTICE

Find the mean and the median of each data set.

19. the first five positive even numbers

20. the first six positive odd numbers

21. $-42, -16, -24, 2, -6, 10, 0, 18$

22. A running back has run for 8, 3, -2, 20, 5, -6, and 13 yards. What was the mean run (also called the *average gain*)? What was the median run?

23. Describe how you would find the median of 17, 41, 41, 56, 60.

24. Describe how you would find the mode of 61, 17, 41, 41, 56, 60.

25. A field biologist studying amphibians collected the following data on the lengths of frogs: 4.7 cm, 4.2 cm, 5.1 cm, 3.5 cm, 5.0 cm. Find the mean and median of the data.

Estimate.

26. the mean number of minutes it takes for you to get to school

27. the median page number of this chapter

28. the mean number of students in your classes

MORE MATH REASONING

29. A data set contains eight negative numbers and three positive numbers. Can you predict anything about the median? about the mean? Explain.

30. Would you want your overall grade to be calculated by the median or the mean of your five test scores in the following situations?
a. You had one excellent score, and the others were fairly good.
b. You had one poor score, and the others were fairly good.

31. Mean Income? Which do you think is higher, the *mean* U.S. family income or the *median* U.S. family income? Write a paragraph defending your answer.

32. Using a Scientific Calculator Any calculator that allows you to store individual pieces of data can find the mean using the $\boxed{\overline{x}}$ key or a similar option. Find out if your calculator can find the mean. Use an example from this lesson to test it.

33. If doubling each value of a data set leaves the mean unchanged, what must have been true about the mean of the original data set?

Making Connections

← CONNECT → *You will continue to collect and encounter many forms of data in school, at work, and just from reading magazines. The ability to organize, interpret, and summarize these data will help you to work with them effectively wherever they occur.*

The English language is spoken in many countries throughout the world. Even in countries with a different official language, English is often the most common foreign language studied in school. But is English the most commonly spoken language in the world? You'll now investigate this and other questions relating to languages of the world.

EXPLORE: SPEAK UP

There are 12 languages in the world that have more than 100 million speakers. The following table gives data on the total number of native and non-native speakers of each of these languages for 1993.

1. Could these data be displayed effectively in a bar graph? a circle graph? What additional data might help make a bar graph or circle graph more effective?

2. a. Organize the data in a matrix. Could you have organized the data in a matrix with a different dimension? Explain.
   b. Use scalar multiplication to show the effect of a 5% increase in the numbers of speakers of these languages. (Hint: First write 100% + 5% as a decimal.)

3. What is the most commonly spoken language in the world? What are some other questions you could ask related to these data?

Language	Millions of Speakers
Arabic	214
Bengali	192
English	463
French	124
German	120
Hindi	400
Japanese	126
Malay–Indonesian	152
Mandarin Chinese	930
Portuguese	179
Russian	291
Spanish	371

1. Describe a situation where you would prefer each of the following for interpreting or organizing a set of data.
   a. bar graph
   b. circle graph
   c. matrix
2. When is it possible to add two matrices?
3. What does a *measure of central tendency* of a set of data mean? Write a brief description of the three measures of central tendency that you have used.

Self-Assessment

Use the matrices to find each of the sums or differences.

$$A = \begin{bmatrix} -5 & 4 & 10 \\ 1 & -1 & -1 \end{bmatrix} \quad B = \begin{bmatrix} -2 & -7 & -3 \\ -1 & 1 & 2 \end{bmatrix} \quad C = \begin{bmatrix} -3 & 11 & 13 \\ 2 & -2 & -3 \end{bmatrix}$$

1. $A + B$ **2.** $A - B$ **3.** $B - A$ **4.** $A + C$

5. $C - B$ **6.** $B + C$ **7.** $2B - C$ **8.** $A + B - C$

9. **Double Jeopardy** The first-round Jeopardy board looks something like this.
   a. Write the amounts in matrix form as matrix J.
   b. What is the dimension of matrix J?
   c. For the second round, all dollar values are doubled. Write this as a scalar matrix operation.

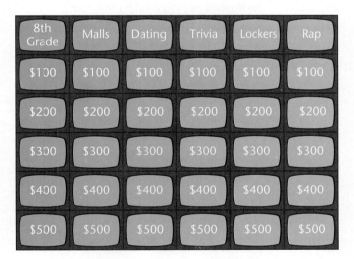

10. For the numbers 1, 4, 5, 3, and 2, the number 3 is the
    (a) mode   (b) median   (c) mean   (d) median and mean   (e) not here

11. What are the factors of 36? [Previous course]

12. How many rows could a 36-entry matrix have?

13. For each of the following, tell whether a bar graph, a circle graph, or neither is most appropriate:

    a. population information for your state for the years 1960, 1970, 1980, and 1990

    b. how you spent your allowance over the summer

    c. your marks on your last five mathematics tests

14. Bye, Bye Vinyl Compare the sales of CDs and LPs.

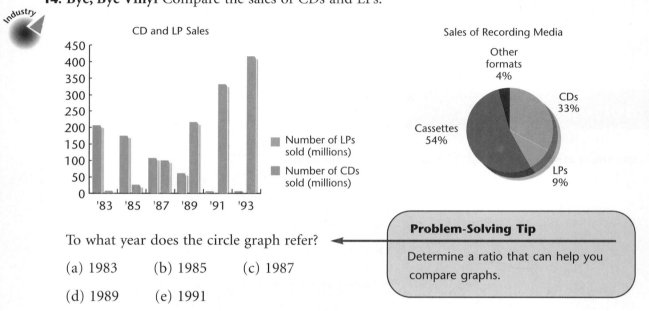

To what year does the circle graph refer?

    (a) 1983   (b) 1985   (c) 1987

    (d) 1989   (e) 1991

Problem-Solving Tip

Determine a ratio that can help you compare graphs.

15. It's a Real Crime The matrix shows crime statistics in the United States, reported per 100,000 people.

	1975	1980	1985	1990
Burglary	1322	1430	1203	1201
Car theft	450	500	421	662
Robbery	193	201	203	247

    a. If it is found that the statistics were underreported and an extra 10% must be added, what matrix operation must be performed? Perform it, and give the result.

    b. What type of graph can be drawn from the original data? Explain.

PS **16. State of the Union** How many presidents were born in your state?
President Clinton was the first president born in the state of Arkansas.

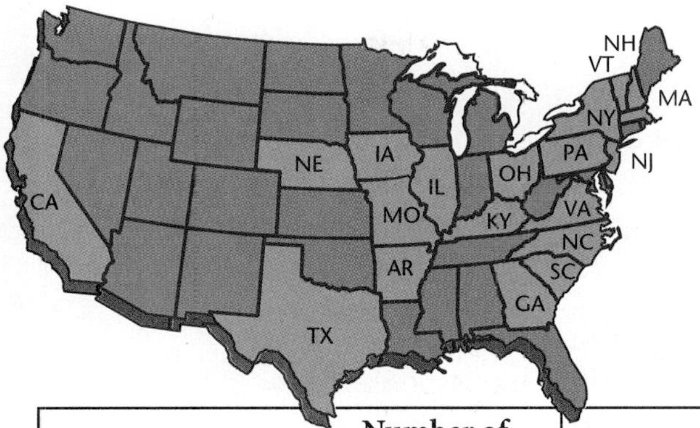

History

State	Number of Presidents	State	Number of Presidents
Arkansas	1	New Jersey	1
California	1	New York	4
Georgia	1	North Carolina	2
Illinois	1	Ohio	7
Iowa	1	Pennsylvania	1
Kentucky	1	South Carolina	1
Massachusetts	4	Texas	2
Missouri	1	Virginia	8
Nebraska	1	Vermont	2
New Hampshire	1		

a. Separate the United States into four or five geographical regions, such as the Midwest and the South, and determine how many presidents came from each region.

Problem-Solving Tip

Make an organized list of the states and regions.

b. Can a circle graph be made from these data? If so, what would the whole circle represent?
c. What is the mean number of presidents from each state of the union?

17. Why can't circle graphs be drawn for all sets of data?

18. How Am I Doing? Pablo has had five tests in each of his subjects so far. These were his scores.

> English: 80, 80, 85, 78, and 92
> History: 85, 95, 92, 75, and 80
> Mathematics: 100, 88, 92, 90, and 95
> Spanish: 88, 95, 85, 80, and 75
> Computer Science: 75, 88, 92, 75, and 85
> Biology: 65, 80, 75, 80, and 88

a. Organize Pablo's scores into two different matrices.
b. Is one way better than the other? Justify your response.
c. Find Pablo's mean score for each subject.

This graph was recently in a local newspaper.

Social Science

19. What does *median hourly wage* mean?

20. Estimate the median hourly wage for women in 1993 and for men in the same year.

21. Is there anything misleading about the graph? Explain.

22. Write a possible headline to go with the article that would accompany this graph.

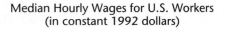

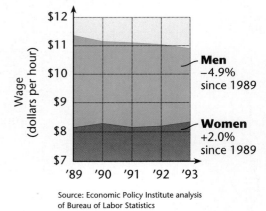

Source: Economic Policy Institute analysis of Bureau of Labor Statistics

23. The following two matrices list the temperatures for a town for three weeks. Matrix *H* gives the daily high temperature, and matrix *L* gives the daily low temperature.

Social Science

$$H = \begin{bmatrix} 50 & 48 & 45 & 47 & 44 & 39 & 42 \\ 42 & 44 & 41 & 38 & 37 & 40 & 41 \\ 35 & 36 & 33 & 38 & 32 & 33 & 30 \end{bmatrix} \quad L = \begin{bmatrix} 41 & 42 & 36 & 36 & 34 & 34 & 31 \\ 33 & 35 & 30 & 31 & 29 & 29 & 28 \\ 22 & 23 & 31 & 26 & 24 & 24 & 19 \end{bmatrix}$$

a. Find the matrix that gives the differences between high and low temperatures each day.
b. Find the matrix that gives the mean temperature for each day.
c. Describe how you could find the median high temperature for these three weeks.

What's Your Number?

During the war in Vietnam in the late 1960s, many people criticized the way in which men were drafted into the U.S. armed forces. (Women were not part of the draft.) Many felt that minorities and the poor would be the first ones sent to war. Congress decided that a draft lottery would be fair.

The first lottery was held in 1970. Each of the 366 possible birth dates was put into a drum. The first date drawn was September 14th. Each man born on that date between 1943 and 1952 was assigned the number 1. The remaining dates were drawn one at a time and given the next numbers.

Soon after, people complained again. There was concern that December dates had been added last, so they were near the top of the drum. Men with December birthdays were more likely to be chosen.

Congress responded by using two drums for the 1971 lottery. One held the 365 dates of 1953. The other held the numbers 1 to 365. The numbers in each drum were mixed, and pairs of numbers were chosen at the same time. This matched a random date with a random number.

The draft was abolished on January 27, 1973, and the lottery was no longer needed.

1. What do you think is meant by a *random* drawing?
2. What data were used in the first draft lottery? Why do you think this was chosen as a basis for the draft lottery?
3. What data were used in the second draft lottery?
4. Was it possible for someone born in December to have a low lottery number in the second drawing?

← C O N N E C T → *You've looked at ways to display data graphically. Now you will learn how to display pairs of data in graphs.*

In many situations, we want to examine how two categories of data, such as heights and weights, are related. The height and the weight of each person in your class can be written as a *pair of data.* In the second draft lottery during the war in Vietnam, pairs of data were used to determine who was drafted.

High school seniors in some states who plan to go to college take a test called the Scholastic Assessment Test, or SAT. When the SATs are graded, each student gets a pair of data—a *verbal* score and a *mathematics* score. The highest possible score on each part of the SAT is 800.

A graph is an excellent tool for studying pairs of data. Locating and marking a *point* on a graph corresponding to a pair of data is called *plotting* the data. The point is represented by a dot. This *plot* shows a student's SAT scores of 480 on the verbal part and 540 on the math part. The verbal score is located using the *horizontal* scale, and the math score is located using the *vertical* scale.

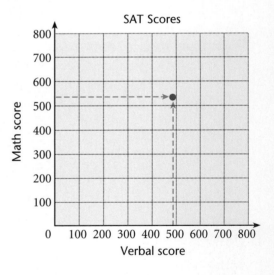

CONSIDER

?

1. In the above graph, why isn't the point representing the pair of scores at the intersection of two grid lines?

EXPLORE: IF THE SHOE FITS . . .

MATERIALS

Tape measure
Graph paper

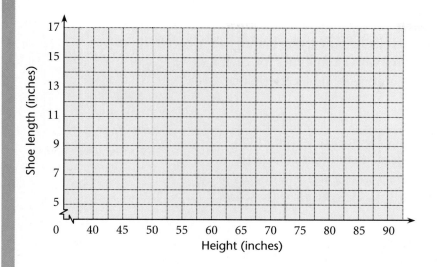

1. Measure and record each student's height and the length of one of his shoes.
2. Copy the grid shown above on graph paper. Plot each student's shoe length and height.
3. Does there seem to be a relationship between shoe length and height? If so, describe it in your own words.
4. Circle all points that do not seem to fit this relationship. Identify the pairs of data that these points represent. Describe how these pairs of data differ from the other pairs.
5. Suppose you found a shoe 14 in. long. How tall do you think the owner of the shoe is? Is she more likely to be shorter or taller than 60 inches? Explain how you decided.

The graph you drew in the Explore is called a **scatter plot.**

A graph showing a set of points, each based on a *pair of data,* is called a **scatter plot.**

Scatter plots help you to notice associations between data.

1. Ms. Waldman gave her American History class a midterm exam last week. She asked each student how long each had studied. She paired test scores with study times for each student and made this scatter plot.

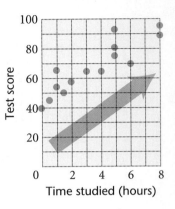

A scatter plot often shows that two quantities are related. In this graph, *more* hours of study are associated with *higher* scores, and *fewer* hours of study are associated with *lower* scores.

When two quantities increase or decrease together, there is a **positive association** of the data.

2. Ms. Waldman also looked at the number of unexcused absences for each student. Describe any relationship between the quantities shown in the graph.

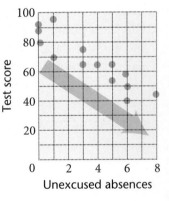

Higher numbers of unexcused absences are associated with *lower* scores.

When one quantity decreases as the other increases, there is a **negative association** of the data.

3. Ms. Waldman also examined whether students' extracurricular activities, such as clubs and sports, were related to their test scores. Describe any relationship between the quantities shown in the graph.

Extra curricular activities and test scores appear to be unrelated.

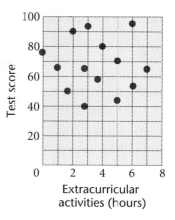

When two quantities are unrelated, there is **no association** of the data, and the quantities are **independent**.

TRY IT

Explain whether you would expect a positive association, a negative association, or no association between the following sets of data.
a. the sizes of countries and their populations
b. the distances of stars from Earth and the amount of light we see from them
c. the lengths and weights of newborn infants

CONSIDER

2. Does positive association mean that for any two points on a scatter plot, the point farther right must also be farther up?

REFLECT

1. How can a scatter plot help you to see if there is an association between two quantities or categories of data?
2. Give an example from your life of two quantities that have a negative association.
3. If you graph a set of data and then switch the quantities you plotted horizontally with the quantities you plotted vertically, what effect would this have on the graph?

Exercises

CORE

1. Getting Started
   a. As Quantity 1 increases, what seems to happen to Quantity 2?
   b. Is the association between the quantities positive or negative, or is there no association?
   c. Which point does not seem to fit?

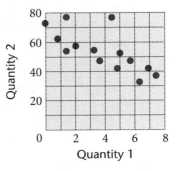

2. Use the list at the right to complete these sentences.
   a. A graph showing a set of points, each based on a pair of data, is called a _____.
   b. When two quantities increase or decrease together, we say there is a _____ of the data.
   c. When one quantity increases as the other decreases, we say there is a _____ of the data.
   d. When two quantities seem to be unrelated, we say that there is _____ or that they are independent.

   i. negative association
   ii. no association
   iii. positive association
   iv. scatter plot

Write the type of association for each scatter plot.

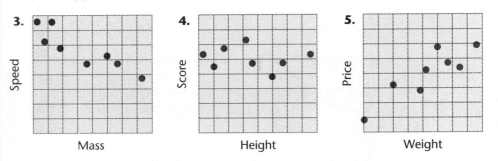

3. Speed / Mass

4. Score / Height

5. Price / Weight

Explain whether you would expect a positive association, a negative association, or no association between each set of data.

   6. temperatures of cups of tea and the time that has passed since they were poured

   7. driving time and distance traveled

   8. a person's age and the remaining number of years that person expects to live

   9. the amount of money a newspaper carrier earns and the weight of the newspaper

   10. the amount of rain in a day and the average temperature

11. "The bigger they are, the harder they fall" is a common expression. What would this look like on a scatter plot?

12. Vital Statistics These were the birth rates and death rates (per 1000 population) for the regions of the United States in 1992.
a. Plot them using the scale shown, and determine the type of association.
b. What real-world factors might explain your answer?

Birth and Death Rates

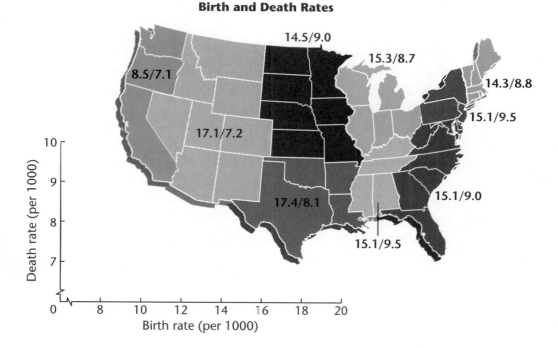

13. This is the graph of Example 1. The dotted line that approximates the graph is called a **trend line.** We use a dotted line to emphasize that not every pair of data from the original set is on the line itself and vice versa—not every point on the line is part of the original set of data.

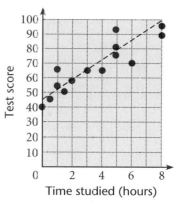

a. How many points are above the trend line? below it? on it?
b. Use the trend line to estimate a student's score on the test if she studied six hours the night before.
c. Describe how the trend line would look for the scatter plot in Example 2.
d. Is it possible to draw a trend line for Example 3? Explain your answer.

14. Where There's Smoke . . . Many studies link cigarette smoking with various diseases. Draw a scatter plot based on the following data from a study.

- **a.** Is there a positive or negative association or no association between the data?
- **b.** Write a sentence that gives your conclusion about the relationship between the two columns of data for those who were studied.
- **c.** Does this set of data suggest any association between smoking and age at death?

Daily Average Number of Cigarettes Smoked	Age at Death	Daily Average Number of Cigarettes Smoked	Age at Death
12	75	38	62
15	72	42	61
22	69	46	58
30	66	55	56
35	64	60	51

15. Weight Up! The following chart appeared over the free-weights at one national sporting goods store in January 1994.

- **a.** Plot as many ordered pairs (weight, price) as you need to see a pattern.
- **b.** Make a conjecture about the relationship between price and weight.
- **c.** Is there one thing you would change to fit the conjecture? What is it?

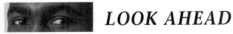

Weight	3 lb	5 lb	8 lb	10 lb	12 lb	15 lb	20 lb	25 lb	30 lb	35 lb	40 lb	45 lb
Price	1.79	2.95	4.72	5.90	7.08	8.85	11.80	14.75	19.00	20.65	23.60	26.55

LOOK AHEAD

Write each as a percentage.

16. $\frac{3}{5}$ **17.** 0.45   **18.** $2\frac{1}{2}$ **19.** $\frac{7}{10}$ **20.** 0.8   **21.** 0.005

MORE PRACTICE

Write the type of association for each scatter plot.

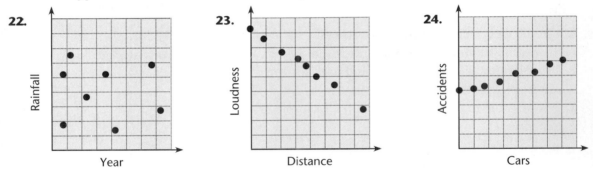

22. Rainfall vs. Year

23. Loudness vs. Distance

24. Accidents vs. Cars

Explain whether you would expect a positive or a negative association or no association between the following.

25. the pace of a jogger and the steepness of a hill

26. the temperatures of lakes and their depths

27. the amount of pollutants in a river and the number of fish in it

28. the number of children in a family and the weekly food bill

29. people's ages and the number of phone calls they make per day

30. the number of cold days in Florida during the growing season and the cost of orange juice

MORE MATH REASONING

31. Outreach Do people's arms get longer as they get taller?
a. Measure the height of 10 people, and then measure their arm span (fingertip to fingertip with arms out at shoulder height).
b. Make a scatter plot of the data pairs, and describe the association.
c. Does it matter whether height is plotted horizontally and arm span vertically or vice versa? Explain.
d. Would it matter whether you used inches for one measurement and centimeters for the other? Explain.

32. Reaching, Writing, and 'Rithmetic In earlier times, a child who could reach over her head with one arm and touch the opposite ear was considered old enough for school.
a. Tell how you would gather data to find out if this was a reasonable practice.
b. What quantities would be plotted on the graph?
c. What would you expect the graph to look like?
d. What assumptions were being made about a child's readiness for school?

33. Fits Like a Glove To see if some socks on sale in a department store would fit his son Jaime, Mr. Gutierrez asked Jaime to make a fist and then wrapped the sock around it heel to toe. Describe how you would collect data to see if measuring fists is a good way to measure feet.

34. Rachel says that number pairs in which the second number is half the first number must have a negative association because the second number is less than the first number. What do you think? Explain your answer with a scatter plot.

1-2 PART B Graphing Data on a Coordinate Plane

← CONNECT → ***You have seen that the relationship between pairs of data can be viewed by making a scatter plot. Now you will look at pairs of numbers that have a predictable relationship, and you will see that relationships may hold even when negative numbers are involved.***

A sequence of diagrams can be the source of a predictable numerical pattern. In the following Explore, you will look at a geometric pattern.

EXPLORE: MAY I HAVE YOUR AUTO GRAPH?

MATERIALS

Graph paper

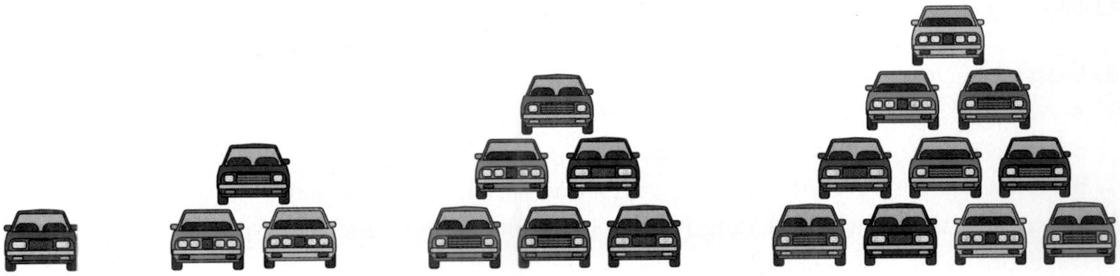

1. Copy the table below. Use the patterns you see above to complete it. Describe the numerical patterns you see in the table.

Cars on bottom row	1	2	3	4	5	6
Total cars	1					

2. Make a scatter plot of the data in your table. Plot the number of cars on the bottom row on the horizontal scale (the *term*) and the total number of cars on the vertical scale (the *value*). Describe what the graph looks like.

3. Use the graph to determine how many cars fit the pattern when there are 12 cars along the bottom row. Explain how the graph helped you decide.

So far, you've looked at positive data, but in many situations, quantities can have any real-number values. To represent the values for these quantities in a graph, we need a system for plotting pairs of data with both positive *and negative* values.

A bank sign flashed the temperature in Duluth, Minnesota. A driver passed the sign four times that day. Certainly the temperature was falling. What is the relationship between the Fahrenheit temperature and the Celsius temperature?

First, we can organize the ordered pairs in a **data table.**

We can plot these pairs of data in a manner similar to those in Part A and see that there does appear to be a pattern.

°F	°C
35	2
26	-3
11	-12
-4	-20

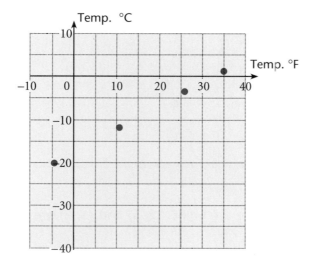

The system used in mathematics for graphing number pairs is called the **Cartesian coordinate system.** It is named after the French mathematician René Descartes (1596–1650).

The two **axes** of this system are **perpendicular** (form right angles) and divide the **coordinate plane** into four **quadrants,** labeled counterclockwise I, II, III, and IV.

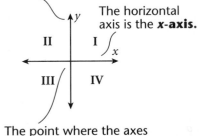

The vertical axis is the **y-axis.**

The horizontal axis is the **x-axis.**

The point where the axes intersect is the **origin.**

Every point in the plane can be described by an **ordered pair** of values—the **coordinates** of the point. The first value is the **x-coordinate,** and the second is the **y-coordinate.**

A is 3 units to the right and 4.5 units up from the origin. The coordinates of A are (3, 4.5)

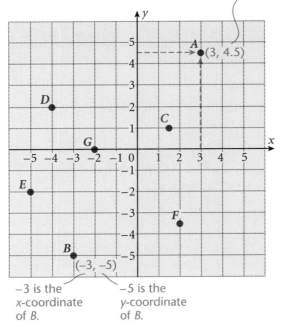

−3 is the x-coordinate of B.

−5 is the y-coordinate of B.

CONSIDER

?

1. **Explain how the points (2, 5) and (5, 2) are different.**

From the coordinate system on page 48, give the coordinates of each of these points, and name the quadrant in which it is located.
a. C **b.** D **c.** E **d.** F **e.** G
f. What are the coordinates of the origin?

REFLECT

1. Compare the seats in a theater to points in a coordinate plane. Explain how they are similar and how they are different.
2. Explain how you would decide which is the correct quadrant in which to plot an ordered pair.
3. How could a ship report its position using a coordinate system? In what other ways do we use coordinate systems in the real world?
4. Think of a situation in which you might plot points. Draw a grid and label the axes. Plot a reasonable point and label the ordered pair.

Exercises

CORE

1. Getting Started
   a. Draw coordinate axes.
   b. Begin at the origin. Move 4 units to the left and 3 units up to plot the point $(-4, 3)$.
   c. Move 5 units down to plot the point $(-4, -2)$.

2. Determine whether the statement is true or false. In quadrant IV, both the x- and y-coordinates are negative.

3. Match the term with the phrase that best describes it.
   a. intersecting lines that form right angles
   b. system used in math for graphing pairs of numbers
   c. horizontal axis
   d. vertical axis
   e. four regions formed by axes
   f. point of intersection of axes
   g. ordered pairs of numbers assigned to a point
   h. table used to organize coordinates

   i. coordinates
   ii. coordinate plane
   iii. origin
   iv. perpendicular
   v. quadrants
   vi. data table
   vii. x-axis
   viii. y-axis

4. The coordinates of P are $(2, -3)$.
   a. What is P's x-coordinate?   **b.** What is P's y-coordinate?
   c. In which quadrant is P?

Give the coordinates of each point in the coordinate plane, and name the quadrant in which it is located.

5. A **6.** B **7.** C **8.** D **9.** H **10.** F

Give the number of the quadrant in which each point lies.

11. $(0.1, 5)$

12. $(-1, -501)$

13. $(1.00, -1.05)$

14. $(-1,000, 0.005)$

15. $(-5,000,000, -1,000,000)$

16. $(5.5555, -0.0001)$

17. What line goes through the points $(-2, 0)$ and $(5, 0)$?

18. Write five ordered pairs of points in which the x- and y-coordinates are equal. Plot them on a coordinate grid. Describe the graph in your own words.

19. Make a data table to represent the points shown in the graph at the right.

20. Draw a coordinate plane. Plot and label these points.

  a. $A(2, 4)$ **b.** $B(-2, 5)$ **c.** $C(3, 0)$

  d. $D(0, 3)$ **e.** $E(-4, 2)$ **f.** $F(2, -4)$

  g. $G\left(1\frac{1}{2}, 3\right)$ **h.** $H(-1.5, 3.5)$ **i.** $I\left(-\frac{1}{2}, 1\frac{1}{2}\right)$

Draw a scatter plot, and write a sentence about the association of the number pairs in each table.

21.

x	y
1	2
2	5
3	8
4	11
5	14

22.

x	y
1	3
1	2
2	4
4	5
5	12

23.

x	y
-2	4
-1	3
0	1
1	-2
2	-4

24. Yeast Beast Clare's science class examined the yeast cell population in a culture over a 10-day period, generating the following data.

Day	0	1	2	3	4	5	6	7	8	9	10
Number of yeast cells	20	28	40	55	63	70	72	70	62	50	30

  a. Make a graph comparing the *change* in the number of cells from the previous day and the day number.

  b. Predict the number of yeast cells for Day 11. Predict the number for Day 12.

Problem-Solving Tip

Make an organized list of the changes in the numbers of cells.

 **LOOK BACK**

The matrices A and B are given. [1-1]
25. Find $A + B$.   **26.** Find $A - B$.   **27.** Find $3A$.

$$A = \begin{bmatrix} -1 & \dfrac{1}{2} \\ 14.6 & -15 \end{bmatrix} \qquad B = \begin{bmatrix} -3 & 1\dfrac{1}{4} \\ -10.1 & 2.5 \end{bmatrix}$$

28. If 1 in. on a map represents 100 miles, what distance is represented by $7\frac{1}{2}$ in.? [Previous course]

29. If 1 cm on a map represents 2.5 km, what distance is represented by 14 cm? [Previous course]

What is the next number in the pattern? [Previous course; 1-1]

30. 0, 10, 210, _____   **31.** 9, 5, 1, _____   **32.** 8, 4, 2, 1, _____

MORE PRACTICE

Copy the graph shown. For each point below, name the point if it is on the graph. If not, plot the point.

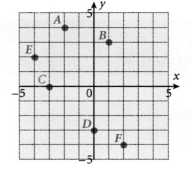

33. $(1, 3)$ **34.** $(-2, 4)$ **35.** $(0, -3)$

36. $(4, -2)$ **37.** $(-4, -3)$

Draw a coordinate plane. Remember to label the axes. Plot and label these points.

38. $M(1, 1)$ **39.** $N(3, -2)$ **40.** $R(-4.5, -2.5)$

41. $S\left(0, \dfrac{1}{2}\right)$ **42.** $T(-1, 6)$ **43.** $U(7, 0)$

Give the number of the quadrant in which each point lies.

44. $(7, 2)$ **45.** $(3, -20)$ **46.** $(-0.01, -0.01)$

47. $(-120, 256)$ **48.** $(25,000, -1,000)$ **49.** $\left(-\dfrac{2}{3}, \dfrac{1}{15}\right)$

MORE MATH REASONING

50. For each table draw a scatter plot and write a sentence about the association of the number pairs in that table.

x	y
0	0
2	-1
4	-2
6	-3
8	-4

x	y
0	0
1	1
2	4
3	9
4	16

x	y
0	0
1	-1
4	-2
9	-3
16	-4

51. The coordinates of a point add up to 0. Is the point always, sometimes, or never in quadrant IV? Explain with some examples.

52. The x-coordinate of point P is negative. Is P always, sometimes, or never in quadrant II? Explain with some examples.

53. The table shows the relationship between education and average income. Decide whether the data show a positive or negative association or no association.

Years of Education	Average Income
Less than 8	$16,000
8 years	18,000
1–3 years of high school	21,000
4 years of high school	29,000
1–3 years of college	35,000
4 years of college	42,000
More than 4 years of college	51,000

54. Explain how you would graph a triangle on the coordinate plane so that the origin is inside the triangle.

1-2 PART C Making Connections

← **CONNECT** → *You've seen how to graph and find associations in pairs of data. Finding associations helps us to connect quantities and categories of data that occur in the real world.*

To locate places on earth, we use a system of latitude and longitude.

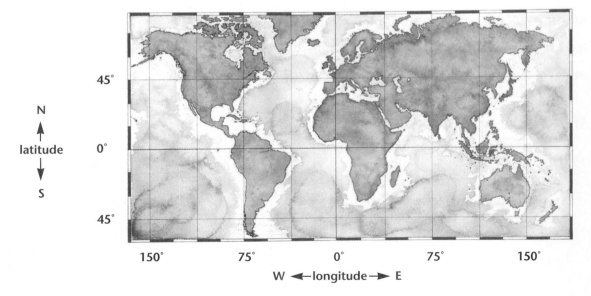

EXPLORE: LATITUDE ATTITUDE

Use an almanac or reference book to find the latitudes of some of the world's major cities. Use the cities below, your city, *and at least 10 others.* You may round to the nearest degree. (Since there are 60 minutes in 1°, 45° 29′ rounds down to 45°, and 45° 30′ rounds up to 46°.)

MATERIALS

World almanac
Current newspaper
Graph paper

Ho Chi Minh City, Vietnam	Latitude 11° N
Sydney, Australia	Latitude 34° S
Moscow, Russia	Latitude 55° N

In a current newspaper, find yesterday's low temperature for each city.

Set up a coordinate plane with latitude on the x-axis and temperature on the y-axis. (Consider south latitudes as negative. For example, for 20° S, use −20.)

Make a scatter plot of the latitudes and temperatures. What kind of association is there between latitude and low temperature?

Recognizing relationships in data is an important skill that can help you make predictions and decisions. Graphing data on a coordinate plane is a powerful technique for recognizing these relationships.

REFLECT

1. Explain how to plot an ordered pair when the x-coordinate is negative and the y-coordinate is positive. What would you do differently if the signs of each were reversed?
2. How do you know whether there is an association between two sets of data?
3. Was the goal in the draft lottery to have positive association, negative association, or no association between birthdates and lottery numbers? Why?

Self-Assessment

Explain whether you would expect a positive association, negative association, or no association between the following sets of data.

1. heights of students and the number of letters in their last names

2. the amount of time a car is parked in a garage and the amount of money the owner will pay

3. the height of a TV antenna and the number of stations the television gets clearly

For Exercises 4 and 5, draw a set of axes. Label them with descriptions and numbers.

4. Students were surveyed for their ages and heights.

5. Adults were surveyed to find out the number of years they had been driving and the number of accidents they had last year.

6. Choose the letter of the answer that best completes the following sentence. On the coordinate plane, the point (−20, 16) is
   (a) 20 units down and 16 units left of the origin
   (b) 16 units down and 20 units left of the origin
   (c) 20 units up and 16 units left of the origin
   (d) 16 units up and 20 units left of the origin
   (e) not here

7. **Big Picture or Home Alone?** Do older people tend to go to more movies than younger people or do younger people tend to go to more movies than older people? In one survey, people were asked how many times they went to the movies last year. The chart below shows the results.
   a. Draw a scatter plot for the chart.
   b. Is it possible to draw a trend line?
   c. Explain whether or not the data in this survey support the claim that older people tend to go to the movies more often than younger people.

The Chicago Theater

Age	13	15	12	13	17	19	22	18	14	16	12	15	18	21	23
Movies	26	22	25	27	21	18	15	17	29	21	25	20	16	15	12

8. That's Not So Cold

a. Make a scatter plot for the low extreme temperatures for the following cities. (Consider south latitudes as negative.)

b. At what latitudes would you expect the low extreme temperature to be zero?

City	Latitude	Low Extreme Temperature
Bogotá, Colombia	5° N	30°F
Toronto, Canada	44° N	−26°F
Manila, Philippines	15° N	58°F
Sydney, Australia	34° S	35°F
Berlin, Germany	52° N	−15°F
Buenos Aires, Argentina	35° S	22°F

9. Whatever Became of...

A teacher had a third-grade class that he kept in touch with for many years. Twenty-five years after he taught this class, he held a class reunion. A survey was taken to compare how many years of education each student had and how much money each earned last year. The results of the survey are summarized in the scatter plot.

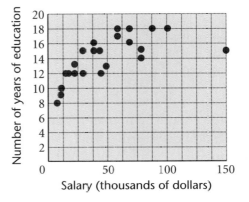

a. How many in the survey had 12 years of education?

b. How many had fewer than 12 years of education?

c. How many were earning about $60,000 per year?

d. How many students were included in the survey?

e. What was the highest salary earned?

f. What was the lowest salary earned?

g. Write a sentence describing the association that you notice.

h. One of the dots in the scatter plot seems to be far away from the others. A point like this is known as an *outlier*. Give the information about salary and education for this outlier.

10.
Which word pair is the best match for the first word pair?
x-axis is to *y*-axis as: (a) horizontal is to vertical, (b) vertical is to horizontal

11.
Finish this sentence so that it describes a positive association.
"The farther I am from home..."

12. This graph shows the net profits for a company over a four-year period.

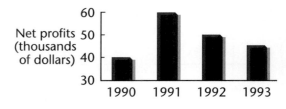

a. Are the net profits for 1992 twice the net profits of 1990? Explain how you know.

b. In what year were net profits $\frac{2}{3}$ of net profits for 1991?

c. How much are the net profits for all four years combined?

13. Hits & Runs Here are the hits and runs from five National League baseball games played on the same day. On the basis of these data, if a pitcher allowed 11 hits, how many runs could the other team expect to score? Explain how you got your answer.

Hits	7	12	18	8	7	5	8	4	9	13
Runs	2	7	12	3	5	3	4	0	5	7

14. Find the mean number of runs in the table in Exercise 13.

15. A point is not located in any of the four quadrants. What is the product of its *x*-coordinate and its *y*-coordinate?

16. At a large corporation, some employees were concerned about annual vacation time. The human resources department did a random check of vacation days earned for 12 employees. Scatter plot 1 shows the number of vacation days compared to salary. Scatter plot 2 shows the number of vacation days compared to the number of years worked.

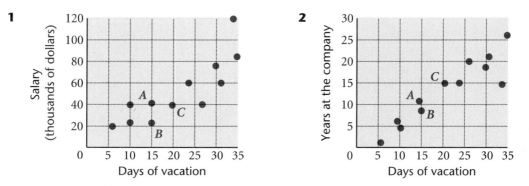

a. Does the company seem to pay more attention to a worker's salary or to a worker's length of service when allotting vacation days?

b. Draw a trend line for each set of data. Is it reasonable to compare the lines to each other? Why or why not?

c. *A*, *B*, and *C* represent the same workers on each graph. Which of them has the greatest cause to complain about vacation time? Explain your answer.

RED *flowers* & BLACK *cats*

Did you know that a pair of gray cats can have a litter of kittens in which one is black? Did you know that two plants with pink flowers can be cross-bred to produce a plant with red flowers?

Colors and other physical traits are passed on from parents to offspring through the parents' genes. The actual traits that will appear in offspring can't be predicted. But probability theory can help us decide how likely it is that a trait will appear.

For example, pink snapdragons carry genes for both red and white flowers. If you cross two pink snapdragons, it's likely that only half the offspring will be pink snapdragons. Of the rest, we would expect half to be red and half to be white.

Many of the first experiments into these exciting ideas were carried out by the monk and botanist Gregor Mendel in the 1870s. His painstaking studies of genetics opened up a whole new field relating mathematics and biology.

THE OFFSPRING OF
TWO PINK SNAPDRAGONS

RED PINK
PINK WHITE

?

1. When two pink snapdragons are crossed, is it more likely that the offspring will be pink or not pink?
2. Of 12 offspring plants from a crossing of two pink snapdragons, how many would you expect to be red?
3. We could say that we expect 25% white snapdragons from a crossing of pink snapdragons. What percentage of yellow snapdragons would you expect?
4. What percentage of the offspring of two pink snapdragons would you expect won't be yellow?

← **C O N N E C T** →   *Probability describes the chance that an uncertain event will occur. You've examined patterns and relationships that occur in data. Now you will use data to gain insight into probabilities.*

Suppose a couple is planning to have two children. How *likely* are they to have two girls? two boys? a girl and a boy? In the eighteenth century, there were two theories that claimed to have the answers.

One theory claimed that, of all two-child families, *half* would have children of the same sex and *half* would have children of different sexes.

The second theory claimed that a *third* of these families would have two girls, a *third* would have two boys, and a *third* would have a girl and a boy.

To investigate these theories, the French mathematician Jean Le Rond d'Alembert (1717–1783) gathered a great deal of data on families with two children. In the following Explore, you will make a similar investigation.

EXPLORE: YOU'RE KIDDING

1. Think of families you know with two children. How many of these families have two girls? How many have two boys? How many have a girl and a boy? Copy and complete the following table of data. Be sure you count each family only once.

	Number of families	Percentage of total	Ratio of number to total
2 girls			
2 boys			
1 girl and 1 boy			
Total			

2. Compare your results with those of your classmates. Do you think these results support either of the theories d'Alembert investigated? Do you have a different theory? Explain.

3. Suppose a couple is planning to have two children. In your own words, describe how *likely* they are to have

a. two girls　　　　　**b.** two boys　　　　　**c.** a girl and a boy

The **probability** of an event, such as a family having two girls, is the *portion* of time the event is expected to occur. The portion can be expressed as a ratio, a fraction, a decimal, or a percentage.

EXAMPLE

A tack is tossed 100 times. It lands on its side 81 times and on its back the rest of the times. Based on this experiment, what is the probability that the tack will land on its side? on its back?

The probability that the tack will land on its side is the ratio $\frac{81}{100} = 0.81 = 81\%$.

The probability the tack will land on its back is the ratio $\frac{19}{100} = 0.19 = 19\%$.

1. What is the probability that the tack in the example will land on its back or side?

The probability of an event is a number from 0 to 1. An event that has no chance of occurring has a probability of 0. An event that is certain to occur has a probability of 1.

Probability

0	0.25	0.5	0.75	1
Virtually impossible	Unlikely	Equally likely as unlikely	Likely	Virtually certain

Probabilities found by collecting data or running an experiment, like those in the preceding Explore and the example, are called **experimental probabilities**.

a. In order to test for defects, a tennis-ball manufacturer checks out 300 tennis balls at random. Five defective balls are found. On the basis of this experiment, find the probability that a ball will be defective. Express your answer as a fraction, a decimal, and a percentage.

Whether a probability comes from a theory or an experiment, it gives a numerical value describing the *chance* or *likelihood* that an event will occur.

REFLECT

1. What is the probability that the next baby born anywhere will be a girl?
2. Name some events that have probability 0.
3. Name some events that have probability 1.
4. Choose a probability that you think reasonably describes each term or phrase.
  a. doubtful   **b.** sure   **c.** 50–50
  d. probable   **e.** extremely unlikely   **f.** not possible

Exercises

CORE

1. Getting Started Explain which of these numbers can be used to express a probability.

a. $\frac{1}{2}$ **b.** $\frac{5}{7}$ **c.** $-\frac{5}{7}$ **d.** 100%

e. 3   **f.** $\frac{5}{5}$ **g.** 0   **h.** 1

i. 50%   **j.** $\frac{7}{5}$ **k.** 150%   **l.** 0.01%

2. Arrange these probabilities from least to greatest.

$\frac{2}{3}$ $\frac{9}{12}$ 0   70%   0.68 $\frac{7}{7}$ 0.95%

3. A coin is tossed 50 times and it comes up heads 31 times. Based on this experiment, what is the probability that the coin will land heads up? tails up? What is the probability that it will land on either heads or tails?

4. Draw a Dozen Wanda takes a dozen gumdrops from the candy tin without looking to choose a particular type. She gets four lime-flavored pieces. Based on this experiment, if she takes one more piece, what is the probability that it will be lime?

5. **A Rose Is a Rose Is a Yellow Rose** Cliff and Elaine are conducting an experiment as part of their science project. Of the 25 people they ask, 13 prefer the yellow rose over the red, pink, or coral variety shown in their pictures. Based on their findings, what is the probability that someone will not choose the picture of the yellow rose?

6. **The Right One** Leon asks 20 classmates to draw any triangle. Sixteen of them draw right triangles. Use probability, and give two different ways that Leon could report the findings of his experiment.

7. **No Winner!** One mail-in sweepstakes illegally threw out all entries that did not include a magazine subscription. What was the probability of winning if you did not include a magazine subscription?

8. **Baseball Probabilities** In baseball, batting averages are reported for every hitter. Pat is batting 0.250.
   a. Explain how Pat is batting in terms of experimental probability.
   b. How many hits would you expect Pat to have in 24 times at bat?

9. Choose one of the following to describe the probability for each event.
   i. 0   **ii.** between 0 and 0.5   **iii.** between 0.5 and 1   **iv.** 1
   a. choosing the one blueberry muffin from a bag of 12 assorted muffins without looking
   b. having school tomorrow
   c. a pearl diver finding a pearl in a particular oyster
   d. two zebras having identical stripes
   e. jumping 35 ft on flat ground
   f. when the TV is turned on, a commercial will be on
   g. a random spot on the earth will be covered with water

10. **On the Road Again** Suppose your family is leaving for a long car trip.
    a. What happens to the probability that you will return home for something as you get farther from home?
    b. What happens to the probability that you will *not* return home for something as you get farther from home?
    c. Skip says, "We'll either return home, or we won't." What is the probability that one of these things will happen? Explain.

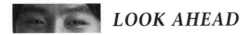 *LOOK AHEAD*

11. Ignoring the edge, what fraction of the checkerboard is black? How did you decide?

12. What is the area of a square that measures $\frac{1}{2}$ in. on a side?

MORE PRACTICE

13. Which of these numbers can be used to express a probability?

    a. $\dfrac{5}{4}$ **b.** 0.000012   **c.** 0.142857   **d.** -1 **e.** 99.9%

Write each fraction or ratio as both a percentage and a decimal.

14. $\dfrac{5}{16}$ **15.** 12 out of 17   **16.** 5 heads in 12 tosses

17. A coin is tossed 100 times and lands heads up 76 times. Based on this experiment, what is the probability that the coin will land heads up? tails up? What is the probability that it will come up either heads or tails?

18. Button Button Ronnette takes a handful of buttons from a bag. Of the 18 buttons, 3 have two holes. Express the probability of withdrawing a two-holed button from the bag as a fraction and as a percentage.

19. What is the probability of an event that cannot occur? that must occur?

20. What is the probability of an event that has an equal chance of occurring or not occurring? Explain.

MORE MATH REASONING

21. If you flipped a coin 100,000 times, how many times would you expect it to land on its edge? Explain.

22. During archery practice, Judy uses two different targets. One has a bull's eye that is 3 inches in diameter, and the other bull's eye is 6 inches in diameter. If she shoots with the same skill from the same distance, is she twice as likely to hit a bull's eye on the second target? Justify your answer.

23. What's the Difference? Statisticians used a computerized data base to predict the likelihood that a person would win a personal injury case and the amount of money the jury would award. Do you think the awards are fair? Explain why or why not.

Case 1: An 18-year-old man suffers a severe injury by diving into a partially filled swimming pool.

    Probability of winning: 55%   *Award:* $3,369,251

Case 2: A 60-year-old man suffers a severe injury in the same kind of swimming-pool accident.

    Probability of winning: 55%   *Award:* $2,817,885

← **CONNECT** → *You've seen how data from experiments can give you an understanding of probability. Now you will examine the theory of probability.*

If you toss a coin 100 times and it comes up heads 47 times, the experimental probability of heads is $\frac{47}{100} = 0.47$. If the coin is *fair*, heads and tails should be *equally likely*, each with a **theoretical probability** of $\frac{1}{2} = 0.5$.

> An **outcome** is any possible result of an experiment or activity. The set of all possible outcomes is the **sample space** of the experiment or activity. A set of outcomes is an **event.**

For families with two children, the four equally likely *outcomes* are GG, GB, BB, and BG, where G represents a girl, and B represents a boy. The *sample space* can be written as follows.

$$\{GG, GB, BB, BG\}$$

For two-child families, the *event* that both children are the same sex is the set of outcomes

$$\{GG, BB\}.$$

This event contains half the outcomes, so we would expect it to happen half the time.

> If all outcomes are equally likely, the **probability** of an event, indicated by $P(\text{event})$, is
>
> $$P(\text{event}) = \frac{\text{number of outcomes in the event}}{\text{number of outcomes in the sample space}}$$

The probability of there being two children of the same sex in a two-child family is

$$P(\text{same sex}) = \frac{2}{4} = \frac{1}{2} = 0.5.$$

a. If each of five outcomes has an equal chance of occurring, what is the probability of any outcome occurring?

b. A CD player is set for random play. If there are 16 tracks on a CD, what is the probability that your favorite song will play first?

EXAMPLE

1. A total of 1250 raffle tickets for a quilt were sold at $1 each. Harlan bought one ticket. Guillan bought the most tickets, 50. One winning ticket will be selected at random. What is the probability that Harlan will win the quilt? What is the probability that Guillan will win? What is the probability that neither Harlan nor Guillan will win?

Outcomes: Ticket #1 wins, ticket #2 wins, . . . , ticket #1250 wins.

Sample Space: The set of 1250 equally likely outcomes, one for each ticket sold.

Harlan bought one ticket, so
P(Harlan wins) $= \frac{1}{1250} = 0.0008$.

Guillan bought 50 tickets, so
P(Guillan wins) $= \frac{50}{1250} = \frac{1}{25} = 0.04$.

Neither Harlan nor Guillan will win if any of the other 1199 tickets sold is chosen.

P(neither Guillan nor Harlan wins) $= \frac{1199}{1250} = 0.9592$

CONSIDER

1. What is the sum of the probabilities of the three events considered in Example 1? Why do you think the probabilities add to this number?

You will now investigate the probability of finding the correct order for an arrangement of trays of photographic chemical solutions.

EXPLORE: DARKROOM MIX-UP

Suppose you are developing a black-and-white print. You must place the exposed print paper in three different chemical solutions in the correct order before the print is ready for washing. The order is developer (D), stop bath (S), and then fixer (F). Someone has mixed up the order of the trays containing the solutions. What is the probability that you can put the trays in correct order on your first try?

1. Suppose you arrange the three trays in a random order. List the possible outcomes. How many outcomes are there? What is the probability that you'll find the correct order on your first try?
2. Suppose you also have a wash (W) tray. Someone has mixed up the D, S, F, and W trays. You must arrange them in correct order. How many outcomes are there? What is the probability that you'll find the correct order on your first try?
3. Examine your answers. Can you see a way to calculate the number of outcomes when arranging any number of trays?

You may have noticed in the Explore that when outcomes have parts, like ingredients, you can multiply the number of choices for each part to find the total number of outcomes. This is called the **counting principle.**

EXAMPLE

2. Alyce has two shirts, two skirts, and three sweaters that match. How many outfits of a shirt, skirt, and sweater can she make?

Using the counting principle, she can make 2 • 2 • 3 = 12 outfits. You can also draw a *tree diagram* to see Alyce's choices.

3. There are nine justices of the Supreme Court. An official portrait of the justices is taken each year. How many different ways could the justices line up for the portrait?

Any of the nine justices could be at the far left. Any of the eight remaining justices could be next, and so on. Using the counting principle, the number of ways they can line up is expressed as follows.

$9 \cdot 8 \cdot 7 \cdot 6 \cdot 5 \cdot 4 \cdot 3 \cdot 2 \cdot 1 = 362,880$

This number is called 9 **factorial** and is written **9!**.

c. If Alyce buys a new skirt and new sweater, she'll have two shirts, three skirts, and four sweaters. How many different outfits can she make now?

d. How many students are in your algebra class? If you all line up across the front of the class, how many different arrangements of students are possible?

The counting principle gives you a quick way to find the number of outcomes in a sample space or event. This makes it easier to find theoretical probabilities.

Understanding experimental and theoretical probabilities is vital for meteorologists, insurance companies, stockbrokers, and anyone who must deal with uncertainty.

1. What is meant by a *fair* coin?

2. What is the difference between experimental probability and theoretical probability?

3. What is the difference between an outcome and an event? an event and a sample space?

4. How does the number of outcomes relate to the probability of an outcome?

Exercises

CORE

1. **Getting Started** William has two vests, five shirts, and three pairs of pants. All are clean and all match. How many different outfits of a vest, shirt, and pants can he make?

2. Use the list at the right to complete these sentences.
   a. A(n) _____ is any possible result of an experiment or of an activity.
   b. The collection of all possible outcomes of an experiment is called the _____.
   c. A(n) _____ is a set of outcomes that matches the type of information that we want to know.
   d. _____ assigns a number to an event. The number measures the event's chance of happening.
   e. When you collect data or run an experiment, you generate _____.

   i. event
   ii. experimental probability
   iii. outcome
   iv. probability
   v. sample space

3. Scientific calculators usually have a key marked $\boxed{x!}$.
   a. Calculate 7!.
   b. Use a calculator to find 12!.
   c. What is the largest factorial your calculator can find?

4. If there are 5 equally likely outcomes in an event and 13 equally likely outcomes in the sample space, what is the probability of the event?

5. Roger finds that 9! = 362,880. Explain how he could use this to calculate 10!.

6. **Musical Medals** Erica has won five medals in the state musical festivals for her clarinet playing. Her mom is arranging them in a line on the den wall. How many different arrangements are possible? Explain your answer.

7. Sven has three sweaters. Two are gray, and one is green. Consider the probable color of the sweater he will choose to wear.
   a. What are the possible outcomes? What is the sample space?
   b. What is the probability that he will wear the green sweater?
   c. What is the probability that he will wear a gray sweater?
   d. What is the probability that the sweater will be red?

8. **Who's Fourth?** At the student body assembly honoring author and Nobel Prize winner Toni Morrison, four different students will read excerpts from her writings. How many different arrangements of these students are possible if each goes to the microphone only once?

Literature

> **Problem-Solving Tip**
>
> Make an organized list.

9. **Draft Lottery** In the 1972 draft lottery, each birthday had an equal chance of being chosen. Every 18-year-old man with a lottery number of 1 to 100 had to report for a physical examination.

a. What was the probability that one of these men had his number drawn and thus had to report?

b. The birthday March 13 had draft lottery number 271. What was the probability of someone with this birthday having to report?

10. **Does It Pay to Guess?** Mr. Mundan gives only multiple-choice tests. Each question has four choices.

a. What is the probability of guessing a correct answer to a question?

b. If a test contains 40 of these questions, how many should Ellen expect to get right if she did not study?

c. Explain whether or not it is possible for Ellen to get a mark of 50% if she just randomly guesses without even reading any of the 40 questions on the test.

11. **Flipping for You** How could you verify by experiment that the probability of getting heads on a flip of a coin is $\frac{1}{2}$?

12. **Carnival** A carnival event consists of trying to throw a dime onto a grid so that it does not touch any of the four border lines.

Center of dime

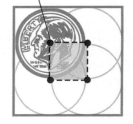

The large grid square is 1 in. by 1 in.

The pink square is $\frac{5}{16}$ in. by $\frac{5}{16}$ in.

a. The center of the coin must land in the pink area of any one square box to win. Why?

b. What is the probability that the coin will be a winner?

13. **Out of Control** In the manufacturing world, *quality-control* experts are hired to check for inferior merchandise. In the Boltnuts plant, a quality-control expert examines 100 bolts at a time to see how many do not meet minimum standards. The following is a list of the number of inferior bolts found in each group of 100 bolts one morning:

3, 7, 2, 1, 4, 4, 5, 2, 7, 4, 8, 1, 15, 3, 2, 1, 0, 4, 4, 0, 2, 4, 6.

a. How many bolts were examined that morning? How many were found to be inferior?

b. Use the above data to estimate the probability that a bolt will not meet the standards.

c. If government standards dictate that no more than 4% of the bolts should be below standards, does this company meet the requirement?

d. If company standards dictate that no more than 3.5% of the bolts should be below standards, does this company meet its requirement?

14. **Variety Is the Spice of Life** Lee Anne has a reversible jacket and three different hats she can wear with her jacket. Is this enough to wear a different hat and jacket combination each day of the week? Explain.

15. **Head of the Class!** A class tried the following experiment. Each student tossed a coin 12 times and recorded the number of times it came up heads. The following are the data from the class:

    5, 6, 6, 4, 6, 7, 6, 5, 9, 6, 7, 6, 6, 5, 4, 5, 6, 6, 3, 7, 8, 6, 8, 5, 4, 6, 6.

    a. Copy and complete the following chart for organizing the data.
    b. Which outcome is most probable?
    c. Find the average number of heads that came up.
    d. Make a conclusion about what to expect when tossing a coin 12 times.

    Use the chart to estimate the probability that in 12 tosses of a coin, you get the following.

    e. three heads   **f.** four heads
    g. five heads   **h.** six heads
    i. six tails

Number of Heads	Frequency
3	
4	
5	
6	
7	
8	
9	

16. **Three Dice** Your mission is to get a good idea about the probability of getting a sum less than 10 when you throw 3 dice.
    a. Explain what you would do to get an *excellent* estimate for this probability.
    b. Explain what you would do to get the *exact* answer to this problem.

LOOK BACK

Use the graph for Exercises 17–22. [1-2]

17. Name a point in the third quadrant.

18. Which point has the coordinates $(0, 0)$? What do we call this point?

19. Which point has the coordinates $(2, -4)$?

20. Is B in the first quadrant? Explain your answer.

21. What percent of the given points are on an axis?

22. What is a name for the system in this graph?

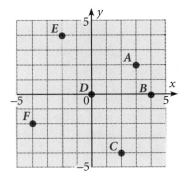

MORE PRACTICE

23. Calculate 5!.

24. Which is greater?

    a. $\frac{2}{3}$ or $\frac{7}{10}$
        b. $\frac{8}{13}$ or $\frac{13}{21}$
        c. $\frac{1}{16}$ or 0.07

    d. 29% or $\frac{2}{7}$
        e. $\frac{1}{2} \times \frac{1}{2} \times \frac{1}{2}$ or 13%

25. A coin is tossed twice. Use H and T to list the possible outcomes.

26. a. What are the equally-likely outcomes of rolling a fair die?
    b. What is the probability that a number less than 5 will turn up on a roll?
    c. What is the probability that the number 5 *won't* turn up on a roll?

27. Selma has 5 pairs of earrings, 2 bracelets, and 3 necklaces. How many different jewelry combinations can Selma make with one pair of earrings, one bracelet, and one necklace?

28. Jim has 6 ties, 5 shirts, and 3 pairs of pants. All are clean and all match. How many different outfits of a shirt, tie, and pants can he make?

29. If an event will occur during the year and is equally likely to occur in any month, what is the probability that it will occur by March 31?

30. A spinner can land on any of the numbers 1 to 6 with equal likelihood.
    a. What are the outcomes?
    b. What is the probability that the spinner will land on 4?

MORE MATH REASONING

31. a. Design an experiment to help you estimate the mean number of heads when seven fair coins are tossed.
    b. Explain how you would get this probability mathematically.
    c. What do you believe is the mean number of heads when seven fair coins are tossed? Explain.

32. I Got a Million of *M* A computer can simulate probabilities using random numbers. Suppose a program is designed to generate alphabetic letters, and calculate the probability that the letter chosen is *M*. When it generated 130 letters, 8 were *M*s. When it generated 1,300,000 letters, 50,219 were *M*s.
    a. What was the experimental probability in each case?
    b. What seems to happen to experimental probability in the long run?

Making Connections

← CONNECT → *Probability gives you a measure of what is likely or not likely to happen. You can collect data or run an experiment to estimate a probability. You can also use outcomes and a sample space to find the theoretical probability. In either case, probability is a useful tool for dealing with uncertainty.*

In the following Explore, you will use probabilities to investigate families with three children.

EXPLORE: THREE-CHILD FAMILIES

MATERIALS

One coin

There are three children in the Petranov family: two girls and one boy.

1. Without doing an experiment or calculation, guess what the probability is of a three-child family having two girls and a boy.

Now you'll find an experimental probability and the theoretical probability and check your guess.

2. Experimental Probability Let one side of a coin represent a girl (G), and the other side a boy (B). You will need to flip the coin three times to represent the children in each family. Simulate data for at least six families, and pool the data from your class or group.

Family	1st child	2nd child	3rd child
1			
2			

Find the experimental probability of a three-child family having two girls and a boy.

3. Theoretical Probability List all possible three-child families, such as GBG representing a girl, then a boy, and then a girl. Find the theoretical probability of a three-child family having two girls and a boy.

4. Write a brief paragraph comparing the ease and accuracy of the experimental and theoretical methods. Explain any significant differences between your guess, the experimental probability, and the theoretical probability.

1. Choose a probability that you think reasonably describes each term or phrase.
   a. probably not   **b.** even chance   **c.** never happen
   d. guaranteed   **e.** iffy   **f.** possible

2. Thinking of it as a ratio, explain why a probability can't be greater than 1.

3. Briefly describe an experiment you could perform to find the probability that a litter of six kittens will consist of three males and three females.

Self-Assessment

1. Arrange these probabilities from least to greatest.

   $\frac{3}{16}$ $\frac{2}{11}$ $\frac{7}{39}$ $\frac{0}{1}$ 1.0   9%   0.1895   0.21%

2. Heather has homework in five different subjects. She likes to finish one assignment before going to the next. How many different ways might she organize the order of her work?
   (a) 5   (b) 15   (c) 20   (d) 120   (e) not here

3. **Alphabet Soup** The 26 letters of the English alphabet are placed in a bag. Josephine closes her eyes, puts her hand in the bag and pulls out a letter.
   a. How many vowels are in the bag? Find the probability that Josephine's letter is a vowel.
   b. How many different letters are in the word *EQUATION*? Find the probability that her letter is in the word *EQUATION*.
   c. How many different letters are in the word *MISSISSIPPI*? Find the probability that her letter is in the word *MISSISSIPPI*.

4. Which is greater, $5 + 4 + 3 + 2 + 1$ or $4!$? Tell how you know.

5. Write the letter of the second pair that best matches the first pair.
   experimental probability: theoretical probability as
   (a) event: outcome   (b) doing: thinking
   (c) pattern: formula   (d) chances: winning

6. **Spinning Wheel** The spinner at the right has four sectors of equal area and one sector twice as large as each of the others.

   Find the probability that a spinner will land in each region.
   a. red   **b.** blue   **c.** not blue   **d.** red or green   **e.** purple

7. An experimental robot will move randomly in any of four directions: left, right, forward, or backward. For the robot's next move,

a. What are the possible outcomes?

b. What is the probability that the robot will go backward?

c. There is a wall directly in front of the robot. What is the probability that the robot will avoid the wall?

8. Do You Believe the Weather Report? Suppose that the newscaster predicts that the probability of rain for tomorrow is 75%.

a. What is the probability that it will *not* rain?

b. Explain how you can find the probability of something not happening if you know the probability that it will happen.

9. Rock and Roll In the game *Rock, Paper, Scissors,* two players put out either a fist (rock), a flat hand (paper), or two fingers (scissors). Here are the possible results.

Player 1	Player 2	Result
Rock	Paper	Paper wins (paper covers rock)
Rock	Scissors	Rock wins (rock dulls scissors)
Scissors	Paper	Scissors wins (scissors cut paper)

Use this game to design an experiment that will give a fifth-grade class an idea of probability.

10. May I Have a Moment Surveys such as Gallup polls often consist of data collected from 1500 respondents. The results usually state that the poll is accurate, plus or minus 3%. Explain whether 1500 respondents provide enough data to get close to the theoretical probability.

11. A restaurant owner wants her employees to wear a uniform of a jacket, shirt, and pants. Four styles of shirts, two pairs of pants, and one jacket are available. How many different versions of the uniform might be worn by an employee?

12. Phony Card Deck A deck of 52 cards has four kinds—red hearts, red diamonds, black clubs, and black spades. Each of the four kinds has one card each of 2, 3, 4, 5, 6, 7, 8, 9, 10, jack, queen, king, and ace. Janet's deck is missing all four aces. She shuffles the deck and removes one card randomly. Find the probability that she gets the following.

a. the three of clubs   b. the king of hearts   c. a five

d. a red card   e. a heart   f. an ace

g. a jack, queen, king, or ace   h. a card showing a number less than five

Explain whether or not each line of reasoning is correct. If it is incorrect, explain the correct line of reasoning.

13. The United States has 50 states. The probability that a U.S. citizen lives in Illinois is $\frac{1}{50}$.

14. Three hundred raffle tickets have been sold, and one winning ticket will be selected randomly. Janet bought three tickets. The probability that she will win is $\frac{1}{100}$.

15. When rolling two dice, the possible totals are 2, 3, 4, 5, 6, 7, 8, 9, 10, 11, 12. The probability of getting a sum of seven is $\frac{1}{11}$.

16. A person is asked to pick a number from 1 through 10. The probability that the number is 7 is $\frac{1}{10}$.

17. **Bead Work** A jar contains 500 beads colored blue, pink, yellow, and green. No one in the class knows how many beads there are of each color. Each student closes his eyes and pulls out a bead, writes down its color, replaces it, and repeats this for 10 beads. The following chart contains the class's results:

Blue	Pink	Yellow	Green	Blue	Pink	Yellow	Green
3	2	3	2	2	2	5	1
4	1	5	0	1	3	5	1
3	3	4	0	1	3	4	2
3	1	3	3	3	1	5	1
5	3	1	1	2	2	5	1
2	4	3	1	1	3	6	0
3	1	4	2	3	0	4	3
3	1	5	1	0	2	6	2
3	2	4	1	4	1	5	0
3	1	6	0	3	3	4	0
4	1	5	0	3	2	4	1
3	0	4	3				

a. Find the totals in each column.
b. Use these results to find the experimental probability for each color that a randomly chosen bead will be of that color.
c. Use your answer from **17a** to estimate how many of each color were in the jar.
d. How many ties were there?
e. Was each result equally likely? Explain.

Chapter 1 Review

An important part of dealing with information is being able to organize it. In this chapter, you have begun your study of data and algebra. Graphs are already familiar to you, but matrices are a new way of organizing data. Probability provides tools for interpreting uncertainty in the world.

KEY TERMS

bar graph [1–1]	integer [1–1]	positive association [1–2]
central tendency [1–1]	matrix (plural: matrices) [1–1]	probability [1–3]
circle graph [1–1]	mean [1–1]	quadrant [1–2]
coordinate [1–2]	median [1–1]	sample space [1–3]
coordinate plane [1–2]	mode [1–1]	scalar multiplication [1–1]
data [1–1]	negative association [1–2]	scalar product [1–1]
dimension [1–1]	no association [1–2]	scatter plot [1–2]
entries [1–1]	opposites [1–1]	theoretical probability [1–3]
event [1–3]	origin [1–2]	trend line [1–2]
experimental probability [1–3]	outcome [1–3]	x-axis [1–2]
factorial [1–3]	perpendicular [1–2]	y-axis [1–2]

Determine whether each statement is true or false.

1. All integers are whole numbers.

2. A sample space lists all possible outcomes.

3. The mode measures probability.

Choose the word that best completes each sentence. [1-1]

4. Median is to middle as mode is to ____.
   a. near   **b.** extreme   **c.** most   **d.** true

5. The intersection of the x-axis and y-axis is called the ____.
   a. origin   **b.** quadrant   **c.** center   **d.** source

6. A table of data is called a ____.
   a. matrix   **b.** factorial   **c.** coordinate plane

CONCEPTS AND APPLICATIONS

The two graphs below represent the number of acres set aside for Federal Indian Reservation and Trust Lands across the United States. [1-1]

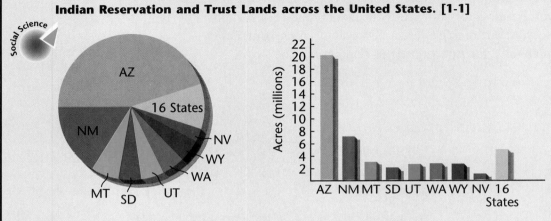

7. Which graph best shows that one state has almost half of all the Reservation and Trust Lands?   (a) the circle graph   (b) the bar graph

8. Approximately how many acres are set aside for Reservation and Trust Lands nationwide? Which graph did you use? Explain why.

Use the matrices for Exercises 9–11. [1-1]

$$A = \begin{bmatrix} 2 & -7 & 15 \\ -4 & 6 & 12 \\ 16 & -20 & -9 \end{bmatrix} \qquad B = \begin{bmatrix} 9 & 6 & -5 \\ -7 & -6 & -8 \\ -20 & 10 & -13 \end{bmatrix}$$

9. Find $A + B$.   **10.** Find $B - A$.   **11.** Find $-2B$.

12. Find the mean, median, and mode for these temperatures. [1-1]

$10°, -2°, 15°, 40°, 55°, 78°, 81°, 95°, 87°, 55°, 39°, 20°$

The graph at the right shows one-way Amtrak fares and distances between San Francisco and eight other cities. [1-2]

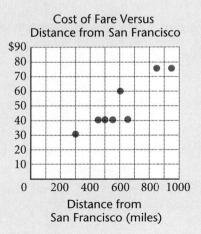

13. Is there a positive association or a negative association between the fares and the distance between the cities?

14. What prediction could you make about a trip of 1400 miles?

This coordinate plane shows points A–E.

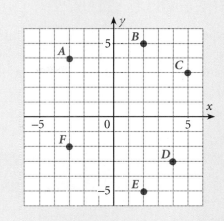

15. Give the coordinates for each of the points on the graph.

16. Which points are in the third quadrant?

17. Which points are in the second quadrant?

18. In which quadrant does a point lie if both its coordinates are negative?

19. If the signs of both of the coordinates for point *A* are changed, in which quadrant would point *A* appear? Explain how you know.

20. Which of the following situations has a probability of 0? [1-3]
   a. rain in the Sahara
   b. a round square
   c. an 8-hour school day
   d. winning the state lottery

21. There are blue, yellow, and red cubes in a bag. Each student removes a cube, records its color, and returns it to the bag. The results were 8 blue, 9 yellow, and 15 red cubes.
   a. Give the experimental probability of getting each of the three colors.
   b. Explain how you would estimate how many of each color there were in the bag if it contained 100 cubes. [1-3]

CONCEPTS AND CONNECTIONS

22. Science The table shows the rate of movement between locations on the earth's surface. A negative number means the distance between the two places is decreasing.

Locations	Movement (cm/yr)
Hawaii–Japan	−11
Hawaii–Alaska	−4
Florida–Germany	1
Florida–Sweden	1
Alaska–California	−8

   a. What is the meaning of a positive number in this situation?
   b. Is Hawaii moving faster towards Japan or towards Alaska?
   c. Does the addition of integers make sense with this use of integers? Give an example and explain.

SELF-EVALUATION

Write a summary about what new things you learned in this chapter.
Discuss the different ways you have seen to display and interpret data.
Be sure to mention areas where you had trouble, and describe how
you plan to review these areas. Be as specific as possible.

Chapter 1 Assessment

TEST

1. A circle is given, as well as the percentages that correspond to the sectors. Write the correct percent for each sector.

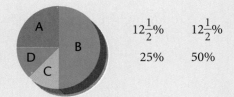

$12\frac{1}{2}\%$ $12\frac{1}{2}\%$

25%   50%

2. When is a circle graph a useful way to represent data?

Use the following matrices for Questions 3 and 4.

$$R = \begin{bmatrix} 0 & -1 & 6 \\ -3 & 4 & 5 \end{bmatrix} \qquad U = \begin{bmatrix} -3 & 1 & 4 \\ 7 & -4 & -2 \end{bmatrix}$$

3. Find the difference $U - R$.

4. Find the product $-\frac{2}{3}U$.

5. This table and graph represent the same relationship. The letter D is assigned to the ordered pair $(1, 1)$. Copy the graph and label points A, B, C, E, and F.

	A	B	C	D	E	F
x	$\frac{3}{2}$	2	3	1	-2	-1
y	-1	0	-2	1	3	1

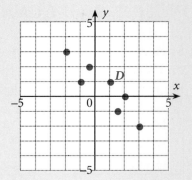

6. Furball has had her very first litter! Are her three kittens male or female?
   a. What are the outcomes?
   b. What is the probability that the litter will have two males and one female?
   c. What is the probability that the litter will *not* have two males and one female?

7. Find the mean for 16, 13, −18, 6, −4, and 29.

8. Scientists have been keeping track of solar activity since the year 1970. Below is a table of the number of sunspots seen each year between 1970 and 1990.

Year	Sunspots	Year	Sunspots	Year	Sunspots
1970	105	1977	28	1984	46
1971	67	1978	93	1985	18
1972	69	1979	155	1986	13
1973	38	1980	155	1987	29
1974	35	1981	140	1988	100
1975	16	1982	116	1989	158
1976	13	1983	67	1990	142

a. Miriam wants to design a chart to display the information about sunspots from 1970 to 1990. Which type graph should she use? Explain.

b. Miriam thinks she can use this information to predict how many sunspots there might be this year. Do you agree or disagree with her thought? Explain.

c. Why do you think scientists need to study the atmosphere over a number of years?

9. Mr. Thomas surveyed his class to determine how many of his students were involved in skiing. Of the 30 students in his class, 20 were involved in downhill skiing, 15 in water skiing, and 8 in cross-country skiing.

a–f. Label the graph. Use numbers on the horizontal axis and words on the vertical axis.

g. Would a pie graph work for this information?

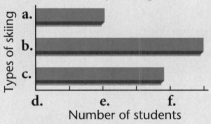

PERFORMANCE TASK

As a staff member of the school paper, you have been assigned to report the findings of a school-wide survey to determine student interest in establishing an intramural sports program. Use the concepts of this chapter to design the format for your article.

Chapter 2

Patterns, Change, and Expressions

Project A
It's Elementary!
How do chemists come up with their formulas?

Project B
You Can Tell by Touch
How do people read if they are visually handicapped?

Project C
Let's Dance
Why can one kind of rhythm make you dance and another kind put a baby to sleep?

I liked math in high school because all the problems had answers.

Math is part of literacy and the framework of science. For instance, film speed depends on chemical reactions. I use math to model problems and design experiments. I like getting results that I can publish and share.

**Diana Garcia
Prichard,Ph.D.**
Chemical Physicist,
Eastman Kodak Company
Rochester, New York

Chapter 2

GETTING READY

Patterns, Change, and Expressions

2-1
Exploring Change

In 2-1 you will learn how changes in one quantity are related to changes in another. You will need ideas about distance and speed to see related changes. You will also need to know some math operation words.

Use *distance traveled* = *speed* × *time* to find the missing information.
[Previous course]

1. Speed: 65 mi per hr   Time: 3.5 hr   Distance: _____

2. Distance: 320 km   Speed: 25 km per hour   Time: _____

3. Time: $\frac{3}{4}$ hr   Distance: 42 mi   Speed: _____

Match the words with the numeric expression. [Previous course]

4. What is *twice* as much as 16?   **a.** $16 + 2$ **b.** $16 - 2$

5. What is *half* of 16?   **c.** 16×2 **d.** $16 \div 2$

2-2
The Language of Algebra

In 2-2 you will learn how algebra is used as a language for solving problems and describing patterns. You will need to know words that denote math operations.

Find the values. [Previous course]

6. product of 6 and 8   7. quotient of 3 and 15

8. difference between 11 and 13   9. 6 less than 28

10. the square of 7   11. 3.2 decreased by 1.8

2-3
The Grammar of Algebra

In 2-3 you will learn about the order we agree to use when performing arithmetic operations so that everyone gets the same results. You will need arithmetic skills and ideas about area and perimeter.

Write two expressions for the perimeter of each shape. [Page 783]

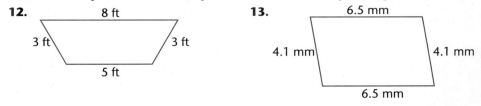

12.
8 ft
3 ft   3 ft
5 ft

13.
6.5 mm
4.1 mm   4.1 mm
6.5 mm

THE DIFFERENCE BETWEEN NIGHT & DAY

In winter I get up at night
and dress by yellow candle-light
In summer quite the other way,
I have to go to bed by day.
Robert Louis Stevenson, *Bed in Summer*

Unless you live near the equator, you may have noticed that days seem longer in summer than in winter. There are actually more hours of daylight in a summer day than in a winter day everywhere except near the equator. Do you know why?

The cause is the tilt in the earth's axis. As the earth turns, some locations get sunlight *more* than half the day while others get sunlight *less* than half the day.

The actual number of daylight hours in a day depends on the latitude where you live. During summer in the northern hemisphere, the further north of the equator you live, the more daylight hours there are. On June 21st, there are 13.5 hours of sunlight in Havana, Cuba, but 20 hours of sunlight in Fairbanks, Alaska. And near the north pole there are 24 hours of daylight—the sun never sets!

AXIS

EQUATOR

Northern Hemisphere Summer

Southern Hemisphere Winter

AXIS

EQUATOR

Northern Hemisphere Winter

Southern Hemisphere Summer

?

1. **Why is it summer in Australia when it's winter in North America?**
2. **How many hours of daylight would the south pole get on June 21?**
3. **How is your life affected by the amount of daylight in a day? Name some occupations or industries you think are affected by the amount of daylight.**

← C O N N E C T → *Earlier, you graphed pairs of data to decide if real quantities were related. Now you'll consider quantities whose values change and quantities whose values stay the same in a given situation.*

Change is all around you. To understand change, you must have an idea of what things change and what things stay the same. If you travel north or south from the equator, your distance from the equator changes, and so does the number of hours of daylight in a day. The distance from the equator and the number of hours of daylight in a day are both real **quantities** that can be described by **values,** such as 1500 mi and 15 hr.

CONSIDER

?

1. What are some words we use to mean *change*?

2. What are some words we use to mean *stay the same*?

A **quantity** is anything that can be measured or counted. The **value** of the quantity is its measure or the number of items that are counted.

Your age, your height, and the number of moons of Mars are all examples of quantities. Their values could be 15 yr, 5 ft 7 in., and 2.

EXPLORE: AS THE WORLD TURNS

Make a chart showing quantities that change and quantities that stay the same in our solar system. Give the value of each quantity that stays the same if you know it. Use these quantities to get started. Then add some of your own.

1. the time it takes for the earth to make a full rotation about its axis

2. the distance of the earth from the sun

3. the number of hours of daylight in a day

4. the number of rotations the earth makes about its axis in a week

5. the number of planets in the solar system

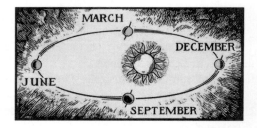

Sometimes the value of a quantity stays the same. The time it takes the earth to make a complete rotation about its axis is about 24 hr, or one day. In this case, time is a **constant.**

> Quantities whose values do not change are called **constant quantities,** or simply, **constants.**

Sometimes other factors in a situation can affect the value of a quantity. The distance from the earth to the sun depends on the time of year. In this case, distance is a **variable.**

> Quantities whose values change or vary are called **variable quantities,** or simply, **variables.**

A lot of your work in algebra will be with variable quantities. When you work with these quantities, it is important to think about the possible values they can have. For example, the distance from the earth to the sun varies from 91 million mi to 95 million mi throughout the year.

EXAMPLES

Give a range of reasonable values for each of these quantities.
1. the length of a movie   1 to 4 hr
2. the internal temperature of a healthy human   98.0°F to 99.5°F
3. the wind speed at the surface of the earth   0 to 240 mi/hr

TRY IT

Decide whether each quantity is constant or variable.
a. the number of sides of a square
b. the number of eggs in a dozen
c. the amount of sales tax you pay

Give a range of reasonable values for each of these quantities.
d. the weight of a professional football player
e. the number of students in a math class

1. What is the difference between a quantity and the value of a quantity? Give two instances of each.
2. Explain the difference between variable and constant quantities. How can you tell one from the other?
3. The height of the arch in St. Louis is 630 ft. Another book says it is 192 m high. Is the height of the arch a variable? Explain.

Exercises

CORE

Getting Started   Decide whether each quantity is constant or variable.

1. the distance around the earth along the equator

2. the number of times you inhale and exhale each minute

3. the time it takes to travel from Chicago to New York

4. the measure of any right angle

Determine whether each statement is true or false. If the statement is false, change the underlined word or phrase to make it true.

5. A quantity is anything that can be measured or counted.

6. Quantities whose values change in a given situation are called constant.

7. Anita's watch ticks once every second. Her heart beats faster than that.
   Health
   a. Does the rate of ticking of her watch change depending on whether she wears it while walking or while running?
   b. Is the rate of ticking of her watch constant or variable?
   c. Does Anita's heart rate change depending on whether she walks or runs?
   d. Is Anita's heartbeat constant or variable?
   e. Is there any situation when the rate of ticking of a watch is variable?

Give a unit of measure that would be appropriate for each quantity.

8. the distance between cities   9. the height of a building   10. the weight of a pear

Give a reasonable range of values for each of these quantities.

11. the amount of water you drink in one day

12. the life span of humans   13. the number of lanes on a highway

14. Housecall The table at the right shows the number of senators and representatives in the U.S. Congress from several states.

  a. What can you say about the number of senators from each state in Congress?

  b. What can you say about the number of representatives from each state in Congress?

  c. The number of representatives in Congress from a given state depends on what other quantity?

15. Stretching It Kelly measured the length of a table and reported to the class that it was $6\frac{1}{2}$ ft long. Huong measured the same table and reported that its length was 1.98 m. Since the numbers were different, several students concluded that the length of the table was a variable quantity. Was this a valid conclusion or not? Explain.

State	Number of Senators	Number of Representatives
Idaho	2	2
California	2	52
Nevada	2	2
Georgia	2	11
Vermont	2	1
Indiana	2	10
Texas	2	30
Michigan	2	16

16. Career Path Jerome's father is a bus driver. His route is the same every day, so his mileage is a constant. His number of riders varies, and so do the bus fares, depending on the age of the rider. Choose a job and imagine a day at work.

  a. What is your job?

  b. Name three quantities related to your job that could vary, and tell what they depend on.

  c. Name two quantities that would be constant, and tell why they stay the same.

17. Easy Rider On average, it takes a city bus five minutes to travel from one bus stop to the next all along its route.

  a. What other quantities would you need to know to figure out how long it takes the bus to complete one full route?

  b. Explain how you would figure out how long it takes the bus to complete its route if you knew the values of the quantities in **17a**.

LOOK AHEAD

Look for a pattern, and complete the table. Describe the y value as increasing or decreasing.

18.

x	−1	0	1	2	3
y	3	1	−1		

19.

x	−1	0	1	2	3
y	−4	−1	2		

MORE PRACTICE

Decide whether each quantity is constant or variable.

20. the cost of a book

21. the number of faces on a cube

22. how far it is from Paris to the equator

23. the length of a yardstick

24. the number of keys on computer keyboards

25. the measure of acute angles

Give a reasonable range of values for each of these quantities.

26. the cost of admission into a movie theater

27. the temperature on a typical summer day where you live

28. the amount of time you spend on homework per week

29. the number of phone calls you make in one day

30. Let's Go Camping Jasper and Roland are going camping for three days, but their plans are uncertain. Two other friends might join them, and they might decide to extend the trip. Make an organized list of some things they'll need, and include the following.
   a. quantities that will vary if four people go instead of two
   b. quantities that will vary if the trip lasts two weeks instead of three days
   c. quantities that will vary depending on the weather they expect
   d. quantities that are constant

MORE MATH REASONING

31. Tropical Topic There are ninety degrees of latitude between the North Pole and the equator. The distance around the earth through the poles is 24,860 miles.
   a. How far is it from the equator to the North Pole in miles?
   b. How far in miles is one degree of latitude?
   c. If you know the latitude of a place, how can you determine how far it is from the equator?
   d. Is one degree of latitude a constant or a variable distance?

0° longitude

Equator

32. Globe Trotter *Longitude* lines begin in Greenwich, England. Greenwich and places directly north and south of it have a longitude of 0°. There are 180° of longitude east, starting from 0°, and 180° west from 0°. The distance around the earth at the equator is 24,902 miles.
   a. How many miles is one degree of longitude along the equator?
   b. Is one degree of longitude a constant or a variable distance?
   c. Is one degree of longitude along the equator the same distance as one degree of longitude along the Arctic Circle? Why or why not?
   d. Explain in your own words the differences between latitude and longitude.

Describing Change

← CONNECT →
You've seen that some quantities are constant and others are variable. Sometimes changes in the values of two variable quantities can be related. Now you will describe these related changes.

Two quantities are *related* if a change in the value of one corresponds to a predictable change in the value of the other. For example, the farther you are from the equator, the greater the number of daylight hours in a summer day. The number of daylight hours in a summer day is *related* to the distance from the equator.

EXPLORE: A FIT OF FITNESS

Frank and Freda are fitness fanatics. They live in the same apartment building and go to the same school by the same route.

1. Frank walks to school. Freda runs. Who takes longer to get to school? Why?
2. Suppose Freda runs twice as fast as Frank walks. If you know how long it takes Freda to get to school, how would you figure how long it takes Frank?
3. What quantities influence how long it takes Freda or Frank to get to school?
4. Wednesday it took Frank five times as long as Freda to get to school. What can you conclude about the speeds at which they traveled?
5. Describe how the speed at which you travel a given distance is related to the time it takes to travel that distance. Write down your description, and discuss it with a classmate.

CONSIDER

Freda ran with Felipe one afternoon. They ran for the same amount of time.
1. Freda ran faster than Felipe. Who ran more miles?
2. Felipe ran slower than Freda. Who ran fewer miles?

Quantities can be related in two ways: directly and inversely.

As her speed **decreases**, the distance **decreases**.

Speed and distance are **directly related.**

As her speed **decreases**, the time **increases**.

Speed and time are **inversely related**.

EXAMPLES

Name the two quantities in each situation. Tell whether they are directly or inversely related. Explain your answer.

1. Miles driven are related to gas left in the tank.
2. Water pressure on a submarine depends on depth.
3. Circle diameter is related to circumference.
4. Soil nutrients affect the time it takes a plant to grow an inch.

The solutions are organized in the following chart.

	Quantity 1	Quantity 2	Related how?	Explanation
1.	Miles drive	Remaining gas	Inversely	As the miles driven *increase*, the amount of gas *decreases.*
2.	Pressure	Depth	Directly	The pressure *increases* as the depth *increases.*
3.	Diameter	Circumference	Directly	As the diameter *decreases*, the circumference *decreases.*
4.	Soil nutrients	Growth time	Inversely	The *more* soil nutrients, the *less* time it takes to grow an inch.

TRY IT

Name the two quantities in each situation. Tell whether they are directly or inversely related. Explain your answer.

a. The number of tickets sold for a fund-raiser is related to the amount of money raised.
b. The number of people sharing a frittata is related to the size of the slice each gets.

1. Can two variable quantities be directly and inversely related at the same time? Explain.
2. How is the length of your step related to the number of steps you take to walk 10 yd?
3. Name at least two quantities that affect the time that you arrive at school. Decide if each is directly or indirectly related to that time.

Exercises

CORE

1. **Getting Started**   **Decide if the second quantity increases or decreases.**
   a. As the area of a circle decreases, the circumference of the circle _____.
   b. As the population of a state increases, the number of representatives from that state in Congress _____.
   c. As the earth's rate of rotation decreases, the length of a day _____.

Write the word or phrase that correctly completes each statement.

2. When an increase in the value of one variable quantity corresponds to a decrease in the value of another, the two quantities are _____ related.

3. When an increase in the value of one variable quantity corresponds to an increase in the value of another, the two quantities are _____ related.

4. When a decrease in the value of one variable quantity corresponds to a decrease in the value of another, the two quantities are _____ related.

Name the two quantities in each situation. Tell whether they are directly or inversely related. Explain your answer.

5. The number of people ahead of you in line at the box office determines how long you'll have to wait.

6. The area of a wall is related to the amount of paint needed to cover it.

7. The age of a used car is related to the price the owner can get for it.

8. The area of a face of a cube is related to the volume of the cube.

9. **Rural Route** Miranda jogs along a road where mailboxes are one-fifth of a mile apart. As she jogs, she counts how many mailboxes she passes.
   a. How can she figure out how far she has jogged?
   b. Name the two related quantities in this problem, and explain whether they are directly related or inversely related.

10. **Threadbare** The Shreds, a juniors' clothing store, is advertising a sale. There is a sign that reads

a. Is it true that the more shirts you buy, the less you have to pay? Explain.

b. What do you think the people might have had in mind when they wrote the sign?

c. Are the number of shirts and their total cost directly related or inversely related?

d. Are the number of shirts and the cost per shirt directly related or inversely related?

e. How would you change the top line in the sign to avoid confusing the customers?

11. **Spandora's Box** Imagine a box that is stretchable in every dimension. What happens to the *volume* of this elastic box if you stretch it in the following ways?

a. You increase the box's height but keep the base the same.

b. You increase the base but keep the height the same.

c. You increase both height and base.

d. You increase the base and decrease the height.

12. **Observe the Limit** Suppose you travel at a constant speed of 55 mi/hr. Are the amount of time you travel and the distance you travel directly related or inversely related? Explain.

> **Problem-Solving Tip**
>
> Make a table showing different times and distances.

LOOK BACK

Draw a scatter plot, and write a sentence about the association of the number pairs. [1–2]

13.

x	−3	0	3	6	9
y	4	7	10	13	16

14.

x	−3	0	3	6	9
y	6	0	−6	−12	−18

15. If a circle graph represents 96 ants, what does a sector labeled 25% represent? [1-1]

MORE PRACTICE

For each quantity, name another quantity that is related to it.

16. the monthly loan payment on a house

17. the time it takes to read a book

18. the amount of homework you have

19. the number of leaves on a tree

20. how long it takes to fill a container with water pouring out of a faucet

Name the two quantities in each situation. Tell whether they are directly or inversely related. Explain your answer.

21. The age of a car determines the amount charged for car insurance.

22. The time it takes to shovel the driveway depends on how much snow has fallen.

23. The cost of life insurance depends on the age of the insured person.

24. The time a teacher spends grading papers is related to her number of students.

25. The average per-capita income of a country is related to the infant mortality rate (how many babies per thousand die before age 2).

26. Population growth of a country is slower when the education level is higher.

MORE MATH REASONING

27. Stream On Water pours out of a faucet at a steady rate. It takes twice as long to fill Container A as Container B with water coming out of that faucet. What can you conclude about the capacity of each container?

28. Planetary Poser While reading about the solar system, Aaron noticed that Pluto is the smallest of the nine planets and that it is also the farthest from the sun. He concluded that the farther a planet is from the sun, the smaller its size. Here are the reasons three classmates gave for why Aaron was wrong.

Joanne: Uranus is closer to the sun, and it is bigger than Pluto.

David: It is not safe to jump to conclusions.

Luis: Jupiter, the largest planet, is not the closest to the sun.

Which of the three reasons proves Aaron's conclusion was not valid? Why?

29. Roll or Stroll Nicole, Daniel, Micah, Ivonne, and Daryl all travel to school along the same country road every morning. Daryl rides to school in a car and Micah walks. The others walk, ride a bike, or go by car.

a. It takes Ivonne and Daryl the same amount of time to get to school, but it takes Ivonne half as long as it takes Micah to get to school. How does Ivonne get to school?

b. It takes Nicole three times as long as it takes Ivonne to get to school. How does Nicole get to school?

c. How does Daniel get to school if it takes him twice as long as it takes Ivonne? Explain.

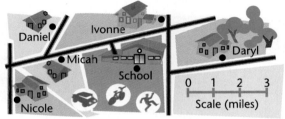

Adapted from Swan, M., *The Language of Functions and Graphs: An Examination Module for Secondary Schools,* Joint Matriculation Board, Shell Centre for Mathematical Education, Nottingham, England.

← C O N N E C T → *You've learned about quantities that are related to one another and how to describe those relationships. Now you will explore how a relationship between two quantities can be represented by a graph.*

In the following Explore, you'll collect data and draw a graph to show the relationship between the volume and height of the contents of a jar.

EXPLORE: THIRST QUENCHER

1. Before collecting any data, guess whether the *volume* of water and the height of water in a jar are directly related or inversely related quantities.

2. Pour 2 oz of water into an empty jar and measure the height. Record the data for volume and height in a table. Add 2 oz more, measure the height, and record the new data. Repeat until you have data for at least three different volumes of water.

3. Graph the data on a coordinate plane with axes for volume and height. Does your scatter plot of the data show positive association, negative association, or no association?

4. Recall that a dotted line approximating a scatter plot is called a *trend line.* Draw a trend line for your scatter plot, and use your graph to describe the relationship between volume and height. Was your guess in Step 1 correct?

5. How could you use your graph to estimate what the height would be for a volume of 3 oz?

MATERIALS

A clear jar or bottle
Two-ounce measuring cup
Water
Ruler
Graph paper

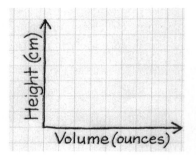

1. What kind of association will you see in a scatter plot of data if the two quantities are directly related? if the two quantities are inversely related?

A trend line or other curve can be a valuable tool for seeing and describing a relationship between quantities. Sometimes there isn't a simple direct or inverse relationship.

This graph shows the relationship between the temperature of a room with the thermostat set at 65° and the time since the heater was turned on.

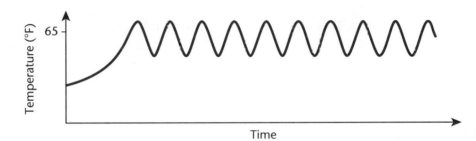

Room Temperature Since Turning on Heater

Once the heater is turned on, the temperature rises towards 65°. The wiggly part of the graph shows how the temperature goes up and down slightly as the thermostat maintains the temperature near the setting.

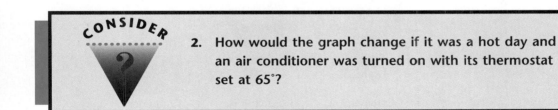

2. How would the graph change if it was a hot day and an air conditioner was turned on with its thermostat set at 65°?

If two quantities are directly related, their data will show a positive association. If two quantities are inversely related, their data will show a negative association.

For each graph, tell whether the two quantities are directly related, inversely related, or neither. Also state whether one quantity stays constant as the other varies.

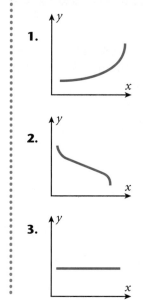

1. The graph goes up from left to right, so as one quantity increases, the other also increases. The quantities are directly related.

2. The graph goes down from left to right, so as one quantity increases, the other decreases. The quantities are inversely related.

3. The graph is flat, so the quantity represented on the vertical axis neither increases nor decreases—it stays constant. The quantities are neither directly nor inversely related.

TRY IT

Each graph relates the volume and the height of water in one of the containers.
a. Match each container to its corresponding graph.
b. Which of the graphs shows a direct relationship between volume and height?

Container A   Container B   Container C

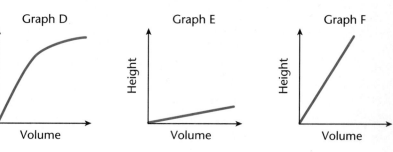

Graph D   Graph E   Graph F

1. How can you tell from a graph that two quantities are inversely related?
2. What does the point where the axes intersect represent in a graph of the volume and height of water in a container?
3. Explain how the graph of room temperature and time since the heater was turned on shows that these quantities are neither directly nor inversely related.
4. How would you explain to a young child how a graph is a picture of change?

Exercises

CORE

1. **Getting Started** Luis was testing the effect of using a fertilizer on the growth rate of a plant. He measured the height of the plant every morning for several days and recorded his observations as shown.
   a. What does each dot represent?
   b. If Luis had measured the height of the plant on the afternoon of the third day, where would the corresponding dot be?
   c. What does the graph tell you about the relationship between time and plant growth?

Plant Growth Over Time

Height of plant (cm) vs. Time (days)

2. **Less Is More** Use the diagram to help you answer these questions.
   a. If Container B is wider than Container A and water drips into both containers at a constant rate, in which container will the water level rise faster?
   b. What would the graph look like for the relationship between height and volume in Container B?

A   B

3. **Rise and Shine** Sketch a rough graph to show the relationship between the time since sunrise and the height of the sun above the horizon. Show sunrise, noon, and sunset as points on the *x*-axis.

Sketch graphs for each story. Label your axes with quantities.

4. Nine to Five My sister says the closer she lives to work, the more free time she has after work. Use distance from work and free time as the quantities.

5. Sorry, I Can't Hear You When I got home from school, I turned on my radio and played it really loud for a while. Then the phone rang, so I turned it way down. Use radio volume and time as the quantities.

6. Step On It The graph shows the relationship between distance and time for a car moving at different speeds. For what time intervals was the speed greatest? slowest? Explain how you know.

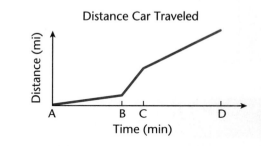

7. Divvy It Up! Bill made a pie and invited a friend over to share it. More and more friends showed up for a piece.
  a. Draw and label a pair of axes for the relationship between the number of people sharing a pie equally and the fraction of the pie that each gets.
  b. Plot several points. (Hint: If there are 3 people, each gets $\frac{1}{3}$.)
  c. Does it make sense to connect the dots with a solid line? Why or why not?
  d. How can you tell from just looking at the set of dots you plotted whether the two quantities are directly or inversely related?

8. On the Road Again Five students travel to school along the same road. Daryl goes in his dad's car, Nicole rides her bike, and Micah walks. Daniel and Ivonne vary how they travel from day to day. The map shows where each student lives. Use the graph to find out how each student traveled to school Friday.

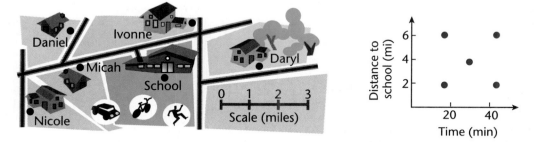

  a. Copy the graph and label each point with the name of the student it represents.
  b. How did Daniel and Ivonne travel to school on Friday? How do you know?
  c. Daryl's father drives 30 mi/hr on straight sections of the road but slows down for the corners. Sketch a graph that shows how the car's speed varies along the route.

  Adapted from Swan, M., *The Language of Functions and Graphs: An Examination Module for Secondary Schools,* Joint Matriculation Board, Shell Centre for Mathematical Education, Nottingham, England.

9. The perimeter of an equilateral triangle is 3 times its side. The circumference of a circle is π times its diameter. (An approximate value for π is 3.14.) Compare and contrast the graphs of these two relationships.

For each graph, tell whether the two quantities are directly related, inversely related, or neither. Also state whether one quantity stays constant as the other varies.

10. **11.** **12.** **13.**

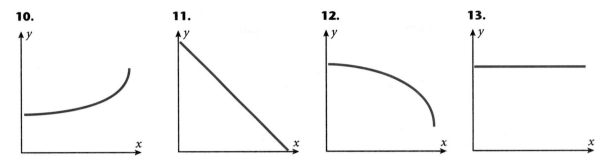

 *LOOK BACK*

Tell whether the scatter plot shows a positive or a negative association or no association. Tell how you know. [1-2]

14. **15.** **16.**

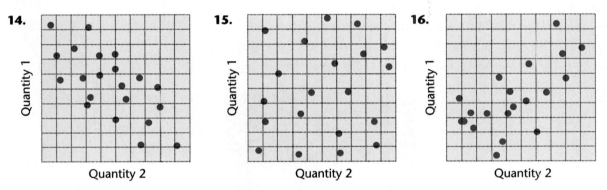

Quantity 1 · Quantity 2 · Quantity 1 · Quantity 2 · Quantity 1 · Quantity 2

17. Dick wears a hat every day. He has three hats with baseball team emblems and two with football designs. What is the probability that on a given day he will wear a hat with a baseball emblem? [1-3]

MORE PRACTICE

18. Maribeth was testing the effect of artificial light on the growth rate of a plant. She measured the height of the plant every morning over a period of several days and recorded her observations as shown.

   a. What does each dot represent?

   b. If Maribeth had measured the height of the plant on the afternoon of the fourth day, where would the corresponding dot be?

   c. What does the graph tell you about the relationship between time and plant growth?

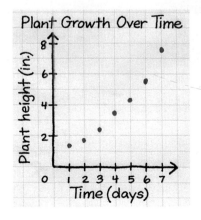

For each graph, tell whether the two quantities are directly related, inversely related, or neither. Also state whether one quantity stays constant as the other varies.

19.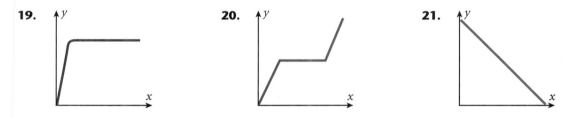

20.

21.

MORE MATH REASONING

22. It's All the Same Legend has it that by dropping lead weights from a tower, Galileo discovered that objects of different weights dropped from the same height take the same amount of time to hit the ground. Sketch a graph that illustrates his discovery. Remember to label the axes.

23. The Hurdles Race This graph shows the progress of 3 athletes in a 110-m hurdles race. Imagine that you are the race commentator. Describe what is happening, using as much detail as you can. The clock is running!

Adapted from Swan, M., *The Language of Functions and Graphs: An Examination Module for Secondary Schools*, Joint Matriculation Board, Shell Centre for Mathematical Education, Nottingham, England.

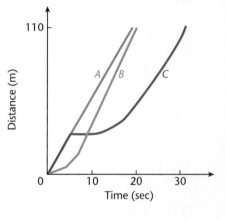

2-1
PART D **Making Connections**

· ·

← CONNECT → *People, technology, and even the earth itself are always undergoing change. Understanding quantities and relationships between quantities is at the heart of understanding and describing change.*

The greatest number of daylight hours in a day occurs on the first day of summer—the summer solstice—around June 21 in the Northern Hemisphere and December 21 in the Southern Hemisphere. Near the equator, the number of hours of daylight in a day remains almost constant.

EXPLORE: A PLACE IN THE SUN

The following graphs show the number of hours of daylight in a day from June 21 through December 21 for four cities.

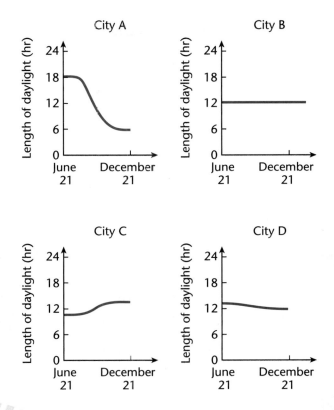

Use the information and graphs given above to answer these questions.

1. What is the approximate range of the number of hours of daylight in a day from June 21 through December 21 in each city?
2. For each city, decide whether the quantities graphed are directly related, inversely related, or neither. Explain how you decided.
3. Decide whether each city is in the Northern Hemisphere, Southern Hemisphere, or near the equator. Explain how you decided.
4. Each graph corresponds to one of the following cities. The latitude of each city is given. Match each city to its graph. Explain how you decided.
   a. Sydney, Australia; 24° S   b. Moscow, Russia; 56° N
   c. Ho Chi Minh City, Vietnam; 11° N   d. Quito, Ecuador; 0°
5. The word *equinox* comes from the Latin word meaning *equal night*. One equinox occurs around September 22. What do you notice about the number of hours of daylight on this date in each graph?

REFLECT

1. What role do quantities play in helping us understand the changes we observe around us? Use an example to help explain.
2. Can you talk about a quantity without knowing its value? Explain with an example.
3. What is the difference between constant and variable quantities?
4. Describe how you can tell whether two quantities are directly related, inversely related, or neither.

Self-Assessment

Decide whether each of the quantities described below is constant or variable.

1. the number of students per math class

2. the diameter of the sun

3. the number of faces in a pyramid

4. the temperature of a room

5. Stay Cool Wondering whether her refrigerator would fit in a new apartment, Hilary measured its width and got 30 in. Her roommate Alicia measured it and got $29\frac{13}{16}$ in. Explain whether the width of the refrigerator is a variable or a constant. If you think it is a constant, how do you explain the difference in measurements?

6. Study the diagram, which shows how the distance from the earth to the sun varies during the year. Describe how the distance between the earth and the sun compares for June and December.

Science

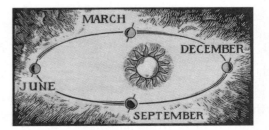

7. Erin gets paid an hourly wage for the work she does at a car wash.

Careers

a. What quantities would you need to know in order to figure out how much she should get paid at the end of the week?

b. How are the two quantities related, inversely or directly? Explain how you know.

c. From week one to week five, the number of hours Erin worked increased by a factor of two and one-half. How did the amount she got paid change from week one to week five?

8. Which of these situations does this graph represent?
   (a) the relationship between two quantities that are inversely related
   (b) the relationship between two quantities that are directly related
   (c) a quantity whose value stays constant as the value of the other quantity varies
   (d) none of these

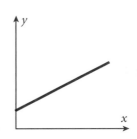

9. The Dorsey family is flying from Santa Fe, New Mexico to Fairbanks, Alaska on the first day of summer. What is the probability that they will arrive during daylight? (See chart on page 103.)

10. Water pours into a tank at a steady rate from a faucet at the top of the tank, and it flows out of the tank at a different but also steady rate from a faucet at the bottom of the tank. At any given time, either faucet can be opened or shut. The graph shows the amount of water in the tank over a period of time.

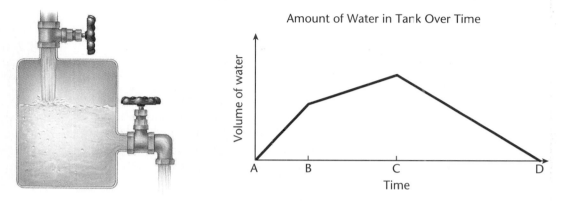

Amount of Water in Tank Over Time

a. Identify the time intervals during which the following are true.
  i. only the top faucet is open   **ii.** only the bottom faucet is open
  iii. both faucets are open
b. Through which of the two faucets does water flow at a faster rate?
c. Summarize what happens from the starting time, A, to the ending time, D, explaining how the amount of water in the tank varies.

11. This chart shows several cities, their latitudes, and the approximate number of daylight hours on the first day of summer, the longest day of the year. Study the data in the chart, and look for a relationship between latitude and daylight hours.

City	Latitude	Daylight Hours (First Day of Summer)
Quito, Ecuador	0°	12
Manila, Philippines	15° N	12.7
Maputo, Mozambique	24° S	13.5
Melbourne, Australia	38° S	15
Paris, France	49° N	16.3
Fairbanks, U.S.A.	64° N	20
Havana, Cuba	24° N	13.5

a. Which city in the chart is farthest from the equator? Which one is nearest? Which one has the longest first day of summer? Which has the shortest?
b. The latitude of Nairobi, Kenya, is 2° S. The latitude of Rome, Italy, is 42° N. Which of these two cities would you expect to have more hours of daylight on its first day of summer? Why?
c. Which person comes from which city? Justify your decision.

12. The Bases Are Loaded The area of a triangle is given by the following formula.

$$A = \frac{1}{2}bh$$

a. What happens to the area of a triangle if the base stays the same but the height is increased?

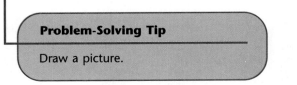

Problem-Solving Tip

Draw a picture.

b. Are the area and height of a triangle directly related or inversely related?

c. What happens to the area of a triangle if the base increases and the height decreases? What can you conclude about the area in that case?

13. Which graph best shows the relationship between the number of congressional districts in a given state and the number of representatives from that state in the U.S. Congress? Explain your choice.

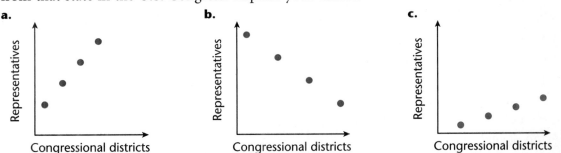

14. Uta lives in Texas. It is 7 hr later in Switzerland where her grandmother lives.

a. If Uta wants to reach her grandmother at 1:00 p.m. Swiss time, when (Texas time) must she call?

b. If her grandmother wants to reach Uta at 7:30 a.m. Texas time, when (Swiss time) must she call?

15. The graph describes Teresa's speed while on a bike ride. Describe what happened to her speed during each of the time intervals marked on the horizontal axis.

a. from 0–20 min

b. from 20–40 min

c. from 40–60 min

d. For part of her ride, Teresa went up a steep hill and got really tired. Which segment of the graph probably reflects that part of her ride?

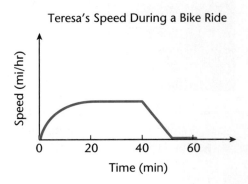

Teresa's Speed During a Bike Ride

THE *Phrase* IS FAMILIAR

Have you ever wondered about the meaning of some of the expressions people use everyday? Here are three well-known phrases, their meanings, and the stories behind them. Each of these familiar phrases was first used by someone. Somehow they continued to be used by people and have become a part of our common language. Phrases are also used in algebra to connect real-world quantities, values, and relationships.

THE LION'S SHARE

is a greedily large portion. This phrase comes from an Aesop's fable in which a lion goes hunting with a cow, a goat, and a sheep. When the animals catch a deer, the lion divides it into four portions—then takes them all!

THE BOONDOCKS

refers to a very remote area. *Bundock* is the Filipino word for mountain. U.S. soldiers brought the term back from the Spanish-American War.

NOT WORTH HIS SALT

means overpaid. Before the invention of money, the Romans paid their soldiers in portions of salt, then a very valuable commodity. It was believed to have magical properties. They'd throw it over their shoulder for luck or sprinkle it on food they suspected might be spoiled or poisoned, which explains another salt phrase—Take It With A Grain Of Salt.

1. Why do you suppose phrases like these have stuck with people for such a long time?
2. What is the advantage of using them instead of expressing their actual meaning?
3. What problems can arise when you use phrases like these to communicate with others?
4. Who is John Doe? What is Brand X? When do people use these expressions?

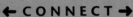
Using Variables and Expressions

← **CONNECT** → *In many real-world situations, the value of one quantity depends on the value of other quantities. Often you can write an expression that relates the values of one quantity to the values of other quantities.*

EXPLORE: A LION'S SHARE

At Marine World Africa USA, in Vallejo, California, each male lion eats 7 lb of fortified horsemeat a day. The lions are fed 6 days a week, for a total of 42 lb of meat a week. (Lions in the wild don't eat every day, so captive lions fast—don't eat—one day a week.) The director of the park must plan ahead to prepare the food budget for the lions.

MATERIALS

Graph paper

1-Week Food Budget	
Number of male lions	Amount of meat(lbs)
1	42
2	84

1. Copy and complete the table to show six pairs of values.
2. Write each pair of values as an ordered pair, beginning with (1, 42). Plot the ordered pairs on a coordinate plane.
3. Are the quantities *number of male lions* and *amount of meat eaten per week* directly related or inversely related? How did you decide?
4. In your own words, describe how to find the amount of meat needed for one week if you know the number of male lions.

People use different expressions to describe relationships between quantities.

Each female lion is fed 5 pounds of meat a day, 6 days a week, for a total of 30 pounds per week. Here are three expressions for the *amount of meat eaten per week* depending on the *number of female lions.*

Rudi's expression: Multiply 30 lb by the number of female lions.

Zoe's expression: 30 lb × (number of female lions)

Jorge's expression: $30 \times L$

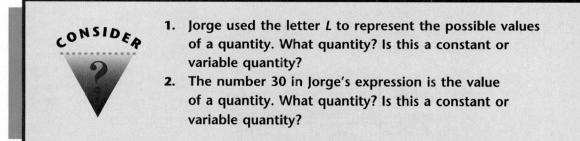

CONSIDER ?

1. Jorge used the letter *L* to represent the possible values of a quantity. What quantity? Is this a constant or variable quantity?
2. The number 30 in Jorge's expression is the value of a quantity. What quantity? Is this a constant or variable quantity?

In spoken languages, letters and punctuation are used to create words and phrases. In the language of algebra, letters along with numbers and operation symbols are used to create expressions.

> An **algebraic expression** is a mathematical phrase involving letters, numbers, and operation symbols. A **variable** is any letter, such as *L*, *n*, *x*, *P*, *a*, *y*, and others, that we use in an expression to represent possible values of a variable quantity.

In Jorge's algebraic expression, he used the variable *L* to represent possible numbers of female lions.

When **expressing products** in algebra, you can write them in several ways.

For 30 × *L*, you can write → $30 \cdot L$
→ $30(L)$
→ $30L$

The form without symbols, like $30L$, is most commonly used for expressing the product of a constant and a variable.

When **expressing quotients** in algebra, we use a fraction more often than ÷ to represent division.

Just as the quotient $3 \div 4$ is $\frac{3}{4}$,

the quotient $x \div y$ is $\frac{x}{y}$.

Write an algebraic expression for each quantity.

1. the amount of change you get back from $100 after buying something.

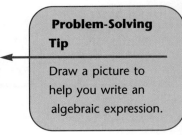

Problem-Solving Tip

Draw a picture to help you write an algebraic expression.

Let y stand for the amount you spend, in dollars. The amount of change you get back, in dollars, is $100 - y$.

2. the price of three equally priced CDs, discounted $5.00.

Let c stand for the price of each CD, in dollars. Before the discount, the price of all three CDs is $3c$. Then $5.00 is subtracted. We use parentheses to indicate that the operation inside is done first. The discounted price is $(3c) - 5$ dollars.

When we say, "Let c stand for the price of each CD, in dollars," we are identifying a quantity—*price of each CD*—and choosing a variable to represent its possible dollar values. When we make this kind of statement, we are **defining a variable.**

In algebra, we use **powers** and **exponents** to write repeated multiplication.

A **power** is a number that can be written as a product of equal factors.

$2 \cdot 2 \cdot 2 \cdot 2 = 16$, so 16 is the 4th power of 2. You can write powers like this in a shorter form using **exponents.**

$$2 \cdot 2 \cdot 2 \cdot 2 = 2^4 \quad \longleftarrow \text{Exponent}$$
$$\longleftarrow \text{Base}$$

The factors in a power can also be variables.

For this power:	Write:	Say:
$x \cdot x$	x^2	"x squared"
$x \cdot x \cdot x$	x^3	"x cubed" or "x to the third power"
$x \cdot x \cdot x \cdot x$	x^4	"x to the fourth power" or "x to the fourth"

3. Why do you think we say *x squared* for x^2? Why do we say *x cubed* for x^3?

EXAMPLE

3. Yolanda is a swimming-pool contractor. She builds rectangular pools of different sizes, but each pool is 1.5 times as long as it is wide. Define a variable, and then write an algebraic expression for the area of any of Yolanda's pools.

> **Problem-Solving Tip**
>
> Draw and label a diagram of a pool.

Let x represent the width of a pool in feet. Then $1.5x$ represents the length in feet. The area of a rectangle is the product of its length and width. Therefore, the area of a pool, in square feet, is given by the expression $1.5x \cdot x$ or $1.5x^2$.

TRY IT

a. Write $3p^3$ without using exponents.

b. Write $0.5(yyyyy)$ using exponents.

c. Assuming you can buy m apples for exactly \$2, write an expression for the cost of one apple.

REFLECT

1. What does a letter in an algebraic expression represent?

2. Why do we use a letter instead of numbers to represent the values of a variable quantity?

3. Sean said, "It doesn't make sense to talk about multiplying two letters, like xy." Do you agree or disagree with Sean? Explain.

Exercises

CORE

1. **Getting Started** The number of keys on a piano is 88.
   a. The number of keys on 2 pianos is 88 _____.
   b. The number of keys on 3 pianos is _____ (_____).
   c. The number of keys on n pianos is _____ (_____).

2. Choose the correct comparison to complete the following statement. Variable: algebraic expression as
   (a) $3{:}25x$ (b) $x{:}25x$ (c) $3{:}25$ (d) $3x{:}25x$

Romare Bearden, *The Piano Lesson*, 1983

Write each expression without using the × or the ÷ signs. Use exponents where appropriate.

3. $7 \times a$

4. c times a

5. $x \div 3$

6. zzz

7. $5 \div (2b)$

8. $4nn$

9. $(3y) \div 2$

10. $x \div (y \times z)$

11. $(a + b) \div c$

Write without using exponents.

12. t^4

13. $2w^3$

14. $1000y^5$

For Exercises 15–21, choose the correct algebraic expression for each phrase.

15. 17 times a number all divided by 3

16. 17 decreased by a number

17. 3 less than the product of 17 and a number

18. 17 less than some number

19. 17 more than 3 times a number

20. 17 decreased by the product of 3 and a number

21. 3 times the sum of a number and 17

A. $(3n) + 17$

B. $m - 17$

C. $\dfrac{17b}{3}$

D. $17 - y$

E. $17z - 3$

F. $3(s + 17)$

G. $17 - 3x$

22. Find an expression that will give the perimeter of each figure.
   a.   **b.**

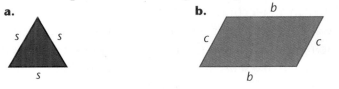

23. Let a stand for the digit in the tens place of a two-digit number, and let b stand for the ones digit. Write an expression using a and b that gives the value of the number.

Write an expression that gives the value of each quantity.

24. the number of yards of material purchased for r dollars at $3.50 a yard

25. the height of a flag that is d meters below the top of a 30-m flagpole

26. the time it takes to read a book that is x pages long at a rate of y pages per hour

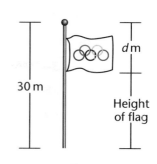

30 m

d m

Height of flag

27. the number of sheets of paper left in a copy machine from a ream of 500 sheets after making 3 copies of a document that is x sheets long

28. She's Worth Her Salt! After Kelly had worked at an hourly rate for six months, her boss was so pleased that she decided to give Kelly a raise. Kelly's new pay rate is $4.50 per hour plus an additional $25 each week.

a. Make a table showing how much Kelly will earn after the raise if she works one hour, two hours, three hours, and so on.

b. How much will she make if she works fourteen hours? twenty hours?

c. Describe in words how Kelly can calculate how much she should get paid per week now, if she knows how many hours she has worked.

d. Let t give the number of hours Kelly works in any given week. Write an expression that gives the amount of money she should get paid for working t hours.

e. What does each part of your expression stand for? Which part is constant, and which part is variable? Explain.

f. Sketch a graph that shows the relationship between hours worked per week and amount earned per week.

g. Are these two quantities directly or inversely related? How is this reflected in your graph?

LOOK AHEAD

Here are three diagrams and the expressions they represent.

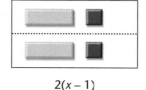

$2x + 3$

$2(x - 1)$

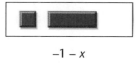

$-1 - x$

Draw diagrams to match each expression.

29. $x + 1$ **30.** $1 - x$ **31.** $3x - 2$ **32.** $3(x - 2)$

MORE PRACTICE

Write each expression without using the × or ÷ signs. Use exponents where appropriate.

33. $d \times 5$

34. $r \times s \times t$

35. $n \times k \times 6$

36. -2 times y

37. xx

38. $aaaa$

39. $(h)(h)(h)(h)(h)(h)$

40. $-7ww$

41. $(x - y) \div z$

42. $(5m) \div 2n$

43. $b \div (-2a)$

44. $r \div (7s \times t)$

Find an expression that gives the value of each quantity.

45. three degrees cooler than the current temperature of x degrees Fahrenheit

46. the capacity of a movie theatre with b rows of seats and 14 seats per row

47. the volume of a cube with an edge of a cm

48. the average percent score for three tests whose scores are a%, b%, and c%

49. the taxi fare for a ride x mi long, if the base charge is $1.75 and 80¢ is charged for each mile over 2 mi

Industry

Write an algebraic expression for each of the following phrases.

50. 7 more than a number

51. twice a number plus 3

52. a number increased by 19

53. the sum of a number and -12

54. 1 less than a number

55. 2 less than 3 times a number

56. a number decreased by -3

57. the difference between a number and 2

58. the product of -5 and a number

59. seven times a number, divided by 2

60. A board ten meters long is to be cut into two parts of different lengths. If the length in meters of one of the parts is given by x, what expression would give the length of the other part?

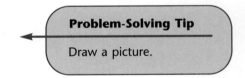

Problem-Solving Tip

Draw a picture.

For Exercises 61–63, use the given variables to write an expression that gives the value of the quantities asked for.

61. If t gives the number of hours a jet has been flying at an average speed of 540 mi/hr, what distance has the jet flown?

62. If h gives the height in centimeters of different triangles with a base of 5 cm, what is the area of any of the triangles?

h

5 cm

63. A cub is fed 1 lb of meat every single day, an adult male lion is fed 7 lb of meat 6 days a week, and adult female lions are fed 5 lb of meat 6 days a week. If there are m adult males, f adult females, and c cubs, how much does the whole pride of lions eat in a week?

64. Find an expression that will give the perimeter of each of these figures.

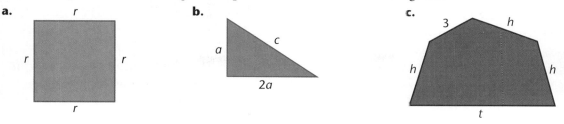

a.

b.

c.

MORE MATH REASONING

65. A Typing Contest Gina types at a rate of 47 words per minute. Evan types at a rate of 55 words per minute. Gina had been typing for 5 minutes when Evan arrived at the office and started typing. Let t stand for the number of minutes gone by since Evan started typing, and assume they both type nonstop.

Each of the following expressions gives the value of what quantity?

a. $55t$ **b.** $47t$ **c.** $47(t + 5)$ **d.** $(55t) - (47t)$

e. Will Evan ever catch up with Gina? If so, in how many minutes?

f. Sketch a graph showing the relationship between the number of words Evan has typed and the time he has been typing.

g. On the same coordinate plane, sketch a graph of Gina's typing.

h. Do the two graphs intersect? If so, where?

Women typists at work, 1907.

66. Read All About It! Luz delivers 80 newspapers every day. Her friend Silvia also delivers papers every day, but the number of papers Silvia delivers varies from day to day. Let s represent the number of papers Silvia delivers on any given day.

a. Write an expression that gives the number of papers Silvia and Luz, together, deliver on any given day.

b. Dave delivers half as many papers as Silvia. Write an expression that gives the number of papers Dave delivers on a given day.

c. Josh delivers three times as many papers as Dave. What expression gives the number of papers delivered by Josh?

d. Tiara delivers as many papers as Luz and Josh combined. What expression gives the number of papers delivered by Tiara?

67. a. Write an expression that will give the total value of any given set of coins. Use variables to represent the number of half dollars, quarters, dimes, nickels, and pennies in the set. The expression you obtained gives the total value in what unit?

b. Modify your expression to obtain the total value of the coins in dollars.

Evaluating Expressions

← C O N N E C T → *You've represented real quantities with variables and algebraic expressions. Now you will learn to evaluate algebraic expressions.*

EXPLORE: WHAT'S MY SCORE?

Ms. Parks is planning to use a spreadsheet on her computer to keep track of her class's scores on the latest test. She would like to have the spreadsheet program give each student's score on the test after she enters just the number of items that a student missed. To do this, she'll need an algebraic expression for the test score.

1. There are 100 points on the test. Each item is worth 4 points. What quantity varies from student to student and could be used to find each student's test score?

2. Define a variable, and write an algebraic expression for the test score.

3. Using your expression, copy and complete the table.

	A	B	C
1	Student	Number of Items Missed	Test Score
2	Darby	3	
3	Yolanda	1.5	
4	Ruben	0	
5	Alicia	5	
6	Yen	4.5	
7	Any student	n	

4. How could this expression help a teacher to compute grades? If you were one of Ms. Parks's students, could you find a use for this expression? Explain.

An algebraic expression is useful because it represents all possible values of a quantity in one convenient expression. In the preceding Explore, you wrote an expression that could be used to find each student's test score. In a spreadsheet program, the *computer* would use the expression to find each score.

> **Substitution** is the process of replacing a variable in an algebraic expression with a number. After substituting, you can do the calculations to find the **value of the expression.** When you find the value of an expression, you are **evaluating the expression.**

EXAMPLES

1. Recall from Part A that the amount of change you get back from $100 after spending y dollars is $100 - y$ dollars. Evaluate this expression to find the change you get back after spending $55.

When $y = 55$: $100 - y = 100 - 55$ Substitute 55 for y.

                $= 45$ Subtract to find the value of the expression.

You get back $45 in change.

2. Enola has time to read about 50 pages of a novel a day. Write an expression for the approximate number of days it will take her to read a novel p pages long. How long will it take Enola to read the 1083-page novel *Chesapeake* by James Michener?

It takes Enola about $\frac{p}{50}$ days to read a novel p pages long.

When $p = 1083$: $\frac{p}{50} = \frac{1083}{50}$ Substitute 1083 for p.

                $= 21.66$ Divide to find the value of the expression.

It will take Enola about 22 days to read *Chesapeake.*

3. The physics formula for the *kinetic energy* of a moving object is $E = \frac{m(v^2)}{2}$, where E is the kinetic energy in joules, m is the mass in kilograms, and v is the velocity of the object in meters per second.

Find the kinetic energy of a 4-kg bowling ball rolling down a bowling alley at 5 m/sec.

$m = 4, v = 5$: $E = \frac{4 \cdot (5^2)}{2} = \frac{100}{2} = 50$

The kinetic energy of the ball is 50 joules.

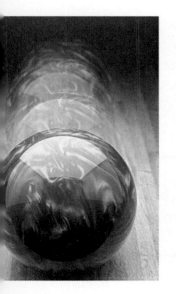

TRY IT

a. Recall from Part A that the price of three CDs that have been discounted $5.00 is $(3c) - 5$ dollars, where c is the price of each CD. Find the total price if the price of each CD is $15.95.

It is often useful to evaluate an expression for different values of the variable. For expressions with fractions, the fraction bar acts like parentheses.

4. Evaluate $\dfrac{x+2}{3}$ for the given values of x.

x	$\dfrac{x+2}{3}$
1	$\dfrac{1+2}{3} = \dfrac{3}{3} = 1$
0	$\dfrac{0+2}{3} = \dfrac{2}{3}$
−1	$\dfrac{-1+2}{3} = \dfrac{1}{3}$
−2.3	$\dfrac{-2.3+2}{3} = \dfrac{-0.3}{3} = -0.1$

Add the numbers above the fraction bar first.

b. Evaluate $\dfrac{x}{3} + 2$ for the given values of x.

x	$\dfrac{x}{3} + 2$
1	
0	
−1	
−2.3	

CONSIDER

?

1. Did the expressions in Example 4 and Try It b have the same values or different values? Explain.

REFLECT

1. What steps do you take to evaluate an algebraic expression for a quantity when you know the values of the variables involved?

2. What are some advantages of knowing an algebraic expression for a quantity?

3. To evaluate an expression with the variables x and y, how many numbers would you have to substitute? Could you substitute the same value for both x and y?

Exercises

CORE

1. **Getting Started** To evaluate expressions, substitute values for the variables.
   a. To evaluate $x + 2$ for $x = 6$, substitute 6 for x: What is $6 + 2$?
   b. To evaluate y^2 for $y = 3$, substitute 3 for y: What is 3^2?

Evaluate the expression for each value of the variable.

2. For $y = 5$ and $y = -4$ **a.** $4y$ **b.** $y - 1$ **c.** $3(y^2)$ **d.** $2y + 10$

3. For $r = 6$ and $r = \dfrac{1}{3}$ **a.** $\dfrac{3r}{6}$ **b.** $9r - 2$ **c.** $10r$ **d.** $2r \times 3$

4. For $p = \dfrac{1}{2}$ and $p = -2$ **a.** $8p$ **b.** $2p + 4$ **c.** $\dfrac{2p}{5}$ **d.** p^2

Evaluate the expression by substituting the given values for each variable.

5. ℓw for $\ell = 9$ and $w = 8$

6. $\dfrac{5}{9}(F - C)$ for $F = 212$ and $C = 32$

7. $\dfrac{1}{2}bh$ for $b = 2.3$ and $h = 6$

8. $\dfrac{1}{4}(a - b)$ for $a = -2$ and $b = 8$

Write the word or phrase that correctly completes each statement.

9. _____ is the process of replacing a variable in an algebraic expression with a number.

10. After substituting, you can then calculate to find the _____.

11. When you substitute into an expression and find its value, you are _____ .

Write an expression that gives the value of the quantities asked for. Then pick a reasonable value for each variable, substitute it into the expression, and evaluate.

Example: In 12, if we let $t = 2$ hr and $k = 8$ km, then the value of the speed $\left(\frac{k}{t}\right)$ is 4 km/hr—a reasonable walking speed!

12. If t gives the number of hours it takes to walk k kilometers, what is the speed in kilometers per hour?

13. If x gives the total for a restaurant bill in dollars, what will a 15% tip be? the total bill including tip?

14. **Mom's Day** Fritzi's Restaurant has special rates for Mother's Day brunch. Mothers' meals are 80% of the regular price, and children's meals are 50% of the regular price. Write an expression that will give the total cost for a family with mother, father, and two children if the price of a regular meal is R.

Industry

Evaluate each expression for the given values of x.

15.

x	−3x + 4
−2	
−1	
0	
1.5	
2	

16.

x	(x)²
2	
1	
0	
−1	
−2	

17.

x	2−(x²)
2	
1	
0	
−1	
−2	

18. Circle the Globe The circumference and area of a circle of radius r are given by $2\pi r$ and πr^2, respectively. Use 3.14 for the constant π.

a. What is the circumference of a circle with a radius of 2 m?

b. What is the area of a circle with a radius of 2 m?

c. The earth has a radius of about 3960 miles. Approximately how long is the equator?

$2\pi r$

19. Manageable Sales Joe bought 80 bottles of shampoo at c dollars per bottle for his beauty supply store. The regular price at his store is 60% over his cost. Write an expression that gives the value of each quantity.

a. the amount Joe spent on the shipment of shampoo

b. the regular price of a bottle of shampoo at Joe's store

c. how much money Joe makes from selling half of the shipment at regular price

d. How many bottles would Joe have to sell at the regular price to begin to make a profit?

e. If the remaining half of the shipment is put on sale at 50% off the regular price, what is the sale price of one bottle of shampoo?

LOOK BACK

20. Complete the sentence. [1-3]

If an event is certain to occur, the probability that the event will occur is _____.

21. Which graph shows 20% shaded? Tell how you know. [1-1]

a.   **b.**   **c.**

22. Would you expect a positive, a negative, or no association between the number of hours of daylight during a day and the number of hours of darkness? [1-2]

MORE PRACTICE

Evaluate the expression for each value of the variable.

23. $6a$ for $a = 3$ and $a = -4$

24. $\dfrac{3m}{5}$ for $m = 20$ and $m = \dfrac{1}{3}$

25. $-2(b^2)$ for $b = 3$ and $b = -3$

26. $(1.8C + 32)$ for $C = 37$ and $C = 0$

Evaluate the expression by substituting the given values for each variable.

27. lw for $l = 5.9$ and $w = 6.5$

28. $\dfrac{b}{a}$ for $a = -2$ and $b = 8$

29. $a(b^2)$ for $a = 5$ and $b = -4$

30. $\dfrac{1}{8}(b - a)$ for $a = 2$ and $b = 10$

Write an expression that gives the value of the quantities asked for. Then pick a reasonable value for each variable, substitute it into the expression, and evaluate.

31. If t gives the number of hours you have hiked at s mi/hr, what is the distance remaining on a hiking trip 28 mi long?

32. If Jane studied a hours and b minutes, how long *in hours* did she study?

In each table, substitute the given values of the variable to find the corresponding values of the expression.

33.

a	$(a^2) - 4$
-3	
0	
0.3	
2	
3	

34.

y	$6 - (y^3)$
-2	
-1	
0	
1	
2	

35.

z	$(6 - z)^3$
-2	
-1	
0	
1	
2	

36.

k	$\dfrac{k + 2}{5}$
-1	
0	
1	
2	
3	

37.

n	$\dfrac{n^2}{n}$
-2	
-1	
1	
2	
3	

38.

u	$\dfrac{100}{u^2}$
-2	
-1	
1	
2	
3	

39. It's a Trap The area of a *trapezoid* is given by the expression $\dfrac{1}{2}h(b_1 + b_2)$, where b_1 and b_2 are the lengths of the bases, and h is the height. Find the area of the trapezoid shown.

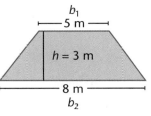

40. Box It A machine is set to make rectangular boxes that are three times as long as they are wide and just as tall as they are wide.
   a. Let x stand for the height of the boxes. Find an expression that will give the capacity of the manufactured boxes.
   b. What is the capacity of a box that is 6.5 inches tall?

41. Recall that when each female lion in an animal park eats 5 lb of meat a day, 6 days a week, the amount of meat eaten by f female lions in a week is $30f$ lb. Evaluate this expression to find the amount eaten by 6 female lions in a week.

MORE MATH REASONING

42. Order the following expressions from least to greatest.
   $n + 1$ $n + 4$ $n - 3$ n $n - 7$

43. Which is greater, $2n$ or $n + 2$? Test your answer with different values for n.

44. If k gives the number of one-dollar bills, q the number of quarters, and d the number of dimes, what is the total value in dollars?

> **Problem-Solving Tip**
>
> Simplify the problem.

45. Worth Its Weight in Leaves? Gold leaf is gold that has been beaten so thin that it can be used for painting or decoration. A standard 3-inch square gold leaf is about $\frac{1}{300,000}$ of an inch thick, and about 2000 leaves weigh an ounce.
   a. Write an equation that relates the thickness of the gold leaves to their weight.
   b. Gold leaf may be sold in books of 25 leaves. How many books should you get if you buy an ounce of gold leaf? How thick will the gold be?

2-2 PART C Making Connections

← C O N N E C T →   *You've learned to describe variable quantities, their relationships, and their values with the phrases and expressions of algebra. The language of algebra helps us to communicate to others the patterns and relationships we discover among quantities.*

Constants and variables are the *words* in the language of algebra, and algebraic expressions are the *phrases*. With this language, you can communicate algebraic ideas and describe the changes you see in the world around you.

EXPLORE: THE PAINTED CUBE

This is a solid cube with edges 3 units long. It's made up of many small, yellow cubes with edges 1 unit long. Imagine the large cube is sprayed with green paint on the outside.

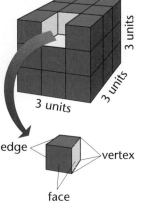

1. If the large cube is taken apart after it is painted, how many small cubes will have exactly three green faces? exactly two green faces? exactly one green face? no green faces? more than three green faces? How many small cubes are there in all?
2. Where in the large cube are the small cubes with three green faces located? Where are those with two green faces? with one green face? with no green faces? with more than three green faces?
3. Answer Steps 1 and 2 again for large cubes with edges of 4 units and of 5 units. Record your results in a table.

> **Problem-Solving Tip**
>
> Draw pictures of the cubes.

Large Cube's Edge (units)	3 Green Faces	2 Green Faces	1 Green Face	0 Green Faces	>3 Green Faces	Total
4						
5						

4. As the edge of the large cube varies from 3 to 4 to 5, which quantities remain constant? Which quantities vary? Do you notice any patterns that could help you predict these quantities for larger cubes?
5. Let *n* be the number of units along the edge of a large, painted cube. For each type of small cube (1 green face, 2 green faces, and so on), give an algebraic expression that tells the number of cubes of that type. Also give an expression for the total number of small cubes. Find the values for a cube with edges of 10 units by evaluating the expressions you found.

REFLECT

1. Why do we use letters in algebra?
2. Does an algebraic expression have a single value? Explain.
3. What does it mean to evaluate an algebraic expression?
4. In your own words, explain how variables and expressions can be used to describe patterns.

Self-Assessment

1. **Orange Juice** A shipment of oranges arrived at the port. There are 2 crates with a lb of oranges each and 7 crates with b lb of oranges each. Write an expression that will give the total weight in pounds of the orange shipment.

2. Which of the following *does not* show the product 14 times q.
   (a) $14q$ (b) $14 \cdot q$ (c) $14(q)$ (d) $14 \times q$ (e) not here

Write each expression without the × or the ÷ signs. Use exponents whenever appropriate.

3. $(x - y) \times 4$

4. $z \div (y - z)$

5. $13 \times (n \times n)$

6. $b \cdot b \cdot b$

7. $3 \div (2 \times y)$

8. $(x + y) \div z$

9. $(p - q) \times (r + s)$

10. $(x + y) \times (x + y) \times (x + y)$

There are one thousand meters in one kilometer. Write an expression for each of the following.

11. the number of meters in x kilometers

12. the sum of x kilometers and y meters if you use meters as the unit

13. the sum of x kilometers and y meters if you use kilometers as the unit

Write an expression that will give the sum of each of the following quantities using the unit in parentheses.

14. x hours and y minutes (hours)

15. a minutes and b seconds (seconds)

16. p yards and q inches (inches)

17. m kilograms and n grams (kilograms)

Write an algebraic expression for each of the following English phrases.

18. $\frac{1}{5}$ of z **19.** 3 times as many as y

20. 3 more than a **21.** 7 less than n

22. 120% of p **23.** the square of w

24. the quotient of a and b **25.** $\frac{1}{2}$ the product of b and h

26. the product of x and x **27.** the cube of the sum of x and y

Write an expression that will give you the value of each quantity.

28. the width of a rectangle whose area is 72 cm^2 and whose length is x cm

29. the number of yards of material purchased for $17.50, tax not included, at d dollars per yard

30. the length of the shaded part in each of these figures

a.

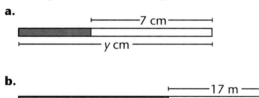

b.

Evaluate each expression in the table for the values of x given.

31.

x	$x - 7$
5	
2	
0	
-2	
-5	

32.

x	$7 - x$
5	
2	
0	
-2	
-5	

33.

z	$3(z^2)$
5	
2	
0	
-2	
-5	

34. On Target The target (recommended) heart rate for exercise, in beats per minute, is given by the expression $0.8(200 - a)$, where a is your age.

a. What is the target heart rate for a 14-year-old?

b. To check your heart rate, you usually measure your number of heartbeats for 10 or 15 sec. If a 45-year-old records 22 beats in 10 sec, is the person over, under, or at the target heart rate? Explain your reasoning.

35. That's Stretching It Weights are hung on the end of a spring, and the stretch of the spring is measured. The data are shown in the table.

s (cm)	3	6	9	12
w (g)	100	200	300	400

a. Write an expression that will give the weight in grams when you know the stretch.

b. Write an expression that will give the stretch in centimeters when the weight is known.

c. Use the expression in **35a** to predict the weight that will cause a stretch of 45 cm.

d. Use the expression in **35b** to predict the stretch caused by 1000 g of weight.

e. Sketch a graph of the relationship between the two quantities.

36. It All Adds Up While exploring polygons, Luis noticed a relationship between the number of sides of a polygon and the sum of its interior angles. He recorded his observations in a table like the one shown. He noticed that the sum of the interior angles of a polygon varied as the number of sides varied.

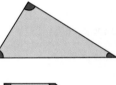

Number of Sides	Sum of Interior Angles
3	180
4	360
5	540
⋮	⋮
12	1800

Interior angles

a. Study the table and try to predict the sum of the interior angles for a hexagon (6 sides) and for an octagon (8 sides).

b. Explain how you can figure the sum of the angles when you know the number of sides.

c. Suppose the letter n gives the number of sides of any polygon. Use n to write an expression that would give the sum of the interior angles.

d. Test your expression, using the data from Luis's table. Do you get the same sums as Luis did?

On the Dot

○ This passage was written by a blind woman named Helen Keller in her book The Story of My Life. Can you read what she wrote? ● If the dots were raised from the surface of the paper, many blind people could read this easily. This is a system invented in 1824 by a blind, 15-year-old French student named Louis Braille. Today, the Braille system has been accepted for all written languages as well as for math and computer science. ● The Braille system uses a "cell" three dots high and two dots wide for each letter and punctuation mark. Some often-used combinations have "shorthand" cells. Braille readers have also agreed to connect the word *to* to the word that follows. ● What would it be like if we did not agree how to start and end sentences or how to spell words? Did you know that the order of words in a sentence can be different in different languages? ● In algebra, as in Braille and other languages, we need to agree how to express ideas so that everyone can understand them. ●

| ed | comma | period | capital letter sign | ch | the | to |

---

1. How many sentences are in the Braille passage? Can you guess any words?
2. If the left-to-right order of written English were suddenly changed to right-to-left, would the ideas being communicated change?
3. What would it be like to read writing without punctuation marks such as commas and periods?
4. Without changing the word order, insert commas, quotation marks, or other punctuation into this phrase to create at least two sentences with different meanings.

   when Pam called Sue Ann was in the shower

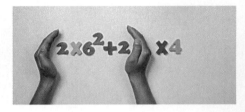

Order of Operations

2-3 PART A

← CONNECT → *You've worked with algebraic expressions and seen how parentheses and fraction bars indicate which operations to perform first. Now you will evaluate expressions with several operations, with or without grouping symbols.*

You've seen that parentheses in an expression show which operations to do first. Does the placement of parentheses really affect the value of an expression? You'll investigate this question in the following Explore.

EXPLORE: LEND A HAND

$$2 \cdot 6^2 + 2 \cdot 4$$

1. Copy this expression several times. Insert one or more pairs of parentheses in each copy to create as many different expressions as you can.
2. Evaluate each expression with your calculator.
3. How many different values did you get? Compare your list of values with a classmate's list. If they are different, try to create expressions whose values you don't have on your list. For example, do you have an expression with a value of 304?
4. Where should you put parentheses to get the expression of the greatest value? Why does that work? What is the greatest value?
5. Where should you put parentheses to get the expression of the least value? Why does that work? What is the least value?
6. Briefly describe how and why an expression's value depends on the order in which the operations are performed.

Problem-Solving Tip

Try working the problem backwards.

To avoid getting different values, we evaluate expressions according to agreed-upon rules. These rules are called **conventions.** This means that people *could* have agreed to different rules, but these are the ones they chose.

CONSIDER

Alma entered the expression $2 + 3 \cdot 4 + 5$ into her calculator and got 25. Wai Lum entered the same expression and got 19.

1. What do you get when you enter $2 + 3 \cdot 4 + 5$ in your calculator?
2. How did Alma's and Wai Lum's calculators evaluate the expression?
3. Which do you think is the *right* value of the expression?

Just as there is an order in which we must perform some daily tasks, there is an order that must be followed for mathematical operations.

ORDER OF OPERATIONS

1. Evaluate what is inside parentheses or above or below fraction bars.
2. Evaluate powers.
3. Multiply and divide in order from left to right.
4. Add and subtract in order from left to right.

EXAMPLES

1. Evaluate $8 + 5 \cdot 4^2$.

$$8 + 5 \cdot 4^2 = 8 + 5 \cdot 16 \qquad \text{Evaluate powers first.}$$
$$= 8 + 80 \qquad \text{Multiply before adding.}$$
$$= 88$$

2. Evaluate $2x^3 - 4x$ for $x = 3$.

$$2x^3 - 4x = 2 \cdot 3^3 - 4 \cdot 3 \qquad \text{Substitute 3 for each } x.$$
$$= 2 \cdot 27 - 4 \cdot 3 \qquad \text{Evaluate powers first.}$$
$$= 54 - 12 \qquad \text{Multiply before subtracting.}$$
$$= 42$$

Computers usually perform one instruction at a time. Keeping track of the correct order of instructions is a key task of computers and computer programmers. Many computers follow *algorithms,* or procedures, based on **expression trees.**

3. Write an expression tree for 4*x*.

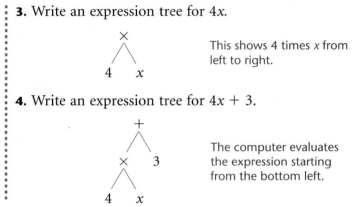

This shows 4 times *x* from left to right.

4. Write an expression tree for 4*x* + 3.

The computer evaluates the expression starting from the bottom left.

a. Evaluate $35 - 4(2^4 - 21)$.
b. Evaluate $5x^2 - 3x + 7$ for $x = 2$.
c. Write an expression tree for $4(x + 3)$.
d. Write an expression for the tree at the right.

A calculator can help you evaluate complicated expressions. A scientific calculator "knows" the order of operations, but *you* have to know that a fraction bar acts as a grouping symbol.

5. Evaluate the expression $1.9 \cdot \dfrac{3.1 + 4}{5.25} - (2.3 + 3)^2$.

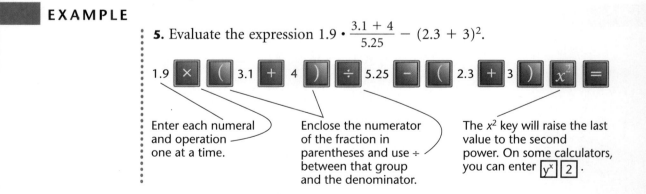

Enter each numeral and operation one at a time.

Enclose the numerator of the fraction in parentheses and use ÷ between that group and the denominator.

The x^2 key will raise the last value to the second power. On some calculators, you can enter y^x 2 .

6. Fireworks are launched at an angle of 70° and a velocity (v) of 240 ft/sec. The fuse is set to go off in 2.5 sec. For safety, we need to know the height at which the fireworks will explode.

The expression for height, in feet, follows.

$$0.94vt + \frac{gt^2}{2}$$

In the expression, t is the number of seconds after launch, and g is the constant acceleration due to gravity, which is -32 feet per second per second (ft/sec^2). At what height will the fireworks explode?

$v = 240;$ $t = 2.5;$ $g = -32$:

$$0.94vt + \frac{gt^2}{2} = 0.94 \cdot 240 \cdot 2.5 + \frac{-32 \cdot 2.5^2}{2}$$

Substitute the values of the variables.

Enter and evaluate on a calculator.

You get the value 464.

The firecracker will explode at a height of about 464 ft.

Evaluate these expressions.

e. $(11 - 9)^2 + \dfrac{6 - 21}{5}$

f. $\dfrac{4.3 \cdot (1.7 - 4)^2}{3.3} + (8.3 + (-3) \cdot 3.2)$

g. What if $v = 275$ and $t = 3$ in the formula in Example 6? At what height will the firecracker explode?

1. How do you show that you want to add two numbers in an expression before raising the sum to a power?

2. What would happen if we did not have conventions about the order of operations? Explain.

3. Explain how an expression tree indicates the order in which operations are carried out.

Exercises

CORE

1. Getting Started To evaluate $(3 + 4 \cdot 5) - 30$, do the following.
   a. Work inside parentheses first. There are no powers, so multiply. What is $4 \cdot 5$?
   b. You now have $(3 + 20) - 30$. What is $3 + 20$?
   c. You now have $23 - 30$. What is this value? You have evaluated the original expression.

Here's a reminder of the commutative and associative properties.

COMMUTATIVE PROPERTIES OF ADDITION AND MULTIPLICATION

For any real numbers a and b,

$$a + b = b + a \qquad \text{and} \qquad a \cdot b = b \cdot a.$$

ASSOCIATIVE PROPERTIES OF ADDITION AND MULTIPLICATION

For any real numbers a, b, and c,

$$a + (b + c) = (a + b) + c \qquad \text{and} \qquad a \cdot (b \cdot c) = (a \cdot b) \cdot c.$$

Evaluate each expression.

2. a. $-11 + 12 + 7 - 8$ **3. a.** $18 - 9 + 3$ **4. a.** $18 \div 9 \div 3$
   b. $(-11 + 12) + (7 - 8)$ **b.** $18 \div (9 \times 3)$ **b.** $18 \div 9 \times 3$
   c. $-11 + (12 + 7) - 8$ **c.** $18 - (9 + 3)$ **c.** $18 \div (9 \div 3)$

5. $\left(-\dfrac{2}{3}\right) + \left(-\dfrac{1}{2}\right) - 1\dfrac{1}{6}$ **6.** $-7.9 - 0.9 + (-2.1)$

7. $\dfrac{17 - 2}{3} - 3^2$ **8.** $6 - 2^2 \times (8 - 6 \div 2)$

9. Choose the statement about order of operations that is *incorrect*.
   (a) Multiplication is performed before subtraction.
   (b) Powers are evaluated before division is performed.
   (c) Evaluation within parentheses is done before multiplication.
   (d) Addition is performed before division.

Insert parentheses in each expression so that you get the value shown.

10. $9 + 6 \div 3 - 1 = 4$ **11.** $9 + 6 \div 3 - 1 = 12$

12. $10 - 2 + 4 \div 2 = 7$ **13.** $10 - 2 + 4 \div 2 = 6$

14. Evaluate each of the following numerical expressions.

a. $3^2 \cdot 4 + 7 \cdot 5$ **b.** $4 \cdot 3^2 + 5 \cdot 7$ **c.** $3^2 \cdot 4 + 5 \cdot 7$

d. $7 \cdot 5 + 3^2 \cdot 4$ **e.** $5 \cdot 7 + 3^2 \cdot 4$

f. Are you surprised by the results? What properties account for the relationship among their values?

Write the expression shown by the expression tree.

15.

16.

17. The expression for the mean of three numbers is $\dfrac{a + b + c}{3}$. Find the mean if $a = -10$, $b = 25$, and $c = 45$.

18. The sales tax rate paid on an item is $8\frac{1}{2}\%$. This can be expressed as $0.085p$, where p is the price of the item. Find the sales tax for a $25 sweater.

19. Fireworks Display Use the formula for fireworks height in Example 6 to determine the height of fireworks when velocity (v) is 250 ft/sec and t is 3.5 sec. How does it compare to the height in the example?

Evaluate each expression for $a = -2$ and $b = 3$.

20. $3a + 5b$ **21.** $5b + 3a$ **22.** $\left(\frac{1}{2}a\right)(-4b)$ **23.** $(-4b)\left(\frac{1}{2}a\right)$ **24.** $\left(\frac{1}{2}\right)(-4)ab$

25. Find the value of each expression for the given values of the variable.

		$2 - x$	x^2	$x^2 - x$	$1 - 4x^2$
a.	1				
b.	-1				
c.	-3				

Write the expression described by each statement.

26. Subtract 3 from x and divide the difference by 2.

27. Multiply 5 by x and 3 by y; then add the two products.

28. Subtract the sum of 2 and x from y.   **29.** Square the sum of a and b.

30. Add the square of a and the square of b.   **31.** Add 3 and z, then multiply the sum by x.

32–35. Write expression trees for Exercises 26–29.

36. While evaluating the familiar formulas for distance and area, Natasha wondered what happens to the units that are part of the quantities she substituted in for the variables. Write the units into your expressions as you evaluate these formulas.
   a. $d = rt$ for $r = 55$ mi/hr and $t = 2$ hr
   b. $A = lw$ for $l = 11.2$ cm and $w = 7$ cm
   c. What happened to the units in your calculations?

LOOK AHEAD

37. Evaluate for $x = -5$ and $y = 5$.
   a. $3(y - x)$ **b.** $3y - 3x$ **c.** $3(x - y)$ **d.** $3x - 3y$
   e. Which of the above have the same value?

MORE PRACTICE

Evaluate each expression.

38. $3 - 4^2$

39. $(3 - 4)^2$

40. 3×4^2

41. $(3 \times 4)^2$

42. $3 + 6 \times 5 - 2$

43. $3 + 6 \times (5 - 2)$

44. $(3 + 6) \times (5 - 2)$

45. $(3 + 6) \times 5 - 2$

46. $-2 + (-7) - (-9) - 4$

47. $3 \times 5 + 6 \times (-3)$

48. $8 \times \left(-\dfrac{3}{4}\right) + 1$

49. $43 - 4 \times 2^3$

Insert parentheses in each expression so that, when evaluated, it gives the indicated result. Check your answer by evaluating the expression.

50. $8 \times 6 - 3 + 1 \times 4 = 32$

51. $8 \times 6 - 3 + 1 \times 4 = 28$

52. $10 \div 2 - 1 \times 3 + 4 = 16$

53. $10 \div 2 - 1 \times 3 + 4 = 28$

Evaluate each expression for the given values of the variables.

54.

	x	$5(x - 2) + (2x + 3)$
a.	2	
b.	0	
c.	3.5	

55.

	a	$\dfrac{a + 2}{5}$
a.	5	
b.	-1	
c.	1.2	

Write the expression described by each statement. Use parentheses and fraction bars only as needed.

56. Subtract z from 7, and add 3 to the difference.

57. Add 7 to a, and divide the sum by b.

58. Add 5 to the sum of the cube of x and 3.

59. Divide y by 3, and multiply the quotient by x.

60. Multiply the difference when 2 is subtracted from x by five.

61. Subtract the product of x and y from 17.

MORE MATH REASONING

62. If the parentheses are not necessary, rewrite the expression without them. Explain why the parentheses are not needed.
  a. $(1 + 2) + (3 + 4)$ **b.** $11 + (4 \times 2)$ **c.** $(6 - 4) \div 5 + 1$ **d.** $(10 \div 2 + 3) - 1$

63. Don't Leave Home Without It Jeff and Sue went on vacation. Jeff took $350 as spending money and spent an average of $32 per day. Sue took $300. She didn't spend any money the first two days, but then she spent an average of $21 per day. Let x be the number of days since Jeff and Sue left on vacation.

> **Problem-Solving Tip**
> Draw a diagram.

  a. Write an expression that will give how much money Jeff has left x days after starting his vacation.
  b. Evaluate the expression to find out how much spending money Jeff has left nine days after he started his vacation.
  c. Write an expression that will show how much Sue has left x days after leaving on vacation. Evaluate the expression to find out how much money Sue has left nine days after leaving on vacation.
  d. Write an expression that will give the difference in the amounts of money Jeff and Sue have left x days after they went on vacation. Evaluate the expression to find out who has more money left seven days after they left on vacation, and how much more.
  e. Who runs out of money first? Explain.

64. Why do you suppose we need to have rules for the order of operations? Why not evaluate expressions from left to right? Think of a situation that justifies the need for conventions.

65. A Braille cell has spaces for two dots across and three dots down.
  a. If only the top four spaces are used, how many unique "letters" can be formed?
  b. If one dot is used in either of the two lower spaces, how many more letters can be formed?

2-3
PART B
The Distributive Property

← C O N N E C T → *You've seen how we agree to evaluate expressions with several operations. Now you will see how you can change an expression into one that gives the same values but may be easier to evaluate.*

EXPLORE: SAME THING, DIFFERENT NAME

The Greenbelt is part park and part nature preserve. Let *x* stand for the length of the park in miles.

1. Use the formula $A = lw$ for the area of a rectangle of length *l* and width *w* to find expressions for
   a. the area of the park
   b. the area of the preserve

2. Use the expressions you found in Step 1 to write an expression for the total area of the Greenbelt.

3. Write an expression for the entire length of the Greenbelt. Use this expression in the formula $A = lw$ to write a second expression for the total area of the Greenbelt.

4. A surveyor finds that the park is 2 mi long. Evaluate the expressions in Steps 2 and 3, and compare the values. What do you notice about these values?

5. Substitute other values for *x* in the two expressions. What do you conclude from your results?

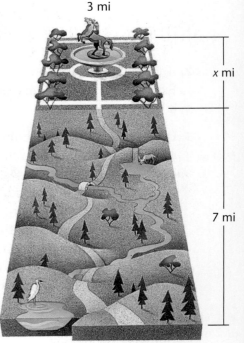

3 mi

x mi

7 mi

3 mi

Two expressions are **equivalent** if they have the same value whenever the same numbers are substituted for the variables in each expression.

To indicate that two expressions are equivalent, we use an equal sign (=).

$$a(b + c) = ab + ac \quad \text{and} \quad a(b - c) = ab - ac$$

This means that for any values of a, b, and c, the expression on the left of the equal sign has the same value as the expression on the right.

$$a = 4 \qquad b = 3 \qquad c = 9$$

$$
\begin{aligned}
a(b + c) = 4(3 + 9), && ab + ac = 4 \cdot 3 + 4 \cdot 9 \\
= 4 \cdot 12 && = 12 + 36 \\
= 48 && = 48 \qquad \text{same value}
\end{aligned}
$$

$$
\begin{aligned}
a(b - c) = 4(3 - 9), && ab - ac = 4 \cdot 3 - 4 \cdot 9 \\
= 4 \cdot {-6} && = 12 - 36 \\
= -24 && = -24 \qquad \text{same value}
\end{aligned}
$$

Transforming the expression $4(3 + 9)$ into the equivalent expression $4 \cdot 3 + 4 \cdot 9$ is called *distributing* the 4 over the sum $3 + 9$. In general, we say that multiplication *distributes* over addition and subtraction.

$$2(x+7)=2x+2\cdot7=2x+14 \qquad -1(3x+5)=-1(3x)+(-1)(5)=-3x-5$$

$$(1+9x)7=1\cdot7+9x\cdot7=7+63x \qquad (1-b)b=1\cdot b-b\cdot b=b-b^2$$

In the last expression we used the fact that $1 \cdot b = b$. Likewise, $-1 \cdot b = -b$. For $-b$ we say, "the opposite of b." We *avoid* saying "negative b" because $-b$ could represent a positive or negative value, depending on the value of b.

DISTRIBUTIVE PROPERTY

Multiplication over addition and over subtraction

For any real numbers a, b, and c,

$$a(b + c) = ab + ac \quad \text{and} \quad a(b - c) = ab - ac.$$

Division over addition and over subtraction

For any real numbers a, b, and c ($a \neq 0$),

$$\frac{b + c}{a} = \frac{b}{a} + \frac{c}{a} \quad \text{and} \quad \frac{b - c}{a} = \frac{b}{a} - \frac{c}{a}$$

CONSIDER

?

1. Is it also true that $(b + c)a = ba + ca$, and $(b - c)a = ba - ca$? Explain.

Use the distributive property and other properties to write an equivalent expression without parentheses. Show all steps.

1. $6x(x + 7) = 6x \cdot x + 6x \cdot 7$ Use the distributive property.

$= 6(x \cdot x) + (6 \cdot 7)x$ Use the commutative property.

$= 6x^2 + 42x$ Multiply, and express $x \cdot x$ as a power.

2. $(2 - y)4 = 2 \cdot 4 - y \cdot 4$ Use the distributive property.

$= 8 - 4y$ Multiply, and use the commutative property.

WHAT DO **YOU** THINK?

Nicole is ordering food for herself and four friends. Each of them wants a burrito, chips, and a drink from the restaurant where Jason works. A burrito costs $2.50, chips cost $0.95, and a drink costs $1.25.

Jason thinks . . .

I'll enter the prices for five burritos, then five nachos, and then five large drinks on the cash register. Then it will total the prices.

$$5(2.50) = 12.50$$
$$5(0.95) = 4.75$$
$$5(1.25) = \underline{6.25}$$
$$= 23.50$$

The bill is $23.50 plus tax.

Nicole thinks . . .

I'll add the prices of the three items and then multiply by 5.

$$5(2.50 + 0.95 + 1.25) = 5 \cdot (4.70) = 23.50$$

The total bill is $23.50 plus tax, the same as Jason's total.

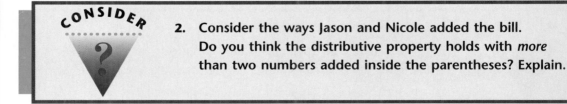

CONSIDER

?

2. Consider the ways Jason and Nicole added the bill. Do you think the distributive property holds with *more* than two numbers added inside the parentheses? Explain.

Recall from your work with integers that subtracting a number is the same as adding its opposite. Also, multiplying by -1 gives the opposite of a number. Since variables and expressions represent numbers, these rules apply to them as well.

EXAMPLES

3. Write an equivalent expression for $-(x + 3)$ without parentheses.

$$-(x + 3) = -1(x + 3)$$ Multiply by -1 to write the opposite of an expression.

$$= -1 \cdot x + (-1) \cdot 3$$ Use the distributive property.

$$= -x + (-3)$$ Write using opposites.

$$= -x - 3$$ Adding the opposite is equivalent to subtracting.

4. A rancher has four fields with the same area and a two-acre homestead. If she divides her land equally among her three children, how much land will each child inherit? Write two equivalent expressions for your answer.

Let $x =$ the area, in acres, of each field. Each child will inherit one-third of the total $4x + 2$ acres, or $\dfrac{4x - 2}{3}$ acres.

To write an equivalent expression, use the distributive property.

$$\frac{4x + 2}{3} = \frac{4x}{3} + \frac{2}{3}$$ Distribute the 3 under the sum in the numerator.

$$= \frac{4}{3}x + \frac{2}{3}$$ Use the associative property of multiplication to write $\frac{4x}{3}$ as $\frac{4}{3}x$.

TRY IT

Use the distributive property and other properties to write an equivalent expression without parentheses.

a. $-(a + 2b)5$ **b.** $-3(2y - z + 1)$ **c.** $\dfrac{5x + 6}{5}$

REFLECT

1. What does it mean for two expressions to be equivalent?

2. When is $-x$ a positive number?

3. What is the *opposite* of the *opposite* of an expression?

4. Joan used the distributive property and got the expression $-3x + 6y - 15$. What expression could she have started out with?

Exercises

CORE

1. Getting Started

    a. Write an expression for the area of the large rectangle (length times width) without carrying out any addition or multiplication. _____(_____ + _____)

    b. Write a different expression for the area of the large rectangle that shows the sum of the areas of the small rectangles. Do not carry out the addition or multiplication. (_____ • _____) + (_____ • _____)

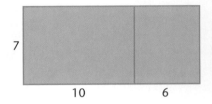

Use the distributive properties to evaluate each expression. Show your work.

2. $-5(500 + 7)$

3. $\dfrac{16 + 88}{-4}$

4. $-3(2 - 0.3)$

Use the distributive, associative, and commutative properties to carry out the operations indicated, leaving no grouping symbols.

5. $-(2m - 3)$

6. $6 - (x + 2)$

7. $10 - 2(4 - 3x)$

8. $(7 - p)6$

9. $(2a - 3b + 4c)(-5)$

10. $8 + \dfrac{2}{3}(18 - 12z)$

11. Evaluate each pair of expressions.

    a. $\dfrac{9 + 6}{2}$ and $\dfrac{1}{2}(9 + 6)$ **b.** $\dfrac{21 + 4}{-5}$ and $-\dfrac{1}{5}(21 + 4)$

    c. Are the expressions in each pair equivalent? Explain.

    d. In 11a above, dividing by 2 has the same effect as multiplying by _____.

    e. In 11b above, dividing by -5 has the same effect as multiplying by _____.

    f. What operation has the same effect as dividing by a given number?

12. Write an explanation for each step.

    a. $-3x(x - 4) = -3x \cdot x + (-3x) \cdot (-4)$

    b. $= -3(x \cdot x) + (-3)(-4) \cdot x$

    c. $= -3x^2 + 12x$

13. Measuring Up One rule of thumb is that a man's adult height in inches will be $21(1 + 0.06a)$, where a is his height at age three. Use a distributive property to write this rule a different way. Then determine the adult height of a man who was thirty-seven inches tall at age three.

14. To find the amount of money you would have in the bank from one interest period to the next, multiply the amount you start with, P, by $(1+ r)$, where r is the interest rate. Use a distributive property to write equivalent formulas. Evaluate each one for $P = \$1000$ and $r = 0.025\%$ daily interest to find the amount of money you would have in one day.

15. How could you use a distributive property to multiply 45 by 98 in your head? (Hint: Think of 98 as a difference.)

Change each expression to an equivalent expression using multiplication. Then use the distributive, associative, and commutative properties to rewrite the expression.

16. $\dfrac{22d - 77}{11}$

17. $\dfrac{20 - 5s + 100}{5}$

18. $\dfrac{x - 5}{x}$

19. On Golden Pond You can get the approximate area of irregular shapes, like this lake, by dividing them into trapezoids of equal height and adding their areas. Write an expression for the area of the lake. Is there more than one way to write it?

$$A= \frac{h}{2}(b_1 + b_2)$$

20. Second Target In 2-2, you used the expression $0.8(200 - a)$ for the target heart rate for exercise in beats per minute, where a is your age. Use a distributive property to rewrite the expression. What is the maximum target heart rate? For what age does this apply?

21. Is the value of $-x$ always negative? For what values of x is $-x$ negative? positive? Is the value of $-x$ ever 0? If so, when?

22. A *trapezium* has no sides parallel. Its area is given by the following expression.

$$\frac{1}{2}(ah_1 + bh_2)$$

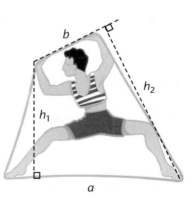

a. Evaluate the expression for $a = 5$ ft 4 in., $b = 2$ ft 8 in., $h_1 = 4$ ft 4 in., and $h_2 = 6$ ft 4 in.
b. If a gymnast stands inside a continuous elastic band to form a trapezium, what do you think is the approximate maximum area that he could form? The approximate minimum area?

23. Evaluate $3x(x + 7)$ and $3x^2 + 7x$ for $x = 8$. Do the two expressions have the same value for the same value of x? Explain.

24. Birds Beware The air intake of a fan jet engine depends partly on the volume of its engine covering. The volume is given by the following expression.

$$\frac{1}{3}\pi d(r_1^2 + r_2^2 + r_1 r_2)$$

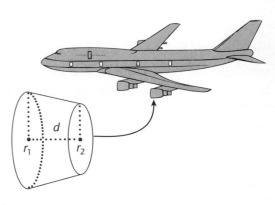

a. Use a distributive property to give an equivalent form for this expression.

b. Evaluate the expression for $d = 81$ in., $r_1 = 32$ in., and $r_2 = 30$ in.

LOOK BACK

What is the nearest integer to each sum or difference? [Previous course]

25. $\frac{7}{8} + \frac{15}{16}$
     26. $-\frac{5}{6} + \frac{11}{10}$
     27. $\frac{12}{5} - 3$

28. Give an example of an ordered pair that is on the x-axis and left of the origin. [1-2]

29. Give an example of an ordered pair that is in Quadrant III. [1-2]

30. In how many ways can the letters ABCD be ordered? [1-3]

MORE PRACTICE

Use the distributive properties to evaluate the following expressions. Show your work.

31. $-6(5 + 3)$
     32. $\frac{5 + 6}{-1}$
     33. $-2(3 - 0.3)$

34. $2.2(2 - 3 - 5)$
     35. $\frac{15 - 8}{3} - 3$
     36. $\frac{1}{3}(300 + 12) + \frac{1}{3}$

Use the distributive, associative, and commutative properties to rewrite the following expressions, leaving no grouping symbols.

37. $3(a + b)$
     38. $3x(1 - x)$
     39. $n(5n - 3)$

40. $2 - 5(b - 6)$
     41. $7 + 2(w + 7)$
     42. $-(2d - 8e - f)$

43. $\frac{x + 5}{5}$
     44. $p - \frac{p - 1}{p}$
     45. $3 + (4F - 5)\frac{3}{4}$

46. What is $-(-x)$?

47. Eat and Run Each of four kids ordered a burger and a soda at a fast-food restaurant. There are two ways to compute the bill. What are they? What property is illustrated by the two methods?

MORE MATH REASONING

48. a. Write two different expressions, both involving the same variables, that will give the perimeter of any rectangle.

b. Substitute numbers for your variables to make sure that the two expressions do give the same values for a rectangle of any specified length and width.

Substitute numbers for the variables in each expression to decide whether or not the expressions in each pair are equivalent. (Hint: A calculator may be helpful here.)

49. $\dfrac{a}{b + c}$ and $\dfrac{a}{b} + \dfrac{a}{c}$

50. $\dfrac{v + w}{z}$ and $\dfrac{v}{z} + \dfrac{w}{z}$

51. $\dfrac{m - n}{p}$ and $\dfrac{m}{p} - \dfrac{n}{p}$

52. $\dfrac{c}{d - f}$ and $\dfrac{c}{d} - \dfrac{c}{f}$

53. $\sqrt{a + b}$ and $\sqrt{a} + \sqrt{b}$

54. $(r - s)^2$ and $r^2 - s^2$

55. $(x \cdot y)^3$ and $x^3 \cdot y^3$

56. $\dfrac{x + y}{y}$ and $x + 1$

57. Is there a distributive property for scalar multiplication and addition of matrices? Check whether $rA + rB = r(A - B)$ for two matrices A and B, with the same dimension and scalar multiplier, r. Show your work.

58. What are different ways to find the mean of a set of numbers if the set has fifty 8s, fifty 12s, and fifty 17s.

59. Nettiquette This cube has an edge of length x, so one face has area x^2. Since a cube has six faces, the whole surface area of the cube is given by the expression $6x^2$. The diagram, called a **net**, shows the cube folded out so you can see all six faces. Here is a box with dimensions a, b, and c. Draw a net to show that its surface area can be given by the expression $2(ab + bc + ca)$.

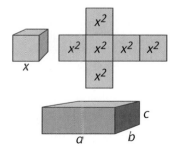

60. Are You Rusty? The following *chemical equation* shows how iron oxide (rust) is formed. A molecule of oxygen (O_2) contains 2 atoms of oxygen, and a molecule of iron oxide (Fe_2O_3) contains 2 atoms of iron and 3 atoms of oxygen.

$$4Fe \quad + \quad 3O_2 \quad \rightarrow \quad 2Fe_2O_3$$

| 4 atoms of iron (Fe) | 3 molecules of oxygen (O_2) | 2 molecules of iron oxide (Fe_2O_3) |

Verify that the numbers of iron atoms and oxygen atoms are the same before and after the reaction. Explain how counting the atoms is related to using the distributive property.

← CONNECT → *You've used the distributive property to write equivalent expressions. Now you'll see more ways to write equivalent expressions, which can make them easier to evaluate.*

By now you are familiar with algebraic expressions. We refer to the *parts* of an expression that are added as **terms.** Numbers and variables, and their products, quotients, and powers, can all be terms of an expression.

Terms This expression has three terms.

$$3x^2 + 2x + 8$$

There are two variable terms.
The first term has **coefficient** 3.
The second term has **coefficient** 2.

There is one constant term

Notice that $3x^2$ is a single term even though it involves two operations—squaring x and multiplying by 3.

The numerical factor of a term containing variables is the **coefficient** of the term.

We can always think of expressions involving subtraction as using only addition. In the expression $4x^2 - 2x - 8$, think of subtracting $2x$ as adding its opposite, $-2x$. The middle term of this expression is $-2x$. The coefficient of this term is -2.

CONSIDER

1. **Which term in the expression $4x^2 - x - 8$ has coefficient −1? How do you know?**

a. How many terms are there in $4x + 3$? in $2x^3 - 3x^2 + x - 2$?

b. What are the coefficients of the variable terms in $4x + 3$?
in $2x^3 - 3x^2 + x - 2$?

Generally, an equivalent expression with fewer terms is easier to evaluate than the original. You must make sure, however, that the simplified expression is actually equivalent to the original one. Here is another look at equivalence.

Algebra tiles are useful for *modeling* algebraic expressions visually. Each tile is a geometric model of a term.

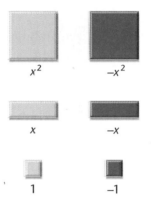

A combination of algebra tiles is a model of an expression.

This is a model of the expression $x^2 + 2x + 3$.

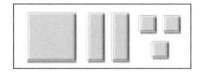

This is a model of the expression $2(-x - 5)$.

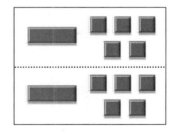

CONSIDER

2. What equivalent expression for $2(-x - 5)$ can you *see* just by looking at the model above?

3. What one-term expression is equivalent to the model at the right?

Algebra tiles can also be used to add expressions.

1. Add $x^2 + 2x + 3$ and $2(-x - 5)$ using algebra tiles.

$$x^2 + 2x + 3 \qquad + \qquad 2(-x - 5)$$

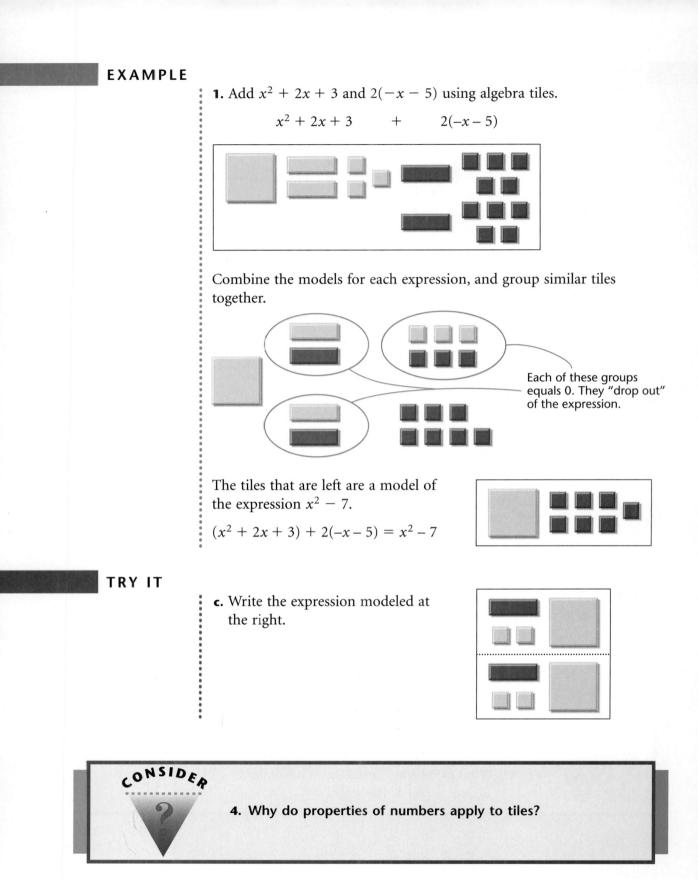

Combine the models for each expression, and group similar tiles together.

Each of these groups equals 0. They "drop out" of the expression.

The tiles that are left are a model of the expression $x^2 - 7$.

$$(x^2 + 2x + 3) + 2(-x - 5) = x^2 - 7$$

c. Write the expression modeled at the right.

CONSIDER

4. Why do properties of numbers apply to tiles?

1. Use algebra tiles to add each expression in the top row of the table to each expression in the left column, a pair at a time. Begin by modeling each expression of a pair.

2. Group similar tiles, removing combinations of tiles that add to 0. Then write the expression modeled by the remaining algebra tiles.

	x	**$2x + 5$**	**$x - 2x^2$**
$-x - 1$			
$2(2 + 4x)$			
$3(1 - x^2)$			

3. Could you have predicted any of the final expressions before modeling? What algebra rules did you use?

When you group algebra tiles that model an expression and remove combinations that add to 0, you are **combining like terms.**

Terms in an expression with the same variable factors are called **like terms.**

You can combine like terms algebraically, using the *distributive property* in reverse.

When you combine like terms, you *simplify* an expression by creating an equivalent expression with fewer terms.

$$2y + 5y = (2 + 5)y = 7y$$

EXAMPLE

2. Simplify $6x + 2x^2 - 3x$.

$$6x + 2x^2 - 3x = 2x^2 + (6x - 3x)$$
Use the commutative and associative properties to gather like terms.

$$= 2x^2 + 3x$$
Combine like terms, using the distributive property.

Notice that $2x^2$ and $3x$ are *not* like terms. Although they have the same variable, their powers are not alike.

EXAMPLE

3. Simplify $3(4s + 2) - (s + 1)$.

$3(4s + 2) - (s + 1) = 12s + 6 - s - 1$ Multiply using the distributive property.

$= (12s - s) + (6 - 1)$ Gather like terms.

$= 11s + 5$ Combine like terms.

TRY IT

Simplify each expression by combining like terms.

d. $-3(2y - 7) + 6y$ **e.** $4z^2 - z(z - 3)$

REFLECT

1. Why is it useful to simplify an expression? Explain with an example.

2. Jill simplified the expression $2x - 2$ and got x. Did she simplify correctly? How could you use algebra tiles to explain?

3. Is it possible to add two expressions using algebra tiles, removing combinations of tiles that add to 0, and be left with no tiles? Explain.

4. Is $a + 3$ the opposite of $a - 3$? Explain.

5. Explain the title of the cartoon.

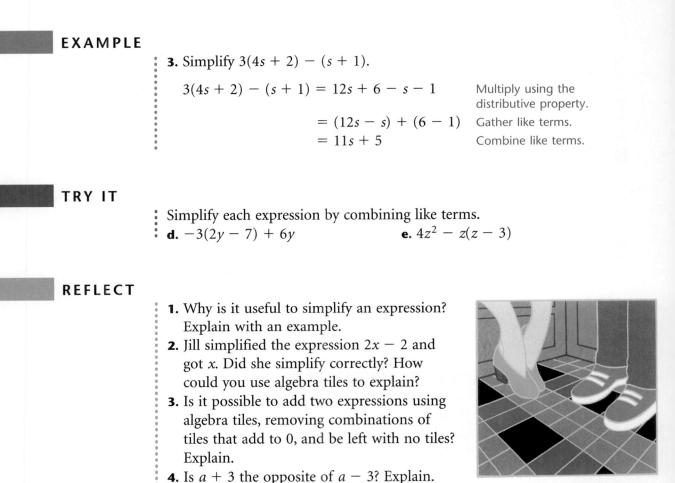

It's called $x^2 - 2x + 8$.

Exercises

CORE

1. Getting Started To simplify $3x - 2x^2 + 3x^2$, ask yourself these questions.

    a. Which terms, or parts of the expression, have the same powers?

    b. What is the sum of those terms?

    c. Can $3x - 2x^2 + 3x^2$ be simplified?

2. Match each word in the second column with its definition.

    a. the numerical factor of a term containing variables   **i.** terms

    b. a term of an algebraic expression that does not contain a variable   **ii.** constant term

    c. the parts of an algebraic expression that are added or subtracted   **iii.** coefficient

    d. terms in an expression with exactly the same variable factors   **iv.** like terms

3. Show an algebra-tile diagram for the following expressions.

    a. $2x - 1$ **b.** $4 - x$

    c. Combine your models to show the following expression.

$$(2x - 1) + (4 - x)$$

Write expressions for the models.

4.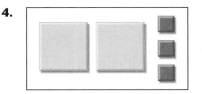

5.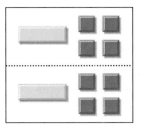

6. Write two different expressions for the model shown.

Substitute $a = -2$ and $b = 3$ for the variables in each expression to decide whether or not the expressions in each pair are equivalent. Explain your results.

7. $3a + 7b$ and $10ab$ **8.** $\dfrac{4a - 6}{2}$ and $2a - 3$ **9.** $6a - a$ and 6

10. $a + a$ and a^2 **11.** $-(a - b)$ and $-a + b$ **12.** $-(b + a)$ and $-b + a$

How many terms are in each expression? What are the coefficients of each term?

13. $2x - 5$?   **14.** $2x^4 - 3x^2 + x$ **15.** 10

Find a simple expression for the perimeter of each figure.

16.   **17.**

Draw algebra-tile diagrams to show whether or not the two expressions in each pair are equivalent.

18. $4(x + 1) - 3$ and $4x + 1$ **19.** $x + x$ and x^2 **20.** $5 + 3x$ and $8x$

Determine whether each expression is sometimes, always, or never positive.

21. y^2 **22.** $-2y^2$

23. a. Copy and complete the table by evaluating the expressions in the top row for the values of x given in the left column.

	$-(x + 2)$	$-x + (-2)$	$-x - 2$	$-(x - 2)$	$-x + 2$
$x = 3$					
$x = -3$					

  b. Write with equal signs all pairs of expressions that appear to be equivalent.
  c. What properties are illustrated by these equivalencies?

24. Copy and complete the table by evaluating the expressions for the given values of x.

  a.

x	-5	-2	0	2	5
$2 - x$					

  b.

x	-5	-2	0	2	5
$x - 2$					

  c. When is $2 - x$ greater than $x - 2$?
  d. How is $2 - x$ related to $x - 2$?

25. Which is greater, $4 + x$ or $x - 4$? Make a table if necessary.

26. Which is less, n^2 or $2n$? ⟵

> **Problem-Solving Tip**
>
> Make a table.

Simplify each expression.

27. $4.3y - 7.2y + 3.1$

28. $-3(2x + 5) - (x - 3)$

29. $\dfrac{4k - 12}{3} - 5k$

30. $8(3x - 2y + 2) - 3(6x - 5y - 1)$

Label the sides of each figure with the given characteristic.

31. a regular hexagon with perimeter $12n - 6$

32. a rectangle with perimeter $4x + 6y$

33. an isosceles triangle (two sides equal) with perimeter $4m + 5$

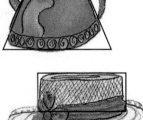

34. Write an expression for the area of each shaded figure.

a.

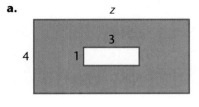

b.

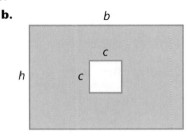

LOOK BACK

The graph shows populations of various ethnic groups in a large city. [1-1]

35. What percent of the circle is represented by each sector, A, B, C, and D?

36. Is the graph an appropriate representation of these quantities?

Add or subtract. [1-1]

37. $\begin{bmatrix} 0 & 1 \\ 1 & 0 \\ 1 & 1 \end{bmatrix} + \begin{bmatrix} -1 & -1 \\ 0 & 0 \\ -1 & -1 \end{bmatrix}$

38. $\begin{bmatrix} 4 & -2 & -1 \end{bmatrix} - \begin{bmatrix} 6 & -1 & 4 \end{bmatrix}$

39. Alpana drove 55 mi/hr for 1 hr, and 35 mi/hr for the next hour. Sketch and label a graph of distance and time. Are the quantities directly or inversely related? [2-1]

40. Find the mean and median for these temperatures. [1-1]

$-7°, -4°, 10°, 6°, -2°, 4°$

MORE PRACTICE

41. Evaluate each expression three different times, with y equal to 0, -3, and 2.

    a. $y - 5$
        b. $3 + (-y)$
        c. $y + 7 + y + y$

    d. $y - y$
        e. $y + y + y + y + y - 5$
        f. $-1 + y + (-1) + y$

    g. Which of the expressions in **41a–f** can be simplified into equivalent expressions? Simplify them.

    h. Test to see that the simpler expressions that you obtained in **41g** above are indeed equivalent to the given ones by substituting numbers for the variables.

State whether or not the following expressions are equivalent. Explain how you know.

42. $11x - 4x$ and 7

43. $\dfrac{x + y}{y}$ and x

44. $-(x + y)$ and $x - y$

45. $y \cdot y \cdot y$ and y^3

46. $(x - y)^3$ and $3x - 3y$

47. $-(3x - 2)$ and $2 - 3x$

48. $5(6 - x)$ and $30 - x$

49. $\dfrac{5x + 2}{5}$ and $x + 2$

50. $x + x + x + x$ and $4x$

51. $\dfrac{3x + 6}{3}$ and $x + 3$

52. The area of a square is given by the expression s^2, where s is the length of a side. Find the area of a square with a side 15 units in length.

53. The service charge in a restaurant is given by $0.15t$, where t is the total bill. Find the service charge for a bill of \$5.79 and for a bill of \$20.00.

How many terms are in each expression? What are the coefficients of each term?

54. $x^3 - 5x + 1$

55. $4x^4 + x$

56. -22

57. $4x^3$

58. $-2x^2 - x + 4$

59. $-x^2 - 1$

Find a simple expression for the perimeter of each figure.

60.

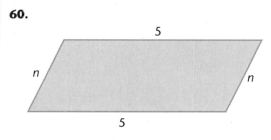

61.

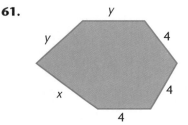

62. Fill in the table by evaluating the expression in the top row for the values of x given in the left column.

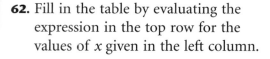

x	$-(x + 3)$	$-x + (-3)$	$-x - 3$
2			
-2			

Simplify each of the following expressions.

63. $5(4x + 3) - 20x - 15$

64. $-4(1.2x - 1) + 5.8x$

65. $8y - (y - 3)$

66. $-2(7z + 5v - 4) + 3(4z + 3v - 2)$

MORE MATH REASONING

67. An expression has three *unlike* terms. The distributive properties are used to multiply it by x and then to divide the result by 2.
   a. How many terms must there be in the resulting expression?
   b. To the resulting expression, 5 is added. Can you predict with certainty how many terms there are in the final result? Explain your reasoning.

Donna used the distributive property of multiplication and ended up with the expressions shown in the table below. In each case, do the following.
   a. Give an expression that Donna could have started out with.
   b. Give the simplest equivalent expression, and tell why it is the simplest.

	Final Expression	Starting Expression	Simplified Expression
68.	$7s - 17s$		
69.	$4x^2 + 5x^2$		
70.	$3xy^2 - 8xy^2$		
71.	$-a + 6a - 11a$		

72. In an algebraic expression in which like terms have been combined, does the term with the largest numerical coefficient always have the greatest value? Explain your reasoning.

2-3 PART D — Making Connections

← C O N N E C T →   *You've seen the order of operations that we agree on in algebra. You've also used the distributive property to write equivalent, often simpler, expressions. Without the common grammar of algebra, the same algebraic expression could mean different things to different people.*

In the following Explore, you will try to spot some of the common mistakes made by people using the *grammar* of algebra.

MATERIALS

Algebra tiles

Here are six expressions that someone simplified.

1. Show which expressions are equivalent and which ones are not by modeling each side with algebra tiles.
2. Correct any errors you find by writing a properly simplified expression on the right side of the equal sign.
3. Choose two values for x, and evaluate your simplified expression to check for equivalence.
4. Explain why someone might make the errors you found. Tell what properties they needed to apply in each case.

> **a.** $4(x - 1) = 4x - 1$
> **b.** $4x + 7x = 11 + x$
> **c.** $3(4 \cdot x) = 12x$
> **d.** $7x - 3x = 4$
> **e.** $2(x + 5) = 2x$
> **f.** $-2(x - 3) = -2x - 3$

REFLECT

1. Why do we need to agree about the order in which operations are to be done when evaluating expressions? What would happen if we didn't agree about this order?
2. What is the point of changing expressions into simpler ones that are equivalent?
3. When simplifying expressions, why is it important to make the simpler expression equivalent to the original one?
4. As x increases, does an expression involving x always increase? Explain.
5. What role does the distributive property play in combining like terms? Explain.

Self-Assessment

Simplify each expression, if possible.

1. $2q + 5q$
2. $2q + 5k$
3. $(r + s) + r$
4. $2q + 5k + q$
5. $(q - k) + k$
6. $3a - (c + a)$
7. $t + 4 + t - 4$
8. $8y - z + y$
9. $(x + y) + (x - y)$

Test each pair of expressions with values for the variables. Tell whether they are always, sometimes, or never equal.

10. $Q + R + S = S + Q + R$

11. $K + J + H = K + G + F$

12. $4 - (p - 3) = 7 - p$

13. $-(x - 5) = (5 - x)$

14. $m(n \div p) = m \cdot n \div m \cdot p$

15. $m \div (n \cdot p) = (m \div n) \cdot (m \div p)$

Simplify.

16. $6 - 6(x + 2)$

17. $3x(2 + 7) - 27$

18. $-(1 - x) - x$

19. $1 + (-1 + 2x) - x - x$

20. $7 + 4(4x + 1) + 3$

21. $x(x + 2y) + 3y$

22. $0.03x + 1.07x - 0.02(x - 1.0)$

23. $x(3x - x^2) + x^3$

24. Choose the correct simplified expression for the algebra tiles shown.
(a) $-x^2 + x - 1$ (b) $x^2 - x - 1$
(c) $x^2 + x - 1$ (d) $-x^2 + x - 3$

25. Write an algebraic expression with three terms and negative variable coefficients.

26. The sum of the three angles of a triangle is 180°. Angle A of triangle ABC is $\frac{1}{3}$ the size of angle B. Write an expression that will give the measure of angle C.

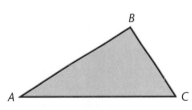

27. Lapping It Up Wanda ran three laps while training. Her time for the second lap was 3.8 sec more than for the first lap. Her time for the third lap was 1.5 sec less than for her first lap.
a. What expression will give her average time?
b. If her first lap took 2 min, what was her average time for the three laps?

28. Code Mode A Braille cell is 2 dots wide and 3 dots high.
a. How is it like a matrix? How is it different?
b. A special sign precedes letters to capitalize them. How is that like scalar multiplication? How is it different?

29. To Insure Promptness Waiters and waitresses are usually tipped 15% of the bill. Suppose the bill for a meal is $16.72. Which of the following is *not* a correct method of calculating the tip?
(a) $10\%(16.72) + 5\%(16.72)$ (b) $15\%(16.00) + 15\%(0.72)$
(c) $\frac{16.72}{10} + \frac{1}{2}\left(\frac{16.72}{10}\right)$ (d) not here

30. Gender Bender At Hairvue Beauty Salon haircuts cost $23 for women and $16 for men. On a typical day, there are one-third as many men as there are women getting a haircut.

   a. Write an expression that will give the total amount collected from haircuts on any given day.

   b. What quantities make up your expression?

31. Apple Algebra Jena and Mark enter an apple-picking contest. Jena picks apples at the rate of twelve pounds per minute. Mark starts picking apples eight minutes after the contest starts and picks at the rate of fifteen pounds per minute. Let x stand for the number of minutes that have gone by since the contest started.

   a. Write an expression that will give the number of pounds of apples that Jena has picked x minutes into the contest.

   b. Write an expression that will give the number of pounds of apples that Mark has picked x minutes into the contest.

   c. Write an expression that will give the total number of pounds Jena and Mark have picked x minutes after the contest started.

   d. Simplify this expression. What quantity does it represent?

$$12x - 15(x - 8)$$

   e. Twenty minutes into the contest, how many more pounds has Jena picked than Mark?

   f. Assume that, on the average, there are 2.6 apples in one pound. Find an expression that will give the total number of apples that Jena has picked x minutes into the contest. Do the same for Mark.

   g. What expression gives the total number of apples the two have picked x minutes into the contest?

   h. The contest is won by whoever picks the most apples in one hour. Who was the winner?

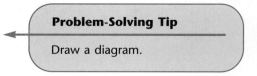

Problem-Solving Tip

Draw a diagram.

Rene Magritte, *Le Fils de l'Homme (Son of Man)*, 1964, Private Collection

Chapter 2 Review

In Chapter 2, some of the important tools of algebra were introduced, including variables and expressions. Variables and graphs can be used to describe how quantities change. Other important tools are the rules that must be followed in computation. The order of operations together with the distributive property allow us to make computations in the same way. You will continue to use these tools of algebra throughout the year as you study relationships and solve problems.

KEY TERMS

algebraic expression [2–2]

coefficient [2–3]

constant [2–1]

conventions [2–3]

directly related [2–1]

distributive property [2–3]

equivalent expressions [2–3]

evaluate an expression [2–2]

exponent [2–2]

inversely related [2–1]

like terms [2–3]

order of operations [2–3]

power [2–2]

quantity [2–1]

substitution [2–2]

term [2–3]

value [2–1]

variable [2–1]

Match the word in Column I to its definition in Column II.

I
1. inversely related
2. terms
3. coefficient
4. constant
5. power
6. variable

II
a. part of an expression that does not change
b. parts of an expression that are added
c. numeric factor in a term
d. The value of one quantity increases as the value of another decreases.
e. a quantity whose value changes
f. product in which the factors are identical

Choose the word that best completes the sentence

7. A quantity whose value changes is called a(n)
   (a) value   (b) like term   (c) variable   (d) expression   (e) none of these

8. A product in which the factors are identical is called a(n)
   (a) term   (b) power   (c) quantity   (d) exponent   (e) none of these

CONCEPTS AND APPLICATIONS

Tell whether each quantity is constant or variable. Explain. [2–1]

9. the distance from your house to school

10. the time it takes you to get to school

11. the distance between the lines of longitude

Write an algebraic expression for each phrase. [2–2]

12. 3 times x, plus 4

13. 3 times the sum of x and 4

Use these values for x to evaluate each expression: 5, 1, –1, and –5. [2–2]

14. $x - 9$

15. $9 - x$

16. $3(x)^2$

State whether the two quantities are directly or inversely related. Explain.

17. the number of minutes a cake has been baking and the time left before it can be served

18. the number of questions on a quiz and the time you will need to take the quiz

19. Which expression best describes the area of the shaded portion of the figure? [2–2]

    a. $(x - a)(y - b)$
    b. $(x - a)(y - a)$
    c. $(xa) - (yb)$
    d. $(xy) - (ab)$
    e. none of these

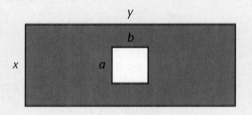

Copy each statement, and insert parentheses so that when you evaluate it, you get a true statement. [2–3]

20. $12 + 6 \div 3 - 8 = 6$

21. $10 - 5 + 1 \div 2 = 7$

Write the expression modeled by each set of algebra tiles.

22.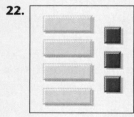

23.

24.

Simplify each expression. [2–3]

25. $-(5 - 3) + 10 \div 2$ **26.** $3(x - 9) - \frac{1}{2}(4 - 2x)$ **27.** $\frac{13 - 4}{6} - 4 \div 8$

28. The Oscar nominations have been announced for the 66th Academy Awards. Movie X received 12 nominations. What is wrong with this conclusion: The probability that Movie X will win an Oscar is $\frac{12}{66}$ or $\frac{2}{11}$? [1-3]

CONCEPTS AND CONNECTIONS

29. Geometry Find the areas of the shaded regions in terms of the variables.

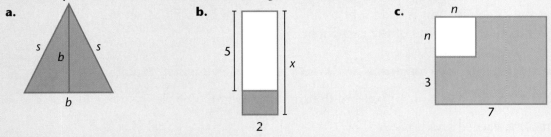

a.   **b.**   **c.**

30. Science The calories you are used to seeing on the back of food packages are actually what scientists call kilocalories. One Calorie is the same as 1000 calories. Scientists use a capital C for the calorie you are familar with. Use the algebra in this chapter to describe the relationship between Calories and calories.

SELF-EVALUATION

Write a paragraph about the language and rules of algebra you've learned in this chapter. Indicate how you think they will be helpful to you in future lessons. Write down what parts of the chapter were difficult for you and what sections you need to study further in order to better understand the chapter.

Chapter 2 Assessment

TEST

1. Tell whether each quantity is constant or variable.
     a. the number of meters in a kilometer
     b. the distance across the Mackinac Bridge
     c. the time it takes to cross the Mackinac Bridge
     d. the number of sides in a triangle

Evaluate or simplify the following expressions.

2. $-(4 - 1) + 6 \div 3$ **3.** $4(x - 2) + 2(4 - x)$ **4.** $\dfrac{8 - 4}{2} - 6 \cdot 4$

In the term $3x^2$,

5. 3 is the _____ **a.** exponent

6. x is the _____ **b.** coefficient

7. 2 is the _____ **c.** variable

8. Both Theo and Mateus have swimming pools. Water pours into their pools at the same rate, but it takes 3 hr to fill Theo's and 6 hr to fill Mateus's. Compare the volumes of the two pools.

State whether the two quantities are directly or inversely related. Explain.

9. the amount of soda in a glass and the amount left in the bottle

10. income earned and taxes paid

Match the phrase on the left with the appropriate algebraic expression on the right.

11. 2 less than the product of 5 and a number **a.** $2(5 + n)$

12. 5 decreased by a number times 2 **b.** $5n - 2$

13. 2 times the sum of 5 and a number **c.** $5 - 2n$

14. Leah used her algebra tiles to make this diagram. Which algebraic expression did she represent?
(a) $3x - 3$ (b) $3(x - 1)$ (c) $-3 + 3x$
(d) all of (a), (b), and (c) (e) not here

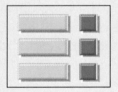

15. Find an expression that will give the distance around (perimeter of) the figure.

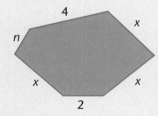

Use these values for x to evaluate each expression: $-2, -1, 0, 1, 2$.

16. $5 - x$ **17.** $x + 5$ **18.** $2(x)^2$

Find the value of each expression by substituting the given numbers for the variables.

19. $\frac{5}{9}(F - 32)$ for $F = 113$

20. $\frac{9}{5}C + 32$ for $C = 45$

21. Insert parentheses in the expression on the left of the equal sign so that you get the answer shown.

$$21 - 6 \div 3 + 2 = 3$$

22. Write an expression for the shaded area of the figure.

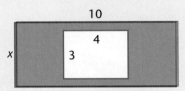

23. When simplifying the expression below, Pete got 42, and Soo Lee got 34.

$$\frac{4 \cdot (7 - 3)^2}{2} + (8 + (-3) \cdot 2)$$

a. Who is right?

b. Describe what common error might have led to the wrong answer.

PERFORMANCE TASK

Science The following paragraph, from *Rainbows, Curve Balls and Other Wonders of the Natural World Explained,* describes a wave in the ocean. Identify as many quantities as you can. Give an example of a direct relationship or an inverse relationship that is described. Sketch a graph of your relationship.

Wave size depends on wind speed, wind duration, and fetch, the distance of water over which the wind blows. The longer the distance the wind travels, the higher the waves will be. The greater the wind speed, the more powerful the waves.

Chapter 3

**Project A
Get in Line**
Should every person get the same
amount if there's a water shortage?
a food shortage? a gas shortage?

**Project B
My, How You've Grown**
How does plant growth
vary with rainfall?
Is this a good year
for corn?

**Project C
It's in the Mail**
How much does it
cost to send a letter to
Louisville? a package
to Pittsburgh?

DAVE SANFILIPPO

I didn't do well in high school mathematics. I didn't think I would use it.

Packages have weight and dimension limits. Time and distance determine my delivery route. When I make a delivery, I enter tracking information on a pocket computer. My job performance is measured by how well I manage my route. I definitely use more math than I thought I would.

Dave Sanfilippo
Driver
United Parcel Service
Menlo Park, California

David Sanfilippo

CALIFORNIA
C1431

3-1
Functional Relationships

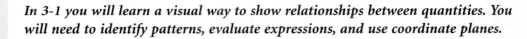

In 3-1 you will learn a visual way to show relationships between quantities. You will need to identify patterns, evaluate expressions, and use coordinate planes.

Draw a coordinate plane. Plot and label these points. [1-2]

1. $A(0, -3)$ **2.** $B\left(1\frac{1}{2}, 5\right)$ **3.** $C(3.5, 0)$ **4.** $D(-2, 1)$

Find the pattern and complete the table. [2-2]

5.

x	1	2	3	4	5	6
y	-1	-3	?	-7	-9	?

Evaluate the given expressions for x = -5. [2-3]

6. $9 - x$ **7.** x^2 **8.** $x + 5$ **9.** $x - 3$

3-2
Linear Functions

In 3-2 you will learn about linear functions and how to identify them from equations and a table of values. You will need to identify points on a plane and to evaluate expressions.

Give the coordinates of the following points. [1-2]

10. A

11. B

12. C

13. D

Complete each table. [2-2]

14.

x	-3	-1	0	1	3
$\frac{2x}{3}$					

15.

x	-4	-1	0	3	5
$x^2 - 3$					

162

UNSTABLE DOMAIN

Sometimes we find it hard to think of our planet Earth as something to be cared for—like an endangered species. We think of tremendous mountain ranges and the powerful waves. Given the awesome size of this planet, it is easy to forget how fragile the environment is.

Yet many of our human activities pollute the ground we walk on, the water we drink, and the air we breathe. Burning fossil fuels can increase carbon dioxide in the air to dangerous levels and the destruction of forests reduces the level of oxygen in the air.

One positive action we can take is to save energy.

The book *30 Simple Energy Things You Can Do to Save the Earth* describes energy conservation: "Conserving energy makes your air easier to breathe, improves visibility on a smoggy day, and helps keep acid rain from ruining the pristine lakes where you fish and swim."

1. How does the Pollutant Standards Index measure air pollution?
2. If the total amount of carbon dioxide in the atmosphere has increased 25% in the past two centuries, do you think it will take another two centuries for it to increase by another 25%? Explain.
3. Even if the 25% rate of increase remained constant over the centuries, does the increase in the actual amount of carbon dioxide remain constant?
4. What does the term "stable climate" mean? If it were a "thing of the past," how might life be different?

163

3-1
PART A
Relationships as Equations

← C O N N E C T → *Now you will continue to explore relationships between quantities. You will see that tables can show relationships and learn to write equations that express these relationships.*

Do you leave the water running while you brush your teeth, do the dishes, or wash the car? If you do, you are wasting a lot of water! An average household wastes 20,000 gallons of water in a year. Imagine how high 20,000 gallons of water would rise in your classroom. If the room measures 20 feet by 30 feet, 4500 gallons would be 1 foot deep.

EXPLORE: SPLISH SPLASH, TURN OFF THE BATH

This table shows how the number of households affects how much water is wasted, based on the rate of 20,000 gal per household.

Water Wasted (in thousands of gallons)										
H	1	2	3	4	5	6	7	8	9	10
G	20	40	60		100	120				200

H is the number of households. *G* is the water wasted in a year, given in thousands of gallons.

1. Copy and complete the table.
2. How much water would 11 households waste? What pattern did you use to decide?
3. Suppose 300,000 gallons were wasted in a year. How many households would be involved? How did you decide?

> **Problem-Solving Tip**
>
> Solve a problem involving smaller numbers, then use the same process to solve this problem.

4. If you are given the number of households, how can you find the number of gallons of water that is wasted? How are the values of *G* related to the values of *H*?

Cesar Rubio, *The Beginning Or The End,* 1994

When you write a statement like $T = 3K$, you are writing an *equation*.

An **equation** is a mathematical sentence with two expressions separated by an equal sign.

The equal sign in $T = 3K$ means that T and $3K$ have the same value.

In many relationships, the value of one variable *depends* on the value of another variable. In Chapter 2, you saw several examples of this. Three of these relationships expressed with equations follow.

- Suppose the total number of pounds of meat needed to feed the lions in a week (M) is $42L$, where L is the number of lions to be fed. The amount of meat needed *depends* on the number of lions to be fed. An equation for this relationship is $M = 42L$.
- Suppose the number of cars (C) you can wash at one time is $\frac{1}{2}S$, where S is the number of students working at the carwash. The number of cars washed *depends* on the number of students working. The equation for the relationship is $C = \frac{1}{2}S$.
- For many Iowa ballot proposals, R is $\frac{2}{3}V$, where V is the number of voters and R is the number of votes required to pass the proposal. The number of votes required depends on the number of voters. The equation for this relationship is $R = \frac{2}{3}V$.

When the value of y depends on the value of x, y is called the **dependent variable,** and x is called the **independent variable.**

CONSIDER

?

1. What are the dependent and independent variables for the relationships in the preceding paragraphs?

1. Write an equation that describes how the perimeter of each figure depends on the number of rectangles that make up the figure. Then find the perimeter of a strip that is made up of 15 rectangles.

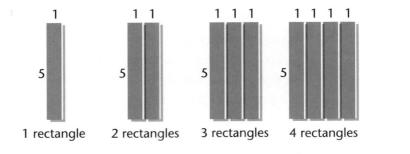

| | 1 rectangle | 2 rectangles | 3 rectangles | 4 rectangles |

> **Problem-Solving Tip**
>
> Make a table and look for a pattern.

We complete the table by examining each figure.

Let R = the number of rectangles.

Let P = the perimeter of the figure.

R	1	2	3	4	5
P	12	14	16	18	20

To find a pattern, notice two things:

- For each figure, the total length of the left and right sides is $5 + 5$, or 10.
- The length of the top or bottom side is the same as the number of rectangles.

With these clues, we see that $2R + 10$ is an expression for the perimeter. But so is P. So, $P = 2R + 10$ is an equation for this relationship.

To find the perimeter when $R = 15$, substitute 15 for R in the equation.

$P = 2(15) + 10 = 40$

The perimeter of the 15-rectangle figure is 40.

CONSIDER

?

2. **What are the lengths of the sides of the figure made up of 15 rectangles?**

a. Write an equation that describes the relationship between the number of triangles in each figure and the perimeter of the figure. Predict the perimeter for a figure made up of 20 triangles.

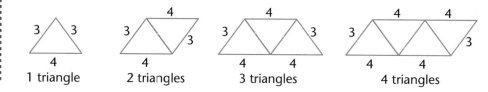

1 triangle 2 triangles 3 triangles 4 triangles

In Example 1, P is increased by 2 when we add another rectangle. But often such an increase is not constant.

EXAMPLE

2. Write an equation that describes the relationship between x and y for the table shown.

x	1	2	3	4	5	6
y	4	7	12	19	28	39

If you look only at $x = 1$ and $x = 3$, you might think y is equal to $4x$. But the correct equation must work for all values.

Notice how the y-values increase quickly, first by 3, then by 5, 7, and so on. This suggests that a power of x is in the equation. Compare x^2 with the y-values.

x	1	2	3	4	5	6
y	4	7	12	19	28	39
x²	1	4	9	16	25	36

The y-values are always 3 more than x^2. The equation is $y = x^2 + 3$.

TRY IT

Find an equation in the form "$y =$ _____" for each table. Then use the equation to find the value of y when $x = 100$.

b.

x	1	2	3	4	5
y	9	18	27	36	45

c.

x	1	2	3	4	5
y	-10	-20	-30	-40	-50

d.

x	1	2	3	4	5
y	4	7	10	13	16

e.

x	1	2	3	4	5
y	-1	-4	-9	-16	-25

We have two ways of describing relationships between quantities—tables and equations. In 3-1 Part B, we will see how graphs of equations also represent these relationships.

REFLECT

1. Describe an example of a dependent variable in a relationship studied in Chapter 2.
2. Describe an example of an independent variable in a relationship studied in Chapter 2.
3. How does an equation demonstrate a relationship between quantities?
4. Can you see relationships between quantities more easily in a table or a graph? Explain your reasoning.

Exercises

CORE

1. **Getting Started**
   a. What is the relationship between y and x in the table?
   b. Write an equation $y = $ _____ x for this relationship.

> **Problem-Solving Tip**
>
> Look for a pattern.

x	-2	-1	1	2	3	4	10	50	x
y	-12	-6	6						

Determine whether the statement is true or false. If the statement is false, change the underlined word or phrase to make it true.

2. The amount of air pollution <u>depends</u> on the number of cars on the roads.

yes

A relationship exists between the x and y quantities shown in each table. Look for a pattern, and complete each table. Then give the equation for each relationship.

3.

x	1	2	3	4	5	10	50	x
y	0.5	1	1.5	2				

4.

x	1	2	3	4	5	10	50	x
y	2	8	18	32				

(Hint: Compare y to x^2.)

5. a. Look for a pattern, and complete the table.

x	1	2	3	4	5	10
y	5	8	11			

b. Write an equation in the form $y = \underline{\quad} x + \underline{\quad}$ by replacing the blanks with the numbers you found in 5a.

Find an equation in the form $y = \underline{\quad}$ for each table. Then use the equation to find the value of y when $x = 100$.

6.

x	1	2	3	4	5
y	6	11	16	21	26

7.

x	1	2	3	4	5
y	6	9	14	21	30

8. The graph at the right represents a relationship between x and y.
  a. Make a table of values for the relationship.
  b. Write the equation for the relationship.

9. Use words to describe the relationship between x and y, shown in the equation $y = 4x + 2$.

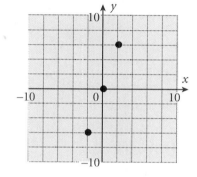

10. Make a table of values for the equation $y = 3x - 2$. Include at least five entries.

11. Out on a Limb It takes one tree that is 15 to 20 years old to make 700 grocery bags!
  a. Write an equation that tells how to find the total number of grocery bags that can be produced when you know the number of trees that will be used.
  b. How many grocery bags can be made from a mature forest of 100 trees?
  c. About how long does it take a grocery store with 4 checkstands operating to use 700 grocery bags? How did you decide?

> **Problem-Solving Tip**
>
> Make a table of values.

12. Warm Ups Draw a graph that might show the relationship between the number of cups of hot chocolate sold at a football stadium and the outside temperature at game time. Are these quantities directly or inversely related? Explain.

13. Hex Wrench Find an equation for the relationship between the number of hexagons and the figure number. Then predict the number of hexagons that would appear in the tenth figure.

Figure 1   Figure 2   Figure 3

14. Spare Change A recycling center advertises prices for returning aluminum cans.

   a. Define two variables in this situation. Which variable depends on the other?

   b. Write and use an equation to find the total amount due when you are given the number of cans returned.

   c. How much would be due to someone who brought in 100 cans?

LOOK BACK

Add or subtract. [1-1]

15. $-3 + \dfrac{3}{5}$ **16.** $-\dfrac{3}{5} - 3$

Give a range of reasonable values for these quantities. [2-1]

17. the speed of a car on a major highway   **18.** the length of a ladder

MORE PRACTICE

A relationship exists between the _x_ and _y_ quantities shown in each table. Look for a pattern, and complete each table. Then give the equation for each relationship.

19.

x	y
1	−1
2	0
3	1
4	2
5	
10	
20	
x	

20.

x	y
1	1
2	3
3	5
4	7
5	
10	
20	
x	

21.

x	y
1	−5
2	−10
3	−15
4	−20
5	
10	
20	
x	

22.

x	y
2	1
4	2
6	3
8	
10	
20	
x	

23.

x	y
1	0
2	3
3	8
4	
5	
10	
x	

24.

x	y
1	3
2	12
3	27
4	48
5	
10	
x	

(Hint: First, square the value for x.)

25. Suppose B = the number of bottles returned, and A = the total amount received for the bottles. You earn five cents for each bottle returned to the recycling center. The total amount received depends on the number of bottles returned. Write an equation for this relationship.

Use words to describe the relationship between *x* and *y*, shown in each equation.

26. $y = 10x - 2$ **27.** $y = -3x + 6$ **28.** $y = \dfrac{x}{8}$

29. a. Look for a pattern, and complete the table.

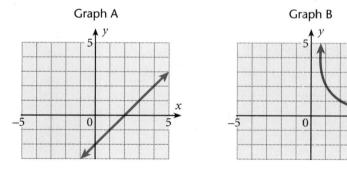

x	1	2	3	4	5	10
y	$\frac{1}{3}$	$\frac{4}{3}$	3			

    b. Tell how to find the value for y when you know the value of x.
    (Hint: First, square the value for x.)
    c. Replace a with an integer in the equation $y = \dfrac{x^2}{a}$.

MORE MATH REASONING

30. Which graph shows that x and y are directly related? Explain your answer.

Graph A

Graph B

31. a. Describe a reasonable situation that would explain the relationship shown in the graph at the right.

    b. Do you think you could find an equation for heart rate based upon minutes of exercise? Why or why not?

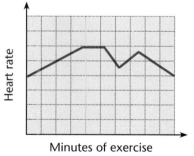

32. Draw a picture that shows $2(x + y) = 2x + 2y$.

33. Look for a pattern, and complete the table.

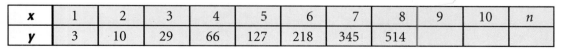

x	1	2	3	4	5	6	7	8	9	10	n
y	3	10	29	66	127	218	345	514			

Relationships as Graphs

You have found equations using tables. Now you will graph equations and determine whether to connect the points of the graph to identify patterns. Patterns can help you to find equations for relationships.

The face of each side of a cube is a square. All faces are **congruent**—they are the same size and the same shape.

A cube has 6 faces and 12 edges. The surface area is the total area of its faces.

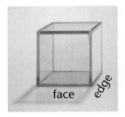

EXPLORE: CUBISM

MATERIALS

Graph paper

1. Copy and complete the table for cubes of different sizes. To see patterns, it may help you to draw a picture of the perimeters and surface areas.

Edge Length	Perimeter (cm) of a face	Surface Area (cm^2) of the cube	Volume (cm^3) of the cube
1 cm			
2 cm			
3 cm			
4 cm			
n cm			

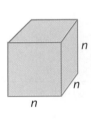

2. Copy and complete the graphs below, plotting the data from your table. Describe each graph in your own words.

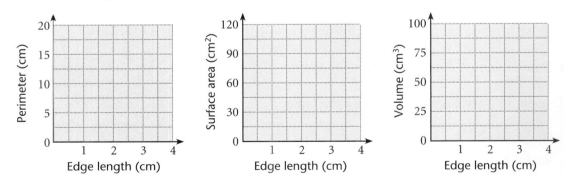

3. Do equal changes in edge length result in equal changes in perimeter? Describe the relationship between perimeter and edge length. Write an equation that describes this relationship. Then use your equation to find the perimeter for an edge length of 10 cm.

4. Do equal changes in edge length result in equal changes in surface area? Describe the relationship between surface area and edge length. Write an equation that describes this relationship. Then use your equation to find the surface area for an edge length of 10 cm.

5. Do equal changes in edge length result in equal changes in volume? Describe the relationship between volume and edge length. Write an equation that describes this relationship. Then use your equation to find the volume for an edge length of 10 cm.

6. Should the points on each graph be connected? Why or why not?

7. Which relationships have straight lines as their graphs?

In graphing, we use the horizontal axis (x-axis) for the independent variable and the vertical axis (y-axis) for the dependent variable.

EXAMPLE

1. Graph the equation $y = \frac{2}{3}x + 1$.

   Choose a value of x and substitute it into the expression $\frac{2}{3}x + 1$ to find the value of y. (Hint: Use multiples of 3 for x.)

   You now have the ordered pairs $(0, 1)$, $(3, 3)$, $(6, 5)$, $(9, 7)$, and $(12, 9)$.

   Plot these points. Notice that they lie on a straight line. An infinite number of ordered pairs will satisfy this equation, so connect the points and extend a line through them in both directions.

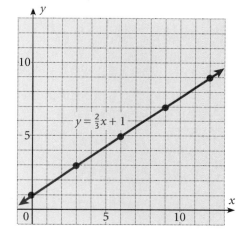

1. Which, if any, quadrants contain no points of the graph of $y = \frac{2}{3}x + 1$?

TRY IT

a. Graph the equation $y = -2x - 3$.

b. Graph the equation $y = \frac{1}{2}x^2$.

WHAT DO **YOU** THINK?

If you write a check without having enough money in the bank, the store owner charges you a 5% penalty on the amount of the check, and a fee of $10. Describe a method for finding the total charge for a returned check. Then use your method to find the total charge for a returned check for $75.90.

Esteban thinks . . .

Let $x =$ the amount of the returned check in dollars.

Let $y =$ the total charge (penalty and fee) in dollars.

I made a table to show some special cases. I chose some values for x, and then I found the values for y by multiplying each value of x by 0.05 (for the 5% penalty) and adding 10 (for the service fee).

x	y
10	$0.05(10) + 10 = 10.50$
15	$0.05(15) + 10 = 10.75$
25	$0.05(25) + 10 = 11.25$
30	$0.05(30) + 10 = 11.50$
60	$0.05(60) + 10 = 13.00$

I wrote $y = 0.05x + 10$.

Then I substituted $75.90 for x, and used my calculator to find the value for y.

$y = 0.05(75.90) + 10$

$y = 13.795$

Rounded to the nearest cent, the total charge is $13.80.

Derrick thinks . . .

I did something like Esteban. But after I found the equation, I entered it into my graphing utility. I used the tracing feature and found these values:

When $x = 75.789474$, $y = 13.789474$.

When $x = 76.842105$, $y = 13.842105$.

:Y1 = 0.05X + 10
:Y2 =
:Y3 =
:Y4 =

X = 75.789474 Y = 13.789474

X = 76.842105 Y = 13.842105

I decided that for $x = 75.90$, the value for y would be about 13.8. So I estimated the total charge to be $13.80.

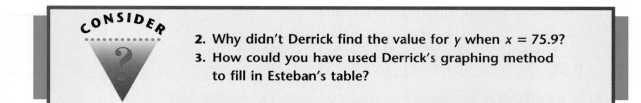

CONSIDER

?

2. Why didn't Derrick find the value for y when $x = 75.9$?
3. How could you have used Derrick's graphing method to fill in Esteban's table?

The solutions given by Esteban and Derrick show that an equation or a graph can be used to solve a problem.

REFLECT

1. How do you decide whether to connect the points for an equation you have graphed?
2. Do you have to write an equation in order to graph a relationship? Explain.
3. How do you know whether the graph of an equation for a situation should continue beyond the first quadrant?

Exercises

CORE

1. **Getting Started**
   a. Graph the points $(1, 2)$, $(2, 4)$, $(3, 6)$, and $(4, 8)$.
   b. How is the y-coordinate related to the x-coordinate for each ordered pair?
   c. What equation $y = \underline{\quad} x$ would relate y to x?
   d. Graph the equation from c. by drawing a line through the four points.

Make a table of ordered pairs using $x = 1, 2, 3, 4$, and 5. Then graph each equation.

2. $y = \dfrac{1}{2}x$ **3.** $y = -x + 1$ **4.** $y = 1.5x - 0.5$

5. Look for a pattern, and complete the table.

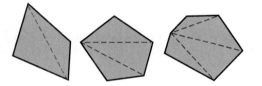

No. of sides	4	5	6	7	10	n
No. of triangles	2	3				

6. a. Look for a pattern, and complete the table.

x	1	2	3	4	5	10
y	0	1	4	9		

b. As x increases at a constant rate, does y increase at a constant rate?
c. Tell in your own words how to find the value for y when you know a value for x. (Hint: You must first subtract something from x.)
d. In $y = (x - a)^2$, replace a with an integer that describes the relationship shown in the table.

Replace a or b in each equation with a number that expresses the relationship in the table. Use the equation to copy and complete the table. Graph the equation.

7. $y = ax - 1$

x	y
1	1
2	3
3	5
4	7
50	

8. $y = 4x + b$

x	y
1	6
2	10
8	34
10	42
20	

9. $y = ax^2$

x	y
2	-8
4	-32
6	-72
10	
20	

10. Define two variables for the situation below. Write an equation, then use it to find the number of dots that would appear in the tenth figure.

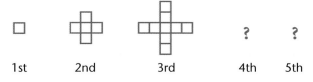

1st   2nd   3rd   4th   5th   6th

11. Chances Are The quality control people at a light bulb company collected the data at the right.

N = the number of bulbs tested
D = the number of defective bulbs

a. Use the data to estimate the *probability* that a specific bulb is defective.

b. Write an equation to estimate the number of defective bulbs that might be in any batch being tested.

c. Use your equation to determine how many defective bulbs you might expect out of 5000 bulbs.

Number Tested	Number Defective
100	5
250	13
200	11
150	7
800	42
500	25
180	7

12. Define two variables for the situation below. Write an equation, then use it to find the number of squares that would appear in the tenth figure.

□   ⊞   ⊞   ?   ?

1st   2nd   3rd   4th   5th

13. You Want It When? When you buy an item from one mail order catalog, you pay an 8% sales tax. If you want the item sent immediately by a delivery service, you must pay an additional $15 per order.

a. Define two variables for this situation.

b. Make a table of ordered pairs that shows the relationship between the variables.

c. Would a telephone operator for the catalog company want a table like the one you made? Explain.

d. Write an equation that shows the relationship.

e. What is the cost of an item priced at $59.95 and shipped immediately?

f. What does "per order" mean? Why might you be upset if it were $15 "per item"?

> **Problem-Solving Tip**
>
> Try special cases to build your table of values.

14. You're So Demanding This graph shows a *demand curve* for compact discs—the number of discs that people will buy at different prices.

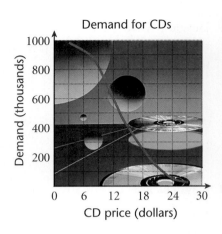

a. At $12, how many CDs would be sold?

b. Describe how demand changes when the price of CDs is reduced.

c. Explain why the graph levels off as the price nears $27.

d. What price would bring in the most income? How do you know?

LOOK AHEAD

15. Determine whether both expressions have the same value for $x = 10$ by substituting and evaluating.

a. x^2 and $10x$
b. $-x$ and $20 - x$
c. $\frac{x}{2} - 10$ and $-\frac{x}{2}$

d. $-2(3 - 5x)$ and $-6 - 10x$
e. $x^2 + 2x + 1$ and $(x + 1)^2$

Fill in the blanks.

16. If $a + b = 37$, then $a + b + 2 =$ ____.

17. If $n - 46 = 89$, then $n - 47 =$ ____.

18. If $a + 1 = 8$, then $a + 0 =$ ____.

19. If $b + 1 = 2$, then $b =$ ____.

MORE PRACTICE

Make a table of ordered pairs, and graph each equation.

20. $y = x + 12$
21. $y = 5x - 2$
22. $y = \frac{x}{4} + 18$

23. $y = -2x - 1$
24. $y = -\frac{1}{2}x$
25. $y = 2(x - 2)$

Copy and complete each table. Then write an equation for each relationship.

26.

x	y
3	5
4	7
6	11
10	19
20	
30	
x	

27.

x	y
2	27
6	31
8	33
10	35
20	
40	
x	

28.

x	y
3	$4.50
4	$6.00
6	$9.00
10	$15.00
20	
30	
x	

29. Running Silly Do you know that a running faucet can waste about 4 gallons of water per minute? The table below shows the relationship between *M*, the number of minutes the faucet runs, and *G*, the number of gallons wasted.

    a. Make a graph that shows the relationship between these quantities. Plot *M* on the horizontal axis.

    b. Use the graph to estimate the amount of water wasted in 10 minutes.

    c. Write an equation that tells how to find the number of gallons wasted when you know the number of minutes the faucet runs.

M	1	3	5	7	9	11
G	4	12	20	28	36	44

MORE MATH REASONING

30. Getting There The relationship between distance (*D*), rate (*R*), and time (*T*), is expressed as $D = RT$. Suppose the distance is 150 miles. Make a rough sketch of a graph that shows the relationship between *R* and *T*. That is, show how the value of *T* changes as the value of *R* increases.

31. Use a Graphing Utility A library charges $15.00 for a lost book, plus $0.20 per day in fines. Graph the total charge for a lost book. Then predict how much you would pay for a book that is reported lost when it is three weeks overdue.

32. Composting vegetable food scraps helps keep trash out of our ever-filling landfills. Suppose you have one bucket of compost, about 24 cups, to spread around the rosebushes in your yard.

    a. Let *B* be the number of rosebushes. Let *C* be the number of cups of compost spread around each rosebush. Which is the dependent variable? Which is the independent variable? How did you decide?

    b. Complete a chart of values for *B* and *C*.

B	4	5	6	10	12	24
C						1

    c. If you know the number of rosebushes, how do you find the number of cups of compost spread around each rosebush? Write an equation that expresses *C* in terms of *B*.

    d. Use matching values of *B* and *C* from the table to make ordered pairs. Graph the ordered pairs.

    e. How would you describe the shape of this graph?

    f. Use the graph to find the value of *C* when *B* = 16.

← C O N N E C T →   *Now you should be able to find ordered pairs for relationships using combinations of tables, graphs, and equations. Next you will investigate dependent relationships in problem situations using equations and graphs to model problems.*

Which bags do you ask for at the checkout counter: paper or plastic? Do you believe one is better for the environment than the other? Actually, both types of bags require natural resources, whether they are made from trees or petroleum.

EXPLORE: PAPER OR PLASTIC?

MATERIALS

Graphing utility or graph paper

The sign at the right shows an alternative to paper and plastic bags.

Let x = the number of string bags ordered.
Let y = the total cost of the bags in dollars.

1. What is the total cost of one bag? two bags? three bags?
2. Write an equation that tells the value of y in terms of x. Use the equation to find the value of y when $x = 120$.

> **Problem-Solving Tip**
>
> Look for a pattern.

3. Use a graphing utility to graph the equation. Then use the graph to find the value of y when $x = 120$. Explain how you found it.
4. What is a reasonable range of values for x? What is a reasonable range of values for y? Are there other numbers within these ranges that do not make sense for this situation?

You have seen many relationships in which the value of one quantity depended on the value of another quantity. A **function** is a consistent, predictable relationship between the dependent and independent variable. Functions let us find the value of the dependent variable if we know the value of the independent variable.

Some examples of real-life functions follow.

- The distance an object falls is a function of the time it has been falling.
- The number of times Gear 2 turns is a function of the number of times that Gear 1 turns.
- The amount of income tax you pay is a function of your taxable income.

If one value of *x*, the independent variable, can result in more than one value of *y*, the dependent variable, then *y* is *not* a function of *x*.

EXAMPLE

1. At a checkout counter, Hassan is charged $1 for a 3-lb bag of apples. Jina is charged $2 for a 3-lb bag of apples. Is the price a function of the weight of the apples? Why or why not?

Let *x* be the independent variable, the weight of the apples. Let *y* be the dependent variable, the price of the apples.

For price to be a function of weight, there must be a single, consistent price for a specific weight. In this situation, for the weight, 3 lb, the price could be $1 or the price could be $2. Therefore, price cannot be a function of the weight of the apples.

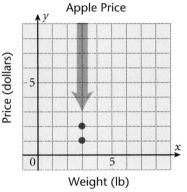

Apple Price

TRY IT

a. Is the height of a tree a function of its age? Why or why not?
b. Is the area of a circle a function of its radius? Why or why not?

> If two quantities, *x* and *y*, are related so that there is *only one* value of the dependent variable (*y*) associated with any value of the independent variable (*x*), then *y* is a **function** of *x*.

The **domain** of a function is the set of all possible values of the independent variable. The **range** of a function is the set of all values that result for the dependent variable.

2. A car travels 55 miles in one hour. At this rate of speed, it can go 385 miles without refueling. Write and graph an equation that relates distance to time. Is the relationship between time and distance a function? If so, what are its domain and range?

Let t = time traveled in hours. Let d = distance in miles.

Pick values for t, and compute the matching values for d. Note that for each additional hour, the car goes 55 miles farther.

Record your results in a table, write the equation, and make a graph.

t	0	1	2	3	4	5	6	7
d	0	55	110	165	220	275	330	385

The equation is $d = 55t$.

For each value of t, there is only one possible value for d. So this relationship, given by $d = 55t$, is a function.

The domain of this function for this problem is any number from 0 to 7. The range of this function is any number from 0 to 385.

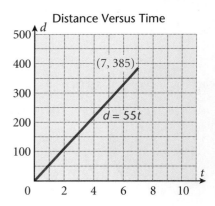

Distance Versus Time

CONSIDER

1. In Example 2, is time a function of distance? Explain.

In Example 2, the domain and range are limited by the amount of gas the car can hold. If we were looking at the function $d = 55t$ separate from any real-world application, we should describe the domain and range as *all* numbers.

REFLECT

1. In your own words, explain what makes a relationship a function.
2. Does any straight-line graph represent a function? Explain.
3. Can a function have more than one value of the independent variable (x) for one value of the dependent variable (y)? Explain.

Exercises

CORE

1. **Getting Started** The cost of electricity in one part of the country is $0.074 per kilowatt-hour (kWh).
   a. Find the cost of electricity for 10 kWh, for 50 kWh, for 100 kWh.
   b. Is the cost always the same for 10 kWh?
   c. Is the cost a function of the number of kWh used? Why or why not?

2. A rollerblader rolls quickly down a board set up as a steep ramp. When the board is set up as a less steep ramp, the rollerblader rolls down it more slowly. Is the speed of the rollerblader a function of the steepness of the ramp?

3. Is the time it takes to open a combination locker a function of the numbers in the combination? Why or why not?

4. Is the area of a rectangle a function of its width? Why or why not?

5. This scatter plot shows the systolic blood pressures of people of different ages. Is systolic blood pressure a function of age?

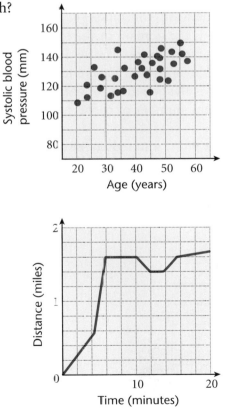

6. This graph shows Ronnie's bicycle trip to school. Tell a story about his trip that explains the patterns in the graph.

7. Match each table of values with the correct graph (the scales on the graphs are missing). Tell how you made your decision.

A.

x	5	10	15	20	25	30	35	40	45	50	55
y	12.50	25	37.50	50	62.50	75	62.50	50	37.50	25	12.50

B.

x	2	4	6	8	10	12	14	16	18	20	22
y	85	94	103	110	110	110	110	104	96	86	79

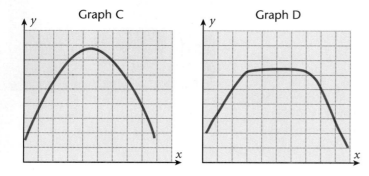

Graph C　　　　Graph D

8. Cookie Care Dwayne is the cook at a day-care center. When he makes cookies, he bakes 2 cookies per child and a total of 12 for the teaching staff.

　a. What is the independent variable in this function? the dependent variable? Are there any constants?

　b. What is the domain of the function? the range?

　c. Give an expression for the number of cookies needed for x children.

　d. Give an expression for the total number of cookies needed.

　e. What is the equation for the relationship between total cookies and children?

　f. Find the number of cookies needed for a day when 34 children attend day care.

For Exercises 9–11, a function exists for the x and y quantities in each table.

　a. Look for a pattern, and complete the table.

　b. Replace a with a number to show the equation.

　c. Draw a rough sketch of the graph.

　d. Is y a function of x? Why or why not?

9. $y = ax + 2$

x	y
1	5
2	8
3	11
4	14
5	17
6	

10. $y = ax^2$

x	y
1	5
2	20
3	45
4	80
5	
10	

11. $y = ax^3$

x	y
1	1
2	8
3	27
4	64
5	
10	

12. a. Write an expression that gives the area of the shaded part of the figure at the right.

b. The area is a function of *x*. Why is this true?

c. What is the domain of the function?

3 2

x – 4

x

13. Show Time The youth symphony has two ticket prices. Orchestra seats are $7.50 each; mezzanine seats are $5.00 each. Copy and complete the table below. Describe all of the patterns you see.

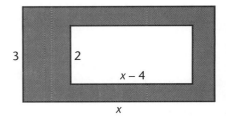

Orchestra seats sold	60			45	37	
Total $		435	300			412.50
Mezzanine seats sold			26	64		54
Total $	200	250			370	

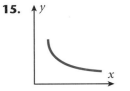 **LOOK BACK**

14. Multiply or divide. [1-1]

a. $-0.01(-1000)$ **b.** $-2(-1-3)$ **c.** $\dfrac{-6}{-2-(-5)}$

Tell whether the two quantities are directly related, inversely related, or neither. Also state whether one quantity stays constant as the other varies. [2-1]

15.

16.

17.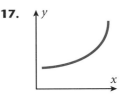

18. Write an expression for the area of the shaded figure. [2-3]

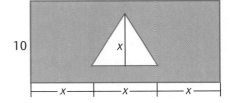

10

x

x   *x*   *x*

MORE PRACTICE

Do you think *y* is a function of *x*? Why or why not?

19.

x	1	3	5	3
y	2	4	6	5

20.

x	1	5	2	4
y	5	1	4	4

Is y a function of x? If it is not, tell why. If it is, give the domain and range.

21.

Hours (x)	Miles traveled (y)
1	45
2	90
3	135
4	180
5	225

22.
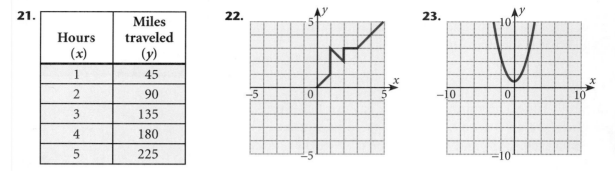

23.

24. A small square of side length *s* is inside a 5-by-5 square. Is the small square's area a function of *s*? If so, what are its domain and range?

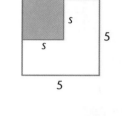

MORE MATH REASONING

25. **a.** Do you think height is a function of age for one person? Explain.
   b. Do you think height is a function of age for several people? Explain.

26. Some airlines offer telephones for passengers. On one airline, the cost of a phone call to the ground is $2 + $2 per minute, charged at the beginning of each minute.
   a. How much does it cost the instant your call is made?
   b. How much does it cost after 30 seconds?
   c. Do you think cost is a function of time? Why or why not?

27. Each of the following represents a function. Describe a point or ordered pair that you could add so that it would no longer represent a function.

   a. (2, 5), (3, 7), (4, 4)

   b.
   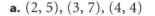

28. Do you think the relationship shown is that of a function? Why or why not?

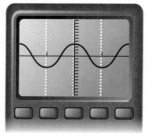

← C O N N E C T → *You have looked at many examples of functions and their equations. You have seen that a function can be represented using a table of values, using a graph, and by writing an equation.*

Here is an opportunity to represent a function in three different ways.

EXPLORE: WASTING AWAY

MATERIALS

Graphing utility or graph paper

There are 80,000 tons of garbage in a landfill that can hold 125,000 tons. Each month, the amount of garbage in the landfill increases by 570 tons despite the fact that some trash decomposes. We want to know how much trash the landfill will contain over the coming months. We also want to predict when it must close.

1. Define two variable quantities for this relationship, and make a table of ordered pairs that shows the relationship between the variables.
2. Write an equation for the relationship.
3. Is the relationship a function? Why or why not?
4. Graph the relationship (with paper and pencil or with a graphing utility). What are appropriate scales for the axes?
5. Use the equation and graph to find the amount of garbage in the landfill at the end of 10 months, 1 year, and 5 years.
6. Estimate the number of years it will take to fill this landfill. Explain your thinking.

Shoreline Amphitheatre in Mountain View, California, is built on land that was once a landfill. The conversion from landfill to usable land takes time, but it assures that much land once considered spoiled can become productive in other ways.

REFLECT

1. What makes a function different from another kind of relationship between variables?

2. What are the different ways to represent a function? What are some advantages and disadvantages of each way?

3. Do you need a table of values to write an equation for a function?

4. Are the graphs of all functions straight lines?

Self-Assessment

1. Use the completed pairs in the table to find the value of a, in $y = ax + 1$, to fill in the blanks of the table.

a. Find the pair $(-1, 3)$ in the table. Substituting these values of x and y into the equation, you get $3 = a(-1) + 1$. What is a?

b. Find the pair $(2, -3)$ in the table. Substitute these values of x and y into the equation. What is a?

c. What value do you get for a when you substitute $(-2, 5)$ into the equation?

d. Describe how to determine y when you know x.

e. Use the equation to copy and complete the table.

x	y
−3	
−2	5
−1	3
0	1
1	
2	−3
3	

Consider the relationship in each table. Find the value of a or b in the equation. Copy and complete the table using the equation. Then graph the equation.

2. $y = ax + 20$

x	y
−10	
−2	
0	
1	25
2	30
3	35

3. $y = ax^2$

x	y
−20	2000
−10	
0	
1	5
2	20
3	45

4. $y = -20x + b$

x	y
−5	80
−4	60
−3	40
−2	
0	
10	

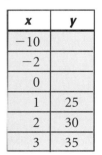

5. A juice drink manufacturer makes a drink that is 8% fruit juice. The plant gets 6000 gallons of juice each day. The amount of drink the plant can produce each day is a function of the amount of juice it uses. The domain of the function is

(a) any number from 0 to 6000   (b) any number from 0 to 48,000

(c) any number from 0 to 75,000   (d) $y = 0.08x$

6. Look for a pattern, and complete the table. Write an equation that describes the relationship between the quantities. Then use your equation to find the number of squares that would appear in the tenth figure.

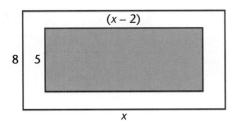

Figure number	1	2	3	4	5	x
No. of blocks	1	4				

7. Table for How Many? A small square table can seat four people. When two tables are pushed together, eight can be seated. Continue the pattern and determine how many people nine tables can seat.

8. Complete the following equation for the area of the *unshaded* part of the figure: $A =$ _____ .

$(x - 2)$

8 | 5

x

9. Complete the following equation for the perimeter of the polygon: $P =$ _____ .

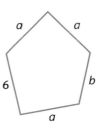

Define two variables for each function. Then write an equation, and graph the function.

10. People in the United States throw away about 2.5 million plastic bottles each hour! (Hint: Use variables for hour and bottles.)

Science

11. By attaching a low-flow aerator to your kitchen faucet, you only use half the normal amount of water.

Science

For each equation, complete the sentence: When you know the value of x, you find y by . . .

12. $y = 6x$

13. $y = -5x$

14. $y = 3x + 8$

15. $y = 25x + 50$

16. Graph the equation $y = -x + 3$.

17. Graph the equation $y = -\frac{1}{2}x^2 + 1$.

18. Watt? This graph shows the lamp life of light bulbs of different wattages.

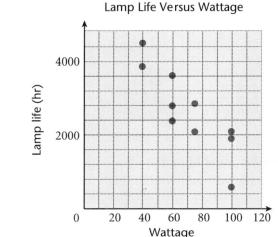

Lamp Life Versus Wattage

   a. Is the association shown positive or negative, or is there no association?
   b. Are the quantities directly related, inversely related, or neither?
   c. Is the lamp life a function of wattage? Justify your answer.

19. Is y a function of x? Why or why not?

x	0	2	0	1	4
y	5	1	5	1	6

20. It's for You!!! The ratio of the number of households that have five or more phones to the number of households that have one phone is 1:4.
   a. Define two variables for this situation.
   b. Make a table of values to show the relationship, using five ordered pairs.
   c. Write an equation.
   d. If there are 250,000 households with one phone, how many might you expect to have 5 or more phones?

21. Let S represent the area of the shaded region. Write two different equations for S. [2-3]

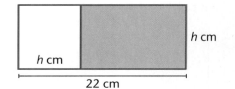

22. Open Sesame A restaurant reserves 1000 hamburger buns for emergencies (in case, say, 20 bus loads of band students came in). An average of 800 buns are used each day.
   a. Write an expression for the buns used in D days.
   b. Suppose the restaurant had no buns on hand. How many should be ordered (remember to order the emergency supply) for 1 day? for 2 days? Make a table for 1 to 7 days.
   c. Write an equation for the table in **b**.
   d. How many buns should be ordered for two weeks?

23. Portrait Français Thirteen of the standard portrait canvas sizes in France are given. The height of the canvas is represented by h, in cm; w represents the width of the canvas, in cm.

h	22	24	27	33	35	41	46	55	61	65	73	81	92
w	16	19	22	24	27	33	38	46	50	54	60	65	73

Vincent van Gogh, *Self Portrait* (detail); Paris; 1887

   a. Is the width of a portrait canvas a function of its height? Explain.
   b. Is the height of a portrait canvas a function of its width?

DOGON ASTRONOMY

The Dogon (Doh GAN´) people live in a remote region of the West African nation of Mali. For thousands of years, these original inhabitants of the Niger valley made their homes in isolated caves in the cliffs of the Hombori Mountains. Their knowledge of astronomy is extensive and, by the standards of modern science, baffling. Anthropologists studying the Dogon in the 1940s reported that without the aid of telescopes or other instruments, the Dogon had discovered that Jupiter has satellites, and that Saturn has rings. Neither fact is apparent to the naked eye.

Dogon natives at work in a village

Even more amazing, the Dogon claimed that an invisible star of enormous density orbits the star Sirius once every 50 years. Not until 1925 had astronomers discovered that a so-called "white dwarf"—a dark, tiny, and incredibly dense star—circled Sirius. In ancient times the Dogon chose a new king when Jupiter and Saturn

	☾ 1 revolution	☾☾ 2 revolutions	☾☾☾ 3 revolutions	☾☾☾☾ 4 revolutions
Jupiter	11.9 years	23.8 years	35.7 years	47.6 years
Saturn	29.75 years	59.5 years	89.25 years	119 years

completed orbits of the sun together. The Dogon calculated Jupiter's period of revolution at 11.9 years and Saturn's at 29.75 years.

1. Some authorities question whether the Dogon discovered the facts cited above. How else could you explain their knowledge of astronomy?
2. How often did the Dogon choose a new king?
3. Find a formula you could use to determine the number of years it takes Jupiter to complete *n* revolutions; the number of years it takes Saturn to complete *n* revolutions.
4. Describe the patterns in the table.

Understanding Linear Functions

← **CONNECT** → *You know that graphs of functions may be straight or curved lines, or even a set of points. Now you will learn more about functions whose graphs are straight lines.*

An important part of math is being able to predict what the graph of a function will look like.

EXPLORE: WHAT'S MY LINE?

Answer the following questions for the equations in a–h.

a. $y = 2x^2$ **b.** $y = \dfrac{x}{2} + 12$

c. $y = \sqrt{x}$ **d.** $y = -3x - 4$

e. $y = 4x$ **f.** $y = 1.5x - 0.05$

g. $y = \dfrac{1}{x}$ **h.** $y = -x^2 + 3$

1. Look for patterns in the equations. Guess which have graphs that are straight lines, then check by entering each equation on a graphing utility.

2. Sketch the general shape of each graph.

3. List the common features of equations whose graphs are straight lines. Discuss how they differ from the other equations.

MATERIALS

Graphing utility
Graph paper

A function whose graph is a straight line is called a **linear function.** The equation of any linear function can be written in the form $y = ax + b$. The letters x and y are used for the independent and dependent variables, respectively. The letters a and b represent the coefficient of x and the constant term, respectively.

1. Determine whether each function is linear.

    a. $y = -5x + 2$ **b.** $y = \frac{x}{10} - 5$ **c.** $y = \frac{5}{x} - 3$

    a. The equation $y = -5x + 2$ is already in the form $y = ax + b$.

$$y = \underset{\underset{a}{\uparrow}}{-5}x + \underset{\underset{b}{\uparrow}}{2}$$

This is the equation of a linear function.

    b. The equation $y = \frac{x}{10} - 5$ can be rewritten as $y = \frac{1}{10}x + (-5)$.

$$y = \underset{\underset{a}{\uparrow}}{\tfrac{1}{10}}x + \underset{\underset{b}{\uparrow}}{(-5)}$$

This is also the equation of a linear function.

    c. The equation $y = \frac{5}{x} - 3$ cannot represent a linear function because x is in the denominator.

We can say that a function using subtraction, like $y = \frac{x}{10} - 5$, is *already* in $y = ax + b$ form, where a is $\frac{1}{10}$ and b is -5.

An equation such as $y = 7x$ represents a linear function ($y = ax + b$, with $a = 7$ and $b = 0$, or just $y = ax$). When two variables are related by $y = ax$, we say y is **proportional** to x.

CONSIDER

1. What is the value of y divided by x for any ordered pairs that satisfy $y = 7x$?

TRY IT

Tell which equations represent linear functions and how you decided.

a. $y = 35x$ **b.** $y = -22x^2 - 20$

c. $y = -22x - 20$ **d.** $y = -\frac{35}{x} + 125$

When the graph of a function is a straight line, we describe the relationship between the quantities by saying, "the relationship is linear." Looking at graphs can help you to understand this more clearly.

Graph 1: Linear Function

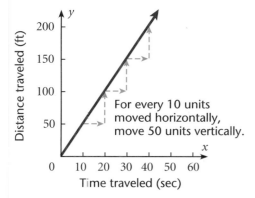

For every 10 units moved horizontally, move 50 units vertically.

Graph 2: Nonlinear Function

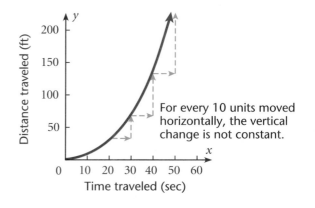

For every 10 units moved horizontally, the vertical change is not constant.

When a relationship is linear, equal changes in the *x*-values result in equal changes in the *y*-values.

Equal changes in the *x*-values do *not* result in equal changes in the *y*-values.

CONSIDER

?

2. Suppose the graphs above represent the distance traveled by two cars. How would you describe each car's motion?

The next examples examine the table of values for the graphs above.

EXAMPLES

2. Is the relationship between time and distance linear? Explain.

equal amounts   10   10   10   10

Time traveled (sec)	10	20	30	40	50	60	70	80
Distance traveled (ft)	50	100	150	200	250	300	350	400

equal amounts   50   50   50   50

Notice that for every 10 seconds of travel time, the distance increases by 50 feet. When time changes by equal amounts, the distance traveled also changes by equal amounts. This means that the relationship between the quantities is linear.

3. Is the relationship between time and distance linear? Explain.

equal amounts   10   10   10   10

| Time traveled (sec) | 10 | 20 | 30 | 40 | 50 | 60 | 70 | 80 |
| Distance traveled (ft) | 10 | 30 | 70 | 130 | 210 | 310 | 430 | 570 |

unequal amounts   20   40   60   80

The table shows that when time changes by equal 10-second amounts, the distance traveled does *not* change by equal amounts. So the relationship between the quantities is *nonlinear*.

CONSIDER ?

3. Which quantity *depends* on the other in Examples 2 and 3?

4. Does the change in the *x*-values have to be the same as the change in the *y*-values for a relationship to be linear? Explain.

TRY IT

e. Is the relationship between pizza diameter and price linear? Why or why not?

| Pizza diameter (in.) | 7 | 9 | 10 | 12 | 14 |
| Price (dollars) | 5.99 | 7.99 | 8.99 | 10.99 | 12.99 |

REFLECT

1. How can you tell by looking at an equation whether the relationship is linear?

2. How can you tell by looking at a table of values whether the relationship is linear?

3. If a relationship is linear, what do you know about the amount of vertical change in the graph when the horizontal change is constant?

4. How can you tell by looking at the equation $y = 3x^2$ that the graph is not a straight line?

Exercises

CORE

1. **Getting Started** Is the equation in $y = ax + b$ form? If so, identify a and b.

   a. $y = 7x + 1$ **b.** $y = x^2 + 4$ **c.** $y = -12x - 9$ **d.** $y = \frac{1}{x} + 1$ **e.** $y = -x$

2. Choose the phrase that best completes the sentence: A linear function
   (a) has a graph consisting of several straight lines.
   (b) has increasing changes in y for equal changes in x.
   (c) can be written in the form $y = x^2 + b$.
   (d) not here

For Exercises 3–4, complete a–c.
a. Is the change in the x-values equal?
b. Is the change in the y-values equal?
c. Is the relationship linear?

3.

x	-3	-2	-1	0	1	2
y	3	5	7	9	11	13

4.

x	2	4	6	8	10	12
y	0.5	0.25	0.17	0.125	0.1	0.08

For Exercises 5–8, complete a–c.
a. Is the relationship linear?
b. If the relationship is linear, write the equation, and determine whether y is proportional to x.
c. If the relationship is linear, graph the equation. Verify your answers to **a** and **b**.

5.

x	-1	-2	-3	-4	-5	-6
y	-4	-8	-12	-16	-20	-24

6.

x	1	2	3	4	5	6
y	3	12	27	48	75	108

7.

x	1	2	5	8	10	11
y	1	3	9	15	19	21

8.

x	-5	-10	-15	-20	-25	-30
y	12	17	22	27	32	37

Without graphing, determine whether each function is linear, and whether y is proportional to x. Explain your reasoning.

9. $y = -x - 5$ 10. $y = 4x + 12$ 11. $y = \frac{3}{x} + 2$ 12. $y = 4 - 7x^2$

13. Make a table for a relationship that you know is linear. Use positive, negative, and zero values for x.

14. Make a table for a relationship that you know is *not* linear. Use positive, negative, and zero values for x.

15. Graph some linear functions of the form $y = ax$. Choose both positive and negative values for a. Make a conjecture about the graphs of these equations.

16. Crash of '29 In October 1929, panic hit the stock market, resulting in millions
 of people trying to sell their stocks. But no one wanted to buy, so stock values
plummeted, continuing to fall until 1932. The table below shows the value of
shares of an average stock for different shareholders from mid-1929 to 1932.

Number of Shares	1929 Value	1932 Value
250	$90,000	$22,500
75	$27,000	$6,750
140	$50,400	$12,600

a. Define your variables and write an equation for the total stock value for
each year shown.
b. Use your equations to find the value of 100 shares of stock for each
year shown.

17. Gearing Up The smaller gear has 6 teeth, the larger gear has
18 teeth.
a. When the larger gear has turned around one time, how
many times will the smaller gear have turned around?
b. Write a function describing this relationship. Is the relationship proportional?

Copy and complete the chart below.

Data Table	Relationship in Words	Equation	Graph
18. x: −2, −1, 0, 1, 2 y: −8, −4, 0, 4, 8			
19.	The number of grams of carbo-hydrates in Marvel Corn Flakes is 23 times the number of ounces the cereal weighs.		
20.		$c = 3w$ w = weight (gm) c = cost (dollars)	
21.			

22. Draw a graph and find an equation for the data shown.

x	5	3	−3	−5
y	4	2	−4	−6

LOOK AHEAD

Evaluate each expression for $x = -20$, $x = -10$, $x = 0$, $x = 10$, and $x = 20$. Substitute values for x that would give each expression a value of 100.

23. $3x + 25$ 　　　　　**24.** $-2x + 150$ 　　　　　**25.** $\frac{1}{4}x + 30$

MORE PRACTICE

For Exercises 26–29, complete a–c.
a. Is the relationship linear?
b. If the relationship is linear, write the equation, and determine whether y is proportional to x.
c. If the relationship is linear, graph the equation. Verify your answers to **a** and **b**.

26.

x	−2	−1	0	1	2	3
y	16	8	0	−8	−16	−24

27.

x	1	3	4	7	8
y	5	10	15	20	25

28.

x	1	2	5	8	10	11
y	1.5	2.5	5.5	8.5	10.5	11.5

29.

x	−5	−10	−15	−20	−25	−30
y	20	30	40	50	50	50

Without graphing, determine whether each function is linear, and whether y is proportional to x. Explain your reasoning.

30. $y = x^2 + 18$ 　　　**31.** $-9x = y$ 　　　**32.** $y = 2x + 3x + 1$ 　　　**33.** $y = 4x^3 + 3x^3$

34. Make a table, an equation, and a graph showing the number of days as we let the number of weeks vary.

MORE MATH REASONING

35. Reel or Spin The ratio of the number of videos rented to the number of laser disks rented at a particular store is 5:2. Write an equation that shows the relationship. Is it linear? Is it proportional?

> **Problem-Solving Tip**
>
> Make a table of ordered pairs to help you identify the relationship between variables.

36. It's a Wrap Graphs are often used to report results in business. This graph, made up of linear segments, shows the sales for a gift-wrap manufacturer for a 14-month period. Tell the story of this company's sales.

37. Marla says that she can graph the equation $y = 5$, and that it's a linear function. Tim says that it can't be done because there's no second quantity. Who do you think is correct? Can $y = 5$ be the equation of a linear function? Explain.

38. Use a graphing utility to graph the linear functions $y = 2x$ and $y = 2x + 4$ on the same axes. Where does each line intersect the y-axis?

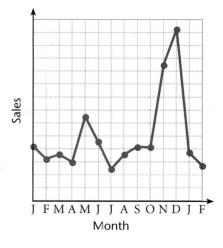

Industry

3-2
PART B Representing Linear Functions

← C O N N E C T →   *You have learned to represent linear functions as a table of values, as an equation, and as a graph. Now you will see that each way of representing a linear function is useful in different situations.*

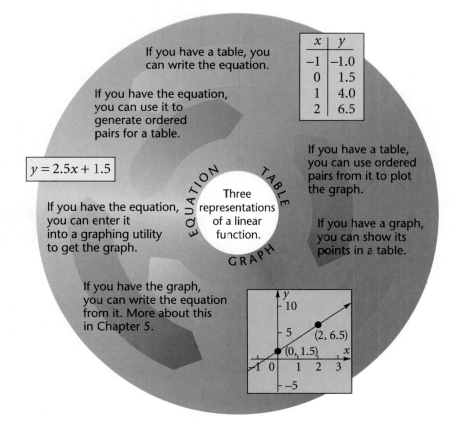

If you have a table, you can write the equation.

If you have the equation, you can use it to generate ordered pairs for a table.

x	y
-1	-1.0
0	1.5
1	4.0
2	6.5

If you have a table, you can use ordered pairs from it to plot the graph.

$y = 2.5x + 1.5$

If you have the equation, you can enter it into a graphing utility to get the graph.

EQUATION   TABLE

Three representations of a linear function.

GRAPH

If you have a graph, you can show its points in a table.

If you have the graph, you can write the equation from it. More about this in Chapter 5.

199

Now you'll see situations where a table, a graph, and an equation are each useful.

EXPLORE: HOLD THAT CALL!

MATERIALS

Graphing utility
Graph paper

The SuperiAire cellular telephone company offers two plans.

Convenience plan:
$0.45 per minute plus a $25 monthly service fee

Executive plan:
$0.25 per minute plus a $50 monthly service fee

1. For each plan, define the variables, then show the linear function as a table of values, as an equation, and as a graph. (Note: Records show that most people talk less than 200 minutes a month.)

2. Which way of representing the linear functions—as an equation, a table of values, or a graph—for the Convenience and Executive plans would be most useful for each of the following people? Explain your reasoning.

Karla: I am the marketing manager. I want to show potential customers that the plan that is best for them depends on the number of minutes of air time they expect to use.

Wilfred: I work in the business office. My job is to calculate the exact charge for a customer's bill.

Juline: I am the sales manager. Most customers want an idea of how much their monthly bill will be for using the car phone. I like to be able to show them, at a glance, some typical charges.

The Explore shows that, depending on the situation, you need to be able to think about and represent linear functions in different ways.

Two linear functions are shown as equations, as tables of values, and as graphs. Which of these represent the same functions? Tell how you decided this.

1

$y = 3x + 5$

2

$y = 4x + 4$

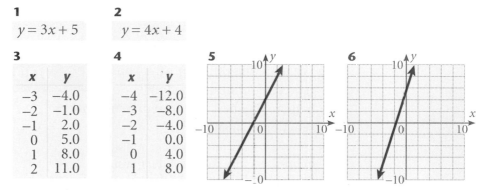

3

x	y
−3	−4.0
−2	−1.0
−1	2.0
0	5.0
1	8.0
2	11.0

4

x	y
−4	−12.0
−3	−8.0
−2	−4.0
−1	0.0
0	4.0
1	8.0

Kirti thinks . . .

I saw that numbers 1, 3, and 6 show the same function. First, I looked at the table of values and used $x = 0$ because that's the easiest to evaluate. When $x = 0$, $y = 5$, so I knew numbers 1 and 3 go together. Then I looked at the graph and saw that (0, 5) is on the graph for number 6.

Keisha thinks . . .

I started by looking at the graph, trying to find ordered pairs that were in the tables. In number 5, the point (0, 4) was easy to see. So I knew that 5 had to go with 4. The equation had to be number 2 because (0, 4) works.

TRY IT

a. Which table, graph, and equation represent the same linear functions? Tell how you decided this.

1

$y = 3x + 1$

2

$y = -2x$

3

x	y
−4	−11.0
−3	−8.0
−2	−5.0
−1	−2.0
1	4.0
5	16.0

4

x	y
−4	8.0
−1	2.0
−5	−10.0
7	−14.0
10	−20.0
12	−24.0

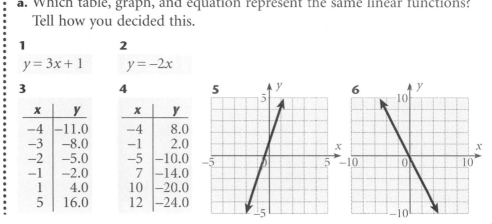

1. How is the origin represented in a table of values? in the graph of a line?

REFLECT

1. What are the different ways you can represent a linear function?
2. Is there one best way to represent a linear function? Explain.
3. Describe a situation where a graph is a helpful way to show a linear function.
4. How do you check whether a graph, a table, and an equation match for a linear function?
5. Explain how the photo represents a linear relationship.

Exercises

CORE

1. **Getting Started**
   a. Does the equation $y = \frac{1}{2}x + 3$ fit the values in the table?
   b. Do the values in the table fit the graph?
   c. Does the equation $y = \frac{1}{2}x + 3$ match the graph?

x	y
0	3
2	4
4	5
5	6

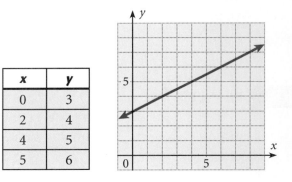

Make a table of values, and graph each equation. Is each the equation of a linear function?

2. $y = 12x + 1$

3. $y = -x + 5$

4. $y = \frac{x}{2}$

5. Randomly select one equation from those below. What is the probability of selecting one whose graph is *not* a straight line?
   a. $y = -12 - 14x^2$
   b. $y = 2x$
   c. $2x + 3 = y$
   d. $y = -\frac{1}{x} + 5$

6. Which table, graph, and equation represent the same linear functions? Tell how you decided this.

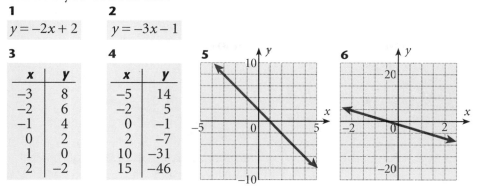

1
$$y = -2x + 2$$

2
$$y = -3x - 1$$

3

x	y
−3	8
−2	6
−1	4
0	2
1	0
2	−2

4

x	y
−5	14
−2	5
0	−1
2	−7
10	−31
15	−46

5

6

7. In each table, the change in the x-value is 1 as you move through the table. Find the corresponding changes in the y-values. What patterns do you notice?

a. $y = 2x + 3$

x	y
1	5
2	7
3	9
4	11
5	13

b. $y = -3x$

x	y
1	−3
2	−6
3	−9
4	−12
5	−15

c. $y = 5x - 2$

x	y
1	3
2	8
3	13
4	18
5	23

d. $y = \frac{x}{2}$

x	y
1	$\frac{1}{2}$
2	1
3	$1\frac{1}{2}$
4	2
5	$2\frac{1}{2}$

Simplify each equation, then tell if it represents a linear function.

8. $y = 3x + 2(x - 5)$

9. $y = -x + 3x^2 + 5x$

10. Look for a pattern, and complete the table. The perimeter (y) depends on the number of squares (x). Show the relationship between x and y as an equation, then sketch the graph.

Number of squares	1	2	3	4	5	10	
Perimeter	4	6					64

11. Don't Talk Too Long! A long-distance telephone company charges a flat monthly rate of $12 plus $0.20 per minute of air time. The total cost (y) for long-distance calls is related to x, the number of minutes of air time. Show the relationship between these variables as a table of values and as an equation. Sketch the graph.

Industry

> **Problem-Solving Tip**
>
> If you use a graphing utility, be sure to check the reasonableness of the graph.

12. Taxi! A taxi costs \$1.75 for the first $\frac{1}{4}$ mile plus \$0.25 for each additional $\frac{1}{4}$ mile. Which graph represents the cost of a taxi ride?

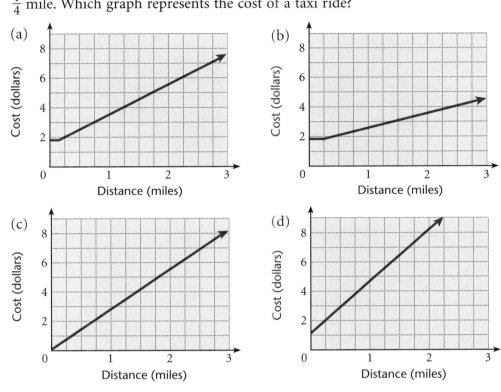

(a)

(b)

(c)

(d)

LOOK BACK

Name the two quantities in each situation. Tell whether they are directly or inversely related. [2-1]

13. The number of songs a radio station plays in an hour is related to the songs' average length.

14. The number of pages a writer completes in a day is related to the number of words on each page.

15. The cost of a 30-sec advertisement on NBC is based on the expected rating, or the number of households expected to be watching.

16. Define two variables for the pattern at right. Write an equation, then use it to find the perimeter of the tenth figure. [3-1]

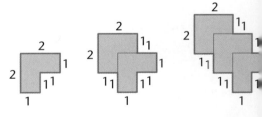

17. The volume of a sphere is given by the expression $\frac{4}{3}\pi r^3$, where r is the radius of the sphere. Use 3.14 for π, and evaluate the expression to find the volume of a field hockey ball with a radius of 1.5 inches. [2-2]

MORE PRACTICE

Make a table of values, and graph each linear function.

18. $y = 2x - 6$ **19.** $y = -x - 25$ **20.** $y = \dfrac{3x}{2} + 1$ **21.** $y = 8 - 2x$

Which table, graph, and equation represent the same linear functions? Explain.

22.

1

$y = x + 4$

2

$y = 4x + 1$

3

x	y
−2	2
−1	3
0	4
1	5
2	6
3	7

4

x	y
−2	−7
−1	−3
0	1
1	5
2	9
3	13

5

6

23.

1

$y = x + 1$

2

$y = x - 2$

3

x	y
−0.10	−2.10
−0.05	−2.05
0	−2.00
0.05	−1.95
0.10	−1.90
0.15	−1.85

4

x	y
−0.10	0.90
−0.05	0.95
0	1.00
0.05	1.05
0.10	1.10
0.15	1.15

5

6

24. Evaluate both expressions for $x = 12$: $(x + 5)(x + 8)$ and $x^2 + 13x + 40$.

MORE MATH REASONING

25. Connie says that even if y is not a function of x, a trend line is the graph of a linear function that approximates the data. Do you agree? Why or why not?

26. You saw that a linear function can be written in the form $y = ax + b$, and that its graph is a straight line. Graph each of the following. Does each represent a straight line? (Hint: $y = 24$ is the same as $y = 0x + 24$.)

  a. $y = 24$ **b.** $x = 8$

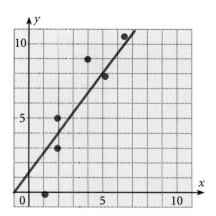

27. A Walk Around the Block Each block has an area of 1 square unit. Write the linear function that shows how the total area (y) depends on the number of the design (x).

Design Number	1	2	3	4	20	x
Total Area						

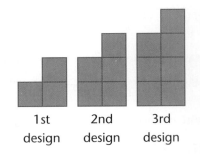

1st design   2nd design   3rd design

28. Tip of the Iceberg An iceberg floats partially submerged in water. M_1 and M_2 represent the mass of the ice above and below the water line, respectively. The data table shows the masses of several icebergs.

Science

a. Write an equation in the form $M_2 = aM_1 + b$ to fit the data in the table.

b. Graph the function. Is it linear? Can the values for either variable be negative? Explain.

c. Find the value for M_2 when $M_1 = 60,000$ tons. Tell how you found the value.

d. Is the ice below the water line or above the water line of more danger to a ship? Explain your reasoning.

Mass above water (tons) M_1	Mass below water (tons) M_2
10,000	125,000
20,000	250,000
30,000	375,000
40,000	500,000
50,000	625,000

3-2 PART C Making Connections

....

←CONNECT→ *You have learned what it means for a relationship between two quantities to be linear. You've also seen how linear functions are represented with tables, equations, and graphs.*

How you represent a linear function—with a table of values, a graph, or an equation—depends on the situation, the person who needs to communicate the information, and the intended audience.

The following Explore gives you an opportunity to see how these ideas work together.

EXPLORE: ARTIFICIAL SATELLITES

Certainly, the Dogons could not have predicted the large number of items that human beings would place in orbit about the earth. Since the former Soviet Union launched Sputnik in 1957, hundreds of satellites have been launched.

Suppose you are the project manager for a satellite launch. It is expected that your company's communications satellite will reach its orbiting height 20 minutes from launch, at which time it should be in direct contact with the company transmitters. It will then complete an orbit every 1.5 hours. At the completion of each orbit, the transmitters will receive the strongest signals from the satellite.

MATERIALS

Graphing utility
Graph paper

1. Make a table comparing the number of orbits to the amount of time since launch. Use time as the dependent variable. You may use minutes or hours, but be consistent.

2. Graph the information from the table.

3. Write an equation for this relationship.

4. Use a graphing utility to make a graph of this situation. Compare it to the graph you made in Step 2.

5. If the launch occurs at 7 a.m., what is the earliest time after 7 a.m. the next day that an orbit will be completed?

REFLECT

1. How would you explain to another student what it means for a relationship between two quantities to be linear?

2. Write an equation that *doesn't* represent a linear function. Explain how you know the relationship isn't linear.

3. When are two quantities proportional to one another?

4. What are some limitations of a graph as a representation of a linear function?

5. What are some limitations of a table as a representation of a linear function?

Decide whether the table of values shows a linear relationship. If the relationship is linear, write the equation.

1.

x	1	2	3	4	5	6
y	3	6	9	3	6	9

2.

x	10	20	30	40	50	60
y	80	75	70	65	60	55

3. Suppose you randomly select one equation from those below. What is the probability of selecting one whose graph is *not* a straight line?

a. $y = -2 - x$ **b.** $y = 2x^2$ **c.** $y = \frac{1}{x}$ **d.** $y = \frac{-x}{2} + 5$

4. A Taxing Situation In the Beatles' song *Taxman*, the tax collector boasts of leaving the worker with only 5% of his income, and sings "that's one for you, nineteen for me." (What does *nineteen* refer to?) Make a table with five ordered pairs that satisfy this relationship, then write an equation.

5. For which equation is y proportional to x?
(a) $y = x^2$ (b) $y = -5x$
(c) $y = 2x + 2$ (d) $y = 9$

6. Which table, graph, and equation represent the same linear functions? Tell how you decided this.

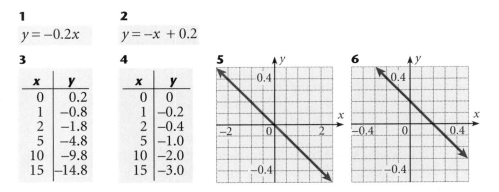

1
$y = -0.2x$

2
$y = -x + 0.2$

3

x	y
0	0.2
1	-0.8
2	-1.8
5	-4.8
10	-9.8
15	-14.8

4

x	y
0	0
1	-0.2
2	-0.4
5	-1.0
10	-2.0
15	-3.0

7. Describe in writing how you can tell by looking at the equation whether the graph of the function is a straight line.

8. Sketch a graph that shows a linear relationship in which the quantities are inversely related.

9. Sketch a graph that shows a relationship that is not linear, in which the quantities are directly related.

Make a table of values, and sketch a graph for each linear function.

10. $y = -x + 1$ **11.** $y = 4.5x + 15$ **12.** $y = \frac{x}{2} - 1$

Define your variables, and write an equation for each relationship. Tell whether one variable is dependent on the other.

13. Copies cost $0.05 each and there is a service fee of $1.00.

14. In a musical piece set in 4/4 time, there are 4 beats to each measure.

15. In the marching band, there are half as many freshman as there are seniors.

16. The number of students at York Suburban is 25 times the number of teachers.

17. In 1992, there were twice as many in-line skates sold as there were skateboards.

18. The chances that an American has appeared on television are one in four.

19. **Dot-'n'-Drop Spot Remover** Jared and his brother put up $20 to buy a license to sell Grandma's Dot-'n'-Drop Spot Remover. They made $0.50 for each bottle they sold.
  a. Define two variables for this situation.
  b. Write an equation for the function.
  c. Guess and check to find how many bottles they need to sell to break even.
  d. Guess and check to find the number of bottles they need to sell to make a profit of at least $25.

20. **Suit in a Bottle** In the United States, we throw away 2.5 million plastic bottles every hour! But it takes 26 recycled plastic bottles to make one polyester suit!
  a. Define the variables.
  b. Write a linear function that relates the total number of polyester suits to the number of hours.
  c. Graph the function.

21. If p is the probability that an event occurs, $q = 1 - p$ is the probability that the event *does not* occur.
  a. What are the domain and range of the function?
  b. Is q a linear function of p? Why or why not?
  c. Graph the relationship. Describe its features.

22. **Stack Flap** This table is from the directions on a Krusteaz® pancake mix box. Is the amount of mix proportional to the amount of water? How did you decide this?

4-in. Pancakes	Mix	Water
8–9	$1\frac{1}{4}$ cups	1 cup
14–15	2 cups	$1\frac{2}{3}$ cups
22–23	3 cups	$2\frac{1}{2}$ cups

Chapter 4

Solving Linear Equations and Inequalities

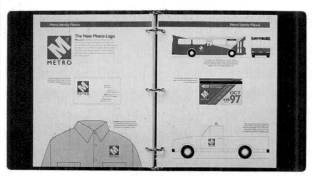

Project A
Leggo my Logo
How do graphic artists design logos? How do they size them up for billboards and down for business cards?

Project B
It's a Fine Line
Where does North Indiana stop and Ohio begin? Where is the Mason-Dixon line?

Project C
Be Your Own Boss
How do you go into business for yourself? Will you succeed or fail?

JOANNA DEAN CLAYTON

Math wasn't one of my better subjects in high school, but I liked the visual side of it. One teacher showed me how straight lines could be used to form a curve, and I could relate to that.

Math helped me get into college. Now I'm surprised how much I need math for page lay-out and other design tasks, especially on the computer. I also do weaving and I need math for that. All my life I wanted to be an artist and now I'm getting paid for my skills. I'm fortunate to be in such a rewarding field.

JoAnna Dean Clayton
Graphic Designer
Bechtel
Whittier, California

Chapter 4

Solving Linear Equations and Inequalities

4-1
Solving Linear Equations

In 4-1 you will use mental math, guess and check, and graphing skills to solve equations.

Solve using mental math or guess and check. [Previous course]

1. $25 + x = 35$ **2.** $6 + x = 66$ **3.** $x - 18 = 20$

4. $15 - x = 10$ **5.** $2x + 4 = 10$ **6.** $x^2 + 2 = 11$

For each function, make a table of values, plot the points, and draw the graph. [3-1]

7. $y = 2x + 1$ **8.** $y = -x + 2$

4-2
Other Techniques for Solving Linear Equations

In 4-2 you will use properties of algebra to solve linear equations. You will need the following algebra skills.

Combine like terms. [2-3]

9. $3x - 2x$ **10.** $x + (-x) + (-x)$

11. $x + \dfrac{x}{2}$ **12.** $7x + x + 4x$

13. $x - 9x$ **14.** $8x - (x - 2x)$

15. $5x + (-2x + 2x)$ **16.** $-x + 6x$

Use the distributive property to simplify these expressions. [2-3]

17. $-3(x + 8)$ **18.** $5(2x - 7)$ **19.** $\dfrac{1}{2}(-6x + 4)$ **20.** $2(-5 - 2x)$

21. $8(x + 2)$ **22.** $-9(-2 + x)$ **23.** $7(x + 10)$ **24.** $4(6x + 4)$

4-3
Relating Equations and Inequalities

In 4-3 you will solve more complicated linear equations and linear inequalities. You will apply the following ideas of order.

Order each set of numbers from least to greatest. [Previous course]

25. $-3, 6, 0, 2.5, -18$ **26.** $-(-7), -7, -3, -30, 20$

27. $2, 2.4, -2, 1.6, -1.8$ **28.** $\dfrac{1}{2}, \dfrac{3}{5}, \dfrac{-5}{3}, \dfrac{-7}{5}, \dfrac{5}{4}$

29. $\dfrac{1}{3}, -1, -\dfrac{2}{3}, \dfrac{2}{3}, -\dfrac{3}{4}$ **30.** $-0.6, 1.3, -1.2, 1, -1.4$

4-1 Solving Linear Equations

HOT stuff

Each year the Oilfield Chili Appreciation Society holds a chili cook-off. Company teams compete to make the hottest and best tasting chili. Every year the ingredients get more exotic.

Recipes sometimes include buffalo, elk, deer, rabbit, squirrel, or alligator meat! When one team heard that their green chili didn't stand a chance of winning, they added red food coloring. (The chili turned orange—the judges were not impressed.)

The most common ingredient in chili recipes is the chili pepper itself. Thousands of years ago, chilis were tiny red berries on vines in the Amazon jungle of South America. Today, chilis are grown throughout the world and come in a wide variety, including bell, cayenne, Tabasco, jalapeño, serrano, and many others.

Some teams in the chili cook-off measure their ingredients exactly to get

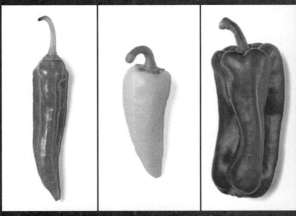

These are three of the most commonly used peppers for general purpose cooking. (Left to right: Jalapeño, Banana, and Bell.)

specific proportions. Others simply add ingredients until they think the proportions are correct. Then they taste the chili and make adjustments if needed. This guess-and-check method has produced some first-place winners.

?

1. The chili cook-off raises money for charity. Describe some ways the organizers could raise money in the cook-off.
2. What is the hottest kind of pepper that you have eaten? People who have tasted them agree that cayenne peppers are hotter than pimento peppers. How would you set up a hotness scale for peppers?
3. Is it a good idea to use a guess-and-check approach in cooking? Why or why not?

Solving Equations Using Number Sense

← CONNECT → *You've seen that a function is a special relationship between quantities and that functions can be represented in different ways. Now you will begin to solve equations that have one variable.*

An equation is *true* when the value of the expression on one side of the equal sign is the same as the value of the expression on the other side of the equal sign.

> The **solutions** to an equation with one variable are the values of the variable that make the equation true. When you find the solutions to an equation, you are **solving the equation**.

To check if a value of the variable is a solution of the equation, evaluate the expressions on both sides of the equation. If the values are equal, then the equation is true, and the value of the variable is a solution. We say, "It checks."

EXAMPLE

1. Determine whether the given value of x is a solution of the equation $24 = 2x + 8$.

   a. $x = 5$

   $24 = 2x + 8$

   $ \overset{?}{=} 2(5) + 8$ Substitute 5 for x.

   $24 \neq 18$ The values are not equal, so $24 = 2x + 8$ is not true when $x = 5$.

   Therefore, 5 is *not* a solution of the equation $24 = 2x + 8$.

   b. $x = 8$

   $24 = 2x + 8$

   $ \overset{?}{=} 2(8) + 8$ Substitute 8 for x.

   $24 = 24$ The equation $24 = 2x + 8$ is true when $x = 8$. It checks.

   Therefore, 8 *is* a solution of the equation $24 = 2x + 8$.

Guess and check means exactly what it says—you guess a value for the variable and then check to see if it makes the equation true. If the value doesn't check, make another guess and check it. Each guess-and-check can help you make a better guess until you find the solution.

Another way to solve equations is using *mental math*—doing calculations in your head.

EXPLORE: SOME LIKE IT HOT

Tom's chili recipe calls for $1\frac{1}{2}$ tablespoons of chili powder for each pound of meat. He always adds "one for the pot"—one more tablespoon to the entire recipe—for just the right "heat."

The linear function $c = 1\frac{1}{2}\,m + 1$ relates c, the number of tablespoons of chili powder, to m, the number of pounds of meat.

When Tom got to the chili cook-off, he realized he had only one box of chili powder. A box holds 46 tablespoons. Substituting this value of c into the equation gives $46 = 1\frac{1}{2}\,m + 1$.

1. Guess a value for m, and check to see if it is a solution of the equation $46 = 1\frac{1}{2}\,m + 1$.
2. If it didn't check, was the value of $1\frac{1}{2}\,m + 1$ too big or too small? Adjust the value of m accordingly, and check your new guess. Continue until you find the solution.
3. Tell what guesses you made as you solved the equation. If you made a guess that didn't check, explain how you chose your next guess.
4. How many pounds of meat will Tom need if he uses the whole box of chili powder?

In the Explore, you probably didn't solve the equation on your first guess. As you guess and check to solve equations, it's important to think about how you can make a better guess with each try.

Sometimes you can solve an equation by breaking the task into simple steps and using mental math.

2. Solve $36 = 3x - 6$ using mental math.

$36 = 3x - 6$

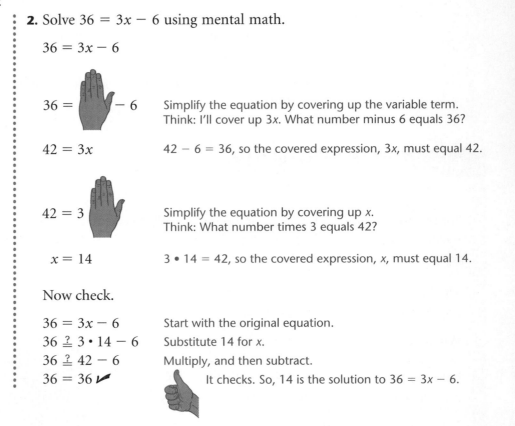

$36 = \boxed{} - 6$ Simplify the equation by covering up the variable term. Think: I'll cover up $3x$. What number minus 6 equals 36?

$42 = 3x$ $42 - 6 = 36$, so the covered expression, $3x$, must equal 42.

$42 = 3\boxed{}$ Simplify the equation by covering up x. Think: What number times 3 equals 42?

$x = 14$ $3 \cdot 14 = 42$, so the covered expression, x, must equal 14.

Now check.

$36 = 3x - 6$	Start with the original equation.
$36 \stackrel{?}{=} 3 \cdot 14 - 6$	Substitute 14 for x.
$36 \stackrel{?}{=} 42 - 6$	Multiply, and then subtract.
$36 = 36$ ✔	It checks. So, 14 is the solution to $36 = 3x - 6$.

Solve each equation using guess-and-check or mental math.

a. $14 = 4x + 26$ **b.** $-6 = 14 - r$

c. $2k + 2 = -10$ **d.** $26 = 40 - 2y$

e. $18 = \frac{x}{4} + 2$ **f.** $25(c + 3) = 100$

1. Would you use guess-and-check or mental math to solve the equation $\frac{x}{3} - 4 = 2$? Explain how you decided this.

2. If you use guess-and-check to solve the equation $\frac{x}{2} + 5 = 45$, what would be your first guess? Explain why you chose this number.

3. If you use mental math to solve the equation $\frac{x}{2} + 5 = 45$, how would you begin?

CORE

1. Getting Started Ella used guess-and-check to solve the equation $2x + 1 = 15$.
  a. Suppose her first guess is $x = 6$. What is the value of $2x + 1$ when x is 6?
  b. Use guess-and-check until you solve the equation.

Write the word or phrase that best completes each statement.

2. The _____ to an equation with one variable are the values of the variable that make the equation true.

3. You are solving an equation when you find the _____ of an equation.

4. Determine whether the given value of x is a solution of the equation $36 = 3x - 9$.
  a. $x = 20$ **b.** $x = 15$

Solve each equation using mental math.

5. $25 + m = 100$ **6.** $8b = -168$ **7.** $\dfrac{63.9}{c} = 21.3$

Use guess-and-check to solve each equation. Tell what number you chose as your first guess and why you chose it.

8. $-14 + 3y = 64$ **9.** $15x + 10 = 235$ **10.** $2b + 24 = 4b + 6$

11. How Much Do I Owe? Spence, Brent, and Trey went to dinner. After a $4 tip was added to the price of the dinner (d), the total cost was $27.
  a. What does the expression $d + 4$ represent?
  b. Write an equation that shows the price of the dinner.
  c. Solve the equation.
  d. If the bill is divided equally, how much money (m) does each boy owe? Tell how you determined this.

12. Best Booth Awards are given for the best decorated booth at the chili cook-off. Booths measure 8 ft by 10 ft. The booths are completely surrounded by railing, except across a 2 ft-wide door. Draw a picture of the booth showing the measurements. Pierre wants to run a crepe-paper border along the railing. If he needs crepe paper twice the length of the entire railing, how much paper does he need to purchase? Remember $p = 2(\ell + w)$.

Solve each equation using guess-and-check or mental math.

13. $4m + 8 = 48$

14. $\dfrac{2d}{3} - 6 = 2$

15. $\dfrac{5k + 6}{4} + 8 = 12$

16. $y + \dfrac{1}{4} = 0.75$

17. $\dfrac{2x}{3} - 10 = 0$

18. $-2p + 5 = 16$

19. Sometimes, substitution is the easiest way to solve an equation. Use substitution to decide which value is the solution of the equation $\dfrac{x}{25} + 1 = 26$.
    (a) 1   (b) 25   (c) 625   (d) 665

20. Richard enjoys making chili. His recipe uses either beef, pork, or turkey. For peppers he can use either jalapeños, habaneros, or mirasol.
    a. How many different kinds of chili can he make from this recipe if he uses one type of meat and one type of pepper? List them.
    b. What is the probability that he will not make turkey chili with mirasol peppers?

 *LOOK AHEAD*

21. Which of these ordered pairs would be found on the graph of the equation $y = 0.25x$?
    (a) $(4, 0)$ (b) $(1, 4)$ (c) $(8, 2)$

Use the graph of the equation $y = -x + 1$ to find the y-coordinate for each point of the line.

22. $(1, ?)$

23. $(0, ?)$

24. $(-2, ?)$

25. $(4, ?)$

MORE PRACTICE

Solve each equation using guess-and-check. Tell what number you chose as your first guess and why you chose it.

26. $a + 83 = 264$

27. $5(y - 100) = 1000$

28. $65c = -2535$

Solve each equation using guess-and-check or mental math.

29. $4c + 24 = 2c + 6$

30. $0.3v = 9.9$

31. $2z - 1 = 4 + z$

32. $\dfrac{3d + 4}{2} = 11$

33. $6(4 - f) = 12$

34. $11g - 1 = 10$

Determine whether 10 would be a good first guess for each equation. Explain your reasoning.

35. $-10s = 110$

36. $4(10 - t) = 2500$

37. $3w - 15 = 15$

38. To solve the equation $6x + 27 = 105$, Ted guessed that x was 15. When he tried it, he found that $6(15) + 27 = 117$. Which would be a better second guess, 14 or 16? Why?

MORE MATH REASONING

39. Desi and Ken are entered in the chili cook-off.
   a. If they begin cooking at 4:45 a.m. and the judging begins at 11:15 a.m., how much time do they have to cook their chili?
   b. At the cook-off, there are 120 teams. All of the team names are put into a hat and the booths are selected by a random draw. Ken and Desi want any of the 8 booths located near the entrance. What is the probability that they will get one of the booths they want?

40. While Judy and Jaime were studying together, Jaime complained that using guess-and-check to solve the equation $3(x - 1) = 2x + 1$ was too difficult. He asked Judy to solve the equation for him. Judy refused to do the work, but she did offer to begin a table that would give Jaime some clues. Here is her table.

x	$3(x - 1)$	$2x + 1$
0	-3	1
1		
2		5
		9
7		
	27	

   a. Copy and complete the table.
   b. What is the solution to $3(x - 1) = 2x + 1$?
   c. Do you think the problem was too difficult to solve by using guess-and-check? Why or why not?

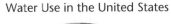

41. Study the chart "Water Use in the United States."
   a. Wanda says that the water used in homes is only about 20% of the water used by factories and businesses. Is she correct? Justify your answer.
   b. Will says that the water used on farms is more than 500% of that used in homes. Is he correct? Justify your answer.
   c. Since the water consumption in homes is only 9%, is water conservation in homes still important? Why or why not?

Water Use in the United States

Solving Equations Using Graphs

4-1 PART B

← **CONNECT** → *You've solved equations by guessing and checking and by using mental math. You can also solve equations visually using graphs of functions. Graphing is sometimes a more efficient method for solving equations.*

EXPLORE: GO FOR THE GOAL

A charity that grants money to families in crisis is planning a fund drive for a new clinic. The planners expect to collect $25,000 per month during the drive and expect expenses for the drive to total $125,000. Their goal is to raise $1 million. The money remaining after expenses are paid will then be available for grants to families.

1. Write an equation that relates x, the number of months of the fund drive, to y, the amount of money available for grants at the end of the drive.

2. Graph the equation on a coordinate plane.

3. How much money will be available for grants to families if the charity's goal is met? Use your graph to decide how long the drive should last to meet this goal.

4. Explain how you found the length of time. Did you read the value directly from the graph or did you have to estimate?

5. If the expenses increase to $225,000, how will this affect the charity's plans?

MATERIALS

Graph paper

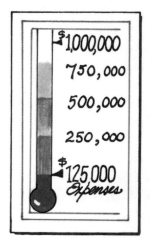

For what value of x is $\frac{1}{2}x + 2$ equal to 5? You can solve an equation such as $5 = \frac{1}{2}x + 2$ or $8 = \frac{1}{2}x + 2$ using the graph of the function $y = \frac{1}{2}x + 2$.

To solve $5 = \frac{1}{2}x + 2$, look for the point on the graph where $y = 5$, and find the corresponding value of x.

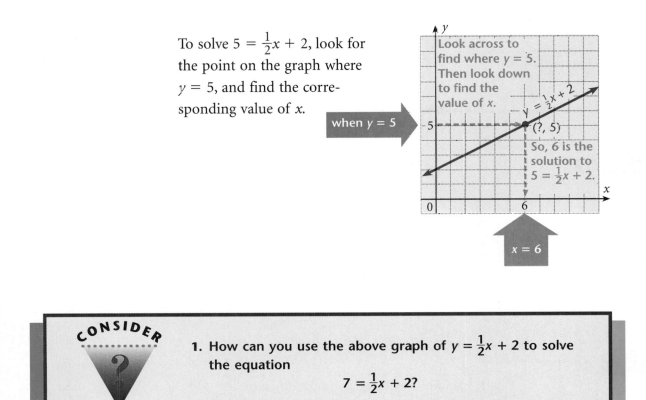

when $y = 5$

Look across to find where $y = 5$. Then look down to find the value of x.

$y = \frac{1}{2}x + 2$

$(?, 5)$

So, 6 is the solution to $5 = \frac{1}{2}x + 2$.

$x = 6$

CONSIDER?

1. How can you use the above graph of $y = \frac{1}{2}x + 2$ to solve the equation
$$7 = \frac{1}{2}x + 2?$$

When graphing, if you use a graphing utility, you may need to adjust the window size to show the x- and y-values that you want to see.

EXAMPLE

Graph the function $y = \frac{1}{2}x + 2$. Then use the graph to solve the equation $24.5 = \frac{1}{2}x + 2$.

Graph the function $y = \frac{1}{2}x + 2$, and adjust the window size so you can see the point where $y = 24.5$. This window shows x-values from -40 to 55, and y-values from -32 to 31.

Use the *trace* feature on the graphing utility to move the cursor along the graph until you find the point where $y = 24.5$. Then read the x-value.

The solution of the equation $24.5 = \frac{1}{2}x + 2$ is 45. Substituting 45 for x and evaluating with a calculator shows that the solution checks.

X=45   Y=24.5

Some graphing utilities use these settings to adjust window size.

Xmin=-40
Xmax=55
Xscl=10
Ymin=-32
Ymax=31
Yscl=10

2. Is there any *y*-value that could be substituted into $y = \frac{1}{2}x + 2$ that would result in *more* than one solution? *no* solutions? Explain.

TRY IT

Use the graph of $y = -2.5x + 1$ to estimate the solution of each equation.

a. $-4 = -2.5x + 1$
b. $-5 = -2.5x + 1$

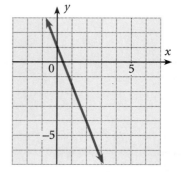

REFLECT

1. Explain how the graph of a function, like $y = 3x + 2$, can be used to solve an equation, like $8 = 3x + 2$.

2. One point on the graph of $y = 2.6x - 9$ has coordinates $(5, 4)$. What does this tell you about the solutions of the equation $4 = 2.6x - 9$?

3. When would solving an equation by using a graph be easier than using other methods? Explain.

Exercises

CORE

1. Getting Started Line *a* is the graph of $y = \frac{2}{3}x - 1$.

a. Trace the arrow on the line $y = 3$. Then use the arrow and the graph of line *a* to solve the equation $3 = \frac{2}{3}x - 1$.

b. Trace the arrow on the line $y = -5$. Then use the arrow and the graph of line *a* to solve the equation $-5 = \frac{2}{3}x - 1$.

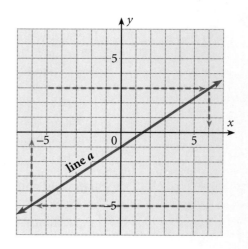

Use the graph of $y = 4x - 1$ to solve each equation.

2. $-1 = 4x - 1$ **3.** $3 = 4x - 1$ **4.** $-5 = 4x - 1$

Graph the function $y = x + 2$. Then use the graph to estimate the solution to each equation.

5. $4 = x + 2$ **6.** $2 = x + 2$

7. $0 = x + 2$ **8.** $-2 = x + 2$

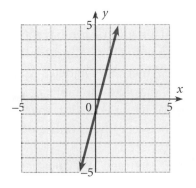

9. Cat Costs When Bryant leaves town, he has to take his cat Smokey to a kennel. The cost of the kennel is \$7 per day. He always has them give Smokey one flea bath that costs \$18. If $c = $ the total cost and $d = $ the number of days, the equation $c = 7d + 18$ shows the relationship between the quantities.
   a. Graph the equation.
   b. When Bryant left Smokey at the kennel in June, the total cost was \$46. Write an equation that can be solved to find how many days the cat stayed at the kennel.
   c. Use the graph to help you make your first guess. Continue guessing until you find the solution.

10. Letitia was assigned to graph the linear function $y = 100x - 1500$, and then to solve the equation $500 = 100x - 1500$. She used the settings shown to create the following graph.
   a. Why do you think Letitia started with Ymin $= -1500$ and Ymax $= 1500$?
   b. The graph is very difficult to see. Which of the settings would you change to make the graph easier to see? How did you determine this?
   c. Why was the domain from 0 to 500 not a very good choice for x?

Xmin=0
Xmax=500
Xscl=50
Ymin=−1500
Ymax=1500
Yscl=500

Solve each equation using guess-and-check or mental math.

11. $\dfrac{3d + 1}{4} = 10$ **12.** $2x - 12 = 5x - 39$

13. Betina bought a new burner to use to cook chili. The burner instructions say that it is not safe to use with a pot that has a circumference of over 35 inches. Betina has a pot labeled in quarts, but the label gives no information about its circumference. She has a ruler, but not a measuring tape. How can she find out if it is safe to use the pot with the new burner?

$C = \pi d$

14. Marina and Glenn have a cousin who has juvenile diabetes. They found that they could raise money for the American Diabetes Association by selling calendars.
  a. Complete the table, using any pattern you observe.
  b. Write an equation that describes the relationship between the number of calendars sold and the proceeds.
  c. If they sell 100 calendars, how much will they make?
  d. Their goal is to raise $500. Estimate how many calendars they must sell to reach their goal.

Calendars Sold (*n*)	Proceeds for Charity (*p*)
5	$15.00
8	$24.00
10	$30.00
13	$39.00
15	
18	
20	

15. Bob has an 8- by 10-inch photo of the Pablo Picasso sculpture in Chicago. He wants to enlarge it and place it in his 18- by 24-inch frame.
  a. Is the ratio of length and width in the photo the same as that of the frame?
  b. Would a 24- by 30-inch frame be better? Explain.

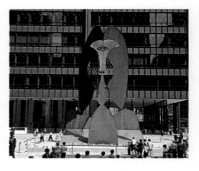

Pablo Picasso, *Untitled*, 1967, Chicago, Illinois

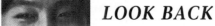

LOOK BACK

Match each phrase with the appropriate algebraic expression. [2-2]

16. 4 less than the product of 13 and a number   **A.** $13 - 4n$

17. 13 decreased by the product of 4 and a number   **B.** $4(13 - n)$

18. 4 times the difference of 13 and a number   **C.** $13n - 4$

19. Make a table of values, and graph the equation $y = -x + 3$. [3-2]

20. Nawel has quiz scores of 98, 93, 80, 85, 97, 78, and 85.   [1-1]
  a. Find her mean score.   **b.** Find her median score.   **c.** Find her mode score.

MORE PRACTICE

Use the graph of the function $y = 2(x - 1) + 3$ to answer the following questions.

21. a. If $y = -1$, what is the value of x?
  b. What is the solution to $-1 = 2(x - 1) + 3$?

22. a. If $y = 1$, what is the value of x?
  b. What is the solution to $1 = 2(x - 1) + 3$?

23. If $y = 7$, what is the solution to $7 = 2(x - 1) + 3$?

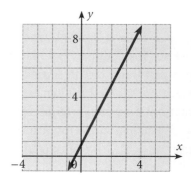

Use the graph of the function $y = -x + 1$ to solve each equation.

24. $-2 = -x + 1$ **25.** $0 = -x + 1$

26. $1 = -x + 1$ **27.** $-3 = -x + 1$

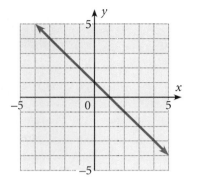

Graph the function $y = -3x + 2$. Then use the graph to solve each equation.

28. $-1 = -3x + 2$ **29.** $8 = -3x + 2$

30. $-7 = -3x + 2$

Graph the function $y = \frac{1}{2}x - 10$. Then use the graph to solve each equation.

31. $12 = \frac{1}{2}x - 10$ **32.** $0 = \frac{1}{2}x - 10$ **33.** $-2 = \frac{1}{2}x - 10$

MORE MATH REASONING

These are linear equations.

$$y = 3x \qquad 4 = 2(x + 5) \qquad y = 7 \qquad \frac{3}{4}m = 0 \qquad 0.5 - 3(2 - h) = g \qquad a = b$$

These are not linear equations.

$$xy = 7 \qquad 3 = j(j + 4) \qquad y = x^2 \qquad \frac{2}{d} = c \qquad v^3 + 1 = w \qquad y > x$$

34. Use the above examples and non-examples to describe some characteristics of linear equations.

35. Ancient Accents Pipian is a sauce made with chili peppers. It was served at the court feasts of the Aztec ruler, Montezuma. Chili peppers and oil are two of the key ingredients. One recipe calls for 3 chilies to 2 tablespoons of oil.

History

a. Copy and complete the table, which describes the numbers of peppers and tablespoons of oil needed to make various amounts of pipian.

Peppers (p)	Tablespoons of Oil (t)
3	2
6	4
9	
15	
	16

b. Write an equation that relates the tablespoons of oil to the number of peppers.

c. Write the resulting equation if the number of tablespoons of oil added to the recipe were 18. What is the solution?

Making Connections

← **C O N N E C T** → *There are many ways to solve equations. You've solved some equations by guessing and checking, some using mental math, and some using graphs. Real-life problems can be expressed by a variety of equations, so it's convenient to know several methods for solving them.*

EXPLORE: HOT PROFITS

MATERIALS

Graph paper

The sponsors of a chili cook-off are debating how much to charge for admission and for sampling the various recipes. They decided to provide free drinks to encourage people to sample more chili. Two plans have been recommended.

1. Define two variables—one for the average number of cups of chili bought per attendee and one for the average amount of money spent per attendee. For each plan, write an equation that relates the variables, and graph the equation.

2. Looking at last year's receipts, one sponsor said that the average attendee spent $8. If that holds true this year, how many cups of chili will the average attendee get with the Jalapeño Plan? with the Habanero Plan? Explain how you determined this.

3. Another sponsor predicted that the average attendee will eat 8 cups of chili. If so, how much money will the average attendee spend with each plan?

4. If the sponsors want attendees to spend at least $10, which plan do you think would work better? Why? Explain how your graphs support your decision.

5. Suppose you go to the cook-off with only $7.50 to spend. Both plans are offered. Which plan would you choose to get the most chili?

6. Devise a plan that you feel would bring in more money than either of these. Why do you think your plan is better? What assumptions are you making about the people who will attend the cook-off?

1. Write a paragraph that explains how you would use guess-and-check to solve $2x + 5 = -3$.
2. Give an example of an equation for which 0 would be a poor choice as a first guess.
3. Give an example of an equation that would be hard to solve by either guessing and checking or using mental math. Would it be any easier to solve using a graph?
4. Describe a way you could use both a graph *and* guessing and checking to solve an equation.

Self-Assessment

1. Max decided to use guess-and-check to solve the equation $\frac{1}{2}(x - 1) = 17$.
   a. Suppose his first guess is $x = 0$. What is the value of $\frac{1}{2}(x - 1)$ when x is 0?
   b. Should he try a larger or a smaller number for his second guess? Why?
   c. Suppose his next guess is 21. What is the value of $\frac{1}{2}(x - 1)$ when x is 21?
   d. Should he try a larger or a smaller number for his next guess? Why?
   e. Use guess-and-check until you solve the equation.

Solve these equations using guess-and-check or mental math. Tell which method you chose and why.

2. $-3c = 27$ 3. $4f + 35 = f + 53$ 4. $15w - 27 = 123$

Use the graph of the function $y = -x + 3$ to solve each equation.

5. $3 = -x + 3$ 6. $-3 = -x + 3$

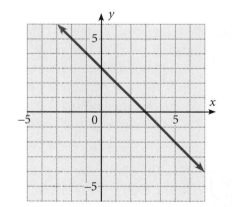

Graph the function $y = 2(x + 1)$. Then use the graph to solve each equation.

7. $4 = 2(x + 1)$ 8. $0 = 2(x + 1)$

9. $-6 = 2(x + 1)$ 10. $2 = 2(x + 1)$

11. Which of the following is a solution of the equation $3 = 2(3 - x) + 1$?
   (a) $x = \frac{3}{2}$ (b) $x = -1$ (c) $x = 4$ (d) $x = 2$ (e) not here

12. Calvin solved the equation $\frac{x - 3}{2} = 10$ using mental math and got a solution of 8. Explain the mistake you think Calvin made.

13. Proceeds Go to Charity The organizer of the cook-off needs to divide the proceeds (p) between two charities. The largest amount (a) will go to the Special Olympics. The American Cancer Society will receive half the amount that the Special Olympics gets.

  a. What quantity does a represent? $\frac{1}{2}a$? p?

  b. Write an equation that relates the proceeds to the amounts given the two charities.

  c. Suppose the proceeds are $24,906. Write an equation that helps calculate how much will go to each charity.

  d. Use guess-and-check to solve the equation. How much money will each charity receive?

14. To graph the function $y = 0.1x - 2$, which values would you select for the range? Why?

  (a) Xmin=−10   (b) Xmin=−10   (c) Xmin=−100   (d) Xmin=−100
      Xmax=10   Xmax=10   Xmax=100   Xmax=100
      Xscl=1   Xscl=10   Xscl=1   Xscl=10

15. Explain why the equation $\frac{x + 4}{5} = 10(x + 1)$ could not be solved easily by using the guess-and-check method.

16. Chili Alternative Akio and Pat want to raise money for the American Red Cross at the cook-off. They decide to sell sandwiches and drinks to those who don't like chili. They buy wheat and white bread, turkey, ham, egg salad, soda, and juice. How many different combinations of a sandwich with one filling and a drink could the customers order? Explain your answer.

17. Fee Figuring The cost of running the cook-off is covered by each team's booth fees. The organizers want to set the amount that they will charge each team. The table at the right shows the relationship between the running costs (c) and the fees (f) paid by the individual teams.

  a. Write an equation that relates the costs to the fees.

  b. If the cost of running the cook-off is approximately $2400, write an equation that relates this amount to the fees charged.

  c. Solve the equation using mental math. How much was charged each team in the table?

c	f
1200	10
1800	15
2400	20
3600	30
4800	40
6000	50

18. Healthy Chili Mary wanted to compare the fat content in the meat contained in the chili recipes. There are 9 calories in each gram of fat, so the percent of fat is the calories from fat divided by the total calories.

  a. Write an expression for the number of calories if there are g grams of fat.

  b. Write an expression for the percent of fat if there are T total calories.

  c. Explain how Mary could use these expressions when she knows the grams of fat and the total calories.

SAVING THE ANIMALS

Zoos have been around for more than 4000 years. The first zoos were random jumbles of animals for people to gawk at. In 1804, scientific study of animals began at the Jardin des Plantes in Paris.

During the nineteenth century, zoos became institutions for educating the public about wildlife. But the main function of zoos has been to entertain visitors in a setting filled with animals.

Recently zoos have taken on another role. The animal world is now faced with problems: destruction of habitat, pressures of population, increased amounts of poisons in the environment, to name a few. These problems have led to the extinction of many species in the wild, and the endangerment of many more. The new role for zoos is to protect and breed endangered species. Zoos have become one of the best hopes for preserving threatened species. Unfortunately, zoos can preserve species only in captivity. Whether those species can be returned to the wild is a question we cannot yet answer.

How fast are species becoming extinct? Biologists

Lorus and Margery Milne have made some estimates for bird and mammal species.

Dates (A.D.)	No. of Extinctions
1–1650	**20**
1650–1850	**40**
1850–1900	**63**
1900–1950	**75**

Since 1950 the rate of extinction has accelerated astronomically. Today, considering all forms of life, we may be losing one species per day.

1. **What role does math play in running a zoo?**
2. **What trends can you spot in the extinction rates? What explanation can you give for those trends?**
3. **If you were responsible for preparing a budget for a zoo, what would be your priorities?**

← CONNECT →
In Chapter 2, you learned to model expressions and simplify them using algebra tiles. Now you will learn to model and solve equations using algebra tiles.

Recall that you can use algebra tiles to model terms and expressions.

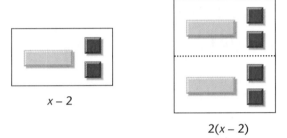

$x - 2$

$2(x - 2)$

The opposite of a number is called its additive inverse. When you add any number and its additive inverse, you get zero. Here are two models of expressions that add to zero.

$1 + (-1)$

$-x + x$

You can also use algebra tiles to model equations.

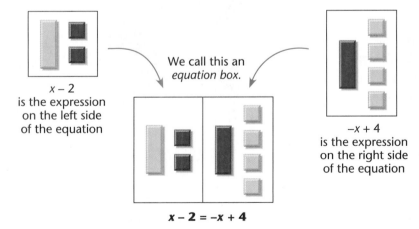

$x - 2$
is the expression
on the left side
of the equation

We call this an
equation box.

$-x + 4$
is the expression
on the right side
of the equation

$x - 2 = -x + 4$

Write the equation modeled in each equation box.

a. 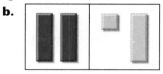   **b.**

EXPLORE: LEFT ALONE

Solve the equation modeled in each equation box using algebra tiles. Follow these rules for working with tiles.

MATERIALS

Algebra tiles

Rules

A. You can add or remove tiles, but whatever you add to or remove from one side of the equation box you must *also* add to or remove from the *other side*.

B. Any pair of additive inverse tiles *on the same side* of an equation box add to zero and can be removed.

C. You can use one or more horizontal dotted lines to divide the equation box into identical equation boxes. Then continue to work with only one of these new boxes.

Write the equation modeled in each equation box. Use the rules to get a single *x*-tile on one side of the equation box and only unit tiles on the other side. The number represented by the unit tiles is the value of *x*.

1.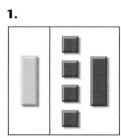

2.

3.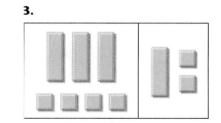

4. Make up your own equation. Then use algebra tiles to model the equation and solve for *x*.

5. Write a paragraph that describes how you applied the rules and any difficulties you had.

1. If the solution to an equation isn't an integer, what do you think will happen when you try to solve it using algebra tiles? Explain.

2. Decide if Monique solved the following equation correctly. Explain how you determined this.

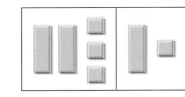

Monique's equation   Monique's solution

Exercises

CORE

1. **Getting Started** What would you have to add to each of these expression models to get 0?

   a.    b.   c.

Write the word or phrase that correctly completes the statement.

2. The opposite of a number is called its _____.

Write the equation modeled in each equation box.

3. 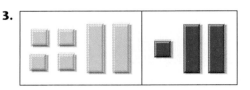   4.   5.

6. Jyotsna added one red unit tile to both sides of the equation box. Renee took away one yellow unit tile from both sides of the box. Who was correct? Explain.

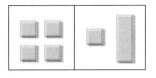

7. Two-thirds of the length of the Mexican iguana is its tail.

a. Write an equation that relates the length of the tail to its body.

b. If an iguana is $4\frac{1}{2}$ ft long, how long is its tail?

8. Making Money At one zoo, zookeepers work 40 hours per week. Which one of the following is needed to determine their weekly salary?

(a) their annual cost-of-living raise
(b) the number of vacation days each person is allowed
(c) their per-hour wages
(d) the number of weeks in a year

9. A bag contains algebra tiles. There are 10 red unit tiles, 10 blue unit tiles, 5 blue x-tiles, and 8 red x-tiles. What is the probability of removing a red x-tile from the bag?

Write the expressions modeled by the tiles.

10.

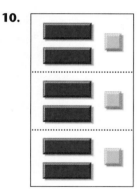

11.

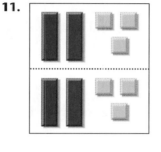

12.

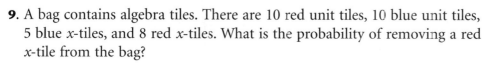

13. Name at least two ways you can begin to solve this equation.

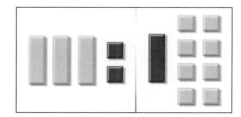

Use tiles or draw diagrams to solve the equations modeled using algebra tiles. Explain what you did.

14.

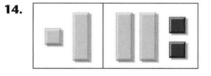

15.

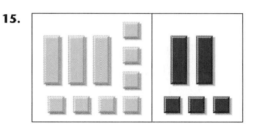

16. Some people think of an equation as a balanced scale. In the Explore, one rule states that if you add or remove any tiles from the equation box, you must add or remove tiles from the other side of the box. Relate that rule to the idea of a balanced scale.

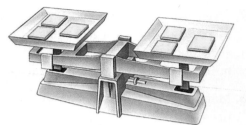

Industry

17. Line of the Zodiac The graph shows the relationship between the part-time (p) and full-time (f) employees at Zodiac Zoo. The ratio of part-time to full-time employees is kept as constant as possible. Part-time employees are hired on the basis of the number of full-time employees. The number of full-time employees usually ranges from 155 to 162.

a. Make a data table showing at least three ordered pairs from the graph.

b. Write an equation that relates the quantities.

c. If in May the number of part-time employees was 483, how many full-time workers would you estimate were employed?

d. What are the domain and range of the function suggested by the relationship between p and f?

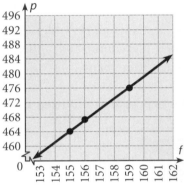

 **LOOK BACK**

Fine Arts

18. Photography, like mathematics, has an order of operations—from inserting the film and composing individual photos, to developing the film and framing the picture. List a logical pattern of steps used by photographers. What are some reasons for agreeing on a sequence in photography or mathematics? [2–3]

19. a. Look for a pattern, and complete the table. [3–1]

x	1	2	3	4	5	6
y	0	3	8	15		

b. Write an equation for the function in the form $y =$ _____.

c. Use the equation to find the value of y when $x = -9$.

20. Determine whether the given value of x is a solution to the equation $8 = 3x - 7$. [4–1]

a. $x = 4$ **b.** $x = 5$

MORE PRACTICE

21. What would you have to add to each of these diagrams to get zero?

a.

b.

c.

22. Write the additive inverse for each expression.

    a. $-4x$ **b.** 16.8 **c.** $5\frac{1}{3}$

Write the equation modeled in each equation box, then solve it.

23.   **24.** 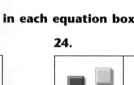   **25.**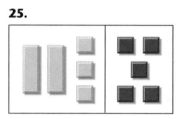

Write the expressions modeled by the tiles.

26.   **27.** 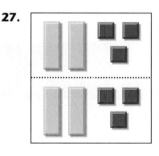   **28.**

MORE MATH REASONING

29. Eggsactly! Tad volunteers at the bird house of the zoo. He keeps the weight records for the ostriches and their eggs.

	Ostrich #1	Ostrich #2	Ostrich #3
weight of mother	160 pounds	180 pounds	150 pounds
weight of egg	3.2 pounds	3.6 pounds	3.0 pounds

    a. Organize his information in a data table, and express the data as an equation.

    b. Pam says she can guess the weight of the mother of an egg that weighs 3.4 pounds without doing any calculations. What do you think she has noticed?

    c. Predict the weight of an egg from a 172-pound ostrich. Explain your thinking.

30. **Around and Around We Go** The cost of a train ride around the zoo is $3.75 for adults and $2.00 for children. The train makes four stops and takes approximately 45 minutes to travel the entire perimeter of the zoo. The conductor collected $7.50 from the Jones family. How many members of the Jones family got on the train? What information is needed to solve this problem?
   (a) train makes four stops
   (b) 45 minutes to travel entire perimeter
   (c) they rode a train
   (d) all of the above are needed

31. An adult giant panda consumes 30 pounds of bamboo per day. Suppose the zoo is able to grow 600 pounds of bamboo per year.

   a. How many pounds of bamboo must they buy for the panda for one year?
   b. How are the amount of bamboo grown and the amount of bamboo purchased related?
   c. If the zoo gets a second panda will this double the amount of bamboo purchased? Explain.

4-2
PART B Connecting Algebra Tiles to Symbols

← **CONNECT** → *You've learned to use algebra tiles to solve equations. Now you will explore the connection between working with algebra tiles and working with algebraic symbols.*

An equation changes as you solve it with algebra tiles. Observing these changes can help you gain insight into solving equations symbolically.

1. When you solve an equation using algebra tiles, why would you try to get a single *x*-tile on one side of the equation box and no *x*-tiles on the other?

MATERIALS

Algebra tiles

1. Use tiles to model the following equation. Record each step, from tiles to symbols, to show how the equation in the right-hand column changes.

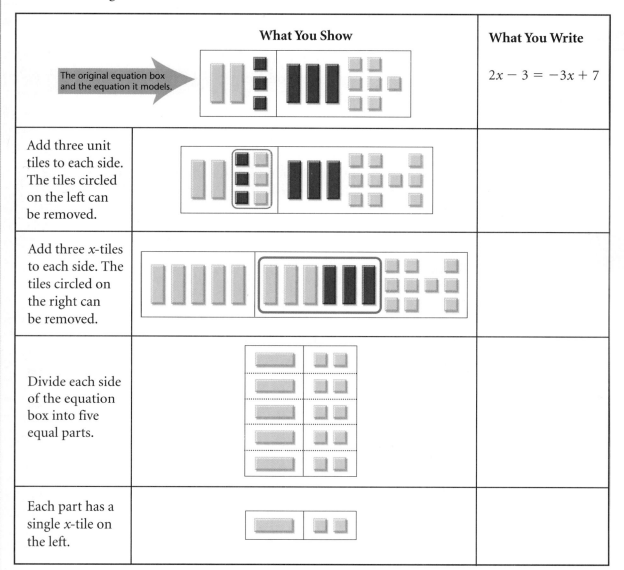

	What You Show	What You Write
The original equation box and the equation it models. →		$2x - 3 = -3x + 7$
Add three unit tiles to each side. The tiles circled on the left can be removed.		
Add three *x*-tiles to each side. The tiles circled on the right can be removed.		
Divide each side of the equation box into five equal parts.		
Each part has a single *x*-tile on the left.		

2. What value of *x* is shown in the last step? Check your solution by substituting this value of *x* into the original equation. Does this value of *x* also solve every other equation in the right-hand column?

3. Start again with the original model and equation. Solve the equation with tiles in a different way. Record your new steps. Did you get the same solution?

a. Write the equation modeled in this equation box. Solve for *x* by *mentally* moving tiles. Record each step by writing only the new equation. Check your solution.

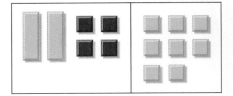

REFLECT

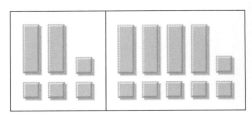

1. Give two first steps toward solving the equation modeled in this equation box.

2. What should be the final step when solving an equation with algebra tiles? with symbols?

3. Why do you think we add tiles to *both* sides of an equation box? Could the solution change if we didn't? Justify your answer.

Exercises

CORE

1. Getting Started Which of these procedures would you recommend as the first step toward solving the equation modeled in this box? Explain your decision.
(a) Divide the tiles into two groups.
(b) Add three red unit tiles to both sides.

Write the equation modeled in each equation box.

2. 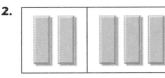   **3.**

Write the equation modeled in each equation box. Solve for *x* by mentally moving tiles. Record each step by writing only the new equation. Check your solution.

4.   **5.**   **6.**

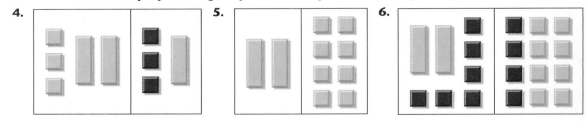

7. The additive inverse property states that $a + (-a) = 0$. How can you use this property when solving equations using the tiles?

8. The equation modeled in the equation box in **8a** is solved using algebra tiles, and the results are shown in **8b, 8c,** and **8d.** Write the equation in each step and explain how the new equation was obtained.

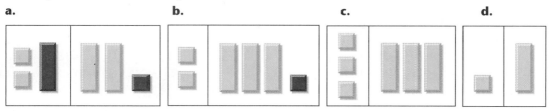

a.   b.   c.   d.

9. Each state has one representative to Congress for about every 520,000 people. Describe how you could estimate the population of a state if you knew the number of that state's representatives to the Congress.

Social Science

10. Copy the table. Draw algebra tile models for each step. Explain each step.

Step	Equation
	$2x + 6 = 12 - x$
a.	$3x + 6 = 12$
b.	$3x = 6$
c.	$x = 2$

11. Preparing the black spider monkey's diet is part of a zookeeper's job. This is the black spider monkey's diet as it appears in *The Zoo Book* (Smithsonian Institution Press, 1976).

Science

A.M. feeding	
ZuPreem Marmoset Diet	$1\frac{1}{2}$ pieces per animal
Purina Monkey Chow	3 oz per animal
Vidaylin pill	1 per animal
Vitamin D	1000 IU per animal
P.M. feeding	
Peas or carrots	2 oz per animal
Kale	2 oz per animal
Cabbage	2 oz per animal
Beans	2 oz per animal

a. Tell how many ounces of food are needed for the p.m. feeding if there are
(i) two monkeys   (ii) four monkeys   (iii) six monkeys   (iv) *n* monkeys

b. Write an equation that relates the number of monkeys to the ounces of vegetables needed to feed them.

c. Describe how you would calculate the pounds of monkey chow needed per animal for one week.

Define two variables for each situation. Express the relationship between the variables as an equation.

12. Overtime pay for zoo employees is $1\frac{1}{2}$ times the regular pay.

13. In the first 56 days of its life, the larva of the polyphemus moth consumes an amount of food that is equal to 86,000 times its birth weight.

14. Shake, Rattle, and Roll The zoo had four diamond-back rattlesnakes. During the year, one died. Which is the percentage of rattlesnakes that died?
(a) 0.25%   (b) 3%   (c) 14%   (d) 25%   (e) 41%

LOOK AHEAD

What number can you add to each number below to get the sum 0?

15. -3 **16.** $-\frac{3}{4}$ **17.** 0.8 **18.** $\frac{6}{5}$ **19.** -1.3

What number can you multiply by each number below to get the product 1?

20. 3 **21.** $\frac{1}{3}$ **22.** -5 **23.** $\frac{6}{5}$ **24.** 0.8

MORE PRACTICE

Write the equation modeled in the equation box. Indicate the first step you would take to solve each equation.

25.

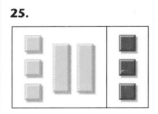

26.

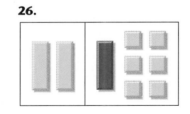

27.

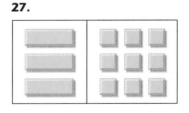

28. Write the equation modeled in the equation box. Solve for x by mentally moving tiles. Record each step, showing the new algebra tile model and the new equation. Check your solution.

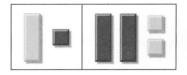

Write the equation modeled in the equation box. Solve for *x* by mentally moving tiles. Record each step by writing only the new equation. Check your solution.

29.

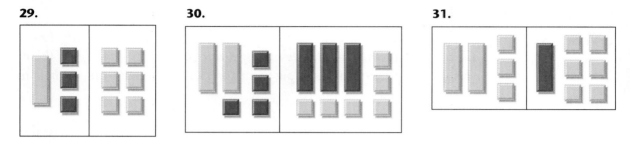

30.

31.

Define two variables for each situation. Express the relationship between the variables as an equation.

32. There are twice as many zebras as camels in the zoo.

33. A zookeeper's hourly wage is one-third that of the head zookeeper.

MORE MATH REASONING

34. Tad's records of the hummingbird eggs are in the table.

	bird #1	bird #2	bird #3	bird #4
Weight of parent	1.44 oz	1.36 oz	1.28 oz	1.52 oz
Weight of egg	0.18 oz	0.17 oz	0.16 oz	0.19 oz

a. What is the mean weight of the eggs? the median weight?

b. Write an equation that describes the relationship between the quantities.

c. Describe what you would do to calculate the weight of a parent hummingbird if you knew the weight of its egg.

d. How does the relative weight of the hummingbird and its egg compare to the relative weight of the ostrich and its egg found in Exercise 29 on page 239?

35. Suppose there are algebra *x*-tiles in a bag. You don't know whether some or none of the tiles are negative.

a. If you pull four from the bag without looking, what are the possible values that you can obtain?

b. What is the probability that the value will be $3x$?

36. Suppose you were asked to model $-(x + 3)$ using algebra tiles. Explain how you would do this.

> **Problem-Solving Tip**
>
> Draw diagrams of the possible results.

Properties of Equality

← **C O N N E C T** → *You've seen how equations change as you solve them with algebra tiles. Now you will investigate the algebraic properties underlying these changes. These properties allow you to work directly with the symbols to solve equations.*

Undoing operations in expressions is the key to solving equations. In the following Explore, you'll work with a partner to investigate a trick involving operations.

EXPLORE: IT'S MAGIC!

1. Try the following number trick with a partner. Can you figure out why the trick works?

   Partner 1 Think of a number and write it down, but don't let your partner know. Follow these steps. Tell your partner the final result only.
   a. Double your number and subtract 1.
   b. Triple the result and add 5.
   c. Divide by 2 and tell your partner the result.

   Partner 2 Follow these steps to find your partner's starting number.
   a. Double the number your partner tells you.
   b. Subtract 5 from the result and divide by 3.
   c. Add 1 and divide by 2. The result is your partner's starting number.
   d. Tell your partner your result. Did you get the correct starting number?

2. Switch partners and repeat the number trick. Discuss the trick with your partner. Can you explain why it works?
3. Work together to create a new trick by altering one step for each partner. Try out your trick to check if it works.

Recall that the conventions for the order of operations tell you to multiply or divide before you add or subtract. When you solve an equation, you generally undo the operations in the reverse order.

To solve the equation $4x + 18 = 66$...

$4x + 18 - 18 = 66 - 18$

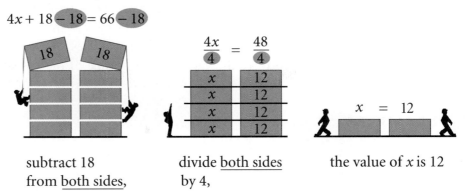

subtract 18
from <u>both sides</u>,

divide <u>both sides</u>
by 4,

the value of x is 12

Undoing means using **inverse operations** to solve equations. Addition and subtraction are inverse operations. Multiplication and division are also inverse operations.

CONSIDER

?

1. What is the inverse of multiplying by 8? of adding −3? of dividing by 1.8? of multiplying by −4?

Recall that when you add algebra tiles to an equation box, you always add the same number of tiles to both sides. Underlying that rule is an important algebraic property.

ADDITION PROPERTY OF EQUALITY

If you add the same number to both sides of an equation, the two sides will remain equal.

For any real numbers a, b, and c, if $a = b$, then $a + c = b + c$.

MULTIPLICATION PROPERTY OF EQUALITY

If you multiply both sides of an equation by the same number, the two sides will remain equal.

For any real numbers a, b, and c, if $a = b$, then $ac = bc$.

Similar properties of equality hold for subtraction and division. (Think of subtracting 3 from both sides of an equation as adding -3 to both sides. Think of dividing both sides by 2 as multiplying both sides by $\frac{1}{2}$.) To solve an equation, use these properties and the idea of inverse operations to isolate the variable on one side of the equation.

EXAMPLES

Solve each equation.

1. $4x + 27 = 63$

$$4x + 27 = 63$$
$$4x + 27 - 27 = 63 - 27 \qquad \text{Subtract 27 from both sides.}$$
$$4x = 36 \qquad \text{Simplify both sides.}$$
$$\frac{4x}{4} = \frac{36}{4} \qquad \text{Divide both sides by 4.}$$
$$x = 9 \qquad \text{Simplify both sides.}$$

Now check.

$$4x + 27 \stackrel{?}{=} 63$$
$$4(9) + 27 \stackrel{?}{=} 63 \qquad \text{Substitute 9 for } x.$$
$$36 + 27 \stackrel{?}{=} 63 \qquad \text{Multiply.}$$
$$63 = 63 \ \checkmark \qquad \text{Add.}$$

It checks.

2. $45.5 = -2.25x - 12.5$

$$45.5 = -2.25x - 12.5$$
$$45.5 + 12.5 = -2.25x - 12.5 + 12.5 \qquad \text{Add 12.5 to both sides.}$$
$$58 = -2.25x \qquad \text{Simplify both sides.}$$
$$\frac{58}{-2.25} = \frac{-2.25x}{-2.25} \qquad \text{Divide both sides by } -2.25.$$
$$-25.78 \approx x \qquad \text{Simplify both sides.}$$

$-25.7777...$ rounds off to -25.78

In Example 2, the answer was rounded off to two decimal places. The sign $\approx$ means *is approximately equal* to.

When you solve equations, the properties of equality produce equivalent equations. Therefore, the solution to your final equation is also a solution to the original equation.

Equations and formulas involving several variables are sometimes called **literal equations.** When solving several similar problems, it is often convenient to rewrite a literal equation so that one variable stands alone. This is called *solving* the equation for that variable.

3. David knows that his truck route from Chicago to Nashville is 440 mi long. He also knows the formula $D = rt$, relating distance (D), rate (r), and time (t).

How long will his route take if he averages a speed of 55 mi/hr? 65 mi/hr? 50 mi/hr?

David can use the formula, but it will be easier if he first *solves* for t, since he is looking for different times.

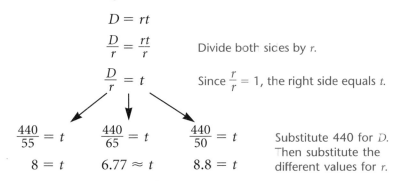

$$D = rt$$

$$\frac{D}{r} = \frac{rt}{r} \qquad \text{Divide both sides by } r.$$

$$\frac{D}{r} = t \qquad \text{Since } \frac{r}{r} = 1, \text{ the right side equals } t.$$

$$\frac{440}{55} = t \qquad \frac{440}{65} = t \qquad \frac{440}{50} = t \qquad \begin{array}{l}\text{Substitute 440 for } D. \\ \text{Then substitute the} \\ \text{different values for } r.\end{array}$$

$$8 = t \qquad 6.77 \approx t \qquad 8.8 = t$$

It would take David 8 hours at 55 mi/hr, almost 7 hours at 65 mi/hr, and almost 9 hours at 50 mi/hr.

Solve each equation. Check your solution.
a. $25 + 4x = -13$ **b.** $16 = \frac{1}{2}x - 2$

c. The speed of a supersonic airplane traveling near or above the speed of sound is often given as a *Mach number*. The Mach number (M) is the quotient of the speed of the airplane (a) and the speed of sound (s).

$$M = \frac{a}{s}$$

Find the speed of an airplane traveling at Mach 1.5 at an altitude where the speed of sound is 680 mi/hr.

1. Indicate the first step you would take to solve the equation $3 + 4x = 32$. Tell how you decided this.
2. Why is it okay to *subtract* a number from both sides of an equation?
3. Why are you allowed to *divide* both sides of an equation by a number other than zero?
4. What is meant by *inverse operations*? Explain, using a few examples.

Exercises

CORE

1. **Getting Started** Follow these steps to solve $6x - 14 = 10$.
   a. Add a number to both sides of the equation to undo the 14. Write the new equation.
   b. Divide both sides of the equation by a number that will undo the 6. Write the new equation.
   c. What is your solution? Check your solution.

2. Match each item from the first column with an item from the second column.
   a. literal equation
   b. Addition Property of Equality
   c. Multiplication Property of Equality
   d. inverse operations

   (i) multiplication and division
   (ii) add the same number to both sides of an equation
   (iii) $I = prt$
   (iv) multiply each side of an equation by the same number

Solve each equation. Check your solution.

3. $x + 18 = 3$ **4.** $22 + a = -2$ **5.** $10 - s = 5$ **6.** $-13 + x = 3$

Write the word or phrase that correctly completes each statement.

7. Multiplying each side of an equation by $\frac{1}{4}$ is the same as dividing each side by ____.

8. Dividing each side of an equation by 3 is the same as multiplying each side by ____.

Solve each equation. Check your solution.

9. $3x = 3$ **10.** $\frac{1}{4}n = 3$ **11.** $\frac{x}{18} = 2$ **12.** $-7d = 1$

13. $\frac{2}{3}b = 16$ **14.** $-\frac{v}{4} = 20$ **15.** $-5w = 21.25$ **16.** $-\frac{3}{4}v = 19$

17. In 1994, the population of Tokyo, Japan, was approximately 30 million. This is about twice the population of New York City.
   a. What was the population of New York City in 1994?
   b. Look up the population of Tokyo and New York City today. What is the ratio of the population of New York City to Tokyo?
   c. What is the ratio of the population of Tokyo to the population of your city?

Define variables for the quantities in each situation. Express the relationship between the variables as an equation.

18. Chimpanzees are fed a mixture of foods that includes fruit. For every three apples, they are fed one banana.

19. An elephant can give birth every six years during its reproductive years.

Indicate the first step you would take to solve each equation. Tell how you decided this.

20. $3w - 4 = 72$ **21.** $8 + 7d = 112$ **22.** $3t + 15 = 65$ **23.** $8 = -10 + 2n$

Solve each equation. Check your solution.

24. $3x + 15 = 18$ **25.** $106 + 4n = 58$ **26.** $34 = 13k - 18$

27. $2c + 2.4 = 8$ **28.** $10 - 6a = 7$ **29.** $25p + 50 = 1500$

30. $3m + 39 = 117$ **31.** $2x + 4 = 6.2$ **32.** $11 + 4d = 3$

33. Jay solves $6x = 1$ by dividing each side by 6. Shelly solves the same equation by multiplying each side by $\frac{1}{6}$. Both students are correct. Why? What is the solution?

34. Lightning quickly heats the air, causing it to expand, which produces the sound waves that we call thunder. Sound travels approximately 1 mile in 5 seconds.
   a. Use the equation $D = rt$, with the distance (D) of 1 mile and the time (t) of 5 seconds, to determine the approximate rate (r) or speed of sound in miles per second.
   b. Substitute the speed or rate of sound for r in the equation $D = rt$.
   c. Use the equation you found in **31b** to determine how far away a thunderstorm is when you notice a 4-sec delay between the flash of lightning and the sound of thunder.

35. Solve each equation. Check your solution.
   a. $\frac{3}{4}a + 13 = 23$ **b.** $-\frac{w}{3} + \frac{2}{5} = \frac{1}{5}$ **c.** $54 - 1.3x = 13$
   d. $32 + 4.2z = 18$ **e.** $27 - 1.5c = 7$ **f.** $\frac{2}{9} - \frac{t}{3} = \frac{4}{9}$

Solve these literal equations for w.

36. $A = \ell w$ **37.** $P = 2\ell + 2w$

38. Solve the formula for the circumference of a circle, $C = \pi d$, for π. A circle whose circumference (C) is 40 inches has a diameter (d) of about 12.7 inches. Find the approximate value of π.

San Francisco

Dallas

39. Alan flew from San Francisco to Dallas to visit his mother.

Social Science

    a. The distance is 1468 miles and his flight took 3 hours and 24 minutes. What is the average speed of the plane? (Hint: Write 3 hours and 24 minutes in hours.)

    b. Alan left San Francisco at 9:25 a.m. Pacific Standard Time. At what Central Standard Time did he arrive in Dallas?

40. Ouch! Have you ever been stung by a jellyfish while swimming? The largest jellyfish, an arctic giant jellyfish, was reported to have a diameter of approximately $7\frac{1}{2}$ feet.

Science

    a. Approximately how big around was the jellyfish?

    b. What area would the jellyfish cover?

 **LOOK AHEAD**

Simplify each expression.

41. $-5(x - 3) + 10x - 1$ **42.** $\frac{1}{2}(4x - 3) - (2 + x)$ **43.** $2(4 - (x + 8))$

MORE PRACTICE

Indicate the first step you would take to solve each equation.

44. $20n - 5 = 16$ **45.** $21 = 14y + 7$ **46.** $4w = 19.5$ **47.** $16 = 3z - 4$

Solve each equation. Check your solution.

48. $3 + x = 2.07$ **49.** $z - 4 = 3.2$ **50.** $10m = 14$

51. $14t - 6.8 = 4.2$ **52.** $3c - 4 = -11$ **53.** $121m + 6.3 = 18.4$

54. For every kilometer beneath Earth's surface, the temperature increases by 10°C.

Science

    a. Write an expression that describes the temperature of the earth at a depth of x kilometers when the temperature on the surface is 21°C.

    b. Use the expression you found in **54a** to find the temperature at the bottom of an oil well 4 km deep.

    c. The bottom of a coal mine is 70°C when the temperature on the surface is 21°C. Write an equation that expresses this relationship. Then solve the equation to find the depth of the coal mine.

Solve each equation. Check your solution.

55. $\frac{3}{4}b + 14 = 38$ **56.** $-\frac{1}{3} = -c - \frac{4}{3}$ **57.** $10 = 1.8 + \frac{h}{4}$

58. $12 - \frac{1}{7}a = -31$ **59.** $\frac{x}{15} - 32 = -40$ **60.** $108 = \frac{1}{12}x + 32$

61. Louise subtracted 6 from both sides of the equation $6 - 3x = 10$ and got $3x = 4$. Explain what Louise did wrong.

Solve each literal equation for the variable indicated.

62. $A = \frac{1}{2}bh$ for b 　　　　　**63.** $I = prt$ for t 　　　　　**64.** $P = 4s$ for s

65. The gas tank of a Chevrolet Cavalier holds approximately 15 gallons of gas,

Industry

and the car is rated to average 30 miles per gallon, or $\frac{1}{30}$ of a gallon per mile.

   a. Write an equation that describes the number of gallons (g) left after driving m miles.

   b. Use this equation to determine how many gallons of gas are left after driving 100 miles, 200 miles, 300 miles. When will the car run out of gas?

   c. In this situation, what are the domain and range of the function defined by this equation?

MORE MATH REASONING

66. Endangered Species In recent years, the Caspian, Bali, and Javan tigers have

Science

become extinct. The graph reveals the populations of the remaining subspecies.

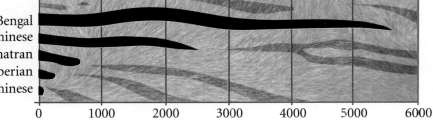

   a. Approximate the number of each subspecies of tigers represented on the graph.

   b. Kamaria says that the information can be represented on a circle graph. Describe how she might do this.

   c. Which is the ratio of Siberian to Indochinese tigers?
   　　(i) 1:25　　　(ii) 1:10　　　(iii) 10:1　　　(iv) 1:100

   d. Which subspecies do you think is in the least danger of becoming extinct?

   e. How might zoos contribute to the survival of tigers?

67. Creative Writing The zoo sponsors a creative writing contest for high school

Science

students. The topic for the essay this year is "Why should we save an endangered species?" The prize winners will split a $9000 scholarship. The prize for first place is three times that of third place. The prize for second place is $1500 more than that for third place.

   a. How much money will be awarded for each place?

   b. If you were in charge of awarding the prizes, would you have awarded the same amounts for the places? Why or why not?

   c. Suppose you are a judge. What would you use as criteria for judging the essay?

← CONNECT →   *You've learned to solve some equations using the properties of equality. In Chapter 2 you learned to simplify expressions. Now you will combine these skills and simplify equations before you solve them.*

Bridges are built in sections that expand as the temperature rises. To allow for this, a small *expansion gap* is left between sections. Engineers must calculate this gap accurately, so that the bridge doesn't buckle on a hot day.

EXPLORE: BRIDGE THE GAP

A bridge engineer decides to leave a gap of 30 mm on a day when the temperature of the bridge sections is 0°C. The sections are known to expand (and the gap, therefore, decrease) 0.5 mm for each 1°C increase in temperature. Let's check the gap at different temperatures.

1. Complete the following table of temperatures and gaps.
2. Define variables, and write an equation showing the expansion gap as a function of the temperature of the bridge sections.

Temperature (°C)	0	1	2	3	4	5	6	7	8
Gap (mm)	30	29.5	29						

3. At what temperature will the gap be completely closed? How did you determine this?
4. Where the bridge is located, on the hottest day the temperature of the sections can reach 95°C. Has the engineer allowed a wide enough gap to keep the bridge from buckling?

> **Problem-Solving Tip**
>
> Look for a pattern.

You may need to simplify the expressions in an equation before you use the properties of equality to solve it. You already know how to simplify expressions and how to solve equations. To put these skills together, first simplify and then solve.

EXAMPLES

Solve each equation.

1. $8a + 7a = 60$

$$8a + 7a = 60$$
$$15a = 60 \qquad \text{Combine like terms.}$$
$$a = 4 \qquad \text{Divide both sides by 15.}$$

2. $5r - 2(2r + 8) + 4 = 25$

$$5r - 2(2r + 8) + 4 = 25$$
$$5r - 4r - 16 + 4 = 25 \qquad \text{Use the distributive property.}$$
$$r - 12 = 25 \qquad \text{Combine like terms.}$$
$$r = 37 \qquad \text{Add 12 to both sides and simplify.}$$

WHAT DO **YOU** THINK?

Solve the equation $\frac{1}{2}x + \frac{1}{2} = \frac{3}{4}$.

Mark thinks . . .

$$\frac{1}{2}x + \frac{1}{2} = \frac{3}{4}$$

$$\frac{1}{2}x + \frac{1}{2} - \frac{1}{2} = \frac{3}{4} - \frac{1}{2} \qquad \text{First, I'll subtract } \tfrac{1}{2} \text{ from both sides.}$$

$$\frac{1}{2}x = \frac{1}{4} \qquad \tfrac{3}{4} - \tfrac{1}{2} = \tfrac{3}{4} - \tfrac{2}{4} = \tfrac{1}{4}$$

$$2\left(\frac{1}{2}x\right) = 2\left(\frac{1}{4}\right) \qquad \text{Multiply both sides by 2.}$$

$$x = \frac{1}{2} \qquad \text{Simplify.}$$

Keisha thinks . . .

$$\frac{1}{2}x + \frac{1}{2} = \frac{3}{4}$$

$$4\left(\frac{1}{2}x + \frac{1}{2}\right) = 4\left(\frac{3}{4}\right) \qquad \text{First, I'll multiply by 4 to clear the fractions.}$$

$$2x + 2 = 3 \qquad \text{Use the distributive property and simplify.}$$

$$2x + 2 - 2 = 3 - 2 \qquad \text{Subtract 2 from both sides.}$$

$$2x = 1 \qquad \text{Combine like terms.}$$

$$\frac{2x}{2} = \frac{1}{2} \qquad \text{Divide both sides by 2.}$$

$$x = \frac{1}{2} \qquad \text{Simplify.}$$

CONSIDER

?

1. Why do you think someone would clear fractions before solving an equation?

TRY IT

Solve each equation.

a. $9x - 2(2x + 6) = 28$ **b.** $0.98 = (0.26 + m) + 3m$ **c.** $\frac{2}{3} - \frac{3}{4}b = 1$

REFLECT

1. Why do we simplify equations before solving them?

2. How could you make sure that the solutions in Examples 1 and 2 are correct?

3. Jim tried to solve the equation $\frac{3}{5}x - 1 = 4$ by taking this first step.

$$\frac{3}{5}x - 1 = 5(4)$$

Do you think Jim's method will give the correct solution? Explain.

Exercises

CORE

1. Getting Started Follow these steps to solve $3(x - 4) + 6 = 15$.

a. Simplify by using the distributive property and combining like terms.

b. Solve as before using the addition and multiplication properties.

c. What is the solution? Check your solution.

Solve each equation. Check your solution.

2. $4z - 12 + 3z + 18 = 20$

3. $45 = 4d - 16 - 10d + 5$

4. $2(3y + 1) = -16$

5. $7f - 2(f + 8) = 29$

Indicate the first step you would take to solve each equation. Tell how you decided this.

6. $4(y - 7) = 1.9$ **7.** $3j - 6(10 - j) = 9.09$ **8.** $\frac{2}{3}h - \frac{1}{3} = \frac{3}{4}$

9. Tina can't decide which way to solve $\frac{3}{4}n - \frac{2}{5} = \frac{1}{10}$. She wants to multiply both sides by 20 or add $\frac{2}{5}$ to both sides. Are both her choices wise? Why?

Solve each equation. Check your solution.

10. $5.4 = 0.09p - 1.8$

11. $\frac{1}{3}v + 2 = \frac{2}{3}$

12. $4\left(\frac{1}{5}f - \frac{1}{2}\right) + \frac{1}{2}f = 11$

13. $-5b + 4(2 + 2b) = -1$

14. $\frac{4}{5} - \frac{2}{3}c = 4$

15. $-\frac{3}{4}(8x - 16) = \frac{3}{4}$

16. For his science project, Corey investigated the incubation periods of several birds. The table shows how many days it took the various eggs to hatch.

    a. Find the mean.

    b. Find the median.

    c. Find the mode.

Bird	Incubation Period
domestic hen	21 days
duck	28 days
turkey	28 days
guinea	28 days
quail	23 days
pheasant	25 days

17. The perimeter of the rectangle is 15. What is the value of x?

    (a) $\frac{60}{13}$ (b) $8\frac{1}{2}$ (c) $6\frac{1}{2}$ (d) $4\frac{1}{4}$

x

$3\frac{1}{4}$

Write the word or phrase that correctly completes the sentence.

18. Multiplying each side of an equation by $\frac{2}{3}$ is the same as dividing each side by _____.

19. Dividing each side of an equation by $\frac{5}{2}$ is the same as multiplying each side by _____.

20. Is It Still Freezing? The zoo personnel were very concerned about the unusually cold weather. The low temperature Wednesday night was $-3°C$. The temperature rose $15°$ during the day on Thursday, but fell $11°$ that night, to its low temperature. What was the low temperature on Thursday? Was it freezing again?

21. A Cub's Share The cost of one week's food (c) for adult polar bears is $50 less than twice the cost of food (b) for the baby polar bears.

    a. Write an equation that describes the relationship between the quantities.

    b. If the cost of feeding the adult animals for one week is $465, write an equation that describes the cost of feeding the babies for one week.

    c. How much does it cost to feed the babies for one week?

    d. Explain how you solved your equation.

22. Which is a solution to $3(x - 1) + 6 = 3$? Tell how you determined this.

    (a) $x = \frac{1}{3}$ (b) $x = 2$ (c) $x = -1$ (d) $x = 0$ (e) not here

23. Let's Go to the Park Marcos works as a camp counselor. He needed to purchase snacks for his group. He bought granola bars for 45¢ each and apples for 32¢ each. He bought 10 more apples than granola bars. The function $45x + 32(x + 10) = y$ can be used to model the problem.

  a. What does $45x$ represent?

  b. What does $32(x + 10)$ represent?

  c. Suppose Marcos spent $8.59 in all. Write and solve an equation to help find the number of apples and the number of granola bars he purchased.

LOOK BACK

24. Consider the table. [3-2]

x	−3	−2	−1	0	1	2	3
y	5	4	3	2	1	0	−1

  a. Is the change in the x-values equal?

  b. Is the change in the y-values equal?

  c. Can you tell for certain that the relationship is linear? Explain.

You can find the solution to an equation by looking at points in a data table. Given the data table for the function $\ell = t + 26.5$, solve these equations. [4-1]

25. $21 = t + 26.5$

26. $20.8 = t + 26.5$

27. $21.2 = t + 26.5$

t	−6.1	−5.9	−5.7	−5.5	−5.3
ℓ	20.4	20.6	20.8	21.0	21.2

MORE PRACTICE

Solve each equation. Check your solution.

28. $4m - 6m - 3 = 9$

29. $3(3y - 2) = 21$

30. $-2 = 2x + 14$

31. $2(x - 3) + 8 = 29$

32. $5(y - 2) = 2.5$

33. $6j - 2(7 - j) = -1.075$

34. $3m - 7 + 6m + 12 = 86$

35. $14y + 7 = 21$

36. $45 = 6g - 14 - 9g + 5$

37. The perimeter of the rectangle at the right is 20 ft. Find the length and the width of the rectangle.

38. Find the length and width of this rectangle if the perimeter is 32.

x

$x + 4$

Solve each equation. Check your solution.

39. $\frac{2}{5}h - \frac{1}{5} = \frac{2}{3}$

40. $8f - 3(f + 8) = 66$

41. $\frac{4}{9} - \frac{2}{5}c = 4$

42. $9.1 = 0.07p - 1.4$

43. $\frac{1}{4}v + 2 = \frac{3}{4}$

44. $\frac{2}{3}(8a - 15) = \frac{7}{9}$

MORE MATH REASONING

45. The board of directors for the zoo has voted to improve the flamingo exhibit. They want to triple the area of the current exhibit.
  a. The shape of the exhibit is a rectangle. Could they just multiply each dimension by 3? Explain.
  b. Suppose the current dimensions are 30 m by 10 m. How might they triple the area?
  c. The San Diego Wild Animal Park is the largest U.S. zoo in terms of area. It covers 1800 acres, or 728 hectares. One acre equals what part of a hectare?

46. In some species of birds, there is a distinct relationship between clutch size and latitude. A clutch is a nest of eggs. Robins living in the Canary Islands have an average clutch of 3.5 eggs; those living in Spain lay 4.9 eggs; in the Netherlands, 5.9 eggs; and in Finland, 6.3 eggs. Describe the relationship between the number of eggs in a robin's clutch and the latitude where she lays the eggs.

Social Science

47. Deliver a Letter, the Sooner, the Better Mercedes spent $5.18 at the post office. She mailed either a postcard or a letter to each of 22 people. Postcards cost 19¢ to mail and letters cost 29¢ to mail. Suppose that $x =$ the number of people she sent letters.
  a. What does $(22 - x)$ represent?
  b. Write an equation that models this problem.
  c. Solve your equation.
  d. How many postcards and letters did she mail?
  e. Suppose we let $x =$ the number of postcards Mercedes sent. Would this change the equation? Would it change the solution?

Industry

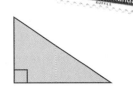

48. Sum Angle The sum of the measures of the angles in a triangle is equal to 180°. Suppose one angle is a right angle and the smallest angle is $\frac{1}{2}$ of the measure of the third angle.
  a. Which equation could be used to represent this problem?
  (i) $\frac{1}{2}(90) + 3 = 180$
  (ii) $\frac{1}{2}x + x + 90 = 180$
  (iii) $\frac{1}{2}x + 90 = 180$
  (iv) $\frac{1}{2}x + x + 90x = 180$
  b. Solve the equation that you chose. What are the measures of the three angles?
  c. How can you tell if your angles are correct?

Making Connections

← C O N N E C T → *You've explored more ways of solving equations, including using algebra tiles. Since not all equations can be modeled and solved with tiles, you also learned to use the properties of equality to solve equations.*

Writing and solving equations can help you to make practical decisions. In the following Explore, you'll use an equation to help decide the most cost-effective plan.

EXPLORE: IT'S ALL HAPPENING AT THE ZOO

Vanna lives in Phoenix with her two children. She and her children love to go to the zoo, which is offering a one-year family membership for $55. Membership allows unlimited family visits to the zoo during the year. At most, Vanna has one free day per month to go to the zoo. She isn't sure she can take her children often enough to make a membership purchase worthwhile.

For nonmembers, the entrance fee for a single day is $7.50 for adults and $2.50 for children.

1. Vanna first decided to determine at what point the cost of membership and the cost of single-day visits will be the same. She used d for days and wrote the equation $7.50d + 2.50d = 55$. Is her equation correct? If not, write a correct equation.

2. Solve the equation you wrote in Step 1. How could your solution help Vanna decide whether to buy a membership or pay for single-day visits to the zoo? Explain.

3. If Vanna thinks they will visit the zoo four times this coming year, should she buy a membership?

4. If Vanna thinks they will visit the zoo once a month this coming year, should she buy a membership?

5. What are some of the other costs of going to the zoo that Vanna should budget for?

1. How do techniques for simplifying expressions help you to solve equations?
2. Describe two ways you might solve the equation $2x - 4 = 7$. In each case, how would *you* start? Give your reasons.
3. What are some of the limitations of using algebra tiles to solve equations?

Self-Assessment

1. Consider the equation box.
   a. What equation is represented by the tiles?
   b. Name two ways to begin solving the equation.
   c. What is the solution to the equation?

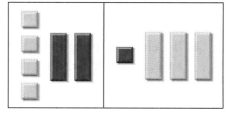

2. Follow these steps to solve $18 = 13x - 21$.
   a. Use the Addition Property of Equality to isolate the x.
   b. Use the Multiplication Property to find the value of x. Check your solution.

3. Students have been assigned to solve the equation $b + 1.5 = 4$. Ida solves the equation by adding -1.5 to each side. Matt subtracts 1.5 from each side. Both get 2.5 as a solution. Explain why this happens.

Which method, graphing, mental techniques, tiles, guess-and-check, or properties, would you use to solve each equation? Give a reason for your choice, and solve.

4. $11n - 1 = 98$
5. $8a - 3 = 15$
6. $0.25x + 3 - 1.5x = 7$

7. $2(c + 1) - 4 = 18$
8. $18 = 13b - 21$
9. $\frac{5}{6}y + \frac{1}{3} = \frac{1}{2}$

10. For which of the following equations is 1 a solution?
    I. $4x - 1 = 0$ II. $2x - 3 + 2x - 5 = 8 - 12$ III. $1 - x = -2$
    (a) I only   (b) II only   (c) III only   (d) II and III only   (e) I, II, and III

11. **Feeding Time** The Zoo Inn sells sandwiches and drinks. There are five kinds of sandwiches: tuna salad, ham and cheese, avocado and bean sprouts, smoked turkey, and roast beef. There are three types of drinks: soda, milk, and apple juice. If Darlene buys one sandwich and one drink, how many different choices does she have and what are they?

12. If $x + y = 10$, which of the following is true? Tell how you determined this.
    (a) $x + y - 6 = 16$ (b) $x + y - 6 = 10$ (c) $x + y - 6 = 6$ (d) $x + y - 6 = 4$

Equations and Inequalities

← **C O N N E C T** → *You've learned to solve equations using the properties of equality. When necessary, you simplified equations before solving them. Now you'll solve equations that have variable terms on both sides. You'll also begin to explore inequalities.*

Suppose you're planning on starting your own business. Can you make a profit? Sometimes solving an equation can help you to decide.

EXPLORE: BUSINESS SOLUTIONS

MATERIALS

Spreadsheet software (optional)

Jan and Shelly are thinking of starting their own custom jewelry business specializing in earrings. Their research shows that their costs will be $500 to get started plus an average of $2.40 per pair. If they make and sell r earrings, their total costs will be

$$500 + 2.40r \text{ dollars}$$

They've decided that a fair and competitive average price for their earrings will be $7 per pair. If they make and sell r pairs, their total income will be

$$7r \text{ dollars}$$

1. Copy and complete the following table. Use a spreadsheet program, if available.

Earrings	Costs	Income
r	$500 + 2.40r$	$7r$
80		
90		
100		
110		
120		

2. Use your table to estimate the solution of the equation $500 + 2.40r = 7r$. Explain how you used the table to estimate.

3. When will Jan and Shelly *break even*, with costs equal to income?

4. When will their costs be *greater* than their income?

5. When will their costs be *less* than their income?

6. Explain how solving an equation can help you to decide whether a business can make a profit or not.

When an equation has variable terms on *both* sides, you can use the Addition Property of Equality to *move* all the variable terms to one side. Then you can solve as before.

EXAMPLE

1. Solve the equation $8x - 1 = 23 - 4x$.

$$8x - 1 = 23 - 4x$$
$$8x - 1 + 4x = 23 - 4x + 4x \qquad \text{Add } 4x \text{ to both sides of the equation.}$$
$$12x - 1 = 23 \qquad \text{Collect like terms and simplify.}$$
$$12x = 24 \qquad \text{Add 1 to both sides.}$$
$$x = 2 \qquad \text{Divide both sides by 12.}$$

WHAT DO YOU THINK?

Solve the equation $6y + 1 = 4 - 4y$.

Kirti thinks . . .

I'll start by getting the $4y$ on the left side.

$$6y + 1 = 4 - 4y$$
$$6y + 1 + 4y = 4 - 4y + 4y \qquad \text{Add } 4y \text{ to both sides of the equation.}$$
$$10y + 1 = 4 \qquad \text{Collect like terms and simplify.}$$
$$10y = 3 \qquad \text{Subtract 1 from both sides.}$$
$$y = 0.3 \qquad \text{Divide both sides by 10.}$$

Elizabeth thinks . . .

I'll start by moving the $6y$ to the right side.

$$6y + 1 = 4 - 4y$$
$$6y + 1 - 6y = 4 - 4y - 6y \qquad \text{Subtract } 6y \text{ from both sides of the equation.}$$
$$1 = 4 - 10y \qquad \text{Collect like terms and simplify.}$$
$$-3 = -10y \qquad \text{Subtract 4 from both sides.}$$
$$0.3 = y \qquad \text{Divide both sides by } -10.$$

CONSIDER

?

1. Would you always begin to solve an equation by moving the variable terms to a particular side, or would it depend on the equation? Explain.

When will two protons collide in a cloud chamber? When will a rocket reach its destination? Equations can often help you to decide when moving objects will meet.

EXAMPLE

Problem-Solving Tip

Draw a diagram of the rocket and comet.

2. Suppose years from now a comet is hurling toward earth at a velocity of 26,000 mi/hr. A rocket is launched to intercept the comet when the comet is 63,000 miles away. It must reach the comet within 2 hours of launch to successfully deflect it away from earth. If the rocket travels at 9000 mi/hr, when will it reach the comet?

Let t = the number of hours since the rocket was launched.

In t hours, the rocket travels $9000t$ miles and the comet travels $26,000t$ miles. The distance of each object from Earth is shown in this diagram.

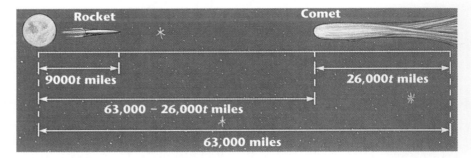

The rocket will intercept the comet when their distances from earth are equal. Solve this equation to find the time when they meet.

$$9000t = 63,000 - 26,000t$$
$$9000t + 26,000t = 63,000 - 26,000t + 26,000t \quad \text{Add } 26,000t \text{ to both sides.}$$
$$35,000t = 63,000. \quad \text{Combine like terms.}$$
$$t = 1.8 \quad \text{Divide both sides by 35,000 and simplify.}$$

The rocket will reach the comet in 1.8 hours, in time to safely deflect it away from earth.

Solve each equation.
a. $4g + 3 = 2g - 7$
b. $2(x + 1) - 6 = 2 + x$
c. $3(1 - b) = 2b - 12$

In the Explore, we were interested in more than when costs and income were equal. Some decisions require knowing when a quantity is *greater than* or *less than* another quantity. Next we'll investigate more situations like this.

REFLECT

1. Why do we collect variable terms on one side of an equation before we begin solving?
2. To solve the equation $5 - 3m = m - 3$, Jerome first subtracted $3m$ from both sides. How would you correct Jerome's mistake?
3. Give two possible first steps to solve the equation $4(c + 10) + 3(c - 2) = 10c - c.$
4. Which equation would you prefer to work with, $-2x = 10$ or $-10 = 2x$? Why?

Exercises

CORE

1. Getting Started Follow these steps to solve $3w + 4 = -2w + 14$.
   a. Use the Addition Property of Equality to move the term $-2w$ to the left side.
   b. Solve as before using the addition and multiplication properties.
   c. What is the solution? Check your solution.

2. Which of the equations have the same solution set as $0.4x + 7 = 4.2 - x$?
   (a) $1.4x + 7 = 4.2$ (b) $14x = -28$ (c) $4x + 7 = 42 - x$

3. Paula began solving the equation $10 - 6m = 11m + 4.5$ by writing $10 = 5m + 4.5$. Then she saw her own error. What was her mistake?

Give two ways you could begin to solve each of these equations.

4. $4 + \frac{1}{2}n = 10 + n$ **5.** $4.3 - 2t = 6.3 + 3t$ **6.** $5(t + 3) - (t - 3) = t + 1$

7. In 1988, small businesses that had one to four employees made up approximately $\frac{1}{4}$ of the total number of businesses in the textile industry. Write an equation that describes this relationship.

8. Spreadsheet Sleuth! Wendy set up a spreadsheet to solve the equation $3x - 9 = 16 - 2x$. Use her spreadsheet to answer these questions.

  a. Does Wendy's spreadsheet show a solution to the equation?

  b. Between which two values of x is the solution to the equation? How do you know?

  c. For what values of x will $16 - 2x$ be less than $3x - 9$?

x	3x − 9	16 − 2x
−4	−21	24
−2	−15	20
0	−9	16
2	−3	12
4	3	8
6	9	4
8	15	0

Solve each equation. Check your solution.

9. $3x = 132 - 8x$

10. $4x + 5 = 6x - 1$

11. $2(v + 6) = 10 + 4v$

12. $3b + 1 - 5b + 3 = 2b$

13. $y = \frac{2}{3}(y + 3)$

14. $2a + (5a - 13) = 47$

15. $45(x + 6) = 35x - 10$

16. $3(y + 7) = 2(y + 9)$

17. $4.6x + 93.1 = 5.6 + 2.1x$

18. Tim's family is on an expedition looking for sunken treasure in the Gulf of Mexico. The boat's crane can bring up a recent find from a depth of 100 ft at the rate of 8 ft per second. Tim can dive down at a rate of 3 ft per second.

  a. Write an expression for the depth Tim will be after s sec of his dive. Write an expression that describes the depth the treasure will be after s sec of being pulled up.

  b. Write an equation that shows when they will be at the same depth.

  c. After how many seconds will Tim and the treasure be at the same depth? At what depth do they meet?

19. When to Order? The table shows some of the stock at Thrifty Mart.

	Blue	Red	Yellow	Green	Orange
T-Shirts	25	45	21	12	10
Shorts	10	12	5	16	12
Warm-ups	5	16	8	4	2

  a. Michael, the owner of Thrifty Mart, likes to keep at least 75 pairs of shorts in stock. Should he place an order now?

  b. Which color of clothing does he have the most of in stock?

  c. If Thrifty Mart triples the entire stock, show the matrix that would illustrate the new amount of stock.

Solve each equation. Check your solution.

20. $2m + 1.6 + m = -2(m - 0.3)$

21. $\dfrac{3}{2}x + \dfrac{1}{5}x = \dfrac{11}{6}x - \dfrac{2}{15}$

22. Use these equations to find the lengths of *a*, *b*, and *c*. Tell how you determined this.

$a + b = 9 \qquad b - a = 1 \qquad a + b - 7 = c$

23. Write two equations that have the same solution as $15 + 2c = 21 - 4c$.

24. The perimeters of both rectangles are the same. What are the length and width of each rectangle? (Hint: Find an expression for the perimeter of each rectangle.)

25. Expanding Matter Rita is responsible for bringing ice to the marathon this Saturday. She plans to freeze water in containers that hold 1 quart, or 32 oz. From her science class, she knows that the volume of water will increase 9% when it freezes. How many ounces of water should she put in each container?

26. A number is selected at random from the numbers 1, 2, 3, 4, 5, and 6.
  a. What is the probability that it is less than 10?
  b. What is the probability that it is greater than 6?
  c. What is the probability that it is less than 3?

27. Shary and Judy are on a business trip in Washington, D.C. Their accommodations and transportation are prepaid. Shary brought $500 and is spending $60 per day. Judy has $375 and is spending $40 per day. If they continue at this rate, on what day of the trip will they have the same amount of spending money? How much money will they have on that day? Tell how you decided.

 *LOOK BACK*

Evaluate each algebraic expression for $a = -1.2$ and $b = 3.6$. [2-3]

28. $(3a)(4b)$

29. $(4b)(3a)$

30. $(3 \cdot 4)(ab)$

Without graphing, tell which are linear functions. Tell how you determined this. [3-2]

31. $y = \dfrac{3}{4}x - 4$

32. $6x - 14y = 35$

33. $3y = x^2 - 5$

Write the equation modeled in the equation box, and solve the equation. [4-2]

34.

35.

MORE PRACTICE

Give two ways you could begin to simplify each of the equations.

36. $-2 + 6x = 5x - 8$

37. $-3(4 - x) + 9 = 10 + 4(x + 2)$

Solve each equation. Check your solution.

38. $14d = 6d - 10$

39. $4(d - 1) + 10 = 16 - 2d$

40. $6 = \frac{2}{5}(w - 10)$

41. $35(m - 2) = 25m - 20$

42. $4.6x - 22.7 = 0.5x + 6$

43. $4a = 6a - 15$

44. The perimeters of these two rectangles are the same. Find the dimensions of each rectangle.

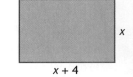

Solve each equation. Check your solution.

45. $3.5(2r - 1) = 6r + 11$

46. $16g + 10 = g - 5$

47. $\frac{4}{b} - 3 = \frac{3}{b} - 5$

48. $\frac{2}{3}t + 12 = 4t - 5$

49. The temperature at Stone Mountain State Park, Georgia, is 73°F and dropping 1.7° per hour. The temperature at Haleakala National Park, Hawaii, is 57°F and rising 2.7° per hour.

  a. Suppose h represents the number of hours since the temperatures were recorded. Write an expression that represents the temperature in Stone Mountain after h hours. Write an expression that represents the temperature in Haleakala after h hours.

  b. Write an equation that sets both locations equal to the same temperature.

  c. Solve to find when both have the same temperature.

  d. What is the temperature when both are the same?

MORE MATH REASONING

50. Split Ends George is a stylist who recently bought his own salon. He feels the salon must make at least $500 per day to stay in business. The charge for a cut and dry is $15.

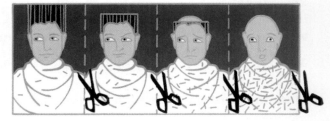

  a. What is the least number of haircuts that must be performed for George to meet his goal?

  b. The salon is open from 9 a.m. until 5 p.m., and the average haircut and blow dry takes approximately $\frac{1}{2}$ hour. If George is alone in the shop, can he meet his goal? Explain.

51. Labor Costs A graph appeared in *USA Today* in 1992 showing that, out of the three major American auto manufacturing companies, Ford needed fewer workers than Chrysler or GM to produce a new car. This gave Ford lower labor costs. In fact, the labor costs for Ford were approximately $\frac{2}{3}$ of the labor costs of GM. If Ford's labor costs were $1563 per car, which is the best estimate of GM's labor costs?

(a) $1600   (b) $2400   (c) $3500   (d) $100,000

52. Is there any value of x that would make $3(x - 4) + 8 = 2(x + 6) - 8 + x$ true? Explain.

4-3 PART B Exploring Inequalities

← CONNECT →

You've written equations and used several effective methods to solve them. Sometimes you need to compare quantities that can't be related by equations. Now you'll explore inequalities and their graphs. You can solve inequalities using rules similar to those you used to solve equations.

In Part A, you considered whether a cost was *equal to, greater than,* or *less than* income. Recall that you can use *inequality signs* to compare values.

Inequality Sign	Meaning	Example
>	is greater than	$25 > -1$
<	is less than	$11 < 13$
≥	is greater than or equal to	$50 \geq -5$
≤	is less than or equal to	$71 \leq 71$

CONSIDER

1. Which inequality sign has the same meaning as the phrase *is at least*? *is at most*?

Just as two expressions separated by an *equal sign* form an equation, two expressions separated by an *inequality sign* form an **inequality.** An inequality can be true or false, just like an equation. The **solutions** of an inequality are the values of the variable that make the inequality true. We often show the solutions of an inequality on a number line.

Inequality	Meaning	Graph
$x > 1$	x is *greater than* 1	
$x \geq 1$	x is *greater than or equal to* 1	
$x < 1$	x is *less than* 1	
$x \leq 1$	x is *less than or equal to* 1	

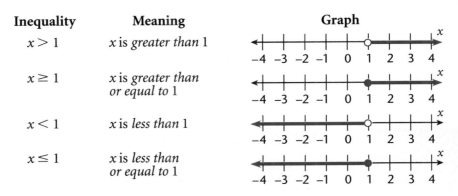

The integer 1 is the **boundary point** of each of these graphs. A solid dot means that 1 is included in the graph. An open dot means that 1 is *not* included in the graph. The boundary point is the solution to the *equation* $x = 1$.

Some inequalities can be solved by guessing and checking or by using mental math. The boundary point is the solution to the *equation,* with an equal sign in place of the inequality sign.

EXAMPLE

1. Write and solve an inequality for the statement "the sum of a number and 4 is less than 6." Graph and check your solutions.

Let x stand for the number: $x + 4 < 6$

The two expressions are equal at the boundary point. Using mental math, $2 + 4 = 6$, so 2 is the boundary point. If x is less than 2, $x + 4$ will be less than 6. If x is greater than 2, $x + 4$ will be greater than 6. The solutions are all values of x less than 2.

$x < 2$

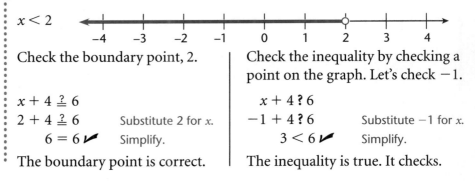

Check the boundary point, 2.

$x + 4 \stackrel{?}{=} 6$
$2 + 4 \stackrel{?}{=} 6$ Substitute 2 for x.
$\quad\; 6 = 6$ ✔   Simplify.

The boundary point is correct.

Check the inequality by checking a point on the graph. Let's check -1.

$x + 4 \,?\, 6$
$-1 + 4 \,?\, 6$ Substitute -1 for x.
$\quad\; 3 < 6$ ✔   Simplify.

The inequality is true. It checks.

Write and solve an inequality for each statement. Graph and check your solutions.

a. The sum of a number and 3 is less than 5.

b. Air temperatures no higher than 70°F are best for pandas.

Some inequalities are too difficult to solve by mental math. In the following Explore, you'll investigate operations on inequalities. By understanding these operations, you'll be able to simplify and solve inequalities much like you did equations.

EXPLORE: DIALOG BOX

Spence is practicing operations on inequalities with a software program. In the screen window at right, he has performed each instruction on the inequality $4 < 8$ and entered his answers.

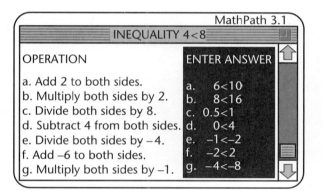

1. Spence's goal is to make each answer true, changing the inequality sign if need be. Which of his answers, if any, should he change? How should he change them?

2. Repeat operations a–g. with the inequality $-8 \le -4$ and at least three other inequalities.

3. Conjecture about which operations require changing an inequality sign. Write your own rules for adding and multiplying a number on both sides of an inequality.

In the Explore, you may have discovered the following properties for operations on inequalities.

ADDITION PROPERTY OF INEQUALITIES

For any real numbers a, b, and c.

If $a < b$, then $a + c < b + c$.

If $a > b$, then $a + c > b + c$.

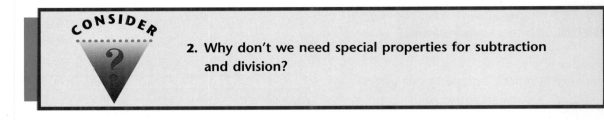

MULTIPLICATION PROPERTY OF INEQUALITIES

For any real numbers a, b, and $c \neq 0$.

If $a < b$, then $ac < bc$, if c is positive;

$ac > bc$, if c is negative.

If $a > b$, then $ac > bc$, if c is positive;

$ac < bc$, if c is negative.

CONSIDER

2. Why don't we need special properties for subtraction and division?

Why do inequalities change when we multiply (or divide) both sides by a negative number? Let's use a number line to look at what happens when we multiply the inequality $-1 < 2$ by -3.

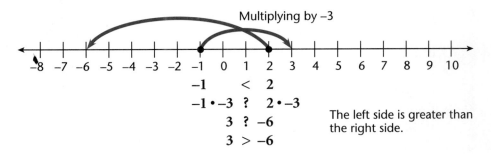

Multiplying by –3

$$-1 \quad < \quad 2$$
$$-1 \cdot -3 \quad ? \quad 2 \cdot -3$$
$$3 \quad ? \quad -6$$
$$3 \quad > \quad -6$$

The left side is greater than the right side.

The order of the points on the number line is *reversed* when you multiply by -3. The same is true when you multiply or divide by any negative number.

CONSIDER

3. What happens if you multiply both sides of an inequality by 0? Explain.

2. Jordy is planning to build a rectangular pen on his animal farm, but the available space and fencing are limited. The pen must be 18 ft wide with a perimeter of at most 198 ft. What are the possible lengths he could make the pen?

> **Problem-Solving Tip**
>
> Draw a diagram of the pen.

Let ℓ = the pen length, in feet.

$2(\ell + 18) \leq 198$	The perimeter is $2(\ell + 18)$ ft.
$2\ell + 36 \leq 198$	Use the distributive property.
$2\ell \leq 162$	Subtract 36 from both sides and simplify.
$\ell \leq 81$	Divide both sides by 2. Since 2 is positive the inequality sign doesn't change.

Here is a graph of the solutions.

The pen can have a length less than or equal to 81 ft. We disregard the values less than or equal to 0 since we know the dimensions of the pen must be positive.

Check the boundary point, 81.

$2(\ell + 18) \stackrel{?}{=} 198$	
$2(81 + 18) \stackrel{?}{=} 198$	Substitute 81 for ℓ.
$198 = 198$ ✔	Simplify.

The boundary point is correct.

Check the inequality by checking a point on the graph. Let's check 10.

$2(\ell + 18) \,?\, 198$	
$2(10 + 18) \,?\, 198$	Substitute 10 for ℓ.
$56 \leq 198$ ✔	Simplify.

The inequality is true. It checks.

TRY IT

Write and solve an inequality to find each unknown. Graph and check your solutions.

c. Three times a number plus 4 is at most 18.

d. The length of the side of a square that has a perimeter no more than 20 centimeters.

1. A student said, "Inequalities are solved exactly the same way as equations." Do you agree or disagree? Explain.
2. Write a brief description of how and why an inequality changes when you multiply both sides by a negative number.
3. Are the solutions to the inequality $2(\ell + 18) \le 198$ the same as the solutions to the inequality $198 \ge 2(\ell + 18)$? Explain.

Exercises

CORE

1. Getting Started Match each statement to its graph.

a. $x > 5$

b. $x = 5$

c. $x \le 5$

d. $x \ne 5$

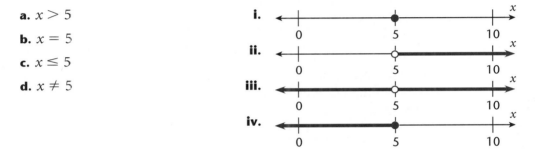

Determine whether the given number is a solution of the inequality.

2. $n = 2; n + 4 > 6$

3. $x = 4; -2x < -10$

4. $m = 4; -3m - 4 < 6$

Solve each inequality. Graph and check your solutions.

5. $3x < -6$

6. $\frac{1}{2}n \ge 8$

7. $-6c > 18$

8. Solve and graph "the sum of a number and 10 is less than 15."

Determine whether each statement is true or false. If the statement is false, change the underlined word or phrase to make it true.

9. The integer 3 is the <u>solution</u> in the graph of $x > 3$.

10. Two expressions separated by an <u>equal sign</u> form an inequality.

Solve each inequality. Graph and check your solutions.

11. $3d - 18 > -6$

12. $\frac{b}{10} + 8 \ge 25$

13. $18 - 2x < 20$

Write and solve an inequality to find each unknown. Graph and check your solutions.

14. The product of a number and -3 is at most 15.

15. 4 less than n is greater than 5.

16. The sum of a number and 10 is at least 12.

17. Keep Your Cool! Rosa's Refrigerator Repair Shop charges $25 per hour plus a flat fee of $20 for the call. Her customer says that the most he is able to pay her is $80. Let x represent the number of hours worked.
   a. Write an inequality that relates the number of hours worked to the total amount the customer is able to pay.
   b. What is the maximum amount of time Rosa has to complete her work?
   c. Can the customer afford to pay Rosa's fee if it takes her two hours to repair the refrigerator? Explain.

Solve each inequality. Graph and check your solutions.

18. $-2a - 3 < 13 + 2(a - 6)$ **19.** $1 - (g + 6) > 3.25$ **20.** $-6(c - 111) < -666$

21. $3x + 1 - 2x < -1$ **22.** $s - 15 \le -525 - 4s$ **23.** $\frac{4}{5}d + \frac{2}{3} \ge \frac{1}{5}$

24. Something to Think About
   a. If $142 + 631 = k$, does $k = 142 + 631$?
   b. If $142 + 631 < f$, is $f < 142 + 631$?
   c. Discuss the differences between these two problems. Explain.

25. Which of the following are solutions of the inequality $n \ge 4.5$?
   (a) 4   (b) 5   (c) $4\frac{2}{3}$ (d) 4.5   (e) 10   (f) 0   (g) -1

Write an inequality for each situation.

26. The down payment (d) for a $110,000 home is at least 10% of the cost.

27. The age (a) of a U.S. senator is at least 30.

28. Lunch Is Calling Magnolia hikes at an average rate of 2.5 mi/hr. She knows that the lodge at Shining Rock is at least 15 miles away. Let $t =$ the number of hours since Magnolia started hiking.
   a. What does $2.5t$ represent?
   b. Write an inequality that shows how long it will take Magnolia to hike to the lodge.
   c. Solve the inequality to find the least number of hours.
   d. It is 7 a.m., and lunch is served between 11 a.m. and 2 p.m. Will she get to the lodge in time for lunch?

29. Trudy is designing a table to display her pottery at the art show. The table must be 4 feet long, and she only has 20 yards of fabric to drape around the edge of the table. What are the possible widths she could make the table?

 LOOK AHEAD

Determine whether each pair of inequalities has the same solutions. Explain.

30. $3 \geq x$, $x \geq 3$ **31.** $x < -1$, $x > 1$ **32.** $5 < x$, $x > 5$

33. Can you draw a triangle with the following dimensions: 3 in. by 2 in. by 1 in.? Explain your results.

MORE PRACTICE

Write an inequality for each statement.

34. One half of my weekly paycheck (p) is less than $150.

35. The total weight of passengers (w) in a certain elevator may not exceed 740 lb.

Social Science

36. In order to run for the presidency of the United States, a person must be 35 years or older.

37. Match each statement to its graph.

a. $x > 7$

b. $x = 7$

c. $x \leq 7$

d. $x \neq 7$

i. [number line: open circle at 7, arrow left, marked 0, 5, 10]

ii. [number line: closed circle at 7, marked 0, 5, 10]

iii. [number line: closed circle at 7, arrow left, marked 0, 5, 10]

iv. [number line: open circle at 7, arrow left, marked 0, 5, 10]

Solve each inequality. Graph and check your solutions.

38. $n + 4 > 6$ **39.** $-2x < -1$ **40.** $-3m - 4 < 6$

41. $2n + 5 \geq 17$ **42.** $-2a - 3 < 13$ **43.** $1 - g > 3.25$

44. $4(x + 5) - 3x \geq 7$ **45.** $4m - 4 > 8 + 2m$ **46.** $24 - 7x \leq 11x - 12$

47. In her algebra course, Robin must get a total of at least 360 points on four tests to earn an A. She got 84, 89, and 93 on the first three tests. What score on the last test will she need to get to earn an A?

Write and solve an inequality for each statement. Graph and check your solutions.

48. The sum of 4 and a number is at least 12.

49. The product of -3 and a number is less than -63.

50. The sum of 32 and a number is at most 100.

MORE MATH REASONING

51. Mom and Pop Make Good Mom and Pop Grocery has grown tremendously in the past few years. They have decided to further expand the business. Now their store has dimensions of 48 ft $\times$ 45 ft. They are looking at different locations. They saw a store advertised as a rectangular shape with a perimeter of 240 feet. The only problem is that they do not know the dimensions of the room.

Industry

> **Problem-Solving Tip**
>
> Draw diagrams.

a. Isn't the perimeter of the new location bigger than the perimeter of the old location? Why are the dimensions of the room important?

b. Find a pair of dimensions that would give a larger square footage than the old place.

c. Find a pair of dimensions that would give a smaller square footage than the old place.

d. Mom and Pop have decided that the square footage must be at least 3000 ft². Give one pair of possible dimensions for the new location.

52. The **greatest integer function** is a special relationship that pairs a real number x with the greatest integer less than or equal to it, written $[x]$. For example when $x = 4.3$, $[x] = 4$.

a. Complete the table of greatest integer functions.

b. Is $x > [x]$ always true? If not, find a counterexample that proves the inequality is sometimes false.

c. Is $x < [x]$ always false? If not, find a counterexample that proves the inequality is sometimes true.

x	$[x]$
3.1	
-2.5	
$\frac{1}{2}$	
0.2	

53. The equation $x + 3 = x + 2$ has no solution. Can you assume that the inequalities $x + 3 < x + 2$ and $x + 3 > x + 2$ have no solutions? Explain.

The Triangle Inequality

←CONNECT→ *You've learned to solve inequalities. Now you'll investigate a connection between inequalities and geometry described by the Triangle Inequality.*

Inequalities can arise in surprising places. The following Explore reveals an interesting connection between inequalities and the geometry of triangles.

EXPLORE: HOW DID SHE KNOW?

MATERIALS

String or paper
Ruler
Scissors

In planning the design for a quilt, Dawn drew these triangles, and then measured and labeled the sides. Trudy told her that she must have measured some of the lengths incorrectly because some of the triangles were impossible to construct with the given measurements. How did Trudy know without even measuring?

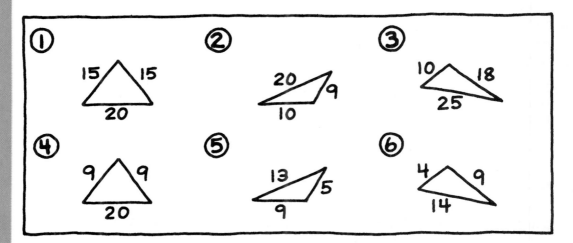

1. Try to construct each of Dawn's triangles using string or paper strips cut to the given lengths. Which triangles are impossible to construct?
2. Why was it impossible to construct some of the triangles? What could you change to make every triangle possible?
3. In your own words, describe the difference between three numbers that *can* be side lengths of a triangle and three numbers that *cannot*.

In the Explore, you may have discovered your own wording of the following theorem.

THE TRIANGLE INEQUALITY THEOREM

The sum of the lengths of any two sides of a triangle is greater than the length of the third side.

These three inequalities are another way of stating the Triangle Inequality Theorem.

$$x + y > z \qquad x + z > y \qquad y + z > x$$

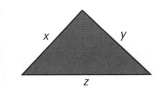

1. Can you use these inequalities to say anything about $z - y$? Explain.

EXAMPLE

1. Use the Triangle Inequality to decide if a triangle can have side lengths of 3.5 feet, 6 feet, and 1.5 feet.

Check the three inequalities.

$3.5 + 6 \, ? \, 1.5$	$3.5 + 1.5 \, ? \, 6$	$6 + 1.5 \, ? \, 3.5$
$9.5 > 1.5 \; ✔$	$5 < 6$	$7.5 > 3.5 \; ✔$

The middle inequality doesn't check. The fact that $3.5 + 1.5 < 6$ means that a condition of the Triangle Inequality is not met. Therefore, a triangle cannot have side lengths of 3.5 feet, 6 feet, and 1.5 feet.

The Triangle Inequality cannot give you the exact length of an unknown side of a triangle, but it can give you a *range* of possible lengths. This can be very useful for solving mathematical problems.

2. Roni lives 13 mi from school and Jo lives 10 mi from school. They think it will be practical to carpool if they live within 5 mi of each other. How far could it be from Roni's house to Jo's house?

We can represent the distances between Roni's house (R), the school (S), and Jo's house (J) with a triangle.

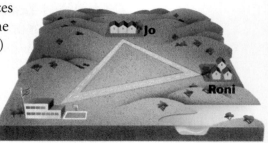

$RS = 13$

$JS = 10$

$RJ = x$

Write the inequalities that result from applying the Triangle Inequality.

$RS + JS > RJ$	$13 + 10 > x$	$23 > x$
$RS + RJ > JS$	$13 + x > 10$	$x > -3$
$JS + RJ > RS$	$10 + x > 13$	$x > 3$

All lengths are positive, so eliminate the inequality $x > -3$. This leaves two inequalities. Both must be true.

$23 > x$ and $x > 3$

We can *flip* the first inequality, rewriting it as $x < 23$. Then, to be concise, we can write both inequalities together in one statement.

$3 < x < 23$

So x is greater than 3 and less than 23. We can also say, x is *between* 3 and 23.

Roni and Jo live more than 3 mi apart, but less than 23 mi apart. They need more information before deciding whether to carpool.

TRY IT

a. Use the Triangle Inequality to determine whether a triangle can have side lengths of 6 cm, 8 cm, and 15 cm.

b. Write these two inequalities in one statement: $x \leq 5$ and $x > 2$.

c. Rewrite the statement $-2 \leq y < 0$ as two inequalities.

d. The lengths of two sides of a triangle are 11 ft and 3 ft. What lengths are possi▮ for the third side?

1. In Example 2, could x have been equal to 1? 2? 3? Why or why not?
2. **a.** Explain why a triangle can't have side lengths of 1 cm, 3 cm, and 5 cm.
   b. What would happen if you tried to use sticks of these lengths to form a triangle? Explain.
3. In your own words, explain how to find the range of lengths possible for the third side of a triangle when you know the lengths of the other two sides.

Exercises

CORE

Getting Started   Complete the following inequalities.

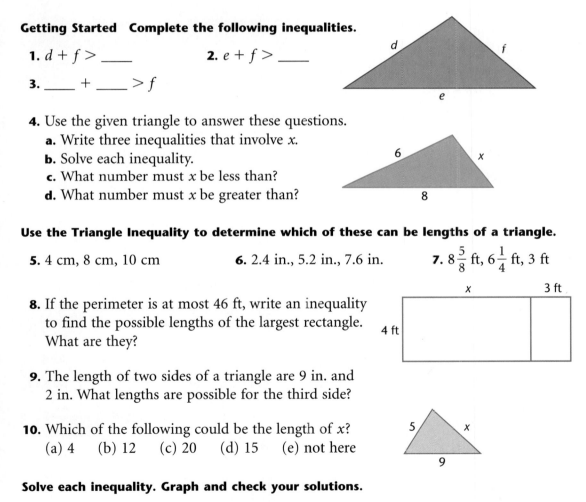

1. $d + f >$ ____   **2.** $e + f >$ ____

3. ____ + ____ $> f$

4. Use the given triangle to answer these questions.
   a. Write three inequalities that involve x.
   b. Solve each inequality.
   c. What number must x be less than?
   d. What number must x be greater than?

Use the Triangle Inequality to determine which of these can be lengths of a triangle.

5. 4 cm, 8 cm, 10 cm   **6.** 2.4 in., 5.2 in., 7.6 in.   **7.** $8\frac{5}{8}$ ft, $6\frac{1}{4}$ ft, 3 ft

8. If the perimeter is at most 46 ft, write an inequality to find the possible lengths of the largest rectangle. What are they?

9. The length of two sides of a triangle are 9 in. and 2 in. What lengths are possible for the third side?

10. Which of the following could be the length of x?
   (a) 4   (b) 12   (c) 20   (d) 15   (e) not here

Solve each inequality. Graph and check your solutions.

11. $18b + 7 + 7b \geq 107$ **12.** $7(2 - c) < 3(c + 8)$ **13.** $3s - 2s > 4s + 1$

14. Bowling Scores After bowling two games, Monica's average score was 98. What score does Monica need in her third game to have an average of 100?
(a) 102   (b) 104   (c) 106

15. Plumbing Particulars Jay owns a plumbing company. He must be very careful in cutting the pipe he uses to avoid waste. He has a piece of pipe $3\frac{3}{8}$ feet long. He needs to cut it into pieces 6 inches long. Suppose n equals the number of pieces.
a. What does $6n$ represent?
b. How many inches are there in $3\frac{3}{8}$ feet?
c. Write an inequality that shows the number of pieces he can cut from this pipe.
d. Solve the inequality. How many pieces can he get from the pipe?

16. How Close Is Close? Rapid City, Casper, and Cheyenne represent the vertices of a triangle. The distance between Rapid City and Cheyenne is approximately 295 mi and the distance between Rapid City and Casper is approximately 260 mi. Which of the following could be the possible distance between Casper and Cheyenne?
(a) 180 mi   (b) 32 mi   (c) 455 mi

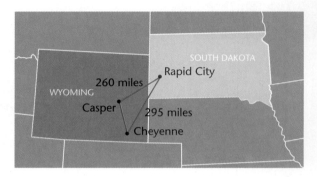

17. Sticks of length 1 in., 2 in., 3 in., 4 in., and 5 in. are put in a box and two are drawn randomly. If the 2-in. and the 3-in. sticks are drawn, what is the probability that the third stick forms a triangle with them? Tell how you decided.

18. Write $x > 3$ and $x < 10$ in one statement.

19. Write $2 \leq x < 5$ as two separate inequalities.

20. If $x < y$, is x^2 always less than y^2? If not, give a counterexample to prove that x^2 is sometimes greater than y^2.

21. Pat wrote the expression "15 less than x" for $x < 15$. Explain why this is wrong.

22. Kitchen Corner The three main work centers in the kitchen are the refrigerator, the sink, and the stove. Imagine them as the vertices of a triangle. It is recommended to you that the three sides of the kitchen triangle add up to more than 12 ft and less than 22 ft, with the shortest side between the sink and the stove. Determine whether each kitchen triangle in the table is possible. Then state whether it follows the recommendation.

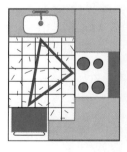

	a.	b.	c.	d.	e.
Stove /sink	5 ft	10 ft	6 ft	4 ft	5 ft
Stove/refrigerator	4 ft	13 ft	8 ft	9 ft	10 ft
Refrigerator/sink	9 ft	8 ft	7 ft	6 ft	4 ft

23. If $x \geq y$ and $-x \geq -y$, what can you conclude about x and y?

24. Do Greater Numbers Mean Larger Receipts? These circle graphs appeared in *The State of Small Business: A Report of the President.* The circle graph on the left shows the number of businesses by type. The one on the right shows the receipts brought in by each type of business.

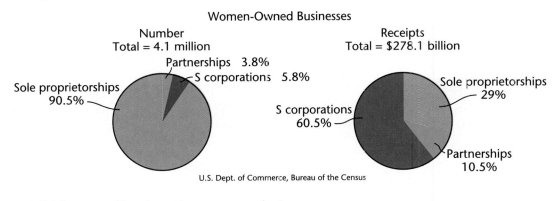

Women-Owned Businesses

Number
Total = 4.1 million

Partnerships 3.8%
S corporations 5.8%
Sole proprietorships 90.5%

Receipts
Total = $278.1 billion

Sole proprietorships 29%
S corporations 60.5%
Partnerships 10.5%

U.S. Dept. of Commerce, Bureau of the Census

a. Which type of business is most popular?
b. Does that type of business bring in the most receipts?
c. The U.S. population, according to the 1990 census, was 248,710,000. Find the ratio of total receipts to persons in the United States. Comment on the receipts per person.

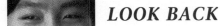

LOOK BACK

Simplify each expression.[2-3]

25. $-(8 - 3m)$ **26.** $4.3 - (4t - 7.9)$ **27.** $25 + \frac{2}{3}(27 - 18d)$

28. Make a table of values for the equation $y = 4x - 6$. Include at least five pairs. [3-1]

29. Solve $\frac{x}{5} + 20 = \frac{2x}{5}$. [4-2]

MORE PRACTICE

Complete each inequality.

30. $a + b >$ _____

31. $a + c >$ _____

32. _____ $+$ _____ $> a$

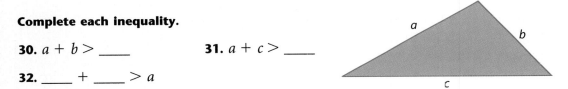

Use the Triangle Inequality to determine which of these can be lengths of a triangle.

33. 1 ft, 1 ft, 2 ft   **34.** 9.4 cm, 0.7 cm, 10 cm   **35.** $3\frac{1}{2}$ in., $5\frac{5}{8}$ in., $6\frac{1}{4}$ in.

The lengths of two sides of a triangle are given. What lengths are possible for the third side?

36. 4 ft, 12 ft **37.** 10 cm, 12 cm **38.** 10 m, 10 m

Solve each inequality. Graph and check your solutions.

39. $\frac{1}{2}d - 5 > 7$

40. $5(x + 2) - 3x \le 22 + x$ **41.** $21 \ge 2k + 5$

42. $\frac{-2}{3}m + 1 < 9$

43. $0 \le 2(3 - 2p) + 7p$ **44.** $2.4 + 1.5b > 2.4$

45. Diving to Win Leah scores 9.3, 9.8, 9.2, 9.6, and 9.7 in the diving competition. She has one dive left. The leader of the competition has already completed her last dive and has a score of 57.2. What is the lowest score Leah can make on her last dive to win the competition?

46. Write the statement $-7 \le x < 2.1$ as two inequalities.

47. Write $x > 4$ and $x < 122$ as one statement.

MORE MATH REASONING

48. How can you tell just by looking at the inequality $3x + 1 < 3x$ that it has no solutions?

49. Mix and Mingle At a meeting, Raoul has told his employees that they must mix and mingle. He is insisting that they shake hands with every person at the meeting. If there are eight people, how many handshakes will take place?

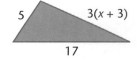
Problem-Solving Tip

Solving a simpler problem may help you to see a pattern.

50. If $x > 0$, which is greater, $x + 1$ or 1? Tell how you determined this.

51. Write three inequalities for the lengths of the sides of the triangle.

52. Suppose a triangle is made up of 12 chain linkages. List the lengths of the sides of the possible triangles. Assume each link is one unit.

53. In the Doghouse Marta's dog ate a very important part of her homework. She had worked a complicated inequality through three steps and had gotten to this point: $x < -6$. Her teacher will not accept papers that don't show the work, and not only could she not show her work, she didn't even know the original inequality. Which one of the following could have been her original inequality?
(a) $4 - x > (10 - x) + x$ (b) $-6x + 1 > 31 - x$
(c) $2(x + 1) < 4x + 14$

Making Connections

← C O N N E C T → *While continuing to solve equations, you've written, solved, and graphed inequalities. The rules for operating on inequalities are similar to the rules you use to solve equations. Often in mathematics, the skills you learn for one concept can be applied to other concepts.*

In this Explore, you'll use your skills with expressions, equations, and inequalities to make practical decisions for a small business.

EXPLORE: CRITTER CLIPPERS

Bonnie recently opened her own business, *Critter Clippers*. Each month she orders supplies. Two local companies supply flea shampoo. Pet Pantry charges $4 per quart bottle plus a $5 handling fee for the whole order. Canine Corner charges only $3 per quart bottle, but charges a $25 handling fee per order.

Let x = the number of quart bottles of flea shampoo Bonnie buys per month.

1. Write an expression that represents the cost of purchasing the bottles from Pet Pantry and an expression that represents the cost of purchasing the bottles from Canine Corner.

2. Bonnie will order at least 5 bottles but no more than 35 each month. Calculate what an order will cost from Pet Pantry for several different values of x. Compare them to the same size order from Canine Corner.

3. Summarize your findings. For which values of x does Pet Pantry offer a better deal? Canine Corner? Did you find a value of x for which each charges the same?

4. The inequality $4x + 5 > 3x + 25$ is true when Canine Corner offers the better (lower) price. Solve the inequality. Draw a graph to show when Canine Corner offers the better price.

5. Suppose you were the owner of a third company, Kibbles & Stuff. Make Bonnie an offer that you think will get her business. (Don't go too low. The flea shampoo costs you $1.75 per bottle wholesale.) Compare your offer with your competitors' offers. Who do you think will get Bonnie's business?

REFLECT

1. When you graph an inequality, how do you know which direction to draw the arrow? How do you know whether to use an open or closed dot? Explain.

2. What would be your first step to solve the equation $3x - 1 = x - 5$? Would the same first step work to solve the inequality $3x - 1 \leq x - 5$?

3. Compare and contrast the processes of solving equations and inequalities.

Self-Assessment

1. Use the expression $3x + 5$ in each problem.
   a. Find x if the expression is equal to 41.
   b. Find x if the expression is greater than 41.
   c. Find x if twice the expression is at most 15.
   d. Find x if one third of the expression is at least 5 less than the expression.

2. **Déjà vu??** Margo is solving the equation $4x - 5 = 2(8 - x)$. Dan is solving the inequality $4x - 5 > 2(8 - x)$. In comparing their work, they notice that they used exactly the same steps. Why did this work?

3. Which of the following inequalities have the same solution set as $3 > x$?
   (a) $x < -3$ (b) $x < 3$ (c) $x > 3$ (d) $-x > -3$

Solve and graph each inequality.

4. $3x - 4 \geq 2.3$ 5. $4 - 3x > 2.3$ 6. $3(x - 4) < 2.3$

7. Which is a solution to $3(x - 1) = 7 - 2x$? Tell how you determined this.
   (a) $x = \dfrac{6}{5}$ (b) $x = -1$ (c) $x = 2$ (d) 8   (e) not here

8. **Relax and Buy More** Arthur likes to play music in the background for his customers. Yesterday, he paid $13.50 each for compact discs and $7.00 each for tapes. He bought 5 more tapes than discs and the total amount he spent was less than $94.00. Let $d =$ the number of discs he purchased.
   a. What does the expression $13.5d$ represent?
   b. What does the expression $d + 5$ represent?
   c. What does the expression $7(d + 5) + 13.5d$ represent?
   d. Write and solve an inequality to determine the number of discs that he could have purchased for less than $94.00.

9. Why are there no triangles with sides of lengths of 1 cm, 4 cm, and 9 cm?

10. If $x - 4 < 0$, which is greater, x or 4? Why?

11. The perimeter of a triangle is 13 cm. The sides are all different lengths and all are whole numbers. What are the possible combinations of lengths of the sides?

Problem-Solving Tip

Make a table.

12. Write an inequality for the fact that a person must be at least 25 years old to be elected a representative to the United States Congress.

13. Publish or Perish Renelee and Kathy own a small publishing company named Mathematics Is Everywhere. One of their first decisions was to select a printing company. Some of the things that they had to consider were price, quality, promptness, and reliability. Price was their first consideration.

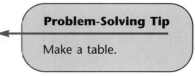

  a. Suppose b equals the number of books. Write an expression that shows the cost of having b books printed by each of the printers.
  b. Write an equation that shows both printers' costs to be equal.
  c. For what number of books would the printers charge the same amount? What would that charge be?

Choose *sometimes*, *always*, or *never* to fill in each blank.

14. Since $5 > 3$, $5 + z$ is _____ greater than $3 + z$.

15. Since $\frac{1}{4} < \frac{1}{3}$ and $\frac{1}{3} < \frac{1}{2}$, $\frac{1}{4}$ is _____ greater than $\frac{1}{2}$.

16. If $x \leq y$, then x is _____ equal to y.

17. If $x > y$, then $x \div z$ is _____ greater than $y \div z$.

18. Just How Far Is It? The distances between Dry Gulch, Wet Creek, and Soggy River can be represented by a triangle. The distance between Dry Gulch and Wet Creek is 524 mi and the distance between Dry Gulch and Soggy River is 325 mi. The distance between Wet Creek and Soggy River is unknown and can be represented by x.

  a. Write three inequalities that represent the distance between Wet Creek and Soggy River.
  b. Solve each inequality.
  c. If Trapper John can travel only 100 mi per day, is it possible for him to reach Soggy River on the same day if he leaves Wet Creek at dawn?

19. How many different triangles can you construct on this geoboard? Tell why you think you have found them all.

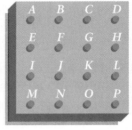

Social Science

20. In 1982, the Department of Transportation mandated the maximum speedometer reading to be 140 km/hr and 85 mi/hr.

    a. Which reading, 140 km/hr or 85 mi/hr, is faster (1 mi ≈ 1.6 km)? Explain.

    b. Write your answer as an inequality.

    c. The same law requires that the speed 55 mi/hr, or its equivalent, be highlighted. What number would be highlighted in km/hr?

Industry

21. Just Raise the Price The average cost of printing *Mathematics Is for Everyone* is $3.50 per book. The selling price of each book is $14.95. The operational costs for last year amounted to $2565.00. Let b = the number of books printed.

	Budget 1995	Projected Expenses	Budget 1996
Computer leasing	1,200	1,200	1,200
Computer paper	360	390	390
Phone	480	450	450
Supplies	250	275	275
Postage	275	275	275
Total	2565	2590	2590

    a. Write an inequality to show the number of books that the company must sell to at least cover the operational costs plus the cost of each book produced.

    b. What is the least number of books they need to sell?

    c. When the company first began, they charged $12.95 per book, but the operational costs were the same. At that time, what was the least number of books that they had to sell in order to cover their operational costs?

    d. Why do you think the company does not just continually raise prices?

History

22. The table shows the effect of the Bubonic Plague (1347–1350) on some European cities. The disease began in Asia and spread across Europe, killing about one third of Europe's population.

	Avignon, France	Barcelona, Spain	Florence, Italy	London, England	Nuremberg, Germany
Before	46,000	50,000	80,000	50,000	18,000
After	23,000	28,000	20,000	28,000	16,000

    a. Which city suffered the greatest loss in the number of people? in percent of population?

    b. Which city suffered the least loss in the number of people? in percent of population?

    c. The epidemic spread from Asia to Greenland in four years. How do you think this happened so fast?

Chapter 4 Review

In Chapter 4, you have become skilled at using an important tool of mathematics—the equation. You have also learned to solve inequalities. These tools can be used to model situations from other fields such as science and industry, so that problems can be defined and solved.

KEY TERMS

Additive inverse [4-2]   Inequality [4-3]   Literal equations [4-2]

Boundary point [4-3]   Inverse operations [4-2]   Solution [4-1, 4-3]

1. Which of the following is an example of a literal equation?
   (a) $3 = (x + 1)(x - 5)$ (b) $5 = 2x + 1$
   (c) $A = lw$ (d) $x = 1 - 5$
   (e) not here

2. Which of the following are inverse operations?
   (a) addition and multiplication   (b) division and fractions
   (c) multiplication and division   (d) subtraction and fractions
   (e) commutative and associative

3. Write the word or phrase that best completes the statement.
   In the graph of the inequality $x < 9$, 9 is called the _____.

CONCEPTS AND APPLICATIONS

4. Which of the following is a solution of the equation $45 = 6x + 3$? [4-1]
   (a) $x = 5$ (b) $x = 0$ (c) $x = 7$ (d) $x = 55$ (e) not here

Solve each equation. In each case, tell whether you guessed and checked, used mental math, or used another method. Explain your choice. [4-1]

5. $3 = x + 1$ **6.** $\dfrac{2x + 5}{3} = 7$ **7.** $2x + 1 = 10$

8. $4x = 4$ **9.** $\dfrac{1}{3}x = 4$ **10.** $-2p + 3 = 14$

11. Which of the following is a solution of the equation $\frac{1}{3}x - 1 = 2x - 6$? [4-1]
   (a) $x = 0$ (b) $x = 1$ (c) $x = -1$ (d) $x = 3$ (e) not here

Use this graph of $y = \frac{3}{5}x - 2$ to solve each equation. [4-1]

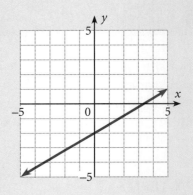

12. $-5 = \frac{3}{5}x - 2$

13. $1 = \frac{3}{5}x - 2$

14. $-2 = \frac{3}{5}x - 2$

15. To raise $500 for their trip to the state championships, the drum and bugle corps decided to have a car wash. The owner of the local gas station has agreed to let them use the station for a fee of $20. They plan to charge $4 for each car. [4-2]

  a. Let c = the number of cars washed. Write an algebraic expression to represent the income.

  b. How much money must they raise to have $500 for their trip?

  c. Write an equation to represent this situation.

  d. Solve your equation to find how many cars they will need to wash.

  e. Is this a reasonable number of cars to expect to wash in one day?

16. Write the equation modeled in each step and explain how the new equation was obtained. [4-2]

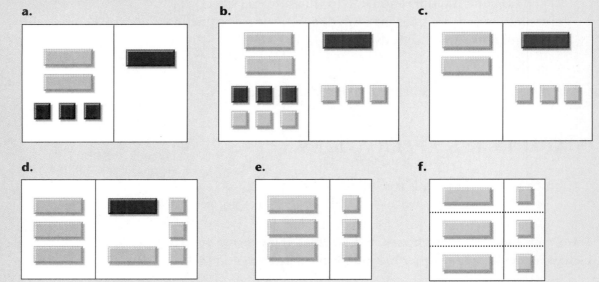

a.

b.

c.

d.

e.

f.

17. Solve the literal equation $I = prt$ for r. [4-2]

Solve each equation. [4-2]

18. $9x - 0.3 = 0.30$

19. $5 - 3x = -31$

20. $\frac{1}{3}x - \frac{5}{6} = \frac{1}{6}$

21. $x + 3(4x - 3) = 30$

22. $-1(-x + 5) = 2x + 12$

23. $\frac{1}{3}x + 2\left(\frac{1}{3}x - \frac{5}{6}\right) = \frac{1}{6}$

24. The perimeters of these two figures are equal. [4-3]

    a. Write an expression that represents the perimeter of the triangle.

    b. Write an expression that represents the perimeter of the rectangle.

    c. Write an equation that shows that the two expressions are equal. Solve your equation.

    d. What is the perimeter of the triangle? of the rectangle?

25. Match the graph with the correct inequality. [4-3]

    (a) $x < -3$ (b) $x \leq -3$ (c) $x > 0$

    (d) $x > 0$ (e) $x > -3$

Solve each inequality. Graph and check your solutions. [4-3]

26. $x - 7 \leq 12$ **27.** $3n > 9$

28. Use the Triangle Inequality to answer these questions. [4-3]

    a. Write three inequalities that involve x.

    b. Solve each inequality.

    c. What number must x be less than?

    d. What number must x be more than?

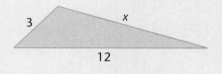

CONCEPTS AND CONNECTIONS

29. Social Studies Abraham Lincoln's 1863 Gettysburg Address refers to the year 1776 as "four score and seven years ago." Write an equation and solve for a *score*.

30. Industry Jon has a business in which he sponsors dances. The cost of printing a flyer to advertise the upcoming dance is 3¢ per copy. The relationship between the total cost (c) of printing the flyer and the number of copies (n) can be represented by the linear function $c = 0.03n$.

    a. Draw a graph of this function.

    b. Find the number of copies run if the total cost is $36.

    c. Suppose Jon has budgeted $45 to spend on advertising the dance. To make any money on the dance, he feels that he must pass out at least 2000 flyers to get enough people to attend. Is his budget large enough?

SELF-EVALUATION

Discuss the different ways you've learned to solve and apply equations and inequalities. Give examples of real-life situations where you need to solve an equation. For each situation, indicate which method you would use. Write down which parts of the chapter were difficult for you and which sections you need to study further in order to better understand these topics.

TEST

Write an algebraic expression that represents each of these models, and write what you would add to each expression to get zero.

1.

2.

3.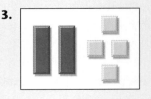

4. Which of the following is a solution of the equation $\frac{1}{3}x + 7 = 5$?
   (a) $x = -9$ (b) $x = -3$ (c) $x = 3$ (d) $x = 9$ (e) not here

Solve each equation.

5. $12x = 30$

6. $12 + x = 30$

7. $12 - x = 30$

8. $\frac{1}{12}x = 30$

9. $x - 12 = 30$

10. $-3m + 4 = -19$

11. Write the equation modeled in each step and explain how the new equation was obtained.

a.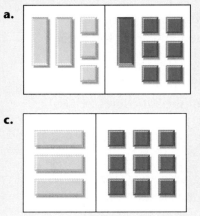

b.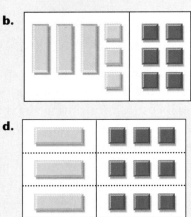

c.

d.

12. Simplify the expression $-4(x + 6) - (4 - 2x)$.

Solve each equation.

13. $2(3x + 7) = -(4 - x)$

14. $\frac{7}{9}x + \frac{7}{45} = \frac{4}{5}x - 2$

15. Solve the literal equation $D = rt$ for r.

16. Which of these inequalities are equivalent to $x \le -2$?
   (a) $-2 \le x$ (b) $-2 \ge x$ (c) $2 \ge -x$ (d) $2 \le -x$

17. Luellen wants to arrive at Londa's house by 5 p.m. Londa lives 225 mi away. Luellen thinks she can average 50 mi/hr. How much time must she allow herself for the trip? Use the formula $D = rt$.

  a. Let t represent Luellen's travel time. What is the distance (D)? What is the rate (r)? Write an equation that describes this relationship.

  b. Solve your equation. How long will the trip take?

  c. How early must Luellen leave home to arrive at Londa's by 5 p.m.?

18. Cook's Careful Count Kyle and Drew are entering the chili cook-off. They need a new $35 pot. The ingredients for their recipe cost $14 per batch.

  a. Define the variables, and write an equation that relates the cost of their chili and the number of batches. (Don't forget to include the cost of the new pot.)

  b. Since they have a budget of $100, what is the greatest number of batches they can make?

  c. Each batch makes 20 one-cup servings. How many servings of chili can they make?

19. Which graph shows the solutions of $10 - 3x < 7(x + 2)$? Tell how you determined this.

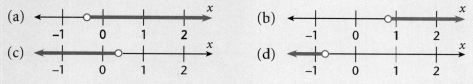

(a)   (b)   (c)   (d)

20. In 1993, the federal government of the United States set a limit on the amount of money an employee would have to pay into Social Security. A tax rate of 6.20% would be applied to all income up to $60,600. For higher incomes, the amount of social security tax is the same as that for $60,600.

  a. Would an employee who earns $23,000 pay less than a person who earns $30,000?

  b. Would an employee who earns $70,000 pay less than a person who earns $80,000?

  c. Let S = the total social security tax that an employee could pay. Express S as an inequality.

Social Science

PERFORMANCE TASK

Careers

As the owner of a new business, you need to consider whether to pay a salesperson a commission or a combination of salary and commission. Choose a business that involves sales, and choose numbers that make sense for your business. Use variables and an equation to analyze which choice you should make. Prepare a proposal for your future salesperson that will show that your choice is in his or her best interest.

Chapter 5

Project A
What's the Bottom Line?
What is a balance sheet? When does a business pass the "acid test" of good financial health?

Project B
It's All Uphill
Did you ever wonder why some stairs are safe and comfortable to use while others are inconvenient going up and dangerous going down?

Project C
My Other Car Is a Mach 5
How do automobile engineers measure and compare acceleration in cars?

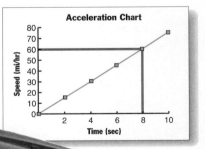

GERI SAKEAGAK

Math was my favorite subject in high school. I thought I'd use it to invest in my future.

Math has helped me to understand economics. Using math, you can deal with a lot of theories at once and explain the variables in a situation. Now I use math to project the earnings my company will need in the future in order to maintain jobs and services.

Geri Sakeagak
Personnel Manager
Arctic Slope Regional Corporation
Barrow, Alaska

5-1
Exploring
Applications
of Slope

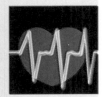

In 5-1 you will learn about rates of change and how to describe slopes of lines mathematically. You will need skills with integers, order of operations, equations, and coordinate geometry.

Simplify. [2-3]

1. $\dfrac{1-2}{3-(-4)}$

2. $\dfrac{12-(-7)}{23-17}$

3. $\dfrac{-1.5-3}{13-10}$

4. $\dfrac{14-10}{26-20}$

Use the graph at the right. [3-2]

5. What is the ordered pair for *A*?

6. What is the *x*-coordinate for *B*?

7. On line *k*, what is the ordered pair for the point where line *k* crosses the *y*-axis?

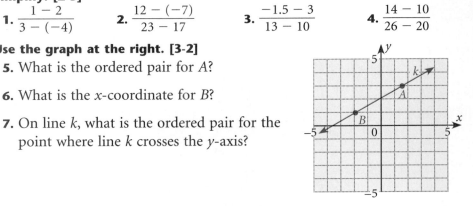

5-2
Connnecting
Slope and
Linear Functions

In 5-2 you will explore the connections between equations and linear functions and examine real-world data that are approximately linear. You will use unit conversion, equation solving, and coordinate geometry skills.

Convert each amount to the given units. [Pages 748 and 784]

8. 38 in. = ____ ft ____ in. = ____ ft

9. 4.5 lb = ____ oz

10. 2500 g = ____ kg

11. 6600 ft = ____ mi

12. 22,850 mm = ____ cm = ___ m = ____ km

Solve each equation for *y*. [4-2]

13. $5 + 3y = 9$

14. $\dfrac{y}{2} - 4 = 0$

15. $-3 + 2y = 6$

16. $2(y + 2) - 3 = 19$

17. $11y - 3 = 96$

18. $12y + 6 = 18$

19. $5(y - 2) = 20$

20. $4 = -3y + 10$

21. $4y = 12 - (6 - 2)$

GREAT PYRAMIDS

I n the Old Kingdom of Egypt a new pharaoh began his reign by planning for the end of it—the construction of his burial tomb. For
Khufu's tomb, the Great Pyramid at Giza, armies of workers, citizens, and slaves were drafted to assemble more than two million
stone blocks. Most blocks weighed about two-and-a-half tons,
although some were six times as heavy. The workers used ramps
and rollers to haul the stones out of the quarries. Then they guided
them in barges along the Nile to the building site.

   In 2600 B.C., engineers had only the simplest tools—even the wheel
had not yet been used in building. Yet the calculations were so exact
that, on a 13-acre site, opposite corners differ in height by at most one-
half inch! The mystery of how the Egyptians built this pyramid rivals
the splendor of the finished monument.

Unless architects made sure
the slope of each side was
the same over the entire
face, the pyramid might have
looked like this!

Unless all the faces had
the same slope, the pyramid
might have looked like this!

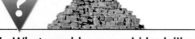

1. What would a pyramid look like if you flew directly above it?
2. What are some other words you could use for slope? Do they convey the same meaning? What is a word for more slope? less slope?
3. What do we mean by the slope of a roof?
4. What are some other real-world examples of slope?

Without correct alignment,
the Great Pyramid of Giza
might have looked like this!

← **C O N N E C T** → *In Chapters 3 and 4, you studied the relationship between linear functions and straight lines. In this part, you will investigate ways to express the slope of a line in the Cartesian plane. You will also calculate the slopes of lines in simple situations.*

In everyday language, we use words like *slope*, *slant*, *steep*, and *tilt* to describe objects that are not perfectly flat or perfectly upright.

This *slope* is for advanced skiers.

The highway was *tilted* by the earthquake.

The steep *pitch* of the roof allows snow to slide off.

The *grade* of the road is about 6%.

The gutter does not *slant* enough to drain well.

A line can also have *slope*. Think of the slope of a line as a measure of its tilt or steepness. Just as some surfaces slant more than others, the slope of one line can be greater than the slope of another line.

EXPLORE: AERIAL ACROBATICS

MATERIALS

Graph paper
Straightedge

Imagine that these takeoff and landing paths of an acrobatic flying team match graphs of linear functions.

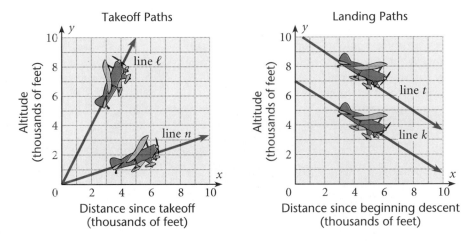

1. Which is steeper, line *l* or line *n*? line *k* or line *t*? How could you explain the idea of steepness using numbers?

2. Find a method to describe the slope of line *l*. Does your method apply to finding the slopes of lines *n, k,* and *t*?

3. Draw any line on a coordinate plane. Without showing the line or telling coordinates, have a classmate draw a line of exactly the same slope on blank graph paper using your description.

4. When your classmate is finished, compare the two graphs. Do the lines have the same slope? Are they in the same location in the coordinate plane?

In the first graph of the Explore, the quantities *x* and *y* are *directly* related, and the line slants *upward* from left to right. Lines like *l* and *n* have **positive slope.**

In the second graph, the quantities *x* and *y* are *inversely* related, and the line slants *downward* from left to right. Lines like *k* and *t* have **negative slope.**

It is possible to describe the slope of a line using a single positive or negative number. Choose any two points on the line. As you move from the left point to the right point, the *ratio* of the *change in y* to the *change in x* is the slope of the line.

$$\text{slope} = \frac{\text{change in } y}{\text{change in } x}$$

EXAMPLES

Find the slope of each line.

1. Calculate from left to right, from point *C* to point *D*.

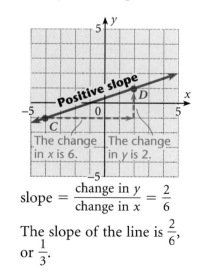

$$\text{slope} = \frac{\text{change in } y}{\text{change in } x} = \frac{2}{6}$$

The slope of the line is $\frac{2}{6}$, or $\frac{1}{3}$.

2. Calculate from left to right, from point *E* to point *F*.

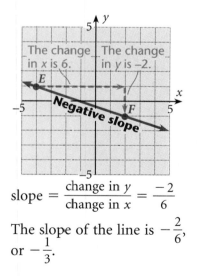

$$\text{slope} = \frac{\text{change in } y}{\text{change in } x} = \frac{-2}{6}$$

The slope of the line is $-\frac{2}{6}$, or $-\frac{1}{3}$.

Notice that you must use a negative number when you move *down* to find the change in *y* or move *left* to find the change in *x*.

Slope has been defined as the ratio of the *change in y* to the *change in x* as you move from one point to the other. We also refer to slope as the ratio of **rise** to **run.**

$$\text{slope} = \frac{\text{change in } y}{\text{change in } x} = \frac{\text{rise}}{\text{run}}$$

Notice that these definitions automatically assign positive slopes to lines that slope upward, and negative slopes to lines that slope downward.

TRY IT

a. In line *v*, what is the change in *y* from *J* to *K*? What is the change in *x*? What is the slope of line *v*?

b. How much does line *w* rise from *P* to *Q*? How far is the run between these points?

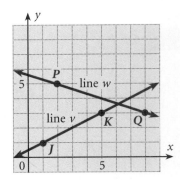

In the next few parts, you will see how to calculate slope directly from the ordered pairs of a linear function.

REFLECT

1. Explain the difference between positive slope and negative slope.
2. How is a ratio used to describe slope?
3. Give three possible slopes for a very steep line. Give three possible slopes for a line with only a slight incline.
4. Do you think it is possible for a line to have a negative slope if it passes through the points (1, 4) and (8, 5)? Why?

CORE

1. **Getting Started** Tell whether the slope of each line is negative or positive.
   a. line *a*   **b.** line *b*
   c. line *c*   **d.** line *d*

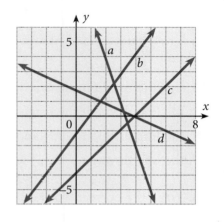

2. Answer these questions about line *r*.
   a. What are the coordinates of *C*?
   b. What are the coordinates of *D*?
   c. Calculate the change in *y* from *C* to *D*.
   d. Calculate the change in *x* from *C* to *D*.
   e. What is the slope of line *r*?

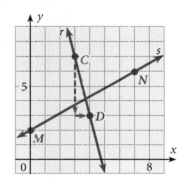

3. Find the slope of line *s* using the ratio of rise to run from *M* to *N*.

4. **American Artistry** Step designs are used in many places in Navajo rugs. If any one "step" rises one unit as it runs two units, what are the slopes of these three designs?

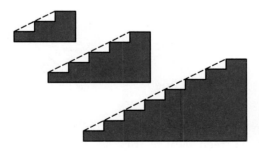

5. What are the slopes of the five segments that make up the sides of this star?

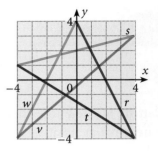

On a coordinate plane, sketch each line and determine its slope.

6. the line through the origin and $(-2, -5)$

7. the line through the origin and $(2, 5)$

8. the line through $(1, 5)$ and $(5, 1)$

9. the line through $(-1, 5)$ and $(5, -1)$

10. Write the correct word or phrase to complete this sentence. Vertical change is to rise as horizontal change is to _____.

11. The slopes of these four lines are -1, $\frac{2}{3}$, 3, and -4. Match each line with its slope.

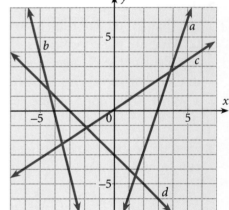

12. Order these fractions from least to greatest.
$$\frac{1}{2}, \frac{2}{1}, \frac{1}{3}, \frac{1}{5}, \frac{5}{6}, \frac{1}{1}$$

13. Determine the slope of each line. Then determine whether each statement is true or false.

a. A line with a slope of $\frac{1}{2}$ is steeper than a line with a slope of 2.

b. A line with a slope of $\frac{1}{3}$ is steeper than a line with a slope of $\frac{1}{5}$.

c. A line with a slope of $\frac{5}{6}$ is steeper than a line with a slope of 1.

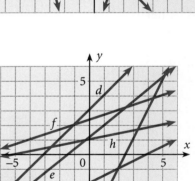

14. Compare the slope of a line with a steep slant to the slope of a line that is more nearly horizontal. Describe the relationship you see.

15. Praiseworthy Pyramids Some of the most famous "pyramids" throughout the world are beautiful structures, but they are not true pyramids. The Mayan pyramids in Mexico are an example. Their sides are stepped, with stairs that go up the center to flat tops.

   a. In this picture of El Castillo, tell which of the following slopes is steeper: the slope of a side or the slope of the stairs that go up the center of that side. Explain how you decided.

   b. Why would a different slope be needed for the stairs?

16. Scope the Slope Egyptian pyramid builders may have used ramps to carry materials to increasingly higher levels. The ramps would have become longer as the construction progressed and the pyramids stood taller. What would you estimate the slope of the large ramp to be? of the small ramp?

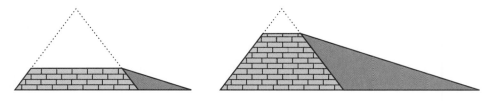

17. A "Slopey" Argument A logical fallacy in an argument is a step that is not necessarily true. One example is called *slippery slope.* "If I don't get a new car, I'll always be late for work. The boss will be angry and I'll get fired." Why is someone who thinks this way on a "slippery slope"?

Give a reasonable slope for each situation.

18. a hill in San Francisco

19. a slide in a children's playground

20. the front window of a car

21. a dump truck dumping gravel

22. Slope Sleuths Lew, Sue, and Hugh disagreed on the value of the slope of a certain line. Lew said the slope was $\frac{4}{6}$ because the line rose 4 units as it ran 6 units. Sue said the slope was $\frac{2}{3}$ because it rose 2 units as it ran 3 units. Hugh used the negative direction and said the slope was $\frac{-2}{-3}$. Help them resolve this argument.

23. Building up Health In 1992, the U.S. Department of Agriculture created a
Food Guide Pyramid to make its advice on nutrition more visual and easier
to understand.

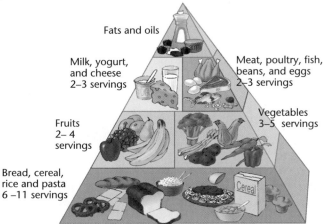

a. How would the pyramid be changed if the slope of its sides were different?
Explain your reasoning.
b. USDA wants to convey information about the proportion, moderation, and
variety of nutritional foods. Can you find these ideas in the pyramid?
c. Could a pie chart, line graph, or histogram convey this information as well
as the pyramid?

LOOK BACK

Write each sentence as an equation. Define your variables. [4-1]

24. Terri burns 40 more calories per hour walking than she does
mowing the lawn.

25. There are 500 times as many species of sac fungi as species of
bread mold.

Sac fungi

26. Darla traveled 295 miles in 5 hours. [4-3]
a. Express the time she traveled in terms of distance and rate.
b. Express the distance she traveled in terms of time and rate.
c. Express the rate she traveled in terms of distance and time.
d. Which equation makes it easy for you to find Darla's average
speed? Explain.

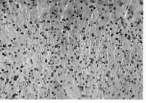

Bread mold

Solve for h. [4-2]

27. $-h = -0.7$ **28.** $-(3h + 1) = -4h$ **29.** $A = \left(\dfrac{b_1 + b_2}{2}\right)h$

MORE PRACTICE

30. Tell whether the slope of each line is positive or negative.

    a. line p **b.** line q **c.** line r **d.** line s **e.** line t **f.** line n

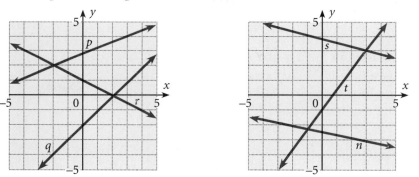

31. Find the slope of lines a and b by using the ratio of rise to run.

32. Find the slope of lines c and d by using the ratio of change in y to change in x.

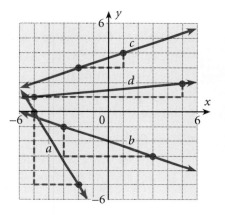

Graph each pair of points and determine the slope of the line through them.

33. $(3, 1)$, $(1, 3)$ **34.** $(5, 2)$, $(7, 6)$

35. $(-3, 6)$, $(-8, 4)$ **36.** $(-2, 1)$, $(-6, 3)$

37. $(4, 3)$, $(-1, 2)$ **38.** $(7, 1)$, $(7, -1)$

Find the slopes of the lines in each of these designs. Which lines have the same slope?

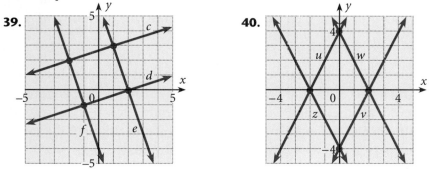

Give a reasonable slope for each situation.

41. the back of a chair   **42.** the slope of the hood of an automobile   **43.** a stairway

MORE MATH REASONING

44. Super Slope If the Great Pyramid of Giza is 463 feet tall, and one side of its square base is 770 feet, what is the slope of each face? (Assume that each face has the same slope.)

History

45. According to Formula The volume of a pyramid with a square base is found by taking one-third of the product of the base area and the height of the pyramid. Define your variables and write a formula for calculating the volume of a pyramid.

46. Northern Exposure The word *climate* comes from the Greek word *klima* meaning "to lean" or "to slope." The ancients believed that the earth north of the Mediterranean Sea "sloped" away from the sun and that the earth south of it "sloped" toward the sun. This explained why it was cold to the north and hot to the south. Do you agree or disagree with this reasoning? Explain.

Science

47. Flip Out Suppose you reverse the horizontal and vertical change in finding the slope. Then you realize your mistake. What can you do to your wrong answer to find the true slope?

5-1 PART B Rate of Change

← CONNECT → *You've begun to investigate slopes of lines. Because lines are models of relationships between real-life quantities, slopes have real-world meanings. One of these meanings is related to the rate of change of quantities.*

Time and rates are important elements in our world. Salespeople can measure their success by the number of customers they serve *per* year. Divers know that they must rise to the surface only a few feet *per* second to avoid the *bends*. Government analysts must calculate the number of dollars *per* person a new program may cost. Rates compare the way quantities vary.

No one knows how long it took to build the Great Pyramid. Imagine that Pharaoh Khufu has appointed you to direct the work. The pyramid will be 480 feet high and you have 20 years to get the work done. The pharaoh has suggested the work schedule shown in the graph.

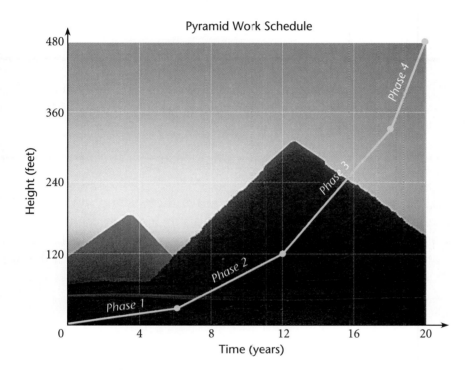

1. How much time has been allotted in each phase?
2. In which phase does the height of the pyramid increase most quickly? most slowly?
3. How high does the pharaoh expect the pyramid to be after 10 years of work? after 12 years?
4. What is the increase in height per year during Phase 3?
5. Calculate the rate the pyramid is rising during each phase.
6. Calculate the slope of the graph during each phase. Compare the slope and the rate of change for each phase. What relationship do you see?
7. Do the workers have an easier schedule at the beginning of the project than at the end? Is there less work to do when the rate of change is less?

The ratio of the change in a quantity, *A*, to a change in a related quantity, *B*, is called the **rate of change** of *A*. Calculate the rate of change of *A* by dividing the change in *A* by the change in *B*.

The rate of change is very important in analyzing functions. You will continue to work with rates of change throughout your courses in mathematics.

CONSIDER

1. **In the Explore, what connections do you see between the rate of change for each phase and the slope of the graph for that phase?**

The graph shows the Phase 2 portion of the pyramid work schedule in greater detail. Subscripts are used to distinguish between the coordinates (*x*, *y*) of different points. The change in *y* is the difference between the two *y*-coordinates. The change in *x* is the difference between the two *x*-coordinates.

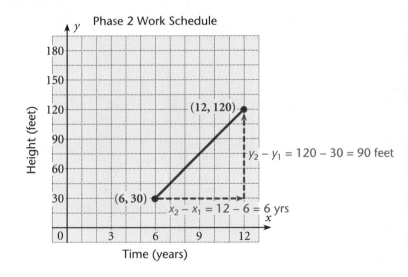

The rate of change $= \dfrac{\text{change in } y}{\text{change in } x} = \dfrac{y_2 - y_1}{x_2 - x_1} = \dfrac{90 \text{ ft}}{6 \text{ yr}} = \dfrac{15 \text{ ft}}{1 \text{ yr}}$, or 15 ft/yr.

When you graph a function, be sure to mark each axis and the scales of your graph correctly. When reading a slope or rate of change from the graph, make sure to express the rates in appropriate units.

EXAMPLE

A 20-gallon tub full of water and flowers is resting on a florist's work table. The total weight on the table is 200 pounds. (The tub and the flowers weigh 30 pounds.) Because this is a dangerously heavy load, the tub must be drained. How does the weight on the table change as the water drains?

You can find the rate at which the weight changes without graphing. Let x stand for the number of gallons drained. Let y stand for the weight on the table. Make two ordered pairs from the information that is given.

$(x_1, y_1) = (0, 200)$ When 0 gallons are drained, the weight is 200 lb.

$(x_2, y_2) = (20, 30)$ When 20 gallons are drained, the weight is 30 lb.

$$\text{rate of change} = \frac{y_2 - y_1}{x_2 - x_1} = \frac{(30 - 200) \text{ lb}}{(20 - 0) \text{ gal}} = \frac{-170 \text{ lb}}{20 \text{ gal}} = -8.5 \text{ lb/gal}$$

The negative number indicates a decreasing weight. The weight is decreasing at the rate of 8.5 pounds per gallon drained.

A graph of these data would show that the slope of the line between (0, 200) and (20, 30) is −8.5, the same as the rate of change we found. From your science class, you may recall that the weight of water is about 8.5 pounds per gallon.

TRY IT

Without graphing, find the rate of change in each situation.
a. It is −2 degrees at 5 a.m. and 7 degrees 4 hours later. What is the rate of change in degrees per hour?
b. An auto that has gone 125 miles in the first 3 hours of a trip continues on and goes a total of 420 miles in 9 hours. At what rate did the distance traveled change during the last 6 hours?
c. The cycle club had biked 24 miles after 2 hours and 42 miles after 5 hours. What was their rate of change in the last 3 hours expressed in miles per hour?

Velocipede race in Paris, 1868.

311

Find the slope of the segment through C and D.

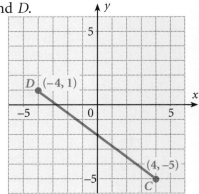

Norma thinks . . .

I'll use the left point, D, as (x_1, y_1) and I'll use C as (x_2, y_2).

So the slope, $\frac{y_2 - y_1}{x_2 - x_1}$, is

$$\frac{-5 - 1}{4 - (-4)} = \frac{-6}{8} = -\frac{3}{4}.$$

Taktuk thinks . . .

I'll use the points in alphabetical order. So, I'll use C for (x_1, y_1) and D for (x_2, y_2).

The slope, $\frac{y_2 - y_1}{x_2 - x_1}$, has to be $\frac{1 - (-5)}{-4 - 4} = \frac{6}{-8} = -\frac{3}{4}.$

By calculating $\frac{\text{rise}}{\text{run}}$ you have found the slope of lines that slant either up or down from left to right. But do horizontal and vertical lines also have slope?

Consider the horizontal line that passes through $(2, 5)$ and $(8, 5)$. The line does not rise at all.

$$\frac{\text{rise}}{\text{run}} = \frac{0}{6} = 0$$

The slope of a horizontal line is 0.

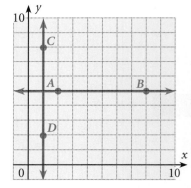

Consider the vertical line that passes through $(1, 2)$ and $(1, 8)$. It does not run at all.

$$\frac{\text{rise}}{\text{run}} = \frac{6}{0}, \text{ which is undefined.}$$

The slope of a vertical line is undefined.

TRY IT

Determine the slope of each line, if possible, using $\frac{y_2 - y_1}{x_2 - x_1}$.
d. the line through the origin and $(-2, 0)$
e. the line through $(1, 5)$ and $(4, 5)$
f. the line from $(-4, 3)$ to $(-4, 6)$
g. the line from $(5, -3)$ to $(-3, 5)$

REFLECT

1. An investment group is thinking of buying one of these companies.
   a. Which one is more profitable?
   b. Which one might be more profitable in the future? Why?
2. How is rate of change related to slope?
3. What does a negative rate of change mean?

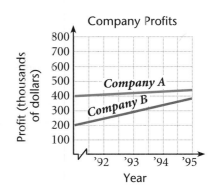

Company Profits

Profit (thousands of dollars)

Company A

Company B

'92 '93 '94 '95

Year

Exercises

CORE

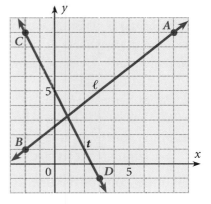

1. **Getting Started** Use A as (x_1, y_1) and B as (x_2, y_2).
   a. What is $y_2 - y_1$?
   b. What is $x_2 - x_1$?
   c. What is the slope of line l?

2. Use C as (x_1, y_1) and D as (x_2, y_2).
   a. What is $y_2 - y_1$?
   b. What is $x_2 - x_1$?
   c. What is the slope of line t?

Science 3. A tree's height is 62 inches on March 1 and 100 inches on October 31. Express the rate of change in inches per month.

Science 4. A snow sculpture is 150 cm high at 10:00 a.m. and 35 cm high at 5:00 p.m. Express the rate of change in cm per hour.

Find the slope of the line through each pair of points. Watch for 0 slopes and undefined slopes.

5. $(-5, 3)$ and $(-5, 12)$ 6. $(7, -3)$ and $(-7, 3)$ 7. $(0, 5)$ and $(-3, 5)$

Careers 8. From years of experience, a hotel chef knows that 2.5 cups of coffee are needed for every 4 people at a dinner party.
   a. How much coffee will be needed at a dinner for 360 people?
   b. What is the rate of change?

Industry 9. Alexandra paid $208 for 32 hours of child care last week.
   a. What rate per hour did she pay?
   b. At this rate, how much will she pay this week for 41 hours of child care?

10. It's the Law Kepler's Third Law of Motion says that the time it takes a planet to go around the sun (orbital period) depends on its average distance from the sun. Earth's average distance from the sun is 92,960,000 miles. It takes 365.25 days to go around the sun. What is the average rate or speed that Earth is traveling?

11. Paka decides to rent a horse for a ride through the park. The cost is $10 per half-hour for the first hour and $5 for each additional half-hour.

a. Copy and complete the table.

b. Use $5 intervals on the *y*-axis and half-hour intervals on the *x*-axis to graph the ordered pairs.

c. What is the rate of change during the first hour?

d. What is the rate of change during the third hour?

e. He has saved $38 for this horseback ride. How long can he ride?

Time	Rental Cost
$\frac{1}{2}$ hr	
1 hr	
$1\frac{1}{2}$ hr	
2 hr	
$2\frac{1}{2}$ hr	
3 hr	

12. Paper Chase Each day Mrs. Austen, a math teacher, has about 30 students in each of her 5 classes. One month she used 3600 sheets of copying paper.

a. How many sheets of paper per student were used during that month?

b. How many sheets of paper might she expect to use in a nine-month school year at this rate?

c. Paper comes in packages of 500 sheets called a ream. How many reams will Mrs. Austen use this school year? Express your answer as a rate.

d. Find other ways to express the rates given in this situation, such as reams per student, sheets per class, etc.

13. Find the slope of the line through each pair of points.

a. $L(-3, 4)$ and $M(4, -6)$ **b.** $C(-4, -4)$ and $D(10, 10)$

c. $R(-1, -4)$ and $S(2, 3)$ **d.** $A(-3, -2)$ and $B(0, -5)$

14. Pure Percentage *Percent* means "for each hundred." Explain how percentage can be thought of as a rate of change in each situation.

a. The population of Fairfax increased 10% last year.

b. Sales at Bikes, Inc., fell 15% from July to September.

15. Plane Sense Three small airlines may merge to become more profitable. The graph shows their current profits.

a. Which airline shows the greatest rate of improvement?

b. Which airline is showing the greatest profit overall?

c. Which airline is showing a decrease in profits?

d. The price for stock in these companies is proportional to current profits. If the current trends continue, which stock is the best buy? Explain.

e. If merging will improve profits for all three airlines, which stock is the best buy now? Explain.

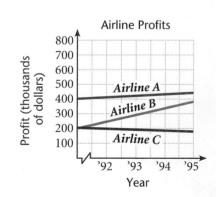

16. **Cabin Cruising** Jered usually travels from Detroit to his cabin in $2\frac{1}{2}$ hours. His cabin is 120 miles from his home.

   a. What is his average rate in miles per hour?
   b. What is his average rate in miles per minute?
   c. Explain the differences in the rates.
   d. At his average rate, how long will it take him to travel the last 15 miles of his journey?

LOOK AHEAD

17. Find the slope for each line, and tell where the graph crosses the y-axis.

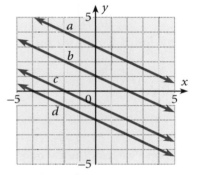

18. Substitute 0 for x in each equation. What is the value of y?

   a. $y = 2x - 5$ b. $y = -2x - 5$

   c. $y = 1.7x + 3.1$ d. $y = 2000x - 1$

   e. $y = \frac{2}{3}x$ f. $y = ax + b$

19. Solve for y.
   a. $3x + 4y = 20$ b. $12y - 3x = 4$ c. $2x - y = 1$

MORE PRACTICE

20. Use A as (x_1, y_1) and B as (x_2, y_2).
   a. What is $y_2 - y_1$?
   b. What is $x_2 - x_1$?
   c. What is the slope of line t?

21. Use C as (x_1, y_1) and D as (x_2, y_2).
   a. What is $y_2 - y_1$?
   b. What is $x_2 - x_1$?
   c. What is the slope of line v?

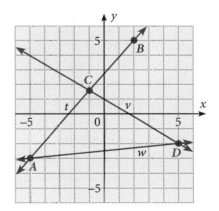

22. Use A as (x_1, y_1) and D as (x_2, y_2).
   a. What is $y_2 - y_1$?
   b. What is $x_2 - x_1$?
   c. What is the slope of line w?

Find the rate of change of y between E and F in each graph.

23.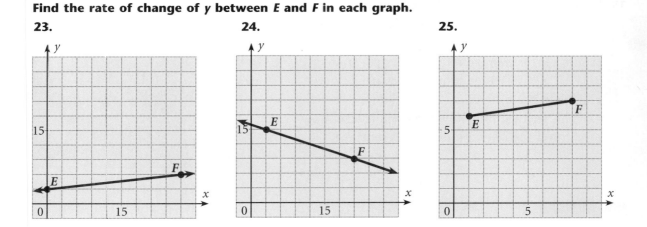

24.

25.

Find the rate of change indicated by each situation.

26. Fido weighed 2 pounds on January 1 and 5 pounds on May 31.

27. Mimi was 6 miles from home at 2:00 p.m., but was only 1 mile from home at 4:00 p.m.

28. Nine cups of chili will serve 5 people, but 90 cups are needed for 50 people.

Find the slope of the line through each pair of points. Watch for 0 slopes and undefined slopes.

29. $(-4, 3)$ and $(-4, 12)$

30. $(12, -3)$ and $(-12, 3)$

31. $(0, 5)$ and $(-3, 5)$

32. $(16, 2)$ and $(2, 16)$

33. Zoom! After flying at a constant altitude, a pilot decides to zoom upward. The graph shows the change in altitude each second.
  a. What ordered pair shows the altitude at 2 seconds?
  b. What ordered pair shows the altitude at 10 seconds?
  c. What are the change in altitude and change in time for your ordered pairs in **33a** and **33b**?
  d. What is the ratio of the change in altitude to the change in time?
  e. What is the rate of change of altitude?
  f. What is the slope of the line?

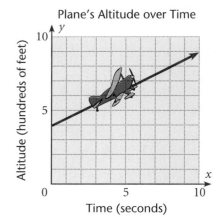

Plane's Altitude over Time

34. Charlene was trying to find the slope of a line segment on a coordinate grid. She found that the horizontal distance was 9, the vertical distance was 6, and the segment slanted upward from left to right. What was the slope of the segment?

35. Nat's Sport Shop paid $280 for 2 dozen baseballs.

Industry

   a. At this rate, what is the cost of one baseball?

   b. How much would Nat's expect to pay for 5 dozen baseballs?

36. Soup's On George uses 8 tablespoons of a secret ingredient in his soup recipe that makes 10 servings.

   a. How much of the secret ingredient is in each serving?

   b. How much of this ingredient would George need if he makes enough soup to serve 100?

MORE MATH REASONING

37. A Pyramid with Ears The Transamerica building in San Francisco is a modern-day pyramid. It was designed in this shape so that more light would reach the street. The earlike appendages on two sides provide elevator access to the upper floors. The base of the Transamerica Pyramid is a square, 145 feet per side. The total height of the pyramid is 786 feet. What is the slope of a side?

Industry

The environment is changing. Do you think the following rates of change are positive or negative? Explain why.

Science

38. acres of rain forest per year

39. arctic temperatures per year

40. tons of garbage per year

41. animal species per year

42. world population per decade

43. new cases of measles per decade

44. Examine the graph.

   a. Which car is going faster?

   b. How much faster?

   c. At what rate is the distance between cars changing each hour?

45. Examine the graph.

   a. Which car is going faster?

   b. How fast is Car C going?

   c. How do you normally the describe the speed of a car?

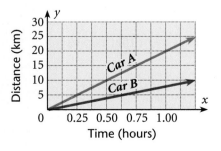

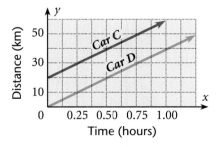

The Geometry of Slope

You've seen that slope is related to rate of change and you've learned to find slopes. Now you will investigate the connection between slope and similar geometric figures.

Remember that a **line** extends infinitely in both directions. A **line segment** is part of a line from one point on it to another.

Line segment $\overline{AB}$

A **line segment** with endpoints A and B is written $\overline{AB}$. Its length measure is written AB.

The line through A and B is written as $\overleftrightarrow{AB}$ or as $\overleftrightarrow{BA}$.

A triangle is labeled by its three vertices: $\triangle ABC$.

In this Explore, you will see that there is a relationship between the slope of a line segment and the slope of the line that contains it.

EXPLORE: TRIANGLE TANGLE

1. How many *different sizes* of triangles are there?
2. How many *of each size* are there?

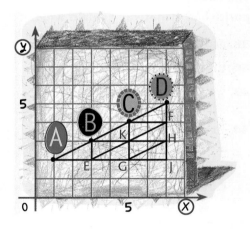

> **Problem-Solving Tip**
>
> Make an organized list to help you keep track of the triangles.

3. What is the slope of $\overline{AB}$? of $\overline{BC}$? of $\overline{CD}$?

4. In lowest terms, what is the slope of $\overline{BD}$? of $\overline{AD}$?

5. What can you conclude about the slope of a line and a segment that is part of that line?

6. Compare the slopes of $\overline{EF}$ and $\overline{AD}$. What do you notice about the relative position of different line segments that have the same slope?

Geometric figures that have the same shape (but not necessarily the same size) are called **similar.** All of the triangles in Triangle Tangle are **similar triangles.** Look again at $\triangle AJD$.

Triangles $\triangle AEB$ and $\triangle AJD$ are similar. The symbol $\sim$ is used to show similar figures.

$$\triangle AEB \sim \triangle AJD.$$

In these similar right triangles, the rise and run may differ but the ratio of the rise to the run is the same.

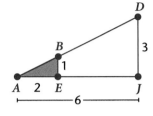

$$\text{slope of } \overline{AB} = \frac{BE}{AE} = \frac{1}{2}$$

$$\text{slope of } \overline{AD} = \frac{DJ}{AJ}$$

$$= \frac{3}{6} = \frac{1}{2}$$

WHAT DO **YOU** THINK?

Find the slope of $\overline{AB}$.

Minh thinks . . .

I'll use the point A as (x_1, y_1) and B as (x_2, y_2), and go from left to right.

So the slope of $\overline{AB}$ is $\dfrac{14 - (-2)}{6 - (-6)} = \dfrac{16}{12} = \dfrac{4}{3}$.

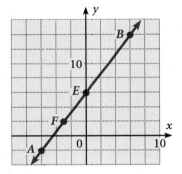

Mark thinks . . .

I'll use the points that are closer together, and go from right to left. E can be (x_1, y_1) and F can be (x_2, y_2).

So the slope of $\overline{AB}$ is $\dfrac{2 - 6}{-3 - 0} = \dfrac{-4}{-3} = \dfrac{4}{3}$.

Even though Minh and Mark used different points and moved in different directions, they both found the correct slope.

TRY IT

a. The following points lie on the same line. Use any two points to find the slope of the line.

$(-10, 5), (0, 3), (10, 1), (15, 0)$

1. What two points would you use to find the slope of this line? Why?

2. In your own words, describe what it means for two triangles to be similar.

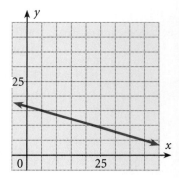

Exercises

CORE

1. Getting Started Use the graph to answer these questions.

a. Name three triangles that are exactly the same size and shape as △*ABE*.

b. Name three triangles that are **similar** to, but larger or smaller than △*ABE*.

c. Find the slope of $\overleftrightarrow{AD}$.

d. Consider △*AJD*. Find the ratio of *DJ* to *AJ*.

e. Consider △*AGC*. Find the ratio of *CG* to *AG*.

f. How do the ratios compare to the slope of $\overleftrightarrow{AD}$? Explain.

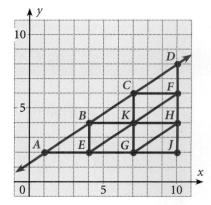

Find the slope of each line. Then determine whether each statement is true or false.

2. Lines *l* and *d* do not have the same slope.

3. Lines *l* and *t* have the same slope.

4. The slope of line *w* is the negative reciprocal of the slope of line *l*.

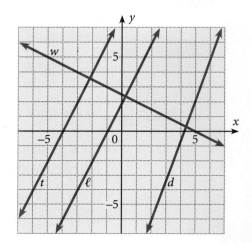

Find the slope of the line through each pair of points. Calculate these algebraically using $\frac{y_2 - y_1}{x_2 - x_1}$. For 5–8, graph points to check your answers.

5. $(2, 3)$ and $(-1, -3)$ **6.** $(-1, 3)$ and $(3, 2)$ **7.** $(-2, -1)$ and $(3, -1)$

8. $(-2, 4)$ and $(-2, -1)$ **9.** $(50, 13)$ and $(75, 63)$ **10.** $(-55, -150)$ and $(-125, 200)$

11. Picture This Masako returned from his tour of the Egyptian Pyramids with eight rolls of film to develop, each with 24 pictures. He compared costs at two stores.

Fast Film	Photo Phormat
$4 service charge and 25¢ per picture	$7.50 per roll of 24

a. Complete charts like these to show how developing costs are related to the number of rolls of film.

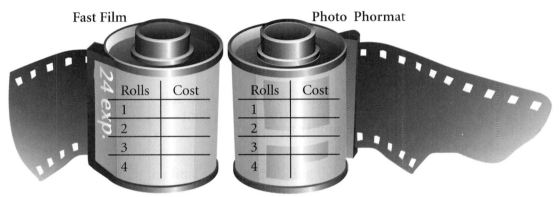

Fast Film

Rolls	Cost
1	
2	
3	
4	

Photo Phormat

Rolls	Cost
1	
2	
3	
4	

b. Graph the relationship between the cost and the number of rolls for each store.

c. What is the slope of each line?

d. How does the slope of each line relate to the information in the problem?

e. Which store offers the better price for developing eight rolls of film?

12. Up and at 'Em Suppose Chio knows the slope of a line is 3. He counts 6 units up from a point on the line. What should he do next to find another point on the line? Explain.

13. The slope of segment AB is $\frac{1}{2}$. P is a point on segment AB. What is the slope of segment AP? of segment PB?

14. Artist's Choice Artists seem to prefer rectangular shapes for their pictures, and so frame shops stock frames in many standard sizes (inches): 8 by 10, 10 by 14, 16 by 20, 20 by 30, 24 by 30, etc. One rectangle is similar to another rectangle if the ratios of their width to length are the same. Are any of these rectangular frames similar?

← CONNECT →
You already know that ordered pairs (x, y) describe points on a coordinate plane, and that equations describe lines. Now you will see that the equation of a line tells its slope and its position in the plane.

A line in the coordinate plane can be located exactly if we know two things:

1. the slope of the line
2. where the line crosses the *y*-axis

slope = 1
(0, 3)

The *y*-coordinate where the line crosses the *y*-axis is the **y-intercept.**

Line *l* crosses the *y*-axis at (0, 3). The *y*-intercept of line *l* is 3.

CONSIDER

?

1. Can you find a *different* line from the one shown above with slope 1 that goes through (0, 3)? If so, describe or graph it.

The slope and *y*-intercept of a line can be seen on the graph. The same information is hidden in its equation!

EXPLORE: EQUATIONS REVEALED

MATERIALS

To find the slope of a line on a graphing utility, move or *trace* to any point on the line. (Integer values of *x* are usually easiest to use.) Write down or store the *x*- and *y*-coordinates of the point. Then move or *trace* to another point on the line and calculate $\frac{y_2 - y_1}{x_2 - x_1}$.

Graphing utility or Graph paper and Straightedge

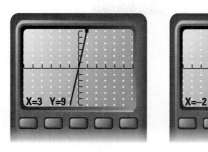

1. Graph these equations using a graphing utility, or using graph paper and pencil. Copy and complete the table and answer the questions.

Line	Slope	y-intercept
$y = 3x$		
$y = 3x + 2$		
$y = 3x - 4$		
$y = 2x + 1$		
$y = -2x + 1$		

2. What relationship do you see between these equations and the slopes and y-intercepts on the graph? Write a brief description.

3. Consider the equation $y = 4x - 5$. Without plotting points, what would you expect the slope to be? the y-intercept? (Check by graphing. Are the slope and y-intercept what you expected?)

4. Write the equation of a line with slope -2 and y-intercept 4. Use the equation to graph the line.

When a linear equation is written in the form $y = ax + b$, we can see certain information about its graph at a glance. The coefficient of x is the slope, and the constant term is the y-intercept.

Since the coefficient of x is the slope, we usually denote slope by the letter m (for *monter*—the French word meaning "to climb").

$$y = \boxed{\text{slope}}\, x + \boxed{\text{y-intercept}}$$
$$y = mx + b$$

The equation of a line can be written in the form $y = mx + b$, where m is the slope, and b is the y-intercept. This is called the **slope-intercept** form of a linear equation.

Find the slope m and y-intercept b for each linear equation.

a. $y = -5x + 7$ **b.** $y = -x - 3$ **c.** $y = \frac{1}{4}x$

Slope and y-intercept provide a quick way to graph a line. First plot the y-intercept, b, on the y-axis. Then use the slope, m, to locate other points.

EXAMPLE

1. Use the slope and y-intercept to graph $y = -5x + 2$.

To sketch a line from its equation (without plotting ordered pairs), find the y-intercept first.

Then locate a second point by counting *up* the necessary number of *rise* units (or *down* if it is negative), and *over* the necessary number of *run* units (right if positive, left if negative). Connect these points and extend the line.

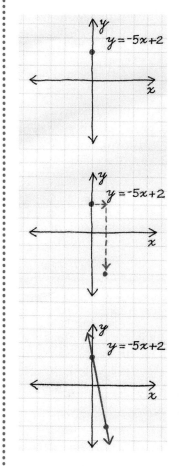

To graph $y = -5x + 2$, note that $m = -5$ or $\frac{-5}{1}$ and $b = 2$.

Since $b = 2$, the point $(0, 2)$ is on the line. Plot $(0, 2)$ on the y-axis.

Then move 1 unit to the right (run = 1) and move vertically -5 units (rise = -5) for a second point.

Connect these two points and extend the line. (As long as you keep your $\frac{\text{rise}}{\text{run}}$ ratio the same, you can locate another point on the line. You can find as many points as you need to draw the line accurately.)

2. **Could you have drawn the graph by moving *left* 1 unit and *up* 5 units from the *y*-intercept? Explain.**

TRY IT

Use the slope and *y*-intercept to graph each equation. Explain how you drew each graph.

d. $y = 2x - 6$ **e.** $y = -\dfrac{2}{3}x + 1$

Linear equations can have many forms. If a linear equation is not in the slope-intercept form you can use the Properties of Equality to transform it into the slope-intercept form.

EXAMPLE

2. Write the linear equation $\dfrac{1}{2}x + 3y - 6 = 0$ in slope-intercept form. Find the slope and *y*-intercept.

$\dfrac{1}{2}x + 3y - 6 = 0$

$3y = -\dfrac{1}{2}x + 6$ Use the Addition Property of Equality to get the *y*-term on left, and the *x*-term on right.

$\left(\dfrac{1}{3}\right)(3y) = \left(\dfrac{1}{3}\right)\left(-\dfrac{1}{2}x + 6\right)$ Use the Multiplication Property of Equality to make the coefficient of *y* equal to 1.

$y = -\dfrac{1}{6}x + 2$

The slope is $-\dfrac{1}{6}$ and the *y*-intercept is 2.

TRY IT

Write each linear equation in slope-intercept form. Find the slope and *y*-intercept.

f. $2y = 4x - 1$ **g.** $\dfrac{x}{2} - 4y = 0$

REFLECT

1. Explain how to graph any linear equation of the form $y = mx + b$.
2. Suppose the *y*-intercept of a line is 0. How does the equation $y = mx + b$ show this? Suppose the slope of a line is 0. How does the equation $y = mx + b$ show this?

Exercises

CORE

1. Getting Started The graph of the linear equation
$y = -\frac{1}{2}x + 3$ is shown.
   a. Use the graph to find the slope of the line.
   b. How is this shown in the equation?
   c. At what value of y does the line cross the y-axis?
   d. How is this shown in the equation?

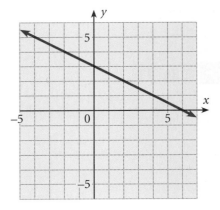

2. Which is the best description of the y-intercept?
   (a) The value of x where the graph of an equation crosses the x-axis.
   (b) The value of y where the graph of an equation crosses the x-axis.
   (c) The value of x where the graph of an equation crosses the y-axis.
   (d) The value of y where the graph of an equation crosses the y-axis.
   (e) The point on a graph where $y = 0$.

Find the slope m and y-intercept b for each linear equation.

3. $y = 3x + 2$ **4.** $y = \frac{1}{2}x - 3$ **5.** $y = -4x$

6. $y = 5$ **7.** $y = -x$

Social Science

8. Sloping Wonder The Leaning Tower of Pisa stands about 54 meters tall and leans about 5 meters out of line. That is, the top of its center line is about 5 meters from its original straight-up position. What is the approximate slope of the Leaning Tower of Pisa?

Write an equation for each line given the slope and y-intercept.

9. $m = 2, b = \frac{1}{3}$ **10.** $m = -4, b = -3$

11. $m = -200, b = 0$ **12.** $m = 0, b = 127$

13. slope $= -\frac{2}{3}$, y-intercept $= 1$

14. What is the equation of the line with slope 1 that goes through the origin?

15. Use the graph of $y = -2x + 3$ to answer these questions.
   a. What is the slope of the line?
   b. What is the y-intercept?
   c. Find x if $y = 7$.
   d. Find the value of y for $x = 0$.
   e. Which answers are the same? Explain why.
   f. If you had to find y for $x = 100$, what would you do?

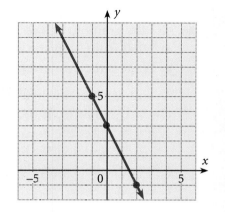

16. Find the slope and the y-intercept for each linear equation.
   a. $2y - 2x = 4$ **b.** $20 - 4y = 3x$
   c. $36x = 6y$

Use the slope and y-intercept to graph each line.

17. $y = 2x - 4$ **18.** $y = -\dfrac{3}{5}x + 2$

19. $y = -2x$ **20.** $y = -3.5$ **21.** $y = x$

Write the linear equation in slope-intercept form.

22. $8y + 2x - 6 = 0$ **23.** $\dfrac{1}{4}x = 3y$ **24.** $0.4x + 0.5y - 10 = 0$

25. Water Line The Swim Club uses the Municipal Pool which has a $10 fee to join. Then, each visit costs only 50¢.
   a. Make a chart showing the relationship between cost and number of visits.
   b. Graph the relationship.
   c. Write an equation to describe the graph.
   d. Explain how slope and y-intercept relate to real-world situations.

26. Car Toon Rent-a-Car rents cars for $79 plus 5¢ per mile. Otto's Autos charges $58 plus 15¢ per mile. (Hint: Choose the scale for your graph carefully.)
   a. Graph the cost of renting a car from each company.
   b. What is the meaning of each y-intercept? of each slope?
   c. Describe the domains and ranges of the functions that the graphs represent.

27. Line Up! Chane did his work on a graphing utility but forgot to match the graphs with the equations. His assignment was to graph $y = 0.5x$, $y = \dfrac{1}{2}x + 1$, and $y = 0.5x - 2$.
   a. Match the equations with the screens.
   b. What is the same in each line?   **c.** What is different in each line?

```
Xmin=-6
Xmax=6
Xscl=1
Ymin=-6
Ymax=6
Yscl=1
```

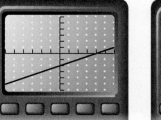
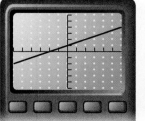
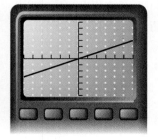

28. Use the graph to answer these questions about line l.

　a. What is the slope of line l?

　b. What is the y-intercept of line l? Is 0 the y-intercept?

As you can see, this line cannot be represented in $y = mx + b$ form. It must be written differently.

　c. If $y = -2$ is the equation for line h, what would be a logical equation for line l?

　d. What is the x-coordinate of all points on line l?

　e. Graph $y = 3$.

　f. Graph $x = -1$.

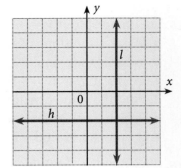

29. Steady Rollers The city of Oakland, California, *recommends* that wheelchair ramps have a slope of $\frac{1}{15}$ and *requires* that the slope not exceed $\frac{1}{12}$. It also requires a flat platform at least 5 feet square in front of the door. The height of Andrea's front-door entrance is 18 inches above the level of the sidewalk. The distance from the front door to the sidewalk is 26 feet. Can a ramp be built that meets the recommended standards? If not, will it meet the required standards?

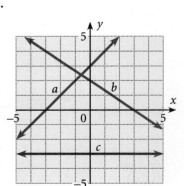

LOOK AHEAD

Simplify each expression.

30. $2 - (-4)$

31. $-3 - 6$

32. $\dfrac{4}{-6}$

33. $\dfrac{-8}{-2}$

34. Evaluate $y_2 - y_1$ for $y_1 = 5$ and $y_2 = -2$.

35. Evaluate $\dfrac{y_2 - y_1}{x_2 - x_1}$ for $y_1 = -3$, $y_2 = -6$, $x_1 = 9$, and $x_2 = -4$.

Use the graph of lines *a*, *b*, and *c*.

36. Find the slope of line a.

37. Find the slope of line b.

38. Find the slope of line c.

Solve each equation for *b*.

39. $-4 = \dfrac{1}{2}(-3) + b$

40. $10 = -3(-4) + b$

41. $0 = \dfrac{-3}{4}(12) + b$

MORE PRACTICE

42. Consider the line represented by the equation $y = 2x + 3$.
    a. What is its slope?
    b. Where does it intercept the y-axis?
    c. Sketch it on a coordinate plane.

Write an equation for each line given the slope and y-intercept.

43. $m = \dfrac{2}{3}, b = \dfrac{3}{4}$ **44.** $m = -6, b = 0$ **45.** $m = 0, b = -4$

46. Slope $= 2$, y-intercept $= -2$

47. Slope $= -0.5$, y-intercept $= 5$

Write the linear equation in slope-intercept form.

48. $3y - 4x + 1 = 0$ **49.** $\dfrac{3}{5}x = 2y$

50. $1.5x + 0.25y + 4 = 0$ **51.** $2 - 3x = 5y + 5$

Use the slope and y-intercept to graph each line.

52. $y = 2x - 6$ **53.** $y = 4x$ **54.** $x + 2y = -6$

55. $y = 3x + 2$ **56.** $y = -4$ **57.** $y = -x$

58. $y = -\dfrac{1}{2}x - 3.5$ **59.** $y = 1.25x$ **60.** $y = -x + 4$

MORE MATH REASONING

61. Solve $y = mx + b$ for x. Use the result to find x in $y = 3x - 5$ when y is 6.

62. Find three more points with integer coordinates that lie on the line through $(6, 5)$ with slope $\dfrac{2}{3}$.

63. Plot each line on the same coordinate plane. What is the area of the geometric figure bounded by the lines?
$$y = -2x + 3 \qquad x = -1 \qquad x - 2y = 4$$

64. To conserve paper, a small graph has been used to show a line. Name the other point on the line, given only one of the coordinates.
    a. $(-16, \underline{\quad})$ **b.** $(\underline{\quad}, -60)$
    c. $(\underline{\quad}, 60)$ **d.** $(10.2, \underline{\quad})$

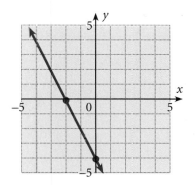

Two-Point Equation of a Line

← C O N N E C T → *You know how the concepts of slope and y-intercept are used to graph linear equations. Now you will see how to graph a linear equation if you only know two points on the line.*

So far, you have been using the equation of a line to find ordered pairs. But suppose you know only the coordinates of two points. How could you find the equation of the line that contains them?

There is only one line that passes through two given points. In other words, two points *determine* a line.

EXPLORE: WHAT'S MY LINE?

MATERIALS

Graph paper
Straightedge

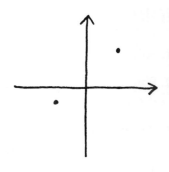

1. Choose two random points in a coordinate plane. Draw the line through your points.
2. Use your graph to find the slope and *y*-intercept. Write the slope-intercept equation of the line.
3. Explain the procedure you used to find the equation of the line.

To write the equation of a line through two given points, use the form $y = mx + b$.

Find *m* from the given coordinates. Then, find *b* by solving an equation.

1. Write an equation of the line through the points $(-2, 2)$ and $(3, 1)$.

First, find the slope of the line.

$$m = \frac{y_2 - y_1}{x_2 - x_1} = \frac{1 - 2}{3 - (-2)} = \frac{-1}{5} = -\frac{1}{5}$$

Substitute this value into $y = mx + b$.

$$y = mx + b$$

$$y = -\frac{1}{5}x + b$$

Now, find the y-intercept.

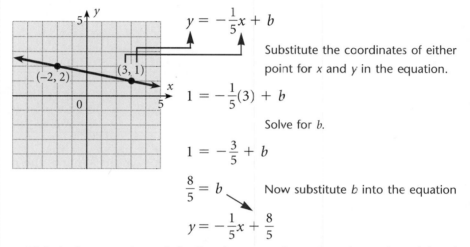

$$y = -\frac{1}{5}x + b$$

Substitute the coordinates of either point for x and y in the equation.

$$1 = -\frac{1}{5}(3) + b$$

Solve for b.

$$1 = -\frac{3}{5} + b$$

$$\frac{8}{5} = b$$

Now substitute b into the equation

$$y = -\frac{1}{5}x + \frac{8}{5}$$

This is the equation of the line between the points $(-2, 2)$ and $(3, 1)$.

Check your equation. If both points are on the line, both ordered pairs are solutions to the equation. Since we used $(3, 1)$ to find the equation, we use $(-2, 2)$ to check.

$$y \stackrel{?}{=} -\frac{1}{5}x + \frac{8}{5} \qquad \text{Start with the equation.}$$

$$2 \stackrel{?}{=} -\frac{1}{5}(-2) + \frac{8}{5} \qquad \text{Substitute } -2 \text{ for } x \text{ and } 2 \text{ for } y.$$

$$2 \stackrel{?}{=} \frac{2}{5} + \frac{8}{5} \qquad \text{Multiply.}$$

$$2 = 2 ✔ \qquad \text{The solution } (-2, 2) \text{ checks.}$$

Since both points are on the line and only one line can go through two points, the equation is correct.

Write an equation of the line through each pair of points.

a. $(0, 6)$ and $(2, -4)$ **b.** $(-4, 5)$ and $(2, 8)$

In many applications such as economics, the rate of change and *y*-intercept of a linear function have real-world meaning. Costs may be broken down into *fixed costs* and *variable costs*. For example, if you own a car, you pay fixed costs for insurance, registration, plates, and so on. Variable costs result from miles driven—for gasoline, oil, tires, and so on.

For linear models $y = mx + b$, fixed costs are determined when $x = 0$.

EXAMPLE

2. A college has included its fixed room and board fees for first-year students into its total cost schedule. In a brochure, they list typical costs for tuition and room and board for a semester. The tuition cost for each credit is constant.

Credits	Total Cost
12	$4,810
15	$5,350
18	$5,890

What is the tuition cost per credit? What is the room and board cost?

$$\overbrace{\text{variable costs}} \qquad + \qquad \overbrace{\text{fixed costs}}$$

total cost = tuition per credit · number of credits + room and board

Let y = total cost and x = the number of credits.

Since tuition cost per credit is constant, total cost is a linear function of the number of credits. So we can use the function $y = mx + b$. Use any two rows of the table to find two ordered pairs. We can use (12, 4810) and (15, 5350).

$$\frac{y_2 - y_1}{x_2 - x_1} = \frac{5350 - 4810}{15 - 12} = \frac{540}{3} = 180$$

Substitute 180 into $y = mx + b$ to get $y = 180x + b$.

Substitute one of the ordered pairs: $4810 = 180(12) + b$.

$$4810 = 2160 + b$$
$$2650 = b$$

The linear function is $y = 180x + 2650$.

The cost per credit is $180. The cost for room and board is $2650.

CONSIDER

?

1. Suppose you evaluate the linear function in Example 2 by substituting 18 credits and do not get $5890. What are the possible implications?

REFLECT

1. How many different lines can be drawn through two points?
2. If $(-2, 14)$ is a point on the line $y = 2x + b$, how would you find b?
3. Explain how to find the slope and y-intercept of a line if you know the coordinates of two points on it.

Exercises

CORE

1. **Getting Started** Use these steps to find the equation of the line through the points $(3, 4)$ and $(1, 6)$.
   a. Find the slope of the line segment between the two points using $m = \dfrac{y_2 - y_1}{x_2 - x_1}$.
   b. Rewrite the equation $y = mx + b$ using your value for m.
   c. Substitute either $(3, 4)$ or $(1, 6)$ for x and y into the new equation. Solve for b.
   d. Substitute m and b into the equation $y = mx + b$.
   e. Check to see that both points are solutions to the equation.

Write an equation of the line through each pair of points.

2. $(-5, 2)$ and $(-6, 0)$
3. $(-3, 0)$ and $(0, -4)$
4. $(64, -32)$ and $(52, -28)$
5. $(-3, -9)$ and $(0, -9)$

Write the equation of each line.

6. the line with slope 7 passing through $(3, 11)$

7. the line passing through the origin with slope 0

8. Crickets chirp about 30 times per minute when the temperature is 48°F, but 110 times per minute when the temperature is 68°F.
   a. Write an equation for this relationship.
   b. Predict the number of chirps per minute when the temperature is 80°F.
   c. Suppose you hear crickets chirping 200 times per minute. What is the temperature?

9. Regular leaded gasoline at 87.5 octane costs $1.19 per gallon. Super Unleaded at 92 octane costs $1.42 per gallon. Assuming a linear function, how much should the new mid-grade gasoline at 89 octane cost per gallon?

Industry

10. The weight of a volume of water depends on the number of gallons.

Science

  a. What is the equation of the line?
  b. What does C show?
  c. What is the weight of 100 gallons of water? How did you find it?
  d. How many gallons of water would weigh 100 pounds?
  e. A half-gallon of water has a volume of 64 fluid ounces. Does a fluid ounce of water weigh exactly 1 ounce? more than 1 ounce? less than 1 ounce? Defend your reasoning.

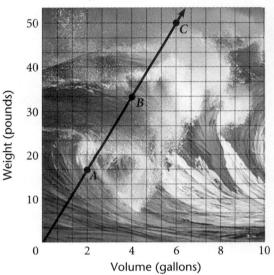

Weight Versus Volume for Water

11. Bruce has played 11 basketball games and has a 17-point average.

  a. How many points would he need to score in his next game to raise his average 1 point? 2 points?
  b. Plot these as ordered pairs: (increase in average desired, points needed).
  c. Write the equation of the line through these ordered pairs.
  d. How are the slope and y-intercept of the linear function related to the number of games Bruce played and his current average?

12. Speed Demons You are the judge in traffic court. A new judge asks you to explain how to determine the fines. What is your explanation?

Social Science

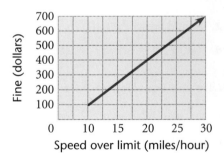

The equation $y - y_1 = m(x - x_1)$ is called the point-slope equation of a line.

13. Verify that $y - 3 = 4(x - 2)$ is an equation of the line through $(2, 3)$ that has slope 4.

14. Using $m = \dfrac{y - y_1}{x - x_1}$, explain how to get the point-slope equation $y - y_1 = m(x - x_1)$.

Write the equation of each line. Show the steps you used.

15. the line with slope 4 through $(2, -6)$ **16.** the line with slope -3 through $(-1, 4)$

 ## *LOOK BACK*

Name the two quantities in each situation. State whether they are directly or inversely related. [2-1]

Social Science

17. The distance you drive on a vacation to Chicago and the amount of money you spend on gasoline.

18. The amount of money you pay for gas and the number of people sharing the cost of the gasoline.

Industry

19. Making Money Ken is a new zookeeper. He is paid by the hour for a 40-hour work week plus a bonus of $20 per week to work the evening shift. The equation $40x + 20 = y$ shows the relationship between Ken's hourly wage and his weekly salary. [4-2]
 a. What does each of the following represent? $40x$; $40x + 20$; y
 b. If Ken earned $310 last week, write an equation and find his hourly wage.
 c. Suppose Ken got a raise after six months of employment. He is still working the evening shift. If his weekly paycheck is now $340, how much of an hourly increase did he receive?

20. Without graphing, find the slope of the line through $(-5, 7)$ and $(6, -10)$. [5-1]

MORE PRACTICE

Write the equation of the line that connects each pair of points.

21. $(1, 5)$ and $(3, 9)$ **22.** $(3, 2)$ and $(5, 10)$

23. $(-1, 4)$ and $(-5, 0)$ **24.** $(3.5, 13)$ and $(8.5, 18)$

25. $(2, 2)$ and $(7, -8)$ **26.** $(-6, -3)$ and $(0, -7)$

27. $(-6, 4)$ and $(-9, 5)$ **28.** $(-2, 0)$ and $(0, -8)$

Assume each situation can be modeled by a linear function.

29. A 9-ounce cup of freshly squeezed orange juice costs $1.25. A 12-ounce cup costs $1.60.
 a. Name two ordered pairs that belong to this function.
 b. Write the linear equation.
 c. How much would a 16-ounce cup cost?
 d. How much would a 5-ounce cup cost?

30. On day 20 of training, Phil can run a quarter mile in 68 seconds. On day 60, he can run it in 58 seconds.
 a. Name two ordered pairs that belong to this function.
 b. Write the linear equation.
 c. How long would it take Phil to run a quarter mile on day 90?

MORE MATH REASONING

31. Patty has been training for a speed-walking race. Throughout her training, her time has always been a function of the number of weeks she has been training. Let x be the number of weeks Patty has been training, and let y be her time in seconds per mile. After 2 weeks of training, Patty's time for walking 1 mile was down to 720 seconds. After 8 weeks, her time was down to 480 seconds.

a. Name two ordered pairs that belong to this function.

b. Express Patty's training program as an equation.

c. What was Patty's time after 3 weeks?

d. What was Patty's time at the beginning of her program?

e. If Patty continues to shorten her walking time, how many weeks will it take for her to reach her goal of 300 seconds per mile?

f. What is the slope of the line that represents Patty's reduction in time?

g. What is the y-intercept of that line? When was Patty's time that amount?

h. The value of x at the point where the line crosses the x-axis is the **x-intercept.** Can Patty ever reach the x-intercept of her training line? Explain.

32. If you have three points, how could you determine without graphing whether they are all on the same line?

33. Kelly found that the number of work stoppages due to labor disputes in 1982 was 96, and that there was a steady drop in the number each year, to 35 in 1992. She found the equation of a line through these two data points and concluded, "This means there will be no more work stoppages after 1997." What is your analysis? Explain in writing.

34. In an area of West Africa, a customer must pay 31 cedis for a portion of soup and 13 additional cedis for each piece of meat he wishes to have in his soup. You could say that the cost of soup is a function of how much meat is in it.

a. Define the variables and express the cost of soup as an expression.

b. What will it cost to have 10 pieces of meat in the soup?

c. For 200 cedis, how many pieces of meat can the customer have in his soup?

Slope and Dimensional Analysis

← C O N N E C T → *In Chapter 1, you may have noticed how changing the scale of a graph gives a different picture of the data. Now you will see how the graph of a line appears different when different scales are used.*

EXPLORE: POWER UP!

MATERIALS

Graphing utility
Graph paper
Straightedge

Anthony, Will, and Jason are still growing, but they are actively working on body strengthening and development as well. Their body masses are increasing, and they have been charting their weight daily. At the end of the first four weeks of their program, each boy made a graph showing the relationship between the number of weeks he had been exercising and his weight in pounds.

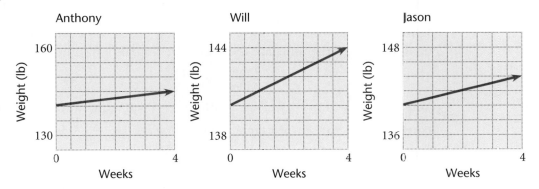

1. At first glance, who *appears* to have gained the most? the least?
2. Copy each graph and complete the labeling of the scales. Use this information to find the slope of each line.
3. What is the equation of each line in slope-intercept form?
4. How much did each boy gain through the four weeks?
5. Why do Will's and Jason's lines look different? Did the scale each boy used have an effect on the slope of the line?
6. If he continues gaining at a steady rate, what will Anthony weigh after eight weeks? When will he weigh 158 pounds?
7. Use a graphing utility to plot each boy's weight using the same window, or plot each boy's weight on one graph, using a different color for each. What is the advantage of this graph over the other three?

As you can see, *scale* has a significant effect on the appearance of graphs. The graph of a linear function can look different depending on the scales used for the coordinate plane. To compare graphs visually, corresponding scales on each graph must be the same.

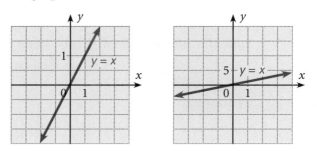

1. If the vertical scales on Will's and Jason's graphs had been the same, but the horizontal scales were different, would the graphs have looked the same? Explain.

Using the units when you solve a problem is called **dimensional analysis.** When the units are the same, the slope is a number:

$$\frac{1 \text{ mm}}{3 \text{ mm}} = \frac{1 \text{ mm}}{3 \text{ mm}} = \frac{1}{3}.$$

You can change units by using a ratio of two equal quantities called a **conversion factor.** For example, multiplying by $\frac{60 \text{ seconds}}{1 \text{ minute}}$ is the same as multiplying by 1 since $\frac{60 \text{ seconds}}{1 \text{ minute}} = \frac{60 \text{ seconds}}{60 \text{ seconds}} = 1.$

EXAMPLE

> **Problem-Solving Tip**
>
> Convert the units one step at a time.

1. A duck hawk can dive $\frac{1}{20}$ of a mile in 1 second. To compare its speed to those of other animals, change this rate to *miles per hour.*

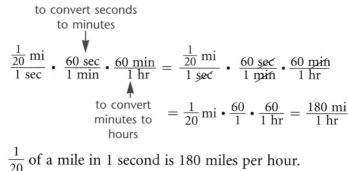

$\frac{1}{20}$ of a mile in 1 second is 180 miles per hour.

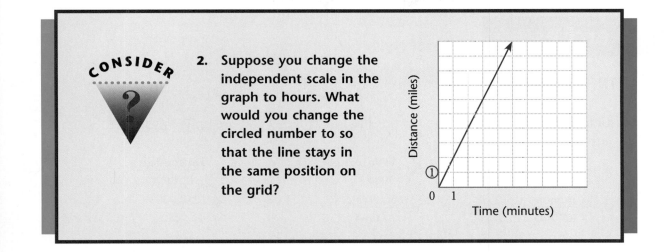

CONSIDER

2. Suppose you change the independent scale in the graph to hours. What would you change the circled number to so that the line stays in the same position on the grid?

TRY IT

Express each rate in pounds per week. Use one or more of the following conversion factors.

$$\frac{7 \text{ days}}{1 \text{ week}} \qquad \frac{1 \text{ year}}{52 \text{ weeks}} \qquad \frac{1 \text{ pound}}{16 \text{ ounces}} \qquad \frac{2000 \text{ pounds}}{1 \text{ ton}}$$

a. 10 pounds in four weeks   **b.** $\frac{1}{2}$ pound per day

c. 20 pounds per year   **d.** 8 ounces per day

e. 2 tons per year   **f.** 104 ounces per year

Conversion factors are widely used in science, when units are used throughout a calculation. Rates are used in many physics and chemistry formulas.

REFLECT

1. If both axes describe quantities with the same units, why doesn't the slope need units?

2. Determine how the appearance of the line will change

     a. if the numbers on both axes are doubled.

     b. if the numbers on both axes are halved.

     c. if the numbers on only the y-axis are halved.

3. Explain how a conversion factor works.

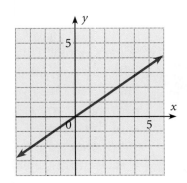

Exercises

CORE

1. **Getting Started** Reduce these fractions to lowest terms and use units in your answer.

   a. $\dfrac{40 \text{ people}}{10 \text{ tables}}$ **b.** $\dfrac{\$495}{5 \text{ weeks}}$ **c.** $\dfrac{121 \text{ modems}}{11 \text{ hours}}$

   d. $\dfrac{\$8 \text{ million}}{12 \text{ months}}$ **e.** $\dfrac{6500 \text{ crates}}{5 \text{ days}}$ **f.** $\dfrac{\$240,000}{16 \text{ years}}$

2. Write the word or phrase that correctly completes the statement. When using dimensional analysis, we use one or more _____ to obtain the appropriate units.

Industry
3. A carat is a unit of weight equal to 200 milligrams. One ounce is approximately 28.35 grams, and there are 1000 milligrams to the gram. The Hope diamond weighs 45.5 carats. What is its weight in ounces?

Science
4. A hummingbird weighs 0.39 ounce; a blue whale 153.5 tons. How many hummingbirds does it take to weigh the same as the whale?

Health
5. Suppose a meal contains 350 calories and 23 grams of fat; 1 gram of fat provides 9 calories. What percent of the calories are from fat?

Convert these rates of change to the units in the parentheses.

6. 12 pounds per year (pounds per month)

7. 6 pounds per week (pounds per month)

8. 2 pounds per month (pounds per week)

9. 32 miles per gallon (miles per quart)

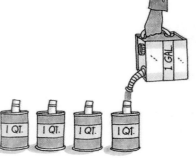

Industry
10. **Sugar Coated?** This is a graph of the annual sales of a popular cereal when it was first introduced many years ago.
    a. What are you able to tell about the sales of this cereal?
    b. What are you *not* able to tell about the sales of this cereal?
    c. How could this graph be improved for a sales presentation?

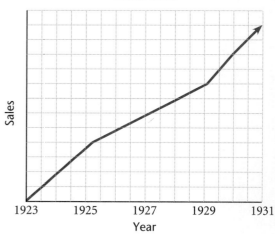

Cereal Sales

11. Use the graphs to answer the questions.

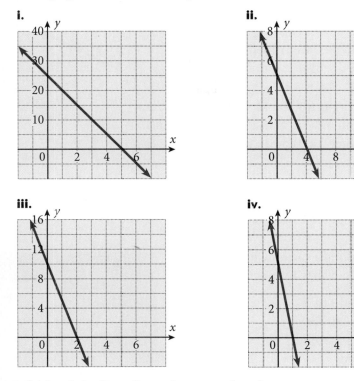

i.

ii.

iii.

iv.

a. Which of the lines have the same slope?
b. What is this slope?
c. What is the slope of the "oddball"?

12. Got Your Goat On the scale at home, Ted's goat weighs 50 pounds. On the scale at the vet's, his goat weighs 22.6 kilograms.

a. If the goat weighed 1 pound (0.453 kg) when it was born 14 weeks ago, at what average rate did it grow in pounds per week?
b. Show the rate of growth in lb/wk on Graph A.
c. At what average rate did the goat grow in kilograms per week?
d. Show the rate of growth in kilograms on Graph B.
e. What is the slope of each line?
f. On which graph does the goat seem to have grown faster? Explain why in your own words.
g. What is the weight of Ted's 5-pound cat in kilograms?

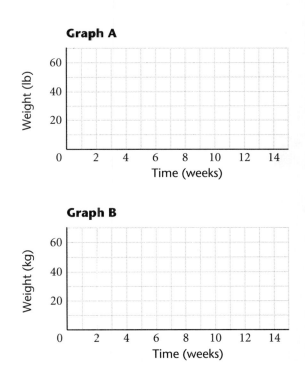

Graph A

Graph B

13. Determine how the appearance of the line will change
   a. if each interval on the vertical axis is 0.5 instead of 1.
   b. if each interval on the horizontal axis is 2 instead of 1.
   c. if the scale numbers on both axes are tripled. How did you decide?

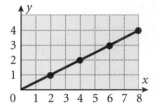

14. I Walk Faster in Feet! Suppose a person walks 4 miles in 2 hours. This is the same as 21,120 feet in 120 minutes. Using $(0, 0)$ and $(2, 4)$ gives a slope of 2. But using $(0, 0)$ and $(120, 21,120)$ gives a slope of 176. Why are these different?

15. Convert 55 feet per second to miles per hour. How could you use world records to determine whether a person has ever run 30 miles per hour?

16. Patwin is reading *Twenty Thousand Leagues Under the Sea*, and wonders how far that is. He charts his research.

Literature

$$1 \text{ league} = 3.45 \text{ miles}$$
$$1 \text{ mile} = 5280 \text{ feet}$$
$$\text{diameter of the earth} = 7927 \text{ miles}$$
$$\text{circumference} = \pi d$$

   a. What is a league in miles? in feet?
   b. How many times could a string 20,000 leagues long wrap around the equator?

Captain Nemo observes a giant octopus. Illustration from Jules Verne, *Twenty Thousand Leagues Under the Sea.*

17. Groundhog Day In chemistry, a *mole* is a unit of measurement that represents the number of particles of a substance. The mass of 1 mole of a compound is found from its atomic formula. One mole of hydrogen has a mass of 1 gram. Oxygen has a mass of 16 grams. So the mass of 1 mole of water, H_2O, is $1 + 1 + 16 = 18$ grams.

Science

   a. Twelve grams of charcoal contain 1 mole of carbon (C). Use the fact that 1 pound is about 454 grams to find how many moles of carbon there are in 50 pounds of charcoal.
   b. Find the mass of 1 mole of table sugar, $H_{12}C_{22}O_{11}$.
   c. How many moles of water are there in 1 kilogram of water? How many moles of table sugar are there in 1 kilogram of table sugar?

Find the slope of each line.

18.

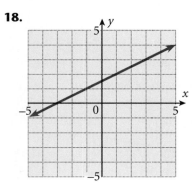

19.

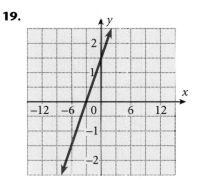

20. Sketch a line with slope -3.

MORE PRACTICE

21. Look again at this graph of annual cereal sales.

Industry

a. Using only the unlabeled *y*-axis, what could you do to the graph to make the improvement in sales appear even better?

b. Using only the unlabeled *y*-axis, what could a competitor do to make the cereal seem less popular?

c. Describe changes to the *x*-axis that would make the cereal seem more or less popular.

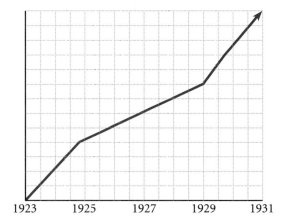

Convert these rates to the units in the parentheses.

22. 84¢ per dozen (each)

23. 320 calories per pint (calories per cup) (Hint: A pint is 16 ounces, a cup is 8 ounces.)

24. 3.5 inches per day (inches per week)

25. 40 calories per ounce (calories per pound)

26. $50 per 1000 (per 25)

27. 7 bushels per day (quarts per week) (Hint: 1 bushel = 4 pecks, 1 peck = 8 quarts)

MORE MATH REASONING

28. Comparison Shopping The graphs indicate a 5-year increase in the prices of Brand X and Brand Y.

  a. What is the rate of increase per year of Brand X?
  b. What is the rate of increase per year of Brand Y?
  c. Explain in your own words what is misleading about these graphs.

Price History of Brand X

Price History of Brand Y

29. This is Pretty Scary! The improper disposal of used motor oil is a serious threat to the environment. This has disastrous effects! *One gallon* of used motor oil poured on the ground, down storm drains, on dirt roadways, or in the household trash can contaminate *1 million gallons* of groundwater—a year's supply for 50 people! The amount of polluted water is a function of the amount of oil disposed of improperly.

  a. Plot this function on a graph. What units have you used on the scale for each axis?
  b. What is the slope of the line?
  c. What is the *y*-intercept of this line? What real-world meaning does the *y*-intercept have?
  d. What is the equation of the line?
  e. Make a second graph, but plot people whose water supply is contaminated on the axis where you had earlier plotted gallons of contaminated water.
  f. What is the slope of this second line?
  g. What is the *y*-intercept of this line? What is its interpretation in the real world?
  h. A rural town of 400 people has 150 vehicles. Each vehicle holds 1.25 gallons of oil. How many careless oil changes will it take in a year before the water supply for the entire town has been contaminated?

30. Meeting Yourself Coming and Going At dawn one morning, a shepherd began to climb a mountain. He followed a path that spiraled up the mountain until he came to a cabin at the very top. At dawn the next day, he started back down, following the same path. He traveled more quickly than before. Is there a point on the path that the shepherd passed at precisely the same time of day?

> **Problem-Solving Tip**
>
> Draw a graph.

← **CONNECT** → *You know that the points of a scatter plot may have a linear association without forming a totally straight line on a graph. Now you will learn how you can "fit" a trend line to this type of data.*

Recall from Chapter 1 that the line that approximates a graph is called a **trend line.** It may also be called a line of best fit, if it is the line that best fits the data points.

In Yosemite National Park, there is a close positive association between the maximum and minimum daily temperatures. That is, high daytime temperatures tend to correspond to high nighttime temperatures. Low daytime temperatures correspond to low nighttime temperatures. A graph shows this positive association. A positive linear trend emerges, even though the data do not fall on a straight line.

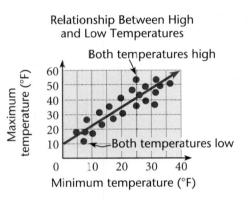

Relationship Between High and Low Temperatures

Both temperatures high

Both temperatures low

Since it rarely rains in summer, rainfall is less when temperatures are high. A graph of daily high temperatures and precipitation—rain or snow— looks like this. The trend line for the data would have a negative slope.

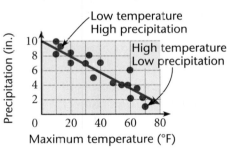

Relationship Between Precipitation and Temperature

Low temperature High precipitation

High temperature Low precipitation

In the following Explore, you will plot points, draw the trend line, and find its equation. Or you may use a graphing utility to do the same thing. Working with pencil and paper first will help you understand what the graphing utility does. It uses an advanced technique to find a trend line.

MATERIALS

Graph paper
Straightedge
Graphing utility (optional)

This chart contains three years of data about eleven U.S. National Parks. For each park, there is information about its size, the number of recreational visits, and the number of overnight stays.

Many questions might be asked. Is the size of the park associated with the number of visits? Are recreational visits associated with overnight stays? Are overnight stays associated in successive years? There are some surprises here!

Area	Federal Acres (1,000)	Recreational Visits (millions)			Overnight Stays (thousands)		
		1985	1986	1987	1985	1986	1987
Blue Ridge Parkway	79	17.2	17.1	18.6	230	249	246
Death Valley Natl. Monument	2049	0.6	0.6	0.7	337	328	314
Glen Canyon Natl. Rec. Area	1194	2.1	2.4	2.9	1628	1965	2062
Golden Gate Natl. Rec. Area	28	18.3	21.6	21.8	99	112	112
Grand Canyon Natl. Park	1179	2.7	3.0	3.5	733	631	866
Great Smoky Mt. Natl. Park	520	9.3	9.8	10.2	479	460	495
Olympic Natl. Park	911	2.5	2.9	2.8	375	366	372
Rocky Mt. Natl. Park	264	2.2	2.4	2.5	201	197	205
Shenandoah Natl. Park	195	1.9	1.8	1.8	430	362	354
Yellowstone Natl. Park	2220	2.2	2.4	2.6	1270	1308	1398
Yosemite Natl. Park	759	2.8	2.9	3.2	2068	1884	2199

1. Make some conjectures about associations you expect to find in the data. For what quantities might you expect to find no association?
2. Choose one conjecture to test. Identify clearly what quantities you need to study to test your conjecture. Make a coordinate grid, indicating the independent and dependent variables. Decide a reasonable scale for each axis.
3. Plot the data and study the associations that you find. If you use a graphing utility, you may enter data and use the *linear regression* option to find a trend line (sometimes called the *line of best fit*).
4. Write your conclusions. How could the National Park Service use your conclusions?

Blue Ridge Parkway

You can use trend lines to make predictions.

EXAMPLE

A company that develops answering machines has tested a model to determine how much time a machine will take to rewind a cassette tape. These are the average rewind times for one side of some standard-length cassettes.

Playback time (minutes)	23	30	45	50	60
Rewind time (seconds)	95	106	124	135	148

Estimate the equation of a trend line. Use the trend line for the data shown to predict the rewind times for a 15-minute side and for a 90-minute side.

Choosing the two convenient points on the graph, the slope is approximately

$$\frac{y_2 - y_1}{x_2 - x_1} = \frac{120 - 62}{40 - 0} = \frac{58}{40} = 1.45$$

The equation of the trend line that we found is about $y = 62 + 1.45x$.

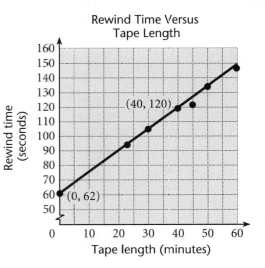

Rewind Time Versus Tape Length

The rewind time for a 15-minute side is about $62 + 1.45(15) = 83.75$, or 84 seconds. The rewind time for a 90-minute side is about $62 + 1.45(90) = 192.5$, or 193 seconds.

TRY IT

a. Use a point other than (40, 120) in the example to estimate the slope and write a different equation. Use this equation to predict the rewind time for a 76-minute side.

CONSIDER

1. If your trend line predicts that y should be 20 when x is 8, but (8, 17) is one of your data points, does this mean that the trend line is incorrect?

1. What does a trend line or line of best fit enable you to do? Give an example.
2. How do you find the equation of a trend line? Explain.
3. For what types of scatter plots would a trend line be inappropriate? Why?
4. What is the difference between a linear function and a set of paired data with a strong linear association?

Exercises

CORE

1. Getting Started
   a. Plot the points (4, 10), (7, 14), and (9, 18.5).
   b. Graph the line $y = 2x + 1$.
   c. Is the graph of the equation a good trend line for these data points? Why or why not?

2. What association would you expect to find between grades and shoe size? Explain.

Find the equation of the trend line between each pair of points.

3. (3, 5) and (7, 11)   **4.** (0, 14) and (36, 2)   **5.** (-3, -1) and (-12, 5)

6. DisSolve This The amount of potassium bromide that will dissolve in 100 grams of water is based upon the water temperature. The graph shows the results of several experiments.
   a. What is the equation of the trend line?
   b. What do the slope and y-intercept tell you about this situation?
   c. Predict the amount of potassium bromide that will dissolve in water that is 90°C.

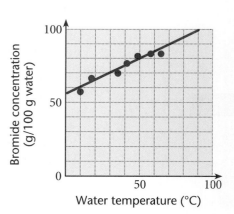

7. A trend line is fit through 50 data points on a scatter plot; 6 points fall exactly on the trend line.
   a. What is the probability that a randomly selected point falls on the trend line?
   b. What would you estimate is the probability that a randomly selected point falls below the trend line? Why?

8. These data are math and science grades at the end of a semester for 10 students.

Student	1	2	3	4	5	6	7	8	9	10
Math	77	90	85	80	95	72	80	92	85	70
Science	83	95	90	90	95	85	80	90	85	80

a. Make a scatter plot of the data.
b. How would you describe the association between math and science grades? (positive? negative? strong? weak? none?)
c. Draw a line through this scatter plot that fits it well.
d. What is the slope of this line?
e. What is the y-intercept of this line?
f. Find the equation of your trend line.
g. Using this equation, what would you predict that a student with a 50% in math will get in science?
h. Using this equation, what would you predict that a student with a 50% in science will get in math?
i. Would you expect your predictions to be absolutely true? Explain.

9. A courier has noticed that it is easy to find the nearest cross street for an address on Michigan Avenue. Estimate the equation of the trend line. Use the trend line for the data shown to predict the cross street for street address 17; for street address 12250.

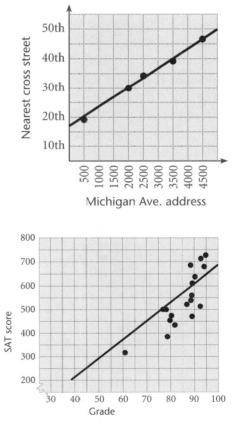

10. SAT Scatter Ms. McMath wanted to know if her students' year-end grades correlated with their SAT scores. This is her scatter plot. The equation for her trend line is $y = 8x - 110$.
a. Use the equation to estimate the score students might expect to get if they have an end-of-the-year grade of 94.
b. Did the student who had a grade of 94 get the exact SAT score predicted by the trend line? Explain.

11. Worldwide Weather Two pen pals wondered about the weather in each other's part of the world. From Minneapolis, Keith sent graph paper with numbered axes to Pak in Singapore. Six months later they traded data. Here are their graphs.

a. Imagine a trend line through the data in each graph. What does the slope of each trend line suggest about the rate of change of temperature during those months in each place?

b. Does it seem reasonable to you that it would be significantly colder in Singapore in the spring than in Minneapolis? Explain your answer.

c. Is anything important missing from these graphs that would clarify the differences in weather in Singapore and in Minneapolis? Explain.

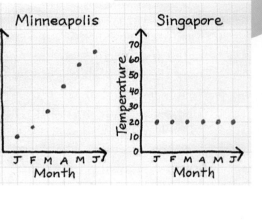

In fact, Keith intended the temperatures on both graphs to be in degrees Fahrenheit, but didn't mention that to Pak. So the numbers on Pak's Singapore graph are in degrees Celsius. To compare the rates of change, Keith has to convert degrees Celsius to degrees Fahrenheit. He can use the thermometer shown at the left or the formula $F = \frac{9}{5}C + 32$.

d. Make a new graph for Singapore (using a Fahrenheit scale) and compare it to the Minneapolis graph.

e. Summarize your finding about the rates of temperature change in these two places.

12. The Plot Thickens Erica and Brian used these scatter plots as part of a science assignment.

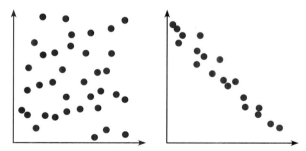

a. For which scatter plot do you think their trend lines are almost the same? Explain.

b. How does the number of data points affect the difficulty of drawing a trend line?

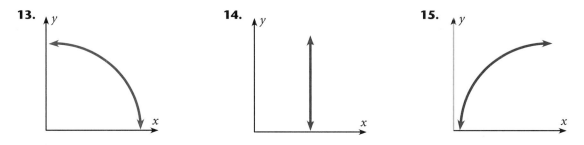

LOOK BACK

For each graph, tell whether the two quantities are directly related, inversely related, or if one is constant as the other varies. Tell how you decided. [2-1]

13.

14.

15.

16. For which equation(s) is 2 a solution? [4-2]
   I. $3x - 4 = 2$ II. $2(x - 4) - 3(8 - 3x) = x - 12$ III. $x - 3 = 1$
   (a) I only   (b) II only   (c) III only   (d) I and II only   (e) I, II, and III

17. An auto that has traveled 135 miles in 3 hours continues on for a total of 465 miles in 9 hours. What is the rate of change in miles per hour during the last 6 hours? Tell how you decided. [5-1]

MORE PRACTICE

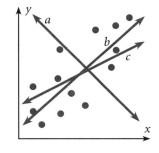

18. Which is the best trend line for the data shown?

19. **Strrreeeetttccchhh** Engineers will tell you that the length to which a 3-inch coiled spring will stretch is a function of the size of the weight attached to the end of it. Consider this graph.
   a. How long will a 3-pound weight stretch the spring?
   b. How much weight will stretch the spring to 7 inches?
   c. What is the slope of this line?
   d. What is the y-intercept of this line?
   e. What is the equation of this line?
   f. To what length would you expect a 16-pound weight to stretch the spring?

Science

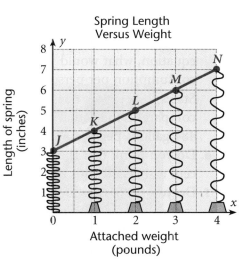

Spring Length Versus Weight

Length of spring (inches)

Attached weight (pounds)

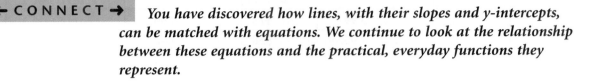

5-2 PART E Making Connections

← **C O N N E C T** → *You have discovered how lines, with their slopes and y-intercepts, can be matched with equations. We continue to look at the relationship between these equations and the practical, everyday functions they represent.*

Real-world data often have function relationships that can be written as equations. The equations can be used to make predictions, with or without graphs.

EXPLORE: KEEP BREATHING!

You know that there is a relationship between the length of time an athlete trains and the athlete's ability to process oxygen. Here are some data for one athlete.

MATERIALS

*Graphing utility or
Graph paper
Straightedge*

Training time (weeks)	0	1	2	3	4	5	6	7	8	9	10
Oxygen consumption (L/min)	3.0	3.2	3.4	3.6	3.7	3.8	3.9	4.0	4.1	4.2	4.3

1. Examine the data in the table. How do you think they were collected? Are the quantities directly related? inversely related? How did you decide?
2. Are there any parts of the graph where the relationship between training and oxygen consumption looks like a function? If so, is it linear? Write an equation for the trend line of the data.
3. During what phase of training does an athlete's ability to process oxygen show the fastest improvement? Express your conclusion as a rate of change.
4. Suppose you are an athletic trainer. Make a graph using the data that would help convince developing athletes that they need to train consistently. Choose scales that will make your presentation more persuasive.

1. Name some ways that you can find the slope and y-intercept of a line.
2. Name some ways that you can find the equation of a line.
3. What is a conversion factor used for?
4. For what types of data does a line of best fit make sense?
5. How can you make a prediction using a trend line? Give an example.

Self-Assessment

1. Consider the line that connects $(-3, -1)$ and $(2, 2)$.
   a. What is its equation in slope-intercept form?
   b. Find y for $x = 12$.
   c. Find x for $y = 5$.
   d. Does $(32, 20)$ lie on this line? Prove your answer without graphing.

2. Use the table to answer these questions.
   a. What is the slope of the line through these points?
   b. What is the y-intercept of this line?
   c. What is the equation of this line?

x	y
12	40
13	43
14	46
15	49
16	52

3. Graph the line $y = 2x - 5$ three ways.
   a. Let the intervals on the x-axis and the y-axis be the same.
   b. Let each interval on the x-axis represent two intervals on the y-axis.
   c. Let each interval on the x-axis represent half an interval on the y-axis.
   d. Comment on how the graphs compare.

4. Which of the following is the y-intercept of the line through $(1, -3)$ and $(5, 7)$?
   (a) -3 (b) 2.5   (c) -5.5 (d) 1

5. Club Medic A medical office is spending $12,000 on a blood-processing machine. It expects to make a revenue of $135 on each patient who uses the machine. Its profit is revenues minus costs.
   a. Graph the relationship between profit and the number of patients.
   b. What is the meaning of the y-intercept? of the slope?
   c. What is the meaning of the x-intercept?
   d. After how many patients will the machine be paid for?

6. Stepping Lightly The graph shows the approximate number of calories burned in an hour
by a 150-pound person walking uphill at
different speeds on various inclines.

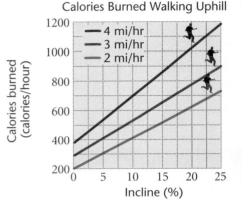

Calories Burned Walking Uphill

a. Estimate the slope of the 2 mi/hr line.
b. Estimate the slope of the 4 mi/hr line.
c. Estimate the number of calories a 150-
pound person would burn off in an hour
of walking 3 mi/hr up a 15% grade.
d. How would the slopes of lines for a person
running up these same hills for an hour (at
faster rates, of course) differ from these?
e. If this were a graph of a 110-pound person walking up these hills at these
rates, how do you think the slopes would differ?

7. Missing Coordinate Sharleen knows the coordinates of A are $(3, 5)$. She also
knows that the x-coordinate of B is 6 and that the slope of $\overline{AB}$ is 2. Describe
how she can find the y-coordinate of B.

Solve and check your answer.

8. $4h + 3 = 6h + 8$
9. $27 - 3(x + 4) = 9(x - 2) - 15$

10. Metabolic Musing The rate at which the human body processes food is called
metabolism. It has two components.

> **Resting Rate** is the energy required simply to keep a body alive in a resting
> state. The resting rate for an average man is about 1700 calories per day
> and for an average woman about 1400 calories per day.

> **Active Rate** is the energy needed for activity. This chart shows the esti-
> mated number of calories used by various activities *per hour.*

50	Sitting at meetings	250	Kayaking
100	Playing the violin	300	Mowing the lawn
150	Skydiving	350	Jogging or bicycling
200	Digging worms	400	Playing tennis

a. Write an equation for the total metabolism of an average woman who
mowed the lawn h hours, but did nothing else that day.
b. Write an equation for the total metabolism of an average man who sat at
meetings for h hours, but did nothing else that day.
c. If each has a total metabolism of 2000 calories for the day, how long did
she spend mowing the lawn? How long did he sit in meetings?
d. Plan an interesting day using the activity chart. Calculate the number of
calories you would use.

11. Health Beat How much exercise is the right amount? Most health experts suggest that you should exercise to the point where the rate at which your heart beats reaches a target level based on your age. Here's a rule that is suggested.

Health

> *To find your target heart rate or pulse . . .*
> *subtract your age from 220 and multiply by 80%.*

a. Define the variables.
b. Make a table that shows the relationship between the variables. Use at least five ordered pairs.
c. Write an equation for the relationship.
d. Find your target rate using the equation.
e. What is the target heart rate for a 50 year old?
f. What is the target heart rate for a 65 year old?

12. Cool Down At a normal temperature of 21°C, a hard-working person uses about 3000 calories per day. As it gets colder, that person uses more calories per day—about 30 calories for every 1°C drop in temperature. In this situation, calorie consumption is a function of outdoor temperature.

Science

a. Let x = the number of degrees below 21°C. Define the dependent variable for this situation.
b. Write an equation that shows the functional relationship between these quantities.
c. Use your equation to determine the temperature at which a hard-working person would burn off 4000 calories per day.

13. Up, Up, and Away A weather balloon rises at a rate of 8 feet per second when the wind is blowing 9.44 miles per hour.

Science

> h = the height of the balloon in feet
> s = the number of seconds the balloon is rising

a. Make a table of values that shows the relationship between h and s. Use at least five ordered pairs in your table.
b. Write an equation for the relationship between h and s.
c. Use your equation to find the height of the balloon after 1 minute.
d. What is the rate in miles per hour?
e. Do you think that the wind speed affects the rate at which the balloon rises? Explain.

14. Use the graph for these questions.
a. Create a problem that has the graph as its solution.
b. Write the equation of the line.

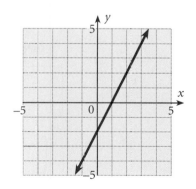

15. Explain why you would or would not find the equation of a trend line for a set of data by finding the equation of a line through two of the data points.

Industry

16. Bolt That Trend Line Down A machine that produces bolts is run at different speeds. The graph shows the number of defective bolts produced at different machine speeds during a test.

a. Why do the *y*-values of the data points fall only on the grid markings?

b. What is the equation of the trend line shown?

c. Is the trend line an accurate predictor for times when the machine is not running? Why or why not?

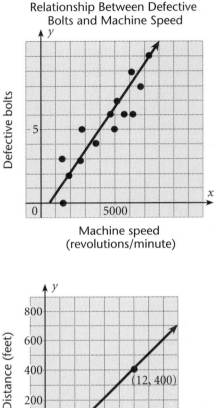

Relationship Between Defective Bolts and Machine Speed

Science

17. Drives Me Crazy This is a graph of the speed of a car, in feet per second, as it drives away from a traffic light.

a. How long does it take for the line to "straighten out"?

b. What does the car do when the line straightens?

c. Find the slope of the segment between the two points.

d. As the time increases by 1 second along this segment, how much does the distance increase?

e. How fast is the car going, in feet per second, over this time? How does this compare to the slope?

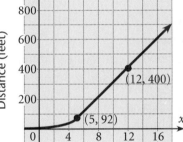

18. Two on the Aisle The slope of the balcony in Chicago's Orchestra Hall is steep. In Long Beach's Crown Theater, the balcony has a gradual rise. What are the advantages and disadvantages of each design?

Fine Arts

Theater with Balcony Seating

Orchestra Hall   **Crown Theater**

Chapter 5 Review

In this chapter, you have been investigating the properties of linear functions. Linear functions are important because they are tools for modeling and understanding relationships in science and business. Slope allows you to quantify the linear relationship between two variables and investigate rate of change. Scatter plots provide the opportunity to look at data and find linear approximations of those data.

KEY TERMS

Conversion factor [5-2]	Positive slope [5-1]	Scale [5-2]
Dimensional analysis [5-2]	Rate [5-1]	Similar triangles [5-1]
Line [5-1]	Rate of change [5-1]	Slope [5-1]
Line segment [5-1]	Rise [5-1]	Slope-intercept form [5-2]
Negative slope [5-1]	Run [5-1]	y-intercept [5-2]

Decide whether the statement is true or false. If the statement is false, change the underlined word or phrase to make it true.

1. The y-intercept is the y-coordinate of the point (<u>b</u>, <u>0</u>).

2. Rate of change is the same as <u>slope</u>.

3. <u>Rise</u> is the measure of the horizontal change.

CONCEPTS AND APPLICATIONS

Determine the slope of each line. [5-1]

4. Line a

5. Line b

6. Line c

7. Line d

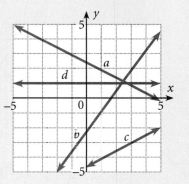

8. On a coordinate plane, sketch the line through (1, 3) and (−2, 5) and determine its slope. [5-1]

9. Express the rate 10 miles per hour in feet per second. [5-1]

10. A swimming pool was 4 feet deep after filling for 3 hours, and 5 feet deep after 5 hours. What was the rate of change? [5-1]

11. Explain why the slope of $\overline{AB}$ is equal to the slope of $\overline{AD}$ and the slope of $\overline{BE}$. [5-1]

12. Name three similar triangles in the figure. [5-1]

13. Are the points $(-6, 6)$, $(0, 2)$, $(-3, 4)$, and $(15, -8)$ on the same line? Explain how you decided. [5-1]

14. Explain the difference between a line with a slope of 0 and a line with an undefined slope. [5-1]

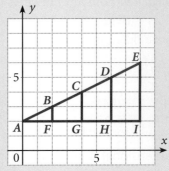

15. Graph the line $2x + 3y = 9$. Then state the slope and the y-intercept. [5-2]

16. Graph the line with slope $\frac{1}{3}$ and y-intercept -1. Then write an equation for the line. [5-2]

17. Write the linear equation $-3x + 2y = 4$ in slope-intercept form. [5-2]

18. Use the points $(-2, 4)$ and $(-6, 8)$. [5-2]
   a. Find the slope of the line through the given points.
   b. Find the y-intercept using $y = mx + b$.
   c. Write an equation for the line through the given points.
   d. Graph the line and label the two given points on it.

19. Graph $y = -2x + 1$. [5-2]

   a. Find x for $y = 0$.   **b.** Find x for $y = -1$.   **c.** Find x for $y = 7$.

20. Which of the graphs represent functions with the same slope? Explain how you decided. [5-2]

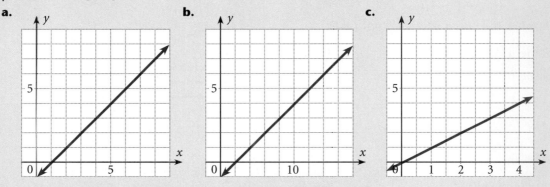

Use the graph to answer the questions. [5-2]

21. What do the numbers on the left side of the graph represent? across the bottom?

22. How would the graph look if the left-hand numbers had gone to 100?

23. Which country shows the greatest difference in its rate of urbanization from the first half to the second half of the century? Which country shows the least difference?

24. How are these lines similar to trend lines on scatter plots?

25. Describe what a graph of the population changes in the rural areas of these countries might look like for the same time period.

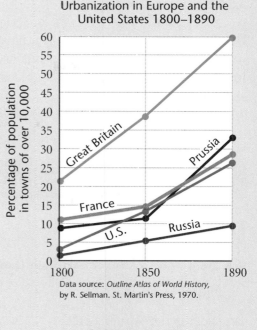

Urbanization in Europe and the United States 1800–1890

Data source: *Outline Atlas of World History,* by R. Sellman. St. Martin's Press, 1970.

The scatter plot shows the change in life expectancy in the United States from 1900 to 1980. [5-2]

26. Copy the graph and draw a trend line through the points. What was life expectancy in 1890? What do you predict life expectancy will be in the year 2000?

27. Estimate the slope and the *y*-intercept of the trend line, then write an equation of the trend line.

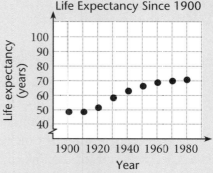

Life Expectancy Since 1900

CONCEPTS AND CONNECTIONS

28. **Food for Thought** Suppose you decide to run a sandwich catering service for the teachers at school. For the first two weeks, business grows slowly but steadily. Encouraged by your success, you expand your service to students. At that point, the rate of business picks up, and continues at that new, higher rate for the next two weeks. Unfortunately, at the beginning of the fifth week, you began to use some cheap, stale bread, and business falls off steadily for your final two weeks. At the end of the second week, you had made a profit of $50. At the end of the fourth week, your profits were up an additional $100. During the fifth and sixth weeks, you made no profits, but rather lost a total of $100.

Draw a graph that describes the success of your business during the time described. Write a paragraph discussing how the rate of change applies to this situation.

SELF-EVALUATION

Describe all the different ways you have learned to find equations of lines. Also write about the various applications of slope you have studied in this chapter. Indicate areas where you had trouble and how you plan to review those areas. Be as specific as possible.

Chapter 5 Assessment

TEST

Use the graph to answer each question.

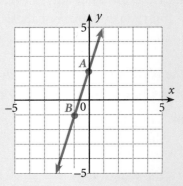

1. Find the slope of $\overleftrightarrow{AB}$.

2. What is the y-intercept?

3. Write the equation of $\overleftrightarrow{AB}$.

4. Explain how a line with a positive slope differs from a line with a negative slope.

5. Graph the line $-4x + 2y = 10$.
   a. What is the slope of the line?
   b. What is the y-intercept of the line?
   c. Use the graph of the line to find x for $y = 1$.

6. Convert the rate $\dfrac{1000 \text{ m}}{3 \text{ min}}$ to $\dfrac{\text{cm}}{\text{sec}}$.

7. Find an equation for the line through the points $(-2, 3)$ and $(6, 9)$.

8. Suppose that the increase in number of visitors for a given park is constant from one year to the next. Project the number of visitors for each park in 1988. (n/a means the information is not available.)

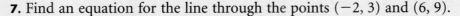

National Park Visitors (millions)				
	1985	1986	1987	1988
Acadia National Park, ME	3.7	3.9	4.1	
Death Valley National Monument, CA	n/a	0.6	0.7	
Grand Teton National Park, WY	1.3	1.3	n/a	

9. A nonprofit organization begins providing services, with $2,455,000 in its checking account. It expects an average income of $50,000 per month in donations and government support.

   a. Which amount, $2,455,000 or $50,000, represents the *y*-intercept?

   b. Which amount represents the slope?

   c. Write an equation for this function.

   d. The director expects expenses to be close to $100,000 per month. Graph both functions on the same coordinate plane.

   e. Will this charity be able to maintain the same level of service indefinitely? Justify your decision.

10. Consider the graph of a line with a slope of -0.8.

   a. If the scale numbers on the *y*-axis are doubled, what is the effect on the slope of the line?

   b. How would the appearance of the line on the graph change?

PERFORMANCE TASK

Suppose you are preparing a report about Yosemite Valley to present to your supervisor. Use the data table to create a scatter plot for average precipitation and temperature. Then use your scatter plot to make conclusions about the relationships between the quantities. Be sure to use the vocabulary from this course that applies.

Average Precipitation and Maximum Daily Temperatures in Yosemite Valley												
	Jan	Feb	Mar	Apr	May	Jun	Jul	Aug	Sep	Oct	Nov	Dec
Max. temp. (°F)	47	55	58	65	71	80	89	89	82	72	57	49
Precipitation (in.)	6.4	6.6	5.9	3.3	1.5	0.5	0.3	0.1	0.6	1.7	3.5	7.1

Use your information and the thermometer (if you need it) to predict the average precipitation for each average daily maximum temperature during the month.

   a. 60°F   **b.** 20°C   **c.** 35°C

Chapter 6

Systems of Equations and Inequalities

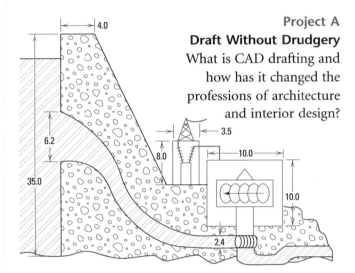

Project A
Draft Without Drudgery
What is CAD drafting and how has it changed the professions of architecture and interior design?

Project B
Tower Power
Why do bridges and towers use triangles for support?

Project C
Picture Perfect
Why do photo studios have white umbrellas? How does lighting create special photographic effects?

PETE DE VASTO

My father was an engineer so I grew up around math. Math helped me earn money for college. I wanted to be a design engineer. Eventually, I turned to economics.

Today I use computers to maintain data and to calculate compensation for management reports. Because I'm blind, I have a machine that reads print one letter at a time and outputs the words in speech or in Braille. I've learned enough to become a trainer. I could not have done this much without a computer.

Pete De Vasto
Senior Programmer,
    Human Resources
Varian Associates
Palo Alto, California

PETE DEVASTO

Chapter 6
GETTING READY

Systems of Equations and Inequalities

6-1
Patterns of Lines

In 6-1 you will study pairs of lines, their equations, and the real-world problems they model. You will need many of the skills you used in Chapters 3 and 5.

Use the slope and y-intercept to graph each line. [5-2]

1. $y = -3x + 2$ **2.** $y = \frac{1}{4}x + 4$ **3.** $y = -x$ **4.** $x = 4$

Write each equation in y = mx + b form. [5-2]

5. $6x + 2y = 8$ **6.** $\frac{1}{2}y - x = 3$ **7.** $x = \frac{2}{3}y$ **8.** $7 = y - x$

9. $\frac{x}{2} - 3y = 18$ **10.** $\frac{x}{3} - y = 5$ **11.** $8y = -4x + 20$ **12.** $-7y = 14 - 2x$

Substitute the given numbers for (x, y) and find b. [5-2]

13. $(3, -1)$ $y = -0.5x + b$ **14.** $(0, 7)$ $y = \frac{2}{3}x + b$

15. $(2, 5)$ $y = -4x + b$ **16.** $(-6, 0)$ $y = -\frac{4}{3}x + b$

6-2
Solving Systems of Equations

In 6-2 you will use algebraic methods to find exact solutions to systems of equations that describe relationships between two or more quantities. You will need to simplify expressions and solve equations.

Simplify and solve each equation. [4-2]

17. $-(3.2 + 0.7x) = 2.4$ **18.** $-x + 4(x - 3) = 5$ **19.** $9 - 2(3 + x) = -5$

20. $2(x + 3) = 3(x - 9)$ **21.** $\frac{3x}{5} - 9 = -11$ **22.** $8 - 5x = 63$

6-3
Solving Systems of Inequalities

In 6-3 you will explore systems of linear inequalities, which are represented by regions in the coordinate plane. You will need to know how to solve and graph inequalities.

Solve each inequality and graph the solution on a number line. [4-3]

23. $3x + 2 \leq 11$ **24.** $-2x + 6 > 7$ **25.** $5 \geq 5 - x$

Solve each expression for y. [4-3]

26. $2y \geq 5x - 7$ **27.** $-y + x < 3$ **28.** $16 > x + 4y$

29. $\frac{y}{4} + 1 > x$ **30.** $x - 3y \leq -15$ **31.** $3y - 2x - 7 \geq 0$

6-1 Patterns of Lines

Fire!

on the line

At this very minute, some part of the American West is probably on fire. In 1992, almost 88,000 fires were reported to the National Interagency Fire Center in Boise, Idaho. The Center helped fight more than 5,700 fires that blazed beyond the control of local fire fighters. Fortunately, 90% of the country's wildland fire-fighting resources are stationed in the West, where there is still a lot of big timber. On a hot summer afternoon in a forested region of Oregon, an observer in Lookout Tower A spots a thread of smoke rising in the distance. With a compass, she can determine that the smoke is due southwest. Somewhere on the line in that direction there is a fire. But where exactly?

Another lookout sees the same smoke from Tower B on a line due northwest from him. Both observers would report their sightings to the National Interagency Fire Center. There workers plot the lines from the towers in the direction the fire was sighted. The exact location of the fire is at their intersection. This method is called triangulation.

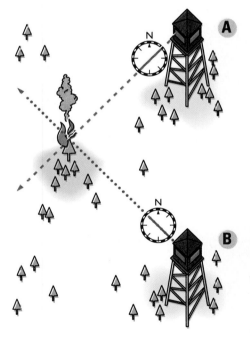

1. Why do you think this method of locating fires is called triangulation?
2. Why might an observer have trouble determining the exact location of a fire from only one tower?
3. In what situation might an observer be able to locate a fire from only one tower?
4. What do we mean by due southwest? by due northwest?

← C O N N E C T → *You've explored linear equations and their graphs. The slopes and y-intercepts you worked with can also be used to relate pairs of lines, including parallel and perpendicular lines.*

So far, you've considered lines and linear equations one at a time. Some situations involve more than one linear equation. In the following Explore, you'll discover some of the ways a pair of lines can be related in the coordinate plane.

EXPLORE: GRIDMATES

MATERIALS

Graphing utility or Graph paper and Straightedge

1. Graph these four linear equations on the same coordinate plane using a graphing utility or graph paper.

$$y = 2x + 1 \qquad y = -3x + 6$$
$$y = \frac{1}{3}x - 2 \qquad y = 2x - 4$$

2. Consider several pairs of lines. How can two lines lie in the same plane? Do they always intersect? How many intersection points can they have?

Summarize the different ways two lines can be related to one another in the coordinate plane.

3. Consider the slopes and y-intercepts of the lines you graphed. Describe any connection you see between the way two lines are related and their slopes or y-intercepts.

Your work in the Explore suggests that two lines in the same plane either intersect in one point or don't intersect at all.

Two lines in the same plane that do *not* intersect are **parallel** lines.

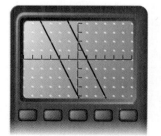

If two lines intersect, they intersect in exactly one point.

Two lines that intersect and form right angles are **perpendicular** lines.

Parallel and perpendicular lines have been used to survey and divide land for hundreds of years.

In 1785, Congress passed the Land Ordinance, the first systematic plan for dividing public lands. This plan called for dividing land using parallel lines running north and south, and lines perpendicular to those running east and west. You can still see the effect of these plans in the layout of many towns and roadways.

The equations in the Explore were given in slope-intercept form, $y = mx + b$. In this form, you can quickly find the slopes of two linear equations. You can then use these slopes to determine whether the graphs intersect or are parallel. If the graphs intersect, you can also tell whether the graphs are perpendicular.

If the slopes of two lines are equal, then the lines are **parallel.**

If the product of the slopes of two lines is -1, then the lines are **perpendicular.**

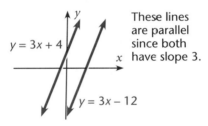

These lines are parallel since both have slope 3.

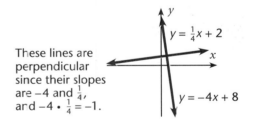

These lines are perpendicular since their slopes are -4 and $\frac{1}{4}$, and $-4 \cdot \frac{1}{4} = -1$.

TRY IT

Determine if the lines are parallel or if they intersect. If they intersect, tell whether they are perpendicular.
a. ℓ and m
b. ℓ and n
c. m and p
d. $y = 2x - 2$ and $y = -2x + 2$
e. $y = 0.5x + 1$ and $y = -2x + 1$

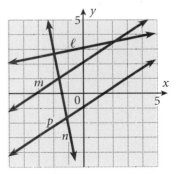

You can use the connection between slope and perpendicular lines to find the line through a given point that is perpendicular to another line.

Write the equation of the line through $(4, 2)$ that is perpendicular to the graph of $y = 2x + 3$.

The slope of the graph of $y = 2x + 3$ is 2. For the product of the slopes to equal -1, the slope of the perpendicular line must be $-\frac{1}{2}$. So the line has an equation of this form.

$$y = -\frac{1}{2}x + b$$

To find b, substitute $(4, 2)$ into the equation.

$2 = -\frac{1}{2}(4) + b$ Substitute 4 for x and 2 for y.

$2 = -2 + b$ Simplify.

$4 = b$ Add 2 to both sides.

The equation of the line through $(4, 2)$ that is perpendicular to the graph of $y = 2x + 3$ is $y = -\frac{1}{2}x + 4$.

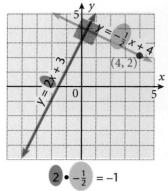

CONSIDER

?

1. **How can you find the equation of a line through a given point that is *parallel* to another line?**

f. Write the equation of the line through $(-1, 2)$ that is parallel to the graph of $y = x + 1$.

g. Write the equation of the line through $(3, 1)$ that is perpendicular to the graph of $y = 4x$.

Although two lines can intersect in at most one point, two linear equations may have more than one point in common. If the equations represent the same line, their graphs will intersect in an *infinite* number of points.

In how many points do the graphs of these two linear equations intersect? none, one, or an infinite number?

$$y = -3x - 2 \text{ and } 6x + 2y = -4$$

Kristin thinks . . .

I'll graph both equations on the same coordinate plane to decide.

I'll graph the first equation by sketching a line with slope -3 and y-intercept -2.

I'll graph the second equation by finding two points and sketching.

The points $(-1, 1)$ and $(-2, 4)$ both satisfy $6x + 2y = -4$.

The lines are the same! So they intersect in an infinite number of points.

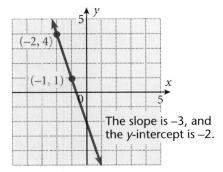

The slope is –3, and the y-intercept is –2.

Esteban thinks . . .

First, I'll write the second equation in slope-intercept form.

$$6x + 2y = -4$$
$$2y = -6x - 4$$
$$y = -3x - 2$$

The second equation written in slope-intercept form is the same as the first equation! So they each have the same graph and intersect in an infinite number of points.

REFLECT

1. Describe four ways that the graphs of two linear equations in the same plane can be related.
2. If two lines intersect at a single point, are those lines necessarily perpendicular? Could they be perpendicular? How could you tell?
3. If two lines do not appear to intersect, are they necessarily parallel? Could they be parallel? How could you tell?
4. Describe any examples of parallel lines you see in the photograph.
5. Describe any examples of perpendicular lines you see in the photograph.

Exercises

CORE

1. **Getting Started** Use the graph to answer these questions.
   a. What is the slope of line ℓ? of line m?
   b. How are the graphs of lines ℓ and m related?
   c. What is the slope of line n? of line m? What is the product of these slopes?
   d. How are the graphs of lines n and m related?
   e. How are the graphs of lines n and ℓ related?

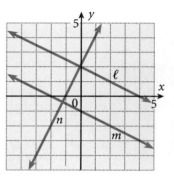

Write the word or phrase that correctly completes each statement.

2. Two lines in the same plane that do not intersect are _____.

3. If two lines intersect, they intersect in exactly _____.

4. Two lines that intersect to form right angles are _____.

5. In a plane, two lines perpendicular to the same line are _____ to each other.

Determine whether the lines are parallel or whether they intersect. If they intersect, tell whether they are perpendicular.

6. c and d

7. a and d

8. b and c

9. $y = 3x - 1$ and $y = -3x - 1$

10. $y = -3x - 1$ and $y = \frac{1}{3}x - 1$

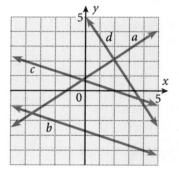

Graph each equation. Then give the slope of a line that is parallel to the original line and the slope of a line that is perpendicular to the original line.

11. $y = 2.5x - 7$

12. $2x - 3y = 5$

13. $y = -4$

14. $27x - 18y = 13$

15. $x = y$

16. $2.3x = 4$

17. The systematic plan used to survey public lands in the United States during the eighteenth century made use of parallel and perpendicular lines. Surveyors used the lines to make sure the land was divided into squares of equal area. Divide a 4-cm by 4-cm square into 16 equal squares to illustrate this plan.

Consider equations A–D.

A. $x - 2y = 3$ **B.** $2x + y = 1$ **C.** $y = \dfrac{1}{2}x - 3$ **D.** $y = -2x + 1$

18. For which pair(s) of equations are the lines the same?

19. For which pair(s) of equations are the lines parallel?

20. For which pair(s) of equations are the lines perpendicular?

This map shows where major fires broke out in San Francisco following a massive earthquake on April 18, 1906. (The arrows show how the fires tended to move.)

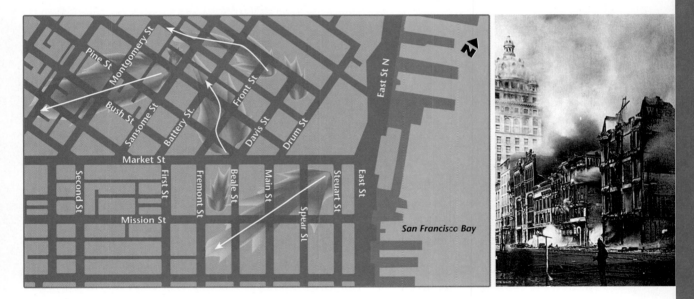

Determine whether each pair of streets intersects or is parallel. If the streets intersect, tell whether they are perpendicular.

21. Main and Spear   **22.** First and Market   **23.** Davis and Front

24. Drum and Market   **25.** Battery and Pine   **26.** East St. and the piers

27. Streets in a city remind us of lines. Identify other real-life examples of parallel, intersecting, and perpendicular lines.

In how many points do the graphs of each pair of equations intersect: none, one, or an infinite number? Tell how you decided.

28. $y = 3x + 5$
$2y = 6x + 10$

29. $y = 3x - 6$
$y = -2x - 1$

30. $y = -x$
$x + y = 4$

31. Use these steps to write the equation of the line through $(2, 7)$ that is parallel to the graph of $y = 3x - 1$.
a. Find the slope of the new line.
b. Find the y-intercept of the new line by substituting $(2, 7)$ and the slope into the slope-intercept formula $y = mx + b$.
c. Use the slope and y-intercept to write the equation of the new line.

32. Use these steps to write the equation of the line through $(2, 7)$ that is perpendicular to the graph of $y = 3x - 1$.
a. Find the slope of the new line.
b. Find the y-intercept of the new line by substituting $(2, 7)$ and the slope into the slope-intercept formula $y = mx + b$.
c. Use the slope and y-intercept to write the equation of the new line.

Write the equation of the line through $(-1, 3)$ that is parallel to the graph of each equation.

33. $y = 2x - 3$ 　　　　**34.** $y = \frac{2}{3}x + 4$ 　　　　**35.** $2x - y = 5$

Write the equation of the line through $(2, -1)$ that is perpendicular to the graph of each equation.

36. $y = -4x + 3$ 　　　　**37.** $y = \frac{1}{2}x - 3$ 　　　　**38.** $3x - 2y = 6$

39. Consider the graphs of $y = 4.5$, $x = -2.5$, and $x = 3$.
a. Give the equations of the parallel lines. What are their slopes? Describe these lines.
b. Give the equations of two perpendicular lines. What are their slopes? Describe these lines.
c. Why are these considered "special cases"?

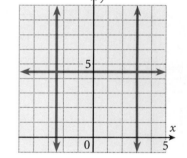

40. The equation of a line in **standard form** is $Ax + By = C$.
a. Rewrite $Ax + By = C$ in $y = mx + b$ form.
b. Give the slope in terms of A and B.
c. How can you tell without graphing that the line represented by $2x + 3y = 6$ is parallel to the line represented by $2x + 3y = 8$?

41. Use this section of the 1993 presidential inaugural poem to discuss what your English teacher calls *parallel sentence structure*. Explain how this is similar to parallel lines in mathematics.

Lift up your eyes upon
This day breaking for you
Give birth again
To the dream.
Women, Children, Men,
Take it into the palm of your hands.
Mold it into the shape of your most
Private need. Sculpt it into
The image of your most public self.
Excerpt from *On the Pulse of Morning*
　　　　　　by Maya Angelou

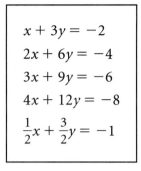
42. The graph of each of these equations is the same line.
    a. Study the equations and describe the patterns you see.
    b. Find the values for a and for b in the equation $10x + ay = b$.

$x + 3y = -2$

$2x + 6y = -4$

$3x + 9y = -6$

$4x + 12y = -8$

$\frac{1}{2}x + \frac{3}{2}y = -1$

Express each equation in slope-intercept form.

43. $6x + 12y = 15$ **44.** $27x - 18y = 3$

MORE PRACTICE

**Determine whether the lines are parallel or intersect.
If they intersect, tell whether they are perpendicular.**

45. s and t **46.** r and t **47.** r and u

48. $y = 5x - 8$ and $y = -5x - 8$

49. $y = 4x - 1$ and $y = -\frac{1}{4}x - 1$

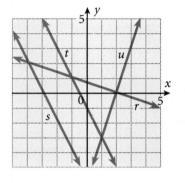

**Consider the graph of each equation, and answer the following
questions.**
    a. What is the slope of a line that is parallel to the graph of this equation?
    b. What is the slope of a line that is perpendicular to the graph of this equation?

50. $y = x - 5.2$ **51.** $2x + 3y = 4$ **52.** $y = x$ **53.** $x = 7$

**Write the equation of the line through (−3, 1) that is parallel to the graph of
each equation.**

54. $y = -4x + 1$ **55.** $y = -\frac{2}{3}x + 1$ **56.** $4x + 2y = 5$

**Write the equation of the line through (6, −2) that is perpendicular to the
graph of each equation.**

57. $y = -x + 1$ **58.** $y = \frac{1}{2}x + 3$ **59.** $3x - 2y = 12$

60. $y = 0.25x + 3$ **61.** $y = 2.5x - 8$ **62.** $0.2x - 0.4y = 3.1$

Consider equations A–E.

    A. $3x + y = 2$ **B.** $x + 3y = 3$ **C.** $y = -\frac{1}{3}x - 1$ **D.** $y = -\frac{1}{3}x + 1$ **E.** $y - 3x = 2$

63. For which pair(s) of equations are the lines the same?

64. For which pair(s) of equations are the lines parallel?

65. For which pair(s) of equations are the lines perpendicular?

In how many points do the graphs of each pair of equations intersect? none, one, or an infinite number?

66. $y = -x + 6$
$y = \frac{9}{4}x - \frac{1}{2}$

67. $x + y = 6$
$x - y = 2$

68. $x + 2y = 5$
$2x + 4y = 1$

MORE MATH REASONING

69. On the corner of a piece of paper, make a fold that has a slope of 2. Describe how you did this. Then make another fold perpendicular to the first one. Describe how you did this. What is the slope of your second fold?

70. Make a table of ordered pairs and plot their points to show that the graph of $xy = 0$ is a pair of perpendicular lines. (Hint: If the product of two numbers is 0, what do you know about the numbers?) What is another name for this graph?

71. This graph shows that the position of the long hand of a clock is a function of the position of the short hand. Notice, for example, that as the short hand moves from the 2 position to the 3 position, the long hand travels the entire distance from 0 to 12. Explain what there is about the operation of this clock that assures that these lines will be parallel.

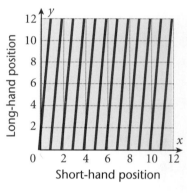

72. Suppose you were given points $C(1, -5)$ and $D(3, -3)$ and asked to write an equation of the line that is parallel to line CD with an x-intercept of -1. Describe the steps you would use to write the equation of this line. Check your answer using a graphing utility.

73. How many lines are there that are parallel to line m that go through at least two of the dots shown? Explain how you got your answer.

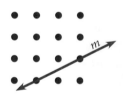

74. Shakespeare's tragedies have a parallel plot development. Consider the elements of a play: setting, acts, character development, heroes, villains, critical decisions, and central themes. Why might someone use parallel plot development? How is the use of *parallel* in this context similar to its use in mathematics?

Scene from *Twelfth Night*.

Systems of Linear Equations

← C O N N E C T →
You've studied how a pair of lines can be related in the coordinate plane. Now you'll investigate and interpret systems of two linear equations. Finding the intersection points of lines is the key to solving systems.

Here is a situation you can model with a pair of linear equations.

EXPLORE: RITZ OR SMITS?

MATERIALS

Graphing utility or Graph paper and Straightedge

1. Define variables and write two equations that relate rental price to length of rental for the two car rental companies.

2. Graph both equations on the same set of axes and find the coordinates of the intersection point.

3. Substitute the coordinates of the intersection point into both equations. Is *neither* equation true, is *one* equation true, or are *both* equations true?

4. For what number of rental days do both Ritz and Smits charge the same price? What is that price? How can you tell the number of days and price from the graph?

5. Cars are rented for business use for two days on average and for recreational use for five days on average. If Ritz wants to be more competitive in the recreational market and Smits wants to be more competitive in the business market, how would you advise each of their managers? Explain using the graphs.

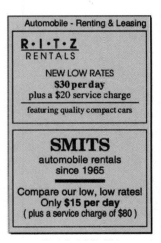

Automobile - Renting & Leasing

R·I·T·Z
RENTALS

NEW LOW RATES
$30 per day
plus a $20 service charge

featuring quality compact cars

SMITS
automobile rentals
since 1965
───
Compare our low, low rates!
Only $15 per day
(plus a service charge of $80)

Two or more linear equations considered together form a **system of linear equations.**

To solve an equation, you find the values of the variables that make the equation true. To solve a system of equations, you find the values that make every equation in the system true.

A **solution to a system** of two linear equations is an ordered pair that makes *both* equations true. Each intersection point of the graphs of the two equations represents a solution to the system.

When you found the intersection point in the Explore you were solving a system of equations.

EXAMPLES

1. Ritz is having a slump in car rentals lately. After looking at the trends in income and expenses, the manager at Ritz produced this graph. If these projections hold true, when will Ritz start making a profit again?

The graphs intersect at about (5.5, 19.5). In about $5\frac{1}{2}$ months, Ritz's income and expenses will both be about $19,500. After that, Ritz will have greater income than expenses. Ritz will start making a profit again in about $5\frac{1}{2}$ months.

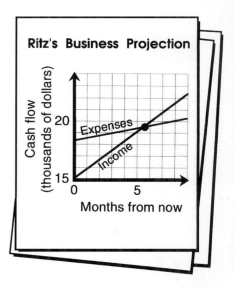

2. Graph and solve the system of equations. Check your solution.

$y = 3x - 1$
$y = -2x + 4$

Graph both equations on a graphing utility, adjusting the window size to see the intersection point. *Trace* along either graph to find the intersection point.

The graphs intersect at the point (1, 2). So the solution to the system of equations is (1, 2).

Substitute $x = 1$ and $y = 2$ into *both* equations to check the solution.

$y \overset{?}{=} 3x - 1$ $y \overset{?}{=} -2x + 4$
$2 \overset{?}{=} 3(1) - 1$ $2 \overset{?}{=} -2(1) + 4$
$2 = 2$ ✔ $2 = 2$ ✔

Both equations are true. The solution checks.

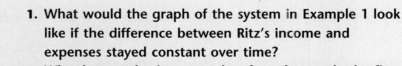
1. What would the graph of the system in Example 1 look like if the difference between Ritz's income and expenses stayed constant over time?
2. Why do most business graphs often show only the first quadrant?

TRY IT

a. The graph shows the income and expenses for Smits's car rental company. When will Smits stop making a profit?

b. Graph and solve the system of equations. Check your solution.

$$y = \frac{1}{2}x + 2$$

$$y = 3x - 3$$

Smits' Business Projection

Cash flow (thousands of dollars)

Expenses

Income

Months from now

REFLECT

1. How is solving a system similar to solving one equation? How is it different?
2. Describe how you check a solution of a system of linear equations.
3. If the graphs of two linear equations are parallel, how many solutions does the system have? Explain your answer.
4. If the graphs of two linear equations are the same, how many solutions does the system have? Explain your answer.

Exercises

CORE

1. **Getting Started** The lines are the graphs of the system of equations $x - 3y = -9$ and $2x + y = -4$.
   a. Which equation has line a as its graph?
   b. Which equation has line b as its graph?
   c. What are the coordinates of the intersection of these two lines?
   d. What is the solution to this system?
   e. Substitute the solution into both equations to check your solution.

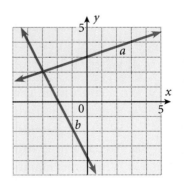

Determine whether each statement is true or false. If the statement is false, change the underlined word or phrase to make it true.

2. Two or more linear equations considered together form a <u>system</u> of linear equations.

3. A solution to a system of two linear equations is a <u>number</u> that makes both equations true.

4. Is $(4, -1)$ the solution to the system $2x - y = 9$ and $x + y = 3$? Justify your answer.

5. **Company Blues** Use the graph to answer these questions.
   a. What was the company's best year?
   b. When did the company break even? Was that "good" news? Explain.

6. Determine the relationship between income and expenses.
   a. when the company breaks even
   b. when it is making a profit
   c. when it is operating at a loss

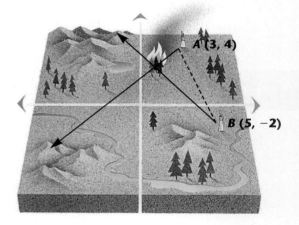

Company Performance

7. Graph the system $3x - y = 3$ and $x - 2y = -4$.
   a. What ordered pair appears to be the intersection of these equations?
   b. Does this ordered pair make both equations true?

8. Fire tower A spots a thread of smoke due southwest from its location at $(3, 4)$ on a giant coordinate system. Fire tower B spots that same thread of smoke on a line due northwest from $(5, -2)$.
   a. What is the equation of the line of sight from A?
   b. What is the equation of the line of sight from B?
   c. What is the relationship of these lines of sight to each other?
   d. Where is the fire?

9. On a coordinate grid, sketch $y = -\frac{3}{2}x + 1$.
   a. Sketch a line through $(0, -3)$ that is parallel to $y = -\frac{3}{2}x + 1$. What is its equation?
   b. Sketch a line through $(0, 2)$ that is perpendicular to $y = -\frac{3}{2}x + 1$. What is its equation?

10. Without graphing, how can you tell that $x + 3y = 4$ and $3x + 9y = 12$ describe the same line?

Graph and solve each system of equations. Check your solution.

11. $y = 2x + 1$
$y = -x + 10$

12. $y = 4x - 1$
$y = -2x - 7$

13. $x - 3y = 6$
$x + y = 2$

14. $x + y = 3$
$x + y = 5$

15. $-\dfrac{1}{2}x + y = 2$
$\dfrac{1}{2}x + y = 4$

16. If two lines in a graph are perpendicular to $x - 4y = 4$, what is their relationship to each other? Explain.

17. Loan Nu used her graphing utility to solve the system $y = x + 5$ and $y = -x - 7$. However, the graph did not show the solution to the system. The settings show the window size Loan used. Tell what she could do to see the solution.

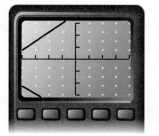

18. Smoke-Jumpers' Challenge In a remote region in northern Idaho, two firefighting smoke jumpers parachuted into the vicinity of a forest fire. On a coordinate grid at command headquarters, one of them landed at $(-3, -2)$ and began walking due north. The other landed at $(5, 2)$ and began walking due northwest. Where would their paths cross?

19. Consider the geoboard design.
   a. What is the relationship between $\overline{AB}$ and $\overline{BC}$? Justify your answer.
   b. What is the relationship between $\overline{AB}$ and $\overline{DC}$? Justify your answer.

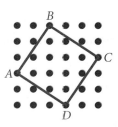

20. Assume the points $(5, 4)$, $(3, 2)$, and $(-2, ?)$ lie on the same line.
   a. What is the y-coordinate of the third point?
   b. What is the equation of the perpendicular line that intersects this line at $(3, 2)$?

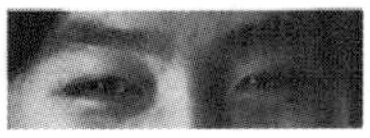

LOOK BACK

21. Match each table with the graph that represents the same function. [3-1]

a.

x	−5	−1	1	5
y	−11	−3	1	9

b.

x	−10	−6	−4	0
y	−2	0	1	3

c.

x	−5	−1	1	5
y	3	3	3	3

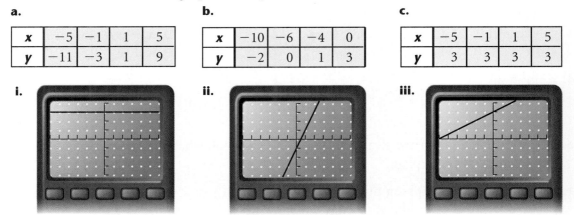

i.

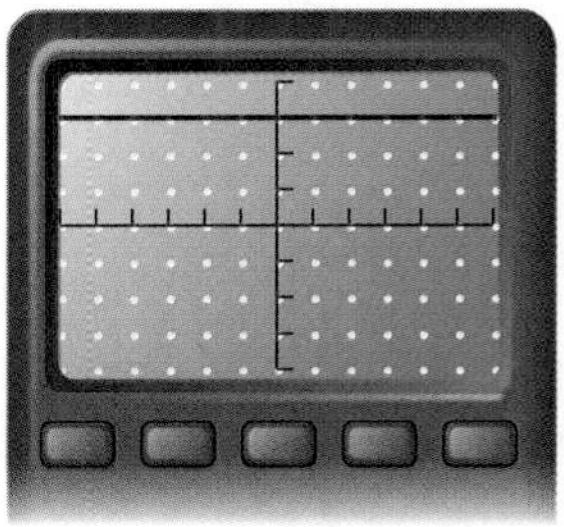

ii.

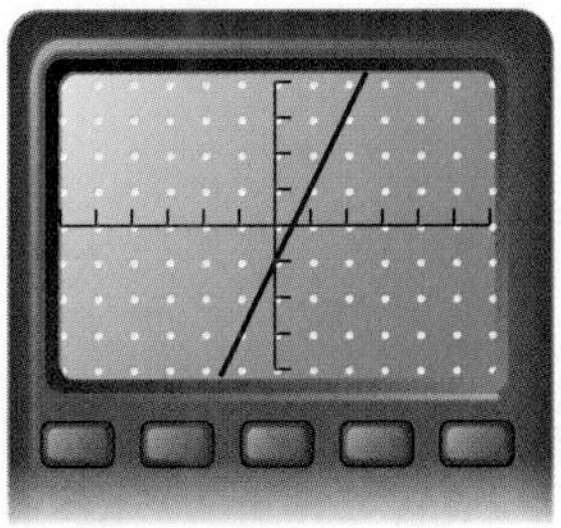

iii.

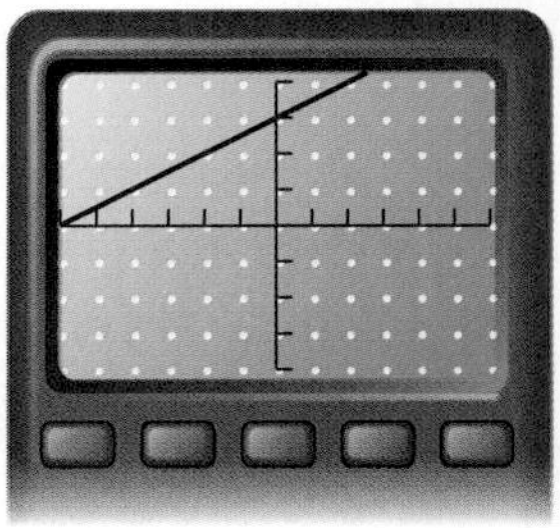

22. Consider the associations between the number of doors on a car and each of the given quantities. Is there a positive, a negative, or no association between the number of doors and the given quantities? Explain your answer. [5-2]

a. the number of passengers it can hold **b.** the miles per gallon it will get

MORE PRACTICE

23. The graph shows the lines in the system $3x - y = 7$ and $x + 3y = -1$.

a. Which equation has line a as its graph?

b. Which equation has line b as its graph?

c. What are the coordinates of the intersection of these two lines?

d. What is the solution to this system?

e. Explain how you could check to see if your solution is correct.

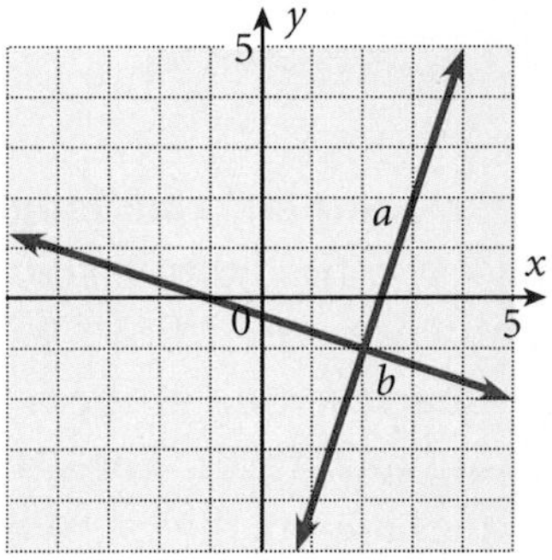

24. Is $(-2, 2)$ the solution to the system $y = x + 4$ and $y = -2x - 2$? Tell how you decided.

Graph and solve each system of equations.

25. $y = \frac{1}{2}x + 2$
$y = -x + 8$

26. $y = 2x - 6$
$y = -x + 4$

27. $y = -\frac{1}{3}x + 1$
$y = 2x - 6$

28. $x + y = 2$
$x = y$

29. $x - y = 2$
$x + y = 6$

30. $x = 3y$
$3y - 6 = 2x$

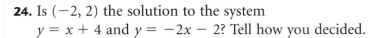

MORE MATH REASONING

31. Quick Work In a national park, a camping party sets out for a day's hike at 7 a.m. Their average walking speed is 3.5 miles per hour. A park ranger arrives at their camp at 8:30 a.m. to warn them about a forest fire. The ranger knows the direction of their hike and can ride on horseback at 12 miles per hour. How soon will he catch up to the hikers? Explain your answer.

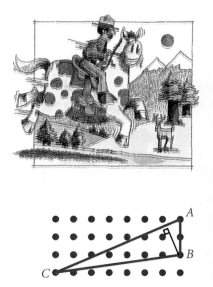

32. The x-axis and the y-axis are perpendicular. Comment on the product of their slopes.

33. Consider the altitude to $\overline{AC}$.
  a. What is its slope?
  b. What is the slope of the altitude to $\overline{AB}$?
  c. What is the slope of the altitude to $\overline{BC}$?

34. Can three lines be parallel to each other? Can three lines in a plane be perpendicular to each other? Explain. (Hint: Use pencils to model the lines.)

35. Stock Search Sal and Nellie are investigating companies. They want to buy stock in the company that is doing better. They consider this report on companies A and B.
  a. Which company shows a profit?
  b. If each company continues as shown, which stock should they buy and why?

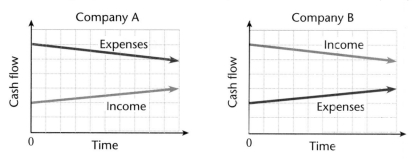

36. Profit Ponders The profits for each of two companies are shown as lines on the same graph. Explain your answer to each question.
  a. If profits are shown as parallel lines, does that mean that one company is doing better in actual profits?
  b. If profits are shown as parallel lines, does that mean that one company is doing better in rate of growth?
  c. If profits over time for two companies show up as perpendicular lines, can they both be profitable?
  d. If profits over time for two companies intersect, what is the significance of the point of intersection?

Making Connections

← C O N N E C T → *You've explored how two lines can be related and how they represent a system of equations. You've also seen that an intersection point of two lines represents a solution to a system and can help you to solve real problems.*

EXPLORE: FLASH EVENT!

MATERIALS

Graphing utility or Graph paper

Most wildfires are caused by lightning. The National Interagency Fire Center uses lightning direction finders (DFs) to find lightning ground strikes, called *flash events*. Two DFs are needed to determine lines to locate the flash event. A computer converts the signals from the DFs to coordinates, using a familiar landmark as the origin.

This map shows two DF locations in relation to a jump station.

N

White Sulfur Springs

100

Three Forks •   • Big Timber

50

MONTANA

100   50   50   100

−50

Yellowstone National Park

IDAHO   WYOMING

0   50   100
miles

The DFs have detected a flash event near White Sulfur Springs. The computer has determined that the event occurred on the lines $y = 1.17x + 105$ and $y = -1.08x + 130$.

1. Why are two DFs needed to locate the flash event?
2. Find the coordinates where the flash event occurred. Describe how you found the coordinates.
3. What is the equation of the line from the jump station to the location of the flash event?
4. In your own words, tell the pilot of a smoke-jumper plane how to get from the jump station to the location of the flash event. Be sure to include both distance and direction in your explanation.

1. How can you tell whether two lines are parallel or perpendicular from their equations?
2. Explain how graphs can be used to solve a system of linear equations.
3. How is it possible for a system of linear equations to have no solutions?
4. Describe a situation that can be modeled with a system of linear equations. Tell what a solution means in this situation.

Self-Assessment

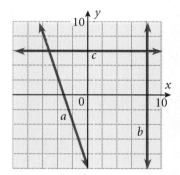

1. Use the graph to answer these questions.
   a. What is the slope of a line that is parallel to line a?
   b. What is the slope of a line that is perpendicular to line a?
   c. What is the slope of a line that is parallel to line c? Is this new line perpendicular to line b? Explain.

2. Which point is the solution to the system $2x + 3y = -4$ and $4x - 3y = -2$? Explain your answer.
   (a) $(-2, 0)$ (b) $(1, -2)$ (c) $\left(\frac{1}{2}, -\frac{5}{3}\right)$ (d) $\left(-1, -\frac{2}{3}\right)$ (e) not here

3. Write the equation of the line through $(2, 3)$ that is parallel to the graph of $2x - 3y = 0$.

4. Write the equation of the line through $(2, 3)$ that is perpendicular to the graph of $2x - 3y = 0$.

5. For which system(s) is the graph of the solution an infinite set of points? Tell how you decided.
   I. $3x + y = 1$ **II.** $3y = -3x + 2$ **III.** $x + 2y = 5$
      $6x + 2y = 2$ $y = -x + \frac{2}{3}$ $x - y = 1$
   (a) I only   (b) II only   (c) III only   (d) I and II   (e) I, II, and III

6. **Trace Thought** Kit used the trace function of her graphing utility to read the solution to the system $y = 3x + 5$ and $y = -2x - 7$. Her screen is shown. Show a method she could use to determine whether the ordered pair is the solution to the system.

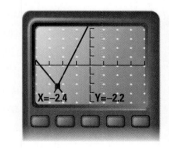

X=-2.4   Y=-2.2

Graph and solve each system. Describe how the lines are related.

7. $y = -\frac{1}{2}x + 1$ 8. $y = -3x + 6$ 9. $x + y = 7$
     $y = x + 4$ $3x + y = -6$ $x - y = 1$

10. **Locate the Buffalo** A lone buffalo survived a fire in Montana. When first sighted, it was due northeast as viewed from the plane. The location of the plane at that time was 4 miles south and 5 miles west of the origin. After the plane traveled for 5 miles due north, the buffalo was again observed due southeast of the plane. The exact location of the buffalo could then be determined.

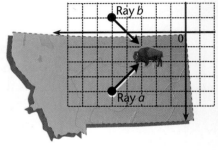

a. A coordinate axis is placed over the map of Montana. Use the northeast corner of the state as the origin. Write the equation for the line of sight along ray *a*.

b. Write the equation for the line of sight along ray *b*.

c. Describe how this information could be used to locate the buffalo.

11. If lightning strikes on the imaginary *baseline* connecting two DFs, a third DF is needed to pinpoint the strike. Why?

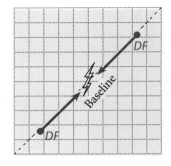

12. **Fire! Fire!** A fire on a line with slope $\frac{2}{3}$ was spotted from a fire tower located at $(-1, -2)$. The same fire was spotted on a line with slope -2 from a second fire tower located at $(0, 4)$. What are the coordinates of the fire?

13. **Lightning Strikes Twice** The placement of lightning direction finders (DFs) takes certain facts into consideration.

a. DFs can only detect lightning within a certain range, usually not more than 350 km. How far apart should two DFs be?

b. DFs should not be placed too close together. Why not?

c. One of the two recommended DF sites is in the center of a field at least 30 m away from any building. The land should be relatively flat without any nearby canyons or mountains. Create an illustration of a good location for a DF. Use scale, buildings, a second DF, and a mountain in your drawing.

14. **Meteor Trails** A person at station *A* takes two photos of a meteor. The photos are of the initial point (*C*) and the final point (*D*) of the meteor's trail. A second person at station *B* takes two photos of the meteor at the same times as the person at station *A*.

a. Tell how this is similar to locating a fire.

b. Describe how you would place this information on a coordinate plane.

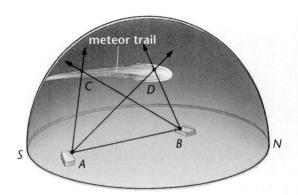

AN AMERICAN EIFFEL TOWER

The Eiffel Tower, designed by French engineer Alexandre Gustave Eiffel, was the main attraction of the World's Fair in Paris in 1890. For the World's Fair in Chicago three years later, Americans wanted a centerpiece to outdo the Eiffel Tower. George Washington Gale Ferris, an architect and bridge-builder, had an idea. He designed a wheel 250 feet in diameter, suspended on twin 140-foot towers. The 32-foot main axle weighed over 45 tons and was the largest single piece of steel that had ever been forged.

For 50¢, people could ride for 40 minutes—twice around the wheel—in an elegantly crafted car. Not only was this the very first Ferris wheel ever built, it was also the largest that has ever been constructed. Though Ferris wheels exist today in many forms and sizes, the original Ferris wheel was not as enduring as the Eiffel Tower. While the tower still stands today, recognized worldwide as a Paris landmark, the original wheel was used only a few more times before it was demolished and sold for scrap in 1906.

1. Why do you think Ferris suggested a wheel instead of a tower taller than the Eiffel Tower?
2. How does the time for a complete revolution of the original Ferris wheel compare to a complete revolution on a present day Ferris wheel? How are the Ferris wheels different?
3. Identify sets of intersecting lines in the Eiffel Tower and the Ferris wheel.

Solving by Substitution

←**CONNECT**→ *You've interpreted and graphed systems of linear equations and their solutions. You can also solve systems symbolically. Now you will discover how to use substitution to solve systems of equations.*

To solve a system of two linear equations, you must find the values of the variables that satisfy *both* equations. Now you'll solve a system and use the solution to help decide how a business can set competitive prices.

EXPLORE: WEEKEND GETAWAY

MATERIALS

Graphing utility or Graph paper and Straightedge

A hotel near an amusement park offers "packaged weekends" to attract business. The hotel offers the *Mad Dash* (1 overnight stay and 2 meals) for $66 and the *Big Bash* (2 overnight stays and 3 meals) for $125. Suppose you manage a new, competing hotel. You want to offer your own packages, so you are curious about the other hotel's pricing method.

1. Assume the other hotel's packages are based on a set price (*s*) per night and a set price (*m*) per meal. Write a system of equations you can use to find each price.

2. Solve your system of equations and compare your solution with classmates' solutions. What are the prices per overnight stay and per meal? Describe how you solved the system, including any difficulties you had. Is your solution exact or approximate?

3. Make up a weekend package for your hotel that differs from the other hotel's packages. Use the solution to the system to help you decide on a competitive price for your package. Explain how you decided.

You cannot always find exact solutions to systems using graphs. Even when a graph does give the exact solution, other methods of solving may be easier.

The **substitution method** allows you to find exact solutions to systems without graphing, guessing, or estimating. If necessary, solve for one variable as an expression of the other using one of the equations. Then substitute the expression for that variable into the second equation.

EXAMPLE

1. Solve this system of equations by substitution. Check your solution.

$$y = 2x - 3 \qquad \text{❶}$$
$$x + 3y = 5 \qquad \text{❷}$$

Equation ❶ tells us that y is equal to $2x - 3$ for any solution to the system. So we can *substitute* $2x - 3$ for y in equation ❷.

$$x + 3y = 5 \qquad \text{❷}$$
$$x + 3(2x - 3) = 5 \qquad \text{Substitute } (2x - 3) \text{ for } y.$$

Now we have an equation with only *one* variable. Solve it for x.

$$x + 6x - 9 = 5 \qquad \text{Use the distributive property.}$$
$$7x = 14 \qquad \text{Add 9 to both sides and simplify.}$$
$$x = 2 \qquad \text{Solve for } x.$$

Substitute the value of x into one of the original equations and solve for y.

$$y = 2x - 3 \qquad \text{❶}$$
$$y = 2(2) - 3 \qquad \text{Substitute 2 for } x.$$
$$y = 1 \qquad \text{Solve for } y.$$

The solution to the system of equations is $(2, 1)$.
Check the solution in both original equations ❶ and ❷.

$$y \stackrel{?}{=} 2x - 3 \qquad\qquad\qquad x + 3y \stackrel{?}{=} 5$$
$$1 \stackrel{?}{=} 2(2) - 3 \qquad\qquad\qquad 2 + 3(1) \stackrel{?}{=} 5$$
$$1 = 1 \; ✔ \qquad\qquad\qquad\qquad 5 = 5 \; ✔$$

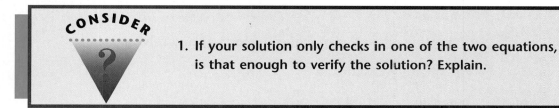

CONSIDER

?

1. If your solution only checks in one of the two equations, is that enough to verify the solution? Explain.

In some systems, you must solve an equation for one of the variables before you can substitute.

EXAMPLE

2. It's time for Joe to paint the Ferris wheel chairs at the amusement park. The park stocks two paints that can be used—a paint with 20% oil and a higher quality paint with 35% oil. To do a quality job and also be economical, Joe plans to combine paints to get 120 gallons of paint with 30% oil. How should he combine the available paints?

> **Problem-Solving Tip**
>
> Make a plan. Decide how many variables and how many equations are necessary to solve the problem.

Let p = the number of gallons of 20% oil paint Joe will use.
Let h = the number of gallons of 35% oil paint Joe will use.

Joe wrote this equation for the total gallons of paint.

$$p \qquad + \qquad h \qquad = \qquad 120 \qquad \mathbf{❶}$$

gallons of 20%   gallons of 35%   total gallons
oil paint   oil paint

Joe then used the percentages to find the total gallons of oil.

$$0.2p \qquad + \qquad 0.35h \qquad = \qquad 0.3(120) \qquad \mathbf{❷}$$

gallons of oil in   gallons of oil in   gallons of oil in
the 20% oil paint   the 35% oil paint   120 gallons of 30% paint

Solve equation **❶** for p.

$p + h = 120$	**❶**
$p = 120 - h$	Solve for p.

Substitute $120 - h$ for p in equation **❷**.

$0.2p + 0.35h = 0.3(120)$	**❷**
$0.2(\mathbf{120 - h}) + 0.35h = 0.3(120)$	Substitute $120 - h$ for p.
$0.15h + 24 = 36$	Simplify.
$0.15h = 12$	
$h = 80$	Solve.

Substitute the value of h into equation **❶** and solve for p.

$p + h = 120$	**❶**
$p + \mathbf{80} = 120$	Substitute 80 for h.
$p = 40$	Solve.

So Joe should mix 80 gallons of the 35% oil paint and 40 gallons of the 20% oil paint.

When you solve by substitution, be sure to solve for a variable in *one* equation and then substitute the expression for it into the *other* equation.

Solve each system of equations by substitution.

a. $x + 5y = 2$ **b.** $x = 3y + 2$ **c.** $2x - y = 2$
   $x = -3y$ $x = 2y - 7$ $x - 2y = 3$

d. Use substitution to solve the system in the Explore.

When you solve a system by substitution, you can start with either equation and solve for either variable. A term with coefficient 1 or -1 often indicates a good equation and variable to begin with.

REFLECT

1. Explain why you check a solution of a system of equations in *both* equations.

2. Substitution is often used when there is a term with a coefficient of 1 or -1. Why?

3. In each system, which variable would you solve for first and using which equation? Tell why in each case.

a. $x = 4y$ **b.** $2x - 3y = 4$ **c.** $x + 2y = 6$
   $5x - 4y = -23$ $x - y = 1$ $x + 4y = 7$

Exercises

CORE

1. Getting Started Consider the system $3x + 6y = 0$ and $y = -5x + 9$.
   a. Which equation tells you what to substitute for y? Why?
   b. Substitute and solve for x.
   c. What is the value of y?
   d. Check your solution in the original system.

Solve each system of equations by substitution. Check your solution.

2. $x + 2y = 14$ **3.** $x - 3y = 6$ **4.** $x = 3y - 4$
   $x = 3y - 11$ $y = x - 28$ $2x + 6y = 4$

5. $x - 4 = y$ **6.** $x = -2y + 5$ **7.** $4x - 3y = 15$
   $4x + 2 = y$ $x = 17 - y$ $x - 2y = 0$

8. Suppose you are collecting the tickets for the school play. You collect 595 tickets. Admission is $5 for adults and $3 for students. The total amount of money from ticket sales is $1951. You want to figure out how many adult tickets were sold.

   a. Define one variable as the number of student tickets. Define a second variable as the number of adult tickets.
   b. Write an expression that represents the money made from student ticket sales. Write another expression that represents the money made from adult ticket sales.
   c. Write an equation that describes the total amount of money made from ticket sales. Write an equation for the total number of tickets sold.
   d. Use the two equations to determine how many adult tickets were sold.
   e. Describe what you did to get the answer.

9. Solve the system $x - 7y = -6$ and $x + y = 3$ two ways, as directed. Show your work.
   a. Begin by isolating x in the first equation.
   b. Begin by isolating y in the second equation.
   c. Should **9a** and **9b** have the same solution? Explain.

10. Detective Darrel Darrel graphed the system $y = 2x + 5$ and $y = -x - 3$. The screen shows the graph of the system with x and y values from -4 to 4.

   a. Describe two different ways he could find the solution to the system.
   b. Darrel says that the lines are not perpendicular. Is he correct? Explain.

11. The sum of two numbers is 70. The difference between these numbers is 24.
   a. Write an equation for the sum of the numbers.
   b. Write an equation for the difference of the numbers.
   c. Solve the system formed by the two equations.
   d. What are the numbers?

12. The difference between two numbers is 18. Twice the smaller number plus three times the larger is 74. Suppose s is the smaller number and ℓ is the larger number.
   a. Write the equation for the difference of the numbers.
   b. Write an expression for twice the smaller number.
   c. Write an expression for three times the larger number.
   d. Write the equation that expresses the sum of twice the smaller number plus three times the larger as 74.
   e. Solve the system to find the numbers.

13. Your cool Uncle Carl is trying to decide between the purchase of a sports car or a station wagon. The sports car is cheaper to buy, but costs more to insure. Specifically, the sports car would cost $5000 plus $2500 each year for insurance, while the station wagon would be $8000 plus $800 per year.

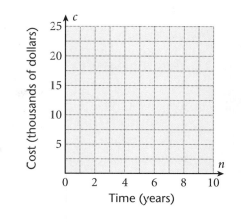

a. Write a system of equations, letting c represent cost in thousands of dollars and n represent years.

b. On a coordinate grid like that pictured, plot each of these equations.

c. After how many years would the amount spent on each car be the same? Can you be certain?

d. Uncle Carl will keep his new car for 5 years. From Uncle Carl's point of view, describe the domains and ranges of the functions that the two equations represent.

14. Kris decides to paint the amusement park booths. She needs to buy the paint. The store stocks paints that are 25% oil and 35% oil. Kris needs 20 gallons of paint but wants to use one that is 31% oil.

a. Let x = the number of gallons of the paint that is 25% oil. Let y = the number of gallons of the paint that is 35% oil. Write an equation that expresses the total number of gallons in the mixture.

b. What quantity is represented by $0.25x$ in this problem? by $0.35y$? by $0.31(20)$?

c. Write an equation that equates the volumes of paint before and after mixing.

d. Solve the system. Tell how many gallons of each type of paint Kris should buy.

15. If the perimeter of the triangle is at most 30, and s must be a positive integer, what are the possible values of s?

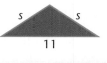

16. **Fun Fee** The price for admission to an  amusement park is different for children and adults. They offer two specials as a savings to families. For 3 children and 2 adults, the price is $21. For 2 children and 1 adult, the price is $12. You are the new manager and want to know how these "specials" were calculated.

a. Write a system of equations using c as the variable for the price for children and a as the variable for the price for adults. Solve this system of equations.

b. What is the price for children's admission? for adult admission?

John Sloan, *Traveling Carnival, Santa Fe*, 1924, National Museum of American Art, Washington, D.C.

 **LOOK BACK**

[6-1]

17. **Motown Mapping** Use this portion of a Detroit map to answer these questions. [6-1]
    a. Name two streets that appear to be parallel.
    b. Name a street that appears to be perpendicular to Gratiot Avenue.
    c. Could you say that Mack Avenue is perpendicular to the Lodge Freeway?
    d. Is Canada south of Detroit? Explain.
    e. Think of Michigan, Grand River, Woodward, and Gratiot as lines. What kind of lines are they?
    f. Detroit is one of the U.S. cities designed with the wheel shape. Explain.

Without graphing, tell which of the functions are linear. Justify your answer. [3-2]

18. $y = \dfrac{4}{x} + 5$

19. $y = \dfrac{3}{4}x - 3$

20. $x = 7.3$

21. $y = 0.2x^2 - 1.9$

22. Write the equation of the line with a y-intercept of 2 and a slope of $\dfrac{1}{3}$. [5-2]

23. Write the equation of the line with an x-intercept of 3 and a slope of $\dfrac{1}{2}$. [5-2]

MORE PRACTICE

Solve each system of equations by substitution.

24. $4x + y = 5$
$x = 2y - 1$

25. $x = y + 8$
$x = -3y + 10$

26. $x - y = -4$
$x + 2y = -5$

27. $2x - 3y = 4$
$y = 2x - 4$

28. $x = 74 - y$
$x = y + 16$

29. $y = 6 - x$
$2x - 3y = 22$

30. $b = -7a + 10$
$2b + 5a = 11$

31. $3x - 4y = 7$
$x + 4y = 5$

32. $a = \dfrac{1}{2}b + 1$
$a = 2b - 2$

33. $8p + 9q = 16$
$q = p - 2$

34. $4w - t = -1$
$t = 6w$

35. $x = y + 8$
$y - 3x = 10$

36. The sum of two numbers is 58, and their difference is 16. Find the numbers using these steps.

    a. Write an equation for the sum of the numbers.

    b. Write an equation for the difference of the numbers.

    c. Solve the system formed by the two equations.

    d. What are the numbers?

MORE MATH REASONING

37. Admission to a certain amusement park is either $6 plus 25¢ per ride or $4 plus 50¢ per ride. Using *c* for cost (of entering the park) and *r* for ride, write a system of equations to determine at what number of rides the cost is the same. Then graph the two equations to verify your findings.

Industry

38. Use the diagram of a wheel to answer these questions. Assume the wheel is a circle.

    a. Find the value of *F* on the *y*-axis. Tell how you found your answer.

    b. Describe how the *spokes* of the wheel are like a system of equations.

    c. Extend several spokes until they intersect the *y*-axis. Will the spaces between the *y*-intercepts be equal? Explain. Is there a pattern? Explain.

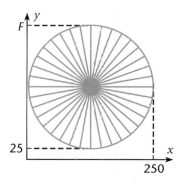

39. Can the graphs of two equations intersect if the quantities in each function are directly related? if the quantities are both inversely related? Explain.

40. Promotional T-shirts were offered by an amusement park at $6 each, or 2 for $10. If 200 T-shirts were sold for a total of $1120, how many shirts were sold as pairs?

Industry

41. An artist attends a conference and learns that a 6% acid solution is the best to use on etchings. He has only a 3% solution, but his partner has a 10% solution. Describe how he could use algebra to calculate the amounts to use from the 3% and the 10% solutions to create 10 milliliters of a 6% solution of acid.

Science

← CONNECT → *You've learned to use substitution to solve systems of linear equations. Another method of solving systems is the linear combination method. You can also use this method to recognize systems with no solutions or an infinite number of solutions.*

The Addition Property of Equality allows us to add or subtract the same quantity on both sides of an equation. It also allows us to add or subtract *equations* in a system, while keeping the original solutions.

For a system with one solution, the graph of the sum or difference of the equations is another line through the solution point of the system.

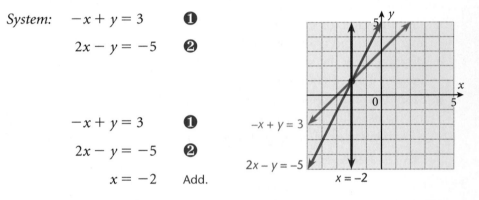

System: $-x + y = 3$ ❶

$2x - y = -5$ ❷

$-x + y = 3$ ❶

$2x - y = -5$ ❷

$x = -2$ Add.

Adding the equations in this system *eliminates* one variable, just as the substitution method does. You can then substitute the value of x into one of the original equations to solve for y.

$$-x + y = 3$$

$$-(-2) + y = 3$$

$$y = 1$$

The solution to the system of equations is $(-2, 1)$.

This method of combining equations to eliminate a variable and solve is called the **linear combination method.** To eliminate a variable, it is sometimes necessary to *multiply* one or both of the equations by constants before adding or subtracting.

1. A paper manufacturer has two factories. One factory produces 800 reams of medium-grade paper and 300 reams of high-grade paper per day. The second factory produces 200 reams of medium-grade paper and 700 reams of high-grade paper per day.

A publishing company has placed an order for 1700 reams of medium-grade paper and 2200 reams of high-grade paper. If both factories work together to fill this order, how many days should each work on the order?

> **Problem-Solving Tip**
>
> Make a table showing the daily paper production of both factories.

Let A = the number of days the first factory works on the order.
Let B = the number of days the second factory works on the order.

Write one equation for the reams of medium-grade paper.

$$800A \quad + \quad 200B \quad = \quad 1700 \quad ❶$$
$$\text{first factory} \qquad \text{second factory} \qquad \text{total reams}$$

Write another equation for the reams of high-grade paper.

$$300A \quad + \quad 700B \quad = \quad 2200 \quad ❷$$
$$\text{first factory} \qquad \text{second factory} \qquad \text{total reams}$$

Multiply both equations so that the terms with the variable B match.

$$7 \cdot ❶$$
$$800A + 200B = 1700 \rightarrow 5600A + 1400B = 11{,}900$$

$$2 \cdot ❷$$
$$300A + 700B = 2200 \rightarrow \underline{600A + 1400B = 4400}$$
$$5000A = 7500 \qquad \text{Subtract.}$$
$$A = 1.5 \qquad \text{Solve for A.}$$

Substitute the value of A into one of the original equations and solve for B.

$$800A + 200B = 1700 \qquad ❶$$
$$800(1.5) + 200B = 1700 \qquad \text{Substitute 1.5 for } A.$$
$$1200 + 200B = 1700$$
$$B = 2.5 \qquad \text{Solve for } B.$$

The first factory should work for 1.5 days on the order and the second factory should work for 2.5 days on the order.

1. What property allows you to multiply an equation by a constant, as in Example 1?

TRY IT

Solve each system using the linear combination method.

a. $x + 2y = -4$
  $2x - 2y = -5$

b. $5x - 3y = 12$
  $2x - 3y = 3$

c. $2x + 5y = 7$
  $3x + 15y = 11$

Recall that not all systems have exactly one solution. If the graphs of the equations are parallel lines, there are no solutions. If the graphs are the same line, there are an infinite number of solutions. In the following Explore, you will investigate these cases using graphs and the linear combination method.

EXPLORE: HOW MANY SOLUTIONS?

MATERIALS

Graphing utility or Graph paper and Straightedge

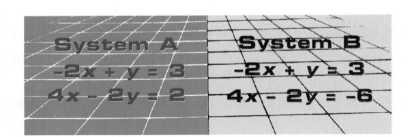

System A
-2x + y = 3
4x - 2y = 2

System B
-2x + y = 3
4x - 2y = -6

1. Graph each system and tell how many solutions the system has.
2. Try to solve each system using the linear combination method. Explain what happened in each system when you tried to eliminate a variable.
3. Compare your results with those of a classmate. Describe a way you can use the linear combination method to tell how many solutions a system has.
4. Make up your own system and decide how many solutions it has using your method. Check by graphing.

A system with an *infinite* number of solutions is a **dependent system.** The graphs of the equations in a dependent system are the same line.

A system with *no* solutions is an **inconsistent system.** The graphs of the equations in an inconsistent system are parallel lines.

In the Explore, you may have discovered how to recognize dependent and inconsistent systems using the linear combination method.

EXAMPLES

Solve each system of equations.

2. $x + y = 4$ ❶
    $4x + 4y = 16$ ❷

$$4 \cdot ❶$$
$$x + y = 4 \rightarrow 4x + 4y = 16 \qquad \text{Multiply both sides of ❶ by 4.}$$
$$4x + 4y = 16 \qquad ❷$$

The equations are the same! So their graphs are the same line. Every point (x, y) on the line is a solution to the system. The system is *dependent*.

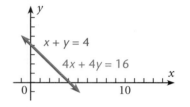

3. $12x - 4y = -20$ ❶
    $-6x + 2y = 16$ ❷

$$12x - 4y = -20 \qquad ❶$$
$$2 \cdot ❷$$
$$-6x + 2y = 16 \rightarrow \underline{-12x + 4y = 32} \qquad \text{Multiply both sides of ❷ by 2.}$$
$$0 \neq 12 \qquad\qquad \text{Adding gives unequal values.}$$

The two sides of the resulting equation are *never* equal! So there is no solution to the system. The graphs must be parallel. The system is *inconsistent*.

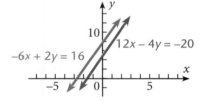

TRY IT

Solve each system of equations.

d. $x + 2y = -4$
    $2x + 4y = -4$

e. $2x - 5y = 10$
    $0.8x - 2y = 4$

REFLECT

1. Describe two ways to combine the equations in this system to eliminate a variable. $x - y = 4$
                                         $4x - y = -2$

2. When you use the linear combination method, how can you tell whether you need to multiply by a constant first?

3. Describe how the graphs of a dependent system are related.

4. Describe how the graphs of an inconsistent system are related.

Exercises

CORE

1. Getting Started Consider the system $x - y = 5$ and $x + y = 7$.
    a. Add the equations. Which variable is eliminated?
    b. Solve for x in the new equation.
    c. Substitute the value of x into one of the original equations. Solve for y.
    d. What is the solution to this system? Check your answer.

Solve each system using the linear combination method.

2. $x + 2y = 7$
   $x - 2y = 11$

3. $2x - 2y = 4$
   $-2x - y = 11$

Write the word or phrase that correctly completes each statement.

4. A system with _____ solutions is a dependent system.

5. A system with _____ solutions is an inconsistent system.

Identify each system as dependent or inconsistent. Tell how you decided.

6. $4x - 10y = 20$
   $-2x + 5y = -5$

7. $3x + 2y = 4$
   $6x + 4y = 8$

8. $8x + 3y = 5$
   $-4x - 1.5y = 3.5$

9. Adam wants to solve each of these systems using linear combination. What would you advise him to use as a first step? Why?
    a. $m + n = -7$
       $3m + n = -9$

    b. $a - 3b = 0$
       $5a - b = -14$

Solve each system. Tell which method you used and why you used it.

10. $7x + 5y = 18$
    $x - 5y = -2$

11. $5c + 6d = 14$
    $3c - 4d = 16$

12. $3v + 4w = -10$
    $4v - w = -7$

13. $4x + 3y = 14$
    $9x - 2y = 14$

14. $2m + 3n = 0$
    $5m - 2n = -19$

15. $3a - b = 8$
    $a + 2b = 5$

16. Fortune Hunting The perimeter of Madame Zelda's Fortune Telling Booth is 32 meters, and the length is 6 meters longer than the width.
    a. Express this in a system of equations, and solve using any method.
    b. What is the area of her booth?

17. Phil has $100 and spends $3 daily. Joe starts with $20 and earns $5 daily.
    a. Write an equation that describes Phil's money (y) over x days.
    b. Write an equation that describes Joe's money (y) over x days.
    c. How many days will it take for them to have the same amount of money? Tell how you decided.

18. Use the tables to write a system of equations. Solve the system.

x	y
−3	2
3	0
6	−1
9	−2

x	y
−2	−8
0	−4
2	0
4	4

19. The perimeter of a rectangle is 12 cm. The length is 1 cm shorter than twice the width. Find the dimensions of the rectangle.

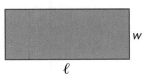

w

ℓ

Problem-Solving Tip

Write a system of equations.

20. Airline schedules allow 3 hours and 10 minutes airborne time to fly from Washington D.C. to Dallas/Fort Worth (D/FW) and 2 hours and 15 minutes from D/FW to Washington D.C. The time difference can largely be attributed to the *jet stream,* a wind that usually blows from west to east. The distance between Washington D.C. and D/FW is 1176 miles. A passenger is curious about the difference in flight times and decides to calculate the speed of the jet stream.

a. The plane's actual speed when flying *with the wind* is the *sum* of the plane's speed (p) and the jet stream speed (w). Express the actual speed of the plane when flying with the jet stream.

b. The plane's actual speed when flying *against the wind* is the difference of the plane's speed (p) and the jet stream speed (w). Express the actual speed of the plane when flying against the jet stream.

c. Write the algebraic expression for the distance flown with the wind in terms of rate and time. Write the algebraic expression for the distance flown against the wind in terms of rate and time.

d. Write and solve a system of two linear equations that represents the flight distances in the two directions. What is the speed of the jet stream?

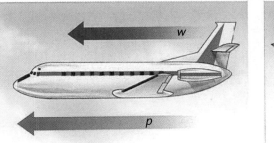
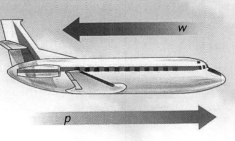

21. We're Off to the Fair Phana and Isaac live on the corner of L and First. They want to go to the fair at the corner of O and Fourth.

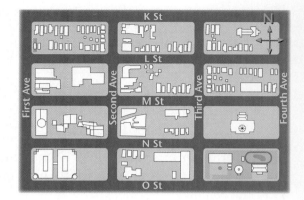

a. How many different routes can they take?

b. Consider two routes. Are there the same number of horizontal and vertical blocks? Explain.

c. Suppose they have to drive. The odd avenues are one way north and the even avenues are one way south. How does this affect the number of routes?

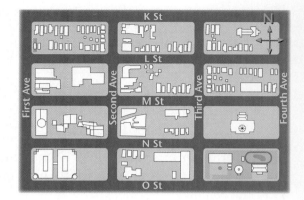

LOOK AHEAD

Let $A = \begin{bmatrix} 7 & -2 & 9 \\ 5 & 6 & 8 \\ -6 & 5 & -7 \end{bmatrix}$ Let $B = \begin{bmatrix} 42 & 76 & -51 \\ 17 & 2.3 & -35 \\ -63 & 57 & 90 \end{bmatrix}$ Let $C = \begin{bmatrix} -75 & 8.2 & -64 \\ 26 & 9 & 17 \\ 5 & -18 & 1.6 \end{bmatrix}$

22. What are the dimensions of these matrices?

Find the following.

23. $A + B$

24. $B - C$

25. $C - A$

26. What is the product of 7 and A?

MORE PRACTICE

Solve each system of equations using the linear combination method.

27. $x - y = 7$
$\quad 2x + y = -1$

28. $x + y = 15$
$\quad -x + y = -1$

29. $2x - 3y = 7$
$\quad x + 3y = 2$

What would be a good first step in solving these systems?

30. $2x + y = -7$
$\quad x + 2y = -2$

31. $\frac{1}{2}x - 3y = 10$
$\quad x + 5y = 3$

32. $3x + 1.6y = 23$
$\quad 7x - 0.8y = 15$

Identify each system as dependent or inconsistent. Tell how you decided.

33. $-3x + y = -2$
$\quad 3x - y = -2$

34. $2x - 6y = 8$
$\quad x - 3y = 6$

35. $x - 3y = 4$
$\quad 3x - 9y = 12$

Solve each system. Tell which method you used and why you used it.

36. $x + y = 4$
$x + 3y = 6$

37. $18a - 5b = 17$
$6a + 10b = -6$

38. $x + 2y = 4$
$3x - y = 5$

39. $4x - 3y = 18$
$2x - y = 8$

40. $2c - 4d = 8$
$-c + 2d = 2$

41. $2x + y = -8$
$1.5x - 3y = -6$

42. $6x + 5y = 9$
$3x - \frac{1}{3}y = -4$

43. $2x - 3y = -11$
$-2x + 3y = -11$

44. $3x - 4y = 1$
$6x + y = 4.25$

MORE MATH REASONING

45. Chirp Calculation It is possible to tell the outdoor temperature (Fahrenheit) by counting the number of chirps a cricket makes per minute, dividing that number by 4, and adding 40. Using a system of equations, determine if there is a temperature at which the number of chirps and temperature are equal.

46. Consider the system of $2x + y = 3$ and _____.
  a. Write an equation that makes the system inconsistent. Tell how you decided.
  b. Write an equation that makes the system dependent. Tell how you decided.

47. If there are three unknown variables, it is usually necessary to have three equations in a system to find a unique solution. Solve the following system. Explain your work.
$x = 3z - 9 \qquad y = z - 1 \qquad 2x + 3y - z = 3$

48. Nomogram Grading Find the grades for these students using the Nomogram. Why does the Nomogram work?
  • Marisa answered correctly 5 out of 10 multiple-choice questions and 23 out of 25 true-or-false questions. Her score was 71%.
  • Sue answered correctly 10 multiple-choice and 21 true-or-false.
  • Lou answered correctly 5 multiple-choice and 25 true-or-false.
  • Stu answered correctly 8 multiple-choice and 23 true-or-false.

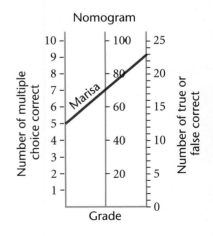

Nomogram

49. Rose needs 10 milliliters of a 3% acid solution to do an experiment. She has only a 5% solution and a 2% solution. Use a system of linear equations to determine how much of each acid she should mix to get her desired 10 milliliters.

Solving with Matrices

← CONNECT →
You've solved systems using graphs, substitution, and linear combinations. Now you'll see how matrices can be multiplied and used to solve systems.

In Chapter 1, you learned addition and scalar multiplication of matrices. In some cases matrices can be multiplied by other matrices. This is called **matrix multiplication.**

Here's how to multiply a 2×2 matrix and a 2×1 matrix. The resulting **product matrix** is another 2×1 matrix.

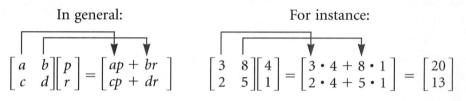

In general:

$$\begin{bmatrix} a & b \\ c & d \end{bmatrix} \begin{bmatrix} p \\ r \end{bmatrix} = \begin{bmatrix} ap + br \\ cp + dr \end{bmatrix}$$

For instance:

$$\begin{bmatrix} 3 & 8 \\ 2 & 5 \end{bmatrix} \begin{bmatrix} 4 \\ 1 \end{bmatrix} = \begin{bmatrix} 3 \cdot 4 + 8 \cdot 1 \\ 2 \cdot 4 + 5 \cdot 1 \end{bmatrix} = \begin{bmatrix} 20 \\ 13 \end{bmatrix}$$

The way we multiply matrices comes from their use in applications.

EXAMPLE

1. Find the value of each store's inventory of polo shirts and dress shirts.

	polo shirts	dress shirts
Downtown store	25	30
Uptown store	18	35

The shirts cost $16 for dress and $12 for polo at each store.

Set up the prices in a 2×1 matrix. Then multiply the matrices to find the values.

Downtown store
Uptown store
$$\begin{array}{c} \text{polo} \quad \text{dress} \\ \begin{bmatrix} 25 & 30 \\ 18 & 35 \end{bmatrix} \end{array} \begin{array}{c} \text{polo price} \\ \begin{bmatrix} 12 \\ 16 \end{bmatrix} \\ \text{dress price} \end{array} = \begin{bmatrix} 25 \cdot 12 + 30 \cdot 16 \\ 18 \cdot 12 + 35 \cdot 16 \end{bmatrix} = \begin{bmatrix} 780 \\ 776 \end{bmatrix} \begin{array}{l} \text{Value of shirts at} \\ \text{downtown store} \\ \\ \text{Value of shirts at} \\ \text{uptown store} \end{array}$$

The value of all shirts at the downtown store is $780.
The value of all shirts at the uptown store is $776.

Find each product matrix.

a. $\begin{bmatrix} 1 & 2 \\ 3 & 4 \end{bmatrix}\begin{bmatrix} 9 \\ 5 \end{bmatrix}$ **b.** $\begin{bmatrix} 4 & -1 \\ -2 & 0 \end{bmatrix}\begin{bmatrix} 3 \\ 1 \end{bmatrix}$

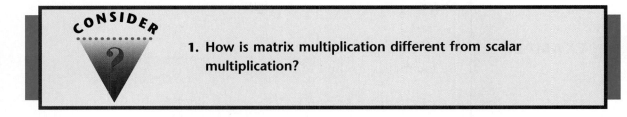

CONSIDER

?

1. How is matrix multiplication different from scalar multiplication?

A graphing calculator or computer program with matrix capabilities can be a useful tool for solving a system of equations if it has exactly one solution.

EXPLORE: JUST MULTIPLY AND SOLVE!

MATERIALS

Graphing calculator or Computer program

You can represent a system of equations in standard form with two matrices.

$3x + y = 5$
$2x + 5y = -1$ $A = \begin{bmatrix} 3 & 1 \\ 2 & 5 \end{bmatrix}$ $B = \begin{bmatrix} 5 \\ -1 \end{bmatrix}$

System   *Coefficient matrix*   *Constant matrix*

1. Enter the matrices A and B into your graphing calculator.
2. To solve the system you need to find a different 2×2 matrix, A^{-1}, called the **inverse matrix** of A. On many graphing calculators, you can find A^{-1} by entering A and then pressing the $\boxed{x^{-1}}$ key. Find the matrix A^{-1}.
3. Use your graphing calculator to multiply the matrices A^{-1} and B. The 2×1 product matrix, $A^{-1}B$, is the **solution matrix.** The entries of this matrix are the values of x and y.

$X = \begin{bmatrix} x \\ y \end{bmatrix}$ $A^{-1}B = \begin{bmatrix} ? \\ ? \end{bmatrix}$ ⟵ The upper entry is the value of x.
⟵ The lower entry is the value of y.

Variable matrix   *Solution matrix*

What is the solution to the system? Check your solution.

4. Repeat this method to solve this system.
$3x + y = 19$
$2x + 5y = 4$

Solving a system with matrices is similar to solving a simple equation.

$$AX = B$$
$$A^{-1}AX = A^{-1}B$$
$$X = A^{-1}B$$

EXAMPLE

2. Use the matrix method to solve this system. $\begin{array}{l} 3x - 5y = -7 \\ 5x - 8y = -11 \end{array}$

$$A = \begin{bmatrix} 3 & -5 \\ 5 & -8 \end{bmatrix} \qquad B = \begin{bmatrix} -7 \\ -11 \end{bmatrix}$$

Coefficient matrix   *Constant matrix*

A graphing calculator will find the inverse matrix, A^{-1}, and the solution matrix, $A^{-1}B$.

```
   [A]⁻¹              [A]⁻¹[B]
[ -8  5]            [  1]
[ -5  3]            [  2]
```

The solution matrix shows that the solution to the system is (1, 2).

TRY IT

Write a constant matrix, and use the inverse matrix in Example 2 to solve each system.

c. $3x - 5y = -9$ **d.** $3x - 5y = 10$
     $5x - 8y = -14$ $5x - 8y = 17$

The matrix method of solving systems is especially useful in this age of technology. This method can also be used to solve the larger systems that are used in operations research and the communications industry.

REFLECT

1. Are all of the entries in a 2×2 matrix and 2×1 matrix used to find the product matrix? Give an example to explain.

2. Why do you think graphing calculators and computers are especially useful for solving systems with matrices?

3. When would you prefer the matrix method to other methods of solving systems? Explain.

Exercises

CORE

1. Getting Started Complete to find the product matrix.

$$\begin{bmatrix} -3 & 4 \\ 5 & 6 \end{bmatrix}\begin{bmatrix} 2 \\ 7 \end{bmatrix} = \begin{bmatrix} -3 \cdot 2 + 4 \cdot \underline{} \\ 5 \cdot \underline{} + \underline{} \cdot 7 \end{bmatrix} = \begin{bmatrix} \underline{} \\ \underline{} \end{bmatrix}$$

2. Use these steps to find the product matrix.

$$\begin{bmatrix} 2 & 3 \\ 4 & 6 \end{bmatrix}\begin{bmatrix} -1 \\ 5 \end{bmatrix}$$

  a. Find the sum of $2 \cdot -1 + 3 \cdot 5$.
  b. Find the sum of $4 \cdot -1 + 6 \cdot 5$.
  c. Write the product matrix.

3. Match the type of matrix with its description.
  a. inverse matrix   **i.** the entries are the values of x and y
  b. product matrix   **ii.** the entries are the coefficients of the variables of a system
  c. coefficient matrix   **iii.** the entries are the constants in a system
  d. solution matrix   **iv.** the answer when two matrices are multiplied
  e. constant matrix   **v.** the matrix by which you multiply the constant matrix to get the solution

Find each product matrix.

4. $\begin{bmatrix} 1 & 2 \\ 0 & 5 \end{bmatrix}\begin{bmatrix} -1 \\ 3 \end{bmatrix}$

5. $\begin{bmatrix} 7 & -3 \\ 11 & 4 \end{bmatrix}\begin{bmatrix} 0 \\ 5 \end{bmatrix}$

6. $\begin{bmatrix} 2 & -9 \\ 6 & 13 \end{bmatrix}\begin{bmatrix} 22 \\ 10 \end{bmatrix}$

For each system, the coefficient matrix is A and the inverse is A^{-1}. Solve each system of equations using matrix multiplication.

$$A = \begin{bmatrix} 5 & -3 \\ -3 & 2 \end{bmatrix} \qquad A^{-1} = \begin{bmatrix} 2 & 3 \\ 3 & 5 \end{bmatrix}$$

7. $5x - 3y = -20$
$-3x + 2y = 14$

8. $5x - 3y = 15$
$-3x + 2y = -9$

9. $5x - 3y = 44$
$-3x + 2y = -28$

10. Algebra Works Overtime Jake works at Musicloud. He is responsible for checking the incoming shipments. An order of 20 AM/FM portable radios and 25 portable CD players arrives, but the invoice is torn, so only the final charge of $1692.50 is readable. He remembers that the CD players were $20 more than the radios. It is too late in the evening to call the company to find the cost of each item. Jake finds their cost by using algebra. Describe what algebra you think he used, and give the cost of each item.

Solve each system. Check your solution.

11. $2x - 3y = 1.5$
$x - y = 1.5$

12. $3a - 2b = 12$
$2a - 2b = 6$

13. $4x - 3y = 11$
$5x - 6y = 9$

14. Solve this problem included in the works of Chinese statesman Ch'ang Ts'ang (c. 250–152 B.C.).

History

Suppose there are a number of rabbits and pheasants confined in a cage. In all, there are 35 heads and 94 feet. How many rabbits and how many pheasants are there?

Rabbit-shaped Jade Pendant, Sui-early Song dynasties, 6th–9th Century, China, Asian Art Museum of San Francisco, The Avery Brundage Collection

15. A pharmaceutical chemist has a 10% solution (by volume) of alcohol and a 25% solution of alcohol. She needs to know how much of each to mix to obtain 1000 ml of a 20% solution. Let x be the number of milliliters of the 10% solution and y be the number of milliliters of the 25% solution in the mixture.

Science

a. Write an equation that expresses the total number of milliliters in the mixture.
b. What quantity is represented by $0.10x$ in this problem? by $0.25y$? by $0.20(1000)$?
c. Write an equation that equates the volumes of alcohol before and after mixing.
d. Solve the system, and describe how much of each solution the chemist should use for the mixture.

16. Use matrix multiplication to find the total value of the inventory for two carnival booths whose prizes are small and large bears worth $2.50 and $5.00. Show your work.

Booth	Small Bears	Large Bears
GatorLand	150	50
Pirate	75	20

LOOK BACK

17. Location, Location, Location!!!!! The information in this chart was compiled by the U.S. Labor Department in 1990. [1-1]

Social Science

a. How many manufacturing jobs are there in the Great Lakes region?
b. Who might be interested in this chart and why?
c. What are some of the factors that contribute to the presence of large numbers of manufacturing jobs in the top two regions?
d. How many of these regions have percentages above the average?

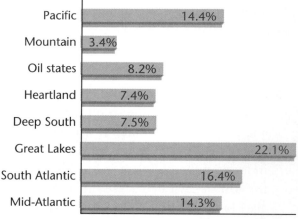

Percent of Total Manufacturing Jobs by Region

Pacific 14.4%
Mountain 3.4%
Oil states 8.2%
Heartland 7.4%
Deep South 7.5%
Great Lakes 22.1%
South Atlantic 16.4%
Mid-Atlantic 14.3%

U.S. employment: 19.1 million

18. Johanna knows the slope of line AB is 3. She knows that the coordinates of A are $(-1, 4)$ and that B lies on the y-axis. Tell how she could find the coordinates of B. [5-2]

19. Final Approach In the time since a plane was cleared to land, 8 seconds have passed and the plane has descended 6400 feet. [5-2]

a. Express the plane's landing path as a rate of change in feet per second.

b. The plane's altitude is now 2500 feet. What was its altitude when it was cleared to land?

c. The pilot wants to land 10 seconds from now. What should the rate of descent be?

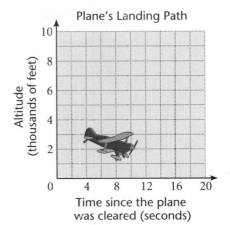

Plane's Landing Path

20. Is $(2, -1)$ a solution to the system $y = x - 3$ and $x + y = 1$? Explain your answer. [6-1]

MORE PRACTICE

Find each product matrix.

21. $\begin{bmatrix} -5 & 12 \\ 7 & 31 \end{bmatrix}\begin{bmatrix} 2 \\ -4 \end{bmatrix}$

22. $\begin{bmatrix} 1 & 3 \\ 5 & 7 \end{bmatrix}\begin{bmatrix} 9 \\ 11 \end{bmatrix}$

23. $\begin{bmatrix} -1 & 0 \\ 0 & -1 \end{bmatrix}\begin{bmatrix} 13 \\ 72 \end{bmatrix}$

For each system, the coefficient matrix is A and the inverse is A^{-1}. Solve each system of equations using matrix multiplication.

$$A = \begin{bmatrix} 10 & -3 \\ 7 & -2 \end{bmatrix} \qquad A^{-1} = \begin{bmatrix} -2 & 3 \\ -7 & 10 \end{bmatrix}$$

24. $10x - 3y = 43$
$7x - 2y = 30$

25. $10x - 3y = -38$
$7x - 2y = -26$

26. $10x - 3y = 15$
$7x - 2y = -11$

For each system, the coefficient matrix is C and the inverse is C^{-1}. Solve each system of equations using matrix multiplication.

$$C = \begin{bmatrix} 25 & 9 \\ 11 & 4 \end{bmatrix} \qquad C^{-1} = \begin{bmatrix} 4 & -9 \\ -11 & 25 \end{bmatrix}$$

27. $25x + 9y = -30$
$11x + 4y = -13$

28. $25x + 9y = 2$
$11x + 4y = 1$

29. $25x + 9y = 59$
$11x + 4y = 26$

Solve each system. Check your solution.

30. $5x - 3y = 3$
$2x - 6y = 30$

31. $2x - 5y = 17$
$6x + y = 3$

32. $x - 3y = 1$
$x + y = 13$

MORE MATH REASONING

33. Think of three lines in space. What are the possibilities for how these three lines might relate to each other? Use the cube to help visualize the answer.

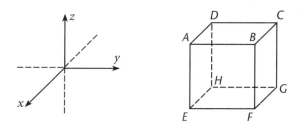

Solve each system using matrices.

34. $3x + 4y + 2z = 6$
$x + 3y - 5z = -7$
$5x + 7y - 3z = 3$

35. $2x + 3y - z = -2$
$-3x - y + z = -2$
$x + y - 3z = -8$

36. Solve this famous Hindu problem adapted from the *Mahavira* (c. 850). Explain your method.

> *The mixed price of 9 citrons and 7 fragrant wood apples is 107. The mixed price of 7 citrons and 9 fragrant wood apples is 101. Oh arithmetician, tell me quickly the price of a citron and of a wood apple, having distinctly separated those prices well.*

37. Bus Baffle The team bus is carrying 15 players. Only sophomores, juniors, and seniors are on the team. There is one more sophomore than juniors. The number of seniors is one more than the sum of the number of juniors and sophomores. How many juniors are there? Explain how you solved this problem.

38. Solve the following problem originally posed by Benjamin Banneker.

> *A gentleman sent his servant with 100 pounds to buy 100 cattle [bullocks and cows] and sheep, with orders to give 5 pounds for each bullock, 20 shillings worth of cows, and 1 shilling for each sheep. What number of each sort did he buy for his master?*
(Hint: There are 20 shillings in a pound.)

> **Problem-Solving Tip**
>
> Try special cases of the number of sheep.

← **CONNECT** → *You've examined systems of equations and their solutions in several ways. The substitution and linear combination methods are symbolic methods of solving systems. They are especially useful for finding exact solutions to systems.*

EXPLORE: BALANCING ACT

MATERIALS

Graphing calculator
Graph paper
Straightedge

Linda got a summer job operating the Giant Gondola Wheel at Fun City. The manager told Linda that overloading the Ferris wheel is very dangerous and that it shouldn't exceed 120 adults or 160 children. Linda wants to figure out what combinations of children and adults can safely ride the wheel.

1. Define variables and write a linear equation that relates the number of adults and the number of children that can safely ride the wheel at one time. (Hint: When there are no children, there can be 120 adults. When there are no adults there can be 160 children.)
2. What do you think is being assumed about the loads placed on the wheel by children and by adults? Explain.

Linda has noticed that the number of adults and the number of children who ride the wheel are usually about the same. She decides just to load equal numbers of adults and children.

3. Write another linear equation that assumes the number of adults and the number of children are equal. Graph both linear equations on the same coordinate plane.
4. Solve the system of two linear equations you wrote. Describe the method you used to solve the system. Why did you choose that method?
5. How many adult-child pairs can safely ride the wheel at one time? Is your answer exact? Does it need to be? Explain.

1. Explain why you want to *eliminate* a variable when you substitute or combine equations in a system.
2. When might the substitution method or linear combination method be preferable to the graphing method for solving a system?
3. Give an example of a system that you would solve using each method. Also describe the first step you would use in each case.
   a. substitution method   **b.** linear combination method

Self-Assessment

1. Solve this system three ways. Show that the solution is the same each way.
$$y = 2x - 6$$
$$x - y = 4$$

Solve each system. Tell which method you used and why.

2. $y = 2x$
   $x + y = 12$

3. $x + y = 6$
   $x - y = 12$

4. $3x + 2y = 14$
   $4 - 2x = y$

5. $5x - 3y = 10$
   $3y = 5x - 10$

6. $x - 3y = 10$
   $y = 5x + 1$

7. $2x - y = 10$
   $2y = 4x - 10$

8. Which ordered pair is the solution to the system $x - 2y = 6$ and $2x - 3y = 5$? Tell how you decided.
   (a) $(-8, 7)$ (b) $(8, 1)$ (c) $(6, 0)$ (d) $(-2, -4)$ (e) not here

9. **My Kingdom for a Parking Space** Before the gates to the County Fair opened one holiday morning, all 250 spaces in the north parking lot had filled. The number of cars was 20 less than twice the number of trucks. How many of each kind of vehicle were there?

> **Problem-Solving Tip**
>
> Write a system of equations.

10. Which system(s) is(are) dependent? Tell how you decided.
   I. $3x + y = 1$
      $6x + 2y = 2$

   II. $3y = -3x + 2$
      $y = -x + \frac{2}{3}$

   III. $x + 2y = 5$
      $x - y = 1$

   (a) I only   (b) II only   (c) III only   (d) I and II   (e) I, II, and III

11. The perimeter of a rectangular garden is 46 meters, and the length is 8 meters longer than the width.

   a. Express this in a system of equations.

   b. Solve the system using any method of your choice.

   c. What is the area of the garden?

12. **Doggie Dilemma** To celebrate the end of school, John's class went to Funland Amusement Park. Before lunch, John took orders and exact change from everyone in the class for either a corn dog or a hot dog. Corn dogs cost $1.50 and hot dogs cost $1.75. His order list blew away in a gust of wind on his way to the refreshment booth, but he had the money he had collected from everyone—$50.25. Since he knew there were a total of 30 students in the class, he was able to figure out how many of each kind of dog to get. How many was that? Tell how you decided.

13. Solve this system. (You may use matrices if you wish.) Explain how to check your solution.

   $2x - y = 6$
   $x - y = 4$

14. Consider the equation $x - y = 4$.

   a. If the equation is multiplied by 2, how is the graph of the resulting equation different from the graph of $x - y = 4$?

   b. If the equation is multiplied by (-1), how is the graph of the resulting equation different from the graph of $x - y = 4$?

   c. What would be true about the graph of any nonzero multiple of $x - y = 4$?

15. **Gondola Wheel Revisited** Suppose Linda received word from the admission window that the specifications state that it can hold 60 adults or 120 children. How many pairs (one adult and one child) could she safely load? Explain.

16. Consider each situation and determine whether there is an algebraic solution and what kind. Then consider the same situation and evaluate it as a real-world solution.

   a. Two planes fly on parallel courses.

   b. Two planes fly on the same course.

   c. Two planes fly on intersecting courses.

17. Brother and Sister Act When Ted was 10 years old, he was 4 feet 9 inches tall. He grew at the same rate until he was 15, when he was 5 feet 7 inches. When Ted's sister Casey was 10 years old, she was 5 feet tall, and she grew at the same rate until she was 15, when she was 5 feet 5 inches.
   a. Was there ever a time when Ted and Casey were the same height at the same age? When was this and how tall were they?
   b. What information could help you determine if they were ever the same height at the same time?

18. Moving Along You know the famous story about the Hare and the Tortoise? Basically, they started out on a race that the Hare thought was ridiculous. Of course, he was much faster and got way ahead of the Tortoise early on. But he stopped to take a nap, during which time the Tortoise overtook him—and eventually won the race. Assume the race is 100 yards. The Tortoise moves at a rate of 5 yards per minute. The Hare gives the Tortoise 6 minutes lead time, then he takes off at a rate of 20 yards per minute. After 4 minutes he stops to take a 10-minute nap. Plot all of this on a coordinate plane.

   a. How many minutes has the Hare been running when he overtakes the Tortoise?
   b. How many minutes has the Tortoise been running when he overtakes the Hare?
   c. How many minutes did the race last?

19. The probability that the merry-go-round at Farnum's Amusement Park will work properly on any given day is 0.98. The probability that it will work properly for n days in a row is the value of the power $(0.98)^n$. What is the probability that the merry-go-round will work properly for 2 weeks in a row? 10 weeks in a row?

20. Bikes International Use the graph to answer these questions.
   a. What was the company's worst year?
   b. When did the company start to make a profit?
   c. Describe how you could use the graph to estimate the profits for this company in a particular year.

Company Performance

SHADOW

We often say that something "casts a shadow." Of course, an object does not "throw" darkness. It simply blocks the path of light to a surface, defining a region of darkness. Did you ever make a shadow rabbit on the wall? As a young boy, Prasanna Rao of Mysore, India, was very ill and had to spend long periods of time in bed. To ease his loneliness, he created shadow images of people, birds, and animals on his bedroom wall by using his fingers and hands in increasingly complicated shapes. Shadowgraphy is the art of creating these illusions, sometimes called silhouettes, on a screen. In Shadowplay, the images help to tell a story.

Rao has performed extensively throughout the world, and has appeared on the children's television program *Sesame Street*. As one of the foremost practitioners of this art, he has earned the title "Prince of Shadow."

1. What defines the boundary of the region that looks like a rabbit?
2. In the shadowgraph of two llamas eating, what defines the regions of the llamas heads? What defines the region that looks like a haystack?
3. In the shadowgraph of the flying bird, two hands cast shadows. Why is there only one shadow image?

← C O N N E C T → *You know how to graph linear equations on a coordinate plane. Now you will interpret and graph linear inequalities with two variables.*

Research has shown that some medical problems can be treated with special diets. You will investigate such a diet in the following Explore.

EXPLORE: FOOD FOR THOUGHT

MATERIALS

Graph paper

A nutrition expert has planned a special diet using two foods as sources of calcium. The goal is to meet a daily minimum requirement for calcium from these two items.

Food A
40 units of calcium per ounce

Food B
10 units of calcium per ounce

Minimum daily requirement
for calcium:
360 units

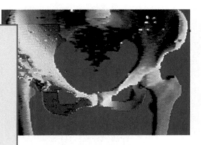

Calcium helps build strong bones.

1. Find five combinations of Foods A and B that *exceed* the minimum daily requirement. Give the number of ounces of each food for each combination.

2. Write and graph an equation that shows that the total amount of calcium in *x* ounces of Food A and *y* ounces of Food B is 360 units.

3. Plot the ordered pairs for the five combinations you found in step 1. What do you notice about the location of these points?

4. How many combinations of Foods A and B contain more than the minimum daily requirement for calcium? What would a graph of the points corresponding to all these combinations look like? Explain.

Phrases like *south of the border* and *out of bounds* describe regions to one side or the other of a *boundary.* When the boundary of a region is a line, the points on one side of it represent **solutions to a linear inequality** with two variables. There are an infinite number of ordered pairs (x, y) that solve the inequality.

Just as we graphed solutions to an inequality with one variable on the number line, we graph solutions to an inequality with two variables on the coordinate plane. The first step in graphing a linear inequality with two variables is to find the boundary line of the solutions by graphing the related equation.

EXAMPLE

Graph the inequality $y \le -x - 2$.

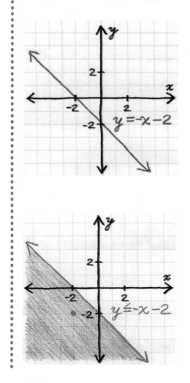

Graph the boundary line $y = -x - 2$.

Solutions of $y \le -x - 2$ include points on the line $y = -x - 2$, so we show the line as solid.

Next determine which region contains solutions of the inequality by testing points on either side of the line.

$(0, 0)$ does not satisfy $y \le -x - 2$.

$(-2, -2)$ does satisfy the inequality.

We shade the region that contains the point that makes the inequality true.

We use a *dotted* line when the inequality symbol is $<$ or $>$ to show that the boundary line is *not* included in the solutions.

Solutions of $y < -x - 2$ would *not* include points on the line, so we would show a dotted line.

1. How many points do you have to test to determine which region to shade?

TRY IT

Write an inequality for each graph. The equation of the boundary line is given.

a. $y = 2x + 1$

b. $y = -0.5x + 1$

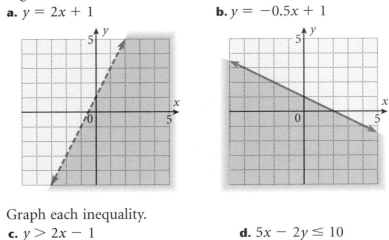

Graph each inequality.

c. $y > 2x - 1$

d. $5x - 2y \leq 10$

We can only show a small portion of the graph of an inequality with two variables. The actual graph extends on and on, covering half of the plane.

REFLECT

1. When you graph an inequality, why does it matter whether or not you include points *on the line* as part of the graph?
2. Why do solutions to an inequality lie on one side of the boundary line but not on the other?
3. Are the solutions to a linear inequality of the form $y < mx + b$ *above* or *below* the boundary line $y = mx + b$? Explain why.
4. Describe how the photo relates to the graph of a linear inequality.

Exercises

CORE

1. **Getting Started** Use these steps to graph $y > x + 1$.
   a. Graph $y = x + 1$ as the boundary.
   b. Should your boundary line be drawn as a solid or a dashed line? Why?
   c. Choose two points on either side of the boundary line. Substitute them into the original inequality. Which point makes the statement true?
   d. Shade the region that contains the solution points.

2. Does the origin satisfy the inequality $x + 2y \leq 2$? Explain.

3. Does $(-1, -1)$ satisfy the inequality $3x - 2y > -2$? Tell how you decided.

Write an inequality for each graph. The equation of the boundary line is given.

4. $x = -2$ 5. $y = x + 1$ 6. $y = -\frac{1}{2}x - 2$

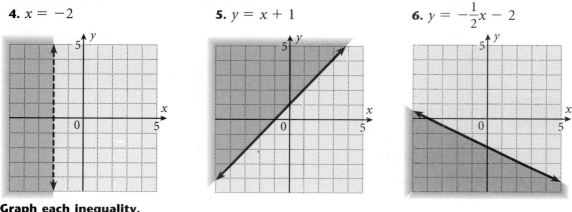

Graph each inequality.

7. $y \leq -3$ 8. $y > -4x - 3$ 9. $3x - 2y \geq 8$ 10. $y \leq 3x$

11. Equivalent inequalities have the same boundaries and the same points as solutions.
    a. Is $x + y < 5$ equivalent to $5 < x + y$? Explain.
    b. Is $5 < x + y$ equivalent to $y < x - 5$? Explain.

12. Graph the line $x + y = 5$.
    a. How many quadrants have solution points for the inequality $x + y < 5$?
    b. How many quadrants have solution points for the inequality $x + y > 5$?
    c. Explain the differences.
    d. What region is described when $x + y = 5$, $x + y > 5$, and $x + y < 5$ are graphed together?

13. Lynn's family just bought a riding stable. It will house no more than 18 animals. They want some ponies and some horses.
    a. Write an inequality that describes the situation.
    b. Which quadrant will hold the solution points to this real-life problem?
    c. Graph the solution. How does it compare to the real-life solution?

Industry

14. Write some English phrases that suggest regions. Explain how they are like linear inequalities.

15. Lake High School makes a profit of $4 on each yearbook bought and paid for in advance. They make a profit of only $2 if a yearbook is bought after publication.
   a. Write an inequality that shows what combinations of advanced sales and after-publication sales are needed to exceed the $2500 goal set by the yearbook staff.
   b. Give three solutions and prove they are solutions.

16. A textile company designs pillow covers on a computer that controls the color of threads used by the weaving machine. The threads on the line $y = 3x - 1$ will be black. The region described by $y > 3x - 1$ will be green and the region described by $y < 3x - 1$ will be blue. Create a model of the pillow cover using a coordinate axis.

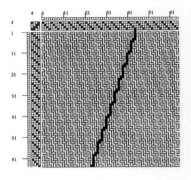

 **LOOK AHEAD**

Write an inequality for each graph.

17.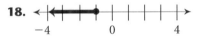

18.

Find the distance between each pair of points on the number line.

19. 4 and 19

20. -2.5 and 7.1

Solve the inequalities and graph their solution.

21. $3x - 7 > 20$

22. $7 - 2x \geq 17$

23. $-2 \leq x - 5 < 3$

24. $x \geq -3$ and $x < 5$

MORE PRACTICE

25. Graph $3x - 2y > 4$.
   a. Graph $3x - 2y = 4$ as the boundary.
   b. Should your boundary line be drawn as a solid or a dashed line? Why?
   c. Choose two points on either side of the boundary line. Substitute them into the original inequality. Which point makes the statement true?
   d. Shade the region that contains the solution points.

Write an inequality for each graph. The equation of the boundary line is given.

26. $y = -2x + 1$

27. $y = \frac{1}{2}x - 2$

28. $y = 3$

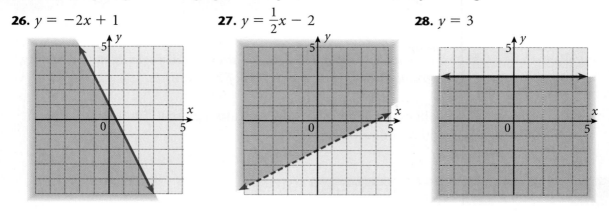

Graph these inequalities.

29. $y \leq -x$

30. $x - 4y \geq 16$

31. $y \leq -4x + 3$

32. $\frac{1}{2}x < -y$

33. $x - 2y < 8$

34. $x < 2$

35. $x + 4y < 16$

36. $3x + 2y > -3$

37. $-2x - y \geq 16$

MORE MATH REASONING

38. Button Button Jason and Wyllie are considering selling homecoming buttons for a fund raiser. The large buttons cost them 50¢ and the smaller ones cost 25¢. There are 650 students at their high school.
  a. What are some considerations they should make regarding price of the buttons and how many of each type to buy?
  b. Make some graphs that might help their planning.

39. Don't Fence Me In Myra has 50 feet of fencing. She wants to build a pen for her pet pigs at the opening of their shelter. Since she wants the pen to be rectangular, what are some possible perimeters for the pen? Explain using diagrams and inequalities.

40. What Was the Question? Write a real-world problem that might be associated with the inequality $1.5x + 0.75y \geq 75$.

Graphing a System of Linear Inequalities

← C O N N E C T → *Now that you've graphed the solutions to a single linear inequality, you'll graph the solutions to systems of inequalities.*

Inequalities are often used in business to represent limitations on time, personnel, and resources.

EXPLORE: SURFING THE ASPHALT

MATERIALS

Graph paper
Straightedge

Urban Surf, Inc. makes two kinds of skateboards. *Curb Cutters* take 2 hours to cut and 4 hours to finish. *Ramp Rodders* take 4 hours to cut and 1 hour to finish.

Urban Surf has 64 hours of production time available for cutting skateboards and 32 hours available for finishing.

Let C = the number of *Curb Cutters* (on the horizontal axis).

Let R = the number of *Ramp Rodders* (on the vertical axis).

1. Write an expression for the total time needed to cut C *Curb Cutters* and R *Ramp Rodders.* Write an inequality that shows that the total cutting time is at most 64 hours.
2. Write an expression for the total time needed to finish C *Curb Cutters* and R *Ramp Rodders.* Write an inequality that shows that the total finishing time is at most 32 hours.
3. Graph both inequalities on the same coordinate plane. Test points and show the region in which *both* inequalities are true.
4. Give the maximum number of *Curb Cutters* Urban Surf can make if it makes only that model. Give the maximum number of *Ramp Rodders* Urban Surf can make if it makes only that model. How can you tell this from the graph?
5. Estimate the coordinates where the two boundary lines to your inequalities intersect. What is the significance of this point to production at Urban Surf?
6. If Urban Surf wants to use all of its possible production time, how many of each board should it make? How can you tell from the graph?

In the Explore, you worked with a system of inequalities. The solution was a region. If you could graph the shadow figures on page 421, you could describe the shaded regions with a system of inequalities.

Two or more linear inequalities considered together form a **system of linear inequalities.** The **solutions** to a system of linear inequalities are the coordinates that make all of the inequalities true.

The graph of the solutions to a system of inequalities is the region where the graphs of the inequalities overlap.

CONSIDER

?

1. **Does every possible ordered pair in the overlapping region in the Explore make sense as a real-world solution? Explain.**

EXAMPLE

Graph this system of inequalities.

$y \geq x - 2$
$x + y < 3$

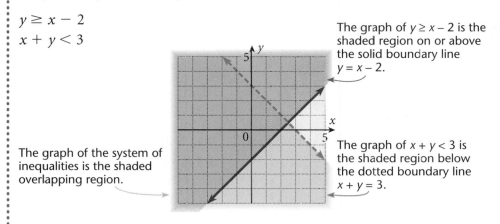

The graph of $y \geq x - 2$ is the shaded region on or above the solid boundary line $y = x - 2$.

The graph of $x + y < 3$ is the shaded region below the dotted boundary line $x + y = 3$.

The graph of the system of inequalities is the shaded overlapping region.

Part of the line $y = x - 2$ satisfies both inequalities and so is included in the graph of the system. The point where the boundary lines intersect does not satisfy $x + y < 3$ and so is not a solution to the system.

Graph each system of inequalities.

a. $y > 9$

  $y < 2x$

b. $x - 2y > 6$

  $x + 2y \le 4$

Every business faces limitations. Solving a system of inequalities can help businesses decide how to get the best use out of their limited time and resources.

REFLECT

1. How is a system of inequalities like a system of equations? How is it different?

2. For a system of linear inequalities, what is true of all the ordered pairs in the overlapping region?

3. Explain how business limitations can lead to a system of inequalities.

4. Do you think it is possible for a system of inequalities to have no solutions? If no, explain. If yes, sketch a graph of an example.

The number of employees that can work in a given shift is one limitation that must be considered in business planning. Photo courtesy of the Ford Archives, Dearborn, Michigan.

Exercises

CORE

1. Getting Started Use these steps to graph the system $y < x + 2$ and $y \ge -x - 1$.

  a. Graph the boundary line $y = x + 2$. Is it solid or dotted? Why?

  b. Choose two points on either side of the boundary line. Substitute them into the original inequality. Which point makes the statement true? Shade the region that contains the solution points.

  c. Graph the boundary line $y = -x - 1$. Is it solid or dotted? Why?

  d. Choose two points on either side of the boundary line. Substitute them into the original inequality. Which point makes the statement true? Shade the region that contains the solution points.

  e. Describe the region that contains the solution points.

This is the graph of the system $x - 3y > -9$ and $2x + y \geq 3$. Tell whether each point is a solution.

2. $(3, -1)$ **3.** $(2, 2)$ **4.** $(-3, 0)$

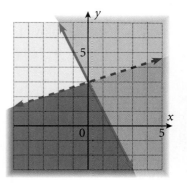

Write the word or phrase that correctly completes each statement.

5. Two or more linear inequalities considered together form a ____.

6. The solutions to a system of linear inequalities are the ____ that make all of the inequalities true.

Graph each system of inequalities.

7. $y > 3$
$x \leq -2$

8. $x + 2y \leq 4$
$3x - y > 6$

9. $y < x + 1$
$y < -x + 3$

10. $x > y$
$y < 4$

11. $y \geq 2x - 3$
$y < -2x + 1$

12. $y < 2x + 1$
$y \geq -x + 1$

13. Write a system of inequalities that describes all of the points in each quadrant, not on an axis.

    a. Quadrant I   **b.** Quadrant II
    c. Quadrant III   **d.** Quadrant IV

14. It is important to be alert to possible avalanche conditions on snowy mountain slopes in the winter time. The diagram indicates the risks at varying slopes. Small slopes obviously do not represent much risk, but very steep ones also do not because the snow is constantly in motion and does not build up precariously; the greatest risk is in between.

    a. Use this diagram (note points on the lines) to write a system of inequalities for the most hazardous (shaded) region.

    b. Write a system of inequalities for the entire region in which one should exercise reasonable caution.

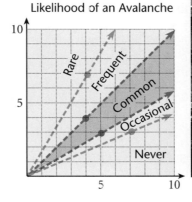

15. Match the solution with its description.

    a. solution to system $x = 0$, $y = 0$ **i.** y-axis

    b. solution to system $x < 0$, $y < 0$ **ii.** origin

    c. solution to system $x \geq 0$, $x \leq 0$ **iii.** none

    d. solution to system $y > 0$, $y < 0$ **iv.** Quadrant III

Write a system of inequalities for each graph.

16.
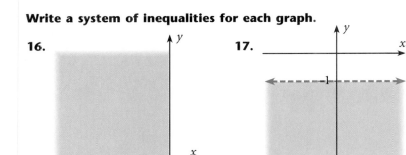

17.

18. The diagram indicates recommended safety slopes for ramps, stairs, and ladders. Ramps should not be too steep, ladders should not lie too flat, and stairs ideally have a slope within a limited range. For each of these, there is a *range* that is preferred, and then a critical slope within which ramps, stairs, and ladders are OK, but not great. Using this coordinate plane, give a system of inequalities for each slope.

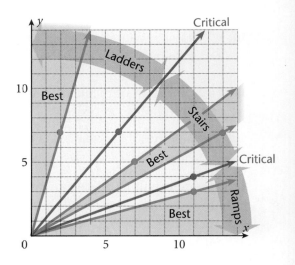

    a. best ladders   **b.** OK ladders

    c. best stairs   **d.** OK stairs

    e. best ramps   **f.** OK ramps

19. Scientists learn that a meteor will crash into the United States. What is the probability that it will hit a nonagricultural region?

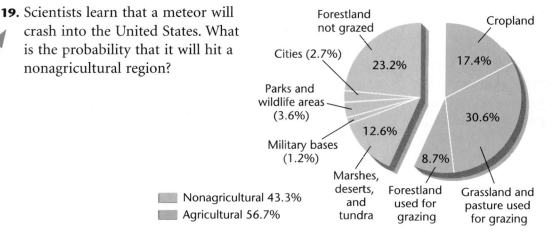

Land Use in the United States

Forestland not grazed

Cropland

Cities (2.7%)

23.2%

17.4%

Parks and wildlife areas (3.6%)

30.6%

Military bases (1.2%)

12.6%

8.7%

Marshes, deserts, and tundra

Forestland used for grazing

Grassland and pasture used for grazing

Nonagricultural 43.3%

Agricultural 56.7%

20. Restaurant Recruits Lee and her family are opening a soup and sandwich restaurant at the River Park. They need at least 3 full-time employees and up to 8 part-time employees. They want no more than 10 employees. What are some of the possible combinations of part-time and full-time persons they might hire? Explain your method of solution.

 **LOOK BACK**

21. A Million Tall The dimensions of a cassette tape are 9.5 by 6 by 1.25 centimeters. [5-2]

   a. If the cassettes are laid flat and stacked one on top of the other, how high will one million reach?

   b. The Sears Tower in Chicago has 110 stories and is approximately 440 meters tall. Would the stacked cassettes be taller or shorter than the Sears Tower? Tell how you decided.

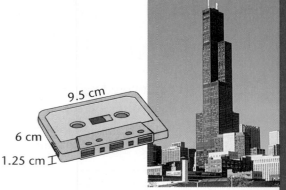

9.5 cm

6 cm

1.25 cm

22. Find the slope of each line. Which line does not belong? Explain why. [5-2]

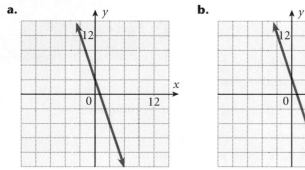

a.

b.

c.

23. Solve the system $y = 3x - 4$ and $3x + 2y = 10$. Which method did you use? Why? [6-2]

MORE PRACTICE

Tell whether each point is a solution of the system $2x + y < 1$ and $x + 2y < 2$.

24. $(0, 0)$

25. $(-2, -1)$

26. $(2, 1)$

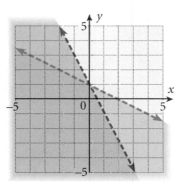

Graph each system of inequalities.

27. $x > y$
$\quad y < -2$

28. $y \geq 2x + 3$
$\quad y < -2x - 1$

29. $y < -2x + 1$
$\quad y \geq x + 1$

30. $y > 4$
$\quad x \leq 2$

31. $x + 2y \leq -4$
$\quad 3x + y > 6$

32. $y > x - 1$
$\quad y < x + 3$

MORE MATH REASONING

33. Flood Fighters A group of 100 people was engaged to help sandbag the Missouri River during the 1993 floods. An adult could handle about 9 bags per minute and an average young person could handle 5 bags per minute. If the group had to position at least 800 sandbags per minute, how many of them needed to be adults?

> **Problem-Solving Tip**
>
> Write a system with an equation and an inequality.

34. If $y = x + 2$ is a line and $y \geq x + 2$ is a half-plane (line included), invent a system to describe the whole plane.

35. Must the boundary lines of the overlapping region of a system of inequalities always intersect? Explain.

36. Does the overlapping region in Graph A have more points than the overlapping region in Graph B? Explain.

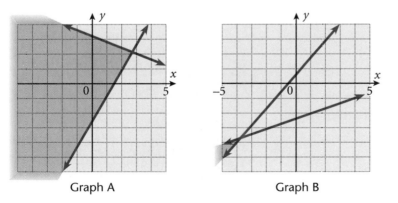

Graph A   Graph B

37. There are three squares that have (2, 4) and (6, 4) as two of their vertices. Give three systems of inequalities that would define those regions.

Making Connections

← **C O N N E C T** → *You've written and interpreted inequalities and explored their solutions graphically. Single inequalities and systems of inequalities have practical applications in a wide variety of businesses and industries.*

Inequalities are not just important in business applications; you can use them to explore graphic designs, such as company logos, as well.

EXPLORE: LOGO LOGIC

Copy this design onto graph paper. It is the logo for Addison-Wesley Publishing Company.

MATERIALS

Graph paper

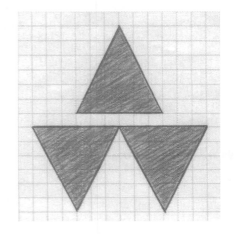

1. Choose a point for the origin and draw coordinate axes on your graph. Mark a convenient scale on each axis.

2. Write the equations of the lines that bound the triangular regions. If everyone chooses the same origin, will everyone get the same equations?

3. Use systems of inequalities to describe the triangular regions in the logo. (Hint: You will need three inequalities to describe each region.)

REFLECT

1. To graph a linear inequality, how do you decide which side of the boundary line to shade? How do you decide whether points on the line itself are included?

2. How are the shadowgraphs (page 421) like a system of inequalities?

3. Can you graph a system of inequalities if the boundary lines are parallel? Explain.

1. Use these steps to graph the inequality $y > -2x + 5$.
   a. Graph the boundary line. Is it dotted or solid? Why?
   b. Choose two points on either side of the boundary line. Substitute them into the original inequality. Which point makes the statement true?
   c. Shade the region that contains the solution points.

2. Which system(s) has (have) the origin as a solution?

   I. $x + y > 1$
   $x - 2y \leq 2$

   II. $y \geq -3x - 2$
   $y < -x + \frac{2}{3}$

   III. $x + 2y > 5$
   $x - y \leq 1$

   (a) I only   (b) II only   (c) III only   (d) I and II   (e) I, II, and III

3. Use these steps to graph this system of inequalities.
   $y \geq -2x + 1.5$
   $y \geq x$
   $y \leq 3$
   a. Graph the boundary line for the graph of $y \geq -2x + 1.5$. Which way should you shade? Tell how you decided.
   b. Graph the boundary line for the graph of $y \geq x$. Which way should you shade? Tell how you decided.
   c. Graph the boundary line for the graph of $y \leq 3$. Which way should you shade? Tell how you decided.
   d. Describe the region that contains the solution points.

Graph each system.

4. $y > x - 2$
   $y < -2x + 1$

5. $y \leq \frac{1}{3}x - 1$
   $y > 3x + 1$

6. $x - y \geq 5$
   $y < -x + 1$

7. The region within the dotted lines on the map is traditionally defined as the Bermuda Triangle. It is an ominous region in the Atlantic Ocean where many ships and airplanes have mysteriously disappeared. If the triangle were placed on a coordinate plane with the tip of Puerto Rico at the origin, tell how you would give a system of inequalities that would describe the region.

Social Science

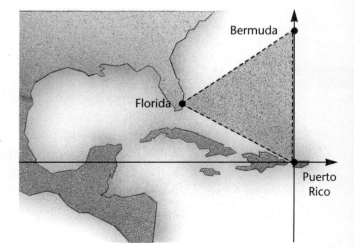

8. The tangram, a geometric puzzle, was invented in China over 4000 years ago by a man named Tan. His most precious possession, a piece of ceramic tile, broke into seven pieces and as he tried to reconstruct the square, he created various shapes. Duplicate each shape using all seven pieces of the tangram, and sketch your solution.

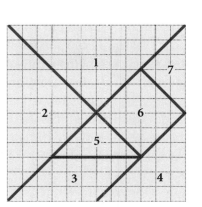

a.

b.

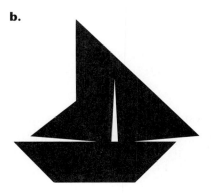

c.

d.

9. Sara wants to construct her own tangram. She uses a piece of graph paper and marks off the first quadrant. Name five pairs of points she must connect to get the tangram puzzle.

10. Graph this system of inequalities.
   a. Identify the geometric figure formed by the system.
   b. Estimate the area of the region.
   c. Give the coordinates of its vertices.

$$y \le \frac{1}{2}x + 2$$
$$y \le -2x + 12$$
$$y \ge \frac{1}{2}x - 3$$
$$y \ge -2x - 3$$

11. The diagram shows what might be called the "geometric states" because all of their boundaries are line segments—rather than rivers, mountain ranges, seacoasts, or other natural borders. The approximate latitudes and longitudes that define them are indicated in the diagram. How might you describe these regions using systems of inequalities?

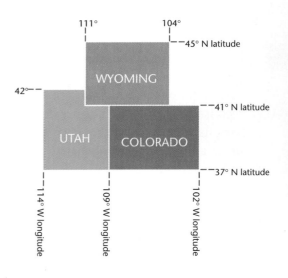

  a. Wyoming (Use W ≤ ?)

  b. Colorado (Use C ≤ ?)

  c. Utah (Use U ≤ ?, but you will need to describe two regions)

  d. Can you explain why the numbering of the longitudes seems reversed?

12. Give a system of inequalities for the figure.

  a. What geometric figure is formed by this region?

  b. What is its area?

  c. What are the coordinates of its vertices?

  d. Can you form such a region using exactly two tangram pieces? Show a diagram.

  e. Can you form such a region using exactly five tangram pieces? Show a diagram.

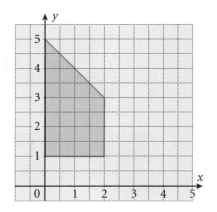

13. Describe the umbra as the solution to a system of inequalities. Use expressions like *under* $\overleftrightarrow{AB}$ instead of inequalities like $3x - 4y \geq 5$.

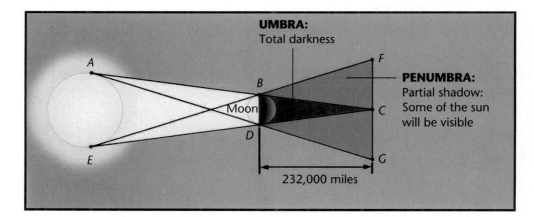

Chapter 6 Review

In Chapter 6, you have extended your knowledge of linear functions by looking at systems of equations. The slope indicates whether the graphs of equations are parallel, intersecting, or perpendicular. By using pairs of equations, you can use new methods for problem solving. Systems of inequalities help in the analysis of business problems.

KEY TERMS

Dependent system [6-2]

Inconsistent system [6-2]

Matrix multiplication [6-2]

Parallel lines [6-1]

Perpendicular lines [6-1]

System of linear equations [6-1]

System of linear inequalities [6-3]

Write the word or phrase that correctly completes each statement.

1. The product of the slopes of _____ lines is -1.

2. The slopes of _____ lines are equal.

3. A system of equations with no solution is a(n) _____ system.

4. A system of equations with an infinite number of solutions is a(n) _____ system.

CONCEPTS AND APPLICATIONS

5. Graph the equation $x - 3y = 6$. [6-1]
   a. What is the slope of a line that is parallel to the graph of this equation?
   b. What is the slope of a line that is perpendicular to the graph of this equation?

6. Graph and solve this system of equations. [6-1]
   $y = 3x + 1$
   $y = -x + 5$

7. Graph this system of equations. [6-1]
   $x - 7y = -6$
   $x + y = 3$
   a. Estimate the solution using your graph.
   b. Solve the system algebraically. [6-2]
   c. If your answers to **7a** and **7b** are exactly the same, explain how you estimated so accurately. If your answers to **7a** and **7b** are not exactly the same, are you satisfied with the accuracy of your answers? Explain.

8. Write an equation of the line through $(1, 2)$ that is parallel to the graph of $y = 2x + 4$. [6-1]

9. Write an equation of the line through $(1, 2)$ that is perpendicular to the graph of $y = 2x + 4$. [6-1]

Science

10. Car A crossed the track marker at 1:00 p.m. traveling 40 miles per hour. Car B crossed the same marker at 1:10 p.m. traveling 60 miles per hour. Assume that the cars maintain a constant speed. [6-2]

   a. Which line on the graph represents Car A's distance? Car B's?

   b. When will Car B overtake Car A?

   c. How far has each car traveled when Car B overtakes Car A?

   d. Can you tell how far apart the cars will be at 2:00 p.m.? Explain your answer.

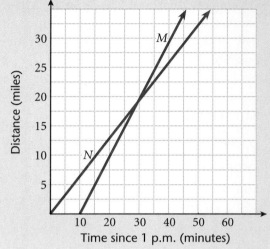

Distance (miles) vs. Time since 1 p.m. (minutes)

Solve each system or state whether it is dependent or inconsistent. [6-2]

11. $3x + 2y = 1$
    $6x + 4y = 2$

12. $x + y = 1$
    $x + y = 2$

13. $y = 3x + 12$
    $3y = x + 4$

14. Find the product matrix. [6-2] $\begin{bmatrix} 7 & -2 \\ 11 & 3 \end{bmatrix}\begin{bmatrix} -1 \\ 4 \end{bmatrix}$

15. On Old MacDonald's farm there are some pigs and some ducks. There are 16 heads and 46 feet. How many pigs and how many ducks does Old MacDonald have? [6-2]

16. Choose the correct solution to this system. [6-2]

$$\frac{1}{3}x + \frac{3}{8}y = \frac{2}{5}$$

$$\frac{1}{6}x + \frac{3}{16}y = \frac{1}{5}$$

   (a) $\left(0, \frac{16}{15}\right)$ (b) dependent   (c) inconsistent   (d) $\left(\frac{6}{5}, 0\right)$ (e) not here

Graph each inequality. [6-3]

17. $y \leq 3x + 12$

18. $-x + y > 12$

19. $-\frac{1}{3}x + \frac{2}{3}y < \frac{1}{6}$

20. Graph this system of inequalities. [6-3]

   $x + y < 2$

     $3y > x + 2$

   a. Choose a test point to check your work.

   b. Explain how your test point helped you decide if your graph is correct.

CONCEPTS AND CONNECTIONS

21. Industry Roxanne pays $20.85 for 15 gallons of Unleaded Plus whenever she fills her car's gas tank. She wondered if she could mix the Premium Unleaded with the Regular Unleaded to get a higher octane percentage than Unleaded Plus for the same price.

a. Define variables for number of gallons of Premium Unleaded and number of gallons of Regular Unleaded. Write an equation that represents total gallons purchased.

b. Write an expression that represents the cost of the Premium Unleaded. Write another expression that represents the cost of the Regular Unleaded.

c. Write an equation that shows the total cost of the mixture.

d. Solve the system of equations.

e. How many gallons of each should Roxanne buy?

f. Does the octane of this mixture exceed the octane in Unleaded Plus? (Hint: Use averaging.)

SELF-EVALUATION

Write a paragraph that describes what you know about systems of equations and inequalities. Describe the kinds of problems you have solved using systems. Write down which parts of the chapter were difficult for you and which sections you need to study further in order to better understand these topics.

Chapter 6 Assessment

TEST

Use the graph to answer these questions.

1. Name two parallel lines. Tell how you decided.

2. Name two perpendicular lines. Tell how you decided.

3. What are the coordinates of the point of intersection of lines *a* and *c*?

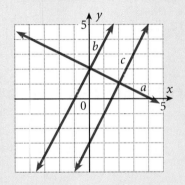

Solve each system. Describe your first step. Explain your method.

4. $2x + y = 7$

   $y = 5x$

5. $y = 2x - 5$

   $y = \dfrac{3}{2}x - 3$

6. $5x + 6y = 7$

   $4x - 3y = 16$

Match each system with the correct number of solutions.

A. An infinite number of solutions

B. No solution

C. One solution

7. $2x + 3y = 10$
   $4x + 6y = 20$

8. $2x + 3y = 10$
   $2x + 3y = 30$

9. $2x + 3y = 10$
   $2x - 3y = 5$

10. Melissa used her graphing utility to solve the system shown on the screen. Estimate her solution. How could you check your estimate?

 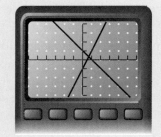

11. Does the graph represent a dependent system? Why or why not?

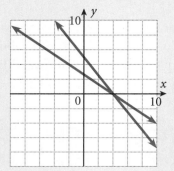

Solve each system or state whether it is dependent or inconsistent. [6-2]

12. $2x - 3y = -2$
   $2x + y = 14$

13. $x + y = 15$
   $-2x - 3y = 15$

14. $0.5x - 1.3y = -1$
   $-7.5x + 19.5y = 15$

15. Least Lakeside Lodging The Harrison family is planning a three-night stay in the Pine Tree Lake Resort. Biggs' Bungalows charge a $50 cleaning bill and $60 per night. Campi's Cabins are priced at $75 per night and a $10 key deposit. Which place is the least expensive to stay for three nights? Justify your answer.

Industry

16. Business Bonus The graph shows income and expenses from June 1990 to June 1996. The accounting department prepared the graph based on records and on projections.
a. When is the company making a profit?
b. When is the company suffering a loss?
c. What happened in the middle of 1993?

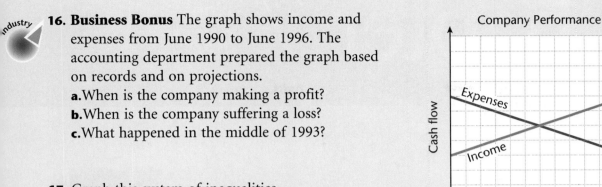

Company Performance

Cash flow

Expenses

Income

92   94   96

Time

17. Graph this system of inequalities.

$2x + y \leq 4$

$x > -1$

$y > -1$

a. Identify the geometric figure formed by the system.
b. Give the coordinates of the vertices.
c. Find the area of the figure. Explain how you know this is the correct area.

PERFORMANCE TASK

The Medical Center needs to upgrade a piece of equipment. The administration has narrowed the field to two models that have the following characteristics.

	Model A	Model B
Purchase price	$1,000,000	$2,000,000
Revenue per test	$200	$200
Expense per test	$90	$70
Number of tests per year	5000	5000
Useful life	5 years	8 years

The administration has asked you to create a graph of the information on the chart and *make a recommendation.* Here are some of the things you might want to show on your graph:
• purchase price
• end of useful life
• profit line
• when each model has paid for itself
• when the two models generate the same profit

Tell which model you would choose and why.

Would your recommendation change if you knew that the hospital may invest any extra money at 5% per year? Explain.

Chapter 7

Lines and Distance

Project A
Flatten the Globe
How can a flat map be an accurate representation of a round planet?

Project B
Move the Masses
Why do people drive to work alone? How do transit authorities plan routes?

Project C
Climb Every Mountain
Are the Himalayas still growing? How do you measure the height of a mountain?

GARY HUFSTEDLER

I enjoyed math in high school because it was logical and dependable. I liked abstract concepts—ones that aren't intuitively obvious. I could see that math had practical applications.

Today I use math to analyze data. We constantly adjust our service to meet the needs of riders. We have to think about passengers, routes and mileage, salaries, and vehicle price and maintenance costs. Hardly any aspect of today's world can be managed without mathematical ability.

Gary Hufstedler
Senior Manager of
    Service Planning
Dallas Area Rapid Transit
Dallas, TX

7-1
Distance on a Number Line

In 7-1 you will use absolute value to describe number line distances. You will graph absolute value functions and solve absolute value equations. You will use graphing skills and knowledge of inequalities.

Graph each pair of lines on the same coordinate axes. [5-1]

1. $y = x$; $y = -x$ **2.** $y = 2x - 3$; $y = -2x - 3$ **3.** $y = \frac{1}{5}x$; $y = -\frac{1}{5}x$

7-2
Square Roots

In 7-2 you will learn about functions and equations involving square roots. You will be using a variety of skills from Chapters 1 to 3.

Copy and complete the table. [2-2]

4.

x	-5	-3	-1.1	0	2.3	4	20
x^2							

7-3
Distance in a Plane

In 7-3 you will learn how to find the distance between points in a coordinate system. You will be using skills from Chapters 1 and 2.

Evaluate. [2-3]

5. $(-8 - 3)^2$ **6.** $(4 - 3)^2 + (-1 + 6)^2$ **7.** $(-5 - 1)^2 + (12 - 2)^2$

8. $(10.3 - 11.8)^2$ **9.** $(-1 - 0)^2 + (8 - 9)^2$ **10.** $\left(\frac{1}{2} - \frac{1}{4}\right)^2 + \left(-2\frac{1}{2} - \frac{1}{2}\right)^2$

11. $a^2 + b^2$ for $a = 0.8$ and $b = -0.6$ **12.** $a^2 + b^2$ for $a = -5$ and $b = 12$

7-4
Indirect Measurement

In 7-4 you will use proportions to enlarge or reduce shapes. Special properties of right triangles will be explored. You will need proportion solving skills and some geometry ideas.

13. Name the right triangles. [Previous course]

Solve and check each proportion. [Page 747]

14. $\frac{x}{4} = \frac{5}{10}$ **15.** $\frac{x}{6} = \frac{1.5}{12}$ **16.** $\frac{38}{10} = \frac{x}{25}$ **17.** $\frac{7}{x} = \frac{2.8}{14}$

Take The [A] Train

When an Australian traveler in the United States got back to Melbourne, he described what he had seen—Chinatown in San Francisco, the night life in Las Vegas, the beauty of Mount Rushmore, the monuments in Washington D.C., the Statue of Liberty in New York Harbor. To his surprise, what impressed his friends most was that he had ridden the New York City subway!

In fact, New York's subway system is the most extensive in the world. With 714 miles of track connecting 469 stations, New Yorkers can really get around. People often try alternate routes before they discover the best ones to their destinations. According to the *Guinness Book of World Records*, the record for traveling the whole system, including every train station, is 21 hours, $8\frac{1}{2}$ minutes, set in October 1973.

© 1993 New York City Transit Authority.

?

1. What do most people mean by the "shortest" route on a subway map?
2. Who would say it is important to know the shortest route between two points?
3. What are some ways to measure the distance between two stops on a subway map?
4. Explain how one route can be shorter than another yet, in another sense, be longer.

Absolute Value

← CONNECT → *You know how to find points on a number line and solve inequalities. Now you'll learn to express distances between points mathematically and solve inequalities involving distance.*

Many types of calculations give us negative numbers. When we are interested in real quantities such as distance and location, there is a mathematical way to use these numbers without representing them as signed numbers.

EXPLORE: HOW FAR FROM HERE TO THERE?

▫Presidential Highway ▫

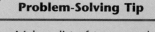

West | East

Presidential Highway is a straight two-way road. All exits from the road are equally spaced, and there is one town at each exit. This information is known about the towns.

• Buchanan is two exits east of Clintonville.
• Lincoln is one exit west of Clintonville.
• Roosevelt is one exit west of Jackson, but two exits east of Hooverville.
• Hooverville is one exit west of Buchanan.

1. Copy the map and determine where each of the six towns is located.

2. If each exit is 1 mile from the next exit, how far apart are Lincoln and Buchanan?

3. What is the longest one-way trip someone could take along this road? Is there more than one longest trip? Explain your answer.

4. Could the distance between two points be negative? Explain.

> **Problem-Solving Tip**
>
> Make a list of towns and rearrange it.

Distance is always a positive value (or zero). Mathematicians use **absolute value** to describe **distance** on a number line.

The **absolute value** of a number is the distance between the number and zero on the number line. We write $|x|$ to mean the absolute value of x.

The absolute value of 3 is the distance from 0 to 3. So $|3| = 3$. The absolute value of -5.2 is the distance from 0 to -5.2. So $|-5.2| = 5.2$.

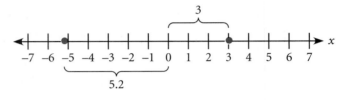

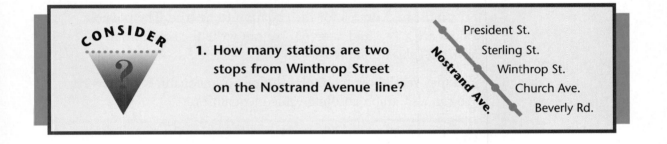

CONSIDER

?

1. **How many stations are two stops from Winthrop Street on the Nostrand Avenue line?**

President St.
Sterling St.
Winthrop St.
Church Ave.
Beverly Rd.

Nostrand Ave.

The absolute value of zero or a positive number is the number itself. We have seen that the absolute value of a negative number is its opposite. We can now build a definition for absolute value that applies to any real number.

$$|x| = x, \text{ if } x \geq 0$$
$$|x| = -x, \text{ if } x < 0$$

TRY IT

Evaluate.

a. $|2.7|$ **b.** $|-0.5|$ **c.** $|0|$

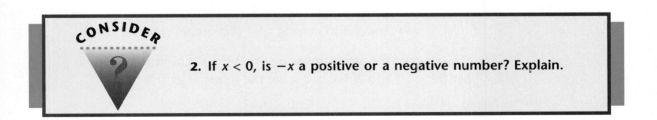

CONSIDER

?

2. **If $x < 0$, is $-x$ a positive or a negative number? Explain.**

Until now you have solved equations with one solution. Absolute value equations often have *two* solutions, since there are *two* numbers on either side of zero that are the same distance from it.

1. Graph and solve $|x| = 3$. (Hint: What are the possible values for x when $|x| = 3$?)

This means that the distance from x to 0 is 3.

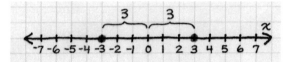

So x must be 3 **or** -3 for the equation to be true. The possible values are $x = 3$ and $x = -3$. We can write the solution as $x = \pm 3$ (*plus or minus* 3).

You may recall how to graph solutions of inequalities, like $x < 2$. We can also graph absolute value inequalities.

2. Graph and solve $|x| < 2$.

This means that the distance from x to 0 is less than 2.

Therefore, x can be any number whose distance is less than 2 units from 0, either to the left or to the right. So x can be any point between -2 and 2.

Both $x > -2$ **and** $x < 2$ must be true for a value to be a solution.

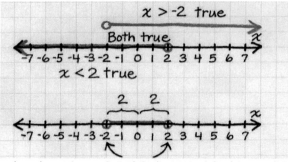

Notice that the points -2 and 2 *do not* satisfy this condition. We show this by drawing open dots at these points.

We can see from the number line that the solution is any point between -2 and 2. We can write the solution as $-2 < x < 2$.

3. Graph and solve $|x| \geq 2$.

This means that the distance from x to 0 is greater than or equal to 2. So x can be any number whose distance is greater than or equal to 2 units from 0, to the left or to the right. We darken the line and use arrows to show that there are an infinite number of points on either side of 2 and -2 that satisfy this condition.

Notice that the points -2 and 2 also satisfy this condition. We show this by drawing solid dots at these points.

Either $x \geq 2$ **or** $x \leq -2$ must be true for a value to be a solution.

CONSIDER

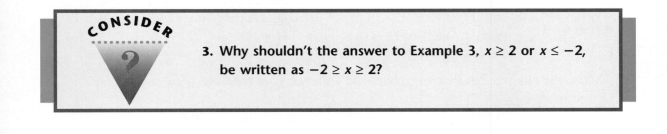

3. Why shouldn't the answer to Example 3, $x \geq 2$ or $x \leq -2$, be written as $-2 \geq x \geq 2$?

TRY IT

Graph and solve.

d. $x = |-2.5|$ **e.** $|x| = 4$ **f.** $|x| > 2$ **g.** $|x| \leq 0.5$

REFLECT

1. Can the absolute value of a number ever be negative? Why or why not?

2. Suppose you know that the absolute value of a number is 3. What do you know about the number? Why?

3. Maria says, "The absolute value of a number is just the number without the sign." Do you agree or disagree? Why?

4. Do all absolute value equations with one variable have exactly two solutions? Explain.

Exercises

CORE

1. **Getting Started** Points O, P, Q, R, and S represent integers.
   Find the distance between the points.
   a. O and P b. P and P c. S and O
   d. O and R e. Q and S

2. Match each equation or inequality with the graph it describes. Remember that a closed dot means that point is a solution. An open dot means the point is not a solution.

   a. $|x| = 4$
   b. $x = |4|$
   c. $|x| < 4$
   d. $|x| > 4$
   e. $|x| \leq 4$

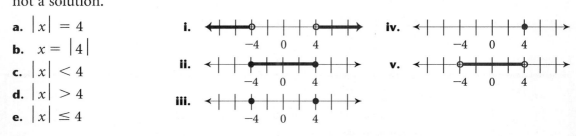

3. Choose the answer that best completes the sentence: The absolute value of a number is _____.
   (a) the distance of the number from its opposite on the number line
   (b) the opposite of the number, if the number is positive
   (c) just the number itself
   (d) the number itself, or its opposite if the number is negative

Find the absolute value of each expression. Explain what each means in terms of *distance* on a number line.

4. $|-4|$ 5. $|100{,}000|$ 6. $-|-5|$ 7. $|a|$

Graph and solve.

8. $|x| \leq 5$ 9. $|x| \geq 3$ 10. $|x| < 1.5$

11. $|x| > 8.1$ 12. $|x| \leq 2.3$ 13. $|x| > 3.3$

14. Use a separate number line for each graph.
    a. Graph $|x| \leq 6$.   b. Graph $x \leq |-6|$.
    c. How are the graphs different? the same?

15. a. Which point represents the opposite of T?
    b. Which point represents the number with the largest absolute value? the smallest absolute value?
    c. Suppose the coordinate of N is 12, what is the coordinate of M?
    d. Suppose the coordinate of M is $-\frac{2}{3}$, what is the coordinate of L?

16. Zero Consideration

   a. What is the absolute value of 0? Why?

   b. Graph $|x| \geq 0$. Describe your answer.

   c. Graph $|x| < 0$. Describe your answer.

17. When is the absolute value of a number the *same* as the number? Explain.

18. When is the absolute value of a number *different* from the number? Explain.

19. Write an inequality that describes this graph. Use x and absolute value.

20. Subway System The map shows a portion of the New York Subway System that contains the Broadway/7 Avenue (Red) and the 8 Avenue (Orange) routes. (Note: In this section of New York, there is a street for every number.)

   a. How many stations on the Broadway/7 Avenue route are 7 blocks from the 79 Street station? 10 blocks? Discuss the difference in your answers.

   b. How many blocks are there between the 103 St. station and the 72 St. station on the 8 Avenue route?

   c. Suppose you design a bus route to connect the 72 Street station on 8 Avenue to the 103 Street station on Broadway/7 Avenue. You want to limit the driver to one left turn and one right turn. How many different paths could you design? Is there a path with only one turn? If so, describe it.

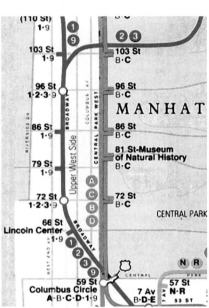

Copyright © 1993 New York City Transit Authority.

Simplify these expressions.

21. $|18 - 28|$

22. $23 + |-4|$

23. $|4 \cdot -5|$

24. $-6 + |-1|$

25. $|(-3)^2 + (-4)^2|$

26. $|(-2)^3| + 5$

27. $\dfrac{|-2.53|}{|2.53|}$

28. $\left|-\dfrac{1}{20}\right| \cdot |20|$

29. $|3^2| - |-14|$

Determine which is greater. Explain.

30. -8 or $+3$

31. $|-6|$ or $|2|$

32. $|9|$ or $|(2-11)|$

33. $+10$ or -15

34. $|4 - 9|$ or $|2^2|$

35. $|7 - (-5)|$ or $|7 + (-5)|$

36. Make up an expression that involves absolute value and the numbers -8 and 2, resulting in each of the following.

   a. 6   **b.** 10   **c.** -6 **d.** 4   **e.** 64   **f.** 256

37. Calculate each sum. Describe your method for adding integers.
    a. $(+12) + (+3)$ **b.** $(-3) + (+12)$ **c.** $(-9) + (+8)$ **d.** $(-8) + (-9)$
    e. Rewrite your rules for adding integers using absolute value notation.

38. Pitch One In Many famous vocalists have absolute pitch, the ability to sing a given tone without having any identified pitch sounded beforehand. How is "absolute pitch" like absolute value? How is it different?

Kathleen Battle

39. Calculate each difference. Describe your method for subtracting integers.
    a. $(+12) - (+3)$ **b.** $(+3) - (+12)$
    c. $(-9) - (-8)$ **d.** $(-8) - (-9)$
    e. Rewrite your rules for subtraction using absolute value notation.

LOOK BACK

40. Tell whether the quantities are variable or constant. [2-1]
    a. the number of days in a week
    b. the amount of change you get back from a dollar
    c. the number of pennies in a dollar

Determine whether the lines are parallel or intersect. If they intersect, tell whether they are perpendicular. [6-1]

41. c and d **42.** a and d **43.** b and a

44. Graph the system and describe the solution. [6-3]

$$y > 2x - 1$$
$$y < -\frac{1}{3}x + 4$$

MORE PRACTICE

45. Points S, T, U, V, and W represent integers. Find the distance between the points.
    a. S and T **b.** T and T
    c. W and S **d.** S and V
    e. U and W

Determine which is greater.

46. $\left|6 - (-1)\right|$ or $\left|-1 - (-6)\right|$ **47.** $\left|-8 + (-1)\right|$ or $\left|-8 - (-1)\right|$

48. Match the equation or inequality with the graph it describes.

a. $|x| = 6$

i. a number line from −6 to 6 with open circles at −6 and 6 and a solid segment between them, marked −6, 0, 6

b. $x = |6|$

ii. a number line with open circles at −6 and 6 and rays extending left from −6 and right from 6, marked −6, 0, 6

c. $|x| < 6$

iii. a number line with a solid dot at 6, marked −6, 0, 6

d. $|x| > 6$

iv. a number line with solid dots at −6 and 6, marked −6, 0, 6

Graph and solve.

49. $|x| > 4$

50. $|x| = 0.75$

51. $|x| \leq 0$

52. $|x| > 0.75$

53. $|x| < 5.1$

54. $|x| = 1.65$

55. $|x| \geq 3.05$

56. $|x| < 1.2$

57. Graph. Use a different number line for each.

a. $|x| = 1$

b. $x = |-1|$

c. $|x| < 1$

Evaluate. Explain what each means in terms of *distance* on a number line.

58. $|-6|$

59. $|-1.25|$

60. $|+4|$

61. $|0|$

62. $|-400|$

Evaluate.

63. $|6| - |+8|$

64. $|6 - 8|$

65. $||-2| - |-4||$

66. $|-3| - |9|$

67. $|-3 - 9|$

68. $||-3| - |9||$

MORE MATH REASONING

69. Temperature Thoughts On the Kelvin scale, the boiling point of water is 373 and the freezing point is 273. A change of one unit on the Kelvin scale is the same as a change of one degree on the Celsius scale.

a. What is the boiling point of water on the Celsius scale? the freezing point?

b. Absolute zero (0 Kelvin) is the hypothetical point at which a molecule would have no motion or heat. What would absolute zero equal on the Celsius scale?

c. Does the word *absolute* have the same meaning in "absolute zero" and "absolute value"? Explain.

d. Write an equation that would change a temperature given in Celsius to an equal temperature in Kelvin.

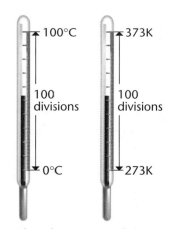

These thermometers show a comparison of the Celsius and Kelvin temperature scales.

70. Solve Smaller Kerry wants to solve the equation $|m - 2| = 4$. Lori suggests that he begin by solving $|x| = 4$ and then let $x = m - 2$. Will Lori's suggestion work? Explain.

71. Mach My Words The speed of supersonic aircraft is given in terms of the ratio of the speed of the aircraft (*v*) to the speed of sound (*s*). This speed is called the Mach number, named after Austrian physicist Ernst Mach. An aircraft is designed to operate between Mach 1.5 and Mach 2.5.

  a. Write an inequality in terms of the aircraft speed *v* in miles per hour and the Mach numbers 1.5 and 2.5.
  b. Solve the inequality in **71a** for *v*.
  c. Write an inequality for the speeds in which it is *not* designed to operate. Is there something strange about this answer?

72. Consider the number line from -10 to 10. If one point is selected at random, what is the probability that the number it represents would be a solution of $|x| \le 5$? Explain.

7-1 PART B Graphing Absolute Value Function

← **CONNECT** → *In Part A, you learned to find solutions of equations like $|x| = 5$. This is a special case of $y = |x|$, which is called the **absolute value function**. Now you will see what the graphs of the absolute value function and related functions look like.*

> The **absolute value function** is a relationship that can be represented by the equation $y = |x|$, where *x* is any real number.

Here is the graph of $y = x$.

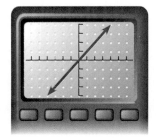

The graph of $y = x$ is in Quadrant I and Quadrant III.

Here is the graph of $y = |x|$.

Notice that the Quadrant III "arm" of the graph $y = x$ is now flipped over into Quadrant II.

This is a data table for $y = |x|$.

x	y
-3	3
-2	2
-1	1
0	0
1	1
2	2
3	3

CONSIDER

1. If $x = -3$, what is the y-value of $y = x$? of $y = |x|$? How does your answer help explain the "flip" of the arm of the $y = x$ graph?

In the next Explore, you will compare the equations and graphs of other absolute value functions to $y = |x|$ and its graph.

EXPLORE: VIVID VARIATIONS

MATERIALS

Graphing utility
Graph paper

Sketch the graph of each function, using a graphing utility or a table of values.

$y = |x|$

$y = |2x|, y = |3x|, y = |4x|$

$y = |-2x|, y = |-3x|$

$y = -|2x|, y = -|3x|$

$y = |x| + 2, y = |x| + 5, y = |x| - 1$

$y = |x + 2|, y = |x + 5|, y = |x - 1|$

Use $y = |x|$ as a basis of comparison to form conjectures about the effects of each variation on the graph of $y = |x|$.

1. What happens when the coefficient of x increases from 1 to 2? from 1 to 3? In general, what happens when the coefficient of x increases?

2. What happens when the coefficient of x is negative? What happens when the negative sign is outside the absolute value bars?

3. What happens when the constant 2 is added to $|x|$ (outside the absolute value bars)? when 5 is added? when -1 is added? In general, what is the effect of a constant added to $|x|$?

4. What happens when the constant 2 is added to x (inside the absolute value bars)? when 5 is added? when -1 is added? In general, what is the effect of a constant added to x inside the absolute value bars?

CONSIDER

2. How are the graphs of $y = |-x|$ and $y = -|x|$ different?

EXAMPLE

A computer-game designer uses the function $y = |x - 3|$ to graph the path of a creature as it bounces off the bottom of the screen. Graph the possible locations of the creature.

Problem-Solving Tip

Make a table to help you graph the locations.

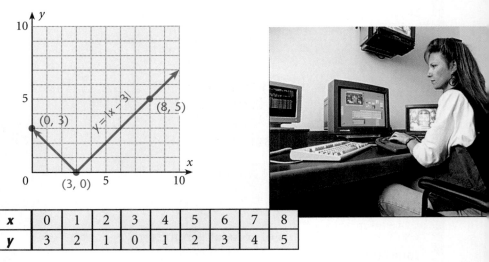

x	0	1	2	3	4	5	6	7	8
y	3	2	1	0	1	2	3	4	5

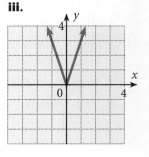

TRY IT

The graphs have identical scales. Match each equation with the graph it describes.

a. $y = |x - 1|$ **b.** $y = |3x|$ **c.** $y = |3x| - 3$

i.   **ii.**   **iii.**

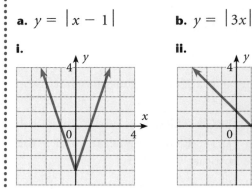

1. How does the constant a affect the graph of $y = |ax|$?
2. How is the equation $y = |x|$ similar to other equations you have graphed? How is it different?
3. Explain how to move the graph of the absolute value function up from the origin; down from the origin; right from the origin; left from the origin.

Exercises

CORE

1. Getting Started

a. Copy and complete the table to find points for the graph of $y = |x + 1|$.

b. Sketch the graph.

c. How is your graph different from the graph of $y = |x|$?

x	$x + 1$	$|x + 1|$
-3	-2	2
-2		
-1		
0		
1	2	2
2		

2. Match each equation with the graph it describes. Explain your choice in each case.

a. $y = |4x|$ b. $y = \left|\frac{1}{4}x\right|$ c. $y = |x|$

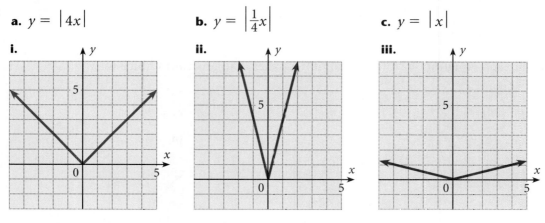

i.

ii.

iii.

3. How is the linear equation $y = 4x$ similar to the equation $y = |4x|$? How is it different?

4. Match each equation with the graph it describes. Explain your choice in each case.

a. $y = |x| + 4$ **b.** $y = |x| + 1$ **c.** $y = |x| + 2$

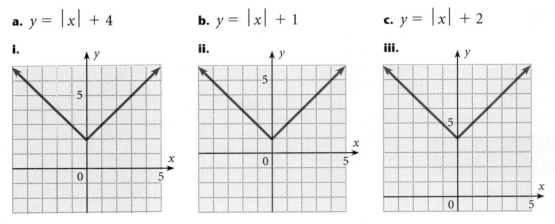

i.   **ii.**   **iii.**

5. How are the graphs of $y = x + 2$ and $y = |x| + 2$ similar? How are they different?

Write the equation for each graph. Explain the procedure you used to obtain it.

6.   **7.**

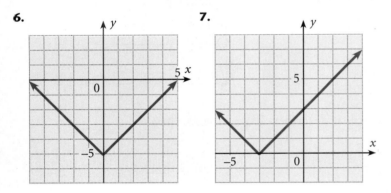

8. Match each equation with the graph it describes. Explain your choice in each case.

a. $y = |x - 1|$ **b.** $y = |x + 2|$ **c.** $y = |x - 2|$

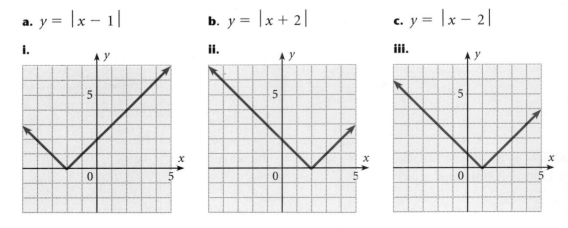

i.   **ii.**   **iii.**

9. A computer-game designer uses the function $y = 15 - |5x|$ to graph the path of a creature as it bounces off the top of the screen. Graph the path of the creature.

Careers

Problem-Solving Tip

Make a table.

10. Timely Transit The New York City Transit Authority operates 24 hours per day, 7 days per week, but it does vary its service. During rush hours (7–9 a.m. and 4–7 p.m.), trains run every 2 to 5 minutes. During the day, they run every 10 to 15 minutes. At night, they run about every 20 minutes.

Social Science

a. What is the range of time between trains during rush hour? What is the range of time between trains during the day?

b. Harold just misses a train at 10:53 p.m. When should the next train come?

c. Tokens to board the train cost $1.25. What is a way to calculate mentally how many tokens you can get for $20?

Problem-Solving Tip

First, determine how many tokens you can get for $5.

11. Graphing Guestimates Tina says the graph of $y = |5x|$ is the same as $y = 5|x|$, so $y = |-5x|$ must have the same graph as $y = -5|x|$. Use a graph or graphing utility to test her theory. Is she right? Explain.

12. Can You Get There from Here? The graph in this problem refers to a set of points called *vertices* and of line segments called *edges*. This graph represents train routes. The vertices O, D, C, S, P, and F represent the cities Oakland, Denver, Chicago, St. Louis, Pittsburgh, and Fort Worth, respectively. The edges tell whether the train company has express connections between these cities.

Social Science

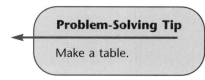

a. Is there an express route from Pittsburgh to Denver? Explain.

b. Use the train graph to find all the possible routes from Oakland to Pittsburgh. (Don't visit a city more than once on a given route.)

13. A New Woof Richard is designing the roof for Cezanne's doghouse. Which algebraic equation could he use to obtain this graphic representation? Justify your answer.

(a) $y = -|10x|$

(b) $y = 10 - |x|$

(c) $y = |x| - 10$

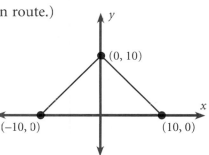

14. Find the distance between each pair of points. You may need to draw a graph first and plot the points.

a. $A(5, 0)$ and $B(8, 0)$ **b.** $C(3, 0)$ and $D(-3, 0)$

c. $G(5, 2)$ and $H(8, 2)$ **d.** $M(-200, 400)$ and $N(-100, 400)$

e. $Q(\pi, 2)$ and $R(2\pi, 2)$

f. What is special about these examples that makes it easy to find these distances?

Evaluate the expression $a^2 + b^2$ using each pair of values.

15. $a = -3$ and $b = 4$ **16.** $a = 1.5$ and $b = 0.8$ **17.** $a = 0.05$ and $b = 0.12$

MORE PRACTICE

18. Match each equation with the graph it describes.

a. $y = \left|\frac{1}{5}x\right|$ **b.** $y = \left|5x\right|$ **c.** $y = \left|x\right|$

i.   **ii.**   **iii.**

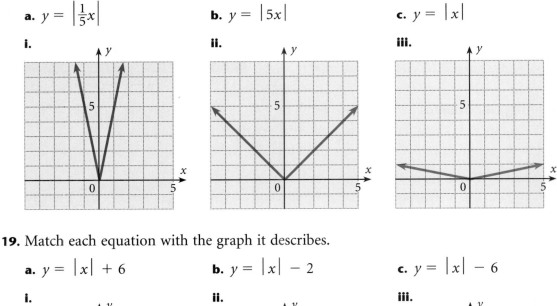

19. Match each equation with the graph it describes.

a. $y = \left|x\right| + 6$ **b.** $y = \left|x\right| - 2$ **c.** $y = \left|x\right| - 6$

i.   **ii.**   **iii.**

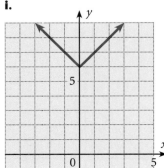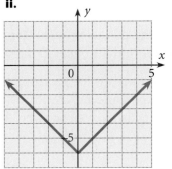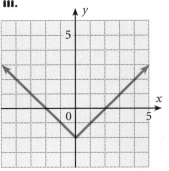

20. Which equation would give this graph?

(a) $y = |x - 3|$

(b) $y = |x| - 3$

(c) $y = |x + 3|$

(d) $y = |x| + 3$

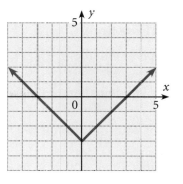

21. Match each equation with the graph it describes.

a. $y = |x - 4|$ **b.** $y = |x + 4|$ **c.** $y = |x - 5|$

i.   **ii.**   **iii.**

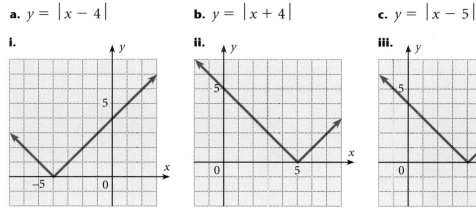

MORE MATH REASONING

22. Watch Those Bars!

  a. Explain whether $|3 + 4| = |3| + |4|$.

  b. Explain whether $|-3 + (-4)| = |-3| + |-4|$.

  c. Explain whether $|3 + (-4)| = |3| + |-4|$.

  d. Can you find numbers x and y for which $|x + y| = |x| + |y|$?

23. Watch Those Bars Again!

  a. Explain whether $|5 - 3| = |5| - |3|$.

  b. Explain whether $|-5 - (-3)| = |-5| - |-3|$.

  c. Can you find numbers x and y for which $|x - y| \neq |x| - |y|$?

24. What Bars?

  a. Explain whether $|6 \cdot 4| = |6| \cdot |4|$.

  b. Explain whether $|6 \cdot (-4)| = |6| \cdot |-4|$.

  c. Explain whether $|(-6) \cdot (-4)| = |-6| \cdot |-4|$.

  d. Can you find numbers x and y for which $|x \cdot y| \neq |x| \cdot |y|$?

25. Oh, Those Bars!

a. Explain whether $\left|\dfrac{-8}{+4}\right| = \dfrac{|-8|}{|+4|}$.

b. Explain whether $\left|\dfrac{-16}{-2}\right| = \dfrac{|-16|}{|-2|}$.

c. Can you find numbers x and y for which $\left|\dfrac{x}{y}\right| \neq \dfrac{|x|}{|y|}$?

26. Consider the graph of $y = |x|$. Are the quantities directly or inversely related? Explain.

27. Complete a table of values for $y = |x + 3|$ and $y = |x| + 3$. Then draw the graph of each function. (If you can, check using a graphing utility.) Describe the differences and similarities.

28. Write a system of inequalities that has this graph. (Hint: Use the top and bottom of the figure.)

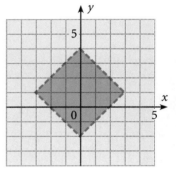

Absolute Value Equations

← **CONNECT** →   *In Part B, you learned to graph absolute value functions. Now you will see the connection between absolute value functions and equations.*

Consider the function $y = |x|$. For what value(s) of x is $4 = |x|$ true?

We can read the solution from the graph of the function $y = |x|$.

The solution of $4 = |x|$ is -4 or 4.

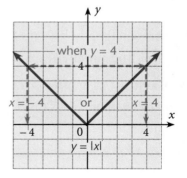

Recent research shows that the average healthy human body temperature is 98.2°F, not 98.6°F as previously thought.

1. Of $|x| - 98.2$, $|x| + 98.2$, $|x - 98.2|$, and $|x + 98.2|$, which represents the distance of any temperature from 98.2°F? Why?

2. Use the correct absolute value expression to determine the distance of 102°F from 98.2°F; the distance of 96.9°F from 98.2°F.

3. Suppose that a difference from the average of 1.5°F is still considered healthy. Is a body temperature of 101°F healthy?

4. What are the maximum and minimum healthy body temperatures? How would you describe these temperatures using absolute value?

5. Let x be a patient's body temperature. How would you describe the range of healthy body temperatures using absolute value?

6. How would you describe the range of unhealthy body temperatures using absolute value?

7. These graphs trace the function that represents the distance of any temperature from 98.2°F. Assume that the scale on both axes is 1, and supply the value of x for each screen. Tell how you decided.

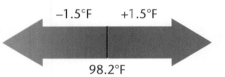

Most people would find a healthy temperature range easier to remember than a formula. But for health research, the absolute value function is a tool for use in computer study of a large amount of temperature data.

This Example reminds you that there are usually two solutions of an absolute value equation.

1. Solve and check $|x + 5| = 6$.

Think 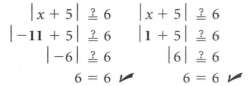 $= 6$.

We know $|-6| = 6$ and $|6| = 6$. So the covered quantity must be either -6 *or* 6.

We can write two equations, $x + 5 = -6$ or $x + 5 = 6$

Solve each equation.
$x = -11$ or $x = 1$

To check, substitute each solution into the original equation.

$$|x + 5| \stackrel{?}{=} 6 \qquad |x + 5| \stackrel{?}{=} 6$$
$$|-11 + 5| \stackrel{?}{=} 6 \qquad |1 + 5| \stackrel{?}{=} 6$$
$$|-6| \stackrel{?}{=} 6 \qquad |6| \stackrel{?}{=} 6 \qquad \text{when}$$
$$6 = 6 ✔ \qquad 6 = 6 ✔ \qquad y = 6$$

You can also see the solutions from the graph of the function $y = |x + 5|$.

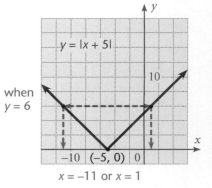

$x = -11$ or $x = 1$

2. Solve and check $|3x - 5| = 4$.

Think 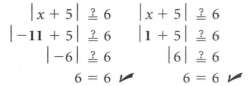 $= 4$. So $3x - 5$ can be -4 *or* 4.

Solve each equation.

$$3x - 5 = -4 \qquad\qquad\qquad 3x - 5 = 4$$
$$3x = 1 \qquad\qquad\qquad\qquad 3x = 9$$
$$x = \frac{1}{3} \qquad\qquad \text{or} \qquad\qquad x = 3$$

To check, substitute each solution into the original equation.

$$y \stackrel{?}{=} |3x - 5| \qquad\qquad\qquad y \stackrel{?}{=} |3x - 5|$$
$$4 \stackrel{?}{=} |3 \cdot \tfrac{1}{3} - 5| \qquad\qquad\qquad 4 \stackrel{?}{=} |3 \cdot 3 - 5|$$
$$4 \stackrel{?}{=} |1 - 5| \qquad\qquad\qquad\qquad 4 \stackrel{?}{=} |9 - 5|$$
$$4 = |-4| \qquad\qquad\qquad\qquad\qquad 4 = |4|$$

Both solutions check.

The equation $|3x - 5| = 4$ is the same as $4 = |3x - 5|$. Using this form of the equation, we can look at the graphs of the solutions.

Use the graph of $y = |3x - 5|$ to solve each equation. Check your solution.

a. $|3x - 5| = 5$ **b.** $|3x - 5| = 2$ **c.** $|3x - 5| = -1$

Graph $y = |2x + 3|$ to solve each equation. Check your solution.

d. $|2x + 3| = 3$ **e.** $|2x + 3| = 0$ **f.** $|2x + 3| = 7$

CONSIDER

1. When is there only one solution of an absolute value equation?

You can simplify absolute value equations using properties of equality to isolate the absolute value expression. Then solve as before.

EXAMPLE

3. Solve and check $-2|x + 5| + 2 = -10$.

$$-2|x + 5| + 2 = -10$$
$$-2|x + 5| = -12 \quad \text{Subtract 2 from each side.}$$
$$|x + 5| = 6 \quad \text{Divide each side by } -2.$$

This is the same equation we had in Example 1. You can verify that -11 and 1 are also solutions of this equation.

TRY IT

Solve and check.

g. $|x + 4| = 9$ **h.** $3|2x - 6| = 12$

REFLECT

1. Explain why you do not need to evaluate to solve $|x + 1| = -6$.

2. Compare the methods of solving $(2x + 1) = 7$ and $|2x + 1| = 7$. How are they alike? How are they different?

3. If you find two solutions of an absolute value equation, must one be positive and one negative? Explain.

Exercises

CORE

1. Getting Started Use these steps to solve $|x - 4| = 7$.
  a. Cover $x - 4$. Determine which two values $x - 4$ equals.
  b. Using "or," write two equations equivalent to $|x - 4| = 7$.
  c. Solve each equation.
  d. To check, substitute each solution into the original equation. What is the solution of $|x - 4| = 7$?

Solve and check.

2. $|x - 2| = 4$ **3.** $|2 - x| = 7$ **4.** $|5 - x| = 3$ **5.** $|x - 5| = 6$

6. Use the graph of $y = |x - 4|$ to solve each equation.
  a. $|x - 4| = 2$
  b. $|x - 4| = 5$
  c. $|x - 4| = -3$

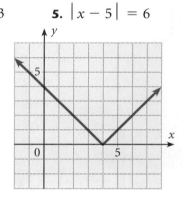

Write an absolute value inequality for each situation.

Industry

7. Free Freeze If you guess the cost (c) of your yogurt within 5¢, you get it free. You guess $1.10 and get your yogurt free. How much would you have had to pay?

Industry

8. Not Eggsactly The USDA requires that the weight (w) of a dozen large eggs be within 1.5 ounces of 25.5 ounces. Describe another real-world situation where it is important to know the numbers within a certain range.

9. Describe a real-world situation where it is important to know the values outside a certain range.

10. You can use a graph to solve an equation.
  a. Draw the graph of $y = |2x - 4|$.
  b. Explain how you can use the graph to solve the equation $|2x - 4| = 0$.

Social Science

11. Poll Fault The polls predict that a measure will pass because 76% of the voters surveyed are in favor of it. In reporting these findings they add, "The margin of error is plus or minus 3%."
  a. What are the highest and lowest percentages of people in favor of the measure?
  b. Explain this using absolute value.
  c. Suppose the measure involved needs a three-fourths majority. Is the measure a "sure thing"? Explain.

Solve each equation. Describe your first step.

12. $|m - 3| + 8 = 18$

13. $3|a - 3| = 12$

14. $2|x + 2| - 2 = 10$

15. Graph each equation on the same coordinate plane.

    a. $y = 0.5|x|$ **b.** $y = 1.5|x|$ **c.** $y = 3|x|$

    d. As the value of a increases, describe what happens to the graph of $y = a|x|$.

16. Reflecting on Graphs Graph each equation.

    a. $y = 2|x - 1|$ **b.** $y = -2|x - 1|$ **c.** $y = \frac{2}{3}|x|$ **d.** $y = -\frac{2}{3}|x|$

    e. Explain how you can determine the graph of $y = -a|x + b|$ if you have already graphed $y = a|x + b|$.

17. Stardates Judy made this time line for her astronomy class to demonstrate how the times of early astronomers relate to other significant dates in history.

History

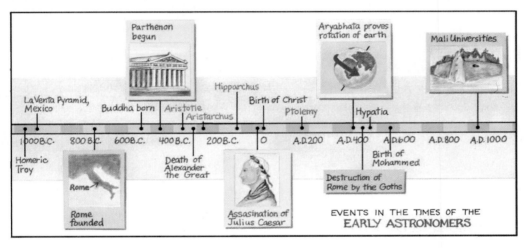

    a. How is the time line like a number line?

    b. Explain how absolute value could relate to the time line.

18. In an absolute value inequality of the form $|x - a| \leq b$, where a and b are constants, what number represents the midpoint of the range of solutions? What number represents the maximum distance a solution point can be from the midpoint?

LOOK BACK

19. The Color Purple Alice Walker is a Pulitzer-Prize winning author. Is the time it takes to read an Alice Walker novel always a function of the number of pages? Why or why not? [3-1]

Literature

20. Trade and Jobs These charts are from a 1990 U.S. Department of Labor Report. They show that jobs in some areas of the United States rely on imports from or exports to foreign countries. [1-1]

a. Which region is closest to the mean number of import-dependent jobs?

b. What are some reasons why the Mountain region is so low on both of the reports?

c. Find your own region. Does it have a greater than average percentage of jobs that are dependent on exports?

d. Do more U.S. jobs depend on exports or on imports?

e. Do the percentages in the import-dependent jobs chart total 100%? Explain your answer.

f. If you were going to start an import-export firm, in what region would you choose to set up business? Justify your decision.

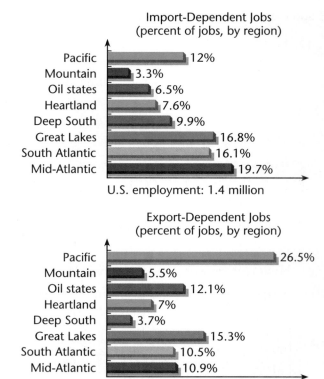

Import-Dependent Jobs
(percent of jobs, by region)

Pacific 12%
Mountain 3.3%
Oil states 6.5%
Heartland 7.6%
Deep South 9.9%
Great Lakes 16.8%
South Atlantic 16.1%
Mid-Atlantic 19.7%

U.S. employment: 1.4 million

Export-Dependent Jobs
(percent of jobs, by region)

Pacific 26.5%
Mountain 5.5%
Oil states 12.1%
Heartland 7%
Deep South 3.7%
Great Lakes 15.3%
South Atlantic 10.5%
Mid-Atlantic 10.9%

U.S. employment: 2.1 million

Note: Pacific region includes California, Washington, Oregon, Alaska, and Hawaii.

MORE PRACTICE

21. Use these steps to solve $|x + 5| = 7$.

a. Cover $x + 5$. Determine which two values $x + 5$ equals.

b. Using the word *or*, write two equations equivalent to $|x + 5| = 7$.

c. Solve each equation.

d. To check, substitute each solution into the original equation. What is the solution of $|x + 5| = 7$?

Solve and check.

22. $|x - 9| = 14$ **23.** $|5 - x| = 8$ **24.** $|x - 6| = 10$ **25.** $|8 - x| = 3$

26. $|x - 3| = 12$ **27.** $|7 - x| = 2$ **28.** $|x - 4| = 8$ **29.** $|9 - x| = 7$

Solve each equation.

30. $|r + 3| + 7 = 10$ **31.** $2|m - 3| - 4 = 6$ **32.** $3|w + 1| - 5 = 1$

33. $|n - 6| + 3 = 7$ **34.** $3|d - 1| = 21$ **35.** $2|c + 2| - 7 = 11$

36. Use the graph of $y = |x - 6|$ to solve each equation.

    a. $|x - 6| = 3$

    b. $|x - 6| = 1$

    c. $|x - 6| = -1$

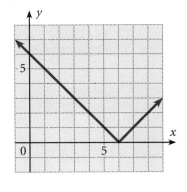

MORE MATH REASONING

37. Graph each equation on a separate coordinate plane.

    a. $y = 2|x|$ **b.** $y = 2|x| + 1$ **c.** $y = 2|x| - 2$

    d. Explain the cause of the differences in these graphs.

38. Police Patrol The city streets form a square grid. Each block is 100 meters long. A police officer can survey a maximum of 100 meters in one direction, that is, 400 meters in all. What is the least number of officers needed to see this 2 × 2 array of blocks? Explain your answer.

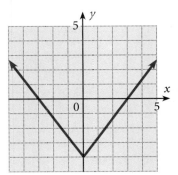

39. Consider the graph.

    a. Write an equation using absolute value.

    b. Describe how you can find the value of x when $y = 4$.

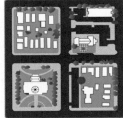

40. Graphing Wizard V. J. solved $|x - 2| = 6$ graphically. These are the screens from his graphing calculator.

    a. What two functions did he use? Why?

    b. How many solutions are there? How do you know? Name the solutions.

    c. V. J. thinks solving $|x - 2| = 6$ means finding the values of x that have a distance of 6 from 2 on a number line. Do you agree? Explain.

Making Connections

← **C O N N E C T** → *You have learned to solve equations and graph functions involving absolute value. Now you will apply what you have learned to a practical problem.*

EXPLORE: RUSH HOUR

The posted speed limit on a test section of turnpike is 55 mi/hr. At various check-points, the license plate, date, and time are recorded on video. Upon leaving the turnpike, the driver gets a computer readout of his or her speeds between check-points. Citations are given for "out-of-compliance" (too fast or too slow) on any stretch. The transit authority needs to set a "compliance range"—a range of legal speed that gives some leeway to allow for traffic flow and equipment errors.

Here are the data for several cars.

123 ABC   GO 4 IT   IM2KOOL   TC 2 ALC   AYZ 784   PAID 4

✓ Pt	Speed	✓ Pt	Speed	✓ Pt	Speed	✓ Pt	Speed	✓ Pt	Speed	✓ Pt	Speed
A	0	A	0	A	0	A	0	A	0	A	0
B	54	B	62	B	68	B	48	B	62	B	58
C	57	C	68	C	70	C	47	C	61	C	59
D	55	D	66	D	72	D	43	D	62	D	55

1. Study the data. How does the computer figure out a car's speed? Why are all the Checkpoint A entries zero?
2. Choose a reasonable compliance range. Does 55 mi/hr have to be the midpoint of the range? Explain why your range is reasonable.
3. Let S be the speed of a car. Write your range as an absolute value inequality.
4. Which drivers should be cited for driving too fast? for driving too slow?
5. Should a driver get a citation for noncompliance in one stretch, or only on the basis of *average* speed? If you base it on average speed, which figures should be averaged? Why?
6. Using your rules, is there a chance that a driver who is not really traveling too fast or slow could be cited? Could someone who was speeding avoid getting a ticket? If so, describe the "loophole" in the system.

1. Can the absolute value of a number be less than the original number? greater than the original? equal to the original? Explain.

2. If $|x - a| = b$ has no solution, do you know anything about a or b?

3. Compare $|x - a|$ and $|a - x|$, where a is any real number.

4. How can you use the graph of the function $y = |expression|$ to solve $5 = |expression|$? Explain.

Self-Assessment

1. Match each equation with the graph it describes. Explain your choice.

   a. $|x| = 4$

   i. ![number line with closed dots at -4 and 4]

   b. $|x| < 4$

   ii. ![number line with open dots just inside -4 and 4]

   c. $|x| \leq 4$

   iii. ![number line with closed dots just outside -4 and 4]

   d. $|x - 1| = 4$

   iv. ![number line segment open dots from -4 to 4]

   e. $|x + 1| = 4$

   v. ![number line segment closed dots from -4 to 4]

2. Name two numbers that are $\frac{5}{3}$ from -2. Explain using a number line.

Solve and check.

3. $|x - 5| = 20$

4. $2|v + 1| + 6 = 14$

5. **Range for Accuracy** A lathe operator is making pipe connections. The specifications require that the diameter (d) of each connector satisfy the equation $|d - 1| \leq 0.011$ centimeters.

   a. What two quantities could be equal to $d - 1$?

   b. Write two inequalities equivalent to $|d - 1| \leq 0.011$.

   c. What are the acceptable dimensions for the connector?

Describe each situation using an absolute value inequality.

6. The amount of precipitation in a tropical rain forest is between 200 and 500 centimeters.

7. The precipitation in a desert ranges from 0 to 20 cm.

8. **Flag on the Play** The referee marked off 10 yards from the spot of the foul, placing the ball on the 19-yard line.

9. Which equation(s) have the solutions -1 and 5?

I. $|x - 2| = 3$ II. $|2 - x| = 3$ III. $3|x - 2| - 12 = -3$

(a) only I   (b) only II   (c) only III   (d) I and III   (e) I, II, and III

10. What Do You See?

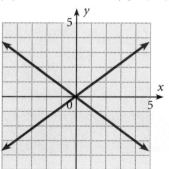

   a. Give the equation of the line in the first and third quadrants.

   b. Give the equation of the line in the second and fourth quadrants.

   c. Give the equation of the figure in the first and second quadrants.

   d. Give the equation of the figure in the third and fourth quadrants.

11. Match each equation with the graph it describes. Explain your choice in each case.

   a. $y = |x|$
          b. $y = |x| + 1$
          c. $y = -|x|$

   d. $y = |2x|$
          e. $y = |x| - 1$
          f. $y = |0.5x|$

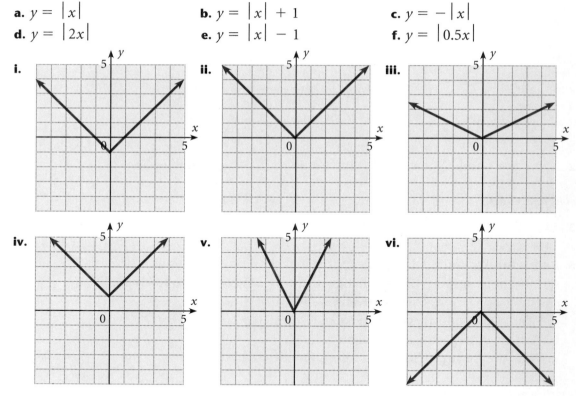

12. Describe how you could use a graph to explain why $-3 = |4x + 1|$ has no solution.

13. Phew A pH scale is used by chemists to show the hydrogen ion concentration. A strongly acidic solution could have a pH of 0, 1, 2, or 3, while a strongly basic solution could have a pH of 14, 13, 12, or 11. A neutral solution has a pH of 7. Use absolute value to describe a strong acid or base.

Irrational

More than 2500 years ago in Greece, followers of the famed mathematician Pythagoras were fascinated by integers. They studied arithmetic, geometry, music, astronomy, and philosophy. They believed that every number could be

mathematics secrets to themselves. They were not even permitted to write anything down! Their motto was:

All is Number

But they were troubled by numbers like pi and square roots of integers like 2 and 3 and 5. There was no ratio they

Secrets

written as the ratio of two integers. Even in music, they found that string lengths in simple ratios produced harmonious sounds.

Then they formed semi-religious societies to keep these

could find to equal these numbers. Admitting that non-rational or irrational numbers had to exist upset their philosophical belief in a universe in which everything depended on integers.

1. Is zero a rational number? Explain.
2. Is π the same as $\frac{22}{7}$? If not, explain how it is different.

3. What do we mean by a rational argument? by rationing?
4. What do we mean by irrational behavior? by an irrational fear?

3.1415926

Square Roots

← **C O N N E C T** → *You have probably squared numbers many times. In this part, we look at reversing this process to find the number that was squared. You'll find that your knowledge of absolute value will help with this task.*

A square is a figure with 4 right angles and 4 equal side lengths. To find its area, we multiply the length of the side *by itself.* That is, we square the number that represents the length of the side. So 64 is the square of 8.

We call 8 a **square root** of 64, because 8 squared is 64.

8

8

$A = 8 \times 8 = 8^2 = 64$

The number *c* is a **square root** of *a* if $c^2 = a$.

EXPLORE: SQUARE DEAL

1. Identify squares that have these areas: 1, 4, 9, 16, 25, 36. How long is the length of the side of each square?

2. Now identify shaded squares that have these areas: 2, 8, 32. (Hint: Look diagonally.) How do you know that these figures are squares?

3. How long is the side of each square in Step 2? Is it a whole number? If not, use estimation.

4. Square the number you found for each length. Do you get 2, 8, 32? Compare your answers with those of other students.

MATERIALS

Dot paper, Geoboard, or Graph paper

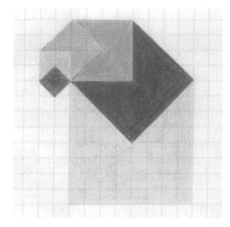

Another square root of 64 is −8, since $(−8)^2 = 64$. Every positive number has two square roots—one positive and one negative.

We use the **radical symbol,** $\sqrt{}$, to denote the *positive* or **principal square root** of a number. For example, $\sqrt{64} = 8$. Pressing 64 $\boxed{\sqrt{}}$ will display 8 on a scientific calculator.

CONSIDER

?

1. **Can you find the square root of a negative number? Explain.**

Remember that a number is **rational** if it can be expressed as the quotient of two integers. We know that 4 is the square of a rational number. We cannot find two integers whose quotient is $\sqrt{2}$. So $\sqrt{2}$ is not a rational number. We call it an **irrational number.**

Here are a few examples of rational numbers with squares close to, but not exactly equal to 2.

$$\left(\frac{17}{12}\right)^2 = \frac{289}{144} \approx 2.007 \qquad \left(\frac{577}{408}\right)^2 \approx 2.000006 \qquad \left(\frac{665857}{470832}\right)^2 \approx 2.000000000009$$

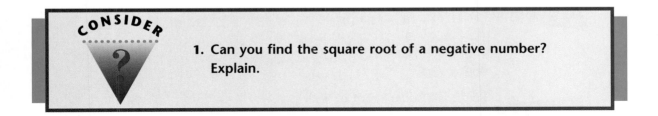

Rational numbers
can be written as a ratio of two integers.

Irrational numbers
cannot be written as a ratio of two integers.

$\sqrt{4}$ 2
Integers

$\sqrt{5.76}$ 2.4 $= \frac{12}{5}$
Terminating decimals

$\sqrt{\frac{1}{9}}$ 0.3333333333333 $= \frac{1}{3}$
Repeating decimals

π   3.1415926535897

$\sqrt{2}$ 1.4142135623730

The Real Numbers

Squaring and finding a principal square root are inverse processes.

Mrs. Yee asked her students to find *a* square root of 900.

Jason thinks . . .

$$900 = 9 \cdot 100$$
$$= 3 \cdot 3 \cdot 10 \cdot 10$$
$$= (3 \cdot 10) \cdot (3 \cdot 10)$$
$$= (3 \cdot 10)^2$$
$$900 = (30)^2$$

So 30 is a square root of 900.

Kristin thinks . . .

Since a negative times a negative is positive, and $(-30) \cdot (-30) = 900$, -30 is a square root of 900.

To use the symbol $\sqrt{}$ to indicate the negative square root of 36, we write $-\sqrt{36}$, which is -6. To use the symbol $\sqrt{}$ to indicate both the positive and negative square roots, we write $\pm\sqrt{36}$.

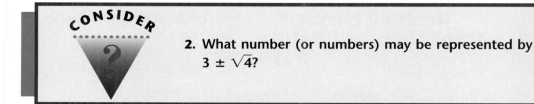

CONSIDER

?

2. What number (or numbers) may be represented by
   $3 \pm \sqrt{4}$?

TRY IT

Evaluate each square root.
a. $\sqrt{100}$ **b.** $-\sqrt{169}$ **c.** $\pm\sqrt{625}$

Which are squares of rational numbers?
d. 5   **e.** 29   **f.** $\frac{16}{9}$ **g.** 48   **h.** 2.56
i. Estimate $\sqrt{54}$.

In Chapter 4, you learned to solve for a variable in a linear equation or formula. Many important formulas involve variables that are squared. You may need to solve for the variable that is squared.

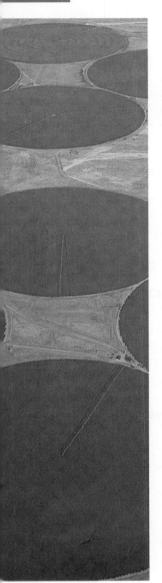

What is the length of a sprinkler arm, in feet, of a central pivot irrigation system that can water a circular field of 125 acres?

The area of a circle is given by $A = \pi r^2$. One acre $= 43,560 \text{ ft}^2$.

Sprinkler arm

$A = \pi r^2$

You know the area of the circle, so solve the formula for r.

$\pi r^2 = A$

$r^2 = \dfrac{A}{\pi}$

$r = \pm \sqrt{\dfrac{A}{\pi}}$

Use $\pm$ because both the positive and negative values are square roots.

$= \pm \sqrt{\dfrac{125 \text{ acres}}{3.14159\ldots}}$

Substitute the value of A. Use the π key on your calculator.

$= \pm \sqrt{\dfrac{125 \text{ acres} \cdot \dfrac{43,560 \text{ ft}^2}{1 \text{ acre}}}{3.14159\ldots}}$

Multiply 125 acres by the conversion factor $43,560 \text{ ft}^2$/acre, so the solution (after you take the square root) will be in feet.

$= \pm \sqrt{\dfrac{5,445,000 \text{ ft}^2}{3.14159\ldots}}$

Multiplying, $125 \text{ acres} \cdot \dfrac{43,560 \text{ ft}^2}{1 \text{ acre}} = 5,445,000 \text{ ft}^2$.

$= \pm \sqrt{1,733,197.33 \text{ ft}^2}$

Use your calculator to simplify the expression and to find the square root.

$r \approx \pm 1316.51 \text{ ft}$

The negative square root does not make sense in the problem. So the length of the sprinkler arm is 1316.51 feet.

Check your result by substituting it into the original formula.

1. If a number can be expressed as a decimal, is it rational? If a number is *approximated* by a decimal, is it necessarily rational?

2. Why don't we use the negative root for some real-world problems?

3. What is the relationship between squares and square roots?

4. Can all numbers of the form $\sqrt{n}$ be modeled as the side lengths of squares? If so, what is the area of the square in each case?

5. What number or numbers have two square roots? one square root? no square roots?

CORE

1. **Getting Started** Use these steps to estimate $\sqrt{130}$.
   a. Find the squares of 9, 10, 11, 12, and 13.
   b. Determine which two squares (n^2) 130 lies between.
   c. Determine which two numbers (n) $\sqrt{130}$ lies between. Which number is it closer to?
   d. Estimate $\sqrt{130}$ to the nearest tenth. Check your estimate on the calculator.

n	9	10	11	12	13
n^2					

2. Name three numbers between 0 and 10 that are squares of integers.

Evaluate.

3. $\sqrt{25}$ 4. $\sqrt{81}$ 5. $\sqrt{100}$ 6. $\sqrt{225}$ 7. $\sqrt{121}$

8. $\sqrt{49}$ 9. $\sqrt{\dfrac{4}{9}}$ 10. $\sqrt{\dfrac{9}{16}}$ 11. $\sqrt{0.04}$ 12. $\sqrt{1.44}$

13. Find the area of each square.   **a.**   **b.**   **c.**

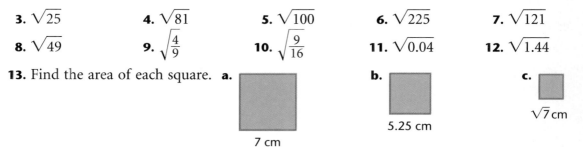

7 cm

5.25 cm

$\sqrt{7}$ cm

Find the length of a side of each square with the given area. Tell whether your answer in each case is a rational number.

14.

100 in.^{2}

15.

17 in.^{2}

16. **Squaring Off** The DeCosta family has budgeted $500 to replace the 12- by 12-foot carpet in their family room.
   a. What is the area in square feet? square yards?
   b. What is the ratio of 1 yard to 1 foot?
   c. What is the ratio of 1 *square* yard to 1 *square* foot? Explain.
   d. Super-release carpet sells for $28.75 per square yard plus a $40.00 installation fee. Can they afford this carpet? Explain your answer.

17. Tell whether each is a square of a rational number. Explain how you know.

   a. 64   **b.** $\dfrac{49}{25}$ **c.** 39   **d.** 1.21

18. The answer is $\sqrt{49}$. Which question is the best choice?

    (a) What is the square root of 49?   (b) What is the principal square root of 49?

    (c) What are the square roots of 49?   (d) What number squared is 49?

19. The surface area of a sphere is given by the formula $A = 4\pi r^2$. Solve for r.

Use mental math to estimate each square root.

20. $\sqrt{50}$ **21.** $\sqrt{12}$ **22.** $\sqrt{140}$

23. $2\sqrt{3}$ **24.** $5\sqrt{20}$ **25.** $4\sqrt{50}$

26. Explain the difference, if any, between $-\sqrt{35}$ and $\sqrt{-35}$.

27. Prove or disprove that $\sqrt{50} = 25\sqrt{2}$.

28. Which has a larger value, $\sqrt{125}$ or $6\sqrt{5}$? Explain how you know.

Industry **29.** What is the length of a sprinkler arm of a central pivot irrigation system that can water a circular field of 110 acres?

Industry **30. Book by the Rule** Adolpho's cookbook is 7.5 by 10 inches. For the second edition, the book will be square. The design costs will stay the same because the pages and cover of the new edition will have the same area. What will the trim size—the outside measurements—of the new book be?

31. Square to Square The small square has an area of 1 square unit. Show that the area of the larger square is 2 square units and its side (s) is $\sqrt{2}$.

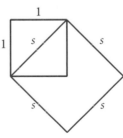

> **Problem-Solving Tip**
>
> Trace and cut out the small square.

32. Anti-Anti Lock When the brakes lock, a car traveling at a velocity of 50 miles per hour will skid 4 times as far as a car traveling at a velocity of 25 miles per hour. This is an example of *kinetic energy* at work, and it can be expressed in the equation

$$\text{kinetic energy} = \tfrac{1}{2}mv^2,$$

where m is mass and v is velocity. Car A has a velocity of 20 miles per hour and Car B has a velocity of 60 miles per hour. Both cars have the same mass. How much farther will Car B skid on ice than Car A? 4 times, 6 times, 9 times, or 12 times? Explain your answer.

33. Half Court In a computer simulation of a basketball game, the designers wanted the probability of a player making two free throws to be 0.5, so they began with $p \cdot p = 0.5$. Solve this for p.

LOOK AHEAD

34. Copy and complete the table and describe the patterns you observe.

1	3	4	5
2	6	8	10
3	9	12	
4	12		
5			
n			

Use your calculator or estimate to copy and complete the tables.

35.

x	0	1	2	3	4	5	6	8	9
$\sqrt{x}$									

36.

x	0	1	2	3	4	5	6	8	9
$2x$									
$\sqrt{2x}$									

MORE PRACTICE

Evaluate.

37. $\sqrt{900}$

38. $\sqrt{400}$

39. $\sqrt{0.0009}$

40. $\sqrt{0.0049}$

41. $\sqrt{\dfrac{16}{25}}$

42. $\sqrt{\dfrac{9}{64}}$

Use mental math to estimate each square root.

43. $\sqrt{90}$ **44.** $\sqrt{1.12}$ **45.** $\sqrt{54}$ **46.** $\sqrt{160}$ **47.** $\sqrt{0.32}$

48. $\sqrt{128}$ **49.** $5\sqrt{3}$ **50.** $3\sqrt{2}$ **51.** $2\sqrt{6}$

52. Evaluate $\sqrt{971}$ to the nearest tenth; to the nearest hundredth.

53. Find the length of a side of the square to the nearest tenth of a foot.

500 ft^2

54. Find the area of the square to the nearest tenth of a square inch.

3.7 in.

55. Between what consecutive integers is the principal square root of 115? Explain your answer.

56. Between what consecutive integers is $\sqrt{92}$? Is $\sqrt{92}$ a rational number?

57. Use a calculator to find $\sqrt{568}$ to the nearest tenth; to the nearest hundredth. Is $\sqrt{568}$ rational or irrational?

MORE MATH REASONING

58. The Pressure's On The study of *hydraulics*, the science of flowing liquids, is a crucial part of training to become a firefighter. The first hydraulics formula, $v = 12.2\sqrt{P}$ ft/sec, relates the pressure (P) of water pumped, in pounds per square inch (psi), to the velocity (v) of the water stream produced. Convert units to rewrite the velocity in inches per minute. Explain your work.

59. Square Roots Forever and Ever You can use your calculator to analyze square roots. (If you don't have a calculator, choose square numbers.)
   a. Choose any number larger than one. Enter it into a calculator and press the square root button repeatedly until you notice a pattern. Describe and explain the pattern.
   b. Choose any number between zero and one. Enter it into a calculator and press the square root button repeatedly until you notice a pattern. Describe and explain the pattern.
   c. Under what conditions is the principal square root of a number larger than the number itself?

60. The Root of the Problem The cube root of 8, written $\sqrt[3]{8}$, means "what number to the third power is 8?" Evaluate.
   a. $\sqrt[3]{8}$ **b.** $\sqrt[3]{-8}$ **c.** $\sqrt[3]{64}$ **d.** $\sqrt[4]{16}$ **e.** $\sqrt[5]{-32}$

← CONNECT → *In your work with linear functions, you learned to think about lines as they relate to the line $y = x$. In 7-1, you compared the graphs of absolute value functions. Now you will see what the graphs of $y = \sqrt{x}$ and related functions look like.*

You can graph **square root functions,** such as $y = \sqrt{x}$. The value of x can be any real number greater than or equal to zero.

Here is a data table for $y = \sqrt{x}$.   Here is the graph of $y = \sqrt{x}$.

x	y
0	0
1	1
2	1.414...
3	1.732...
4	2
5	2.236...
6	2.449...

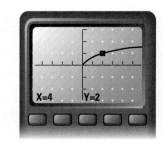

X=4   Y=2

EXPLORE: THE ROOT OF THE MATTER

MATERIALS

Graph each function using a graphing utility or table of values.

Graphing utility or Graph paper

> **Problem-Solving Tip**
>
> Use your table of values to determine which quadrant(s) each graph is in.

$y = \sqrt{x}$

$y = \sqrt{2x}, y = \sqrt{3x}$

$y = 2\sqrt{x}, y = 3\sqrt{x}, y = -\sqrt{x}$

$y = \sqrt{x} + 2, y = \sqrt{x} + 5$

$y = \sqrt{x + 2}, y = \sqrt{x + 5}$

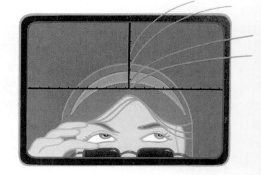

Use $y = \sqrt{x}$ as a basis of comparison to form conjectures about each variation.

1. What happens when the coefficient of x (under the $\sqrt{}$ sign) increases from 1 to 2? from 2 to 3? In general, what happens when the coefficient of x increases?

2. What happens when a factor such as 2 or 3 appears in front of the $\sqrt{}$ sign? What if the factor were increased to 4? In general, what happens when this factor increases? What happens when this factor is negative?

3. What happens when a positive number is added to $\sqrt{x}$?

4. What happens when a positive number is added to x (inside the $\sqrt{}$ sign)?

5. Explain how to move the graph of $y = \sqrt{x}$ up from the origin; down from the origin; right from the origin; left from the origin. Illustrate your conjectures with sketches of your graphs.

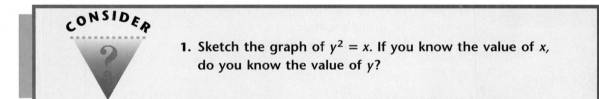

CONSIDER

?

1. Sketch the graph of $y^2 = x$. If you know the value of x, do you know the value of y?

TRY IT

Match each equation with the graph it describes. The graphs have identical scales.

a. $y = \sqrt{x}$ **b.** $y = \sqrt{3x}$ **c.** $y = \sqrt{3x} - 3$

i. **ii.** **iii.**

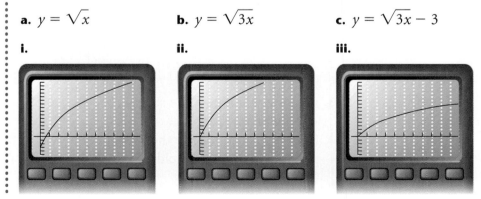

A graph can be used to model real-life situations in which square roots are useful.

EXAMPLE

If an object falls to the moon from a height of h feet, the time it takes to fall in seconds is given by $t = \sqrt{0.370h}$. Graph this function to determine the time it takes a golf ball dropped from a height of 50 feet to fall to the surface of the moon.

To use a graphing utility, use X for the height h and Y for the time t. Trace to evaluate the function.

The golf ball takes approximately 4.3 seconds to fall from a height of 50 feet to the moon's surface.

TRY IT

Solve by graphing.

d. How long would it take a golf ball to fall to the earth from 50 feet above the earth's surface? Use $t = \sqrt{0.0622h}$.

e. How long would it take a golf ball to fall from 1000 feet above the moon's surface? from 1000 feet above the earth's surface?

REFLECT

1. How does the graph of $y = x$ compare to the graph of $y = \sqrt{x}$? Why does the roundest part of the graph of $y = \sqrt{x}$ occur where $0 < x < 1$?

2. How does the graph of $y = \sqrt{x + 1}$ compare to the graph of $y = \sqrt{x} + 1$?

3. Which graph rises more steeply, $y = \sqrt{2x}$ or $y = 2\sqrt{x}$? How do you know without graphing?

4. How could you modify the function $y = \sqrt{x}$ so that some of the points of the graph would lie in Quadrant II? in Quadrant III? in Quadrant IV?

Exercises

CORE

1. Getting Started Copy and complete the table for $y = \sqrt{x} + 4$.

x	0	4	9	16	25
$\sqrt{x}$		2			
$\sqrt{x} + 4$		6			
(x, y)		$(4, 6)$			

a. Use the data in the table to graph part of $y = \sqrt{x} + 4$.
b. Explain the effect of the $+ 4$ on the graph.

2. Copy and complete the table and use it to graph $y = \sqrt{x + 4}$. Explain the effect of the $+ 4$ on the graph.

x	-4	-3	0	4	9
$x + 4$					
$\sqrt{x + 4}$					
(x, y)					

3. Describe the similarities and the differences in the graphs of Exercises 1 and 2. How are these differences related to the equations?

4. Find the y-value of $y = -\sqrt{x} + 4$ when $x = 4$.

5. Use the graph of $t = \sqrt{0.370h}$ to determine how long it would take a golf ball to fall from 100 feet above the moon's surface. *(Science)*

6. Can $-x$ be a perfect square? If so, what would the graph of $y = \sqrt{-x}$ look like?

7. True or false: $y = \sqrt{2x}$ is a linear function. Justify your answer.

8. Graph $y = |x|$ and $y = \sqrt{x}$ together. Where do they intersect? Why?

9. Lost Cause The high school Wall Street Club invested $150 in a new stock and lost the entire investment. All members shared the loss equally. If each person lost $10, which equation shows how many people are in the club? Explain your choice. *(Industry)*

(a) $150 - 10 = x$ (b) $150 = 10x$
(c) $150 = \dfrac{x}{10}$ (d) $150 = x - 10$

10. Match each equation with the graph it describes. The graphs have identical scales. Explain your choice in each case.

   a. $y = \sqrt{x}$
   b. $y = \sqrt{5x}$
   c. $y = \sqrt{5x} + 5$
   d. $y = \sqrt{5x} - 5$

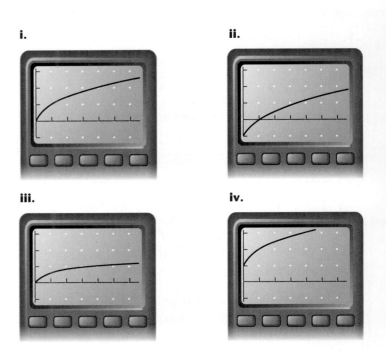

i.

ii.

iii.

iv.

Industry

11. **Cool Heads Prevail** Mr. Tomaso was trying to figure out how much wrapping paper he needed to wrap a new refrigerator he had purchased as a surprise for the family. His daughter, Serina, used a ruler to measure the box. She entered the numbers in her calculator and arrived at a total of about 11,000 square inches. Her father knew the refrigerator's dimensions were about 3 × 2.5 × 5.5 feet. He told Serina that he thought she had made a mistake because he got a total of about 75 square feet. Serina insisted that she had not made any mistakes. Who is right? Explain your answer.

12. Graph $y = \sqrt{6x}$ and $y = 6\sqrt{x}$ on the same coordinate axis. Describe the difference.

Science

13. **Beyond the Blue Horizon** The distance to the horizon is approximately $\sqrt{2Rh}$, where R = the radius of the earth and h = the height above sea level. If h is measured in feet, then the distance to the horizon is $\sqrt{1.5h}$ miles. Calculate the distance to the horizon from Byron's home at 300 feet above sea level. (If you are working without a calculator, estimate your answer.)

14. If, instead of graphing the areas of squares on the x-axis and their sides on the y-axis, you graphed the areas on the y-axis and the sides on the x-axis, what function would you be graphing?

15. A fiber artist is designing a carpet. The shaded area is half of the total area of the carpet. It is centered on an 8- by 10-foot carpet as shown. What is the radius of the inner circle?

10 ft

8 ft

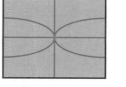

16. What combination of square root functions makes a design like this?

17. Glenda is working some problems and using radicals. She reasons that since $\sqrt{2} \cdot \sqrt{2} = 2$, $\dfrac{2}{\sqrt{2}}$ must equal $\sqrt{2}$. She uses the fact that $3 \cdot 3 = 9$ to illustrate her point. Write an explanation of Glenda's argument.

18. *History* Heron of Alexandria, who lived sometime between 150 B.C. and A.D. 250, is generally credited with this formula for finding the area of a triangle (K) with sides a, b, and c.

$$K = \sqrt{s(s - a)(s - b)(s - c)}$$

with $s = \frac{1}{2}(a + b + c)$

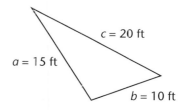

The triangular area between the overpass and the freeway exit is to be covered with redwood chips. The workers need to know the area of the region so they can order the chips. Show how they could use Heron's formula to find the area of the region.

LOOK BACK

19. *Fine Arts* **Music and Math** Pythagoras discovered a mathematical basis for the scale used in music. He was attracted by the diverse tones blacksmiths made when they struck anvils of different lengths. Through experiments, he was able to show the 2:1 ratio between the lengths of lyre strings which produced the "C" notes at either end of an octave. In the Andes of South America, musicians play a flute made from a bundle of bamboo pipes. They also use the ratio of 2:1 for the length of their pipes for the "C" notes at either end of an octave.

Fine Arts **Copy and complete the table. Give lengths to the nearest hundredth. [3-1]**

Pitch	C	D	E	F	G	A	B	C
Length ratio	1	$\frac{8}{9}$	$\frac{4}{5}$	$\frac{3}{4}$	$\frac{2}{3}$	$\frac{3}{5}$	$\frac{8}{15}$	$\frac{1}{2}$
Length	10 cm							5 cm

Write an inequality for each situation. [4-3]

20. The candidate is only accepting campaign contributions not exceeding $1000.

21. The manager posts a sign reading, "Riders must be at least 3 feet tall."

22. Jorge's parents budgeted at most $500 for the rehearsal dinner. [4-3]

What is the largest number of people they can invite and still be within their budget?

Number of Guests	Cost of the Meal
1	$18.75
2	$37.50
3	$56.25
10	$187.50

23. Solve the system $2n - 3m = 6.5$ and $n + 2m = 9$. Describe your first step. [6-2]

MORE PRACTICE

Copy and complete each table. Then graph the equation.

24. $y = \sqrt{x} + 2$

x	0	4	9	16	25
$\sqrt{x}$		2			
$\sqrt{x} + 2$		4			
(x, y)		$(4, 4)$			

25. $y = \sqrt{x} - 3$

x	0	4	9	16	25
$\sqrt{x}$					
$\sqrt{x} - 3$					
(x, y)					

26. $y = \sqrt{x + 9}$

x	-8	-5	0	7	16
$x + 9$					
$\sqrt{x + 9}$					
(x, y)					

27. $y = \sqrt{x + 16}$

x	-12	-7	0	9	20
$x + 16$					
$\sqrt{x + 16}$					
(x, y)					

28. Match the equation with the graph it describes. The graphs have identical scales. Explain your choice in each case.

a. $y = \sqrt{x}$

b. $y = \sqrt{7x}$

c. $y = \sqrt{7x} + 7$

d. $y = \sqrt{7x} - 7$

i.

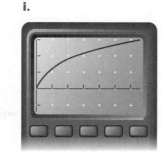

ii.

iii.

iv.

MORE MATH REASONING

29. Gravity Can Be Useful After seven years of drought the New Melones Reservoir was again a summer playground. For a science project, Kaili and Lydia need to find the depth of the water. The Stevenot Bridge rises about 240 feet from the bottom of the reservoir. The distance covered by a falling object can be calculated from Galileo's formula $d = \frac{1}{2}gt^2$, where $g = 32\ \frac{\text{ft}}{\text{sec}^2}$. Lydia timed the rock that Kaili dropped from the bridge. The splash appeared 3.5 seconds after Kaili released the rock.

a. How far above the water is the bridge?

b. How deep is the water?

c. How far would the rock have fallen in 2 seconds?

d. If the reservoir were empty, how long would it have taken to hit the bottom?

30. Irrigation Interrogation

The Midwest has many circular irrigation systems. In this one, an arm moves in a circle sprinkling plants. How much of a field remains unwatered? Are longer arms more cost effective than several smaller ones? Explain.

Fields as viewed from above

← C O N N E C T → *Evaluating and graphing are important tasks in problem solving. In Part B, you learned to evaluate and simplify square roots and graph square root functions.*

Pythagoras noticed that laying out pebbles geometrically uncovered interesting logic in numbers. For instance, the series of odd integers $(1 + 3 + 5...)$ led to squares $(1, 9, 25, ...)$.

This Explore will help you understand the concept of square root in a visual way.

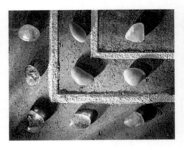

EXPLORE: SQUARING OFF

MATERIALS

Calculator, Graph paper, Ruler, Scissors

If you had 16 small squares you could build a larger square with side $\sqrt{16}$, or 4. If you could build a square from 17 squares, its side would be $\sqrt{17}$. Estimate $\sqrt{17}$ this way.

1. Carefully draw a 4- by 4-inch (4×4) square.

2. Draw one additional 1-inch square. Cut this 1-inch square into 8 equal-sized strips. What is the width of each strip?

3. Arrange the strips along adjacent sides of the 4×4 square. Is the new square complete? If not, exactly what area is missing?

4. Write an inequality that *traps* the exact value of $\sqrt{17}$ between two numbers. Why is your inequality true? Use your calculator to make sure that $\sqrt{17}$ is a solution of your inequality.

5. Can you continue to cut and arrange to estimate $\sqrt{17}$ more accurately? Explain.

1. Why are numbers like $\sqrt{17}$ called irrational?
2. Describe the distinction between a square root and a principal square root.
3. How could a solution of an equation with a square root not make sense in the problem?
4. How would you solve $y = ax^2$ for x? What types of situations have you seen that use this form as a model?
5. If a number inside a radical represents area, what does the square root represent? What happens to units when you solve a square root problem? Illustrate with an example.

Self-Assessment

Find the square of each number.

1. 6   **2.** 5.5   **3.** -4 **4.** 16

Find the principal square root of each number.

5. 0   **6.** 16   **7.** 20   **8.** 0.0009

9. List all numbers between 90 and 300 that are the square of an integer.

10. Which of the following numbers is *not* rational? Explain how you know.
    a. $\sqrt{25}$ **b.** $\sqrt{35}$ **c.** $\frac{3}{5}$ **d.** $\frac{\sqrt{32}}{\sqrt{8}}$

11. Find the square of each number.
    a. 11   **b.** 111   **c.** 1111   **d.** 11111
    e. Describe a pattern you observe as a result of these four exercises.

12. a. Find the length of a side of a square with area 81 cm^2.
    b. Find the area of a square with side length 81 millimeters.
    c. Are the sizes of the squares in the diagram helpful? Are they misleading? Explain.

81 cm^2

81 mm

13. Between what two consecutive integers will $\sqrt{407}$ lie? Explain how you know.

14. Which Is Largest? Without using a calculator, determine which of these *must* have the largest value. Explain your choice.

$$\sqrt{\frac{1}{27}}, \sqrt{\frac{1}{7}}, \sqrt{\frac{1}{275}}, \text{ or } \sqrt{\frac{1}{95}}$$

15. The area of a circle is 75 square inches. Find the length of a radius of this circle to the nearest tenth of a foot.

Remember: $A = \pi r^2$.

16. See the Solution Vince used his graphing calculator to solve these systems.

Screen   System   Screen   System

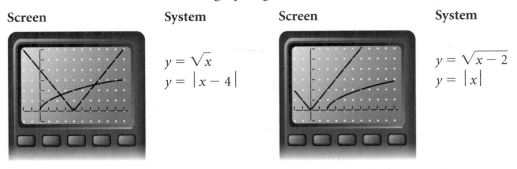

$y = \sqrt{x}$
$y = |x - 4|$

$y = \sqrt{x - 2}$
$y = |x|$

a. Use his graph to determine how many values of x satisfy the equation $\sqrt{x} = |x - 4|$. Explain.

b. Use his graph to determine how many values of x satisfy the equation $\sqrt{x - 2} = |x|$. Explain.

17. On the same set of axes draw the graphs of $y = \sqrt{x}$ and $y = x - 2$. Use your graph to determine how many value(s) of x satisfy the equation $\sqrt{x} = x - 2$.

18. Fast Fall Rheta is calculating the time it will take for a ball to fall from a 1-meter high table. She uses the formula $d = \frac{1}{2}gt^2$. Since the height of the table is given in meters she uses $g = 9.8\frac{m}{sec^2}$ for the acceleration due to gravity.

a. Solve $d = \frac{1}{2}gt^2$ for t.

b. How long does it take for the ball to fall from the table?

c. Show that the solution is in seconds.

19. I Never Promised You a Square Garden Can a 150-square foot square garden be constructed with rational dimensions? Why or why not?

20. Round and Round The force (F) required to move a mass (m grams) in a circular path (of radius r meters) with a constant speed (v meters per second) is given by $F = \frac{mv^2}{r}$.

a. What is the unit dimension of force? Explain how you know.

b. Solve the formula for v.

21. Graph $y = \sqrt{2x}$ and $y = -\sqrt{2x}$ on the same coordinate plane. Describe the differences and the similarities.

22. A downhill skier is traveling at 25 miles per hour (v). The temperature is 20°F (F). Find the windchill on her face.

$$\text{windchill} = 91.4 - \frac{(10.45 + 6.69\sqrt{v} - 0.447v)(91.4 - F)}{22}, \text{ for } 4 \le v \le 45$$

A TALE OF TWO CITIES

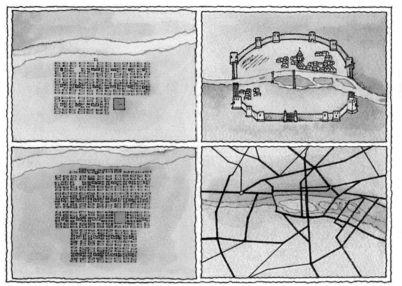

Hundreds of years ago, cities developed differently from today. Paris began as a medieval walled city around the River Seine. It grew as new structures were built. These included landmarks such as the Bastille and the Louvre Museum. Savannah was also built around a river, but it has a cell-like structure. Each cellular unit has a central square or park surrounded by twelve blocks. Gradually, more cells were added until 1856, when the map resembled a grid. The grid design of a modern city lets us calculate distances and travel between key places more easily. As cities like Paris and Savannah continue to grow, architects have been challenged to create designs for the convenience and pleasure of their citizens.

1. Which of the two designs—Paris or Savannah—does your town resemble more?
2. Which of the two cities would have a more complicated map today?

3. For which city should it be easier to give directions?

← **CONNECT** → *In 7-1, you found distance on a number line. Now you will look at distances on a grid, moving horizontally and vertically.*

In the real world, our routes are often limited. Imagine a taxi traveling from one street intersection to another. The passenger wants the shortest, most direct route. We call this the grid distance or **taxi distance** between points. Informally, we call the process of finding this distance *taxicab geometry.*

EXPLORE: ALL AROUND THE TOWN

MATERIALS

Graph paper

Welcome to Our Town! It isn't very big and everybody knows everyone else. For easier reading, we use a coordinate plane with Main Street as the *x*-axis.

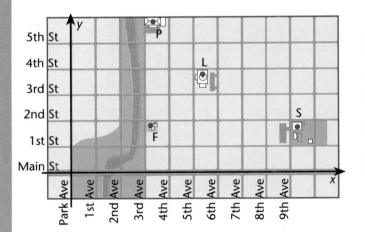

The post office, **P**, is located at 3rd Avenue and 6th Street.

The high school, **S**, is located at 9th Avenue and 2nd Street.

Florence, **F**, lives at 3rd Avenue and 2nd Street.

Larry, **L**, lives at 5th Avenue and 4th Street.

1. How far is it from Florence's house to school? (She must stay on the horizontal and vertical streets.)
2. How many different routes can Florence take to Larry's without backtracking?
3. The map shows the route Florence took one day, stopping at Larry's house on the way to school. How long is this route? Is there a shorter route that connects all three places? Explain.

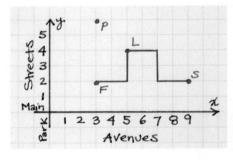

4. Using graph paper, draw two routes Florence can use to stop at the post office on the way to school. How long are these routes? How long is the shortest route? Is there more than one shortest route?

5. Using your previous answers, describe how to find the taxi distance between two points on a grid.

Using a portion of the plane from the Explore, here are three routes Larry can take to school.

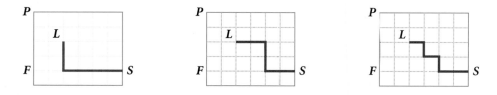

Larry needs to go four blocks over and two blocks down, a total of six blocks, regardless of which route he takes to school. We can summarize the calculation of the taxi distance.

The **taxi distance** from (x_1, y_1) to (x_2, y_2) is $|x_2 - x_1| + |y_2 - y_1|$.

EXAMPLE

Find the taxi distance between $(10, -3)$ and $(-2, 4)$.

The horizontal distance is $|10 - (-2)|$, or 12. The vertical distance is $|-3 - 4|$, or 7.

The total distance is $12 + 7$, or 19 units.

CONSIDER

?

1. Why do we need absolute value in the taxi-distance formula?

TRY IT

Find the taxi distance between these points.
a. (4, 4) and (12, 4)
b. (8, −2) and (6, −4)
c. A and B

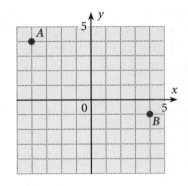

REFLECT

1. Write a brief comparison of number-line distance and taxi distance.
2. Does the direction of travel between two points affect the taxi distance between them?
3. How do the taxi and straight-line distances between two points differ? Can they ever be equal? Explain.
4. Suppose someone interchanged x_1 and x_2 in the taxi-distance formula. How would the result compare with the correct answer if everything else was done correctly?

Exercises

CORE

1. Getting Started Use the grid to answer these taxi-distance questions.
  a. Trace the grid to find the horizontal distance from D to E. What is the vertical distance?
  b. Give the coordinates of D and of E.
  c. Which coordinates would you subtract to determine the horizontal distance? the vertical distance?

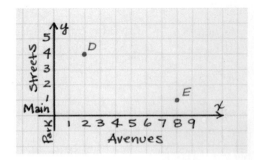

Find the taxi distance between each pair of points.

2. $P(3, 5)$ and $Q(12, 5)$

3. $A(4, 6)$ and $B(-2, 6)$

4. $O(x + 2, y + 4)$ and $W(x - 4, y - 5)$

5. $R(-5, -3)$ and $S(-4, -3)$

6. What does the Triangle Inequality tell you about the straight-line distance from Larry's house to school?

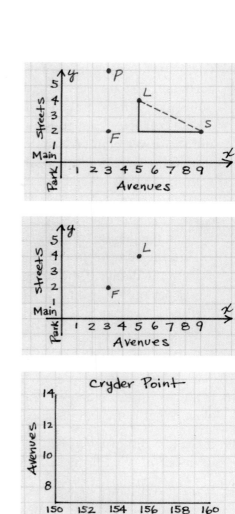

7. Let's Meet Midway! Locate all points that are as far from Florence's house as they are from Larry's house. Describe these points.

The diagram shows part of a town called "Cryder Point." The avenues run east and west and the streets run north and south. All streets and avenues are two-way. We will use coordinates such as (155, 12) to stand for 155th Street and 12th Avenue.

Find the distance a taxicab would travel between each pair of points.

8. (150, 10) and (153, 8)   **9.** (159, 12) and (160, 14)

10. If you drove three blocks from (155, 12), what would be the coordinates of all possible points of intersection you would pass on your trip? Explain.

Recently, a park was built in Cryder Point. Vehicles are *not* allowed in the park. Find the taxi distance between each pair of points.

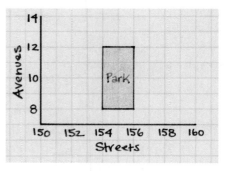

11. (151, 13) and (154, 10)

12. (151, 7) and (158, 11)

13. (153, 10) and (157, 10)

14. The dispatcher for the Cryder Point Police Department gets a report of an accident at 157th Street and 13th Avenue. She knows there is one police car at 153rd and 11th and another at 158th and 9th. Which car should she send to the accident? Why?

15. The map shows a small county with three major highways. Mileages measured north and east are used to designate the highways and streets. A truck leaves from (35, 146) and travels east along Highway 146 to make a delivery at (58, 147). There is a detour along Highway 146, and the driver *must* take Highway 50 south.

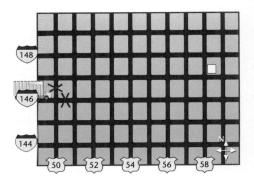

a. Find the shortest distance the truck would go from (35, 146) to (58, 147) according to the original plan.

b. Find the shortest distance the truck can go using the detour.

c. Find the additional shipping charge resulting from the detour if the company charges 30¢ per mile. Explain.

Solve for x.

16. $|10 - x| = 8$

17. $|x - 4| = 6$

18. If the taxi distance between $A(5, 12)$ and $B(5, m)$ is 7, find all possible values of m. What if the taxi distance is 9?

19. If the taxi distance between $A(-5, 12)$ and $B(n, 12)$ is 3, find all possible values of n. What if the taxi distance is 5?

20. If the taxi distance between $A(5, 12)$ and $B(m, n)$ is 4, find all possible values of m and n, if $\overline{AB}$ is horizontal. What if it is vertical?

LOOK BACK

What is the slope of the line through each pair of points? [5-1]

21. $(-4, 1)$ and $(3, -1)$

22. $(6, 3)$ and $(-3, -1)$

23. $(-5, -2)$ and $(6, 8)$

Graph each inequality. [6-3]

24. $y < 2x - 5$

25. $y > -x + 3$

26. $y \geq 3x - 2$

27. The volume of a cylinder with height (h) and radius (r) is found using the formula $V = \pi r^2 h$. [7-2]

a. Solve the formula for volume of a cylinder for r in terms of V, π, and h.

b. The volume of a cone is $\frac{1}{3}$ the volume of the cylinder with the same height and radius. Write the formula for the volume of a cone and solve for r.

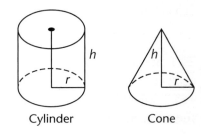

Cylinder   Cone

MORE PRACTICE

Find the taxi distance between each pair of points.

28. $A(3, 2)$ and $B(7, 2)$

29. $C(4, 5)$ and $D(4, -1)$

30. $E(-2, 6)$ and $F(-7, 6)$

31. $M(-5, -3.5)$ and $N(-5, -23.5)$

32. $R(-1, 3)$ and $S(8, -3.6)$

33. $T(-6.3, 5)$ and $U(-1.2, 1.4)$

34. $W\left(-\frac{1}{2}, 4\right)$ and $X\left(\frac{2}{3}, -5\right)$

35. $Y(1.4, 6)$ and $Z\left(-\frac{1}{5}, -4\right)$

36. Problem for Squares! A square is a four-sided figure whose sides all have the same length and whose angles all have the same measure.
  a. Draw three *taxi squares* whose sides have a length of 5, starting at $(0, 0)$.
  b. Draw three *taxi squares* whose sides have a length of 5, starting at $(2, 4)$.

37. In a city, the streets are $\frac{1}{20}$ of a mile apart, and the avenues are $\frac{1}{5}$ of a mile apart. What is the taxi distance between the intersections?
  a. 74th Street/3rd Avenue and 34th Street/8th Avenue
  b. 59th Street/10th Avenue and 125 Street/2nd Avenue
  c. A driver mistakenly drove to 5th Street/19th Avenue instead of 19th Street/5th Avenue. How far will the driver need to go to get to the right place?

38. If the taxi distance between $P(3, 0)$ and $Q(x, 5)$ is 9, find all possible values of x. Show your answers on a graph.

39. If the taxi distance between $A(5, 10)$ and $B(5, m)$ is 3, find all values of m.

40. If the taxi distance between $A(-2, 12)$ and $B(n, 12)$ is 4, find all values of n.

MORE MATH REASONING

41. Find the coordinates of all points that are the same taxi distance from $A(0, 0)$ and $B(10, 6)$.

42. What can you say about two points that are a taxi distance of zero apart?

43. Going Around in Circles On your graph paper, plot all points that are 4 units away from $(0, 0)$. The result is called a *taxi circle* with center $(0, 0)$ and radius 4. Explain why we use this terminology.

  In each case, first draw a taxi circle with the center at point C with the given radius. Then find the "circumference" of the taxi circle you drew.
  a. $C(1, 1)$ and radius 5
  b. $C(1, 2)$ and radius 3
  c. $C(-1, 5)$ and radius 1
  d. $C(-2, -2)$ and radius 2
  e. Draw a geometric figure that can be considered both a taxi square and a taxi circle.

44. Would taxicab geometry apply to your neighborhood? Explain why or why not.

← CONNECT →
In Part A, you found taxi distance. Now you will explore one of the most fundamental ideas of mathematics—the Pythagorean Theorem.

A and B are two points on the coordinate plane.

From the taxi-distance formula we know that the taxi distance between them is $AC + CB$.

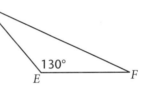

When A and B are not on the same vertical or horizontal line, the length of the straight-line segment between them runs diagonally. Its length is shorter than the taxi distance.

Notice that angle C is a right angle.

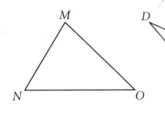

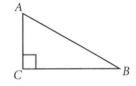

An **acute triangle** has only angles measuring less than 90°.

An **obtuse triangle** has an angle measuring more than 90°.

A **right triangle** has a 90° angle.

The longest side of a right triangle is called the **hypotenuse.** It is always opposite the right angle. The other two sides are called the **legs** of the right triangle.

CONSIDER

?

1. When is the straight-line distance between two points equal to the taxi distance between them?

2. How do you know that in all other cases, the straight-line distance between two points is less than the taxi distance?

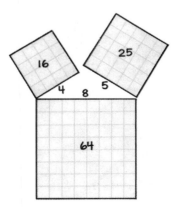

MATERIALS

Graph paper
Scissors

1. Cut out 13 squares from graph paper, with these dimensions.

3×3	6×6	9×9	12×12
4×4	7×7	10×10	13×13
5×5	8×8	11×11	14×14
			15×15

2. Using three squares at a time, arrange them to form a triangle as shown.

3. Determine the type of triangle formed in each case. Keep track of your results in a table like the one below. Form at least ten triangles using the 13 squares.

Length of the Side of Each Square			Area of Each Square			Type of Triangle
a	b	c	a^2	b^2	c^2	
4	5	8	16	25	64	Obtuse

4. Focus on cases where a *right* triangle was formed. Write a conjecture about the areas of the squares that form right triangles.

Problem-Solving Tip

Look for a pattern.

Egyptians used the relationship you saw in the Explore to survey land in 2000 B.C. The Greek mathematician Pythagoras, who was born on the island of Samos in 580 B.C., is credited with proving the relationship true for right triangles.

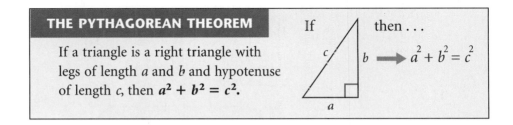

THE PYTHAGOREAN THEOREM

If a triangle is a right triangle with legs of length a and b and hypotenuse of length c, then $a^2 + b^2 = c^2$.

If ... then ... $a^2 + b^2 = c^2$

The **converse** of a statement that has an *if-then* form reverses the *if* and *then* parts. For example, the converse of "*If* Jake is a collie, *then* Jake is a dog" is "*If* Jake is a dog, *then* Jake is a collie." You can see that the converse of a true statement is not always true.

The converse of the Pythagorean Theorem *is* true, however.

THE CONVERSE OF THE PYTHAGOREAN THEOREM

If a triangle has side lengths a, b, and c, and $a^2 + b^2 = c^2$, then the triangle is a right triangle.

If $a^2 + b^2 = c^2$, then...

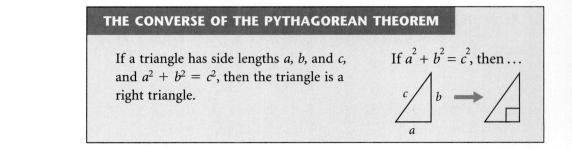

TRY IT

$\triangle ABC$ is a right triangle. Use the Pythagorean Theorem to find c.
a. $a = 9$, $b = 12$
b. $a = 5$, $b = 12$

EXAMPLES

1. Our Town's chamber of commerce is laying out a baseball field. It should be a square with 90 feet between bases. To double-check that they have a square layout, the mayor suggests measuring the distance from home plate to second base. How long should this distance be?

The diagram shows that, if the field is square, the line segment between home plate and second base is the hypotenuse of two right triangles.

$$a^2 + b^2 = c^2 \qquad \text{Use the Pythagorean Theorem.}$$

$$90^2 + 90^2 = c^2 \qquad \text{Substitute number values for the legs and square them.}$$

$$8100 + 8100 = c^2$$

$$16{,}200 = c^2 \qquad \text{Take the square root of each side of the equation.}$$

$$\pm\sqrt{16{,}200} = c$$

$$\pm 127.3 \approx c$$

Problem-Solving Tip

Check to see if your solution is reasonable.

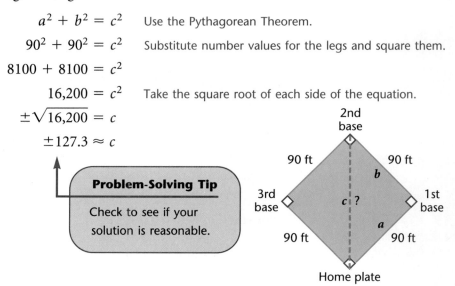

The negative solution does not make sense in the problem, since distance cannot be negative.

Converting, 0.3 foot = $0.3 \cdot \dfrac{12 \text{ inches}}{1 \text{ foot}}$ = 3.6 inches. So the distance between home plate and second base should be approximately 127 feet 4 inches. The solution is reasonable because the length should be more than 90 feet but less than 180 feet.

2. XuXia has let out all 300 feet of kite string, and her kite is directly above the park entrance 150 feet away. A nearby airport requires that kites be flown no higher than 250 feet. How high above ground is XuXia's kite?

> **Problem-Solving Tip**
>
> Use a right triangle to model the situation.

A right triangle is formed by XuXia, the park entrance, and the kite.

$$a^2 + b^2 = c^2$$
Use the Pythagorean Theorem.

$$150^2 + b^2 = 300^2$$
Substitute values for the leg and the hypotenuse and square them.

$$22{,}500 + b^2 = 90{,}000$$
Solve for b^2. Then take the square root of each side of the equation.

$$b^2 = 67{,}500$$

$$b = \pm\sqrt{67{,}500} \approx \pm 259.81$$

A kite cannot have a negative height, so the negative number is not a solution. The kite is about 260 feet above ground. The solution is reasonable because $150 + 260 > 300$. But the kite is higher than regulations permit.

CONSIDER

?

3. If there is some slack in the kite string, is XuXia's kite more or less than 260 feet up? Why? What other assumption is she making?

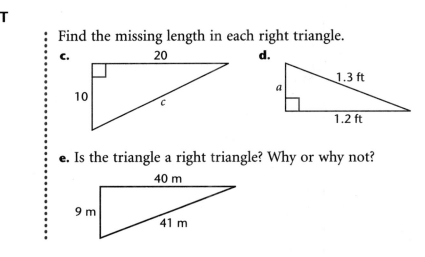

Find the missing length in each right triangle.

c. 20, 10, c

d. 1.3 ft, a, 1.2 ft

e. Is the triangle a right triangle? Why or why not?

40 m, 9 m, 41 m

1. With what type of figure(s) do we use the Pythagorean Theorem?
2. Does your work in the Explore illustrate the Pythagorean Theorem or its converse? Explain.
3. Why can the Pythagorean Theorem be considered a rule involving squares? involving diagonal lines? How is measuring the diagonal of a four-sided figure helpful in showing that it is a square?
4. How do you know from side lengths of a triangle whether it contains a right angle?
5. Why are the Pythagorean Theorem and its converse important?

Exercises

CORE

1. Getting Started $\triangle RST$ is a right triangle.
  a. Name the hypotenuse.
  b. Name the legs.
  c. Use the Pythagorean Theorem to solve for the length of segment RT.

R, 10 in., S, 24 in., T

**If the lengths of the legs of a right triangle are represented by
a and b and the length of the hypotenuse is represented by c,
find the missing length.**

2. $a = 3, c = 5$ **3.** $b = 1, c = 2$ **4.** $a = 1, b = 1$

c, a, b

Find the missing length.

5.

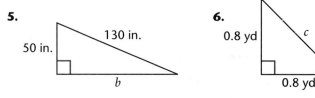

130 in.

50 in.

b

6.

0.8 yd

c

0.8 yd

7.

1.0 m

0.6 m

b

T

2 cm   4 cm

R   3 cm   *S*

8. Is △*RST* a right triangle? Justify your answer.

9. Write the converse of the statement, "If you are a registered voter, then you can sign this petition." Is the converse a true statement? Explain.

10. Save Me! A building is on fire. Firefighters need to use a 50-foot ladder to save someone who is 40 feet above street level. How far from the bottom of the building must the ladder be placed in order to reach this person?

Careers

Problem-Solving Tip

Draw a diagram.

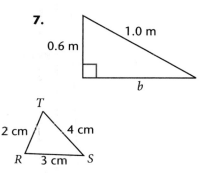

11. Rain, Rain Go Away Will a 40-inch-long umbrella fit flat on the bottom of a suitcase that has dimensions 36 by 27 inches? Explain.

12. Getting into the Swim of It Hilda swims diagonally across a rectangular swimming pool. The pool is 45 feet wide and 60 feet long. How much farther did she swim than if she had just swum the length of the pool?

13. A Couch-Potato Problem When a television set is advertised as a 27-inch model, the screen is a rectangle with a diagonal of 27 inches. The screen has a height of 15 inches. Find the length, to the nearest tenth of an inch.

Industry

14. Pythagorean Triples Three *positive integers* that satisfy the equation $a^2 + b^2 = c^2$ are called "Pythagorean Triples." One such triple is (3, 4, 5) since $3^2 + 4^2 = 5^2$.

Find another Pythagorean Triple. Justify your answer.

15. Root, Root, Root for the Home Team A baseball diamond is a square with 90 feet on a side. Roslyn says the distance from first base to third base is 127.28 feet. Maile says it is 127 feet and $3\frac{3}{8}$ inches. Who is right? Justify your answer.

16. **More Triples** These similar triangles show a pattern used to generate Pythagorean Triples.
    a. Find values of x, y, and z.
    b. If there were a fourth similar right triangle with legs 36 and 160, could you find the length of the hypotenuse? Explain.
    c. Describe how to find a fifth Pythagorean Triple using these similar triangles.

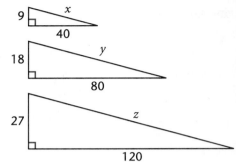

17. **Stair Safety** The fire department wants the manager of an apartment building to line the underside of the wooden flight of stairs with plywood because trash is stored below and a fire could block escape from upstairs apartments. The stairs are 4 feet wide and plywood comes in 4- by 8-foot sheets. Each step has a rise of 7 inches and a run of 12 inches.
    a. How much plywood is needed?
    b. Is there an easier way to measure? Explain.
    c. If the same contractor installs a new banister, how long a piece of metal will he or she need?

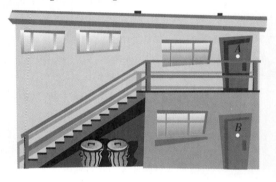

18. In the 1939 film *The Wizard of Oz*, the scarecrow says:

    "The sum of the *square roots* of *any* two sides of an *isosceles* triangle is equal to the *square root* of the remaining side. Oh, joy, rapture! I've got a brain!"

    Isosceles triangles

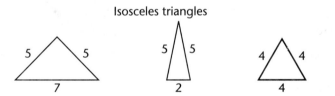

    Isosceles triangles have at least two sides of the same length.
    a. Is the scarecrow's statement about isosceles triangles true? Defend your reasoning.
    b. Why does the scarecrow think he now must have a brain?
    c. How could you change the italicized words to make a different, true statement?

19. **Larger Than Life** Feng Qiao is shopping for a new television set. She found that the screen of a "25-inch" television had a length of 20 inches. She also found a large screen model with double the dimensions of this set.
    a. What is the width of the screen of the smaller television set?
    b. How many times bigger is the area of the larger screen model than the smaller one?

20. An airplane is flying north with an airspeed of 96 kilometers per hour in a strong wind that is blowing 40 kilometers per hour east. The diagonal of the rectangle in the illustration gives the groundspeed of the plane in a northeasterly direction. Find the groundspeed of the plane.

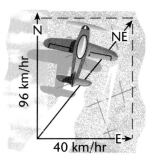

21. Climb Your Way to Success A 40-foot ladder is placed against a building. If the bottom of the ladder is placed 12 feet away from the foot of the building, will the top of the ladder reach the third floor 35 feet above ground? Use a diagram to illustrate your answer.

LOOK AHEAD

Evaluate.

22. $(5 - 3)^2 + (7 - 1)^2$ **23.** $\sqrt{4 + 12}$ **24.** $\sqrt{6^2 + 8^2}$ **25.** $\sqrt{5^2 + 12^2}$

Evaluate for $a = 6$, $b = 8$, and $c = 10$.

26. $a^2 + b^2$ **27.** $c^2 - a^2$ **28.** $c^2 - b^2$

MORE PRACTICE

If the lengths of the legs of a right triangle are represented by a and b and the length of the hypotenuse is represented by c, find the missing length.

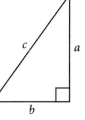

29. $a = 9$, $c = 15$ **30.** $a = 6$, $b = 6$ **31.** $b = 24$, $c = 25$

32. $a = 0.3$, $b = 0.4$ **33.** $b = 21$, $c = 75$ **34.** $a = 0.1$, $b = 0.24$

Find the missing length.

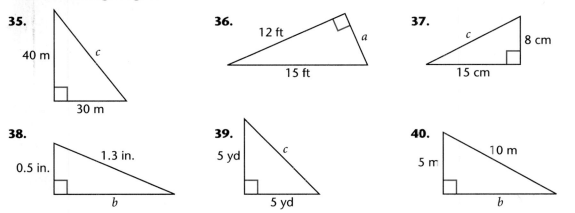

41. Treephone To get away from her eavesdropping brother, Jean climbed a tree to use a cordless telephone that can be used up to 100 feet from its base. The tree is 70 feet from the base, and she is 40 feet up. Can she use the phone?

MORE MATH REASONING

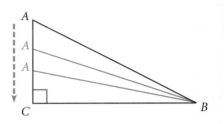

42. As point *A* slides down to point *C*, what happens to the length of $\overline{AB}$? to the size of $\angle B$? Will *AB* ever equal *CB*? What happens to $\triangle ABC$? Explain.

43. Tell whether or not a right triangle is formed with the lengths of the three sides equal to $\frac{3}{4}$ inch, 1 inch, and 1.25 inches. Explain how you know.

44. Deep-Sea Design Use this diagram to create a real-world problem that could be solved by applying the Pythagorean Theorem.

45. a. Write positive values of *a*, *b*, and *c* that sum to 12. Repeat until you have 10 sets of values.
  b. What was the experimental probability that the numbers could represent lengths of a triangle?
  c. What was the experimental probability that the numbers could represent lengths of a *right* triangle?

46. The force (*F*) applied to the lawnmower is the result of the horizontal component (*x*) and the vertical component (*y*). How could you express *F* in terms of components *x* and *y*? Explain.

7-3
PART C · Finding Coordinate Distances

← CONNECT → *Now that you know the Pythagorean Theorem and how to find taxi distances, you are ready to find straight-line distances on a grid, even for segments that lie diagonally.*

EXPLORE: MISSION POSSIBLE

During a parade in downtown Savannah, a police helicopter hovering over Chatham Square is called to an emergency at the Maritime Museum near Warren Square.

Your mission is to find the helicopter distance from Chatham Square to Warren Square.

1. What are the coordinates of Chatham Square? of Warren Square?

2. Copy the grid and draw a right triangle containing the segment from Chatham Square to Warren Square. Find the lengths of the legs of this triangle.

3. Use the Pythagorean Theorem to find the straight-line distance the helicopter must fly from Chatham Square to Warren Square.

4. How does the straight-line distance compare to the taxi distance between these points?

5. Write an explanation of how to find the straight-line distance between any two points whose coordinates you know without using the words *Pythagorean Theorem.*

MATERIALS

Graph paper

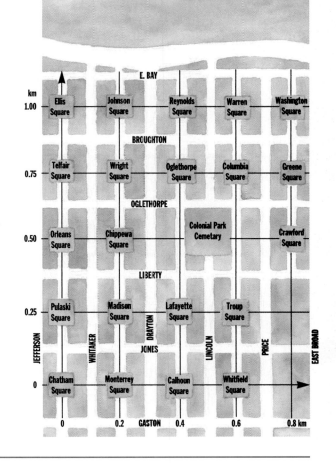

The straight-line distance you found is the *shortest* possible distance between the two points.

To find the distance between any two points P and Q, think about the right triangle formed by the points and the horizontal and vertical legs.

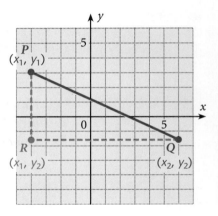

Using the taxi-distance formula, we can find the length of each leg. So $PR = |y_2 - y_1|$ and $QR = |x_2 - x_1|$.

We use the Pythagorean Theorem.

$PQ^2 = QR^2 + PR^2$ These represent distances, not variables.

$PQ^2 = |x_2 - x_1|^2 + |y_2 - y_1|^2$

$PQ = \sqrt{|x_2 - x_1|^2 + |y_2 - y_1|^2}$ Distance cannot be negative, so $\pm$ is not used.

THE DISTANCE FORMULA

If P has coordinates (x_1, y_1) and Q has coordinates (x_2, y_2), then the distance d from P to Q is given by

$$d = \sqrt{(x_2 - x_1)^2 + (y_2 - y_1)^2}.$$

CONSIDER

1. Why were the absolute value bars dropped in the Distance Formula box? Why were the parentheses inserted?

Just as when we calculated slope, the order of the points is unimportant.

EXAMPLE

1. Find the distance between the points $(2, 8)$ and $(5, 4)$.

$\sqrt{(2 - 5)^2 + (8 - 4)^2} = \sqrt{(-3)^2 + (4)^2} = \sqrt{9 + 16} = 5 \ or \dots$

$\sqrt{(5 - 2)^2 + (4 - 8)^2} = \sqrt{(3)^2 + (-4)^2} = \sqrt{9 + 16} = 5$

Either point can be (x_1, y_1), and the distance is 5.

Find the distance between $(5, -3)$ and $(10, 9)$.

Norma thinks . . .

I will just substitute the coordinates into the Distance Formula.

$$d = \sqrt{(x_2 - x_1)^2 + (y_2 - y_1)^2}$$
$$d = \sqrt{(10 - 5)^2 + (9 - (-3))^2}$$
$$= \sqrt{5^2 + 12^2}$$
$$= \sqrt{25 + 144}$$
$$= \sqrt{169}$$
$$= 13$$

Derrick thinks . . .

I'll use a right triangle.

The legs of the triangle give me the horizontal distance $|5 - 10| = 5$ and the vertical distance $|-3 - 9| = 12$. I can use the Pythagorean Theorem to find the straight-line distance.

$$a^2 + b^2 = c^2$$
$$5^2 + 12^2 = c^2$$
$$169 = c^2$$
$$13 = c$$

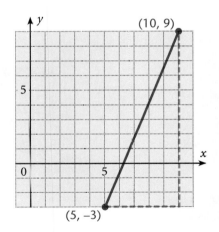

Derrick might have subtracted in a different order. No matter which way you subtract, you will get the same *solution* because you square the numbers when you apply the Pythagorean Theorem.

TRY IT

Use the Distance Formula to find the distance between each pair of points.

a. $(0, 0)$ and $(-6, -8)$ **b.** $(1, 1)$ and $(-2, -3)$

We can use the Distance Formula to illustrate facts in geometry. When you study geometry more formally, you will see that the Distance Formula is used in coordinate geometry to actually prove facts about geometric figures.

2. Write a convincing argument for each statement.

a. Opposite sides of the four-sided figure *ABCD* are *congruent* (have equal lengths).

The coordinates of the four vertices follow.

$A(-1, 7)$ $B(2, 8)$ $C(4, 2)$ $D(1, 1)$

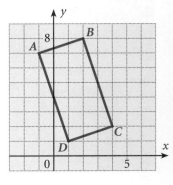

Use the Distance Formula, $d = \sqrt{(x_2 - x_1)^2 + (y_2 - y_1)^2}$, to find the length of each segment.

$AB = \sqrt{10}$ $CD = \sqrt{10}$ $BC = \sqrt{40}$ $AD = \sqrt{40}$

Since $AB = CD$ and $BC = AD$, the opposite sides of *ABCD* are congruent.

b. Side *BC* is twice *AB*.

Since $BC = \sqrt{40} \approx 6.32$ and $AB = \sqrt{10} \approx 3.16$, *BC* is twice *AB*. A property of square roots shows the solution to **2b** must be true.

> For any real numbers $a \geq 0$ and $b \geq 0$, $\sqrt{a \cdot b} = \sqrt{a} \cdot \sqrt{b}$.

For *BC*, $\sqrt{40} = \sqrt{4 \cdot 10} \stackrel{?}{=} \sqrt{4} \cdot \sqrt{10} = 2\sqrt{10}$.

3. Show that $\sqrt{54} = 3\sqrt{6}$.

$\sqrt{54} = \sqrt{9 \cdot 6}$ Rewrite 54 as 9 • 6 since
$\quad\ = \sqrt{9} \cdot \sqrt{6}$ 9 is the square of a whole
$\quad\ = 3\sqrt{6}$ number.

4. Simplify $\sqrt{5} \cdot \sqrt{15}$.

$\sqrt{5} \cdot \sqrt{15} = \sqrt{5 \cdot 15}$
$\qquad\quad\ = \sqrt{5 \cdot 5 \cdot 3}$
$\qquad\quad\ = 5\sqrt{3}$ The square root of 5 • 5 is 5.

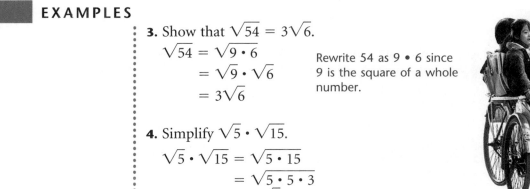

TRY IT

c. Show that $\sqrt{72} = 6\sqrt{2}$.   **d.** Show that $\sqrt{500} = 10\sqrt{5}$.

e. Multiply $\sqrt{10} \cdot \sqrt{2}$.   **f.** Multiply $\sqrt{5} \cdot \sqrt{5}$.

2. Looking at the slopes in Example 2, what kind of figure do you think *ABCD* is? How could you check?

3. If you could give a convincing argument using the Distance Formula that all sides of a four-sided figure are congruent, would that prove that the figure is a square?

REFLECT

1. Compare and contrast taxi distance and straight-line distance between two points.

2. Explain why we need a formula to find the distance between two points when we could draw a diagram and measure the distance.

3. When using the Distance Formula, why doesn't it matter which *x*-coordinate you choose for x_1?

Exercises

CORE

1. Getting Started Find the distance from *A* to *C* by using the Distance Formula,
$$d = \sqrt{(x_2 - x_1)^2 + (y_2 - y_1)^2},$$ and answering the following.

a. From *A:* $x_1 =$ _____ and $y_1 =$ _____

b. From *C:* $x_2 =$ _____ and $y_2 =$ _____

c. Substitute the values into the Distance Formula and find the distance from *A* to *C*.

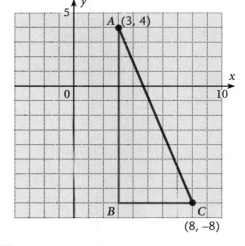

2. Find the distance from *A* to *C* by using the graph and answering the following.

a. What are the coordinates of *B*?

b. What is the length of $\overline{AB}$? of $\overline{BC}$?

c. Use the Pythagorean Theorem to find the length of $\overline{AC}$.

3. Which method of finding the distance from *A* to *C* do you prefer? Why?

Use the Distance Formula to find the distance between each pair of points.

4. $(0, 0)$ and $(0, 8)$ **5.** $(1, 5\frac{1}{2})$ and $(1, -3)$ **6.** $(2.3, 7)$ and $(-8, 7)$

7. **Country Roads** The diagram shows the mileage markers on a system of two-way country roads.

   a. Find the distance by car between A and B.

   b. Find the distance by helicopter between A and B.

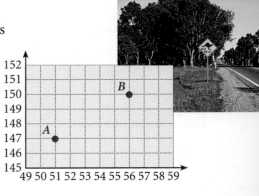

Complete each statement.

8. $\sqrt{200} = \sqrt{100 \cdot \underline{}} = \sqrt{100} \cdot \sqrt{\underline{}} = 10\sqrt{\underline{}}$

9. $\sqrt{50} = \sqrt{\underline{} \cdot 2} = \sqrt{\underline{}} \cdot \sqrt{2} = \underline{}\sqrt{2}$

10. $\sqrt{75} = \sqrt{\underline{} \cdot 3} = \sqrt{\underline{}} \cdot \sqrt{3} = \underline{}\sqrt{3}$

Multiply.

11. $\sqrt{2} \cdot \sqrt{3}$

12. $\sqrt{2} \cdot \sqrt{10}$

13. $\sqrt{11} \cdot \sqrt{11}$

14. Cassandra says $\sqrt{150} = 5\sqrt{6}$. Describe how she could check her answer. Is she correct?

15. **Oh Canada!** Use the map of Canada and the scale to approximate the coordinates of Juneau, Alaska, if the coordinates of Windsor, Newfoundland, are $(0, 0)$. Use your answer and the Distance Formula to approximate the distance between these two points.

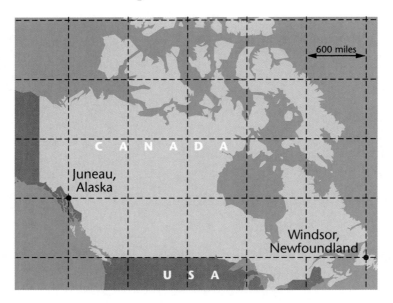

16. Recall that a triangle is isosceles if two of its sides have the same length.

    a. Plot $D(5, -1)$, $E(-1, 2)$, and $F(11, 2)$ and connect them to create a triangle.

    b. Find the lengths of the three sides of the triangle.

    c. Tell whether or not the triangle is isosceles.

17. The point (3, 4) is a distance of five units from the origin. Find the coordinates of seven other points that are five units from the origin. What figure do these points suggest?

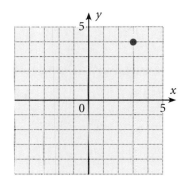

18. In using the Distance Formula, you must first *subtract* two *x*-values, then *square*. You then have to repeat this procedure for two *y*-values. Suppose when she used the Distance Formula, Selma first *squared* and then *subtracted* each time.

  a. Give an example in which she will not get the correct answer.

  b. Give an example in which she will get the correct answer, even though she made an error.

19. Over or Under? Considering the distance from *A* to *B*, Coty drew △*ABC*. Dwayne drew △*ABD*. Will each student get the same answer? Justify your response.

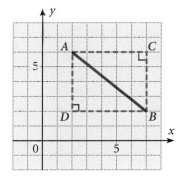

![eyes icon] **LOOK BACK**

20. Training and Time Eighteen students in Mr. Campos's P.E. class run a 2-mile course. The scatter plot compares their time to the months they trained. [5-2]

  a. Is the association positive, negative, or non-existent? Explain.

  b. Find an equation for a trend line of this scatter plot.

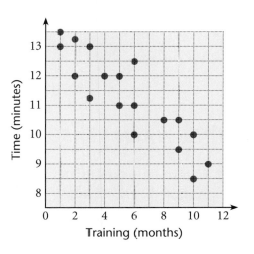

Graph these systems of inequalities. [6-3]

21. $y > -2$
 $x < 3$

22. $y < -x + 2$
 $y > \frac{1}{2}x - 3$

23. More Conversions The average American consumes about 2000 calories of energy per day from food. How many calories per second would this be? Tell how you made the conversion. [5-2]

Health

MORE PRACTICE

Use the Distance Formula to find the distance between each pair of points.

24. $(5, -2)$ and $(-4, 1)$

25. $(5, 4)$ and $(20, 24)$

26. $(-6, 4.5)$ and $(-9, 8)$

27. $(-3.1, -0.2)$ and $(6.1, 3.5)$

28. $\left(-\frac{1}{2}, 0\right)$ and $\left(\frac{3}{4}, -\frac{7}{8}\right)$

29. $(4.1, 3.8)$ and $(-7.3, -4.1)$

Complete each statement.

30. $\sqrt{32} = \sqrt{16 \cdot \underline{\quad}} = \sqrt{16} \cdot \sqrt{\underline{\quad}} = 4\sqrt{\underline{\quad}}$

31. $\sqrt{18} = \sqrt{\underline{\quad} \cdot 2} = \sqrt{\underline{\quad}} \cdot \sqrt{2} = \underline{\quad}\sqrt{2}$

32. $\sqrt{500} = \sqrt{\underline{\quad} \cdot 5} = \sqrt{\underline{\quad}} \cdot \sqrt{5} = \underline{\quad}\sqrt{5}$

33. $\sqrt{128} = \sqrt{\underline{\quad} \cdot 2} = \sqrt{\underline{\quad}} \cdot \sqrt{2} = \underline{\quad}\sqrt{2}$

34. $\sqrt{98} = \sqrt{49 \cdot \underline{\quad}} = \sqrt{49} \cdot \sqrt{\underline{\quad}} = 7\sqrt{\underline{\quad}}$

Multiply.

35. $\sqrt{15} \cdot \sqrt{5}$

36. $\sqrt{6} \cdot \sqrt{7}$

37. $\sqrt{3} \cdot \sqrt{3}$

38. $\sqrt{6} \cdot \sqrt{12}$

39. $\sqrt{7} \cdot \sqrt{7}$

40. $\sqrt{10} \cdot \sqrt{5}$

41. The diagram shows two points.
   a. Find the distance by car between points A and B.
   b. Find the distance by helicopter between points A and B.

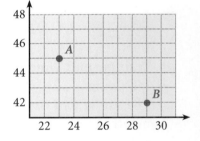

MORE MATH REASONING

42. Can you use the Distance Formula to find horizontal or vertical distances? Justify your answer.

43. When will the Distance Formula give the same result as the taxi-distance formula? Illustrate your answer.

44. **Line Up** Suppose you want to calculate the distance from a pole (P) to the river ($\overleftrightarrow{RV}$). PX denotes the distance from the pole to the river. Outline a method for finding the coordinates of X and the distance PX.

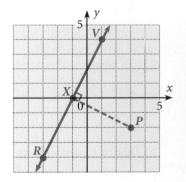

Making Connections

← **C O N N E C T** → *In Part C, you learned how to find distances on a coordinate plane. Real distances can also be found in this way.*

EXPLORE: PARADE PATROL

According to plans, the last marching band of the Independence Day parade should pass by Chatham Square when the first one reaches Reynolds Square. For good reception, a radio patrol should park halfway between these two points. At what street intersection should the radio patrol park?

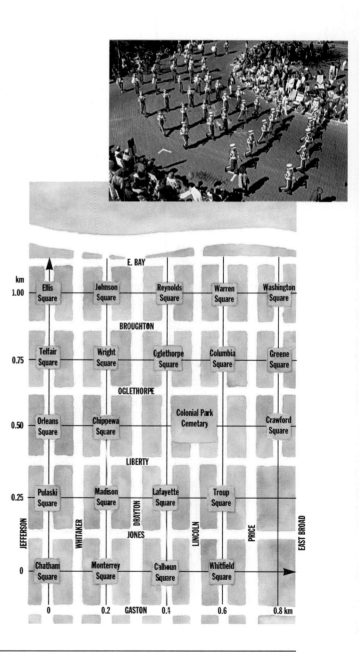

1. What are the coordinates of Chatham Square? of Reynolds Square?

2. What is the straight-line distance between Chatham Square and Reynolds Square? What is half of that distance?

3. Just by looking at the map, can you tell which point is halfway between Chatham Square and Reynolds Square? What are its coordinates? (The halfway point is the **midpoint** of a segment.)

4. Use the Distance Formula to verify that the point you chose as the midpoint is exactly halfway between Chatham Square and Reynolds Square.

5. How do the x-coordinates of the three points compare? How do their y-coordinates compare? Explain how you might have figured out the coordinates of the midpoint without using the Distance Formula.

1. How are the Pythagorean Theorem and the Distance Formula related?
2. In what real-world situations is taxi distance important? When is straight-line distance more important?
3. Why does the Distance Formula involve a square root when the horizontal and vertical distances are equal?

Self-Assessment

1. $\triangle ABC$ is shown on the graph.
   a. What is the distance from A to B? How do you know?
   b. What is the distance from A to C? Tell how you decided.
   c. What special type of triangle does $\triangle ABC$ seem to be? Justify your answer.

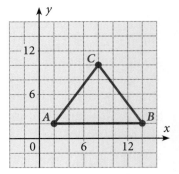

2. **Let's Go Downtown** The map shows places Ellen often visits.
   a. What is the *taxi distance* from Gerry's Video Palace to Jan's Deli?
   b. What is the *distance* from Gerry's Video Palace to Faride's Diner?
   c. If Josephine wishes to open a laundry that is the same distance from Noel's Meat Market as from Jan's Deli, give the coordinates of every possible intersection where she may locate her business.

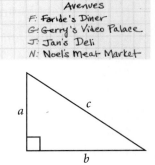

F: Faride's Diner
G: Gerry's Video Palace
J: Jan's Deli
N: Noel's Meat Market

If the lengths of the legs of a right triangle are represented by a and b and the length of the hypotenuse is represented by c, find the length of the missing side.

3. $a = 24, c = 30$ 4. $b = 15, c = 39$ 5. $a = 8, b = 8$

6. Find the square root of 500.
   I. $5\sqrt{10}$ II. $10\sqrt{5}$ III. about 22.36
   (a) only I   (b) only II   (c) only III   (d) II and III   (e) I, II, and III

7. Plot $P(0, 0)$, $Q(2, 4)$, and $R(10, 0)$. What special type of triangle does $\triangle PQR$ seem to be? Justify your answer.

8. **Back to the Point** Earlier we visited Cryder Point.
   a. If Adam's house stands on the midpoint of line segment *PB*, where does Adam live?
   b. If Adam's taxi distance to Brenda's house is more than his taxi distance to the post office but less than his taxi distance to the supermarket, find all possible locations for Brenda's house.

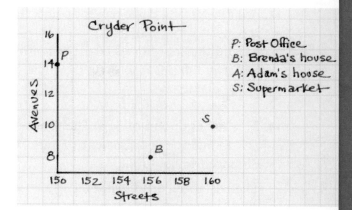

9. **Merry Andrew** Danny Kaye sang this song to his students in the film *Merry Andrew*. "The square of the hypotenuse of a right triangle is equal to the sum of the squares of the two adjacent sides . . ." while they played lawn croquet. Compare this to the Pythagorean Theorem. Is it true? Explain.

10. **Incan Midpoints** Use the map of Peru to answer the questions.
    a. Name three cities that lie on the same line, in which one of them is located at the midpoint of the line segment joining the other two cities.
    b. Use the scale to approximate the distances between the cities you named in **10a.**
    c. Repeat **10a** and **10b** using a different set of three cities.

The capital **delta** (**Δ**), the fourth letter of the Greek alphabet, is used to express change in mathematics. For example, Δx is written to mean $x_2 - x_1$.

11. Rewrite each of the following formulas using the "delta" notation.
    a. the slope formula
    b. the formula for the distance between two points

12. A diameter of a circle has endpoints $A(6, -4)$ and $B(3, 4)$.

   a. Find the coordinates of the center of the circle.

   b. Use graph paper to draw the circle, its center, and the diameter.

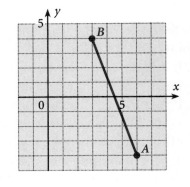

13. M is the midpoint of $\overline{AB}$. The coordinates of A are $(12, 8)$ and the coordinates of M are $(10, 9)$. Find the distance from A to B.

   The Distance Formula is $d = \sqrt{(x_2 - x_1)^2 + (y_2 - y_1)^2}$.

14. Plot $A(0, 0)$, $B(5, 0)$, $C(5, 4)$, and $D(0, 4)$. Is $ABCD$ a square? Justify your answer.

15. Use $\triangle KLM$ to answer these questions.

   a. What is the length of $\overline{LN}$? of $\overline{NM}$?

   b. What is special about point N?

   c. A *median* of a triangle is a segment whose endpoints are a vertex of the triangle and the midpoint of the opposite side. What segment is a median of $\triangle KLM$? How can you be sure?

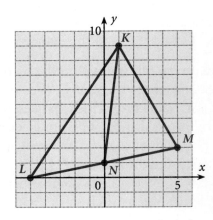

16. An airplane is flying north at 100 miles per hour in a strong wind that is blowing east at 75 miles per hour. The diagonal of the rectangle in the illustration gives the groundspeed of the plane in a northeasterly direction. Find the groundspeed of the plane.

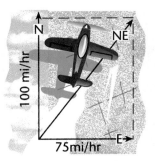

17. The Last Straw Terri has responsibility for ordering new straws for the family drive-in. Should she order 8-inch straws? Will a straw stick out of the cup without a lid? with a lid that has a hole in the center? Explain your answer.

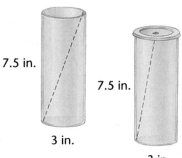

7.5 in.

7.5 in.

3 in.

3 in.

7-4 Indirect Measurement

Early television screens had the same 4:3 width-to-height ratio as movies. When we watch movies from that era on TV, nothing is cut from view. In an attempt to compete with the growing popularity of television, Hollywood began releasing films shot in Panavision in 1954. Panavision films have a screen ratio of 7:3. Unfortunately, when a Panavision film is reduced to fit vertically on a television screen, the sides of the film are cut off.

A common conversion method to show Panavision movies on TV, called *Pan-and-Scan*, cuts a portion of the original image to fit the reduced screen ratio of TV.

A second method, called *Letterboxing* was introduced in the 1980s. To fit a 7:3 movie on a 4:3 TV screen, the entire film image is reduced to fit horizontally. Nothing is cut, but the image is smaller and the top and bottom of the TV screen are unused.

Early in 1993, *wide-screen* TV was introduced. Not as wide as Panavision, but wider than traditional TV, the 16:9 format shows most of the original picture.

1. To compare the shapes of traditional TV, Panavision, and wide-screen formats, would it be convenient to use common fractions? decimals? some other method?
2. When you buy a 25-inch television, 25 is the length of the screen's diagonal. What might the other dimensions of the screen be? Why don't advertisers mention them?

← C O N N E C T → *In 5-1, you learned that triangles with the same shape (but not necessarily the same size) are called **similar triangles**. We now extend this idea to all figures.*

EXPLORE: AUTO ROW

Here are three drawings of cars.

MATERIALS

Ruler, Protractor

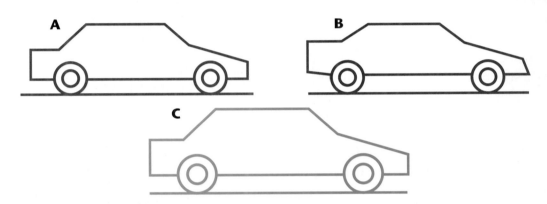

1. Measure individual parts of each car. Copy and fill in the table.
   a. Measure the lengths of some shapes on each car (for example, length of the hood).
   b. Measure the angles of some shapes on each car (for example, the angle between the rear window and trunk).
2. Copy and complete the table with the ratios of lengths that you measured.

	Car Part	A	B	C	$\frac{A}{C}$	$\frac{B}{C}$	$\frac{A}{B}$
Lengths	1.____						
	2.____						
	3.____						
Angles	4.____						
	5.____						
	6.____						

3. Decide which drawings might be illustrations of the same model car. Explain your conclusion using the information from your table.

In the Explore, you used some important concepts. Parts of shapes that match up are called **corresponding parts.** Two figures are **similar** when they have the same shape. Using ratios, we can define the "same shape" more precisely. Remember that a *ratio* is a comparison of two quantities using division, and an equation stating that two ratios are equal is a **proportion.**

In **similar figures,** corresponding angles have the same measure and corresponding side lengths have the same ratio.

ABCD ~ MNOP means *ABCD* is similar to *MNOP.*

$m\angle B = m\angle N$ means angle B and angle N have the same measure.

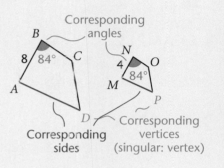

$A \leftrightarrow M$

means *A corresponds to M*

Vertices	Angles	Sides
$A \leftrightarrow M$	$m\angle A = m\angle M$	$\overline{AB} \leftrightarrow \overline{MN}$
$B \leftrightarrow N$	$m\angle B = m\angle N$	$\overline{BC} \leftrightarrow \overline{NO}$
$C \leftrightarrow O$	$m\angle C = m\angle O$	$\overline{CD} \leftrightarrow \overline{OP}$
$D \leftrightarrow P$	$m\angle D = m\angle P$	$\overline{AD} \leftrightarrow \overline{MP}$

EXAMPLE

1. Is $\triangle ABC \sim \triangle WXY$? Justify your answer.

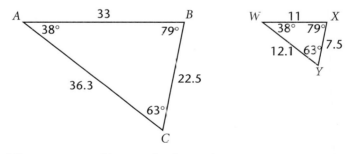

The corresponding angles have the same measures.
Comparing ratios of corresponding side lengths, we get the following.
$$\frac{AB}{WX} = \frac{33}{11} = 3 \qquad \frac{BC}{XY} = \frac{22.5}{7.5} = 3 \qquad \frac{AC}{WY} = \frac{36.3}{12.1} = 3$$
Corresponding angles have the same measure and corresponding side lengths have the same ratio, so $\triangle ABC \sim \triangle WXY$.

1. To show that two *triangles* are similar, is it necessary to show *both* that corresponding angles have the same measure *and* that corresponding side lengths have the same ratio? Explain.

If two figures are similar, we can write a proportion to find a missing dimension.

EXAMPLE

2. $\triangle ABC \sim \triangle DEF$. Find the value of x.

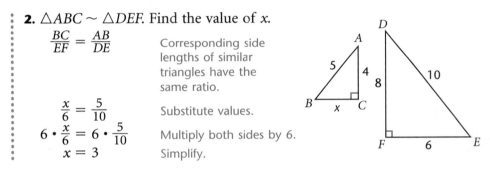

$$\frac{BC}{EF} = \frac{AB}{DE}$$ Corresponding side lengths of similar triangles have the same ratio.

$$\frac{x}{6} = \frac{5}{10}$$ Substitute values.

$$6 \cdot \frac{x}{6} = 6 \cdot \frac{5}{10}$$ Multiply both sides by 6.

$$x = 3$$ Simplify.

Since you can write several true proportions using corresponding sides of similar triangles, there is often more than one way to find a missing dimension.

2. What other proportion for $\triangle ABC$ and $\triangle DEF$ would help you find x?

TRY IT

$\triangle ABC \sim \triangle DEF$.

a. Find AC.
b. Find DE.
c. Is $\triangle GHI \sim \triangle ABC$?
Justify your answer.

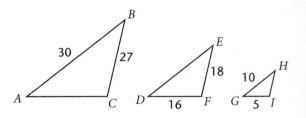

1. Are two congruent figures similar? Explain.
2. How does proportion relate to similar triangles?
3. What do we mean by *corresponding* angles and *corresponding* sides of similar figures?
4. Identify as many similar figures as you can in the photograph.

Joan Miro, *Personage And Birds,* 1970,
Houston, Texas. Polychrome bronze.

Exercises

CORE

1. Getting Started $\triangle ABC \sim \triangle DEF.$
   a. Use the lengths of corresponding sides to complete the proportion $\frac{12}{6} = ?$
   b. Find the value of x.
   c. Is your solution reasonable? Explain.

In each case, the figures are similar (the arcs indicate congruent angles). Find the value of each variable.

2.

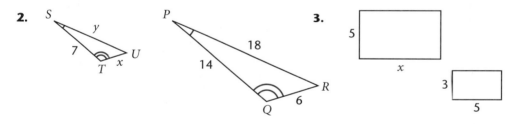

3.

Use each proportion to find the value of x.

4. $\frac{5}{10} = \frac{x}{4.3}$

5. $\frac{x}{3} = \frac{1.5}{9}$

6. $\triangle RST \sim \triangle WXY.$
   a. Find $RT.$ **b.** Find $WX.$
   c. Is $\triangle RST \sim \triangle LMN$? Justify your answer.

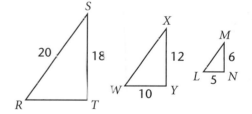

Write the word or phrase that correctly completes each statement.

7. Parts of shapes that match up are called _____ parts.

8. Two figures are _____ when they have the same shape.

9. In similar figures, _____ have the same measure and _____ have the same ratio.

In each case, tell whether the figures are similar. Justify your answer.

10.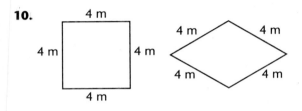

11.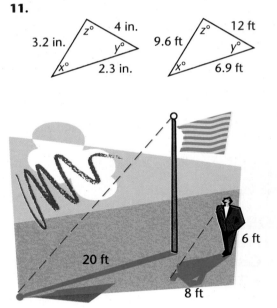

12. Dark Shadows If you have the lengths of two shadows measured at the same time and the height of one object, similar triangles can help you find the height of the second object.

 a. Use the similar triangles shown in the picture to find the height of the pole.

 b. Draw a diagram to show that similar triangles are *not* formed if shadows are measured at different times of the day.

Fine Arts

13. Write a plan for finding the height of the Clothespin sculpture in the city of Philadelphia using shadows and your height.

Claes Oldenburg, *Clothespin*, 1976, Philadelphia, Pennsylvania. Cor-Ten and stainless steel.

14. $\triangle ACD \sim \triangle BDC$. $\triangle RST \sim \triangle UTQ$. Copy and complete the table showing corresponding angles and sides.

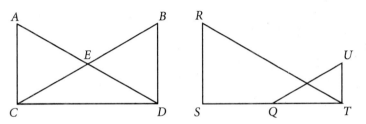

Angles	Sides
a. $m\angle A =$	**b.** $\overline{BD} \leftrightarrow$
c. $m\angle R =$	**d.** $\overline{QT} \leftrightarrow$
e. $m\angle Q =$	**f.** $\overline{BC} \leftrightarrow$

15. The Apartment A realtor makes a diagram of the floor plan for an apartment she hopes to rent. The dining room measures 15 by 12 feet in actuality, but measures 5 by 4 inches on the diagram.

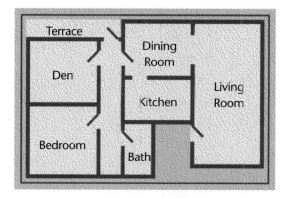

  a. Find the actual dimensions of the kitchen if it measures 5 by 3 inches on the diagram.

  b. Find the actual dimensions of the living room if it measures 10 by 5 inches on the diagram.

  c. Find the dimensions of the den on the floor plan if it actually measures 13 by 15 feet.

16. Now That's Big! The big 50-inch diagonal of this new TV is twice as long as the 25-inch diagonal of the old TV. In fact, the dimensions of anything appearing in the new TV are twice those in the old TV.

  a. An advertisement says a television with a 50-inch diagonal is four times as big as a 25-inch set. Is this accurate? Why or why not?

  b. Suppose the diagonal of the new set was three times the length of the diagonal of the old set. How would their areas compare?

17. Find the lengths of the sides of each triangle. Decide whether $\triangle ABC \sim \triangle DEF$. Explain your reasoning.

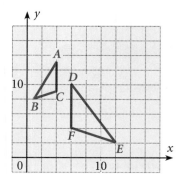

18. Find the lengths of the sides of each triangle. Are the triangles similar? How do you know?

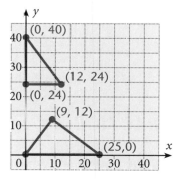

19. Undersea Radio The radiolarian is a deep-sea, single-celled animal with a perforated skeleton of silica. Since this photo of a radiolarian is magnified 700 times, what is the actual size of this sea creature? How is this like similar figures?

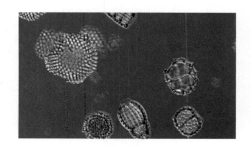

20. Copycat Car Curved shapes can be enlarged or reduced if you see them as geometric shapes.

See if you can enlarge this curved shape. Describe your method of using similar geometric shapes.

LOOK BACK

21. Based on the Triangle Inequality Theorem, is a triangle with sides 9 by 5 by 16 centimeters possible? Explain. [4-3]

Solve each system of equations. Tell which method you used. [6-2]

22. $y = x$
$x + 2y = 18$

23. $x + 2y = 11$
$x - y = 5$

24. $3x - 2y = 7$
$2y - x = 6$

25. The graph shows the range of temperatures of certain reptiles. Express each range in terms of absolute value. [7-1]

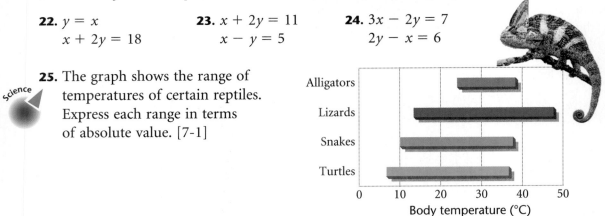

MORE PRACTICE

In each case, the figures are similar. Find the value of each variable.

26. **27.** **28.**

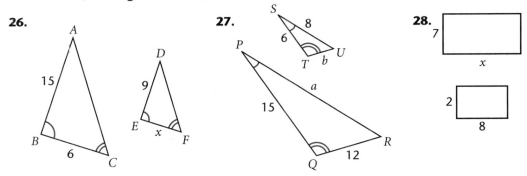

Use each proportion to find the value of x.

29. $\frac{1}{3} = \frac{x}{9}$

30. $\frac{x}{2} = \frac{15}{6}$

31. $\frac{x}{5} = \frac{20}{30}$

32. $\frac{3}{4} = \frac{x}{6}$

33. $\frac{6}{9} = \frac{x}{3}$

34. $\frac{x}{12} = \frac{2}{3}$

MORE MATH REASONING

35. The River Runs Through It To find the width of a river, point A is sighted from a tree. Three measurements are made as shown. $\triangle ABC \sim \triangle TRC$. Find the width of the river.

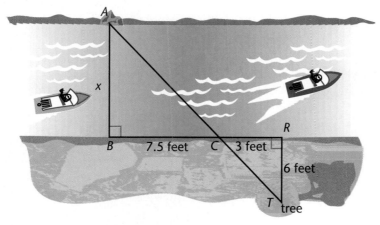

36. The sides of a triangle have length 6, 11, and 14. If the smallest side of a similar triangle has length 4, find the perimeter of the smaller triangle.

37. Blow Up A **dilation** is a function that changes all the dimensions of a geometric figure by a factor k. This factor is called the **scale factor.** Enlarging a picture, making wallet-size pictures, and making scale models are all examples of dilations.

    a. If an enlargement scale factor is always greater than 1, what is the scale factor for a reduction of a picture? Why?

    b. Draw a triangle whose sides measure 5 by 12 by 13. Draw a dilation of this triangle using a scale factor of 1.5.

38. Recall that *quadrilaterals* are four-sided figures.

    a. Which pair of quadrilaterals shows that the angles of one can have the same measures as the angles of the other, even though the *quadrilaterals* are *not* similar? Explain.

    b. Which pair of quadrilaterals shows that the sides can be proportional to one another, even though the *quadrilaterals* are *not* similar? Explain.

Quadrilaterals

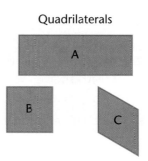

Right Triangle Trigonometry

←CONNECT→ *Now you will learn how right triangles can also be used to measure other right triangles indirectly.*

In many real-life situations, it is impractical to measure a distance directly. To find the height of a building or the width of a river, a surveyor uses *indirect* procedures—calculation instead of measurement. Right triangles are often useful for modeling these situations. We can represent distance as the lengths of legs of a right triangle. **Trigonometry** literally means "triangle measurement."

EXPLORE: RAMPING UP

Plans for a highway ramp call for a 3% grade—a rise of 3 feet for a run of 100 feet.

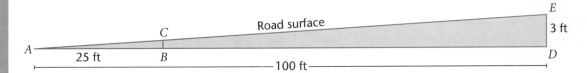

1. After grading a run of 25 feet, the engineer wants to make sure that the amount of rise is correct. How is $\overline{CB}$ related to $\overline{AB}$? What kind of triangles are △ABC and △ADE? Are △ABC and △ADE similar?

2. How high should the road surface be after the first 25 feet of run? after 50 feet? after 65 feet? What is the *ratio* of the rise to the run at each stage of construction?

3. What can you conclude about the ratios of the legs of similar right triangles?

In △*ABC*,

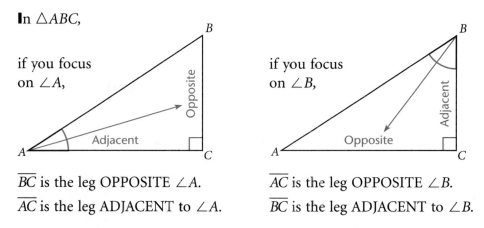

if you focus
on ∠*A*,

if you focus
on ∠*B*,

$\overline{BC}$ is the leg OPPOSITE ∠*A*.

$\overline{AC}$ is the leg ADJACENT to ∠*A*.

$\overline{AC}$ is the leg OPPOSITE ∠*B*.

$\overline{BC}$ is the leg ADJACENT to ∠*B*.

As you may have seen in the Explore, the ratio of the legs of each triangle is the same.

Recall from 5-1 that △*AEB* ~ △*AJD*, and that in similar right triangles, the rise and run may differ, but the ratio of the rise to the run is the same.

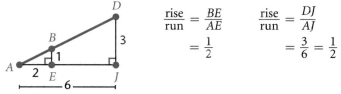

$$\frac{\text{rise}}{\text{run}} = \frac{BE}{AE}$$

$$= \frac{1}{2}$$

$$\frac{\text{rise}}{\text{run}} = \frac{DJ}{AJ}$$

$$= \frac{3}{6} = \frac{1}{2}$$

In fact, for any right triangle that has an angle with the same measure as ∠*A*, the length of the opposite leg will always be $\frac{1}{2}$ the length of the adjacent leg.

$$\frac{\text{the length of the leg } \textbf{OPPOSITE } \angle A}{\text{the length of the leg } \textbf{ADJACENT to } \angle A}$$

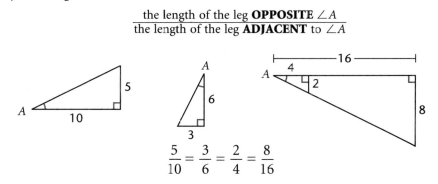

$$\frac{5}{10} = \frac{3}{6} = \frac{2}{4} = \frac{8}{16}$$

Each ratio is the quotient of two lengths of the sides of a right triangle.

In a right triangle, the **tangent** of ∠*A* = $\dfrac{\text{the length of the leg } \textbf{OPPOSITE } \angle A}{\text{the length of the leg } \textbf{ADJACENT to } \angle A}$.

For the **tangent** of ∠A we can write **tan** A.

Remember that the sum of the measures of the three angles of a triangle is 180°. In the diagram, each triangle has ∠A and a right angle.

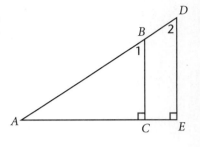

CONSIDER

?

1. Why is $m\angle 1 = m\angle 2$?

The tangent of any particular angle is the same, whether the triangle is large, or small, whether you measure the sides in inches, centimeters, feet, or miles!

EXAMPLE

1. Find tan B.

The leg opposite ∠B is $\overline{AC}$.

The leg adjacent to ∠B is $\overline{CB}$.

$$\tan B = \frac{\text{the length of the leg OPPOSITE } \angle B}{\text{the length of the leg ADJACENT to } \angle B}$$

$\tan B = \frac{3}{4}$

TRY IT

a. Find tan R.
b. Find tan P.

c. Find tan D.
d. Find tan F.

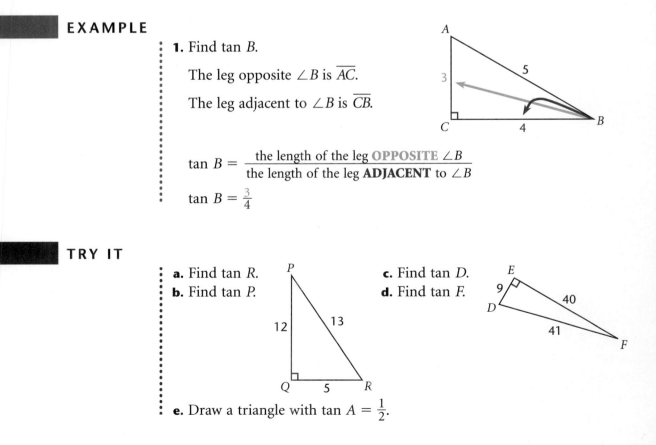

e. Draw a triangle with tan $A = \frac{1}{2}$.

2. At noon, when the sun is directly overhead, the shadow of a building extends 8 meters from the base of the building. A meter stick perpendicular to the ground can touch the side of the building 0.2 meters from its base. How tall is the pedestal?

> **Problem-Solving Tip**
>
> Draw a picture. Use the important information even if the picture cannot be drawn to scale.

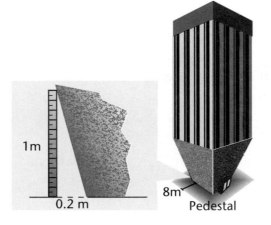

8m
Pedestal

The large triangle is similar to the small triangle. The tangent of the angle from the building base must be equal for each.

$$\frac{\text{length of leg opposite } B}{\text{length of leg adjacent to } B} = \frac{1 \text{ m}}{0.2 \text{m}} = \frac{x \text{ m}}{8 \text{ m}}$$

Solve the proportion.

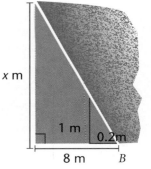

$$\frac{1 \text{ m}}{0.2 \text{ m}} = \frac{x \text{ m}}{8 \text{ m}}$$

$$0.2x = 8$$

$$x = 40$$

The pedestal is approximately 40 meters high.

REFLECT

1. What does the word *adjacent* mean?

2. What ratio can you remember to find the tangent of an angle?

3. To use the tangent ratio, what kind of triangle must be involved? What special sides of the triangle must be involved?

4. Explain why you cannot find the tangent of a right angle.

5. The height of the totem pole is *x* meters. How far away from the totem pole would you have to stand so that the tangent of the angle formed by a line drawn from your feet to the top of the totem pole is 1?

Exercises

CORE

1. Getting Started In $\triangle ABC$, name each of the following.
   a. the leg opposite $\angle A$
   b. the leg opposite $\angle B$
   c. the leg adjacent to $\angle A$
   d. the leg adjacent to $\angle B$
   e. the angle opposite $\overline{AC}$

Write the word or phrase that correctly completes each statement.

2. $\overline{BC}$ is the leg _____ $\angle A$.

3. $\overline{AC}$ is the leg _____ $\angle A$.

4. Tan B is the ratio of the length of the leg _____ $\angle B$ to the length of the leg _____ $\angle B$.

In each case, write tan A as a ratio.

5. **6.** **7.**

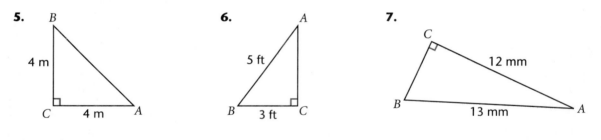

8. What happens to the value of tan A in each of the following?
   a. as a increases
   b. as b increases

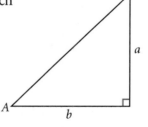

9. Use $\triangle RST$ to answer the following.
   a. Name the leg opposite $\angle T$.
   b. Name the leg adjacent to $\angle T$.
   c. Complete the statement: tan $T = \frac{RS}{?}$.
   d. Find tan T to the nearest tenth.

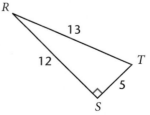

Getting Tenths Find the tangent of the marked angle to the nearest tenth.

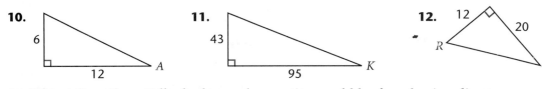

10.

11.

12.

13. Direct Questions Tell whether each quantity would be found using direct measurement or indirect measurement. Explain.
a. your height
b. the height of a building
c. the height of a tree
d. the length of a ladder
e. the width of a river
f. the height of the ceiling in your classroom
g. the distance you travel on an automobile trip
h. the distance you travel on an airplane trip

14. Name two similar triangles. Give two ratios for tan *A*.

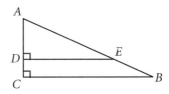

15. In a new horror movie, the director wants a monster to appear 40 feet tall standing next to a house 24 feet tall. To film the monster, artists will build models.
a. Find the height of the model monster if the model house is 3 feet tall.
b. Suppose a 4-foot-tall model of a monster is actually used. How tall would the monster appear to be in the film?

16. North by Northwest A movie theater is having an Alfred Hitchcock Filmorama. The size of Mount Rushmore on the film is 2 centimeters. What is the size of its picture on the screen?

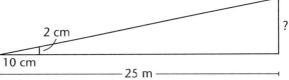

17. See How the Mainsail Sets The Pequod, the ship in *Moby Dick*, has a mainsail that is 20 meters wide and 12 meters high. Several scale models of the ship have been made. Use the tangent ratio to determine whether each scale model of the mainsail is similar to the actual mainsail.
a. 5 cm high and 3 cm wide
b. 18 cm wide and 12 cm high
c. 2 ft high and 3 ft 4 in. wide
d. 0.1 m high and 6 cm wide

18. $\triangle ABC$ is a right triangle with $m\angle C = 90°$.
    a. Remember that the sum of the angles of a triangle is 180°. Copy and complete the table.

$m\angle A$	10°	20°	30°	40°				
$m\angle B$					40°	30°	20°	10°

    b. Study the data in the table, then write a rule for the sum of the two acute angles of a right triangle.

MORE PRACTICE

19. In $\triangle RST$, name each of the following.
    a. the leg opposite $\angle R$
    b. the leg adjacent to $\angle R$
    c. the leg opposite $\angle S$
    d. the leg adjacent to $\angle S$
    e. the angle opposite $\overline{RS}$

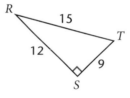

20. Use $\triangle RST$ to answer the following.
    a. Name the leg opposite $\angle R$.
    b. Name the leg adjacent to $\angle R$.
    c. Complete the statement: $\tan R = \dfrac{ST}{?}$.
    d. Find $\tan R$.

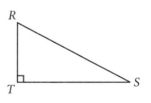

Find the tangent of the marked angle to the nearest tenth.

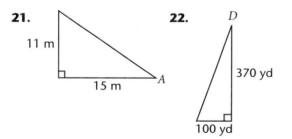

21. 11 m, 15 m, A

22. D, 370 yd, 100 yd

23. 16 cm, 20 cm, M

24. B, 26.4 in., 35.2 in.

25. Name two similar triangles. Give two ratios for tan A.

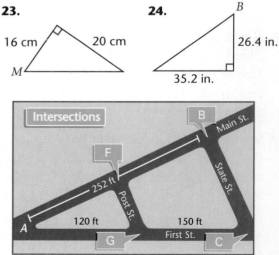

26. A ranger is preparing the outdoor slide show. She knows that the projector produces a 1-foot-tall image when the projector is 4 feet from the screen. How far back should she have them place the table for the projector if the screen is 4 meters tall?

MORE MATH REASONING

27. △*ABC* is a right triangle.
  a. Tan $A = \frac{1}{2}$. Find the value of tan *B*. Tell how you decided.
  b. If tan *A* = tan *B*, what can you say about ∠*A* and ∠*B*? Explain.
  c. Find the product of tan *A* and tan *B*. Why is this true?

28. Hypotenuse Hypothesis Given $\overline{AB}$, how many right triangles can you draw with $\overline{AB}$ as the hypotenuse? Illustrate your answer.

29. Running Rampant The tangent ratio for the shaded angle of this access ramp will be between 0.05 and 0.08. Use guess-and-check to estimate how far out from the building the ramp will extend.

30. The photo shows a model of the Cathedral of Notre Dame in Paris, France. The models show the triangles that make up part of the spire. Describe how you could use a proportion to build a small model of the spire and be sure that *r* is at the correct angle.

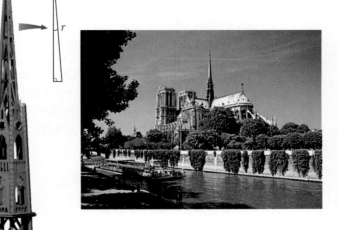

← C O N N E C T → *You have used similar triangles and the tangent ratio to make indirect measurements. Now you will extend these ideas to include other trigonometric ratios.*

Scientific calculators have values for trigonometric functions built in. The following Explore examines the meaning of these values.

EXPLORE: TRIG TRICKS

MATERIALS

Calculator

These three right triangles are similar.

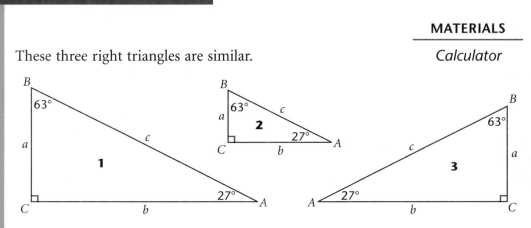

1. Measure the legs a and b and the hypotenuse c of each triangle. Calculate the ratios $\frac{a}{b}$, $\frac{a}{c}$, and $\frac{b}{c}$ for each triangle. Copy the table and enter these values.

△	a	b	c	$\frac{a}{b}$	$\frac{a}{c}$	$\frac{b}{c}$	tan A	tan B	sin A	sin B	cos A	cos B
△1												
△2												
△3												

2. Use your calculator to find sin A, sin B, cos A, cos B, tan A, and tan B. (Be sure your calculator is set for *degrees*.) Round each number to the nearest thousandth. Complete the table.

3. What do you notice in your table about your ratios compared to your calculator results?

> **Problem-Solving Tip**
>
> Look for patterns.

4. Can you define sin *A*, sin *B*, cos *A*, cos *B*, tan *A*, and tan *B* in terms of the side lengths *a*, *b*, and *c* of the triangle? If so, what are they?

In some real-world problems that you can model with triangles, you know the lengths of the legs. In others, you know the length of the hypotenuse. Although you can use the Pythagorean Theorem, to save work you can use trigonometric ratios.

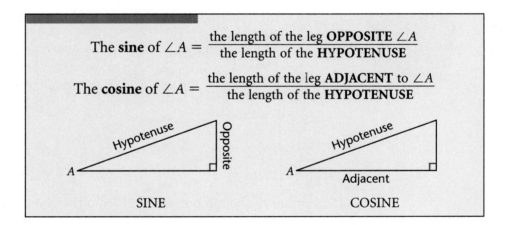

The **sine** of ∠*A* = $\dfrac{\text{the length of the leg } \textbf{OPPOSITE } \angle A}{\text{the length of the } \textbf{HYPOTENUSE}}$

The **cosine** of ∠*A* = $\dfrac{\text{the length of the leg } \textbf{ADJACENT to } \angle A}{\text{the length of the } \textbf{HYPOTENUSE}}$

SINE   COSINE

For the **sine** of ∠*A* we can write **sin** *A*. For the **cosine** of ∠*A* we can write **cos** *A*. We can also write just the words *opposite, adjacent,* and *hypotenuse,* and recognize that these mean the length of these sides in relation to the given angle.

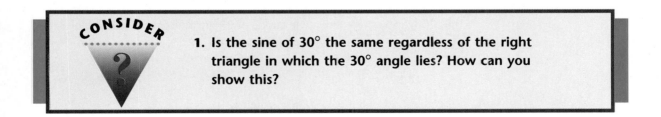

CONSIDER ?

1. Is the sine of 30° the same regardless of the right triangle in which the 30° angle lies? How can you show this?

A 50-foot ramp is used to load cargo onto an airplane. If the ramp makes a 23° angle with the ground, how far away from the plane is the bottom of the ramp?

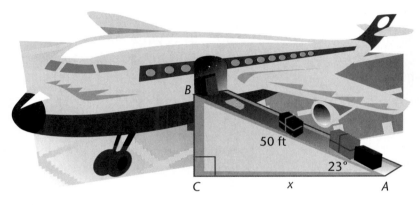

Minh thinks . . .

The sides involved are the *hypotenuse* and the leg *adjacent* to ∠A. I'll use the **cosine** ratio.

$$\cos A = \frac{\text{adjacent}}{\text{hypotenuse}}$$

$$\cos 23° = \frac{x}{50}$$

$$0.920504853 = \frac{x}{50}$$

$$50(0.920504853) = x$$

$$46.02524267 = x$$

The bottom of the ramp is 46.0 feet from the plane.

Taktuk thinks . . .

The missing length is *opposite* ∠B. But we have the measure of ∠A! Since the measures of the three angles of a triangle add up to 180°, ∠B must measure 67°.

$$\sin B = \frac{\text{opposite}}{\text{hypotenuse}}$$

$$\sin 67° = \frac{x}{50}$$

$$0.920504853 = \frac{x}{50}$$ The cosine of 23° is the same as the sine of 67°!

$$50(0.920504853) = x$$

$$46.02524267 = x$$

The bottom of the ramp is 46.0 feet from the plane.

Note that Minh and Taktuk got the same answer using different trigonometric ratios.

CONSIDER

?

2. If ∠A and ∠B are the acute angles of a right triangle, is it always true that sin A = cos B? Explain how you know.

TRY IT

a. Find *AC* using cos *A*.
b. Find *AC* using sin *B*.

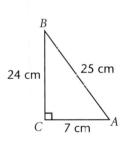

REFLECT

1. Explain which trigonometric ratio you would use to find the missing side in a right triangle if you know the following.
   a. the lengths of both legs
   b. the lengths of the hypotenuse and the leg *adjacent* to ∠A
2. An *equilateral* triangle has sides of equal length and three 60° angles. Do trigonometric ratios work for non-right triangles? Why or why not?
3. Suppose you moved away from the base of a cliff until the angle to the top reached 60°. How could you find the height of the cliff?

Exercises

CORE

1. **Getting Started** Consider △*ABC*.
   a. Which side of the triangle is the hypotenuse?
   b. Which leg is opposite ∠A?
   c. Which leg is adjacent to ∠A?

2. Match each ratio using △*ABC*.
   a. sin *A*   b. cos *A*   c. tan *A*

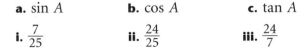

   i. $\frac{7}{25}$ ii. $\frac{24}{25}$ iii. $\frac{24}{7}$

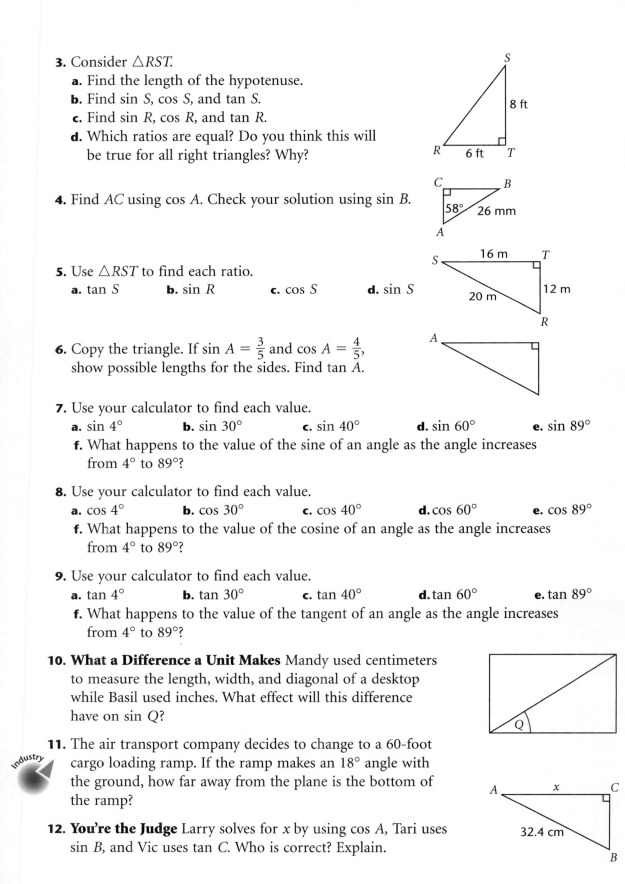

3. Consider △*RST*.
   a. Find the length of the hypotenuse.
   b. Find sin *S*, cos *S*, and tan *S*.
   c. Find sin *R*, cos *R*, and tan *R*.
   d. Which ratios are equal? Do you think this will be true for all right triangles? Why?

4. Find *AC* using cos *A*. Check your solution using sin *B*.

5. Use △*RST* to find each ratio.
   a. tan *S*   **b.** sin *R*   **c.** cos *S*   **d.** sin *S*

6. Copy the triangle. If sin $A = \frac{3}{5}$ and cos $A = \frac{4}{5}$, show possible lengths for the sides. Find tan *A*.

7. Use your calculator to find each value.
   a. sin 4°   **b.** sin 30°   **c.** sin 40°   **d.** sin 60°   **e.** sin 89°
   f. What happens to the value of the sine of an angle as the angle increases from 4° to 89°?

8. Use your calculator to find each value.
   a. cos 4°   **b.** cos 30°   **c.** cos 40°   **d.** cos 60°   **e.** cos 89°
   f. What happens to the value of the cosine of an angle as the angle increases from 4° to 89°?

9. Use your calculator to find each value.
   a. tan 4°   **b.** tan 30°   **c.** tan 40°   **d.** tan 60°   **e.** tan 89°
   f. What happens to the value of the tangent of an angle as the angle increases from 4° to 89°?

10. What a Difference a Unit Makes Mandy used centimeters to measure the length, width, and diagonal of a desktop while Basil used inches. What effect will this difference have on sin *Q*?

11. The air transport company decides to change to a 60-foot cargo loading ramp. If the ramp makes an 18° angle with the ground, how far away from the plane is the bottom of the ramp?

Industry

12. You're the Judge Larry solves for *x* by using cos *A*, Tari uses sin *B*, and Vic uses tan *C*. Who is correct? Explain.

13. S.O.S. An airplane is flying at an altitude of 30,000 feet. If the angle of depression of the airport is 10°, how far must a radio signal travel from the airport to the plane in feet? in miles?

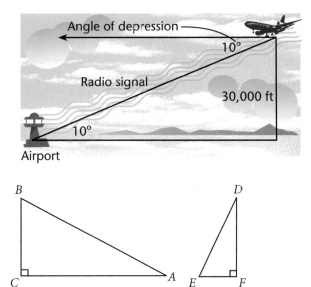

Angle of depression

10°

Radio signal

30,000 ft

10°

Airport

14. Both $\triangle ABC$ and $\triangle DEF$ are right triangles. Explain whether or not they are similar if $m\angle A = 35°$ and $m\angle E = 55°$.

15. Everything Is Looking Up Mr. Puelle and his class went out into the street to find the height of the school building. They made a simple sextant using a board protractor and a tripod. Each of the 18 students in the class measured the angle to the top of the building from a point 15.5 feet from the foot of the building. Their average angle measurement was 78.5°. Find the height of the school building to the nearest foot. Do you think their school was in the country or the city? Explain.

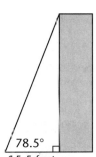

78.5°

15.5 feet

16. Are We Nearly Home Yet? An airplane pilot measures the angle of depression to the airport to be 10°. If the altitude of the airplane at that moment is 15,000 feet, what is the horizontal distance of the plane from the airport in feet? in miles?

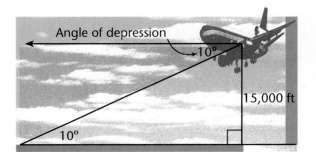

Angle of depression

10°

15,000 ft

10°

17. Bon Voyage From a lighthouse 250 feet above sea level, a ship is spotted using an angle of depression of 8 degrees. Approximately how far out at sea is the ship? Explain your answer.

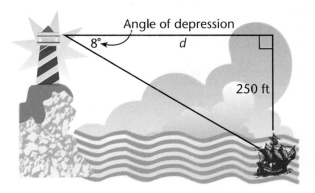

Angle of depression

8°   d

250 ft

18. Can't Get Rid of These Shadows What is the angle measure that a ray from the sun makes with the ground when a 5-foot student has a 5-foot shadow?

Problem-Solving Tip

Use a drawing.

LOOK BACK

19. In 1992, banks collected $4.35 billion in bounced-check fees. [2-2]
   a. How much profit do banks make from bounced checks if 84% of that amount is profit?
   b. How much money per day did banks get from this fee in 1992 (a leap year)?

20. Ruben needs 20 milliliters of a 10% acid solution to do an experiment. He has only a 5% solution and a 27% solution. How much of each acid should he mix to get the amount he needs? [6-2]

Problem-Solving Tip

Write a system of equations.

21. The forest service wants to know how tall the tree was. [7-3]
   (a) 42 ft   (b) 49 ft   (c) 50 ft
   (d) 51 ft   (e) not here

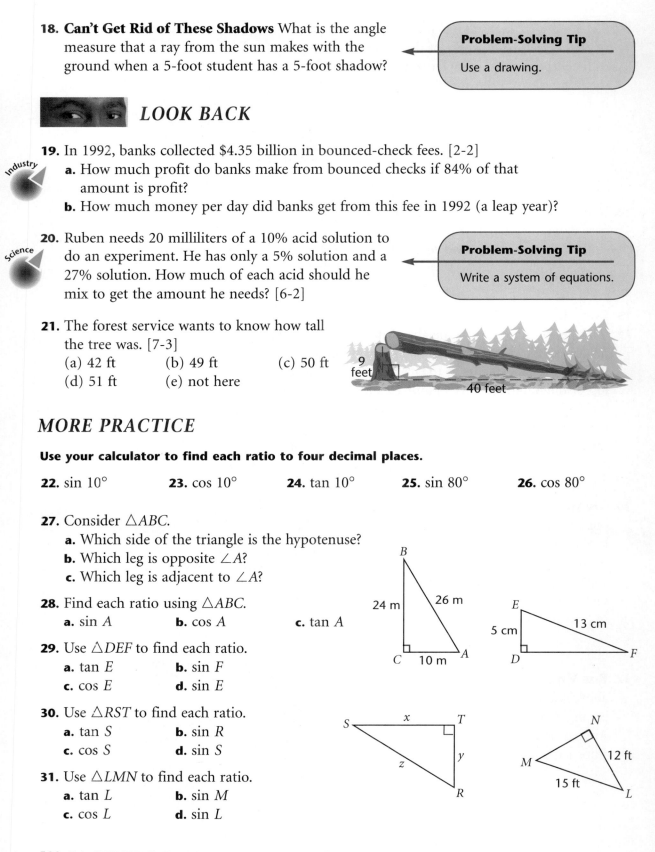

9 feet

40 feet

MORE PRACTICE

Use your calculator to find each ratio to four decimal places.

22. sin 10°   **23.** cos 10°   **24.** tan 10°   **25.** sin 80°   **26.** cos 80°

27. Consider △ABC.
   a. Which side of the triangle is the hypotenuse?
   b. Which leg is opposite ∠A?
   c. Which leg is adjacent to ∠A?

28. Find each ratio using △ABC.
   a. sin A   **b.** cos A   **c.** tan A

29. Use △DEF to find each ratio.
   a. tan E   **b.** sin F
   c. cos E   **d.** sin E

30. Use △RST to find each ratio.
   a. tan S   **b.** sin R
   c. cos S   **d.** sin S

31. Use △LMN to find each ratio.
   a. tan L   **b.** sin M
   c. cos L   **d.** sin L

MORE MATH REASONING

32. Describe a plan for finding cos B in △ABC.

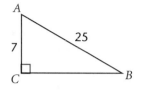

33. In the drawing, ∠C is a right angle. As ∠A increases from 0° to 90°, consider what would happen to each ratio.

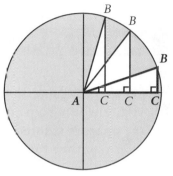

  a. Does sin A get greater or smaller as m∠A approaches 90°?
  b. Does cos A get greater or smaller as m∠A approaches 90°?
  c. Does tan A get greater or smaller as m∠A approaches 90°?
  d. Draw $\overline{AB}$ when tan A = 1. Justify your answer.

34. What limitations are there on the value of the sine of an angle?

35. In △ABC, with m∠C = 90°, sin A = sin B. What is m∠A? m∠B? Tell how you decided.

36. Pattern Probe Use your calculator to find tan 89.9°; tan 89.99°; tan 89.999°. Describe the pattern you observe. Predict tan 89.99999°. Explain your choice.

37. Shoot the Moon?

Tan 0.5° ≈ 0.008727.

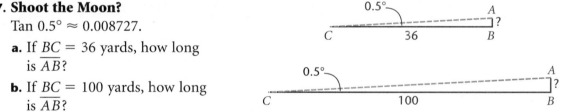

  a. If BC = 36 yards, how long is $\overline{AB}$?

  b. If BC = 100 yards, how long is $\overline{AB}$?

  c. A science technician is aiming a laser at the moon, which is approximately 235,000 miles from the earth with a 1080-mile radius. If the technician makes a 0.5° error when aiming the laser, will the beam still strike the moon's surface? Explain.

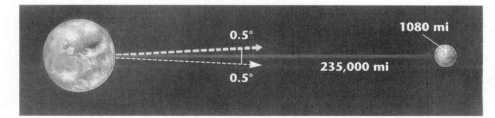

Making Connections

← C O N N E C T → *You have learned to make indirect measurements using the Pythagorean Theorem, similar triangles, and trigonometric ratios.*

EXPLORE: TO BOX OR NOT TO BOX

When a 7:3 Panavision film is shown on television, it is either reduced to fit vertically using a *pan-and-scan* technique that cuts off the sides, or *letterboxed*—the image is reduced to fit horizontally. All of the film appears on the television screen, but the top and bottom of the television screen are not used (dark stripes appear there).

Original image	Pan-and-scan	Letterbox
7:3	4:3	7:3

1. For the pan-and-scan technique, what percentage of the film image is seen on the television screen? What percentage is not seen? What is the probability that a random point on the film image will appear in the pan-and-scan image?

2. For letterboxing, what percentage of the film image is seen on the television screen? What percentage is not seen? What is the probability that a random point on the film image will appear in the letterboxed image?

3. What percent of the television screen is unused in letterboxing? How much is the additional reduction of the letterboxed image compared to the pan-and-scan triangle?

4. Suppose the image, when shown on the large 28- by 12-foot screen in Panavision, has side lengths 10 inches, 2 feet, and 26 inches. It will now appear on a 16- by 12-inch television screen. What are its dimensions if it is a pan-and-scan image? What are its dimensions if it is a letterboxed image? Is its shape similar in each image? Explain.

5. Sometimes, during the opening credits, the film image is reduced more horizontally than vertically, so it actually fits the television screen. Describe the effect on the film image. Would the triangle be similar to the one on the large screen? Explain.

1. When is it *necessary* to use proportional sides of similar triangles rather than trigonometric ratios?
2. What is the difference between direct and indirect measurement?
3. In a right triangle *ABC*, where you know the measure of ∠*A* and the length of a leg, describe how you would find the length of another side.

Self-Assessment

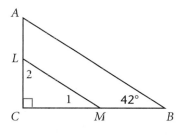

1. △*ABC* ~ △*LMC* and *m*∠*B* = 42°.
   a. Which angle has the same measure as ∠*A*? ∠1?
   b. If the ratio of the sides of △*ABC* to △*LMC* is 2:1, and *LM* = 7, what is *AB*?

2. Glenda's new television has "PIP" (Picture-in-Picture). Her television screen has a 25-inch diagonal, while her PIP screen has a diagonal of 5 inches. The PIP screen is proportional to the television screen. If a figure on the original screen is 12 inches high, how high will it be on the PIP screen?

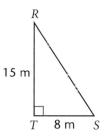

Solve for the variable in each proportion.

3. $\frac{x}{5} = \frac{3}{25}$

4. $\frac{14}{y} = \frac{7}{9}$

5. Consider △*RST*.
   a. Which side of the triangle is the hypotenuse?
   b. Which leg is opposite ∠*R*? adjacent to ∠*R*?

6. Find each ratio using △*RST*.
   a. sin *R*
   b. cos *R*
   c. tan *R*

For each triangle, find sin *A*, cos *A*, tan *A*, sin *B*, cos *B*, and tan *B*.

7.

8.

9. **Vacation Time** At 9 o'clock on Saturday morning, the Stokes family left Albany, Georgia, to begin their annual vacation. They drove 250 kilometers north on Route 19, stopped for 30 minutes for an early lunch, and then drove east 145 kilometers on Highway 20 to Madison.
   a. How far were they from their home in Albany when they arrived in Madison? Tell how you decided.
   b. If they averaged 80 kilometers per hour, how much driving time could they have saved if they had driven directly from Albany to Madison?
   c. Give two reasons for not driving directly from Albany to Madison.

10. Recall that the ratio of the sides of a standard television screen is 4:3. Find the length and width of a standard television with a 27-inch diagonal.

11. Consider $\triangle RST$. Which of these could be used to find the length of $\overline{RS}$?
   I. sin R II. cos S III. tan R
   (a) only I   (b) only II   (c) only III
   (d) II and III   (e) I, II, and III

12. **Need a Lift?** The angle of elevation from the bottom to the top of the mountain has a measure of 60°. Suppose a ski lift to the top is 2000 feet long.
   a. How high is the mountain, to the nearest foot?
   b. If this scene appears on a television, and the ski lift is 15 inches long on the screen, find the measure of the angle of elevation that would appear on the television screen.
   c. Find the height of the mountain on the screen, to the nearest inch.

13. **Observation Pays** The assignment was to solve the proportion $\frac{3}{7} = \frac{x}{15}$. Marcia multiplied the equation first by 7, then by 15. Juan says he just multiplied the 7 by x and 3 by 15 and that those quantities are equal. Is each method correct? Explain. Solve for x.

14. **Ramp Revamp** Lydia is designing an access ramp for the front of her home. Her porch is 4 feet 3 inches from the ground. She sketches two plans, one using an angle of 3° between the ramp and the ground, the other using a 4° angle. Compare the difference in ground distance for each plan. Explain.

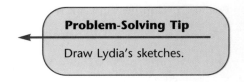

Problem-Solving Tip

Draw Lydia's sketches.

15. **How Likely?** Roberto randomly entered an angle measure into his calculator. Find the probability that the sine of this angle is greater than 1.

16. School Days After the students in
Mr. Shindler's class were shown how to use
a homemade sextant to measure an angle,
they went outside to calculate the height of
a tree. Sasha stood 25 feet from the base of
a tree. Her eyes were about 5 feet above the
ground. The sextant gave her an angle of
35° from the "horizon" to the top of the
tree. Approximately how tall is the tree?
What other method could Sasha have used
to approximate the height of the tree?

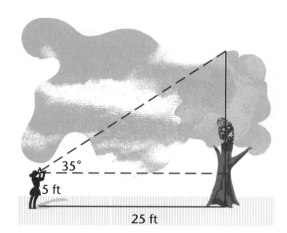

17. On Top of the World When Sonia's family
visited New York, they went to the top of
the World Trade Center, 1368 feet above the
ground. She saw a ship out at sea through a
special viewer. The viewer indicated that the
angle to the ship was 5°. How far away was
the ship from the foot of the World Trade
Center in feet? in miles? Is the drawing close
to scale? Explain.

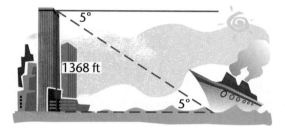

18. Ships Ahoy! Much of what you have studied can be applied to navigation.
Special equipment is used on ships to make some needed measures, but
others must be calculated. In the diagram, ships A and B and an island at
C lie on the same straight line. Another
ship at D has sent an SOS message,
requiring help. Ship B is 32 miles from
C and sights Ship D at an angle of 52°.
Ship A sights Ship D at an angle of 35°.
a. How far is Ship B from Ship D?
b. How far is Ship D from the island
at C?
c. How far is Ship A from Ship B?

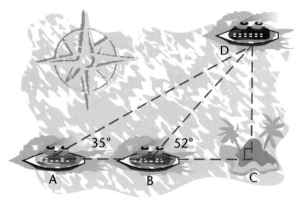

19. Find an object that you could not measure directly. Use a ruler and a piece of
paper to measure it indirectly. Explain how you got your answer.

Chapter 7 Review

In Chapter 7, you have investigated the concept of distance. Absolute value is the distance between two points. Distance on a grid can be calculated with taxicab geometry formulas. The Pythagorean Theorem provides a tool to calculate any distance on a coordinate grid. Distance can also be measured indirectly using similarity and trigonometry.

KEY TERMS

Absolute value [7-1]

Acute triangle [7-3]

Adjacent angle [7-4]

Adjacent leg [7-4]

Corresponding parts [7-4]

Cosine [7-4]

Distance [7-1]

Hypotenuse [7-3]

Irrational number [7-2]

Leg [7-3]

Obtuse triangle [7-3]

Opposite angle [7-4]

Opposite leg [7-4]

Principal square root [7-2]

Proportion [7-4]

Rational number [7-2]

Right triangle [7-3]

Similar figures [7-4]

Sine [7-4]

Square root [7-2]

Tangent [7-4]

Write the word or phrase that correctly completes each statement.

1. In a right triangle, the side opposite the right angle is called the ____.

2. A number that can be written $\frac{a}{b}$, where a and b are integers and $b \neq 0$, is a(n) ____ number.

3. The ____ of 64 is 8.

4. Distance is always a(n) ____.

CONCEPTS AND APPLICATIONS

Solve. [7-1]

5. $x = \left| -5 \right|$

6. $x = \left| 3 \right|$

7. $x = \left| -0.41 \right|$

8. $1 = \left| x + 4 \right|$

9. Match each equation or inequality with the graph that describes it. [7-1]

a. $\left| x \right| = 8$

b. $\left| x \right| < 8$

c. $\left| x \right| \geq 8$

i.
$$\longleftrightarrow \underset{-8 \quad 0 \quad 8}{\circ \!-\!|\!-\! \circ} \longleftrightarrow$$

ii.
$$\longleftrightarrow \underset{-8 \quad 0 \quad 8}{\bullet \!-\!|\!-\! \bullet} \longleftrightarrow$$

iii.
$$\longleftrightarrow \underset{-8 \quad 0 \quad 8}{\bullet \!-\!|\!-\! \bullet} \longleftrightarrow$$

This is the graph of $y = |x - 3|$. Use it to tell how many values of x satisfy each equation. [7-1]

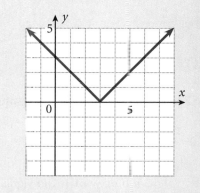

10. $1 = |x - 3|$ **11.** $5 = |x - 3|$

12. $-1 = |x - 3|$

Evaluate. [7-2]

13. $\sqrt{81}$ **14.** $\sqrt{\dfrac{25}{100}}$ **15.** $\sqrt{0.0016}$

Name the two integers between which each square root lies. [7-2]

16. $\sqrt{33}$ **17.** $\sqrt{2}$

18. The formula for finding the volume of a cylinder is $V = \pi r^2 h$. Solve the equation for r. [7-2]

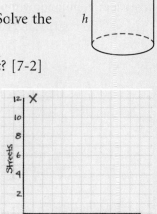

19. How does the graph of $y = x^2$ differ from the graph of $y = \sqrt{x}$? [7-2]

20. The streets and avenues in Model City's downtown area are set out in a grid similar to the one shown. On his first day of work as a bicycle delivery person, Bob accidentally went to 1st Street and 12th Avenue instead of where he wanted to go, 1st Avenue and 12th Street. [7-3]
   a. How far is he, in taxi distance, from where he wants to be?
   b. How far away is he if he could ride there in a straight line?

Find the values of x and y in these right triangles. [7-3]

21.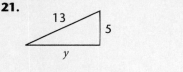

22.

23. Is $\triangle PQR$ a right triangle? Why or why not?

24. Find the distance between $(-1, 4)$ and $(7, 10)$.
   Remember $d = \sqrt{(x_2 - x_1)^2 + (y_2 - y_1)^2}$ [7-3]

25. The vertices of a quadrilateral are $(-5, -2)$, $(-1, -1)$, $(0, -5)$, and $(-4, -6)$. [7-3]
   a. Are the sides all the same length? How do you know?
   b. Approximate the area of the figure. Explain your method of approximation.
   c. Find the perimeter. Give your answer to the nearest hundredth.

Complete each equation. [7-3]

26. $\sqrt{300} = 10\sqrt{\underline{}}$ **27.** $\sqrt{80} = \underline{}\sqrt{5}$ **28.** $\sqrt{162} = \underline{}\sqrt{\underline{}}$

29. The point $(12, 5)$ is 13 units from $(0, 0)$. Plot it on a coordinate plane. Plot and label at least 7 other points that are 13 units from $(0, 0)$. What geometric shape does this set of points suggest? [7-3]

30. Gretchen's company, The Vipers, washes windows on commercial property. Filipa must occasionally fill in for an absent employee. Today she is working on the fourth floor, 40 feet above the ground. She hopes that her cordless cellular phone is within its 100-foot range. She estimates that her truck is 90 feet from the base of the building. Will she be able to receive calls? Explain how you know. [7-3]

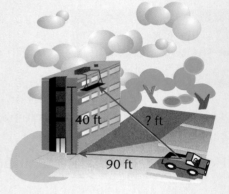

40 ft   ? ft   90 ft

31. Explain what you would do to show that $\triangle ABC \sim \triangle EFG$. [7-4]

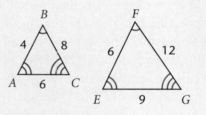

32. Find $\cos A$. [7-4]   **33.** Find $\sin C$. [7-4]

34. Find $\tan C$. [7-4]   **35.** Find $\sin A$. [7-4]

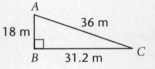

18 m   36 m   31.2 m

36. Find x. [7-4]

37. Find y. [7-4]

Reference
$\tan 58° \approx 1.600$
$\sin 58° \approx 0.8480$
$\cos 58° \approx 0.5299$

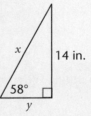

x 14 in.   58° y

38. Chie is attempting to determine the height of an apartment building. Standing 35 feet out from the building, she used her homemade sextant to get the angle from her eye to the top of the building. Explain what she needs to do to finish solving her problem. [7-4]

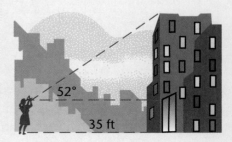

52°   35 ft

39. If $\sin A = \frac{3}{5}$ and $\cos A = \frac{4}{5}$, what is $\tan A$? Express your solution as a ratio. (Hint: Draw and label a right triangle.) [7-4]

40. $\triangle ABC \sim \triangle EDC$. Describe two ways to find x, and then find x. [7-4]

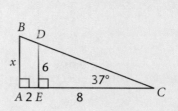

CONCEPTS AND CONNECTIONS

41. Industry ABC Utility Company needs to bring power from the new power plant at the top of the cliff to the Lakefront Development across the lake. The developer is responsible for paying for the installation. They have two options.

Plan A: Run underground cable around the lake and along the cliff at a cost of $50 per running foot. The 80-foot section up the cliff would be suspended cable at $10 per running foot.

Plan B: Suspend a cable from tower to plant, at a cost of $10 per running foot. This plan requires the rental of a helicopter at an estimated cost of $650.

a. Find the length of cable needed for Plan B.
b. Find the cost of each plan.
c. The neighboring subdivision homeowners do not want an ugly bunch of high-tension wires draped across the beautiful lake. As the developer, how would you handle this problem?

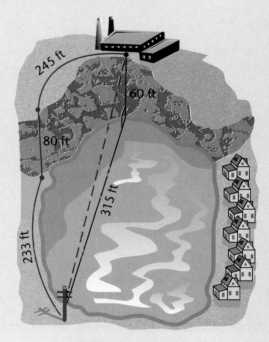

SELF-EVALUATION

Write down the different ways you've learned to find distance. Write about any ideas that became clearer to you because of your work in this chapter. Include a description of what parts of the chapter were difficult for you and what sections you need to study further in order to better understand these topics.

TEST

1. Match the equation or inequality with the graph it describes.

    a. $|x| = 3$ **i.** ⟵┼┼┼┼●┼┼┼┼┼●┼┼⟶
                                            -6   -4   -2   0   2   4

    b. $|x| < 3$ **ii.** ⟵┼┼┼●┼┼┼┼┼┼●┼┼⟶
                                          -6   -4   -2   0   2   4

    c. $|x| \geq 3$ **iii.** ⟵┼┼┼○━━━━━━○┼┼⟶
                                          -6   -4   -2   0   2   4

2. Between what two integers is $\sqrt{90}$? Tell how you decided.

3. Evaluate $\sqrt{121}$.   **4.** Approximate $\sqrt{122}$.

5. The screen shows the graph of $y = |x - 4|$.
How many values of x satisfy the equation
$1.5 = |x - 4|$? Explain your answer.

Xmin=−2
Xmax=10
Xscl=1
Ymin=−4
Ymax=4
Yscl=1

6. Solve $|2x - 4| = 3$.

7. Complete the equation $\sqrt{1200} = \underline{\quad} \sqrt{\underline{\quad}}$.

8. Explain why $\frac{1}{5}$ is a rational number while
$\sqrt{0.2}$ is not.

Use $\triangle XYZ \sim \triangle LMN$ to answer the following.

9. Find x and y.

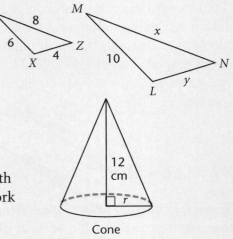

Use the formula for finding the volume of a cone,
$V = \pi \frac{1}{3}r^2 h$, **to answer the following.**

10. If the volume (V) is 300 cubic centimeters and
the height (h) is 12 centimeters, what is the length
of the radius to the nearest tenth? Show your work
and include units of measure.

Cone

11. Is the length of the radius a rational or an irrational
number? Explain how you know.

12. Find the distance between A and B if A is $(-1, 4)$ and B is $(3.5, -7)$.

13. When are taxi distance and straight-line distances equal?

Find the value of *x*.

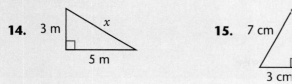

14. 3 m *x* 5 m

15. 7 cm *x* 3 cm

16. 6 m 9 m *x*

17. Is △*ABC* a right triangle? Why or why not?

B 18 24 A 30 C

18. Plot the points *A*(4, 3), *B* (−2, 3), and *C*(1, 7) on a coordinate plane.
  a. Is $\overline{AC}$ the same length as $\overline{BC}$? Explain.
  b. Find the perimeter of the triangle.

19. Building Balance An 11-foot ladder is placed against a building from a point 4 feet from the base of the building. How high on the building will the ladder reach?

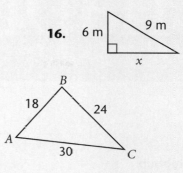

11ft

4ft

20. Find each value using △*ABC*. Express your answer as a ratio.
  a. tan *A*   **b.** sin *B*   **c.** cos *A*

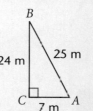

B 24 m 25 m C 7 m A

21. Ramp Rising A theater owner plans to construct a ramp to an entrance that is 2.5 feet above the ground. The ramp should slant up at an angle of 4° from the ground. How far out from the building will the ramp extend? A drawing will help you decide which ratio to use. Show all your work.

Suppose a city inspector requests a less steep ramp. Discuss the changes in the dimensions of the ramp needed to make it less steep.

Reference
tan 4 ≈ 0.0699
sin 4 ≈ 0.0697
cos 4 ≈ 0.9976

Industry

PERFORMANCE TASK

Draw a map showing your home and your school. Mark at least one other landmark. Set up a coordinate grid on your map. Write an explanation for a friend about how to use the distance ideas you've learned in this chapter to find distances between your landmarks. Also, explain how you could find a distance that you could not measure directly (such as a distance across a river). If your map does not work for this problem, look up a map of a city such as the ones shown in the book.

Chapter 8 Polynomials

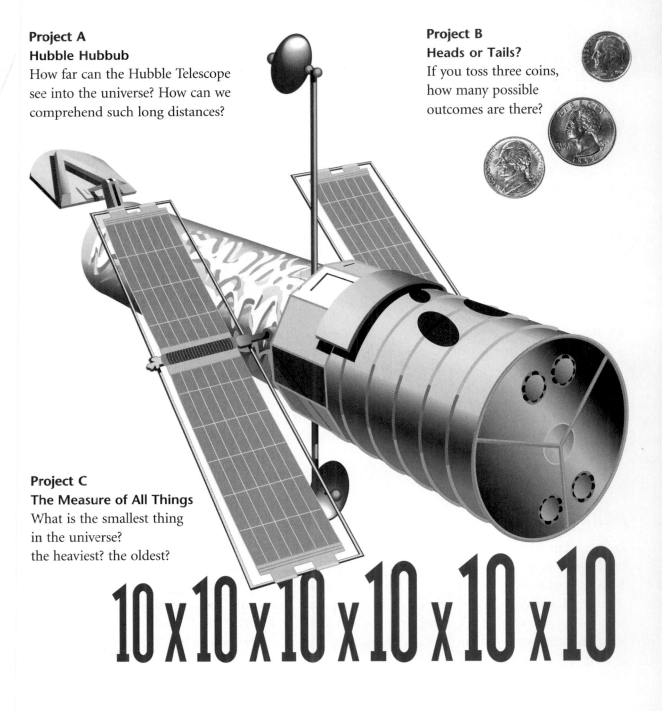

Project A
Hubble Hubbub
How far can the Hubble Telescope see into the universe? How can we comprehend such long distances?

Project B
Heads or Tails?
If you toss three coins, how many possible outcomes are there?

Project C
The Measure of All Things
What is the smallest thing in the universe?
the heaviest? the oldest?

10 x 10 x 10 x 10 x 10 x 10

I loved math in high school. Einstein was one of my role models and he liked math so I liked it, too. I used to think I could use math to make computers intelligent. Now I realize computers only do what they are told to do.

I'm proud that I could use electronics to develop an efficient program called a device driver. To do that I had to understand the old operating system so I could make the driver work on the new system. I also had to know how the hardware worked. There is something in mathematics that is just beautiful.

Javan M. Banks
Electrical Engineer,
    Aerospace Technology
*National Aeronautics and
    Space Administration
    (NASA)*
Kennedy Space Center, FL

8-1
Polynomials and Scientific Notation

In 8-1 polynomials are used to model projectile motion, surface area of planets and business performance. You will see how scientific notation is used for large and small numbers. You will need skills with decimals, fractions, and simplifying algebraic expressions.

Perform each indicated operation. [Previous course]

1. $2.74 \cdot 10{,}000$ **2.** $0.0085 \cdot 100{,}000$ **3.** $508 \div 1000$ **4.** $22.1 \cdot 100$

5. $49{,}328 \div 1000$ **6.** $0.107 \div 100$ **7.** $1.746 \div 100$ **8.** $0.0928 \cdot 1{,}000{,}000$

Write each fraction as a decimal. [Page 749]

9. $\dfrac{3}{1000}$ **10.** $\dfrac{7}{10}$ **11.** $\dfrac{39}{100}$ **12.** $\dfrac{428}{100}$

13. $\dfrac{2.8}{10}$ **14.** $\dfrac{527}{10000}$ **15.** $\dfrac{9}{100000}$ **16.** $\dfrac{11.5}{100}$

8-2
Multiplying and Factoring Polynomials

In 8-2 you will multiply and factor polynomials that are used in computer science, engineering, and business problems. You will be simplifying expressions and using ideas about number and area.

Find all pairs of integer factors. [Pages 757–758]

17. $32 = 1 \cdot \underline{\quad} = 2 \cdot \underline{\quad} = \underline{\quad} \cdot \underline{\quad}$

18. $20 = 1 \cdot \underline{\quad} = \underline{\quad} \cdot \underline{\quad} = \underline{\quad} \cdot \underline{\quad}$

19. $18 = 1 \cdot \underline{\quad} = 2 \cdot \underline{\quad} = \underline{\quad} \cdot \underline{\quad}$

20. $21 = 1 \cdot \underline{\quad} = \underline{\quad} \cdot \underline{\quad}$

Find the greatest common factor (GCF) of each number pair. [Pages 757–758]

21. 3 and 12   **22.** 16 and 12   **23.** 20 and 30   **24.** 9 and 7

Find the area of each of the four rectangles (A, B, C, D). [2-2]

25. A   **26.** B

27. C   **28.** D

7 in.	x
4 in. A	B
1 in. C	D

a trip to Mars

o the ancient Babylonians, Mars was a wandering red light. We know it as the planet next farthest from the sun. In science fiction, we traveled to Mars many times before the Viking 1 lander actually came to rest on the planet's rocky surface in 1976.

Mars has long captured our imaginations. There have been visions of super-intelligent extra-terrestrials building canals, living in huge cities, and touring the universe in flying saucers. How close are these fantasies to the reality of Mars? In 1964, the Mariner IV space probe returned the first close-up pictures of the Red Planet and its two tiny, irregular moons, Phobos and Deimos. We learned that the planet is barren, with fierce dust storms and many huge craters. We were surprised to learn from Viking 1 that Mars has a pinkish sky, but disappointed to learn that Mars is uninhabited.

What is the planet's history? Was it ever inhabited? Is there water in the soil? Until humans land on Mars, we can only analyze the data from space probes and visit there in our imaginations.

1. The distance from Earth to Mars averages between 35 and 248 million miles. Why do you think there is so much difference between the maximum and minimum distances from Earth to Mars ?
2. A Martian year is 687 Earth days. Why does Mars have a longer year than Earth?
3. The temperatures on Mars range from −190°F to 85°F. Why is Mars so much colder than Earth? Which would you expect to be the hottest planet? the coldest planet?
4. Why is exploration of Mars important? If you were the first human to land on Mars, what would you look for?

← C O N N E C T → *In Chapter 2, you added, subtracted, and simplified linear expressions by combining like terms. Combining like terms is also useful for working with polynomial expressions and functions.*

Linear models don't always describe and predict real relationships well. The relationship between the height of a baseball and the time since it was hit is a *nonlinear* function. Likewise for the population of a town and the year.

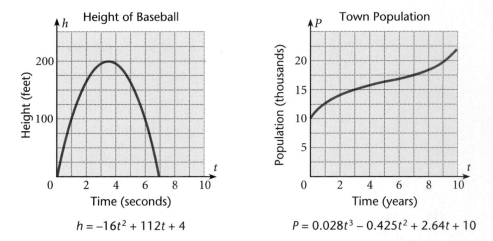

Height of Baseball

$h = -16t^2 + 112t + 4$

Town Population

$P = 0.028t^3 - 0.425t^2 + 2.64t + 10$

Many of the tools you used to explore linear expressions and functions are also useful for studying *nonlinear* expressions and functions.

EXPLORE: OUT OF LINE

MATERIALS

Compare these two expressions using algebra tiles or graphs.

Algebra tiles
Graphing utility or graph paper

$x^2 - 2x + 3$

$-5x + 3x^2 + 3x - 2x^2 + 3$

Use one or both of Steps 1 and 2 to compare the expressions. Then do Step 3.

1. Model each expression with algebra tiles. Use the rules for working with algebra tiles to simplify the second expression as much as possible. What do you notice?
2. Graph the functions $y = x^2 - 2x + 3$ and $y = -5x + 3x^2 + 3x - 2x^2 + 3$ on a graphing utility or a coordinate plane. What do you notice?
3. Make a conjecture about how these two expressions are related.

Recall that *terms* are the parts of an expression that are added. A **monomial** is an expression with a single term, either a constant or a product of constants and variables with exponents that are whole numbers. Monomials do not have variables in the denominators of fractions or under radical symbols.

A **polynomial expression** is a monomial or a sum of monomials.

Some polynomial expressions are classified by the number of terms.

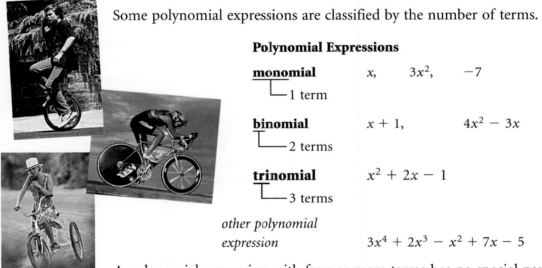

Polynomial Expressions

monomial $x,$ $3x^2,$ -7
└─ 1 term

binomial $x + 1,$ $4x^2 - 3x$
└─ 2 terms

trinomial $x^2 + 2x - 1$
└─ 3 terms

*other polynomial
expression* $3x^4 + 2x^3 - x^2 + 7x - 5$

A polynomial expression with four or more terms has no special name.

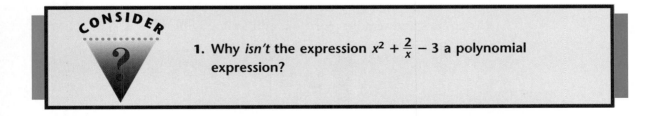

CONSIDER

?

1. Why *isn't* the expression $x^2 + \frac{2}{x} - 3$ a polynomial expression?

The **degree of a polynomial expression** with one variable is the value of the largest exponent of the variable that appears in any term. The degree of the binomial $x^2 + x$ is 2.

A functional relationship between quantities that can be described by an equation where y equals a polynomial expression of x is a **polynomial function.**

Polynomial Functions

A **linear function** is a polynomial function of degree 1.
$$y = 3x + 2$$

A **quadratic function** is a polynomial function of degree 2.
$$y = 5x^2 + 2x + 4$$

A **cubic function** is a polynomial function of degree 3.
$$y = x^3 + 3x^2$$

TRY IT

Find the *degree* of each polynomial expression. Decide whether it is a monomial, binomial, or trinomial.

a. $x^3 + 4x$ **b.** x^2 **c.** $x^5 + 6x^3 + 3$

Determine whether each polynomial function is *linear, quadratic,* or *cubic.*

d. $y = 4x^2$ **e.** $y = x^3 + 1$ **f.** $y = 4x - \frac{1}{2}$

Working with algebra tiles shows that you can simplify polynomial expressions in the same way that you simplify linear expressions—by combining like terms.

You can model the polynomial expression $5 + 2x^2 - 2x - x^2 + x - 3$ using algebra tiles and then use the rules for removing tiles.

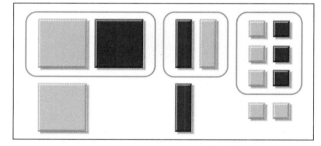

Group tiles and remove pairs that add to 0, leaving $x^2 - x + 2$.

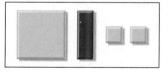

You can also use algebraic properties to group and combine like terms.

$$5 + 2x^2 - 2x - x^2 + x - 3$$
$$= (2x^2 - x^2) + (-2x + x) + (5 - 3)$$ Group like terms using the commutative and associative properties.

$$= x^2 - x + 2$$ Combine like terms using the distributive property.

We often refer to polynomial expressions simply as *polynomials*. We usually write a polynomial with the highest degree term first, the next highest second, and so on. This is called writing the polynomial in *descending order.*

The properties you use to simplify polynomials also allow you to add and subtract polynomials.

EXAMPLES

Add or subtract the polynomials.

1. $(3x^2 + 5x) + (x^2 - 2x - 2)$
$$= (3x^2 + x^2) + (5x - 2x) - 2$$ Group like terms.
$$= 4x^2 + 3x - 2$$ Combine like terms.

2. $(3x^2 - 2x + 5) - (2x^2 + 3)$
$$= (3x^2 - 2x + 5) + (-2x^2 - 3)$$ Subtract by adding the opposite.

$$= (3x^2 - 2x^2) - 2x + (5 - 3)$$ Group like terms.
$$= x^2 - 2x + 2$$ Combine like terms.

TRY IT

Add or subtract the polynomials.
g. $(x^2 + 3x) - (x^2 + 3x - 1)$ **h.** $(3x^2 + 4x - 5) + (3x - 1 + 2x^2)$

REFLECT

1. How is a polynomial function different from a polynomial expression?
2. What do the prefixes *mono, bi,* and *tri,* used to describe polynomial expressions, mean? What are some other words that use these prefixes?
3. What word describes a polynomial function of degree 1? degree 2? degree 3?
4. When you write a polynomial in *descending order,* what is descending?
5. How are subtraction and addition of polynomials related?

Exercises

CORE

1. **Getting Started** Use these steps to simplify the polynomial expression
   $6 + 4x^2 - 5x + 8x - x^2 - 10$.
   a. Group like terms using the commutative and associative properties.
   b. Combine like terms.
   c. Write the result in descending order.

2. Match each word with a polynomial expression. Explain each choice.
a. trinomial	**b.** binomial	**c.** monomial
i. $-4x^3$	**ii.** $x^2 + 6x - 3$	**iii.** $-2x + 3$

Find the degree of each polynomial expression and write the polynomial in descending order.

3. $6 + x^2 + 2x$

4. $x^3 - 10x + x^4$

5. Match each word with a polynomial function. Explain each choice.
a. linear function	**b.** quadratic function	**c.** cubic function
i. $y = 7x^2 + 7x$	**ii.** $y = -2x^3 - 3x + 1$	**iii.** $y = 1 - 3x$

Determine whether each of the following is a polynomial expression or a polynomial function.

6. $y = 3x^2 - 4x + 5$

7. $3x^2 - 4x + 5$

8. $x^2 - 5x^3 + 7x - 13$

9. $y = x^2 - 5$

10. **Mars Musing** The diameter of Mars is approximately
    4200 miles. What is the volume of the planet? The
    function $V = \frac{4}{3}\pi r^3$ represents the volume of a sphere
    of radius r.

11. Copy and complete this table. Use it to determine whether
    any two of the polynomials are equivalent.

x	$2x^2 + x$	$2x^3 + 1$	$3x^2 + x - x^2$
-1			
2			
4			

12. Is $4x$ equivalent to $x^2 + 6x - 2 + 2 - x^2 - 2x$? Explain.

13. Subtract $4x^2 - 3x$ from $5x^2 - 2x + 1$.

Add or subtract the polynomial expressions.

14. $(6x^3 - 2x) + (14 - 3x + 5x^2)$

15. $(6a - 4a^3 + 1) - (-7a^2 + 10a - 15)$

16. $(8 - 2x^3 + x) - (2x^3 - x)$

17. $(d^3 - 2 + 4d^2) + (-4d^3 + 7d)$

18. $(3y^2 - 6 + 5y) + (12 + 6y^2 - 7y)$

19. $(-2x^2 - 6x) - (3x^2 - 10x + x^3)$

20. Answer the following questions about the graphs.
   a. Which represents a linear function? Tell how you decided.
   b. Describe how you can tell if an equation is linear.

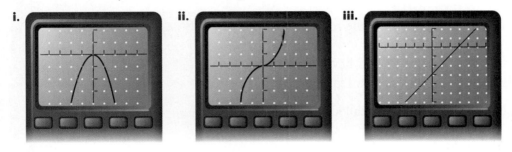

i.   **ii.**   **iii.**

Graph each function.

21. $y = \frac{5}{2}x - 1$

22. $y = |x|$

23. Sum Fun John wanted to make a deal with his boss. Instead of his regular salary of $25 per week, he wanted her to pay him $1 for the first day, $2 for the second day, $3 for the third day and so on. Who would get the better deal? Answering these questions will show you a mathematical idea helpful in studying John's deal.
   a. Find the sum of the numbers 1 to 7. Did you find a quick way to add those numbers? If so, explain what you did.
   b. The expression $\frac{n(n + 1)}{2}$ is an easy way to find this sum. Substitute 7 for n. Did you get the same value?
   c. What would be the sum of the first 30 numbers?
   d. If John gets a salary of $100 per month now, should he try to convince his boss to follow his new plan for a month? Explain.

24. How many different polynomial expressions can you create from these terms? Use each term no more than once for a given polynomial.

   $x^4 \qquad -2x^3 \qquad -5$

25. Grander Than the Grand Canyon Valles Marineris, named for the Mariner 9 that discovered it, is a huge canyon system on Mars. It is over 4000 kilometers long. Given that the distance across the United States from the Pacific Coast to the Atlantic Coast is approximately 3000 miles, would the Valles Marineris *fit* from coast to coast (1 kilometer = 0.62 mile)? Explain.

Determine whether each statement is always, sometimes, or never true.

26. A polynomial is a monomial.

27. A monomial is a polynomial.

28. A trinomial is a cubic polynomial.

29. The probability (p) that a rocket will work properly in a test is 0.99. The probability that the rocket will work properly in n tests is given by the power p^n.
  a. What is the probability that the rocket will work properly in 2 tests? 10 tests? 100 tests?
  b. Estimate when the rocket will have a 50% chance of working properly in each test. Explain your answer.

30. Oblong Numbers The Greeks called the following numbers oblong numbers.
  a. Why do you think they called these numbers oblong?
  b. Do you see a relationship between the figure number and the number of dots? Write this relationship using a complete sentence.
  c. How many dots would be in the 10th figure? the 100th? the nth?

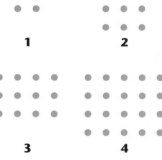

 *LOOK BACK*

Define these quantities as variables and write each sentence as an equation. [4-1]

31. Marci had \$740 in savings, which was \$52.50 less than twice the amount that Amy had in savings.

32. The sale price of the CD player was \$210. This was \$2 less than $\frac{1}{3}$ of the original price.

33. Points L, M, N, O, and P all represent integers. Find the distance between the points. [7-1]
  a. O and P **b.** L and P **c.** P and N
  d. M and M **e.** O and N

Find the value of each variable. In each case, the figures are similar. [7-4]

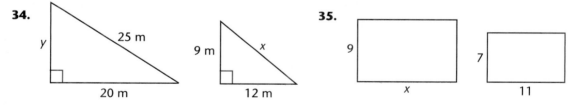

34.

25 m, y, 20 m, 9 m, x, 12 m

35.

9, x, 7, 11

MORE PRACTICE

36. Match each word with a polynomial expression.
    a. trinomial   **i.** $-4x + 2$
    b. binomial   **ii.** $-5x^3$
    c. monomial   **iii.** $x^2 + 5x - 9$

Give the degree of each polynomial expression and write the polynomial in descending order.

37. $1 + 5x - x^2$
                            38. $2x - 3x^5 + 7$

39. Subtract $2x^2 - 5x - 1$ from $7x^2 - 4x + 8$.

Add or subtract the polynomial expressions.

40. $(4x^3 - x) + (1 - 3x + 2x^3)$ **41.** $(5x^2 - 3 - 2x^3) - (6x^3 - 5x^2 + 3)$

42. $(x^3 - x^2) + (5x^2 - x^3 - x)$ **43.** $(5x^2 - 3x + 6) - (6x^2 - 2x - 4)$

44. $(7x^2 - 4 + 6x) - (4x^2 - 3x)$ **45.** $(3x^2 - 4x^3 + 10) + (4x^3 - 2x^2)$

46. $(6 + 5x^2 + 3x) - (3x + 5x^2 - 6)$ **47.** $(5a^3 - 4a + 6a^2) + (4 - 6a^2 + 3a^3)$

48. Which graph represents a linear function?
    (a)   (b)   (c)

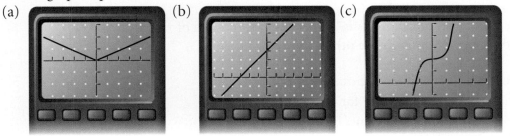

49. The diameter of Pluto is approximately 2330 kilometers. What is the volume of the planet? The function $V = \frac{4}{3}\pi r^3$ represents the volume of a sphere of radius r.

50. Is $2x$ equivalent to $-3x^2 - 2x + 1 + 3x^2 - 1$?

51. Is 4 equivalent to $4x^2 + 6x - 2 + 6 - 4x^2 - 6x$?

52. Copy and complete this table. Use it to determine whether any two of the polynomials are equivalent.

x	$3x^2 - x$	$5x^2 - x - 2x^2$	$2x^2 - x + 1$
-1			
2			
4			

MORE MATH REASONING

53. The table gives values of x and the corresponding values of y.

   a. Is y a linear function of x? Explain.

   b. Which expresses the relationship between x and y shown in the table of values?

x	y
1	1
2	3
3	6
4	10
...	...
...	...
10	55

   (a) $y = x^2 + x$ (b) $y = \dfrac{x + 1}{2}$

   (c) $y = \dfrac{x^2 + x}{2}$ (d) $y = \dfrac{1}{2}x(x - 1)$

54. Cornered Points R and S move simultaneously at the same rate away from vertex A along sides $\overline{AB}$ and $\overline{AD}$ on square $ABCD$. Let y be the area in square centimeters of $\triangle ARS$ and let x centimeters be the length of $\overline{AS}$ and $\overline{AR}$. The lengths of $\overline{AR}$ and $\overline{AS}$ are equal.

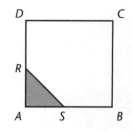

   a. Express y in terms of x.

   b. Make a table that shows the corresponding areas for lengths of 0, 1, 1.5, 2, 3, and 11.2 centimeters.

   c. Show that when $x =$ the length of the side of square $ABCD$, the area of the triangle is equal to half the area of the square.

55. If the sum of two polynomials is $2x^2 + 2x + 3$, and one of the addends is $x^2 + 3$, what is the other?

56. Eighteenth-century mathematician Maria Gaetana Agnesi is responsible for one of the first thorough textbooks on calculus, *Instituzioni Analitiche (Analytical Institutions)*. Her writings include the bell-shaped curve, given by the equation $x^2y = a^2(a - y)$, referred to as *versiera of Agnesi* (curve of Agnesi). The equation can be expressed as $y = \dfrac{a^3}{x^2 + a^2}$.

   a. Write the equation for $a = 2$.

   b. Copy and complete the table of values for the equation when $a = 2$.

x	−3	−2	−1	0	1	2	3
y							

   c. Write the equation for $a = 5$.

   d. Copy and complete the table of values for the equation when $a = 5$.

x	−3	−2	−1	0	1	2	3
y							

   e. Graph each of the equations on the same axis. Describe your results.

Multiplying Monomials

←CONNECT→ *You've added and subtracted polynomials. Now you'll multiply monomials. You'll also learn the notation used in science to express large numbers using powers of 10.*

Recall that a power is a number written as a product of equal factors. Astronomers and other scientists often use powers of 10 to express large numbers in **scientific notation.** In scientific notation, a number is written as a power of 10 multiplied by a number at least 1 but less than 10.

EXAMPLES

1. The average distance from Mars to the sun is 142 million miles. Write this distance in standard notation and in scientific notation.

   In **standard notation,** 142 million miles is written as 142,000,000 miles.

   142,000,000 mi
   $= 1.42 \times 100,000,000$ mi $142,000,000 = \frac{142,000,000}{100,000,000} \times 100,000,000$

   $\downarrow$exponent
   $= 1.42 \times 10^8$ mi $100,000,000 = 10 \cdot 10 \cdot 10 \cdot 10 \cdot 10 \cdot 10 \cdot 10 \cdot 10 = 10^8$
   $\uparrow$base

   On some calculators 1.42×10^8 is shown this way: $\boxed{1.42 \qquad ^{08}}$.

   In **scientific notation,** 142 million miles is written as 1.42×10^8 miles.

2. The Pioneer 10 spacecraft detected radiation from Jupiter when it was 1.55×10^7 miles away from the planet. Write this distance in standard notation.

   1.55×10^7 mi $= 1.55 \times 10,000,000$ mi   Write 10^7 as 10,000,000 and multiply.

   $= 15,500,000$ mi

TRY IT

a. When the Viking I spacecraft sent the first pictures from Mars to Earth, the two planets were 321 million kilometers apart. Write this distance in scientific notation.

In the following Explore, you will use a calculator to explore patterns in powers and exponents.

EXPLORE: POWER PLAY

MATERIALS

Calculator

1. Find the values of 2^{20}, 4^{20}, 2^9, and 4^9 on your calculator. Which power is equal to $2^4 \cdot 2^5$? Make a conjecture about multiplying two powers with the same base.

2. 2^4 raised to the third power is written as $(2^4)^3$. Which of the powers 2^7, 2^{12}, 6^4, or 6^{12} is equal to $(2^4)^3$? Make a conjecture about raising a power to a power.

3. Which of the products $2^3 \cdot 4$, $2 \cdot 4^3$, or $2^3 \cdot 4^3$ is equal to $(2 \cdot 4)^3$? Make a conjecture about raising a product to a power.

4. Test all three of your conjectures for powers of 3 and powers of 10. Do you think your conjectures are always true?

Problem-Solving Tip

Make an organized list.

$\mathbf{S}$implifying powers can also help you multiply monomials.

EXAMPLES

3. Multiply x^2 by x^3.
$$x^2 \cdot x^3 = (x \cdot x) \cdot (x \cdot x \cdot x) = x^5$$

4. Multiply $-3x^6$ by $4x^3$.
$$-3x^6 \cdot 4x^3 = -3 \cdot 4 \cdot (x \cdot x \cdot x \cdot x \cdot x \cdot x) \cdot (x \cdot x \cdot x) = -12x^9$$

5. Raise the monomial $3y^2$ to the fourth power.
$$(3y^2)^4 = 3y^2 \cdot 3y^2 \cdot 3y^2 \cdot 3y^2 = 81y^8$$

TRY IT

Simplify each monomial.
b. $(p^5)^7$ **c.** $(2x^2)^3$ **d.** $3y^4(2y)^2$
e. Find the area of a rectangle with width $4y^2$ and length $5y^4$.

Here is a summary of some patterns you may have noticed.

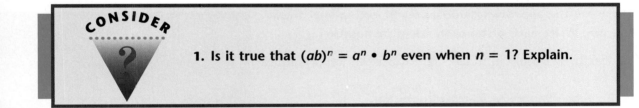

MULTIPLYING POWERS WITH LIKE BASES

For any real number a and for any positive integers m and n,
$a^m \cdot a^n = a^{m+n}$.

RAISING A POWER TO A POWER

For any real number a and for any positive integers m and n,
$(a^m)^n = a^{mn}$.

RAISING A PRODUCT TO A POWER

For any real numbers a and b and for any positive integer n,
$(ab)^n = a^n \cdot b^n$.

Although we don't often have a need to show the exponent for a single variable, like x, its exponent is 1. That is, x^1 means x.

CONSIDER

1. Is it true that $(ab)^n = a^n \cdot b^n$ even when $n = 1$? Explain.

EXAMPLE

6. Albert Einstein's famous energy formula is $E = mc^2$, where m stands for mass and c stands for the constant speed of light, 3.0×10^8 meters per second. Find the value of c^2 you would use in this formula.

$$c^2 = (3.0 \times 10^8 \text{ m/sec})^2 \quad \text{Square the value for } c.$$
$$= (3.0)^2 \cdot (10^8)^2 \quad (\text{m/sec})^2 \quad \text{Square each factor.}$$
$$= 9.0 \times 10^{16} \quad \text{m}^2/\text{sec}^2 \quad (10^8)^2 = 10^{8 \cdot 2} = 10^{16}.$$

REFLECT

1. What value of n will make $6^2 \cdot 6^6 = 6^3 \cdot 6^n$ true? Explain.

2. Why do you *add* exponents when you *multiply* powers with the same base?

3. Are the powers $(3^5)^4$ and $(3^4)^5$ equal? Explain.

4. If a is negative, will a^7 be positive or negative? Will a^{12} be positive or negative? Explain how you know.

Exercises

CORE

1. **Getting Started** Use these steps to write 36 million in scientific notation.
   a. Write 36 million in standard notation.
   b. Give the missing number: 36 million = $3.6 \times$ ____.
   c. Give the missing exponent: 36 million = 3.6×10 ____.
   d. Check your answer by using your calculator.

2. Each length is equal to 1 mile. Which one is expressed in scientific notation?
   a. 52.8×10^2 ft
   b. 1.61×10^5 cm
   c. 1.07×3^{10} in.

3. The average distance between Jupiter and the sun is 778.3 million kilometers. Use these steps to write 778.3 million kilometers in scientific notation.
   a. Write 778.3 million in standard notation.
   b. Give the missing number: 778.3 million km = ____ $\times$ 100,000,000 km.
   c. Give the missing numbers: 778.3 million km = ____ $\times 10$ ____ km.
   d. Check your answer by using your calculator.

These are the approximate distances of each planet from the sun. Write each distance in scientific notation.

4. Earth: 92.9 million miles
5. Saturn: 900 million miles

Write each distance in standard notation.

6. Mercury: 3.6×10^7 miles
7. Pluto: 2.67×10^9 miles

8. Multiply x^{10} by x^3.
9. Multiply $-2y^3$ by $4y^7$.

10. List all factors to show that $(x^2)^3 = (x^3)^2$.

11. Raise the monomial $2y^3$ to the fourth power.

Complete each to make a true statement.

12. $(2n)^3 = 8n^?$
13. $(3x^4y)^2 = 9x^?y^2$

Simplify each monomial.

14. $a^3 \cdot a^3$
15. $-c^5 \cdot c$

16. $(r^2)^3$
17. $(-3w^3)^2$

18. $(x^2y^5)(2y^2)$
19. $(-fg^8)(10fg^2)$

20. $(-a^3b^2)^2(-4a^5b^4)$
21. $(2m^3n^3)^3(-6mn^2)$

Find the perimeter (*P*) and the area (*A*) of each figure. All the angles in the figures are right angles. Remember, for a rectangle, *P* = 2ℓ + 2*w* and *A* = ℓ*w*.

22.
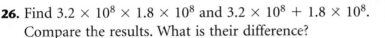
5*xy*

2*xy*

23.
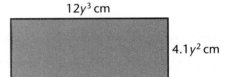
2*x*
x
x x
x
3*x*

24. Multiply 3.2×10^8 by 5.7×10^8. Write your answer in scientific notation.

25. Find the area of the rectangle. Is it reasonable for the value of *y* to be negative? Explain.

12y^3 cm

4.1y^2 cm

26. Find $3.2 \times 10^8 \times 1.8 \times 10^8$ and $3.2 \times 10^8 + 1.8 \times 10^8$. Compare the results. What is their difference?

27. Arrange these numbers from least to greatest.

1.23×10^3 -2.35×10^4 1.75×10^3 1.03×10^4 11.4×10^3

28. Einstein's Energy Gretta used $E = mc^2$ to find the value of *E* in a physics homework problem. Given $m = 1.7$ and $c = 3.0 \times 10^8$, find her numerical solution in scientific notation.

Science

29. Earth to Mars The approximate average distance from Earth to Mars is 142 million miles. Given that 1 mile = 1.6093 kilometers, what is the distance in kilometers? Write your answer in scientific notation.

Science

30. Write $27 \cdot 9 \cdot 3$ as a power of 3.   **31.** Write 4^3 as a power of 2.

32. Real Realty Real estate listings show home prices like 125K or 93K. What do these expressions represent in "real" numbers? How is this like scientific notation? How is it different?

Industry

windows. Priced for quick sale. **88K**

COUNTRY ATMOSPHERE. Well-maintained three-bedroom house with sunroom, veranda and many extras! Take Lakeview Dr. east to Cedar Lane. **93K**

IMMACULATE RANCH. Nice lot, gas heat, plenty of storage with enclosed rear porch. 4 BR 1.5 BA. **125K**

CHARMING BI-LEVEL. Newly remodeled.

33. Astronomical Units A light-year is a unit of distance equal to the distance that light travels in a vacuum during 1 year, about 6×10^{12} miles.

    a. At that speed, how far would light travel in a day? an hour? a second?

    b. If the diameter of Mars is approximately 4200 miles, how many trips around the equator of Mars would equal 1 light-year in distance?

    c. Did you use scientific notation in your calculations? Why or why not?

LOOK AHEAD

34. Which is larger, $\frac{1}{1000}$ or $\frac{1}{10000}$? Tell how you decided.

35. Which is smaller, 1.001 or 1.00001? Tell how you decided.

Write these decimal numbers as fractions.

36. 0.0001   **37.** 0.000001   **38.** 0.00000001

MORE PRACTICE

Simplify each monomial.

39. $-b^3 \cdot b^2$ **40.** $(3y^2)^3$ **41.** $(-a^2)(-a^8)$ **42.** $2c^2 \cdot 3c$

43. $(y^3)(y)$ **44.** $(4x^7)(-3x^5)$ **45.** $(2b^3)^3$ **46.** $(-x)^2(3x^4)^2$

47. $(-2)^2(3x^2)^3$ **48.** $(-x)(-x)$ **49.** $(-1)^3$ **50.** $(2y^3z^5)(4y)$

51. $(-3a^2b)(-6a^3b^2)$ **52.** $(2r^2s^3)^2$ **53.** $(-m^2n^5)^4$ **54.** $(-2)^3(-x)^3(-y^4)^2$

55. Arrange these numbers from least to greatest.

    1.04×10^3 -1.51×10^4 1.07×10^3 1.01×10^4

56. Multiply 1.2×10^6 by 7.3×10^6.

57. Write each number in scientific notation.

    a. 342 billion   **b.** 1.04 million

    c. The weight of the tongue of a blue whale is 128,000 ounces.

58. Write each number in standard notation.

    a. 4.01×10^3 **b.** 5.89×10^8

    c. The mass of Jupiter is approximately 1.9×10^{27} kg.

MORE MATH REASONING

59. If a number in scientific notation is cubed, is the power of 10 in the result three times the power in the original number? Give some examples to support your argument.

60. Picture This The cameras of Viking I provided pictures of Arsia Mons, one of Mars' largest volcanoes.
   a. The diameter of the interior of the volcano is about 19 kilometers. A football field is 120 yards by 160 feet. The area of how many football fields would equal the area of the interior of the crater?
   b. The volcano's edge reaches about 19 kilometers above the surrounding Martian terrain. Mount Everest is about 6 miles high. Which is taller? What is the difference in their heights?

61. While working the following two problems, Pete decided he had discovered a new rule for exponents. Since $4^2 = 2^4$, he felt that $a^b = b^a$. Did Pete make a new discovery? Support your answer with other examples.

62. In engineering notation, which is similar to scientific notation, the exponent for 10 must be a multiple of three. This causes the number to have one, two, or three digits before the decimal, as in 100×10^{12}. Write these numbers in scientific notation and in engineering notation.
   a. 23,246,130   **b.** 107,943,271   **c.** 3,568,410
   d. Will scientific and engineering notations for a number ever be the same? Explain.

63. The Mayan numeral system was based on groups of 20 (vigesimal) instead of the groups of 10 (decimal). The Mayans used place value, but their numerals were stacked instead of in a row. Study and complete the table of Mayan numerals below.

1	•	6	•̱	11	**f.**	16	**j.**
2	••	7	**b.**	12	**g.**	17	**k.**
3	**a.**	8	**c.**	13	•••̳	18	**l.**
4	••••	9	**d.**	14	**h.**	19	**m.**
5	——	10	**e.**	15	**i.**	0	⬯

Dividing Monomials

← CONNECT → *You've discovered patterns when you multiply monomials. Now you will investigate patterns when you divide monomials. You'll also learn to express small numbers using scientific notation and negative exponents.*

Not all powers increase as the exponent increases. Powers can also help you describe quantities that *decrease,* such as the temperature of a dead star or the amount of carbon-14 left in an ancient artifact.

EXPLORE: THE POWER OF PAPER

MATERIALS

Paper

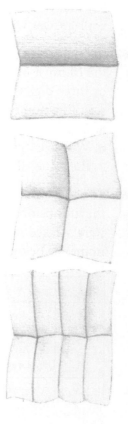

1. Fold a sheet of paper in half. How many regions are formed in the paper?

2. How many regions are formed when you fold the paper in half twice? three times? What pattern do you notice between the number of folds and the number of regions?

> **Problem-Solving Tip**
>
> Make an organized list and look for a pattern.

3. Write an expression for the number of regions formed when the paper is folded in half *n* times. Use it to predict the number of regions formed after 10 folds; 100 folds.

4. Write an expression for the portion of the whole sheet represented by one region after *n* folds. Use it to predict the portion of the whole sheet represented by one region after 10 folds; 100 folds.

5. How are the expressions you wrote in Steps 3 and 4 related? Describe how each quantity increases or decreases as the number of folds increases.

Powers with a base greater than 1 *increase exponentially* as the exponent increases. But powers *decrease exponentially* if the base is between 0 and 1, such as $\frac{1}{10}$. This is the basis for scientific notation for small numbers (numbers close to 0).

Just as 10^6 equals one million, $\frac{1}{10^6}$ equals one *millionth*. In standard notation, one millionth is written as a decimal. In scientific notation, it is written with a *negative exponent*.

Meaning		Fraction		Decimal		Scientific Notation
one millionth	$=$	$\frac{1}{10^6}$	$=$	0.000001	$=$	1.0×10^{-6}

Here are some other powers of 10.

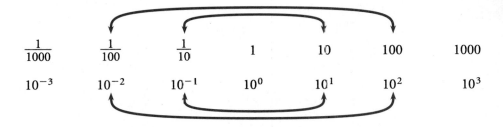

$\frac{1}{1000}$	$\frac{1}{100}$	$\frac{1}{10}$	1	10	100	1000
10^{-3}	10^{-2}	10^{-1}	10^{0}	10^{1}	10^{2}	10^{3}

Notice that powers with opposite exponents represent *reciprocals* (their product is 1). Also, notice that $10^0 = 1$, since $10^0 = 10^{1 + (-1)} = 10^1 \cdot 10^{-1} = 10 \cdot \frac{1}{10} = 1$.

For any nonzero real number a and any integer n,
$$a^0 = 1 \text{ and } a^{-n} = \frac{1}{a^n}.$$

EXAMPLE

1. Express $\frac{10^3}{10^5}$ as a power of 10.

Write out the powers in the fraction and simplify.

$$\frac{10^3}{10^5} = \frac{10 \cdot 10 \cdot 10}{10 \cdot 10 \cdot 10 \cdot 10 \cdot 10} = \frac{1}{10 \cdot 10} = \frac{1}{10^2} = 10^{-2}$$

Check by writing the expression in standard notation before dividing.

$$\frac{10^3}{10^5} = \frac{1000}{100,000} = \frac{1}{100} \text{ or } 0.01 = 10^{-2} \text{ ✔}.$$

All of the rules for powers you use are true for positive and *negative* exponents.

Recall that to multiply powers with the same base you add their exponents. To *divide* powers with the same base you *subtract* their exponents.

DIVIDING POWERS WITH LIKE BASES

For any nonzero real number a and for any integers m and n,
$$\frac{a^m}{a^n} = a^{m-n}.$$

These patterns can help you divide monomials.

EXAMPLES

Simplify each expression.

2. $\dfrac{2x^8}{4x^3}$

$\dfrac{2x^8}{4x^3} = \dfrac{2}{4} \cdot \dfrac{x^8}{x^3}$

$= \dfrac{1}{2}x^{8-3}$

$= \dfrac{1}{2}x^5$

3. $\dfrac{10x^5y^3}{2x^9y}$

$\dfrac{10x^5y^3}{2x^9y} = \dfrac{10}{2} \cdot \dfrac{x^5}{x^9} \cdot \dfrac{y^3}{y^1}$

$= 5 \cdot x^{5-9} \cdot y^{3-1}$

$= 5x^{-4}y^2$ or $\dfrac{5y^2}{x^4}$

4. A bacterium is 10 μm long. A micron (μm) is one millionth of a meter (10^{-6} m). A virus is 100 nm long. A nanometer (nm) is one billionth of a meter (10^{-9} m). Write each length in meters using scientific notation. Which organism is longer?

Bacterium	*Virus*
10 μm $= 10 \times 10^{-6}$ m	100 nm $= 100 \times 10^{-9}$ m
$= 10^1 \times 10^{-6}$ m	$= 10^2 \times 10^{-9}$ m
$= 10^{1+(-6)}$ m	$= 10^{2+(-9)}$ m
$= 10^{-5}$ m	$= 10^{-7}$ m
10 μm $= 1.0 \times 10^{-5}$ m	100 nm $= 1.0 \times 10^{-7}$ m

The bacterium is longer than the virus since 10^{-5} is greater than 10^{-7}.

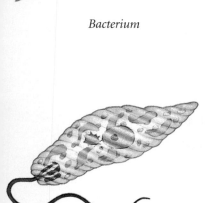

Bacterium

5. A medical illustrator wants an organism 4.8×10^{-5} meters long to appear 4.8 centimeters long in a biology book. In the caption, she needs to say how many times larger the illustration is than the organism. Find the enlargement factor.

Euglena

Let $F =$ the enlargement factor. The illustration is F times larger than the organism.

$(4.8 \times 10^{-5} \text{ m})F = 4.8 \times 10^{-2} \text{ m}$ One centimeter is 10^{-2} m.

$$F = \frac{4.8 \times 10^{-2} \text{ m}}{4.8 \times 10^{-5} \text{ m}}$$ Divide both sides by 4.8×10^{-5}.

$$= \frac{10^{-2}}{10^{-5}}$$ Simplify and solve for F.

$$= 10^{-2 - (-5)}$$ Divide the powers by subtracting exponents.

$$F = 10^{3}$$

The illustration is 10^3 or 1000 times larger than the organism.

CONSIDER

?

1. How can you simplify the fraction $\frac{a^n}{a^n}$ to show that $a^0 = 1$?

You can also simplify powers of fractions using the patterns you've discovered.

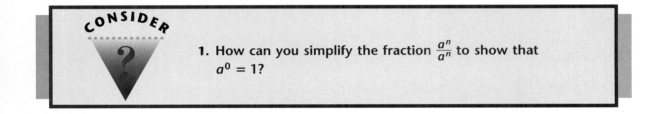

$$\left(\frac{2}{3}\right)^4 = \frac{2}{3} \cdot \frac{2}{3} \cdot \frac{2}{3} \cdot \frac{2}{3} = \frac{2 \cdot 2 \cdot 2 \cdot 2}{3 \cdot 3 \cdot 3 \cdot 3} = \frac{2^4}{3^4} = \frac{16}{81}$$

RAISING A QUOTIENT TO A POWER

For any real numbers a and b, with $b \neq 0$, and for any integer n,

$$\left(\frac{a}{b}\right)^n = \frac{a^n}{b^n}.$$

TRY IT

Simplify each expression.

a. $\dfrac{m^3}{m^6}$

b. $\dfrac{2x^6y^3}{4x^9y}$

c. $10^{-2} \div 10^2$

d. $\left(\dfrac{3}{4}\right)^4$

e. A hydrogen atom is 0.30 nanometer in diameter. A plant cell is 30 microns in diameter. Which is bigger? by what factor?

1. How does scientific notation help you to quickly get a sense of the size of a number?
2. State the rules for multiplying and dividing powers with like bases in your own words.
3. In your own words, explain how you convert powers of 10 with *negative* exponents to decimal form.
4. Is it easier to convert nanometers to meters than inches to miles? Why or why not?

Exercises

CORE

1. **Getting Started** Use these steps to simplify $\dfrac{-12x^4y^2}{3x^2y^3}$.

   a. Simplify $\dfrac{-12}{3}$.
   b. Simplify $\dfrac{x^4}{x^2}$.
   c. Simplify $\dfrac{y^2}{y^3}$.

   d. Write the simplified expression for $\dfrac{-12x^4y^2}{3x^2y^3}$.

Complete each to make a true statement.

2. $\dfrac{x^5}{x^?} = x^3$
3. $\dfrac{a^5}{a^?} = a$
4. $\dfrac{b^3}{b^3} = b^?$

Simplify each expression.

5. $\dfrac{a^3}{a}$
6. $\dfrac{r^5}{r^5}$
7. $\dfrac{d^4}{d^7}$
8. $\dfrac{8b^4}{16b^2}$

9. 1^{-5}
10. $2^0 \cdot 3^1 \cdot 3^{-1}$
11. a^0b^1
12. $x^{-5} \cdot x^{-3}$

13. $\left(\dfrac{2}{10}\right)^3$
14. $\dfrac{m^2n^3}{m^3n}$
15. $\dfrac{2x^3z^2}{-8x^5z}$
16. $\left(\dfrac{3a^3}{7b}\right)^2$

17. **Many Many Molecules** The human body has about 25 trillion blood cells. Each blood cell may contain 250 million hemoglobin molecules. Each hemoglobin molecule can carry 4 molecules of oxygen. Write in scientific notation the potential number of oxygen molecules carried in a person's blood.

Blood cells as viewed through a scanning electromicrograph.

18. Answer these questions to compare the quotients.

   a. Express $\dfrac{10^9}{10^3}$ as a power of 10.

   b. Express $\dfrac{10^3}{10^9}$ as a power of 10.

   c. Which quotient is greater? How many times greater? Tell how you decided.

19. Which shows 10 written as a power of 10?

    (a) 10^{10} (b) 10^2 (c) 10^1 (d) 10^0

20. Which shows 1 written as a power of 10?

    (a) 10^{10} (b) 10^2 (c) 10^1 (d) 10^0

Place parentheses in each expression so that the value of each is 64.

21. -2^6 **22.** 2^{32}

Simplify each expression. Write your answer in standard notation.

23. $(1.2 \times 10^8)(3.6 \times 10^4)$ **24.** $(-1.6 \times 10^3)(2.1 \times 10^5)$

25. Billions of Kilowatts The electrical energy consumption is increasing each year. The expression $1.3(1.07)^n$ can be used to predict the consumption n years from now, in billions of kilowatt-hours used annually.

    a. Approximately how many billion kilowatt-hours will be used annually 10 years from now?

    b. Approximately how many billion kilowatt-hours are used now?

    c. Approximately how many billion kilowatt-hours were used two years ago?

Industry

Each of these problems contains a mistake. Correct the mistake and tell what you think the student who made the error was thinking.

26. $(4n^4)^2 = 8n^8$ **27.** $(4n^4)^0 = n^4$ **28.** $\dfrac{3x^2y^6}{x^3y^4} = 3xy^2$

29. A sheet of paper is approximately 0.003 inch thick. You cut a piece of paper in half and stack one piece on top of the other. You cut those in half and stack all pieces on top of one another. Suppose you do this 22 times. How will your stack compare to the 185-meter-tall Seattle Space Needle? Tell how you decided.

Social Science

30. Is $(a^2)^3$ equivalent to $a^{(2^3)}$? Why or why not?

> **Problem-Solving Tip**
>
> Evaluate the expressions for a few values of a.

31. An illustrator wants a protozoan 1.1×10^{-4} meters long to appear 7.7 centimeters long on a chart. She needs to say how many times larger the illustration is than the organism. Find the enlargement factor.

Careers

32. The HIV virus is 110 nanometers long. How long is that in meters? Write your answer in scientific notation.

Science

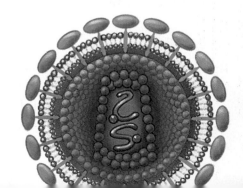

33. Line Up Three thousand polio viruses could fit end to end across a decimal point on this page. Use a millimeter ruler to judge the width of a decimal point and estimate the length of a polio virus in meters using scientific notation. Give its estimated measure in microns (μm) and in nanometers (nm).

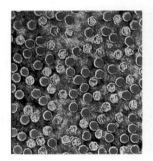

34. Which industries have a daily need to use very large numbers or very small numbers?

LOOK BACK

Write an inequality for each situation. [4-3]

35. The down payment (d) for an $11,000 car is at least 20% of the cost.

36. On Quick Flight Airline, the weight of luggage may not be more than 15 pounds.

Solve and check each equation. [7-1]

37. $|x - 9| = 4$

38. $|9 - x| = 7$

39. $|52 - x| = 36$

40. Mickey, who is $3\frac{1}{2}$ feet tall, had a $2\frac{3}{4}$-foot shadow one morning. At the same time, his sister had a 5-foot shadow. How tall is his sister? [7-4]

MORE PRACTICE

Simplify each expression.

41. $\dfrac{y^2 x}{xy^2}$

42. $\dfrac{-2x^2}{-x}$

43. $\dfrac{-3j^4 k}{-9j^5 k}$

44. $\dfrac{y^{10}}{y^{10}}$

45. $\dfrac{-20y^5}{4y^4}$

46. $\left(\dfrac{2p^3}{3p^2}\right)^4$

47. $\dfrac{150c^3 de^5}{-10c^2 de}$

48. $(-2y^2)^3$

49. $\left(\dfrac{3}{5}\right)^3$

50. 1^{-8}

51. $2^5 \cdot 3^1 \cdot 3^{-1}$

52. $a^9 b^0$

53. $\left(\dfrac{-3}{5}\right)^3$

54. $\dfrac{m^4 n^2}{m^5 n^6}$

55. 1^{-3}

56. $\dfrac{2p^2}{4p^0}$

Simplify each expression. Write your answer in standard notation.

57. $(1.3 \times 10^4)(5.1 \times 10^2)$

58. $(2.6 \times 10^3)(-1.1 \times 10^6)$

59. An illustrator wants a paramecium 7.8×10^{-4} meters long to appear 7.8 centimeters long on a chart. She needs to say how many times larger the illustration is than the organism. Find the enlargement factor.

MORE MATH REASONING

science

60. Light travels 1.86×10^5 miles in 1 second. How far does it travel in 1 year?

61. Calculate $(-1)^n$ for $n = 1, 2, 3, 4,$ and 5.
  a. What is $(-1)^{10}$? **b.** What is $(-1)^{25}$?

62. Find a value for x and a *different* value for n so that $x^n = n^x$.

63. Consider $\left(-\frac{3}{5}\right)^3$ and $\left(\frac{3}{5}\right)^{-3}$. Which is greater? Justify your response.

64. Exponential Growth The growth pattern demonstrated by bacteria is an example of exponential growth. Growth is exponential when the number in each new generation is a multiple of the number in the previous generation.

science

  a. Sketch a curve showing the exponential growth of bacteria.
  b. An assumption in the model is that all bacteria will live and reproduce. Do you think that this assumption is reasonable?
  c. Name something else that you think shows exponential growth. Explain your choice.

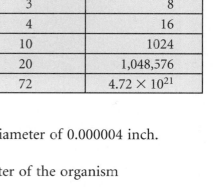

Number of Generations	Number of Bacteria
0	1
1	2
2	4
3	8
4	16
10	1024
20	1,048,576
72	4.72×10^{21}

65. A pneumonia-like organism, *Mycoplasma laidlawii,* has a diameter of 0.000004 inch.

science

  a. Write this number in scientific notation.
  b. Given that 1 inch = 2.54 centimeters, express the diameter of the organism in centimeters.
  c. Cassandra needs to make a diagram of this organism for her science project. Find the enlargement factor, if the diameter of the diagram is 4 inches.

8-1 PART D Making Connections

← CONNECT → *You've learned to use the language of polynomials and polynomial functions. You've also explored monomials, powers, and scientific notation. Economists, astronomers, and many businesspeople use these tools every day to describe, model, and make predictions.*

Modeling with polynomials helped scientists send people to the moon. Someday, it may also help send people to Mars.

You are a scientist in charge of the early planning for a new space mission. The plan is to launch a spacecraft from Earth, which will fly by Mars and Jupiter on its way to Pluto and beyond. Here are some distances you'll need to use.

Mean Distances Between Orbits

Earth and Mars 7.83×10^7 km

Mars and Jupiter 5.504×10^8 km

1. How many times farther is the distance between Mars and Jupiter than the distance between Earth and Mars?
2. Add the mean distances between orbits to find the approximate distance between the orbits of Earth and Jupiter. To add numbers in scientific notation, the powers of 10 must be the same. (Hint: First express the mean distance between Earth and Mars as a number times 10^8.)
3. If you round the distance between Mars' and Jupiter's orbits to 5.50×10^8 kilometers, how many kilometers (in standard notation) are you disregarding? What percent of the mean distance does that represent?
4. Describe some other things about your data, your calculations, or the solar system that could make the actual distance the spacecraft must travel to get to Jupiter different from the distance you found in Step 2.

REFLECT

1. How is using an exponent a shorthand for writing a product?
2. How do you know if a polynomial function is linear, quadratic, or cubic? Are there other types of polynomial functions? Explain.
3. Can you think of quantities that a space scientist would need to express in scientific notation with *negative* exponents? that a micro-biologist would need to express with *positive* exponents?

Self-Assessment

Complete each to make a true statement.

1. $2^3 \cdot 2^? = 2^7$

2. $a^7 \cdot a^? = a^7$

3. $a^5 \cdot a^? = a^0$

4. $(a^5 b^3)^2 = a^{10} b^?$

5. $\dfrac{2^?}{2^5} = 2^2$

6. $\dfrac{2^4}{2^4} = 2^?$

7. $\dfrac{a^4}{a^?} = a$

8. $\left(\dfrac{2^3}{3^4}\right)^2 = \dfrac{2^6}{3^?}$

9. Answer the following questions about the given polynomials.

  i. $(1 + x + 2x^2)$
  ii. $(x^2 - 3x)$

  a. Which polynomial is written in descending order?
  b. Which polynomial is a binomial?
  c. What is the sum of the two polynomials?
  d. What is the difference of the trinomial and the binomial?

Write each expression as a monomial if possible.

10. $m^4 \cdot m^4$

11. $m^4 + m^4$

12. $m^4 + n^4$

13. These five expressions have been simplified by a student.

  a. Which equations are true?
  b. Correct the errors.
  c. Explain why students sometimes make the errors that you found.

  i. $2x^2 + x^2 = 2x^2$
  ii. $5x^2 + 3x - 2x + 1 = 5x^2 + x + 1$
  iii. $(3x^3 + 1) - (x^3 + 1) = 2x^3 + 2$
  iv. $4x^5 - 2x^5 = 2$
  v. $10x^2 - 10x + 10x^2 = 20x^2 - 10x$

Simplify each expression.

14. $3^2 \cdot 2^2 \cdot 6^{-2}$

15. $\dfrac{3x}{x^3}$

16. $(3x^2 - 3x) + (2x^2 - x + 1)$

17. $\dfrac{r^{99}}{r^{99}}$

18. $\dfrac{2z^0}{4z^{-2}}$

19. $\left(\dfrac{2x^2}{3x^1}\right)^4$

20. $(6y^3 - 8y) - (3y)(2y^2)$

21. $(-5g^4)^2$

22. $6^{-2} \cdot 6^3 \cdot 6^0$

23. Thumbs Up It would take about 2000 red blood cells to reach across your thumbnail. Write the diameter of one red blood cell in microns ($1 \; \mu m = 10^{-6}$ m); in nanometers ($1 \; nm = 10^{-9}$ m).

24. Smallville Gets Smaller Scientists have been studying the population of Smallville. It seems that the population is decreasing each year. The population in thousands of people can be represented by $3(0.95)^t$, where t is the number of years from now.

  a. What is the population today?
  b. What is the estimated population in 10 years?
  c. Determine what the population was 2 years ago.

25. BART (Bay Area Rapid Transit) is a commuter train system with 71.5 miles of track and 34 stations.

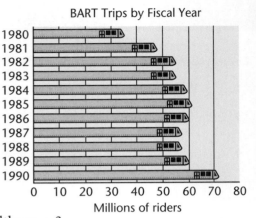

BART Trips by Fiscal Year

Millions of riders

  a. Which year showed the greatest increase in ridership?
  b. What was the average number of riders per day for 1989?
  c. It costs about $20 million annually for the electricity BART runs on. Write this number in scientific notation.

26. The sides of a rectangle have lengths $x + 6$ and widths $x - 3$.
Which equation describes the perimeter (P) of the rectangle in terms of x?
(a) $P = x^2 + 2x + 3$ (b) $P = x^2 + 3x - 18$ (c) $P = 4x + 6$ (d) $P = 2x + 3$

27. Hubble Power The Hubble telescope, launched in 1990, is able to take photos showing stars from galaxies up to 50 million light-years away. Stars once seen as a blur can now be seen clearly. Given that a light-year is approximately 6×10^{12} miles, using scientific notation, write 50 million light-years in miles.

28. Larger Than Life Microscopes are used to study organisms. If the microscope is set at 100×, this means that an organism will appear 100 times larger than its actual size.

  a. If the width of a human hair is 0.02 centimeter, how large would it appear under a microscope set at 100×? Write your answer in scientific notation.
  b. Water fleas measure approximately 9.8×10^{-3} inches long. Write this number in standard notation. How long would a flea appear under a microscope set at 1000×?

29. To Mars and Beyond Again Mars takes approximately 2 earth years to complete its orbit around the sun. Saturn takes almost 30 earth years to complete an orbit. Discuss how these facts might affect any plans made for space voyages to these planets.

30. A strain of H39 bacteria has an estimated weight of 1.0×10^{-16} grams.
  a. Write this number in standard notation.
  b. To find the weight of the H39 bacteria in tons, multiply its weight in grams by $1.1 \times 10^{-6} \frac{\text{tons}}{\text{gram}}$. What is the weight in tons?
  c. It is estimated that a blue whale weighs 1.47×10^{24} times as much as the H39 bacteria. How many tons does a blue whale weigh?

8-2 Multiplying and Factoring Polynomials

Pascal's triangle is an array of numbers that has many applications in mathematics, including multiplication of binomials. It was named for Blaise Pascal, a French mathematician who wrote about the triangle in 1653. However, earlier mathematicians knew about the magic of the triangle. Chu Shih-Chieh, a Chinese mathematician, included an illustration of the triangle in a book in 1303. Chu Shih-Chieh was a resident of Yen-shan, near modern-day Beijing.

Chu Shih-Chieh called the triangle the "old method" for working with binomials. Chinese mathematicians had been using the triangular pattern for multiplying binomials for two centuries before Chu Shih-Chieh.

Pascal's Triangle contains many number patterns that occur in algebra, geometry, and nature. Real-world problems, such as the number of varieties of pizza toppings a resturant needs to offer, can be solved by searching for patterns in Pascal's Triangle.

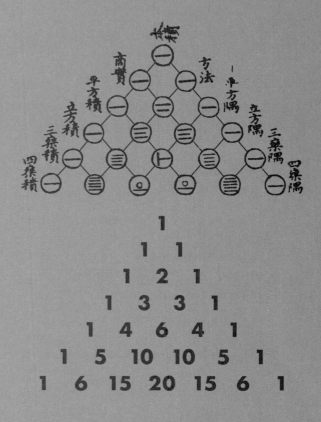

```
              1
            1   1
          1   2   1
        1   3   3   1
      1   4   6   4   1
    1   5   10   10   5   1
  1   6   15   20   15   6   1
```

1. What is similar about the two triangles? What is different?
2. Why do you think Chu Shih-Chieh never achieved the fame of Pascal?
3. Describe at least two patterns that can be seen in Pascal's Triangle.

Multiplying and Factoring

← C O N N E C T → *You've learned to multiply and divide monomials. Now you'll identify common monomial factors in terms of binomials, trinomials, and other polynomials.*

There is more than one rectangle with an area of 36.

Think of the area of a rectangle as a product. When you look for the possible dimensions of the rectangle, you look for *factors* of the product.

Factoring a number means writing it as a product of two or more numbers. You can also factor expressions with variables.

EXPLORE: HOW MANY CAN YOU FIND?

How many different ways can you model the monomial $3x^2y$ as an area of a rectangle?

1. Draw as many rectangles as you can with an area of $3x^2y$ and side lengths represented by monomials. Only use monomials with positive, integer coefficients. Label the dimensions of each of your rectangles.

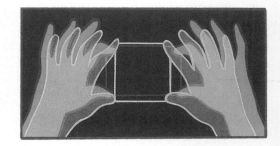

Problem-Solving Tip

Make an organized list.

2. List all the ways you found of expressing $3x^2y$ as a product of monomials.

3. Explain in writing why you think you have found all possible rectangles and products.

You've multiplied monomials together before. Using the distributive property, you can also multiply a monomial by any polynomial.

1. Multiply $3x^2$ by $2x + 5$.

$$3x^2(2x + 5) = 3x^2 \cdot 2x + 3x^2 \cdot 5 \qquad \text{Use the distributive property.}$$
$$= 6x^3 + 15x^2 \qquad \text{Simplify.}$$

TRY IT

Multiply the polynomials.

a. $x(2x^2 + 3)$ **b.** $(3x - 2)x^2$

c. Write the polynomial that represents the area of this rectangle.

In the Explore, you found different ways to factor a monomial. By *reversing* the process of distributing multiplication, you can **factor** polynomials with *more* than one term.

> **Factoring** a polynomial means writing it as a product of two or more polynomials.

Consider the trinomial $2x^3 - 10x^2 + 6x$.

The **common monomial factor** of the terms of the trinomial is $2x$. You can *factor out* the common monomial factor by dividing each term by $2x$ and using the distributive property *in reverse* to write the product.

$$2x^3 - 10x^2 + 6x = 2x(x^2 - 5x + 3)$$

We can model this product with a rectangle like the ones you drew in the Explore.

EXAMPLES

Factor each polynomial.

2. $x^2 + 2x$

The common monomial factor of both terms is x.

$$x^2 + 2x = x(x) + x(2)$$ Factor x out of each term.
$$= x(x + 2)$$ Use the distributive property in reverse.

Check your work by multiplying the factors, using the distributive property.

$$x(x + 2) = x^2 + 2x$$

3. $12x^4 - 8x^3 - 4x^2$

The common monomial factor of all three terms is $4x^2$.

> **Problem-Solving Tip**
>
> Make an organized list of the factors of the terms.

$$12x^4 - 8x^3 - 4x^2$$
$$= 4x^2(3x^2) + 4x^2(-2x) + 4x^2(-1)$$ Factor $4x^2$ out of each term.

$$= 4x^2(3x^2 - 2x - 1)$$ Use the distributive property in reverse.

Always try to factor out a monomial that contains *all* the common integer and variable factors. Such a monomial is called the **greatest common factor** of the polynomial.

 **CONSIDER**

1. Roxanne factored $12x^4 - 8x^3 - 4x^2$ as $2x^2(6x^2 - 4x - 2)$. Did she factor out the *greatest common factor*? Explain how you know.

TRY IT

Factor each polynomial.

d. $2x + 10$

e. $y^2 + 6y$

f. $18x^3 + 4x^2 - 2x$

g. $5x^4 - 20x^3 - 20x^2$

1. In your own words, explain the connection between multiplying using the distributive property and factoring.
2. How can you check whether you've factored a polynomial correctly?
3. How do you know when you've factored out the greatest common factor of a polynomial?

Exercises

CORE

1. **Getting Started** Use these steps to multiply $2x^2$ by $3x - 7$.
   a. Use the distributive property to complete this expression.
      $2x^2(3x - 7) = 2x^2 \cdot \underline{\hspace{1cm}} + 2x^2 \cdot \underline{\hspace{1cm}}$
   b. Simplify each product.

Multiply the polynomials.

2. $5x(3x^2 + 2x)$

3. $6x(8x^2 - 3x)$

4. The rectangle has length $4x + 5$ and width $3x$. Compare these ways of finding the perimeter (P).
   a. Use $P = 2\ell + 2w$. What is two times the length? two times the width? their sum?
   b. Use $P = 2(\ell + w)$. Find the sum of the original length and width. Double that sum.
   c. Is the polynomial expression for perimeter the same no matter which formula is used? Explain.

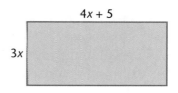

Write the polynomial that represents the area of each rectangle.

5.

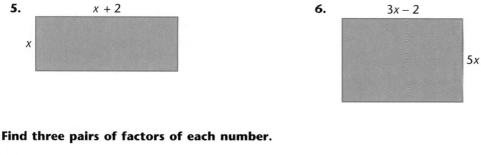

6.

7. 48

8. 1000

9. 64

Find three pairs of factors of each number.

10. Consider the trinomial $2y^3 - 14y^4 - 6y^2$.

   a. List all the factors of each term in the trinomial.

   b. Which factors are common to all three terms?

   c. What is the greatest common monomial factor of the polynomial $2y^3 - 14y^4 - 6y^2$?

   d. Use the distributive property *in reverse* to write $2y^3 - 14y^4 - 6y^2$ as a product.

Problem-Solving Tip

Make an organized list.

11. Which of these trinomials has $2x$ as its greatest common factor?

   I. $6x^2 - 24x + 18x^3$ **II.** $8x^3 + 16x^2 - 12x$ **III.** $6x^4 - 10x + 8x^3$

   (a) I only   (b) II only   (c) III only   (d) I and III   (e) I, II, and III

Factor each polynomial.

12. $x^2 - 10x$ **13.** $5x^3 + 20x^4 - 35x$ **14.** $18x^2 - 24x^4 - 12x^3$

15. Which of the following polynomials cannot be factored? Explain your answer.

   (a) $3x^2 + 13$ (b) $2x^2 + 8x + 12$

16. Find an expression for the area of the shaded region.

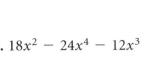

17. Deck the Yard Katrina has been hired to construct a deck in her neighbor's backyard. The deck is to be rectangular with the length twice the width. There is a pond in the middle of the yard that is 3-by-3 feet.

   a. What expression represents the amount of decking she will need to purchase?

   b. If she decides to make the deck 8 feet wide, how much decking material does she need?

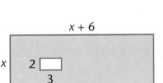

Careers

18. The area of a rectangle is $2x^2 + 10x$. What are the possible dimensions of the rectangle? Write each pair of dimensions as a product of length and width.

19. Water, Water, Everywhere Drink It Up, Inc. is considering changing the size of their water tanks to increase the amount of water stored. The tanks are all 10 meters tall, but the radius (r) varies on the different tanks. The formula for determining the volume (V) of water that the tank holds is $V = \pi r^2 h$.

   a. Since $h = 10$, what is the formula for determining the amount of water that all tanks with a height of 10 meters will hold?

   b. Write a formula to determine the amount of water that a tank could hold if the radius were increased by 3 meters.

   c. The radius of an original tank is 5 meters. How much more water could a new tank hold if the radius is increased by 3 meters?

Industry

LOOK AHEAD

20. Find the sum and the product of each pair of numbers.

	a.	b.	c.	d.	e.
sum					
number	2	8	-5	-1	4
number	12	-1	3	-1	-2
product					

21. Find each pair of numbers with the given sum and product.

	a.	b.	c.	d.	e.
sum	10	3	3	0	-5
number					
number					
product	21	2	-4	-9	-14

22. Factor out the common term.
    a. $a(x + 3) + 2(x + 3)$ **b.** $3(a + 2) + x(a + 2)$
    c. What is similar about the two answers?

23. Find two pairs of factors of each monomial.
    a. x^6 **b.** $4x^5$ **c.** $-x^3$

MORE PRACTICE

Find three pairs of factors of each monomial.

24. 84   **25.** 300   **26.** 144

27. Consider the polynomial $x^2 - 5x$.
    a. What is the greatest common monomial factor of both terms?
    b. Apply the distributive property in reverse to factor out the monomial in **27a**.
    c. Use the distributive property to check your answer.

28. Consider the polynomial $x^2 - 7x$.
    a. What is the greatest common monomial factor of both terms?
    b. Apply the distributive property in reverse to factor out the monomial in **28a**.
    c. Use the distributive property to check your answer.

29. Consider the polynomial $14y^3 - 21y - 7y^2$.
    a. List all the factors of each term that appears in the polynomial.
    b. Which factors are common to all three terms?
    c. What is the greatest common monomial factor of the polynomial
        $14y^3 - 21y - 7y^2$?

30. Which of these trinomials has $3x$ as the greatest common factor?

  I. $6x^2 - 21x^4 + 18x^3$ **II.** $6x^4 - 12x + 9x^3$ **III.** $81x^3 + 54x^2 - 18x$

  (a) I only   (b) II only   (c) III only   (d) I and III   (e) I, II, and III

31. Which of the following polynomials cannot be factored?

  (a) $3x^2 + 18$ (b) $x^2 + 3y$

Factor each polynomial.

32. $3t + 9$ **33.** $6s - 48$ **34.** $8c - 8$

35. $5x^2 - 10x$ **36.** $3b^2 + b$ **37.** $21g^2 + 7g$

38. $20a^3 + 15a^2$ **39.** $3x^2 + 9x$ **40.** $4y + 12$

41. $9h^3 + 27h$ **42.** $4d - 2d^2$ **43.** $5c^4 - 15c^2$

44. $18x^2 - 30x^4 - 12x^3$ **45.** $16f^4 - 4f^3 - 4f^2$ **46.** $6d^2 - 45d^5 - 12d^3$

47. $42k^6 + 14k^3 - 21k^2$ **48.** $54h^4 - 9h + 36h^3$ **49.** $y^3 - 2y^4 - y^2$

50. The area of a rectangle is $4x^2 + 8x$. What are the possible dimensions of the rectangle? Write each pair of dimensions as a product of length × width.

MORE MATH REASONING

51. The area of a rectangle is $x^2 + 3x$. If the width is represented by a monomial and the length is greater than the width, suggest an algebraic expression to describe the length.

52. Find the area of the gray portion of the microscope filter in terms of π. Write your answer in factored form.

53. Can I Stop in Time? The stopping distance, in feet, on certain surfaces, of an automobile can be approximated by using the polynomial $0.05x^2 + x$, where x is the speed in miles per hour.

  a. Write the polynomial in factored form.
  b. If a person is driving 20 miles per hour, how long is the stopping distance?
  c. Dale is driving 60 mi/hr on Interstate 45. He suddenly sees a stalled truck about one-fourth of a mile down the interstate. Can he stop in time?

54. If $x = 8.5$, then $\dfrac{x^2 + 2x}{x} = ?$

  (a) 7.425   (b) 10.5   (c) 17   (d) 74.25   (e) 89.25

  Tell how factoring could make the problem easier to solve.

8-2
PART B Multiplying Binomials

← C O N N E C T → *You have multiplied monomials by polynomials. Now you'll discover how to multiply two binomials with the aid of algebra tiles and other models.*

Earlier, you used algebra tiles to help you add polynomials. They can also help you to *multiply* polynomials.

EXPLORE: ALGEBRA TILE JIGSAW PUZZLE

MATERIALS

Algebra tiles

1. Draw a rectangle with height $x + 2$ and length $x + 5$, where x is the length of an x-tile. The area of this rectangle is $(x + 2)(x + 5)$.

2. Fill in the rectangle using one x^2-tile and as many x-tiles and unit tiles as you need. Be efficient with the tiles, but be sure you fill in the rectangle completely.

3. Write the polynomial modeled by the tiles you used to fill in the rectangle. Check whether this polynomial has the same value as the product $(x + 2)(x + 5)$ for a few values of x. (If not, check whether you filled in the rectangle exactly with tiles.)

4. Repeat this procedure and write polynomials for these products.
   a. $(x + 1)(x + 3)$
   b. $(x + 2)(x + 4)$

5. Describe any relationship you see between the product and polynomial expression for each rectangle.

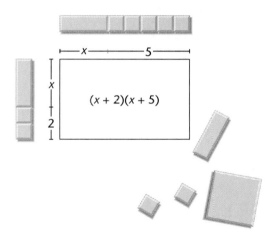

Problem-Solving Tip

Look for a pattern in the constants and coefficients.

Multiply $x + 2$ by $x + 6$.

Nicole thinks . . .

I'll use algebra tiles.

So $(x + 2)(x + 6) = x^2 + 8x + 12$.

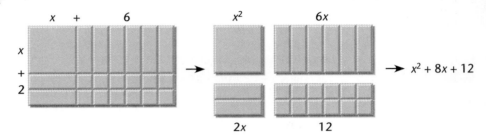

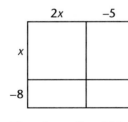

Kirti thinks . . .

I'll use the distributive property twice.

$$(x + 2)(x + 6) = x(x + 6) + 2(x + 6)$$
$$= x^2 + 6x + 2x + 12$$
$$= x^2 + 8x + 12$$

So $(x + 2)(x + 6) = x^2 + 8x + 12$.

You can also use a chart to multiply binomials and organize the terms.

EXAMPLE

Multiply $x - 8$ by $2x - 5$.

Label the terms of each binomial on one side of the chart.

	$2x$	-5
x	$2x^2$	$-5x$
-8	$-16x$	40

$2x^2 - 5x - 16x + 40$
$= 2x^2 - 21x + 40$

The chart should have four parts.　Write a product of terms in each part.　Add the parts.

So $(x - 8)(2x - 5) = 2x^2 - 21x + 40$.

CONSIDER

?

1. Explain how the chart in the Example relates to multiplying binomials using the distributive property.

TRY IT

Multiply the binomials.

a. $(x + 6)(x + 5)$ **b.** $(y + 3)(y - 1)$ **c.** $(r - 4)(r - 100)$

REFLECT

1. When you multiply two binomials, how many terms are there before you combine like terms? Does it depend on which method you use? Explain.
2. Choose any two methods for multiplying binomials (using algebra tiles, a chart, or the distributive property) and write a brief description of how they are related.
3. Which methods do you think would work for multiplying polynomials with *more* than two terms?

Exercises

CORE

1. **Getting Started** Use these steps to simplify $(x + 4)(2x - 3)$.
   a. Use the distributive property to multiply $(2x - 3)$ by x.
   b. Use the distributive property to multiply $(2x - 3)$ by 4.
   c. Combine like terms from the products in **1a** and **1b**.

2. Use this diagram of algebra tiles to find the product of $(x + 3)$ and $(x + 5)$.

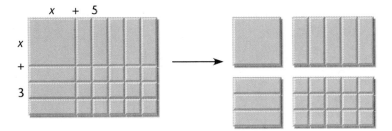

3. Place the proper monomials in each cell to show the multiplication. What is the simplified product of each?

a. $(d + 3)(d - 2)$

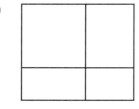

b. $(2x + 5)(3x - 1)$

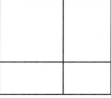

Multiply the binomials.

4. $(3x - 4)(3x - 4)$

5. $(a^2 - 9)(a^2 + 9)$

6. $(p + 4)(p - 5)$

7. $(m - 2)(m - 4)$

8. $(5s + 2)(5s + 2)$

9. $(y + 8)(y - 1)$

10. $(2x + 3.5)(x - 1.5)$

11. $(3c - 2)(-2c + 2)$

12. $(\frac{1}{2}d + 2)(2d - \frac{1}{2})$

13. Which method would you use to find each product? Why? You do not have to solve the problems.

a. $(x + 6)^2$

b. $(2x + 6)(3x + 7)$

14. Don't Invade My Space The office space in Lila's department is being modularized. Previously, it was divided into square spaces. The new plans call for each space to be 2 feet shorter in width and 3 feet greater in length.

a. Write an expression that shows the new size of each space.

b. Write your expression as a polynomial.

c. If the dimensions of each old office space were 12 feet by 12 feet, what will be the area of each new space?

15. Check It Out Blake said that the sum of the first n natural numbers can be found by $\frac{n(n + 1)}{2}$. Patricia said that $\frac{n^2 + n}{2}$ would give the sum. Who is correct? Why?

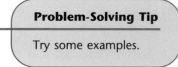

Problem-Solving Tip

Try some examples.

16. Each of these problems contains a mistake. Correct the mistake and tell what you think the student who made the error was thinking.

a. $(x + 3)^2 = x^2 + 9$

b. $(x - 7)^2 = x^2 - 14x - 49$

17. Find the product of $(2x + 5)$ and $(4x + 1)$ and the product of $(4x + 1)$ and $(2x + 5)$. Compare the two products. What algebraic property is illustrated?

18. The expression $(3x^3y^3)^2 = 9x^6y^6$, yet $(3x^3 + y^3)^2 = 9x^6 + 6x^3y^3 + y^6$. Shouldn't they be the same? Why or why not?

19. **Soaring High** The height, in feet, of a model rocket after launching can be found by using the expression $-16t^2 + 114t$, where t is time in seconds.
    a. Can this expression be simplified to $98t$? Why or why not?
    b. At launch time, how high is the rocket?
    c. Two seconds after launching, how high is the rocket?
    d. How high is the rocket after 7.5 seconds? (Be realistic!) Tell how you found your answer.

 **LOOK BACK**

Write the equation of each line with the given slope and y-intercept. [5-1]

20. slope $= -2$, y-intercept $= 5$

21. slope $= \frac{1}{2}$, y-intercept $= -2$

22. Find the intersection of $y = \sqrt{x} + 3$ and $x = 9$. [7-2]

23. Listed in the table are the actual earth-sun distances on the first day of several months of a representative year. [8-1]
    a. Write each distance in standard notation.
    b. Calculate the difference between the earth-sun distance in January and July.

Date	Distance ($\times 10^8$) (kilometers)
1 January	1.4710
1 April	1.4949
1 July	1.5208
1 October	1.4977

MORE PRACTICE

24. Use these steps to simplify $(x + 5)(3x - 1)$.
    a. Use the distributive property to multiply $(3x - 1)$ by x.
    b. Use the distributive property to multiply $(3x - 1)$ by 5.
    c. Combine like terms from the products in **24a** and **24b**.

Place the proper monomials in each cell to show the multiplication. What is the simplified product of each?

25. $(x + 12)(3x - 12)$

26. $(g - 1)(g + 1)$

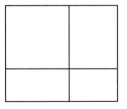

27. Which method would you use to find each product? Why? You do not have to solve the problems.

  a. $(m - 5)^2$ **b.** $(2m + 1)(m + 2)$

Multiply the binomials.

28. $(2x + 3)(x - 5)$ **29.** $(x + 10)(x - 10)$

30. $(x + 2)(x + 1)$ **31.** $(s - 25)(s - 4)$

32. $(2s + 5)(2s - 5)$ **33.** $(3y + 1)(3y + 1)$

34. $(5t + 1)(t + 5)$ **35.** $(6n - 5)(6n - 5)$

36. $(b + 4)(b - 6)$

MORE MATH REASONING

37. Find a pair of binomials whose product has following number of terms.

  a. 2 terms   **b.** 3 terms   **c.** 4 terms

38. If x and y are positive integers, which is greater, $(x + y)^2$ or $x^2 + y^2$? Why?

39. If x and y are both negative integers, which is greater, $(x + y)^2$ or $x^2 + y^2$? Tell how you decided.

40. For what values of x and y would $(x + y)^2 = x^2 + y^2$? Tell how you decided.

41. Does the product $(x + p)(x + q)$, with p and q constant, have a term $2x^2$? When would the value of the term pq be negative?

42. Express the cube of $(x + 1)$ as a polynomial in standard form.

43. Is $2.4 \times 10^2 + 4.6 \times 10^2$ equal to 7.0×10^4? If not, what is the correct answer in scientific notation?

44. How Long Is a Million? The *circumference* of a circle is the distance around. It is given by the formula $C = \pi d$. A compact disc (CD) is approximately 16 inches in circumference.

  a. If one million CDs were placed in a row, do you think the length would be much longer than 1 mile, much shorter than 1 mile, or very close to 1 mile? Find the approximate length.

  b. People listened to *long-playing* records (LPs) before CDs became available. LPs have a circumference of approximately 38 inches. How much farther would 1 million LPs stretch than 1 million CDs? Tell how you decided.

Factoring Trinomials

← CONNECT → *You've explored several ways to multiply binomials. In most cases, the result was a trinomial. Now you'll discover how to reverse the process to factor trinomials.*

When you multiplied polynomials, you started with factors and found their product. To *factor* a polynomial, you *reverse* this process. You start with the polynomial and find its factors.

EXPLORE: FACTOR FIT

MATERIALS

Algebra tiles

1. Use algebra tiles to model the trinomial $x^2 + 5x + 6$.

2. Arrange the tiles to form a rectangle. Be sure to use all the tiles you used to model the trinomial. Don't leave any gaps in your rectangle.

3. What binomials are modeled by the length and width of your rectangle? What is the product of these binomials?

4. Model each trinomial with algebra tiles. Use the same method to write each as a product of two binomials.
   a. $x^2 + 8x + 15$ b. $x^2 + 9x + 14$

5. Do you see any patterns that could help you factor trinomials *without* using algebra tiles? Explain.

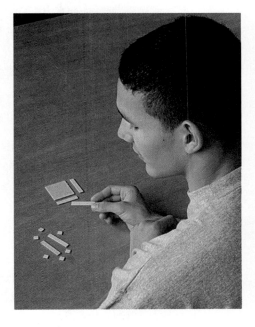

Recall that you can use algebra tiles, a chart, or the distributive property to multiply binomials. These methods can also help you *factor* trinomials.

1. Factor $x^2 - 5x - 6$.

Look for two monomials whose coefficients have a sum of -5 and a product of -6.

$1 + (-6) = -5$ and $1 \cdot (-6) = -6$

The factored trinomial results.

$x^2 - 5x - 6 = (x + 1)(x - 6)$

Check by multiplying the factors.

$(x + 1)(x - 6)$
$\quad = x(x - 6) + 1(x - 6)$
$\quad = x^2 - 6x + x - 6$
$\quad = x^2 - 5x - 6$

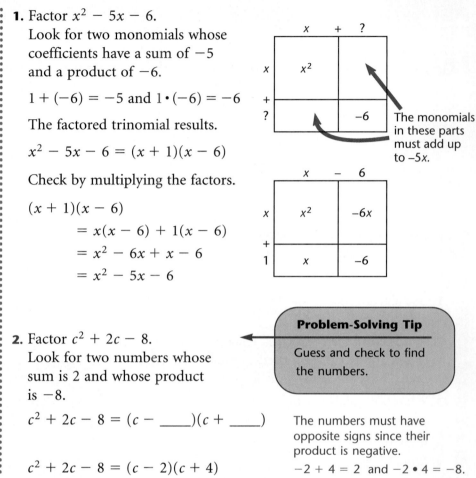

The monomials in these parts must add up to $-5x$.

Problem-Solving Tip

Guess and check to find the numbers.

2. Factor $c^2 + 2c - 8$.

Look for two numbers whose sum is 2 and whose product is -8.

$c^2 + 2c - 8 = (c - \underline{\quad})(c + \underline{\quad})$

The numbers must have opposite signs since their product is negative.

$c^2 + 2c - 8 = (c - 2)(c + 4)$

$-2 + 4 = 2$ and $-2 \cdot 4 = -8$.

When the terms of a trinomial have a common factor, first factor it out.

3. Factor $-2y^2 + 14y - 20$.

$-2y^2 + 14y - 20$
$\quad = -2(y^2 - 7y + 10)$

Factor out the common factor -2.

Look for two numbers whose sum is -7 and whose product is 10.

$-2y^2 + 14y - 20$
$\quad = -2(y - \underline{\quad})(y - \underline{\quad})$

Both numbers must be negative because their sum is negative and their product is positive.

$-2y^2 + 14y - 20$
$\quad = -2(y - 2)(y - 5)$

$-2 + (-5) = -7$ and $-2 \cdot -5 = 10$.

CONSIDER

?

1. How can you use the result of Example 3 to help you quickly factor the trinomial $-2y^3 + 14y^2 - 20y$?

TRY IT

Factor each trinomial.
a. $x^2 + 11x + 30$ **b.** $m^2 - 4m - 45$ **c.** $-3y^2 + 24y + 60$

When you factor trinomials, first factor out the greatest common factor of the terms. Then look for the binomial factors.

REFLECT

1. In your own words, describe how you factor a trinomial using the following.
   a. algebra tiles   **b.** a chart   **c.** the distributive property
2. If two binomial factors are the same, what geometric figure can you use as a model for their product? Why?
3. Briefly compare factoring using a chart with factoring using the distributive property.

Exercises

CORE

1. **Getting Started** Answer the following questions about the given rectangle.
   a. What polynomial is represented by the area of the rectangle?
   b. What are the dimensions of the sides of the rectangle?
   c. Write the area of the polynomial as the product of two factors.

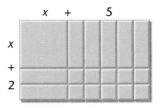

Find three pairs of factors of each product.

2. 42   **3.** 100   **4.** 24

5. Show $x^2 + 7x + 10$ as a rectangle.
Complete the equation: $x^2 + 7x + 10 = (x \underline{\hspace{1cm}})(x \underline{\hspace{1cm}})$.

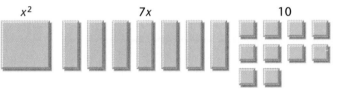

6. Use these steps to factor $x^2 - 7x + 12$.
    a. List all possible pairs of positive and negative factors of 12.
    b. Find the sum of each pair of factors.
    c. Which pair has a sum of -7?
    d. Write the binomial factors of $x^2 - 7x + 12$.

Complete each equation.

7. $x^2 + 8x + 15 = (x + \underline{\hspace{1cm}})(x + \underline{\hspace{1cm}})$
8. $x^2 + 7x - 18 = (x \underline{\hspace{1cm}} 9)(x \underline{\hspace{1cm}} 2)$

9. $x^2 - 3x - 18 = (x \underline{\hspace{1cm}} 6)(\underline{\hspace{1cm}} 3)$
10. $x^2 - 15x - 100 = (x - 20)(\underline{\hspace{1cm}})$

Factor each trinomial. Check by multiplying the factors.

11. $x^2 + 6x + 8$
12. $x^2 + 5x + 6$
13. $e^2 - 24e - 25$

14. $x^2 + 7x + 6$
15. $x^2 - x - 6$
16. $a^2 - 9a + 14$

17. $b^2 + 3b - 40$
18. $c^2 - 10c - 24$
19. $d^2 + 13d + 12$

20. How many values are possible for b if $x^2 + bx - 12$ is factorable?

> **Problem-Solving Tip**
>
> Make an organized list of the integer factors of -12.

21. Suppose you used algebra tiles to factor $x^2 + 4x + 5$ and made these arrangements.

What does this suggest about the polynomial $x^2 + 4x + 5$?

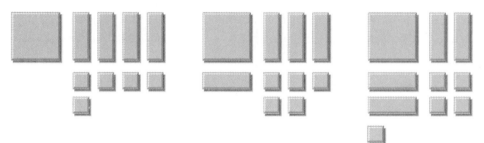

22. Each student in the cooperative group found a different answer when factoring $12 - 7x + x^2$. Who is right? Explain.

Timmy	Janel	Liz	Mitch
$(x - 4)(x - 3)$	$(3 - x)(4 - x)$	$(4 - x)(3 - x)$	$(x - 3)(x - 4)$

23. Snapdragon Genes Pink snapdragons (RW) have a gene for red flowers and a gene for white flowers. Offspring of pink snapdragons can be red (RR), pink (RW), or white (WW), depending on the genes they inherit.

a. Expand $(0.5R + 0.5W)^2$.

b. The coefficients of the square trinomial in **23a** are the probabilities of pink snapdragons having red (R^2), pink (RW), and white (W^2) offspring. Find each probability.

LOOK AHEAD

24. Copy and complete the table.

n	$\frac{1}{2}n$	$\left(\frac{1}{2}n\right)^2$
	1	
	2	
	3	
	4	
10	5	25
	6	
	7	
	8	
	9	

25. Copy and complete the table.

n	$\frac{1}{2}n$	$\left(\frac{1}{2}n\right)^2$
	-1	
	-2	
	-3	
	-4	
-10	-5	25
	-6	
	-7	
	-8	
	-9	

26. Copy and complete the table of values. Which of the expressions in the table are equivalent?

x	$x^2 + 6x + 9$	$(x - 3)^2$	$(x + 3)^2$	$x^2 - 6x + 9$	$x^2 - 9$
-3					
-1					
0					
1					
3					

Multiply the binomials.

27. $(x + 1)(x + 1)$ **28.** $(x - 1)(x - 1)$ **29.** $(x + 1)(x - 1)$

MORE PRACTICE

Find three pairs of factors of each product.

30. 36   **31.** 400   **32.** 54

33. Answer the following questions about the given rectangle.
  a. What polynomial is represented by the rectangle?
  b. What are the dimensions of the sides of the rectangle?
  c. Write the polynomial as the product of factors.

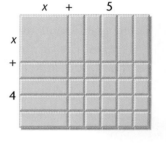

34. Show $x^2 + 8x + 15$ as a rectangle.
Complete the equation: $x^2 + 8x + 15 = (x \underline{\quad})(x \underline{\quad})$.

Complete each equation.

35. $k^2 + 9k + 18 = (k \underline{\quad})(k \underline{\quad})$ **36.** $k^2 + 3k - 18 = (k \underline{\quad} 6)(k \underline{\quad} 3)$

37. $k^2 - 3k - 18 = (k \underline{\quad} 6)(k \underline{\quad} 3)$ **38.** $k^2 - 9k + 18 = (k - 6)(\underline{\quad})$

Factor each polynomial. Check by multiplying the factors.

39. $3t + 9$ **40.** $3b^2 + b$ **41.** $a^2 + 7a + 12$

42. $u^2 - 7u + 10$ **43.** $t^2 + 8t - 48$ **44.** $f^2 - 10f - 24$

45. $h^2 + 13h + 42$ **46.** $a^2 - 23a - 50$ **47.** $x^2 - 0.8x + 0.16$

48. $w^2 + 16w + 64$ **49.** $g^2 - 16g + 64$ **50.** $c^2 - 30c - 64$

MORE MATH REASONING

51. Find the area of any one of the smaller rectangles.
Tell what you did to find your solution.

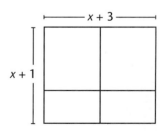

52. In forming a rectangle to factor $x^2 + 7x + 6$ with algebra tiles, how does the number 6 help you decide how to form the rectangle?

53. What is the area of the triangle? of the whole figure?

Area of a triangle

$A = \frac{1}{2}bh$

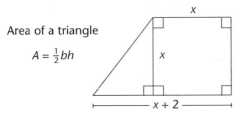

54. If $(x + 2)(x + 3) = x^2 + 5x + 6$ models a rectangle, what is modeled by $(x + 1)(x + 2)(x + 3)$? Explain.

55. Triangular Numbers These figurate numbers are called triangular numbers.

Blaise Pascal (1623–1662)

a. Why do you think the numbers are called triangular numbers?

b. Draw a picture of the next two triangular numbers.

c. Copy and complete the table.

Figure Number (d)	Number of Dots (n)
1	1
2	3
3	6
4	
5	
6	
10	

d. The triangular numbers appear in Pascal's Triangle. Find them.

e. The formula for the sum of consecutive numbers, $d = \frac{n(n + 1)}{2}$, will give you the triangular numbers. Use this formula to find the one-hundredth triangular number.

f. If you add any two consecutive triangular numbers, what kind of figurate number do you get? Rearranging the dots in two of the consecutive triangular numbers may help you see why this happens.

Patterns in Factors and Products

← **C O N N E C T** → *You've explored ways to multiply binomials and factor trinomials. Now you will look at some special patterns and strategies for multiplying and factoring.*

Recognizing *squares*—both geometric and algebraic—can reveal patterns that can help you multiply and factor polynomials.

EXPLORE: PAPER PATTERNS

MATERIALS

Paper, Scissors

1. Choose two convenient lengths, *a* and *b*, with *a* > *b*. Cut out an *a*-by-*a* square, a *b*-by-*b* square, and two *a*-by-*b* rectangles from a piece of paper. What is the total area of all these figures in terms of *a* and *b*?

2. Assemble the shapes into another geometric figure. What shape does it have? What is its area? Explain how you know.

3. What are the dimensions of the new figure? Write a *different* expression for the area in terms of these dimensions.

4. Compare the two expressions you found for the area of the figure. Explain why the expressions are equivalent, using properties of algebra.

5. Trace the *b*-by-*b* square in the corner of the *a*-by-*a* square. Then cut out the traced corner. What is the area of the new figure that remains? Explain how you know.

6. Make a straight cut in the new figure and arrange the two pieces to form a rectangle.

 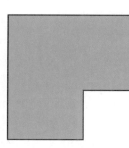 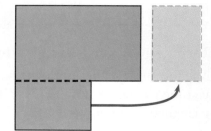

7. What are the lengths of the sides of the rectangle in terms of *a* and *b*? What is the area of the rectangle? How does it compare with the area you found in step 5?

You can see special patterns when you square binomials. The resulting polynomials are called **square trinomials.**

$$(x + 5)^2 = (x + 5)(x + 5)$$
$$= x^2 + 10x + 25$$

The coefficient of the middle term is *twice* the constant term in the binomial.

$$(x - 5)^2 = (x - 5)(x - 5)$$
$$= x^2 - 10x + 25$$

The last term is the square of the constant term in the binomial.

TRY IT

Write each power as a product and multiply.
a. $(x + 10)^2$ 　　　　　　　　　　**b.** $(y - 8)^2$

These patterns are true when you square *any* sum or difference of real numbers.

> For any real numbers a and b,
> $(a + b)^2 = a^2 + 2ab + b^2$ and $(a - b)^2 = a^2 - 2ab + b^2$.

1. How many different ways can you complete the polynomial x^2 _____ + 49 to make a square trinomial?

Another pattern occurs when you multiply binomials with opposite constant terms.

$$(x + 5)(x - 5) = x^2 + 5x - 5x - 25 = x^2 - 25$$

The middle terms cancel.

The result is a **difference of two squares.**

> For any real numbers a and b, $(a + b)(a - b) = a^2 - b^2$.

Factor $12x^2 - 48$.

$12x^2 - 48 = 12(x^2 - 4)$ Factor out the common factor, 12.

$= 12(x + 2)(x - 2)$ Factor the difference of squares.

Check by multiplying the factors.

$12(x + 2)(x - 2) = 12(x^2 - 4) = 12x^2 - 48$

TRY IT

Factor each polynomial.

c. $x^2 + 12x + 36$ **d.** $x^2 - 49$ **e.** $y^2 - 22y + 121$

REFLECT

1. What questions should you ask yourself to determine whether a trinomial is a square trinomial?

2. What questions should you ask yourself to determine whether a binomial is the difference of two squares?

3. If two square trinomials have the same x^2-term but opposite x-terms, what can you say about their constant terms?

4. Explain how this photo models a polynomial.

Exercises

CORE

1. Getting Started Consider the square of the binomial $d - 10$.
   a. Multiply $d - 10$ by $d - 10$.
   b. What is the relationship between the last term of the polynomial and the constant term of the binomial?
   c. What is the relationship between the coefficient of the middle term of the polynomial and the constant term of the binomial?

Write each power as a product and multiply.

2. $(x + 6)^2$ **3.** $(y - 12)^2$

Tell whether each polynomial expression is a square trinomial. Explain how you know.

4. $x^2 - 2x + 1$

5. $s^2 + 18s + 81$

6. $n^2 - 14n - 49$

Tell whether each binomial is the difference of two squares. Explain how you know.

7. $h^2 - 169$

8. $33b^2 - 1$

9. $k^2 + 144$

10. If you factor $2x$ out of $6x^3 + 4x^2$, have you chosen the greatest common factor? Explain.

11. What polynomial multiplied by $x - 2$ equals $x^2 - 4$?

12. What polynomial multiplied by $y + 7$ equals $y^2 + 14y + 49$?

Factor each polynomial completely.

13. $c^2 - 16$

14. $a^2 + 10a + 25$

15. $y^2 - y - 72$

16. $3m^2 - 48$

17. $11p^2 - 66p + 99$

18. $8x^3 - 8x$

19. Batter Up A batter hits a pop fly. The polynomial $96t - 16t^2$ represents the height of the baseball, in feet, at t seconds.
a. Write the polynomial in factored form.
b. How high is the ball after 3 seconds?

20. Kris factored the polynomial $12x^4 - 6x^3 - 18x^2$ into $6x(2x^3 - x^2 - 3x)$. It was marked wrong on her paper. What did she do wrong? Correct her solution.

21. If $a = 3$ and $b = 1$, find the value of each polynomial.
a. $(a - b)^2$
b. $a^2 - 2ab - b^2$
c. $a^2 - 2ab + b^2$
d. Which two expressions are equivalent?

22. Help Is on the Way A flare is launched from a life raft. The expression $128t - 16t^2$ represents the height of the flare, in feet, after t seconds.
a. Write the expression in factored form.
b. How high is the flare after 1 second? after 8 seconds?
c. How did the factored form make the expression easier to evaluate?

23. $(0.56)^2 - (0.55)^2 = ?$
(a) 0.00111   (b) 0.0111   (c) 0.111   (d) 1.11   (e) 11.1

24. Given $x = 501$ and $y = 500$, which is greater, $(x + y)(x - y)$ or 1000? Explain.

25. Which is greater, $0.7x + 0.9y$ or $0.7(x + y)$? Tell how you decided.

Solve each system of equations. Check your solutions. [6-2]

26. $y = -2x + 5$
$y = x + 2$

27. $y = 3x - 6$
$y = 4x - 11$

28. $2x + y = 8$
$4x - 2y = 8$

29. Given A (6, 5) and B (4, 2), answer the following. [7-3]
  a. Find the distance from A to B.
  b. Find the taxi distance from A to B.
  c. Find the midpoint of segment AB.
  d. Find the slope of segment AB.

30. The U.S. federal debt was 4.4747 trillion dollars in January 1994. Write this number in scientific notation and in standard notation. [8-1]

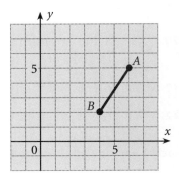

MORE PRACTICE

Write each power as a product and multiply.

31. $(x + 15)^2$

32. $(y - 20)^2$

33. $\left(s + \frac{1}{2}\right)^2$

Factor each polynomial.

34. $m^2 - 144$

35. $x^2 - 18x + 81$

Tell whether each polynomial expression is a square trinomial.

36. $h^2 - 16h - 64$

37. $m^2 + 14m + 56$

38. $x^2 - 22x + 121$

Tell whether each binomial is the difference of two squares.

39. $x^2 - 88$

40. $u^2 - 400$

41. $d^2 + 9$

42. If you factor $3x$ out of $6x^3 + 18x^2$ is the expression completely factored? Explain.

Factor each polynomial.

43. $d^2 - 16$

44. $s^2 + 12s + 36$

45. $z^2 - z - 42$

46. $2x^3 + 18x^2 - 6x$

47. $3m^2 - 75$

48. $15p^2 - 45p + 30$

49. $t^2 - t - 6$

50. $x^2 + x - 6$

51. $3d^2 + 30d + 75$

52. $4y^2 - 4$

53. $2t^2 + 4t + 2$

54. $5x^2 - 15x - 20$

MORE MATH REASONING

55. Factor $x^4 - 3x^2 - 4$.

56. Which polynomial does not belong? Why?
   (a) $x^2 - 1$ (b) $(x - 1)^2$ (c) $(x - 1)(x + 1)$ (d) $x^2 - 1^2$

57. If $x^2 - 9 = (17)(23)$, which of the following could be the value of x?
   (a) 8   (b) 14   (c) 20   (d) 26

58. Factor $x^{2a + 3} + x^{2a}$.

59. Squares, Squares, and More Squares Diophantus, a Greek
mathematician, studied problems that led to equations that
had more than one solution. These problems were later
called Diophantine equations. Here is one such problem
studied by an Egyptian mathematician, Hypatia.

History

    *"Find a number such that it is the sum of two squares
    and its square is also the sum of two squares."*

  a. Would this be true for the number 5? Could you write
    5 as the sum of two squares and its square also as the
    sum of two squares?

  b. Hypatia found that there were many solutions. Some of the solutions took
    the form of $4n + 1$, where $n = 1, 2, 3,$ and so on. If we let $n = 3$, what is
    $4n + 1$? Is this number the sum of two squares? What about its square? Is
    $(4n + 1)^2$ the sum of two squares?

  c. Try another number and substitute it into $4n + 1$ and $(4n + 1)^2$. Does it
    work? (Hint: Try numbers that will make $4n + 1$ a prime number.)

60. Cut Ups Show how each figure can be reassembled into a square with a single
cut. What is the side length of each square?

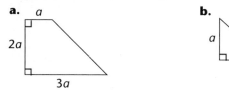
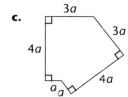

61. Multiply the polynomials.
  a. $(x + 1)(x^2 - x + 1)$
  b. $(x + 1)(x^3 - x^2 + x - 1)$
  c. $(x + 1)(x^4 - x^3 + x^2 - x + 1)$
  d. Without performing the multiplication, predict the product of
    $(x + 1)(x^5 - x^4 + x^3 - x^2 + x - 1)$.
  e. What types of patterns do you see in the factors and the products? Find a
    new product that follows this pattern.

Making Connections

←CONNECT→ *You've learned to multiply and factor polynomials using geometric and algebraic methods. Factoring is one skill that will later help you solve some polynomial equations that arise in engineering and business applications.*

You've used the distributive property to square binomials. You can also use the property to find cubes and higher powers of binomials.

EXPLORE: THE POWER OF PASCAL

1. Use repeated multiplication to find each power of $x + 1$. Record your results in a chart. Write the exponents in one column and the products in another.
   a. $(x + 1)^0$ (Hint: What is a^0?)
   b. $(x + 1)^1$
   c. $(x + 1)^2$
   d. $(x + 1)^3$ (Hint: Multiply $(x + 1)(x + 1)^2$.)
   e. $(x + 1)^4$

2. Look at Pascal's Triangle. Describe the relationship between its entries and the products in your chart.

3. Find the numbers on the next two rows of Pascal's Triangle, using the patterns you see in the triangle itself.

4. Use the relationships that you found to raise each binomial to the power shown.
   a. $(x + 1)^5$ **b.** $(x + 1)^6$ **c.** $(x + 1)^{10}$

5. Describe how you can find the coefficients of $(x + 1)^n$ using Pascal's Triangle.

Anonymous, *Travelers Among Valleys and Peaks,* Jin Dynasty (1115–1234), China. Hanging Scroll, Ink on paper. Asian Art Museum of San Francisco, The Avery Brundage Collection.

1. How many factors can a trinomial have? Give examples to explain your answer.
2. How many terms can the product of two binomials have? Give examples.
3. a. Can a binomial of degree 2 have two binomial factors? If so, give an example.
   b. Can a binomial of degree 1 have two binomial factors? If so, give an example.

Self-Assessment

Describe your first step in multiplying these polynomials.

1. $3x^2(4x - 5)$

2. $(x - 3)(5x - 1)$

3. a. Write a polynomial to represent the area of the pond.
   b. Write a polynomial to represent the area of the pond and the lawn.
   c. Write a polynomial to represent the area of the lawn.

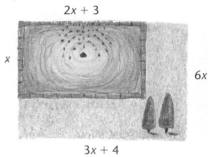

Without actually multiplying, determine how many terms the simplified product will have. Then check your answer by multiplying.

4. $(x + 2)^2$

5. $(x + 2)(x - 2)$

6. $(x - 4)(x - 4)$

7. A rectangle with an area $6x^2 + 13x + 5$ is modeled using algebra tiles. What are the dimensions of the rectangle in terms of x?
(a) $(2x + 5)(3x + 1)$ (b) $(x + 1)(x + 5)$
(c) $(2x + 1)(3x + 5)$ (d) $(2x + 3)(3x + 2)$
(e) not here

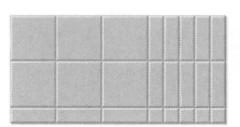

Each problem contains typical mistakes made by students. Determine the mistake(s) made in each problem and then factor it if it can be factored. If not, write "cannot be factored."

8. $x^2 + 6x - 7 = (x - 7)(x + 1)$

9. $x^2 + 9 = (x + 3)(x + 3)$

10. $2x^3 - 6x^2 + 2x = 2x(x^2 - 3x)$

11. $5x^3 - 125x = 5x(x^2 - 25)$

12. Which polynomial does not belong? Why?
(a) $3a + 2ab$ (b) $6c^2 + 3a$ (c) $3a^2 + 3a$ (d) $18b^2 + a$

13. Write the area of the shaded region in factored form.

14. Evaluate the following expressions for the value $x = -5$.
  a. $2x^2 + 8x - 10$ **b.** $2(x^2 + 4x - 5)$
  c. $2(x + 5)(x - 1)$

15. Which shows the correct factorization of $x^2 - 11x - 42$?
Tell how you decided.
  (a) $(x + 14)(x - 3)$ (b) $(x + 6)(x + 7)$
  (c) $(x - 14)(x + 3)$ (d) $(x - 6)(x - 7)$

16. The surface area of a cylinder can be found using the
expression $2\pi r^2 + 2\pi rh$.
  a. Write the expression in factored form.
  b. Use the expression to find the amount of aluminum
    needed to make a can with a radius of 7 centimeters
    and a height of 10 centimeters.

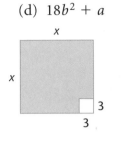

17. Match each expression with the method or methods you would use
to factor the polynomial. You can use a method more than once.
  a. $x^2 + 10x + 25$ **i.** remove a common factor
  b. $12x^2 + 48$ **ii.** factor a trinomial
  c. $x^2 - 1$ **iii.** factor the difference of two squares
  d. $2x^4 - 18x^2$ **iv.** factor a square trinomial

18. Pizza Pizza The local pizza place offers plain pizza or different toppings you

can choose to put on the pizza. Let's look at the number of choices that a
person has when ordering pizza.
  a. Suppose the pizza house offered only plain pizza.
    How many choices would a customer have when
    ordering pizza?
  b. If there was one topping, how many choices would
    there be?
  c. How many choices if the place offered two
    toppings? three toppings?
  d. Can you find the answers from **18a–c** in Pascal's
    Triangle? Use the triangle to help you find the
    number of choices if there are six toppings.
  e. If the pizza place wants to run the advertisement
    "Pizza Palace offers you over 1000 different types of
    pizzas," what is the minimum number of toppings
    they must offer?

19. Arjelia runs a bakery. She is creating a special cake box from a piece of cardboard measuring 20 by 25 centimeters. She cuts out regions of x^2 so that she can fold up the flaps.

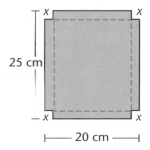

 a. What are the dimensions of the box?
 b. If $x = 2$ centimeters, what is the volume of the box?
 c. Could she use 10-centimeter squares for the corners? Why or why not?

20. Fossil-fuel plants use coal, gas, or oil to produce electricity.

 a. What percent of U.S. electricity came from nonfossil-fuel plants?
 b. Suppose you were testifying before Congress in 1992. Write a brief paragraph to explain how you would use this chart to support your position on energy used to produce electricity in the United States.

Energy Sources for the Production of Electricity in the United States

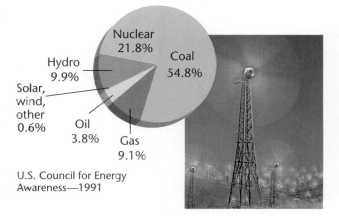

U.S. Council for Energy Awareness—1991

21. The cost (c) to drive a car at (s) mi/hr is given by the function $c = 0.02s^2 - 1.3s + 30$. Use this formula to find the cost of driving at 55 mi/hr and the cost of driving at 75 mi/hr. Who might use this information? Why?

22. Watch the Bouncing Ball A tennis ball bounces up from the ground at approximately 8 meters per second. The expression $8t - 5t^2$ gives the approximate height of the ball, in meters, at t seconds.

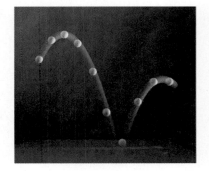

 a. Write the expression in factored form.
 b. At $t = 0$, how high is the ball?
 c. How high is the ball at 1 second?
 d. What would a negative result mean? Try a few values for t. Do you have much time to prepare to hit the ball?

23. Solve this logic problem, which dates back to eighth-century writings.

 A farmer needs to take his goat, wolf, and cabbage across the river. His boat can only accommodate him and either his goat, wolf, or cabbage. If he takes the wolf with him, the goat will eat the cabbage. If he takes the cabbage, the wolf will eat the goat. Only when the man is present are the cabbage and goat safe from their respective predators. How does he get everything across the river?

Chapter 8 Review

In Chapter 8, you began working with functions and expressions that are not linear. Polynomial functions and expressions provide the tools for working with more complicated applications. The rules of exponents and scientific notation help organize the operations of monomials, which are special polynomials.

KEY TERMS

Binomial [8-1]

Common monomial factor [8-2]

Cubic function [8-1]

Degree of a polynomial expression [8-1]

Difference of two squares [8-2]

Factor [8-2]

Greatest common factor [8-2]

Monomial [8-1]

Polynomial expression [8-1]

Polynomial function [8-1]

Quadratic function [8-1]

Scientific notation [8-1]

Square trinomial [8-2]

Standard notation [8-1]

Trinomial [8-1]

Tell whether each sentence is true or false. If it is false, change the underlined word or phrase to make the sentence true.

1. The polynomial $x^2 - 2x - 1$ is an example of a <u>monomial</u>.

2. The polynomial $x^2 - 1$ is an example of the <u>difference</u> of <u>squares</u>.

3. Match each phrase with a polynomial function. Explain your choice.
  a. linear function
  b. quadratic function
  c. cubic function
  i. $y = x^3 + 1$
  ii. $y = -6x^2 - x$
  iii. $y = x + 1$

CONCEPTS AND APPLICATIONS

4. Match each algebraic expression with an equivalent algebraic expression. [8-1]
  a. $5x^2 - x + 1 - 2x^2 + x + 1$
  b. $2x - 1 - x + 2$
  c. $-x^2 + 2x - 3 + 2x^2 - x + 2$
  i. $x + 1$
  ii. $3x^2 + 2$
  iii. $x^2 + x - 1$

5. An object with mass m kg moving at velocity v m/sec has kinetic energy $K = \dfrac{mv^2}{2}$ joules. Find the kinetic energy of a snail with mass 2×10^{-3} kg moving at 6×10^{-4} m/sec. Write your answer in scientific notation. [8-1]

Simplify each expression. [8-1]

6. $(x^3 + 4x^2 - x - 3) + (x^3 + x^2 + x - 5)$ **7.** $(-3x^2 - 6x + 1) - (-2x^2 - x + 1)$

8. $x^9(x^{-7})$ **9.** $-(x^2)(x)$ **10.** $(x^2)^3$

11. $(2x^2)x^0$ **12.** $\dfrac{2xy^2}{x^2y}$ **13.** $(4x^2 - 3) + (2x^3 + 6x)$

14. Which of these algebraic expressions is a binomial? [8-1]
    I. $x^2 - x + 1$ **II.** x^2 **III.** $(x + 1)(x - 5)$ **IV.** $x + 1$
    (a) I   (b) II   (c) III   (d) IV   (e) not here

15. Explain why $(125)(25)(5) = 5^6$. [8-1]

16. Write an algebraic expression for the area of the unshaded part of the square. What is the area if $x = 5$? [8-1]

17. The atomic mass unit (amu) is a unit used in chemistry. One amu $= 1.6605 \times 10^{-24}$ g. Write the value of 1 amu, in grams, in standard notation. [8-1]

18. Write Avogadro's number (N) in scientific notation. [8-1]

$$N = 602{,}210{,}000{,}000{,}000{,}000{,}000{,}000 \, \frac{\text{particles}}{\text{mole}}$$

19. When the sun, moon, and earth line up as shown, the two triangles are similar and a solar eclipse occurs. The ratio of the diameter of the sun to the diameter of the moon is equal to the ratio of the distance (from earth) to the sun and the distance (from earth) to the moon.

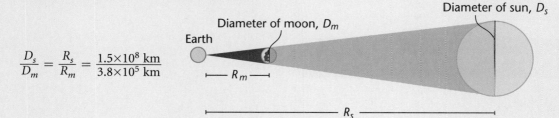

$$\frac{D_s}{D_m} = \frac{R_s}{R_m} = \frac{1.5 \times 10^8 \text{ km}}{3.8 \times 10^5 \text{ km}}$$

Write this ratio in standard notation. [8-1]

Multiply the polynomials. [8-2]

20. $3(12x + 9)$ **21.** $2x(3x^2 - 15x + 1)$ **22.** $(x + 3)(x + 7)$

23. $(x + 1)(x + 1)$ **24.** $(x + 1)(x - 1)$ **25.** $(3x + 1)(4x - 5)$

26. Are $(x + 3)^2$ and $(x^2 + 3^2)$ equivalent expressions? Explain. [8-2]

Factor each polynomial. [8-2]

27. $3x^2 - 6$ **28.** $5x^3 - 50x^2 + 80x$ **29.** $x^2 - 9$ **30.** $x^2 + 16x + 64$

31. Each circular end of this cylinder has area πr^2 and the vertical face has area $2\pi rh$. Which factored expression represents the total surface area of the cylinder? [8-2]

(a) $\pi r(1 + 2h)$ (b) $2\pi r(r + h)$ (c) $\pi r(r + 2h)$ (d) not here

CONCEPTS AND CONNECTIONS

32. Industry Polynomial functions are often used to model costs, sales, and profits. It costs a company $C = 0.5x^2 + 0.4x + 3.2$ dollars to produce a large sheet of plastic film x millimeters thick. The film sells for $S = 0.4x^2 - 0.2x + 6.2$ dollars per sheet.

a. The sales price minus the cost gives the profit (P) the company makes on each sheet of film. Write the profit as a function of x.

b. Find the profits for a sheet 1 mm thick and a sheet 2 mm thick.

c. Can the film be too thick for the company to produce profitably? Explain.

SELF-EVALUATION

Write a paragraph about the language and rules of algebra you've learned in this chapter. Mention how scientific notation might be helpful to you. Write down which parts of the chapter were difficult for you and which sections you need to study further in order to better understand the chapter.

Chapter 8 Assessment

TEST

1. Which of these expressions are equivalent? Explain how you know.

(a) 2   (b) $2x^2$ (c) $x^2 + 1$ (d) $3x^2 + 1 - x^2 - 1$

Answer the following questions about the given polynomials.

2. Which polynomial is written in descending order?   **A.** $-7x^2 - 3x$

3. Which polynomial is a binomial?   **B.** $11 + 5x^4 + 3x^2$

4. What is the sum of the two polynomials?

5. Subtract polynomial A from polynomial B.

6. Find three pairs of factors for the monomial $24xy$.

7. Explain how 10^0 is different from 10^1.

8. Consider the polynomial $4x^3y^2 - 16x^2y^3 + 20x^3y^3$.
   a. List all of the factors of each term of the polynomial.
   b. What is the greatest common monomial factor of the polynomial?

9. Kick Off The height of a football after kick-off is given by the expression $25t - 5t^2$. The height of the football is measured in meters. The variable t represents the number of seconds after the kick.
   a. Write the expression in factored form.
   b. At $t = 0$, where is the ball?
   c. How high is the ball after 1 second?
   d. Evaluate some values of t to estimate when the ball starts downward.

Simplify each expression.

10. $4x(x - 12)$ **11.** $(x + 4)(x + 7)$ **12.** $x^2(3x^3 + 15x^2 - 10)$ **13.** $4x^4(x^7)$

14. $\dfrac{x^0y^5}{y}$ **15.** $\dfrac{-12x^4y^5}{6x^7}$ **16.** $\dfrac{3x(x - 5)}{3x}$ **17.** $\dfrac{-x^4}{3x^2}$

18. Write a polynomial to represent the area of each region.
   a. unshaded rectangle
   b. larger rectangle
   c. shaded region
   d. Find the area of the shaded region if $x = 7$.

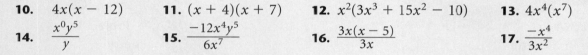

19. Which is the correct factorization of $x^2 - 9x - 36$? Tell how you decided.
   (a) $(x + 12)(x - 3)$ (b) $(x + 9)(x + 4)$ (c) $(x - 12)(x + 3)$ (d) $(x - 9)(x - 4)$

Factor each polynomial.

20. $5x^2 + 15$ **21.** $x^3 + 3x^2$ **22.** $2y^2 + 15y$

23. $x^2 - 9$ **24.** $b^2 - 18b + 81$ **25.** $3x^2 + 15x + 12$

26. Which is greater, $0.9x - 0.7y$ or $0.7(x - y)$? Explain how you know.

27. Tortoise and Glacier A giant tortoise walks 600 times faster than a glacier flows. If the glacier flows at 9×10^{-5} m/sec, how fast does the tortoise walk?

PERFORMANCE TASK

Think of a solid figure for which you can find the volume and surface area. Let x or a polynomial expression of x represent one of its dimensions, such as a width, height, or radius. Write polynomials to model the volume and surface area of your figure. Describe how the volume and surface area change as x takes on different values.

Chapter 9 Quadratic Functions and Equations

Project A

Time in a Bottle

How did people know what time it was before the invention of clocks?

Project B

Poetry in Motion

How is symmetry used in literature, music, and visual art?

Project C

Dish It Up

How does a satellite dish collect radio signals? How is a car headlight like a satellite dish?

EMILY W SHU

I liked math in high school, especially tricky problems. I believed that if I knew math I could learn anything.

I have great flexibility because my training in experimental physics is very broad. I can be working on optical sensors in the morning and analyzing flow from a smoke stack in the afternoon. Designing a telescope lens is a project that involves a lot of math. Just suppose that it can only be x so big and weigh y so much, that it has to go aboard a spacecraft and be able to show the moon very clearly

Emily Y. Shu
Physicist, Research and
    Development
General Electric Co.
Schenectady, New York

Chapter 9 — Quadratic Functions and Equations

GETTING READY

9-1
Exploring Quadratic Functions and Their Graphs

In 9-1 you will investigate quadratic functions by analyzing their graphs and properties. You will need skills in evaluating functions and graphing.

1. Identify the linear function(s). [3-2]

    a. $y = 2x - 8$ **b.** $y = \sqrt{x} + 3$ **c.** $y = \dfrac{1}{x}$ **d.** $y = 3x^2 - 3x$

e.

x	0	2	4	6	8
y	10	20	40	60	80

f.

x	0	5	10	15	20
y	0	3	64	169	324

On the same set of coordinate axes, graph each pair of functions. [7-1; 7-2]

2. $y = |x|;\ y = |x| - 2$ **3.** $y = \sqrt{x};\ y = -\sqrt{x}$

4. $y = \sqrt{x - 2};\ y = \sqrt{x} - 2$

9-2
Solving Quadratic Equations

In 9-2 you will write quadratic equations to represent problems and use graphs, tables, and factoring to help solve the equations. You will need skills in evaluating expressions and factoring.

Factor each expression, if possible. [8-2]

5. $x^2 - 7x + 12$ **6.** $4x^2 - 12x$ **7.** $x^2 - 9$

8. $x^2 - 3x - 4$ **9.** $-15x + 5x^2$ **10.** $9x^4 - 15x^3 + 6x^2$

11. $6x - 3$ **12.** $x^2 - 10x - 75$ **13.** $x^2 - 2x - 2$

9-3
Other Techniques for Solving Quadratic Equations

In 9-3 you will learn additional methods for solving equations and how to pick the most effective solution method. You will need skills in evaluating expressions, solving equations, and square roots.

Solve and check the following equations. [7-1; 7-2]

14. $|x - 9| = 14$ **15.** $|x| - 8 = -7$ **16.** $2|x - 5| + 7 = 9$

17. $2|x| + 6 = 8$ **18.** $|-3x| + 9 = 15$ **19.** $-4|x| = 20$

Simplify each expression, if possible. [7-2]

20. $\pm\sqrt{49}$ **21.** $-\sqrt{25}$ **22.** $\sqrt{-81}$ **23.** $\sqrt{1.21}$

seeing isn't believing

At 25, Galileo (1564–1642), an Italian astronomer, mathematician, and physicist, challenged Aristotle's theory that a heavy object falls faster than a lighter one. According to legend, he dropped two balls—one ten times heavier than the other—from the top of the Tower of Pisa and proved Aristotle wrong.

Galileo studied objects moving in space as well as on earth. He showed that an object shot into the air follows a parabolic path, a special kind of curve. This had practical value at the time but also led to the discoveries that ultimately resulted in our ability to launch satellites and to explore space.

In Galileo's day, some dismissed his science as magic. Others simply did not want to admit that he was right. Today Galileo is credited with starting the age of modern science. He formulated problems clearly and did experiments to test his ideas. He believed in simple explanations and in using proven theories to make predictions. Most importantly, he directed attention to mathematics as the language of physical science.

1. In Galileo's theory, were there any quantities that were directly related? inversely related? What about in Aristotle's theory?
2. What is the difference between a scientific experiment and a magic trick? Do "magic" tricks have physical explanations?
3. Galileo believed that appearances alone do not prove a theory. If you didn't know that Earth revolves around the sun, would watching the sun rise and set prove it to you? What else might explain it?

Graphing Quadratic Functions

← **CONNECT** → *Some of the polynomial functions you explored in Chapter 8 were quadratic functions. Now you will graph quadratic functions of the form $y = ax^2$ and learn to describe the characteristics of their graphs.*

Recall that polynomial functions of degree 2 are called *quadratic functions*. Each of these functions is quadratic.

$$y = x^2 \qquad y = 3x^2 \qquad y = x^2 + x + 1$$

Satellite dishes, radio telescopes, and headlight reflectors all have similar shapes that can be described using quadratic functions.

Every quadratic function can be written in the form $y = ax^2 + bx + c$, where the coefficients a, b, and c are real numbers and $a \neq 0$.

CONSIDER

?

1. **Why must the coefficient a not be 0 for $y = ax^2 + bx + c$ to be a quadratic function? How would you classify the function if $a = 0$?**

When y is a linear function of x, equal changes in the value of x result in equal changes in the value of y. However, when y is a *quadratic* function of x, equal changes in the value of x *do not* result in equal changes in the value of y.

Consider the quadratic function $y = x^2$.

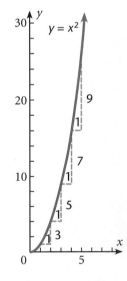

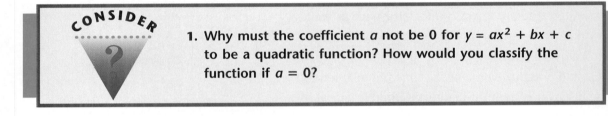

Change in x 1 1 1 1 1

x	0	1	2	3	4	5...
y	0	1	4	9	16	25...

Change in y 1 3 5 7 9 ...

One of Galileo's experiments to study the effects of gravity on moving objects was to roll a ball down a ramp. The relationship between rolling distance (d) and rolling time (t) can be modeled by a quadratic function of the form $d = at^2$.

MATERIALS

Cardboard, Ruler, Ball, Stopwatch, Graphing utility or Graph paper

1. Create a ramp at least 4 feet long using a piece of cardboard. Bend the cardboard lengthwise to make a channel for the ball to roll down. Mark distances along the ramp at regular intervals. Prop up one end to give the ramp a slight incline. Have a stopwatch ready.

2. Release the ball several times from the highest (zero) mark. Note the time (t) it takes to reach each mark at a distance (d) down the ramp. Record your data as ordered pairs of the form (t, d).

3. Find the value of $\frac{d}{t^2}$ for each data pair. Then find the average (a) of these values.

4. Write the equation $a = \frac{d}{t^2}$ using your value of a. Multiply both sides by t^2 and write the quadratic function, $d = at^2$, that models the ball's motion. Graph this function.

5. Choose a new value of the time (t) and use the quadratic function to predict the distance (d) that the ball will roll. Roll and time the ball to check your prediction. What are some sources of error that could affect the accuracy of your prediction?

6. If you made the ramp steeper, do you think the new value of a would be greater or less than your value? Explain.

The graph of each quadratic function is a U-shaped curve called a **parabola.** Quadratic functions of the form $y = ax^2$ form a *family* of functions. The graph of any function in this family is a parabola that goes through the origin. If $a > 0$, the parabola opens upward. If $a < 0$, the parabola opens downward.

The parabola is **symmetric** with respect to the y-axis. The y-axis is the **axis of symmetry.**

Every point on one side of the y-axis has a mirror image or **reflection** on the other side.

The point where the parabola intersects its axis of symmetry is the **vertex.**

$y = -x^2$

Because parabolas are symmetric, you can fold a drawing of a parabola along the axis of symmetry and both halves of the parabola will match.

Graph $y = 0.5x^2$.

a. Find the axis of symmetry.

b. Find the coordinates of the vertex.

c. Find the coordinates of three other points on the graph and their reflections.

Make a table of values and sketch the graph.

x	−3	−2.4	−1	0	1	2.4	3
y	4.5	2.88	0.5	0	0.5	2.88	4.5

The axis of symmetry is the y-axis. The vertex is $(0, 0)$.

The points $(-3, 4.5)$ and $(3, 4.5)$ are reflections.

The points $(-2.4, 2.88)$ and $(2.4, 2.88)$ are reflections.

The points $(-1, 0.5)$ and $(1, 0.5)$ are reflections.

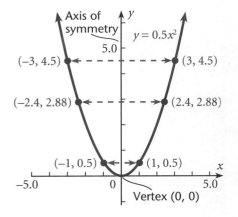

Graph the functions $y = 6x^2$ and $y = -6x^2$.

a. Find the axis of symmetry of each graph.

b. Find the coordinates of the vertex of each graph.

c. On each graph, find the coordinates of one other point and its reflection.

1. How can you tell from the equation whether a function is quadratic? Are all functions whose equations have a squared variable quadratic functions? Explain.

2. How can you tell whether the graph of a function of the form $y = ax^2$ will open upward or downward?

3. Do all functions of the form $y = ax^2$ have the same vertex and axis of symmetry? Explain.

4. How can you tell from the coordinates that two points are reflections of each other across the y-axis?

Exercises

CORE

1. **Getting Started** Use the graph to help you answer the following questions.
   a. Name the coordinates of point *A*. What are the coordinates of its reflection across the *y*-axis?
   b. Name the coordinates of point *B*. What are the coordinates of its reflection across the *y*-axis?
   c. Name the coordinates of point *C*. What are the coordinates of its reflection across the *y*-axis?

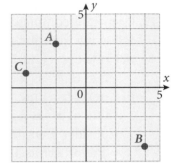

Write the word or phrase that correctly completes each statement.

2. The graph of each quadratic function is called a ____.

3. The point of intersection of the parabola and its axis of symmetry is the ____.

4. Every point on one side of a symmetric figure has a mirror image on the other side of the ____.

5. A mirror image of a point is called its ____.

6. Which points of the figure seem to be reflections of each other across the *y*-axis?

7. The musical use of horizontal reflection (across the *y*-axis) is called *retrogression.* Use this portion of the Shaker song "Simple Gifts" to identify six notes that form a retrogression. Copy the notes and draw the axis of symmetry.

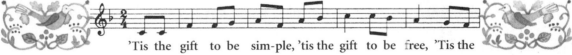

'Tis the gift to be sim-ple, 'tis the gift to be free, 'Tis the

8. Copy the graph of $y = -0.4x^2$.
   a. Find the axis of symmetry.
   b. Find the coordinates of the vertex.
   c. Find the coordinates of three other points on the graph and their reflections.

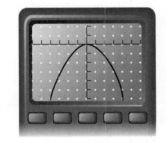

Find the values of *a*, *b*, and *c* for each function of the form $y = ax^2 + bx + c$.

9. $y = -x^2 + 3x + 2$

10. $y = 4x^2$

11. $y = -2 + x^2$

12. Graph the functions $y = 2x^2$ and $y = -2x^2$.
   a. Find the axis of symmetry of each graph.
   b. Find the coordinates of the vertex of each graph.
   c. On each graph, find the coordinates of one other point and its reflection.

13. Copy and complete the table. Then answer the following questions.

x	2x	x²	2x²
0			
1			
2			
3			
4			
5			

   a. Consider x and $2x$. What happens to the value of $2x$ as x increases from 0 to 5?
   b. Consider x and x^2. What happens to the value of x^2 as x increases from 0 to 5?
   c. Consider x and $2x^2$. What happens to the value of $2x^2$ as x increases from 0 to 5?
   d. Consider $x = 10$. What is the value of x doubled? What is the value of x squared? What is the value of $2x^2$?

14. Without graphing, answer the following questions about the given functions.
   i. $y = 2x^2$ **ii.** $y = -3x^2$ **iii.** $y = 0.5x^2$

   a. Which graph(s) will open upward? Explain how you know.
   b. Which graph(s) are symmetric over the y-axis? Explain how you know.
   c. Which graph(s) have a vertex of $(0, 0)$? Explain how you know.

15. Answer the following questions about the given functions.
   i. $y = -\frac{1}{3}x^2$ **ii.** $y = -2x + 5$ **iii.** $y = x^2$
   iv. $y = 3x^2$ **v.** $y = -3x^2$ **vi.** $y = x$

   a. Without graphing, determine which have graphs that pass through the origin $(0, 0)$. Explain how you know.
   b. Which of these graphs are symmetric across the y-axis?
   c. For which of these graphs is it true that as x increases, y always decreases?

16. Sketch the graphs of the functions.
   a. Graph the functions $y = x^2$ and $y = 4x^2$. How are they alike? How are they different?
   b. Graph the functions $y = 4x^2$ and $y = -4x^2$. How are they alike? How are they different?
   c. Graph the functions $y = \frac{1}{4}x^2$ and $y = 4x^2$. How are the graphs alike? How are they different?
   d. Summarize the effects of a on the graphs of quadratic functions.

Match each function with the graph it describes. Tell how you decided.

A. $y = x^2$ **B.** $y = 3x^2$ **C.** $y = \frac{1}{3}x^2$

D. $y = -x^2$ **E.** $y = -3x^2$ **F.** $y = -\frac{1}{3}x^2$

17.

18.

19.

20.

21.

22.

Science

23. The horsepower of a certain engine is calculated using the formula $HP = \frac{nb^2}{2.5}$, with HP as the horsepower, b as the diameter of one of the cylinder bores, in inches, and n as the number of cylinders. Use this formula to determine the amount of horsepower produced by a four-cylinder engine with 1-inch bores.

1930 Model A Ford Roadster

24. Copy the graph and label the axis of symmetry.

25. Without graphing, describe in as much detail as you can the graph of $y = -\frac{1}{2}x^2 + 7$.

26. Describe three ways to tell if a function is linear, quadratic, or neither.

27. $4y - 3 = 12 + y$

28. $2x + 2y = p$

29. $Ax + By = C$

30. Use the graph of $y = |x| - 3$ to solve each equation. Explain what you did.

   a. $-1 = |x| - 3$

   b. $0 = |x| - 3$

   c. $1 = |x| - 3$

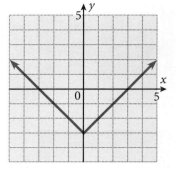

MORE PRACTICE

31. Use the graph to help you answer the following questions.

   a. Name the coordinates of point A. What are the coordinates of its reflection across the y-axis?

   b. Name the coordinates of point B. What are the coordinates of its reflection across the y-axis?

   c. Name the coordinates of point C. What are the coordinates of its reflection across the y-axis?

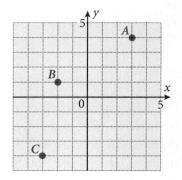

32. $y = -3x + x^2$

33. $y = -5x^2$

34. $y = 1 - 3x^2$

35. $y = \frac{1}{2}x^2 - 3$

36. $y = x^2 - \frac{1}{3}x + 6$

37. $y = -6x + \frac{2}{5}x^2$

38. Which points of the figure seem to be reflections of each other across the y-axis?

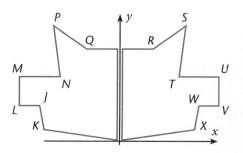

Match each function with the graph it describes. Tell how you decided.

A. $y = x^2$ **B.** $y = 4x^2$ **C.** $y = \frac{1}{4}x^2$

D. $y = -x^2$ **E.** $y = -4x^2$ **F.** $y = -\frac{1}{4}x^2$

39.

40.

41.

42.

43.

44.

45. Copy the graph $y = 0.8x^2$.
    a. Find the axis of symmetry.
    b. Find the coordinates of the vertex.
    c. Find the coordinates of three other points
       on the graph and their reflections.

46. Copy the graph $y = -0.6x^2$.
    a. Find the axis of symmetry.
    b. Find the coordinates of the vertex.
    c. Find the coordinates of three other points
       on the graph and their reflections.

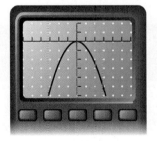

47. Without graphing, answer the following questions
about the given functions.
    i. $y = -x^2$ **ii.** $y = 2x^2$ **iii.** $y = -9x^2$
    a. Which graph(s) will open upward?
    b. Which graph(s) are symmetric with respect to the y-axis?

48. Without graphing, describe in as much detail as you can the graph of $y = -x^2 + 3$.

MORE MATH REASONING

49. The musical use of vertical reflection (across the *x*-axis) is called *inversion.* An inversion occurs in this Old English tune "Greensleeves." Locate and describe the axis of symmetry.

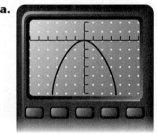 

A - las   my Love you   do me wrong To cast me off   dis - court - eous - ly

50. Which graphs show a reflection across the *y*-axis? the *x*-axis? both? neither? Explain your answers.

a. **b.** **c.**

51. Copy the graph of $y = x^2 - 2x$.
   a. Find the axis of symmetry.
   b. Find the coordinates of the vertex.
   c. Find the coordinates of three other points on the graph and their reflections.

9-1 PART B Modeling with Quadratic Functions

← CONNECT → *You've seen that the graphs of quadratic functions of the form $y = ax^2$ are parabolas. In fact, the graphs of all quadratic functions are parabolas. Now you'll explore more graphs of quadratic functions. Quadratic functions are especially useful for modeling motion.*

The graphs of all quadratic functions are parabolas. Using a graphing utility you can graph several quadratic functions and compare the features of the parabolas.

MATERIALS

Graphing utility or Graph paper

1. Graph each trio of functions on the same screen of your graphing utility. Sketch the graphs shown on each screen.

a. $y = 3x^2$

b. $y = 3x^2 + 4$

c. $y = 3x^2 - 1.5$

d. $y = -x^2$

e. $y = -x^2 + 3$

f. $y = -x^2 - 2$

2. a. Find the values of a, b, and c for each of these functions in the form $y = ax^2 + bx + c$.

b. Find the axis of symmetry.

c. Find the coordinates of the vertex.

3. Briefly describe how the value of c affects the graph of a quadratic function of the form $y = ax^2 + c$.

Problem-Solving Tip

Make an organized list.

You've seen how a and c affect the graph of $y = ax^2 + c$. You may have also noticed that when $a > 0$, the parabola opens upward and the y-value at the vertex is the *minimum* (least) value of y. When $a < 0$, the parabola opens downward and the y-value at the vertex is the *maximum* (greatest) value of y.

EXAMPLE

1. Graph $y = -0.2x^2 + 2$.

a. Find the axis of symmetry.

b. Find the coordinates of the vertex.

c. Find the maximum (greatest) y-value.

The axis of symmetry of the graph is the y-axis and the coordinates of the vertex are $(0, 2)$.

Since the coefficient of x^2 is negative, the parabola opens downward. The maximum value of y is 2, the value at the vertex.

Axis of symmetry

Vertex (0, 2)

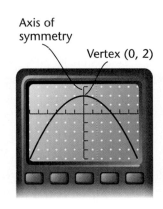

Graph $y = 2x^2 + 5$.
a. Find the axis of symmetry.
b. Find the coordinates of the vertex.
c. Find the minimum (least) y-value.

CONSIDER

?

1. **How is the effect of c on the graph of $y = ax^2 + c$ similar to the effect of c on the graph of $y = a|x| + c$?**

Quadratic functions are also useful for modeling vertical motion of objects. Galileo discovered that the height of an object affected by gravity is a quadratic function of time.

Vertical Motion Formula

The height (h) of an object at time t after being released is

$$h = \tfrac{1}{2}at^2 + vt + s$$

where a is the acceleration due to gravity; v is the upward speed of the object when released ($t = 0$); and s is the starting height of the object.

We usually measure s and h from ground level, but they can be measured from any convenient level. Just be sure to measure both from the *same* level.

On earth, a is approximately -9.8 m/sec^2 in SI (metric) units or -32 ft/sec^2 in customary units. Using these values for a, we can write two formulas for the height of an object.

SI (metric) Units	Customary Units
$h = \tfrac{1}{2}(-9.8)t^2 + vt + s$ meters	$h = \tfrac{1}{2}(-32)t^2 + vt + s$ feet
h and s are in meters	h and s are in feet
t is in seconds	t is in seconds
v is in meters per second	v is in feet per second

2. Marcus dropped a penny into a wishing well and heard it hit the bottom exactly 1.5 seconds later. How deep is the well?

The penny hit the bottom in 1.5 seconds.

$t = 1.5$ sec

Since we don't know the depth of the well, it is convenient to measure s and h from the top, where Marcus dropped the penny. *Dropped* means that the penny started with no upward speed.

$s = 0$ ft; $v = 0$ ft/sec

$h = \frac{1}{2}(-32)t^2 + vt + s$ ft   Use traditional units.

$ = \frac{1}{2}(-32)1.5^2 + (0)(1.5) + 0$ ft   Substitute the values for t, s, and v.

$ = -36$ ft

A *negative* value means a height *below* the starting height. The well is 36 feet deep.

3. A ball is thrown straight up with an upward speed of 10 m/sec, leaving the thrower's hand 2 meters above the ground.
   a. Write the height of the ball as a function of time.
   b. Graph the height function.
   c. Use the graph to estimate the maximum height of the ball. Also, estimate when the ball will hit the ground.

$h = \frac{1}{2}(-9.8)t^2 + vt + s$ m   Use SI units.

$ = \frac{1}{2}(-9.8)t^2 + 10t + 2$ m   Substitute the values $v = 10$ and $s = 2$.

Graph this function using a graphing utility. Let y stand for h and x stand for t. Adjust the window size so you can see the vertex.

Tracing to the vertex shows that the greatest value of y is about 7.

So the ball goes about 7 meters straight up.

The ball hits the ground when $y = 0$. The value of x at that point is about 2.2.

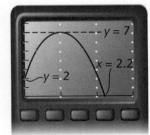

Xmin=0
Xmax=3
Xscl=1
Ymin=0
Ymax=8
Yscl=1

The ball takes about 2 seconds to hit the ground.

It is important not to confuse the graph in Example 3 with the actual *path* of the object. Recall that the object is launched straight up, so its path is straight up and down. The graph shows how the distance above the launching point varies with *time*.

CONSIDER
?

2. Could the height of a falling object have a graph that is a parabola opening *upward*? Explain.

TRY IT

d. A ball is thrown straight up with a starting speed of 10 m/sec, leaving the thrower's hand 1.5 meters above the ground. What function models the height of the ball? Use the graph of the function to estimate how high the ball will go and when it will hit the ground.

Remember that the vertical motion formula is only a model. The actual height of an object, at any moment, may differ from the model due to air resistance and other factors.

REFLECT

1. What are some similarities between the graphs of functions of the form $y = ax^2 + c$? What are some of the ways these graphs differ from each other?

2. How would you change the function $y = ax^2$ to move the graph up? to move the graph down?

3. When two objects are thrown upward, the one thrown with greater speed will go higher and will take longer to hit the ground. How will these facts be apparent in the graphs of the two functions?

4. How does the photo illustrate a quadratic function?

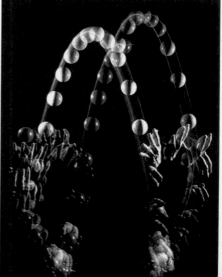

Exercises

CORE

1. Getting Started Use the graph of $y = -x^2 + 4$.
   a. Find the axis of symmetry.
   b. Find the coordinates of the vertex.
   c. Find the maximum (greatest) y-value.

2. Use the graph of $y = x^2 + 1$.
   a. Find the axis of symmetry.
   b. Find the coordinates of the vertex.
   c. Find the minimum (least) y-value.

3. Use the graph of $y = -x^2 + 8$.
   a. Find the axis of symmetry.
   b. Find the coordinates of the vertex.
   c. Find the maximum (greatest) y-value.

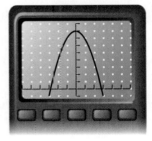

4. Without graphing, answer the following questions about the given functions.

   i. $y = -x^2 - 4$ **ii.** $y = 2x^2 + 5$ **iii.** $y = -9x^2$

   a. Which graph(s) will open upward? Explain how you know.
   b. Which graph(s) are symmetric about the y-axis? Explain how you know.
   c. Which graph(s) have a vertex of $(0, 0)$? Explain how you know.

5. Imagine throwing a golf ball straight up with a starting speed (v) of 28 m/sec from a starting height (s) of 1 meter above the ground.

   a. Substitute these values of s and v into the following formula to write the ball's height (h) as a function of the elapsed time (t).

   $$h = \tfrac{1}{2}(-9.8)t^2 + vt + s$$

   b. Make a table to show the height of the ball after 1, 2, 3, and 4 seconds. Comment on the change in the height.
   c. Graph the function. Use the graph to estimate the maximum height of the ball and when it will hit the ground.

Without graphing, match each function with the graph it describes. Tell how you decided.

A. $y = 3x^2 - 1$ **B.** $y = -x^2 + 4$ **C.** $y = x^2 + 4$

D. $y = 0.2x^2$ **E.** $y = -2x^2 - 1$ **F.** $y = -2x^2 + 3$

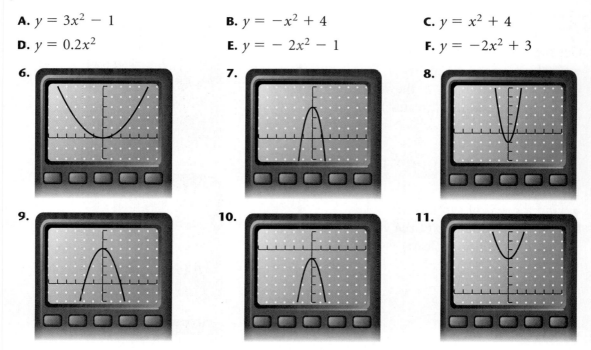

6.   **7.**   **8.**

9.   **10.**   **11.**

12. The graph of $y_1 = rx^2 + 3$ is a parabola that is much wider than that of $y_2 = sx^2 + 3$. Which is larger, r or s? Explain.

13. If the graph of a function of the form $y = 17x^2 + c$ is a parabola with the vertex at the origin, what can you conclude about c?

14. Once in a Blue Moon The maximum height of an object launched straight up, with a starting speed of v ft/sec, is given by the following.

$h = 0.01555v^2$ on earth   and $h = 0.0926v^2$ on the moon

a. Show graphically how the maximum height is six times greater on the moon than on the earth.

b. What is the effect of the two different coefficients, 0.01555 and 0.0926, on the graphs?

15. Sherwood Shoots Maid Marian shoots an arrow into the air. The function $h = \frac{1}{2}(-9.8)t^2 + 25t + 1$ models the height, in meters, of the arrow after t seconds. Graph the function and use it to answer the following questions.

a. How high is the arrow after 2 seconds? 3 seconds?

b. At what time is the arrow at the maximum height?

c. When does the arrow hit the ground?

16. Yikes! A window washer drops a screwdriver while working on a skyscraper. It hits the ground 3 seconds later. How high up was the window washer?

17. **Mail Call** Melinda is a pilot with her own delivery
service. She must drop mail to scientists doing
research on an isolated island. Ignoring wind speed,
how could she calculate the time it will take for the
mail pouch to hit the ground when she drops it
from an altitude of 600 feet?

 *LOOK BACK*

18. Use your knowledge of systems of equations to solve this problem from a
1926 algebra book. [6-1]

> *A grocer has 20 pounds of coffee worth 50 cents per pound. How many*
> *pounds of 35-cent coffee should he mix with it to produce a mixture worth*
> *40 cents per pound?*

Add or subtract the polynomial expressions. [8-1]

19. $(3x^3 + x - 4) + (3 - 5x + 2x^2)$ 20. $(8a - 3a^3 + 2) - (-a^2 - 7a - 9)$

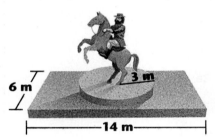

21. Swift Construction has been hired to lay cement around
the base of a Civil War monument in the town square.
How many square meters will they need to cover? What
else do they need to know before they can order the
necessary cubic feet of cement? [8-2]

MORE PRACTICE

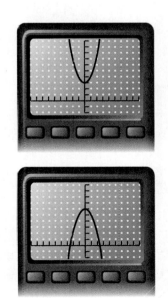

22. Use the graph of $y = x^2 + 3$.
    a. Find the axis of symmetry.
    b. Find the coordinates of the vertex.
    c. Find the minimum (least) y-value.

23. Use the graph of $y = -x^2 + 6$.
    a. Find the axis of symmetry.
    b. Find the coordinates of the vertex.
    c. Find the maximum (greatest) y-value.

24. Use the graph of $y = x^2 + 6$.
   a. Find the axis of symmetry.
   b. Find the coordinates of the vertex.
   c. Find the minimum (least) y-value.

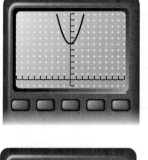

25. Use the graph of $y = -x^2 - 6$.
   a. Find the axis of symmetry.
   b. Find the coordinates of the vertex.
   c. Find the maximum (greatest) y-value.

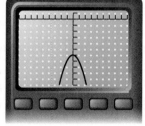

Without graphing, match each function with the graph it describes. Tell how you decided.

A. $y = 8x^2$ **B.** $y = x^2 - 8$ **C.** $y = -8x^2$

D. $y = x^2 + 8$ **E.** $y = -x^2 + 8$ **F.** $y = 0.8x^2$

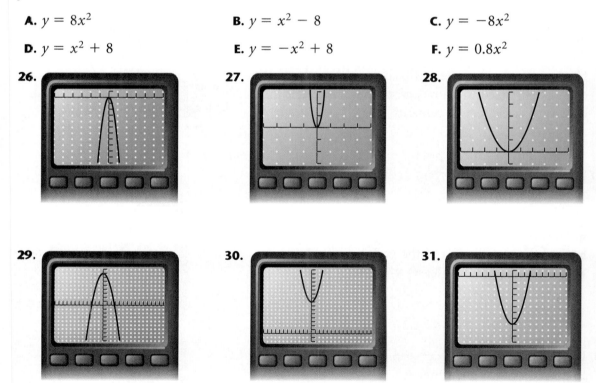

26.   **27.**   **28.**

29.   **30.**   **31.**

32. Yikes 2! A window washer drops a pail while working on a skyscraper. It hits the ground 2 seconds later. How high up was the window washer?

MORE MATH REASONING

33. Use a graphing utility to help you answer the following questions.

   a. Graph $y = 2x^2$ and $y = 2x^2 + 5x$. How are the graphs alike? How are they different? Is the axis of symmetry the same for both parabolas?

   b. Find out what happens to the graph of $y = 2x^2 + bx$ as the value of b varies. Write a description of how the graph changes.

   c. Compare the graph of $y = 2x^2 + 5x$ to the graph of $y = 2x^2 + 5x + 6$. Describe what happens when you add 6 to the right side of the equation.

   d. Describe what happens to the graph of $y = 2x^2 + 5x + c$ as the value of c varies.

34. Write an equation for a quadratic function whose graph is symmetric about the y-axis and has a maximum point.

35. Jack and Jill Imagine Jack rolling down the hill. The distance in meters traveled by Jack can be represented by the quadratic function $y = 2x^2$.

   a. Copy and complete the table to show how far Jack has fallen.

   b. How far does Jack fall between second 2 and second 3? between second 4 and second 5? How does this compare to rate of change of a linear function? Explain.

x (sec)	y (m)
1	
2	
3	
4	
5	

36. Crash Policy The equation $y = 0.008x^2 - 0.72x + 20$ is used by a certain insurance company to predict the number (y) of accidents per million miles driven by groups of drivers (x) of different ages.

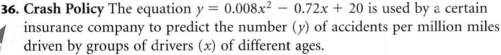

   a. Use a graphing utility to show the graph of this function. Adjust the range and the x and y scales so that you can view the graph for age groups ranging from 16 and 70.

   b. For what age group is the number of predicted accidents minimum? How many accidents are predicted per million miles driven by this age group?

   c. According to the graph, how many accidents per million miles driven are predicted for the 17-year-old age group?

← C O N N E C T →   *You've explored quadratic functions and their graphs. The graph of every quadratic function, $y = ax^2 + bx + c$, is a parabola with features that can be associated with the coefficients of the terms. You've also seen an important application of quadratic functions for modeling vertical motion.*

When Galileo was a medical student, he used a *pendulum* to make a timing device to measure heart rate (pulse). A simple pendulum consists of a weight, called a *bob*, suspended from a string.

EXPLORE: TO AND FRO

MATERIALS

Thread, Hook, Weight, Stopwatch, Tape measure

Tie a weight to a thread at least 0.5 meter long and suspend it from a hook so that it can swing freely.

1. Measure the length (ℓ) of the pendulum from the hook to the center of the bob. Record the length in a table like the one in Step 4.

2. Pull the bob about 10° away from vertical and let it swing. Use a stopwatch to measure the time it takes for the bob to swing back and forth ten times. Record your result in the table.

3. Calculate and record the value of $\frac{\ell}{t^2}$.

4. Shorten or lengthen the pendulum a little and do steps 1–3 again. Repeat this procedure until you have data for at least four different lengths.

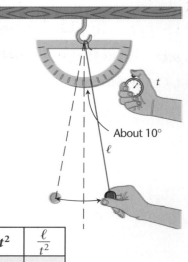

About 10°

Length	Time for Ten Swings	Time for One Swing	t^2	$\frac{\ell}{t^2}$
ℓ	$10t$	t		

5. Find the average (m) of the values of $\frac{\ell}{t^2}$. Write the equation $m = \frac{\ell}{t^2}$ using your value of m. Multiply both sides by t^2 and write the quadratic function, $\ell = mt^2$, that models the relationship between the pendulum length and the swing time.

6. Use your function to predict the length of a pendulum that makes a full swing in 1 second.

7. Heart rate (pulse) is measured in beats per minute. Describe how you could use a 1-second pendulum to take your pulse.

REFLECT

1. If one quantity is proportional to another, what is the shape of the graph of their relationship? If one quantity is proportional to the *square* of another, what is the shape of the graph of their relationship?

2. Describe some of the effects of varying a and c on the graph of $y = ax^2 + c$.

3. Describe a real situation where an object is thrown or dropped vertically in the air. What values would you need to know to write its height as a function of time?

Self-Assessment

1. Use the graph of $y = -0.25x^2$.
   a. Find the axis of symmetry.
   b. Find the coordinates of the vertex.
   c. Find the coordinates of three other points on the graph and their reflections.

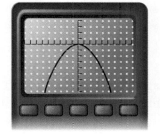

2. Which of these functions has (have) a parabola as its (their) graph?
   I. $y = x^2 + 6$ II. $y = -x^3$ III. $y = 2x^2$

   (a) only I   (b) only II   (c) only III   (d) I and III   (e) I, II, and III

Fine Arts

3. Study this basket from a Shoshone Indian design. Identify lines of symmetry and reflections found.

4. Answer the following questions about the function $y = x^2 + 4$. Explain your reasoning.
   a. Does the graph open upward or downward?
   b. Is the graph symmetric over the y-axis?
   c. Does the graph have a vertex of $(0, 0)$?
   d. Does the graph have a minimum or a maximum value?

5. Without graphing, match each function with the graph it describes.

a. $y = 5x^2$ **b.** $y = x^2 - 5$ **c.** $y = -x^2 - 5$

i. 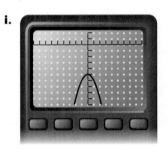 **ii.** 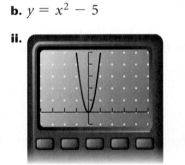 **iii.**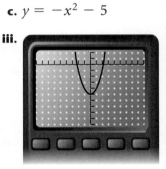

6. a. How does the area of the circle change when its radius is doubled? tripled? halved? made five times bigger? made $\frac{1}{3}$ smaller?

b. How does the circumference of the circle change when its radius is doubled? tripled? halved? made five times bigger? made $\frac{1}{3}$ smaller?

c. Is the circumference of a circle a linear or a quadratic function of its radius? Is the area of a circle a linear or a quadratic function of its radius? Explain.

6 cm

$A = \pi r^2$
$C = 2\pi r$

Tell whether each functional relationship is linear or quadratic. Explain how you know.

7. The amount charged by a taxi is a function of the number of miles driven.

8. The distance it takes a moving car to come to a stop after the brakes are applied is a function of the square of the speed of the car.

9. The amount of tax charged on the sale of an item is a function of the price of the item.

10. Just Drop It Imagine dropping an object from the top of a tall building. Think of the distance the object has fallen 1 second after it was dropped, 2 seconds after it was dropped, 3 seconds, and so on. Use the vertical motion formula $h = \frac{1}{2}(-9.8)t^2 + vt + s$.

a. Is the distance the object has fallen directly or inversely related to the time it has been falling?

b. Does the object fall the same distance each second after being dropped? Explain.

c. How long would it take for the object to fall 120 meters?

11. Write an equation for a quadratic function whose graph opens downward and whose vertex is below the x-axis.

12. How many different quadratic functions, $y = ax^2 + bx + c$, can be formed using each of the following terms at most once in a given function? Explain your answer.

$$3x^2 \qquad 4x \qquad -5$$

A FOOT IN TWO WORLDS

Few people find fame in two different fields. Even fewer build a solid reputation in the academic world and also become famous in the world of popular science fiction. But Isaac Asimov was one of those people. A Russian born biochemist, who died in 1992 at the age of 72, he wrote almost 400 books on science, literature, and history, and was known for the clarity of his explanations. But for most Americans, his fame rests on his outpouring of science fiction stories.

Earlier science ficton fantasized about the marvels of future ages, focusing on the wonders of space travel and futuristic inventions. Typical stories told the plight of inhabitants of distant worlds threatened with destruction by unimaginably horrible invaders.

Isaac Asimov's writing raised science fiction's literary status. His stories, while inventive and clever, involved moral and social issues that typical stories ignored. His legacy is apparent in today's science fiction world where stories revolve around issues important to human society and on relationships that develop regardless of time.

1. Why would a story about space travel be more popular today than in the late 60s?
2. What formula have you used that could be used to describe the height of a space craft?
3. What inventions have been developed in recent years that were science fiction at one time?

← CONNECT →   *In Chapter 4, you used the graphs of linear functions to solve linear equations. Now you will solve quadratic equations in a similar way, using the graphs of quadratic functions.*

Recall that you can solve the linear equation $10 = 2x - 3$ by graphing the linear function $y = 2x - 3$, and looking for the point on the graph where the y-coordinate is 10. The x-coordinate of that point is the solution of the linear equation.

You can use the graph of a *quadratic* function in a similar manner to solve equations of the form $d = ax^2 + bx + c$, called **quadratic equations.** When $d = 0$, the equation is in **standard form.**

An equation of the form $0 = ax^2 + bx + c$, where a, b, and c are real numbers and $a \neq 0$, is a **quadratic equation in standard form.**

EXAMPLE

1. Graph the quadratic function $y = x^2 + 3x - 7$. Use the graph to solve the quadratic equation $3 = x^2 + 3x - 7$.

Graph the function on a graphing utility and trace to find the points where the y-value is 3, or graph the function and the horizontal line $y = 3$ by hand, and find the points where they intersect.

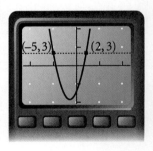

The x-coordinates of the two points are the solutions of the quadratic equation.

The solutions of the quadratic equation are $x = -5$ and $x = 2$.

Check the solutions.

$3 \stackrel{?}{=} x^2 + 3x - 7$ $3 \stackrel{?}{=} x^2 + 3x - 7$

$3 \stackrel{?}{=} (-5)^2 + 3(-5) - 7$ $3 \stackrel{?}{=} (2)^2 + 3(2) - 7$

$3 = 3$ ✔ $3 = 3$ ✔

Graph the quadratic function $y = x^2 + 2x$. Use the graph to solve each quadratic equation.

a. $8 = x^2 + 2x$ **b.** $-1 = x^2 + 2x$ **c.** $3 = x^2 + 2x$

EXPLORE: SOLUTION QUEST

MATERIALS

Graphing utility or Graph paper

1. Graph the quadratic function $y = 2x^2$. Use the graph to solve each quadratic equation.

    a. $8 = 2x^2$ **b.** $-8 = 2x^2$ **c.** $0 = 2x^2$

2. For each equation in Step 1, determine the number of solutions.

3. Graph the quadratic function $y = -2x^2$. Use the graph to solve each quadratic equation.

    a. $8 = -2x^2$ **b.** $-8 = -2x^2$ **c.** $0 = -2x^2$

4. For each equation in Step 3, determine the number of solutions.

5. Group the equations in Steps 1 and 3 by the number of solutions. What do the equations in each group have in common?

6. Briefly describe how a graph can help you determine the number of solutions of a quadratic equation.

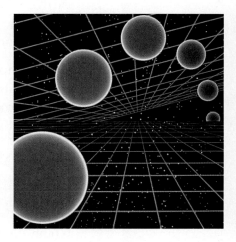

The solutions of $0 = ax^2 + bx + c$ are the values of x where $y = 0$ on the graph of $y = ax^2 + bx + c$. Recall that $y = 0$ describes the x-axis. So the solutions are the values of x where the graph crosses the x-axis.

The values of x where a graph crosses the x-axis are the **x-intercepts** of the graph.

$y = x^2 - 4x + 9$ $y = x^2 - 4x + 4$ $y = x^2 - 4x - 2$

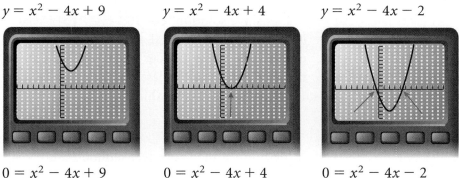

$0 = x^2 - 4x + 9$ has *no* solutions.

$0 = x^2 - 4x + 4$ has *one* solution.

$0 = x^2 - 4x - 2$ has *two* solutions.

1. Why can't a quadratic equation have *more* than two solutions? Explain using a graph.

To solve some real problems involving quadratic equations, you have to determine whether a solution is reasonable.

EXAMPLE

2. A space shuttle craft has just landed on the rim of a crater on the earth's moon. Suddenly, the ground gives way and the shuttle hurtles toward the floor of the crater, 270 feet below. The commander must fire the retrorockets before the shuttle crashes.

Use the moon's gravitational acceleration, -5.4 ft/sec^2, and the vertical motion formula, $h = \frac{1}{2}at^2 + vt + s$, to decide how much time the commander has to fire the retrorockets.

The shuttle starts 270 ft above the crater floor with no upward speed and an acceleration of -5.4 ft/sec^2. So $s = 270$, $v = 0$, and $a = -5.4$.

$h = \frac{1}{2}(-5.4)t^2 + 270$ feet

$h = -2.7t^2 + 270$ feet

Graph the height function.

The solutions of the quadratic equation $0 = -2.7t^2 + 270$ are $h = 0$ when $t = -10$ or $t = 10$.

Both solutions check in the quadratic equation.

The positive solution, $t = 10$, is the solution to the real problem. The commander must fire the retrorockets in less than 10 seconds to avoid crashing.

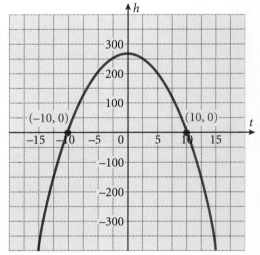

TRY IT

d. If the floor of the crater in Example 2 were 1080 feet down, how much time would the commander have to fire the retrorockets?

1. Briefly describe how a graph of a quadratic function can help you solve a quadratic equation.
2. When you write a quadratic equation in standard form, why is a solution of the equation an x-intercept?
3. Describe the graph of $y = ax^2 + bx + c$ if the quadratic equation $0 = ax^2 + bx + c$ has exactly one solution.

Exercises

CORE

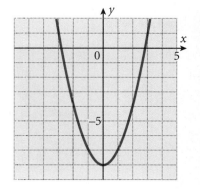

1. **Getting Started** Use the graph of the function $y = x^2 - 8$.
   a. Find the coordinates of the vertex.
   b. How many solutions does the equation $8 = x^2 - 8$ have?
   c. How many solutions does the equation $-10 = x^2 - 8$ have?
   d. Give a value of y in $y = x^2 - 8$ that will result in an equation with only one solution.

Rewrite each quadratic equation in standard form, $0 = ax^2 + bx + c$.

2. $10 = x^2 - 6$ **3.** $5 = 5 - 4x + x^2$ **4.** $0 = (x - 3)^2$

Use the graph of the quadratic function $y = x^2 + 6x$ to solve each equation. Check your solution.

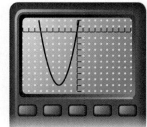

5. $0 = x^2 + 6x$ **6.** $-5 = x^2 + 6x$ **7.** $-9 = x^2 + 6x$

8. Which of these equations is (are) equivalent to $0 = x^2 + 6x - 10$?
   I. $10 = x^2 + 6x - 10$ II. $5 = x^2 + 6x - 5$ III. $10 = x^2 + 6x$

   (a) I only   (b) II only   (c) III only   (d) II and III   (e) II and III

9. If you were to use the x-intercept method to graphically solve the quadratic equation $14 = 10 + x^2$, how would you rewrite the equation? Tell how you would find the solution(s).

10. Explain how you can use the graph of a quadratic equation in standard form to tell if the equation has one, two, or no solutions.

11. **Earth or Moon?** Suppose the shuttle craft in Example 2 had slipped off a
1-mile-high cliff *on earth* instead of a crater on the moon.
  a. Use the formula $h = \frac{1}{2}(-32)t^2 + vt + s$ to write the shuttle's height in feet
  as a function of the time since it slipped. Since 1 mile = 5280 feet, use
  $s = 5280$ and $v = 0$.
  b. After 5 seconds, how far will the shuttle craft have fallen?
  c. Approximately how many seconds will it take the shuttle craft to hit the
  ground?
  d. If you were the commander, would you rather have been on earth or earth's
  moon in such a situation? Explain your choice.

**Without graphing, match each function with the graph it describes. Tell how
you decided.**

A. 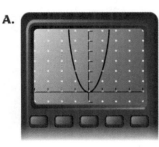   **B.** 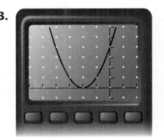   **C.**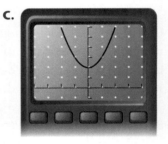

12. $y = x^2 + 2$ **13.** $y = 2x^2$ **14.** $y = (x + 2)^2$

15. **How Much Is Too Much?** A theater seats 500 people.
Since the theater has been sold out for every performance, the owner decides to raise the price of the
tickets. She knows she will lose some customers, but
has decided to raise the price by $5 anyway. The
equation $y = 2500 + 375x - 50x^2$ can be used to
approximate the money (y) she will make by raising
the price x dollars.
  a. How much will she make if she raises the price $5?
  b. If she wants to make $3200, what is the least amount
  she can raise the price?

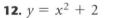 *LOOK AHEAD*

Factor each expression.

16. $x^2 - 16x$ **17.** $-5t^2 - 75t$

18. Copy and complete the table.

    a. For what values of x is the expression $3x(x + 2)$ equal to 0?

    b. For what values of x is the expression $3x(x + 2)$ equal to 9?

    c. For what values of x is the expression $3x(x + 2)$ equal to -3?

x	$3x(x + 2)$
-3	
-2	
-1	
0	
1	
2	

Simplify each expression.

19. $\sqrt{81}$

20. $(\sqrt{10})^2$

21. $\sqrt{64}$

Factor each expression, if possible.

22. $x^2 - 16$

23. $x^2 + 16$

24. $x^2 + 16x + 64$

MORE PRACTICE

Use the graph of $y = 4 - 5x + x^2$ to solve each equation. Check your solution.

25. $-2 = 4 - 5x + x^2$

26. $0 = 4 - 5x + x^2$

27. $-10 = 4 - 5x + x^2$

Rewrite each quadratic equation in standard form, $0 = ax^2 + bx + c$.

28. $8 = x^2 - 2x$

29. $56 = 56 - 3x + x^2$

30. $0 = (x - 5)^2$

31. Use the graph of the function $y = x^2 + 5x - 6$.

    a. How many solutions does the equation $-31 = x^2 + 5x - 6$ have?

    b. How many solutions does the equation $-12 = x^2 + 5x - 6$ have?

    c. Give a value of y in $y = x^2 + 5x - 6$ so there are two solutions.

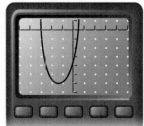

```
Xmin=-10
Xmax=10
Xscl=2
Ymin=-14
Ymax=2
Yscl=2
```

32. Splashdown! Suppose a stone is dropped from Hoover Dam.

    a. Use $v = 0$ and $s = 0$ in the formula $h = \frac{1}{2}(-32)t^2 + vt + s$ to write the stone's height relative to the dam as a function of time.

    b. After 1 second, how far will the stone have dropped?

    c. After 2 seconds, how far will the stone have dropped?

MORE MATH REASONING

33. Write a quadratic equation that has two solutions.

34. Write a quadratic equation that has no solutions.

35. Which equation has 0 as a solution?

    (a) $4x^2 - x = 0$ (b) $x^2 + 2x + 1 = 0$ (c) $2x^2 = 10$

36. Create a quadratic equation that has 0 as a solution.

Use a graphing utility to solve each equation.

37. $15 = x^2 - 2x$ **38.** $0 = x^2 - 12x$ **39.** $-12 = 7x + x^2$

40. Which of these equations would give the same solutions? Explain how you know.

    (a) $-4 = 2x - x^2$ (b) $0 = 2x - x^2$ (c) $0 = 4 + 2x - x^2$

41. Use a graphing utility to help you solve this problem. A skydiver jumps from an airplane with no upward speed at an altitude of 1000 meters.

    a. Use the formula $h = \frac{1}{2}(-9.8)t^2 + vt + s$ to write her height during free fall as a function of the time since she jumped. Graph this function.

    b. If the skydiver has fallen approximately 100 meters, how many seconds have passed? Explain how to use the graph to estimate your solution.

    c. If the skydiver has fallen 400 meters, approximately how many seconds have passed? Tell how you decided.

    d. Can the skydiver wait 15 seconds before pulling the parachute cord? Explain.

42. An object attached to a string and swung in a circle exerts the pull or force of F pounds on the string where $F = \frac{WRn^2}{2933}$. The weight of the object is W pounds, the length of the string is R feet, and the number of revolutions per minute is n.

    a. What is the force on a 1-foot string if a 2-pound object is swung at 100 revolutions per minute?

    b. How fast must the object be swung to exert a force of 20 pounds on the string?

43. According to the American Red Cross, 85 out of every 100 human blood donors are RH positive. Assuming 90% of the 431 crew members on a space-ship are human, what is the probability that a crew member is RH positive? Explain your answer.

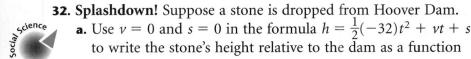

Solving Using Tables and Factoring

← C O N N E C T → *You've solved quadratic equations using the graphs of quadratic functions. You can also use tables of values or factoring to solve quadratic equations.*

EXPLORE: MARTIAN PLAYGROUND

A new children's park is being planned for a Martian spacecraft. The rectangular park will be enclosed on three sides by a force-field barrier and on the fourth side by a wall. If the planners want to use 50 meters of barrier to create a park with an area of 200 square meters, what should the dimensions be?

Let x = the distance the park extends from the wall, in meters.

MATERIALS

Spreadsheet software (optional)
Graphing utility or Graph paper

$50 - 2x$

1. Lt. Beacom says $50 - 2x$ represents the other dimension and $x(50 - 2x)$ represents the area. He also says deciding what the dimensions should be will require solving the equation $x(50 - 2x) = 200$. Explain his reasoning.

2. Lt. Beacom has asked you to make a recommendation. Find the dimensions and areas for values of x from 2 to 24 meters using a table or spreadsheet. Why didn't the lieutenant ask for values of x greater than 24 meters?

Width (m)	Length (m)	Area (m²)
x	$50 - 2x$	$x(50 - 2x)$
2	46	92
.	.	.
.	.	.
.	.	.
24	2	48

3. Use your table or spreadsheet to solve the equation $x(50 - 2x) = 200$. How many solutions are there? Graph the function $y = x(50 - 2x)$ to check your results.

4. What dimensions would you recommend to Lt. Beacom? Explain your choice.

In the Explore, you used values of the factors x and $50 - 2x$ to solve the equation $x(50 - 2x) = 200$. Factoring can also help you solve quadratic equations in standard form. The idea is to factor the polynomial, if possible, and then decide when each factor is 0.

> **THE PRINCIPLE OF ZERO PRODUCTS**
>
> For any real numbers f and g,
>
> if $fg = 0$, then $f = 0$ or $g = 0$; and if either $f = 0$ or $g = 0$, then $fg = 0$.

EXAMPLES

1. Solve $x^2 = 6x$.

$$x^2 = 6x$$
$$x^2 - 6x = 0 \qquad \text{Write the quadratic equation in standard form.}$$
$$x(x - 6) = 0 \qquad \text{Factor the binomial.}$$
$$x = 0 \text{ or } x - 6 = 0 \qquad \text{Use the principle of zero products.}$$
$$x = 0 \text{ or } x = 6 \qquad \text{Solve for } x.$$

The solutions of the equation are $x = 0$ and $x = 6$.

Check both solutions in the original equation.

$$x^2 \stackrel{?}{=} 6x \qquad\qquad x^2 \stackrel{?}{=} 6x$$
$$0^2 \stackrel{?}{=} 6(0) \qquad\qquad 6^2 \stackrel{?}{=} 6(6)$$
$$0 = 0 \; ✔ \qquad\qquad 36 = 36 \; ✔$$

2. Solve $x^2 + 9x + 20 = 0$.

$$x^2 + 9x + 20 = 0$$
$$(x + 5)(x + 4) = 0 \qquad \text{Factor the trinomial.}$$
$$x + 5 = 0 \text{ or } x + 4 = 0 \qquad \text{Use the principle of zero products.}$$
$$x = -5 \text{ or } x = -4 \qquad \text{Solve for } x.$$

The solutions of the equation are $x = -5$ and $x = -4$.

Both solutions check in the original equation.

CONSIDER

1. If your first step in solving the equation in Example 1 were to divide both sides by x, would you still find both solutions?

EXAMPLE

3. If a flare is launched straight up from the ground with an upward speed of 25 m/sec, how long will it take the flare to reach a height of 30 meters? Use the formula $h = -5t^2 + 25t$ for the approximate height, in meters, after t seconds.

$$30 = -5t^2 + 25t \qquad \text{Substitute the value of } h.$$

$$5t^2 - 25t + 30 = 0 \qquad \text{Write the quadratic equation in standard form.}$$

$$5(t^2 - 5t + 6) = 0 \qquad \text{Factor out the common factor, 5.}$$

$$5(t - 2)(t - 3) = 0 \qquad \text{Factor the trinomial.}$$

$$(t - 2)(t - 3) = 0 \qquad \text{Divide by 5.}$$

$$t - 2 = 0 \text{ or } t - 3 = 0 \qquad \text{Use the principle of zero products.}$$

$$t = 2 \text{ or } t = 3 \qquad \text{Solve for } t.$$

Both solutions check in the original equation.

The flare is 30 meters high after 2 seconds (on the way up) and again after 3 seconds (on the way down).

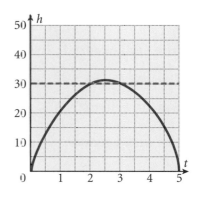

TRY IT

Solve each quadratic equation by factoring.
a. $m^2 - 6m - 27 = 0$
b. $g^2 - 4g = 5$
c. $z^2 - 5z + 7 = 5z - 17$

Factoring to solve a quadratic equation can be the easiest method if you can immediately identify the factors. Using a graph, a table, or factoring can all be effective methods for solving quadratic equations. Deciding what method to use is always the first step in solving equations.

1. Briefly describe the advantages and limitations of using a table or spreadsheet to solve a quadratic equation.
2. When would you choose to solve a quadratic equation by factoring rather than by graphing? When *wouldn't* you choose to solve by factoring?
3. How does the principle of zero products help you solve quadratic equations? What do you have to do to a quadratic equation before you can use this principle?
4. If a quadratic equation for a real problem has two solutions, will both solutions always be meaningful in the context of the problem? Explain.

Exercises

CORE

1. **Getting Started** Use these steps to solve $x^2 - 7x = -12$.
   a. Write the equation in standard form.
   b. Factor the trinomial.
   c. Apply the principle of zero products and solve.

Write each quadratic equation in standard form.

2. a. $9x^2 = 18x - 27$ b. $10x = 5x^2 + 3$ c. $24 = 8x^2 + 4x$

3. a. $3x = 5 - 2x^2$ b. $16 = 4x - 3x^2$ c. $2x^2 = 7x - 8$

Solve each equation.

4. $x^2 + 7x + 12 = 0$ 5. $x^2 + 7x = 0$ 6. $x^2 + 5x + 6 = 0$

7. $x^2 = -3(2x + 3)$ 8. $x^2 = x$

9. $x^2 + 3x = 10$

10. $x^2 + 121 = 22x$

11. **Space in Space** The living space per person on a spacecraft is 110 square meters. Create four different rectangular living spaces with this area. Assume the sides of all the rectangular spaces must be in whole numbers. Which has the maximum perimeter? minimum perimeter?

12. Suppose you solved a quadratic equation and found two values of a height— one positive and one negative. Describe a situation in which only the *positive* solution is meaningful. Describe another situation in which only the *negative* solution is meaningful.

13. Use the spreadsheet to solve the quadratic equation $x^2 - 4.8x - 7.2 = 0$.

   a. What is one solution to the equation?

   b. By looking at the table, how do you know that there is another solution to the equation?

   c. Between which two x-values in the table is the second solution found?

   d. To which of the two x-values will the solution be closer? How does this fact help you estimate the solution?

   e. Estimate the second solution to the nearest tenth.

   f. For which values is $x^2 - 4.8x - 7.2 > 0$?

   g. For which values is $x^2 - 4.8x - 7.2 < 0$?

x	$x^2 - 4.8x - 7.2$
−4	28
−3	16.2
−2	6.4
−1	−1.4
0	−7.2
1	−11
2	−12.8
3	−12.6
4	−10.4
5	−6.2
6	0
7	8.2

14. Which of these equations is (are) equivalent to $x^2 + 0.5x + 0.25 = 0$?

   I. $x^2 = -0.25$ II. $x^2 + 0.5x = -0.25$ III. $x(x + 0.5) = -0.25$

   (a) I only   (b) II only   (c) III only   (d) II and III   (e) I, II, and III

Use the graph of $y = 2(x - 6)^2 - 5$ to approximate the solution(s) of each equation. Explain your solution.

15. $-5 = 2(x - 6)^2 - 5$

16. $-17 = 2(x - 6)^2 - 5$

17. $3 = 2(x - 6)^2 - 5$

18. Which of these is (are) equivalent to $(x + 10)^2 = 0$?

   I. $x^2 + 10^2 = 0$ II. $x + 10 = -(x + 10)$ III. $x^2 + 20x + 100 = 0$

   (a) I only   (b) II only   (c) III only   (d) II and III   (e) I, II, and III

Determine whether each statement is true or false. If the statement is false, change the underlined word or phrase to make it true.

19. An equation that can be simplified to the standard form $0 = ax^2 + bx + c$, where a, b, and c are real numbers and $a \neq 0$, is called a <u>linear equation</u>.

20. The x-intercepts of the graph are the x-coordinates of the points where the graph intersects the <u>y-axis</u>.

Look at the table for each equation. How many solutions do you think each equation has? Explain how you know. If necessary, choose a few more values of *x*.

21. $4 = x^2 - 5$

x	$x^2 - 5$
-4	11
-3	4
-2	-1
-1	-4
0	-5
1	-4
2	-1

22. $-15 = x(x - 6)$

x	$x(x - 6)$
-2	16
-1	7
0	0
1	-5
2	-8
3	-9
4	-8

23. $(x - 3)^2 = 0$

x	$(x - 3)^2$
-2	25
-1	16
0	9
1	4
2	1
3	0
4	1

24. Romping in Space The Martians are planning a larger children's park for their new spaceship. Again, one wall of the ship will be used as one side of the park. There are 60 meters of fencing on board the ship. The crew wants an area of 400 square meters. They need to determine possible dimensions of the park.

Let $x =$ the width of the park. The quadratic equation $x(60 - 2x) = 400$ can be used to solve the problem. Skyler started this spreadsheet so that decisions could be made on the dimensions of this park.

> **Problem-Solving Tip**
>
> Draw a diagram.

Width	Length	Area
x	$60 - 2x$	$x(60 - 2x)$
5	50	250
10		
15		
20		
25		
30		

a. Copy and complete the table.
b. What do the factors x and $60 - 2x$ represent in the equation $x(60 - 2x) = 400$?
c. Why are x and $60 - 2x$ multiplied together in the equation?
d. For what value(s) is equation $x(60 - 2x) = 400$ true?
e. Estimate the value(s) of x if the area desired were 200 square meters. Graphing may help you find the value(s).
f. What is the largest area shown in the table?

25. Is It a Goal? A soccer ball is kicked in the air with an upward speed of 20 m/sec. The function $h = \frac{1}{2}(-9.8)t^2 + 20t$ gives the height (h) in meters t seconds after the kick.

a. When will the ball hit the ground again?

b. Do you think that the ball will go higher than 20 feet? Explain.

26. Brrrrr! The meteorologist for the TV station uses the function $y = -0.15x^2 + t$ as a model for the windchill factor, with windchill (y), wind velocity (x), and the present temperature (t). Use her model to determine whether a change in temperature or a change in wind speed would have a greater effect on the windchill. Explain.

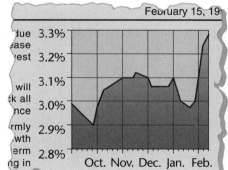

Problem-Solving Tip

Try special cases.

 ## LOOK BACK

27. This is a graph of the interest rate of 3-month treasury bills from September 1, 1993, through February 15, 1994, as reported to the media. [1-1]

a. Does there appear to be a wide or small change in the percent paid on treasury bills?

b. Give the range of percent shown.

c. What would the graph look like if the left-hand column had started at 0.0%?

d. Why do you think the graph was presented as shown?

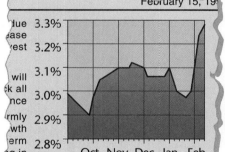

February 15, 19...

3.3%
3.2%
3.1%
3.0%
2.9%
2.8%   Oct. Nov. Dec. Jan. Feb.

Multiply using any method. [8-2]

28. $(x - 3)(x - 3)$

29. $(f^2 - 4)(f^2 + 4)$

30. $(n - 3)(n - 5)$

31. $(g + 2)(g + 2)$

32. Does this seventeenth-century Persian drawing have an axis of symmetry? How many horses do you see? [9-1]

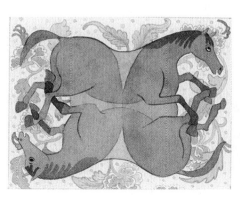

MORE PRACTICE

33. Use these steps to solve $x^2 - 9x = -18$.
  a. Write the equation in standard form.
  b. Factor the trinomial.
  c. Apply the principle of zero products to solve the equation.

Write each quadratic equation in standard form.

34. $3x^2 = 16 - 4x$ **35.** $14 - 3x = -10x^2$ **36.** $5x = 20 - 7x^2$

Solve each equation. Tell which method you used.

37. $x^2 + 9x + 18 = 0$ **38.** $x^2 + 9x = 0$ **39.** $x^2 - 9x = 0$

40. $x^2 + 10x + 25 = 0$ **41.** $x^2 - 9 = 0$ **42.** $x^2 + 11x + 18 = 0$

43. $x^2 + 14x = 32$ **44.** $x^2 - 14x = -49$ **45.** $-3 = x^2 + 2x$

PS
Science

46. Is It a Field Goal? A football is kicked in the air with an upward speed of 25 m/sec. The function $h = \frac{1}{2}(-9.8)t^2 + 25t$ gives the height (h) in meters t seconds after the kick.
  a. When will the ball hit the ground again?
  b. Do you think the ball will go higher than 30 feet? Explain.

By looking at the tables, determine the number of solutions to the equations. If it helps, try a few more values of x.

47. $7 = x^2 - x$ **48.** $-16 = x^2 + 8x$ **49.** $0 = x^2 - x + 2$

x	$x^2 - x$
-5	30
-3	12
-1	2
0	0
1	0
3	6
5	20

x	$x^2 + 8x$
-5	-15
-3	-15
-1	-7
0	0
1	9
3	33
5	65

x	$x^2 - x + 2$
-5	32
-3	14
-1	4
0	2
1	2
3	8
5	22

MORE MATH REASONING

50. To solve the equation $16 = x(x + 3)$ by creating a table, what value would you pick first for x? Why?

51. The product of two consecutive integers is 72. What are the two numbers?

52. Sum Area The sum of the area of square *A* and the area of square *B* is equal to the area of square *C*. What are the areas of each? Explain your method of solution.

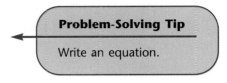

Problem-Solving Tip

Write an equation.

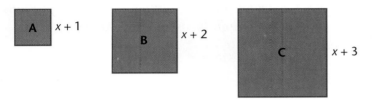

A $x + 1$

B $x + 2$

C $x + 3$

53. Study these numbers and predict the next three numbers in the pattern. Tell how you decided.

0, 1, 3, 7, 15, 31, ...

54. Circulating The Lakeside Park has a circular region with a 20-foot diameter which is covered with rocks. The gardener decides to remove a circular area with a 4-foot radius from the center so that he can plant spring flowers. How much will the radius of the circle increase if he places the stones around the outside of the original circle?

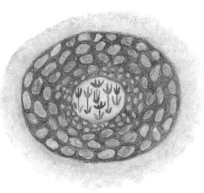

55. Bill has an interest in impact craters, caused by asteroids or comets striking the earth. He has studied a few found in Canada and wants to determine if there is a relationship between the age and the diameter of the crater. Describe how he could examine the data.

Diameter (km)	Age	Diameter (km)	Age
12	100	30	350
13	450	32	290
20	15	37	485
22	290	46	360
23	225	70	210
25	95	140	1840
28	38		

Making Connections

←**C O N N E C T**→ *Quadratic functions describe many relationships in the real world; hence, many real-world problems involve solving quadratic equations. Graphs, tables, and factoring can all be useful tools for solving quadratic equations.*

You can sometimes use quadratic functions and equations to help make better business decisions.

EXPLORE: A DAY IN SPACE

MATERIALS

Graphing utility or Graph paper (optional)

The senior class is sponsoring a Star Trek® Day when they will show 10 favorite Star Trek television episodes. Last year they charged $3 and sold 2500 tickets. The students took a survey and found that, for every 10¢ price increase, they would sell 50 fewer tickets. They want to decide what to charge this year.

1. Let $x =$ the number of 10¢ price increases. Explain why the following expressions represent the expected ticket price, number of tickets sold, and money collected.

Number of Price Increases	Ticket Price	Number of Tickets	Money Collected
x	$3.00 + 0.10x$	$2500 - 50x$	$(3.00 + 0.10x)(2500 - 50x)$

2. Create a table of values for these expressions or graph the function
$y = (3.00 + 0.10x)(2500 - 50x)$.
Use your table or graph to answer each question.

3. How much money will the class collect if the ticket price isn't increased at all?

4. Is it possible for them to collect $7800? $9000? Explain your answers.

5. What is the most money they can expect to collect according to this model, and what is the ticket price? Explain how you used your table or graph to decide.

1. How do you recognize a solution of a quadratic equation of the form $ax^2 + bx + c = 0$ from the graph of the quadratic function $y = ax^2 + bx + c$?
2. Describe a way to determine the number of solutions of a quadratic equation.
3. If you factor a quadratic equation and get a result of the form $(x - a)(x - a) = 0$, what can you say about the solutions of the equation? What would the graph look like if you solved the equation by graphing?

Self-Assessment

1. Use the graph of the function $y = x^2 - 4$.
   a. Find the coordinates of the vertex.
   b. How many solutions would the equation $8 = x^2 - 4$ have?
   c. How many solutions would the equation $-8 = x^2 - 4$ have?
   d. Give a value of y in $y = x^2 - 4$ so there is only one solution. Tell how you decided.

Use the graph of the function $y = x^2 + 4x$ to solve each equation.

2. $0 = x^2 + 4x$

3. $-5 = x^2 + 4x$

4. $-4 = x^2 + 4x$

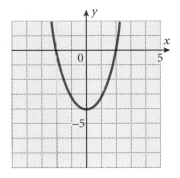

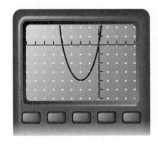

5. **Foxtail** A research scientist for a toy company is experimenting with a new toy called a *Foxtail*. The height (h) in feet, reached by the Foxtail t seconds after it has been thrown, can be modeled by the equation $h = \frac{1}{2}(-32)t^2 + 40t$.
   a. When is the Foxtail at 0 feet? Explain.
   b. Find the height of the Foxtail at $t = 0, 0.5, 1, 1.5, 2$, and 2.5 seconds.
   c. When is the Foxtail at 16 feet?
   d. Between what two values of t does the Foxtail reach its maximum height?
   e. What is the maximum height?

6. Which of these equations is (are) equivalent to $x^2 + 0.4x + 0.16 = 0$?

I. $x^2 + 0.4x = 0.16$ II. $x^2 = -0.16$ III. $x(x + 0.4) = -0.16$

(a) I only   (b) II only   (c) III only   (d) I and III   (e) I, II, and III

7. Copy and complete the table for the function $y = x^2 + 3x$.

x	-5	-4	-3	-2	-1	0	1	2
$x^2 + 3x$								

a. What is the solution to the equation when $y = 0$?
b. What is the solution when $y = 4$?

8. Write a linear equation with a solution of -2.

9. Write a quadratic equation with a solution of -2.

Solve each equation. Tell which method you used.

10. $2 = 2(x - 1)^2$ **11.** $0 = x^2 + 2x + 1$ **12.** $-5 = x^2 + 9x + 9$

13. Increased Circulation *Sci Fi Daily* sells their newsletters for 50¢ per copy and has a circulation of 50,000 people. Because of increased labor costs, the company has decided that it must raise the price of the newsletter. A marketing survey indicated that for every 10¢ increase, the circulation would decrease by 5000 people. The company also sells science fiction merchandise but it feels that it must increase its income to at least $27,000 to stay in business.

a. Let $x = $ each 10¢ increase in price. Write an expression to show the new price per copy. (Think of what the price would be for a 10¢ increase, for two 10¢ increases, x 10¢ increases.)

b. Write an expression to show the reduced circulation. (Remember that for each price increase the circulation goes down by 5000.)

c. *Sci Fi Daily's* income is based on the price times the circulation. Write a function to show the income (I) made from the increased prices.

d. The following is a spreadsheet that the president prepared to help the board of directors make a decision. What price increases would yield an income of at least $27,000?

e. Between what two numbers would the maximum income be found?

f. What would you recommend to the company that the new selling price be? Explain your reasoning.

10¢ Price Increases	Income
1	$27,000
2	28,000
3	28,000
4	27,000
5	25,000
6	22,000

9-3 Other Techniques for Solving Quadratic Equations

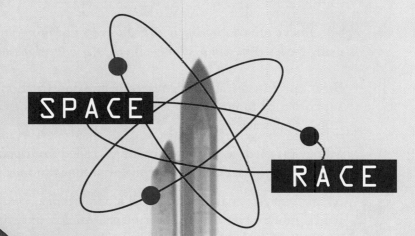

SPACE

RACE

In the 1950s, as the United States powered into the space age with Vanguard, its first missile program, Evelyn Boyd Granville launched her career. She received her doctorate degree in mathematics from Yale University. She worked in the Atomic Energy Commission and later at IBM in Washington, D.C. There she made on-site calculations on computers that guided the Vanguard satellite.

The type of mathematics Dr. Granville performed is called numerical analysis. Her work on the Vanguard program made good use of her study of functions. Later she studied rocket trajectories at Space Technology Labs in California.

Dr. Granville was inspired by the historical physicists Copernicus and Galileo who bravely theorized that Earth revolved around the sun. Dr. Granville credits her family and her teachers for giving her the confidence to study mathematics. After working in the space industry, she became a professor of mathematics at California State University at Los Angeles.

Now living in Texas, she recalls the excitement of many discoveries made by the people working in the early stages of the space program, particularly those that benefited humankind. These discoveries laid the groundwork for today's space explorations including the Space Shuttle program. She hopes that teachers will help students to have confidence in their math ability.

1. There have been many important scientific discoveries since the time of Copernicus and Galileo. Why do you think modern scientists are still fascinated by ideas that are hundreds of years old?
2. The United States government depends heavily on private industry for human and material resources to expand our knowledge of space. Why is private industry interested in space?

Solving with Square Roots

← **CONNECT** → *You've solved quadratic equations by graphing, by factoring, and using tables. You can also solve quadratic equations using square roots.*

Business ventures, scientific research, and construction projects are often supported by money from banks. Much of the money banks loan comes from savings accounts.

Money invested in a savings account is called *principal*. Banks usually pay **interest** on savings making the amount of money grow over time.

Simple interest is paid on principal alone, whereas *compound interest* is paid on interest as well as on principal. An account with interest compounded annually earns more and more each year as the interest is added at the end of each year.

EXPLORE: THAT'S INTERESTING

Suppose you invest a principal of $1000 at an interest rate of 8% per year ($r = 0.08$).

1. How much interest will you earn after one year? What is the total amount of money you will have at the end of one year? How many times greater is the amount at the end of the year than the principal?

2. How much interest will you earn *on this new amount* in the second year? What is the total amount of money you will have at the end of two years? How many times greater is the amount at the end of the second year than the amount at the end of the first year?

3. Will you earn the same amount of interest in the second year as in the first, or will the interest be *compounded*? Will the amount of money increase by the same factor each year?

4. Suppose you invest $1000 at an interest rate of r. Write the amount of money (A) you will have at the end of two years as a function of r. What kind of function is it?

When you apply the Pythagorean Theorem and use square roots to find the length of a side of a right triangle, you are actually solving a simple quadratic equation, such as $c^2 = 49$. Square roots can also be used to solve other quadratic equations.

EXAMPLE

1. Solve $3x^2 + 4 = 18$.

$$3x^2 + 4 = 18$$

$$3x^2 = 14 \qquad \text{Subtract 4 from both sides.}$$

$$x^2 = \frac{14}{3} \qquad \text{Divide both sides by 3.}$$

$$x = \pm\sqrt{\frac{14}{3}} \qquad \text{Find the square root of both sides.}$$

$$x \approx \pm 2.160 \qquad \text{Estimate } \sqrt{\frac{14}{3}} \text{ with your calculator.}$$

Both solutions check in the original equation.

You investigated compound interest in the Explore. If you invest a principal (P) at a compound interest rate (r), the investment will grow by a factor of $(1 + r)$ each year. At the end of two years, the amount of money (A) you will have is $A = P(1 + r)^2$.

Using square roots, you can solve to find the interest rate that will give your money a certain growth over two years.

EXAMPLE

2. What is the interest rate on an account, in which interest is compounded annually, if a principal of $625 grows to $729 in two years?

$$A = P(1 + r)^2$$

$$729 = 625(1 + r)^2 \qquad \text{Substitute the values of } A \text{ and } P.$$

$$\frac{729}{625} = (1 + r)^2 \qquad \text{Divide both sides by 625.}$$

$$\pm\frac{27}{25} = 1 + r \qquad \text{Find the square root of both sides.}$$

$$-1 \pm \frac{27}{25} = r \qquad \text{Subtract 1 from both sides.}$$

$$r = \frac{2}{25} \text{ or } \frac{-52}{25}$$

$$= 0.08 \text{ or } -2.08$$

The interest rate is the positive solution, $r = 0.08$ or 8%.

CONSIDER

?

1. Why isn't a *negative* solution a reasonable interest rate in Example 2?

TRY IT

Solve each quadratic equation.
a. $4g^2 = 16$ **b.** $-3y^2 = -9$ **c.** $2m^2 + 3 = 15$
d. What is the interest rate on an account, in which interest is compounded annually, if a principal of \$400 grows to \$441 in two years?

You can solve any equation of the form $ax^2 + b = c$ using this **square root method** of solving quadratic equations. Just use the properties of equality to get x^2 alone on one side of the equation, and then find the square root of both sides.

REFLECT

1. Give three equations for which solving with square roots would be an effective method.
2. Explain why the square root method is *not* effective for solving equations of the form $ax^2 + bx + c = 0$ when $b \neq 0$.
3. Does the constant term have to be the square of an integer in order to solve a quadratic equation using the square root method? Explain.
4. Why does taking the square root of both sides of an equation usually give *two* mathematical solutions?

If you deposited \$10 at 5% interest per year in this bank during the Gold Rush of 1849, it would be worth over \$15,000 today.

CORE

1. Getting Started Use these steps to solve $5x^2 + 4 = 21$.
   a. Subtract 4 from each side.
   b. Divide both sides by 5.
   c. Find the square root of both sides. Check your solutions.

Tell which method you would use to solve each equation: graphing, using a table, factoring, or taking the square root. Explain your choice.

2. $x^2 + 5x = 24$ **3.** $c^2 - 13c + 36 = 0$ **4.** $0 = g^2 - 28$

5. When $x^2 - 8 = 0$ is solved by using the square root method, $x = \pm\sqrt{8}$. What are the two solutions?

6. Use these steps to calculate the amount (A) in an account if a $2000 principal ($P$) was deposited for a two-year period. Interest was compounded annually at the rate (r) of 4%.
   a. Use the formula $A = P(1 + r)^2$. Substitute the values of the variables.
   b. Simplify within the parentheses and raise to the power before multiplying.
   c. What amount would be in the account after two years?

Solve each quadratic equation. Tell which method you used.

7. $x^2 = 144$ **8.** $s^2 = 10$ **9.** $2w^2 = 32$

10. $-3d^2 = 39$ **11.** $9y^2 - 4 = 0$ **12.** $25n^2 - 125 = 50$

13. Use these steps to find the interest rate on an account in which interest is compounded annually if a principal of $880.00 grows to $919.60 in two years.
   a. Substitute the values of the variables into the formula $A = P(1 + r)^2$.
   b. Divide both sides by 880.
   c. Find the square root of both sides and solve for r.
   d. Write your answer as a percent.

14. Find an equation of the form $x^2 = a$ with the solutions 3 and -3.

15. Solve $x^2 + 8 = 24$ by the square root method.

16. How Fast Will It Grow? Billy's grandparents gave him $324 for graduation. He is checking on different banks for their interest rates. He wants his savings to be at least $400 in two years.
   a. What interest rate compounded annually would make a principal of $324 grow to $400 in two years?
   b. If the best interest rate that he can find is 5.25% compounded annually how much will he have in the account at the end of two years?

17. What is the interest rate on an account in which interest is compounded annually if a principal of $2540 grows to $2698.75 in two years?

18. If the area of the circle in the diagram is 154 square meters, what is the approximate area of the square? Use $\frac{22}{7}$ for π.

19. You Be the Judge Mike says the equation $x^2 + 3 = -22$ can be solved by the square root method. Julita says it cannot. Who is right? How do you know?

Tell whether each statement is true or false. If it is false, give a counterexample to prove it is false.

20. If $x^2 = 26$, then the solution is $x = \sqrt{26}$.

21. The solution of $x^2 = 25$ can be written as $x = \pm 5$.

22. The expression $2 + 3\sqrt{x}$ is equivalent to $5\sqrt{x}$.

23. Answer the following questions about the graph of $y = x^2 - 16$.
  a. What are the x-intercepts?
  b. Solve $x^2 - 16 = 0$. How are the solutions to this equation related to the x-intercepts?
  c. For what values of x is $y = 0$? $y > 0$? $y < 0$?
  d. What are the coordinates of the point when y is a minimum?

24. Look Out Below The equation $h = \frac{1}{2}(-9.8)t^2 + s$ gives the approximate height, in meters, of an object starting at rest at a height of s meters and falling for t seconds.
  a. If an object was accidentally dropped from the top of the Sears Tower in Chicago, about how long would it take it to fall to the ground, approximately 440 meters below?
  b. How far will the object have fallen in 5 seconds?

LOOK AHEAD

25. For the quadratic equation given in standard form, $0 = 2x^2 + x - 6$, $a = 2$, $b = 1$, and $c = -6$. Evaluate $b^2 - 4ac$.

Copy and complete this table.

	Equation	Equation in Standard Form	a	b	c
26.	$(x + 3)^2 = -5$				
27.	$12 = x^2 - 12$				
28.	$2x^2 + 0.5 = x + 0.4$				

MORE PRACTICE

Tell which method you would use to solve each equation: graphing, using a table, factoring, or taking the square root. Explain your choice.

29. $x^2 + 3x = 18$ **30.** $0 = 4g^2 - 8$ **31.** $t^2 + 5t = 0$

Solve each equation by using the square root method.

32. $x^2 = 256$ **33.** $85 = r^2$ **34.** $10 = s^2 + 4$

Solve each quadratic equation by any method.

35. $8y^2 - 16 = 0$ **36.** $-2a^2 = 72$ **37.** $x^2 - 3x = 4$

38. $5p^2 - 40 = 0$ **39.** $k^2 - 18 = 72$ **40.** $z^2 - 3z = 18$

41. $3c^2 - 27 = 0$ **42.** $36 = -9d + d^2$ **43.** $n^2 - 36 = 64$

44. $6f^2 - 42 = 0$ **45.** $42 = -11g + g^2$ **46.** $m^2 - 25 = 144$

47. Use these steps to calculate the amount (A) in an account if a \$4000 principal (P) was deposited for a two-year period. Interest was compounded annually at the rate (r) of 5%.
   a. Use the formula $A = P(1 + r)^2$. Substitute the values of the variables.
   b. Simplify within the parentheses and raise to the power before multiplying.
   c. What amount would be in the account after two years?

MORE MATH REASONING

48. Is solving the equation $x^2 = 9$ the same as finding $\sqrt{9}$? Explain.

49. Explain the meaning of the following statement: If $x^2 = a$, then $x = \sqrt{a}$ or $x = -\sqrt{a}$ for $a \geq 0$.

Some quadratic trinomial equations can be solved by finding the square roots. Remember that a trinomial square can be factored into a binomial squared.

Example   Solve: $x^2 + 8x + 16 = 10$.

$$x^2 + 8x + 16 = 10$$
$$(x + 4)^2 = 10 \qquad \text{Factor into a binomial squared.}$$
$$x + 4 = \pm\sqrt{10} \qquad \text{Find the square root of both sides.}$$
$$x = -4 \pm\sqrt{10} \qquad \text{Subtract 4 from both sides.}$$

The solutions are $-4 + \sqrt{10}$ and $-4 - \sqrt{10}$.

50. Solve $(h + 4)^2 = 12$ by the square root method.

51. Solve $m^2 - 14m + 49 = 16$ by the square root method.

52. Find an equation of the form $ax^2 + b = c$ with the solutions 3 and -3.

53. The process of changing an expression of the form $x^2 + bx$ into a trinomial square is called completing the square; $x^2 + bx + \left(\frac{b}{2}\right)^2$ completes the square for $x^2 + bx$. Complete the square for each of the following. Write the trinomial square in factored form.

    a. $x^2 - 6x$ **b.** $c^2 + 8c$ **c.** $d^2 + 7d$

54. **Some Odd Sums** The sum of consecutive odd numbers can be found by applying the formula $n^2 = S$, where $n =$ the number of consecutive odd numbers and S is the sum.

    a. What is the sum of the first eight consecutive odd numbers?

    b. If the sum of the numbers is 441, how many odd numbers were added?

55. What is the formula for total amount of money after interest is computed on a given principal for three years? in t years? Explain how you know.

56. Evelyn Boyd Granville made use of Pascal's Triangle in her study of probability. You can also do this. Think of the possible outcomes when flipping one coin; two coins; three coins. Compare the numbers of different outcomes in each situation to the numbers in a given row. What is the link between Pascal's Triangle and probability?

```
                1
              1   1
            1   2   1
          1   3   3   1
        1   4   6   4   1
```

9-3
PART B The Quadratic Formula

← **CONNECT** → *You've solved quadratic equations by graphing, by factoring, using tables, and by the square root method. Each of these methods has limitations. The quadratic formula allows you to efficiently solve any quadratic equation.*

The solution of quadratic equations has been of interest to many cultures. The Arab mathematician Mohammed ibn Musa al-Khowarizmi wrote a book published in 825 A.D. in which he showed how to solve equations. One of the methods that he used was geometric models. He ignored negative solutions to quadratic equations because he felt that they had no meaning geometrically.

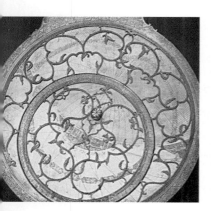

Astrolabe, circa 1712.

Today most people solve quadratic equations using a formula that is based on a geometric model. The **Quadratic Formula** is one of the most important formulas in mathematics.

> **QUADRATIC FORMULA**
>
> If $ax^2 + bx + c = 0$, $a \neq 0$, then $x = \dfrac{-b \pm \sqrt{b^2 - 4ac}}{2a}$.

To apply the quadratic formula, write the quadratic equation in standard form and substitute the values of a, b, and c into the formula.

EXAMPLE

Solve $2x^2 + 3x = -1$.

$$2x^2 + 3x = -1$$
$$2x^2 + 3x + 1 = 0 \qquad \text{Write the equation in standard form.}$$

Use the values $a = 2$, $b = 3$, and $c = 1$ in the quadratic formula.

$$x = \frac{-b \pm \sqrt{b^2 - 4ac}}{2a}$$

$$x = \frac{-3 \pm \sqrt{3^2 - 4(2)(1)}}{2(2)} \qquad \text{Substitute the values } a, b, \text{ and } c \text{ into the formula.}$$

$$x = \frac{-3 \pm \sqrt{1}}{4} \qquad \text{Simplify.}$$

$$x = \frac{-3 + 1}{4} = -\frac{1}{2} \text{ or } x = \frac{-3 - 1}{4} = -1$$

The two solutions are $x = -\dfrac{1}{2}$ and $x = -1$.

Check both solutions in the original equation.

$$2x^2 + 3x \stackrel{?}{=} -1 \qquad\qquad 2x^2 - 3x \stackrel{?}{=} -1$$
$$2(-1)^2 + 3(-1) \stackrel{?}{=} -1 \qquad 2\left(-\frac{1}{2}\right)^2 + 3\left(-\frac{1}{2}\right) \stackrel{?}{=} -1$$
$$-1 = -1 \ ✔ \qquad\qquad\qquad -1 = -1 \ ✔$$

TRY IT

Solve each quadratic equation using the quadratic formula.
a. $x^2 + 2x - 5 = 0$ **b.** $s^2 - 3s = -1$

Recall that a quadratic equation can have zero, one, or two real-number solutions. One way to determine the number of solutions is using a graph. Another way is using the expression under the radical symbol, $b^2 - 4ac$, in the quadratic formula. This expression is called the **discriminant.**

MATERIALS

Graphing utility or Graph paper

1. To determine the number of solutions of each quadratic equation, graph the appropriate quadratic function. Evaluate the discriminant in each case. Copy and complete the table.

Equation	Number of Solutions	Value of the Discriminant $b^2 - 4ac$
$x^2 + 5x - 6 = 0$		
$2x^2 + 5x + 3 = 0$		
$x^2 + 6x + 9 = 0$		
$4x^2 - 28x + 49 = 0$		
$x^2 + x + 5 = 0$		
$2x^2 + 2x + 3 = 0$		

2. Make a conjecture about how you can use the discriminant to determine the number of solutions of a quadratic equation.

3. Make up several quadratic equations in standard form and use your conjecture to determine the number of solutions of each equation. Check by graphing.

Using the quadratic formula is often the most reliable method of solving a quadratic equation. You know it will always work. However, you should use whatever method is fastest and easiest for you.

WHAT DO **YOU** THINK?

Solve $x^2 - 11x + 28 = 0$.

Esteban thinks . . .

I'll use the quadratic formula.

$$x = \frac{11 \pm \sqrt{(-11)^2 - 4(28)}}{2} = \frac{11 \pm \sqrt{9}}{2} = \frac{11 \pm 3}{2}$$

$$= \frac{14}{2} \text{ or } \frac{8}{2}$$

$$= 7 \text{ or } 4$$

The solutions are $x = 7$ and $x = 4$.

Elizabeth thinks . . .

Since -4 and -7 have a sum of -11 and a product of 28, I can factor the equation immediately!

$x^2 - 11x + 28 = (x - 7)(x - 4) = 0$ when $x = 7$ or $x = 4$.

The solutions are $x = 7$ and $x = 4$.

CONSIDER

?

1. If Esteban and Elizabeth had to solve $x^2 - 11x + 29 = 0$, would you suggest that either of them change their method? Why?

The quadratic formula was known to Hindu mathematicians more than a thousand years ago. To this day, it remains one of the most famous formulas in mathematics.

REFLECT

1. Name an advantage of using the quadratic formula over factoring to solve a quadratic equation.
2. What does the discriminant of a quadratic equation tell you about the graph of the related quadratic function?
3. Give an example of a quadratic equation that you can solve using the quadratic formula, but that you *cannot* solve by factoring.

Exercises

CORE

1. **Getting Started** Use these steps to solve $2x^2 + 5x = 3$.
   a. Write the equation in standard form, $ax^2 + bx + c = 0$.
   b. Find the values a, b, and c, and substitute them into the quadratic formula,
   $x = \dfrac{-b \pm \sqrt{b^2 - 4ac}}{2a}$.
   c. What does the value of the *discriminant*, $b^2 - 4ac$, tell you about the number of solutions of this equation?
   d. What are the solutions of $2x^2 + 5x = 3$? Check your solution.

Write each quadratic equation in standard form, $0 = ax^2 + bx + c$. Identify a, b, and c.

2. $5x^2 - 10 = 0$

3. $m^2 = 49m$

4. $j^2 - 6j = 10$

5. Use the quadratic equation $x^2 + 6x = 16$ to answer each question.
   a. Solve the equation by using the quadratic formula.
   b. Solve the equation by factoring. Show your work.
   c. Which method did you find easier?
   d. Solve the equation by one more method. What method did you choose?

Solve each quadratic equation. Tell which method you used and why.

6. $m^2 + 4m - 5 = 0$

7. $6x^2 - x = 15$

8. $3b^2 = 27$

9. $3x^2 + 5x + 2 = 0$

10. $c^2 - 5 = 20$

11. $f^2 + 6f = -8$

12. $5y^2 - 25y + 30 = 0$

13. $2a^2 - 3 = 35$

14. $p^2 + 5p = -6$

15. $d^2 - 2d + 5 = 0$

16. $k^2 + 6k = 6$

17. $2x^2 + 13x = -15$

18. The area of the rectangle is 91 square feet.
   a. What is the value of x?
   b. What are the dimensions of the rectangle?

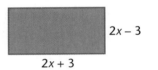

$2x - 3$

$2x + 3$

Find the number of solutions of each equation by using the discriminant $b^2 - 4ac$.

19. $9x^2 - 12x + 3 = 0$

20. $t^2 + 5t = 8$

21. $j^2 = 3 + 5j$

22. If $a = 1$, $b = 7$, $c = -6$, write a quadratic equation using them. How many solutions does your equation have?

23. Given the graph of the quadratic function $y = -x^2 - 8$, what can you say about the value of the discriminant of $-x^2 - 8 = 0$? Explain how you know.

24. If you are told that a quadratic equation has only one real solution, what do you know about the value of the discriminant?

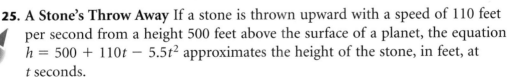

25. A Stone's Throw Away If a stone is thrown upward with a speed of 110 feet per second from a height 500 feet above the surface of a planet, the equation $h = 500 + 110t - 5.5t^2$ approximates the height of the stone, in feet, at t seconds.
   a. When will the rock be 698 feet above the planet's surface?
   b. What method did you use to solve the equation?
   c. Approximately how high is the rock after 8 seconds?
   d. What is the approximate maximum height that the rock reaches?

26. Making Money The amount of money (P) invested at an interest rate (r) will grow to an amount (A) in t years. The formula $A = P(1 + r)^t$ represents the amount A if the interest is compounded annually. What is the approximate interest rate if $1024 grows to $1225 in two years?

27. Which pair of numbers are the solutions of the equation $2x^2 - x = 7$?

(a) $\dfrac{-1 \pm \sqrt{57}}{4}$ (b) $\dfrac{1 \pm \sqrt{57}}{4}$ (c) $\dfrac{-1 \pm \sqrt{57}}{2}$ (d) $\dfrac{1 \pm \sqrt{57}}{2}$

28. Write a quadratic equation that has only one real solution.

29. Write a quadratic equation that has no real solutions.

LOOK BACK

30. Match each function with the graph it describes. Give a reason for your choice. [7-2]

a. :Y1ᴇ abs (2X)
   :Y2 =
   :Y3 =
   :Y4 =

b. :Y1ᴇ 2X
   :Y2 =
   :Y3 =
   :Y4 =

c. :Y1ᴇ √ (2X)
   :Y2 =
   :Y3 =
   :Y4 =

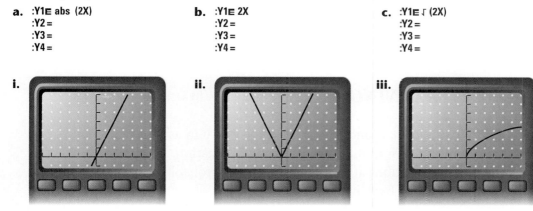

i.   **ii.**   **iii.**

31. How many values are possible for b if $x^2 + bx - 18$ is factorable? [8-2]

> **Problem-Solving Tip**
>
> Make an organized list of the factors of -18.

32. The formula $h = \frac{1}{2}(-32)t^2 + vt + s$ represents the height, in feet, of an object after t seconds. What can you say about a situation where the function $h = \frac{1}{2}(-32)t^2 + 10$ applies? Explain. [9-1]

MORE PRACTICE

For each quadratic equation, identify *a*, *b*, and *c*.

33. $x^2 = 5$

34. $-100 + 4f - 2f^2 = 0$

35. $2x^2 = 3x - 1$

Solve each quadratic equation. Tell which method you used.

36. $s^2 - 45 = 0$

37. $c(c + 3) = 28$

38. $2d^2 + 8d = 21$

39. $3v^2 + 2v - 10 = 0$

40. $m^2 = 6 - m$

41. $2x^2 + 2x = -21$

42. $29 = n^2 - 20$

43. $6k^2 - k = 12$

44. $3w^2 = 5 - 4w$

Find the number of solutions of each equation by using the discriminant $b^2 - 4ac$.

45. $3x^2 + 3x = 3$

46. $d^2 + d - 1 = 0$

47. $f^2 = -25$

48. The area of the rectangle is 99 square feet.
 a. What is the value of x?
 b. What are the dimensions of the rectangle?

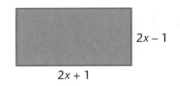

$2x - 1$

$2x + 1$

MORE MATH REASONING

49. Substitute 1, 2, and 3 for *a*, *b*, and *c* in $ax^2 + bx + c = 0$ in as many different ways as you can, using each number once in a given equation. If someone chooses one of your equations at random, what is the probability that the solutions will be integers? Explain your solution.

> **Problem-Solving Tip**
>
> Make an organized list of the equations.

50. For what value(s) of k will the equation $x^2 + kx + 49 = 0$ have only one solution?

51. For what value(s) of k are the solutions of $x^2 + 8x + k = 0$ real numbers?

52. The rectangles have the same area.
 a. Write a quadratic equation in standard form that shows that the two areas are equivalent.
 b. What is the area of each?

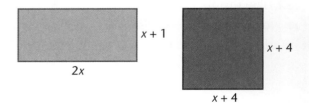

$x + 1$

$2x$

$x + 4$

$x + 4$

53. Evelyn Boyd Granville enjoys solving puzzles like this one. Solve it and explain your reasoning.

> The math club at Vanguard High School held a puzzle solving contest.
> Eight members of the science club were there.
> Ten members of the math club attended.
> Two reporters from the school paper came.
> Three students are members of both the science and the math club.
> One reporter belongs to neither club the other belongs to both.
> Four students came just because they like puzzles.
> The moderator of the math club was there.
> How many people attended the contest?

54. Describe the solutions of the quadratic equation $ax^2 + bx + c = 0$, given the following conditions.

a. $a \neq 0$, $b \neq 0$, $c = 0$ **b.** $a \neq 0$, $b = 0$, $c = 0$

c. $b = 0$, a and c have opposite signs   **d.** $b = 0$, a and c have the same signs

History

55. Brahmagupta, the most prominent Hindu mathematician of the seventh century, wrote an astronomical work, *Brahmasiddhanta*, in which he gave the following solution to equations of the form $x^2 + px - q = 0$.

$$x = \frac{\sqrt{p^2 + 4q} - p}{2}$$

Use the quadratic formula or substitution to show that Brahmagupta's solution is correct. What is the other solution of the quadratic equation $x^2 + px - q = 0$?

9-3 PART C Making Connections

← CONNECT → *You've explored quadratic equations and many methods for solving them. These equations and methods are valuable tools used in science and business.*

Evelyn Boyd Granville's work with rockets and satellites required a clear knowledge of projectile motion in the earth's atmosphere and beyond. Quadratic functions and equations are basic tools of any study of projectile motion.

EXPLORE: BLAST OFF!

MATERIALS

Graphing utility or
Graph paper

Solid rocket boosters separate from a space shuttle two minutes after launch. Then the boosters fall back to earth where they can be retrieved and reused.

Assume that the boosters separate from the shuttle at an altitude of 40,000 feet with an upward speed of 1000 feet per second. The vertical motion formula gives a model of their height, in feet, t seconds after separating from the shuttle.

$$h = \frac{1}{2}(-32)t^2 + 1000t + 40{,}000$$

1. Graph the height function. Use your graph to estimate the maximum height of the boosters and the time when they will reach that height.
2. Write and solve a quadratic equation to find the time when the boosters will reach earth if their parachutes fail to open.

Solid rocket booster

> **Problem-Solving Tip**
>
> Choose an appropriate solution method.

3. If the parachutes open properly, how do you think the actual time it takes the boosters to reach earth will be affected?
4. Besides the parachutes, what are some other possible causes of inaccuracy in using the vertical motion formula as a model in this situation? Explain.

REFLECT

1. If all quadratic equations can be solved using the quadratic formula, why would you ever want to use another method?
2. Can any quadratic equation be solved using the square root method? Explain your answer.
3. Give an example of a quadratic equation you could solve using each method.
   a. factoring   **b.** square root method   **c.** quadratic formula

Self-Assessment

For each quadratic equation, identify *a*, *b*, and *c*.

1. $x^2 + 2x = 0$

2. $3c^2 - 1 = 2c$

3. $4 = x^2$

Find the number of solutions of each equation by using the discriminant $b^2 - 4ac$.

4. $2x^2 - x + 15 = 0$

5. $b^2 + 5b = 10$

6. $j^2 = j - 2.5$

7. Making More Money Use the formula $A = P(1 + r)^2$ to find the interest rate on an account in which the interest is compounded annually if $441 grows to $484 in two years.

Industry

Solve each equation by any method. Explain your choice of method.

8. $x^2 = 9$

9. $c^2 - 15 = 0$

10. $w^2 + 4w = 8$

11. $d^2 + 5d + 6 = 0$

12. $3k^2 + 11k - 4 = 0$

13. $30 = 25n - 5n^2$

14. $y^2 - 12y = 45$

15. $e^2 - 21 = 0$

16. $z^2 = 81$

17. $f^2 + 10f + 9 = 0$

18. $6\ell^2 + 11\ell - 7 = 0$

19. $3h^2 = 39h - 126$

20. Walking to New Orleans Jonathan, a Louisiana contractor, has been hired to complete a diagonal walkway across a rectangular garden that measures 22×36 meters. Approximately how long will the walkway be?

Industry

> **Problem-Solving Tip**
>
> Draw a diagram.

21. Tee Time Chi Chi Rodriquez hit a golf ball into the air with an upward speed of 64 feet per second. The formula $h = \frac{1}{2}(-32)t^2 + 64t$ approximates the height, in feet, of the ball after t seconds.

Science

a. At what time will the ball be 48 feet above the ground?
b. What method did you choose to solve the problem?
c. At what time will the ball hit the ground?
d. Will the ball be in the air for more than 5 seconds? Tell how you decided.

22. After reading Exercise 21, Kerri says the ball must have been hit at a 90° angle because the sine of 90° is equal to 1. Use $h = 0 + 64t - 16t^2$ and the equation $h = \frac{1}{2}at^2 + (\sin A)vt + s$ to explain why her reasoning is correct.

23. Which of the equations, if any, has 5 as a solution?

I. $x^2 - 2x = 15$ II. $u^2 + 5u = -4$ III. $v^3 - v = 0$

(a) I only   (b) II only   (c) III only   (d) I and II   (e) not here

24. There's More Than One Way… Students were asked to determine the number of solutions to the equation $3x^2 + 11x - 4 = 0$.

  a. Sally finds that there are two solutions of the equation $0 = 3x^2 + 11x - 4$ by graphing the function $y = 3x^2 + 11x - 4$. Explain how she could know this by examining the graph.

  b. Salvador finds that there are two solutions of the equation $0 = 3x^2 + 11x - 4$ by using the discriminant $d = b^2 - 4ac$. Explain how Sal used the discriminant.

  c. Sylvia finds that there are two solutions of the equation $0 = 3x^2 + 11x - 4$ by using the quadratic formula $x = \dfrac{-b \pm \sqrt{b^2 - 4ac}}{2a}$. Describe what Sylvia did to solve the equation.

  d. Which way would you approach the problem? Why?

25. This graph of women in the work force spans the years during which Evelyn Boyd Granville worked in the space industry and taught mathematics and computer science at the college level. Study the graph.

  a. Which group of women shows the greatest percent increase in the work force over these 30 years? What is that increase? Why do you think this happened?

  b. Do the lines on the graph represent three distinct groups? Explain.

  c. What would you predict these percentages to be in 2000? Why?

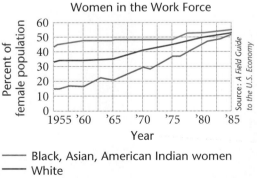

Women in the Work Force

Percent of female population / Year

Source: A Field Guide to the U.S. Economy

—— Black, Asian, American Indian women
—— White
—— Married women with children under 6

Chapter 9 Review

In Chapter 9, you continued working with nonlinear functions and equations. Quadratic functions and equations provide the tools for working with many applications from science such as the vertical motion formula. Solving quadratic equations is an important skill for solving problems.

KEY TERMS

Axis of symmetry [9-1]   Quadratic equation [9-2]   Standard form [9-2]

Discriminant [9-3]   Quadratic formula [9-3]   Vertex [9-1]

Parabola [9-1]   Reflection [9-1] x-intercepts [9-2]

Tell whether each sentence is true or false. If it is false, change the underlined word or phrase to make the sentence true.

1. The <u>discriminant</u> determines how many roots a quadratic function has.

2. A parabola is the graph of a <u>cubic</u> function.

CONCEPTS AND APPLICATIONS

3. Graph $y = 3x^2$. [9-1]
  a. Find the axis of symmetry.
  b. Find the coordinates of the vertex.
  c. Find the coordinates of three other points on the graph and their reflections.

Match each function with the graph it describes. [9-1]

4. $y = x^2$ **5.** $y = 3x^2$ **6.** $y = -x^2 + 3$

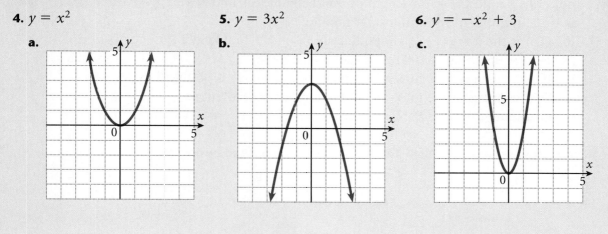

a.   **b.**   **c.**

Determine whether the functional relationship described is linear or quadratic. [9-1]

7. The amount of string needed to tie around a cube as a function of the length of a side.

8. The amount of paper needed to wrap a cube as a function of the length of a side.

9. The amount of asphalt needed to cover the surface of a parking lot as a function of the number of parking spaces.

10. When United Nations relief packages are dropped, one of the things that must be taken into consideration is the time allowed for a container to reach the ground. The formula for calculating the time (t) in seconds it takes to fall from an altitude of h feet is $h = \frac{1}{2}(32)t^2$. If the pilot wants the package to reach the ground 12 seconds after it is released, how high should the plane be when the package is released? Give your answer to the nearest 100 feet.

Write each quadratic equation in standard form, $0 = ax^2 - bx + c$. [9-2]

11. $12 = 3x^2 - 8x + 17$

12. $(x + 1)^2 = 9$

13. Use the graph of the function $y = x^2 + 4x - 5$. [9-2]
   a. Find the coordinates of the vertex.
   b. Find the axis of symmetry.
   c. Find the minimum y-value.
   d. How many solutions does the equation
      $8 = x^2 + 4x - 5$ have?
   e. How many solutions does the equation
      $-9 = x^2 + 4x - 5$ have?
   f. How many solutions does the equation
      $-11 = x^2 + 4x - 5$ have?

14. The formula $F = \frac{WRn^2}{2933}$ is used to calculate the force (F) in pounds, exerted by an object attached to a string and swung in a circle. W = the weight of the object in pounds, R = the length of the string in feet, and n = the number of revolutions per minute. [9-2]
   a. What is the force (F) of a 6-pound object on a 3-foot length of string spinning at 200 revolutions per minute?
   b. What happens to the force (F) if the length of string is doubled?
   c. What happens to the force (F) if the number of revolutions per minute is doubled?

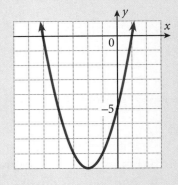

Solve each quadratic equation. Tell which method you used and why. [9-2]

15. $x^2 - x = 0$

16. $x^2 + 6x + 8 = 0$

17. $x^2 + 8x + 15 = 0$

18. $x^2 - 2x + 1 = 0$

19. $x^2 + 24x + 144 = 0$

20. $x^2 + 2x - 15 = 0$

21. Look at the table to help you solve the equation $-6 = x(x + 3)$. How many solutions do you think the equation has? Explain how you know. [9-2]

x	-4	-3	-2	-1	0	1	2
$x(x + 3)$	4	0	-2	-2	0	4	10

22. The formula $c = -0.15w^2 + t$, where c is windchill factor, w is wind speed, and t is temperature, is used by meteorologists to determine windchill factor. [9-2]

Science

a. Find the windchill factor when the temperature is $42°$ with a 12-mile-per-hour wind.

b. Find the windchill factor when the temperature drops to $21°$ but the wind speed doesn't change.

c. Find the windchill factor when the temperature remains stable but the wind speed doubles.

23. Use the formula $A = P(1 + r)^2$ to find the amount (A) a person will have when the interest at a specific rate (r) has been added to the principal (P) for two years compounded annually. What would the amount be on a principal of \$7400, invested at $5\frac{1}{4}\%$ for two years? [9-3]

Industry

24. Solve the equation $F = \dfrac{Wrn^2}{2933}$ for n. [9-3]

For each quadratic equation, find the value of the discriminant and the number of solutions. [9-3]

25. $3x^2 - 18x + 27 = 0$ **26.** $x^2 + 15x + 50 = 0$ **27.** $x^2 + 1 = 0$

28. Which pair of numbers are the solutions of the equation $2x^2 - x = 9$?

(a) $\dfrac{-1 \pm \sqrt{71}}{2}$ (b) $\dfrac{1 \pm \sqrt{71}}{2}$ (c) $\dfrac{-1 \pm \sqrt{73}}{4}$ (d) $\dfrac{1 \pm \sqrt{73}}{4}$ (e) not here

Solve each quadratic equation by any method. Explain your choice of method.

29. $x^2 = 64$ **30.** $x^2 - 12 = 0$ **31.** $4x^2 - 3x - 7 = 0$

32. $30 = -5x^2 + 25x$ **33.** $x^2 + 16 = 0$ **34.** $x^2 + 2x = 0$

CONCEPTS AND CONNECTIONS

35. Science and Health When you dive from a 3-meter diving board, your height (h) above the water, in meters, is described by the function $h = 3 + vt - 5t^2$, where v is the initial velocity in meters per second and t is time in seconds.

Science

a. If you hit the water after 1.6 seconds, what was your initial velocity (v)?

b. How high above the board did you go?

c. If you dive from a 1-meter board with the same initial velocity, when will you hit the water?

Describe what you have learned about quadratic functions and equations, including how they are related. List the different ways to solve quadratic equations. Write down which parts of the chapter were difficult for you and which sections you need to study further in order to better understand the chapter.

Chapter 9 Assessment

TEST

Use the graph of $y = x^2 + 4$.

1. Find the axis of symmetry.

2. Find the coordinates of the vertex.

3. Does y have a minimum or a maximum value? What is that value?

4. What point on the curve is a reflection of $(-1.5, 6.25)$?

5. Write the letter of the second pair that best matches the first pair.
Quadratic function: Parabola as
  (a) Inverse function: Direct function   (b) Linear function: Line
  (c) Direct function: Inverse function   (d) Quadratic formula: Discriminant
  (e) Not here

6. Sketch the graphs of the given functions. Then answer the following questions.
  i. $y = -4x^2 - 2$ **ii.** $y = 3x^2$ **iii.** $y = -\frac{1}{3}x^2$
  a. Which graph(s) open upward?
  b. Which graph(s) are symmetric over the y-axis?
  c. Which graph(s) have a vertex of $(0, 0)$? Explain how you know.

Rewrite these equations in standard form, $0 = ax^2 + bx + c$.

7. $10 = 2x^2 + 6x$ **8.** $4 = (x + 3)^2$

9. Use the graph of $y = x^2 + 6x$ to determine the number of solutions of each equation. Tell how you decided.
  a. $-9 = x^2 + 6x$
  b. $0 = x^2 + 6x$
  c. $12 = x^2 + 6x$

10. Marina has invested \$2400 at $6\frac{1}{4}\%$ to be compounded annually. To find the amount she will have after two years use the formula $A = P(1 + r)^2$.

11. Match each function with the graph it describes.

    a. $y = 2x^2 + 4$ **b.** $y = -2x^2 + 4$ **c.** $y = 2x^2 - 4$

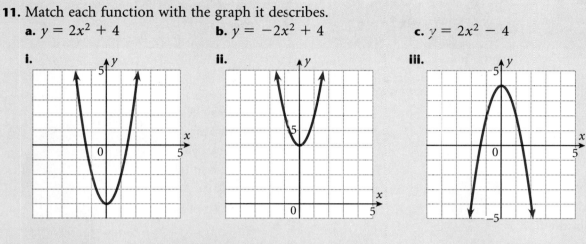

i.   **ii.**   **iii.**

Solve each equation. Tell which method you used and why.

12. $x^2 - 10 = 6$ **13.** $x^2 - 6x + 4 = 0$ **14.** $x^2 = 5x - 6$

15. Solve $x^2 - 9x + 18 = 0$ using two methods. Tell which method you prefer and why.

16. Keith drops a stone from a bridge to the water 100 meters below. Use the height function $h = -4.9t^2$ to find the number of seconds it took for the stone to reach the water.

17. Describe how you would use the discriminant to determine the number of solutions to the equation $2x^2 - 5x - 3 = 0$.

18. Animal Farming Larry and Fatima are planning a rectangular space in their yard for their 4-H animals. They have 20 feet of fence and will use the garage wall for one side of the pen. Larry says that he is sure that they can get 42 square feet of space for the animals. Fatima is not so sure. Use algebra to clear up their disagreement.

PERFORMANCE TASK

Suppose you are going to design a circular theater with a circular row surrounding a central stage. The lot is a square 1400 feet on a side. You are interested in how much area is added each time a level is added. Write a proposal for the width of the rows, taking into consideration the advantages and disadvantages of different widths. The people who will see your proposal are impressed by math, so be sure to include a variable, a quadratic function, tables, and a graph. Include a reason why it would be important to consider rows of different widths.

Chapter 10

Functions and the Structure of Algebra

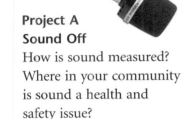

Project A
Sound Off
How is sound measured? Where in your community is sound a health and safety issue?

Project B
Aspire to Spirals
What human-made or natural things have spiral shapes? How are spirals generated mathematically?

Project C
Name That Tune
How are musical instruments tuned? Is all music based on the sounds *do, re, mi, fa, sol, la, ti, do*?

LORINDA JOHNSON

I didn't enjoy math in high school. I liked writing and creating. Now I wish I'd taken more math.

Today I work as a marketing communications specialist for an aviation firm and I have my own company doing freelance writing and designing. I coauthored a book, *Windows Sound Funpack*, about the sound capabilities of Microsoft Windows, a software program. I needed math and physics to explain the digitizing of sound samples in simple terms. When designing, I use math for good page layout.

Lorinda Johnson
Writer/Editor/Designer
The Write Solution
Lincoln, NE

Chapter 10

Functions and Structure of Algebra

GETTING READY

10-1
Real Numbers, Expressions, and Equations

In 10-1 you will explore rational and radical numbers, expressions, and their equations. You will need to know about solving inequalities and quadratics, square roots, and exponents.

Solve each inequality. [4-3]

1. $18 - 3x < 0$ **2.** $0.5x - 3 < 0$ **3.** $0 > \dfrac{3}{4}x - 9$ **4.** $-7x + 11 \geq 60$

Simplify each expression. [7-2; 8-2]

5. $-\sqrt{36}$ **6.** $\sqrt{7} \cdot \sqrt{7}$ **7.** $(-\sqrt{9})(-\sqrt{9})$ **8.** $\pm\sqrt{0.04}$

9. $\dfrac{\sqrt{64}}{\sqrt{100}}$ **10.** $\dfrac{x^2y^5}{xy^3}$ **11.** $(5x^3)^2$ **12.** $-4x^4y \cdot x^3y$

Solve each equation. [9-2]

13. $2x^2 - 18 = 0$ **14.** $x^2 - x - 12 = 0$ **15.** $4x^2 + 4x = -1$

16. $x^2 - 25 = 0$ **17.** $x^2 + 4x + 4 = 0$ **18.** $2x^2 = 12x$

10-2
Exploring Exponential and Logarithmic Functions

In 10-2 you will use technology to explore exponential and logarithmic functions. You will need skills in graphing and evaluating expressions with exponents.

Evaluate the expressions. [2-2]

19. For $x = 3$ **a.** $\dfrac{3}{4}x$ **b.** $0.6(2)^x$ **c.** $2(1.1)^x$

20. For $x = 4$ **a.** $5x^2$ **b.** $7 \cdot 10^{-x}$ **c.** $3(0.1)^x$

Find the missing exponent. [8-1]

21. $1000 = 10^?$ **22.** $32 = 2^?$ **23.** $0.01 = 10^?$

24. $81 = 3^?$ **25.** $10^? = 1,000,000$ **26.** $125 = 5^?$

Find the discriminant of each equation and tell the number of distinct solutions to each equation. [9-3]

27. $x^2 + 6x + 9 = 0$ **28.** $x^2 - 7x - 10 = 0$ **29.** $x^2 + 2 = 0$

30. $x^2 = 0$ **31.** $x(x + 5) = 0$ **32.** $(x - \pi)^2 = 0$

The Golden Ratio

The number π (pi) is certainly one of the most common ratios known. Another commonly known ratio is the *golden ratio*, approximately equal to 1.618.

The golden ratio is most often encountered in the form of a *golden rectangle*—a rectangle with dimensions in the golden ratio. Because golden rectangles are considered to be visually appealing, they have been used by artists and architects for thousands of years.

One famous example of the golden rectangle in classic architecture is the Parthenon in Greece. The golden ratio also influenced Leonardo da Vinci's illustrations for the book *De Divina Proportione* by Luca Pacioli.

Spirals such as this one, constructed in a series of embedded golden rectangles, can be seen in nature in surprising places, such as nautilus shells, sunflowers, and pine cones.

The golden ratio's connections to art, architecture, nature, and mathematics show why it has fascinated people for ages.

1. Why do you think golden rectangles might be more attractive than other rectangles?
2. In what sense is π a ratio?
3. What are some other examples of spirals in nature?

← **CONNECT** → *You have worked with expressions and real numbers throughout this course. Now you will reflect on the connections between these and other mathematical concepts. You will also explore algebraic expressions involving radicals and quotients.*

Writing the exact value of the golden ratio involves integers, a square root, and a ratio.

Golden ratio: $\quad g = \dfrac{1 + \sqrt{5}}{2} \approx 1.618034$

One of the many interesting topics connected with the golden ratio is the *Fibonacci sequence,* a famous pattern of numbers named for the thirteenth-century mathematician Leonardo Fibonacci.

EXPLORE: THE FIBONACCI SEQUENCE

MATERIALS

Calculator

The first seven numbers in the Fibonacci sequence follow.

$$1, 1, 2, 3, 5, 8, 13, \ldots$$

To find each new number in the sequence simply add the previous two numbers. (For example, $3 + 5 = 8$ and $5 + 8 = 13$.)

1. Write the first 15 numbers in the Fibonacci sequence. Then find the ratio of each number to the previous number. Use a calculator to approximate each ratio to six decimal places. (For example, $\dfrac{5}{3} \approx 1.666667$ and $\dfrac{8}{5} = 1.6$.)

> **Problem-Solving Tip**
>
> Make an organized list.

2. Compare the ratios you found with the value of the golden ratio. What do you notice?

Although the golden ratio and $\sqrt{5}$ are both irrational numbers, you can combine them in two surprising expressions to find *any* number in the Fibonacci sequence.

$\dfrac{g^n + g^{-n}}{\sqrt{5}}$ if n is an odd integer

$\dfrac{g^n - g^{-n}}{\sqrt{5}}$ if n is an even integer

3. Evaluate the appropriate expression for $n = 1, 2, 3, 4, 5,$ and 6, and show that you get the first six numbers in the Fibonacci sequence. What are the twenty-ninth and thirtieth numbers in the Fibonacci sequence?

4. Describe some of the integers, rational numbers, and irrational numbers you used in this Explore.

The Explore illustrates how mathematical concepts are often interconnected. At the core of mathematics are the real numbers we use to describe the values of quantities. Here are some of the number sets you've worked with in this course.

Natural numbers: $\{1, 2, 3, \ldots\}$

Whole numbers: $\{0, 1, 2, 3, \ldots\}$

Integers: $\{\ldots, -3, -2, -1, 0, 1, 2, 3, \ldots\}$

Rational numbers: $\{\frac{a}{b},$ for any integers a and b, with $b \neq 0\}$

Irrational numbers: {real numbers not equal to a quotient of two integers}

Real numbers: {all rational and irrational numbers}

This *Venn diagram* shows how these number sets are related within the real number system.

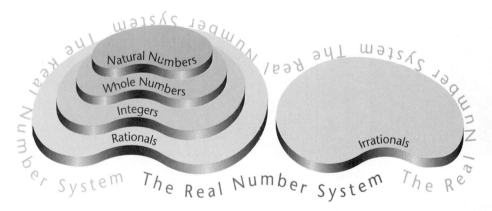

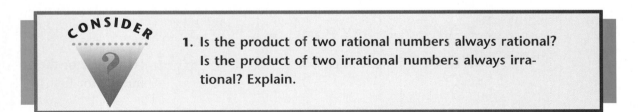

CONSIDER

?

1. Is the product of two rational numbers always rational? Is the product of two irrational numbers always irrational? Explain.

We have seen that an important tool of algebra is the use of variables to represent quantities. By using polynomials in quotients and radicals we can explore new expressions called **rational expressions** and **radical expressions.**

Rational Expressions

$\dfrac{x}{2}, \dfrac{4x^2 + 12x}{x(x-5)}, \dfrac{x^2 - 4}{x + 2}$

Radical Expressions

$\sqrt{2x}, \sqrt{3x - 5}, x^2 + \sqrt{2x}$

You can apply the same properties you've used throughout this course to simplify rational and radical expressions.

EXAMPLES

Simplify each expression.

1. $2(\sqrt{x} + 5) + 5\sqrt{x} = 2\sqrt{x} + 10 + 5\sqrt{x}$ Use the distributive property.

$= \left(2\sqrt{x} + 5\sqrt{x}\right) + 10$ Group like terms.

$= (2 + 5)\sqrt{x} + 10$ Use the distributive property in reverse.

$= 7\sqrt{x} + 10$

2. $\sqrt{x^3} - 3x\sqrt{x}$, when $x > 0$

$\sqrt{x^3} - 3x\sqrt{x} = \sqrt{(x^2)x} - 3x\sqrt{x}$

$= x\sqrt{x} - 3x\sqrt{x}$ $\sqrt{x^2} = |x| = x$, when $x > 0$.

$= -2x\sqrt{x}$ Use the distributive property in reverse.

3. $\dfrac{2x^2(3x - 5)}{4x} = \dfrac{x(2x)(3x - 5)}{2(2x)}$ $2x$ is a common factor of the numerator and the denominator.

$= \dfrac{x(3x - 5)}{2}$ Divide common factors: $\dfrac{2x}{2x} = 1$.

4. $\dfrac{(2x + 1)^2(x - 3)}{(2x + 1)} =$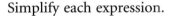

$= (2x + 1)(x - 3)$ Divide common factors: $\dfrac{2x + 1}{2x + 1} = 1$.

TRY IT

Simplify each expression.

a. $3(\sqrt{2x} + 2) - 8\sqrt{2x}$

b. $\dfrac{3x^2 + 5x}{2x^2}$

c. $4x\sqrt{x} + 3\sqrt{x^3}$, when $x > 0$

d. $\dfrac{x^2 + 3x + 2}{x + 1}$ (Hint: Factor the numerator first.)

A fraction $\frac{a}{b}$ is *not defined* when $b = 0$. Similarly, a rational expression is *not defined* for any values of the variables that make the denominator 0.

A radical $\sqrt{c}$ is *not defined* when $c < 0$. Similarly, a radical expression is *not defined* for any values of the variables that make the value under the radical symbol negative.

EXAMPLES

Find the value(s) of x for which each expression is not defined.

5. $\dfrac{8 - 14x}{2x^2 + 4x}$

The expression is not defined when the denominator, $2x^2 + 4x$, equals 0.

$2x^2 + 4x = 0$	Solve to find when the denominator is 0.
$2x(x + 2) = 0$	Factor the binomial.
$x = 0$ or $(x + 2) = 0$	Use the principle of zero products.
$\quad x = 0$ or $x = -2$	

So $\dfrac{8 - 14x}{2x^2 + 4x}$ is not defined when $x = 0$ or -2.

6. $\sqrt{5x - 25}$

The expression is not defined when $5x - 25 < 0$

$5x - 25 < 0$	Solve the inequality.
$\quad 5x < 25$	Add 25 to both sides.
$\quad x < 5$	Divide both sides by 5.

So $\sqrt{5x - 25}$ is not defined when $x < 5$.

TRY IT

Find the value(s) of x for which each expression is not defined.

e. $\dfrac{4x + 5}{x^2 - 16}$ **f.** $\sqrt{x + 17}$

Real numbers, both rational and irrational, and algebraic expressions help us to describe values of quantities. Remember that the properties you've used in this course apply to all of the numbers and expressions of algebra.

: **1.** How are rational expressions different from rational numbers?
: **2.** How are radical expressions different from radicals of real numbers?
: **3.** What are some properties of algebra you use when you simplify
:   rational and radical expressions?
: **4.** What does it mean when a rational or radical expression is *not defined*?

Exercises

CORE

1. Getting Started For each real number, determine whether it is rational
or irrational.

a. $\sqrt{11}$ **b.** 13   **c.** $\frac{5}{9}$ **d.** $-4\sqrt{5}$ **e.** -1.3 **f.** $57\frac{3}{4}$

2. Match each algebraic expression with the best phrase.

a. $\sqrt{3x - 2}$ **b.** $4x^3 - 3x + 2$ **c.** $\frac{4x - 1}{x^2 + 3}$

i. rational expression   **ii.** radical expression   **iii.** polynomial expression

3. Simplify the numbers to find four pairs of equal numbers. For
each pair determine whether the value is rational or irrational.

$2(1 + 2\sqrt{3}) - 2$ $\frac{3}{4}$ $2 + 2\sqrt{3}$ $\frac{3(6 - 2)}{3^2}$

$\frac{8}{6}$ $3\sqrt{3} + 2 - \sqrt{3}$ $\frac{3 \cdot 5}{5 \cdot 4}$ $4\sqrt{3}$

4. Find the perimeter of the trapezoid. Is your answer a rational
number or an irrational number? Describe how you found
your answer.

Simplify each expression.

5. $\sqrt{x} + 2x + 3\sqrt{x}$ **6.** $\frac{5x^2 + 2x}{-2x}$ **7.** $-\sqrt{y^3} + 12y\sqrt{y}$, when $y > 0$

8. $\frac{x^3 - 2x^2}{x^2}$ **9.** $8 - 3\sqrt{x} + 12\sqrt{x}$ **10.** $\frac{(x + 3)(x - 17)}{x^2 - 17x}$

11. These are the frequencies, in hertz (cycles per second),
of four consecutive notes of a synthesizer.

Note	A	A#	B	C
Frequency	880	932.3	987.8	1046.5

a. Find the ratio of the higher frequency to the lower
frequency for each pair of consecutive notes.
b. Estimate the frequency of the next note, C#.

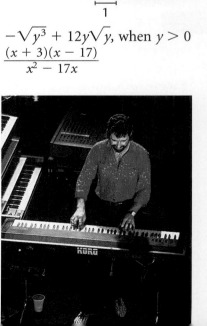

Find the value(s) of x for which each expression is not defined.

12. $\dfrac{2x^2 + 7}{2x - 6}$

13. $\sqrt{x + 1}$

14. $\dfrac{18}{x^2 - 49}$

15. $\sqrt{16 - 2x}$

16. $\dfrac{2x - 3}{(5 - 8x)(x + 3)}$

17. $\sqrt{\dfrac{1}{3}x + 6}$

18. Write a rational expression that is not defined when $x = -4$.

19. Write a radical expression that is not defined when $x < 6$.

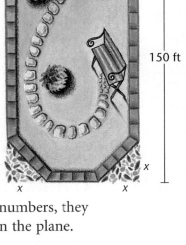

20. City Slicker Alberto was hired to plan a fence for a rectangular-shaped park. Triangular sections at each corner are to be outside the fence for special gardens.

    a. Using the diagram of the park, write an expression, in terms of x, for the length of fencing Alberto will need to surround the inner section.

    b. What is the greatest possible value of x in this situation? Explain. What is the perimeter of the fence for this value of x?

21. Are all decimal numbers rational numbers? Explain.

22. Mr. Lee placed five cards, each with one of the numbers $\sqrt{5}$, -3.7, $\frac{45}{37}$, $3\sqrt{49}$, or π in a box. If he draws a card from the box at random, what is the probability the card will have an irrational number on it?

23. Even though you can't write exact decimal values for irrational numbers, they do represent real points on the number line and real distances in the plane.

Show how a right triangle with integer-length legs can be used to construct line segments with each irrational length.

    a. $\sqrt{2}$

    b. $\sqrt{5}$

    c. $\sqrt{13}$

LOOK AHEAD

Factor each polynomial expression.

24. $x^2 - 9x + 18$

25. $9x^2 - 18x$

26. $x^2 - 9$

27. $x^2 + 16x - 36$

28. $x^2 - 5x - 36$

29. $x^2 + 12x + 36$

Complete each equation with a number or an expression.

30. _____ $\cdot \dfrac{2}{3} = 2$

31. _____ $\cdot \dfrac{3}{7p} = 3$

32. _____ $\cdot \dfrac{3t}{4x} = 3t$

MORE PRACTICE

Simplify each expression.

33. $8\sqrt{3} - 3\sqrt{2} + 5\sqrt{3}$

34. $-\sqrt{5} + 5\sqrt{25} + 3\sqrt{5}$

35. $\sqrt{x^3} - 8x\sqrt{x}$, when $x > 0$

36. $\dfrac{12^2 + 2}{-2}$

37. $\dfrac{8x^3 - 4x^2}{3x}$

38. $\dfrac{(2x + 3)(x + 9)}{(x - 17)(x - 9)}$

39. $\dfrac{x^3 - 5x^2}{x^2}$

40. $14 - 7\sqrt{x} + 32\sqrt{x}$

41. $\dfrac{(x + 6)(x - 13)}{x^2 - 13x}$

Find the value(s) of x for which each expression is not defined.

42. $\dfrac{x^2 + 4x}{5x - 18}$

43. $\dfrac{x^2 + 11x + 30}{2x(x + 5)}$

44. $\dfrac{x + 10}{x^2 - 36}$

45. $\dfrac{x^2 + 5}{3x - 6}$

46. $\sqrt{x + 8}$

47. $\dfrac{8}{x^2 - 64}$

48. $\sqrt{15 - 3x}$

49. $\dfrac{x - 1}{(5 - x)(x + 4)}$

50. $\sqrt{\dfrac{3}{4}x + 6}$

51. Find the perimeter of the trapezoid. Is your answer a rational or an irrational number?

MORE MATH REASONING

52. Evaluate the expression $\sqrt{\dfrac{4.00 \times 10^{14}}{R}}$ for $R = 7 \times 10^6$. Write the value in standard notation and in scientific notation.

53. Write a rational expression using x that is not defined for two values of x.

54. Is this a true or false equation for all real numbers a and b? Explain.

$$\sqrt{a^2 + b^2} \stackrel{?}{=} \sqrt{a^2} + \sqrt{b^2}$$

> **Problem-Solving Tip**
>
> Try special cases.

55. Use a graphing utility to repeatedly multiply the matrix A.

$$A = \begin{bmatrix} 1 & 1 \\ 1 & 0 \end{bmatrix}$$

a. Find A^2, A^3, A^4, A^5, and A^6.

b. Describe the patterns you see in the entries of these matrices.

Repeating Decimals All repeating decimal numbers are rational numbers. This example shows how to write the repeating decimal 0.353535… as a fraction. The *repetend* is the sequence of digits (35) that repeats.

$$x = 0.35353535…$$ (1) Assign a variable to the number.

$$(10^2)x = 35.353535…$$ (2) Multiply both sides by 10^m where m is the number of digits in the repetend.

$$100x = 35.353535…$$ (3) Subtract the first equation from the second.
$$\underline{x = 0.353535…}$$

$$99x = 35$$
$$x = \frac{35}{99}$$ (4) Solve.
$$\frac{35}{99} = 0.35353535…$$ (5) Check by dividing.

Use the procedure shown above to write each repeating decimal as a fraction.

56. 0.333333…   **57.** 0.125125…   **58.** 0.2343434…

10-1 PART B Functions and Equations

← CONNECT → *You've explored numbers and expressions involving quotients and radicals. Now you will investigate functions and equations involving radical and rational expressions. One important kind of function describes* **inverse variation.**

Throughout this course you have explored functions, often described by equations with two variables, such as $y = x^2 + 3x - 4$. In the future you may see this written as $f(x) = x^2 + 3x - 4$. You have also used the graphs of functions to solve equations, such as $6 = x^2 + 3x - 4$.

$$6 = x^2 + 3x - 4, \text{ when } x = -5 \text{ or } x = 2$$

Recall that the *domain* of a function is the set of all possible values of the independent variable. The domains of most of the functions you've studied in this course have been the set of real numbers. However, the domain of a function doesn't have to be all real numbers.

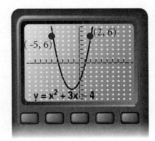

1. What would the graph of $y = x^2 + 3x - 4$ look like if the domain were just integers?

Because rational and radical expressions are not always defined, the domains of functions involving these expressions may not be all of the real numbers.

EXPLORE: SEEING IS BELIEVING!

Consider each function. Think about the domain and the range (values of the dependent variable) as you study each function and graph.

$$y = \frac{1}{x} \qquad y = 3 + \sqrt{x - 2}$$

MATERIALS

Graphing utility

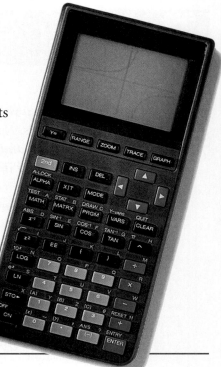

1. Graph each function and describe any unusual features of the graph.

2. Find the value(s) of x for which each function is not defined. Describe how the graph of this function reflects these undefined values.

3. What are the domain and the range of each function? Tell how you decided.

4. Use your graphs to find approximate solutions of each equation.
   a. $-4 = \frac{1}{x}$ **b.** $5 = 3 + \sqrt{x - 2}$

5. Compare the graphs of these functions to the graphs of other functions you've studied, such as linear and quadratic functions. Also compare solving equations using these graphs with solving other types of equations using graphs.

In the Explore, you solved equations involving rational or radical expressions using graphs. These equations can also be solved using properties of algebra, much like you solved other equations in this course.

1. Solve $\dfrac{24}{x} = x + 2$.

$\dfrac{24}{x} = x + 2$

$24 = x^2 + 2x$ Multiply both sides by x.

$0 = x^2 + 2x - 24$ Subtract 24 from both sides.

$0 = (x + 6)(x - 4)$ Factor.

$x = -6$ or $x = 4$ Use the principle of zero products.

Check the solutions in the original equation.

$\dfrac{24}{x} \stackrel{?}{=} x + 2$ $\dfrac{24}{x} \stackrel{?}{=} x + 2$

$\dfrac{24}{-6} \stackrel{?}{=} -6 + 2$ $\dfrac{24}{4} \stackrel{?}{=} 4 + 2$

$-4 = -4$ ✔ $6 = 6$ ✔

To solve an equation with a radical, first isolate the radical on one side of the equation, then square both sides to get an equation *without* a radical.

PRINCIPLE OF SQUARING

For any real numbers a and b, if $a = b$, then $a^2 = b^2$.

---

2. Solve $\sqrt{3x} + 4 = 9$.

$\sqrt{3x} + 4 = 9$

$\sqrt{3x} = 5$ Subtract 4 from both sides.

$3x = 25$ Square both sides.

$x = \dfrac{25}{3}$ Divide both sides by 3.

The solution checks in the original equation.

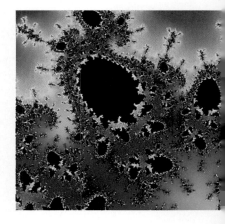

It is especially important to check your results when you solve equations involving rational or radical expressions. Squaring both sides of an equation sometimes produces **extraneous solutions**—values that don't check and so are *not* actual solutions. For example, squaring $x = 2$ gives $x^2 = 4$, then taking square roots gives $x = \pm 2$. The value $x = -2$ is an extraneous solution.

3. Solve $x + 3 = \sqrt{x + 5}$.

$$x^2 + 6x + 9 = x + 5 \qquad \text{Square both sides.}$$
$$x^2 + 5x + 4 = 0 \qquad \text{Subtract } x + 5 \text{ from both sides.}$$
$$(x + 4)(x + 1) = 0 \qquad \text{Factor.}$$
$$x = -4 \text{ or } x = -1 \qquad \text{Use the principle of zero products.}$$

Check the solutions in the original equation.

$$x + 3 \overset{?}{=} \sqrt{x + 5} \qquad\qquad x + 3 \overset{?}{=} \sqrt{x + 5}$$
$$-4 + 3 \overset{?}{=} \sqrt{-4 + 5} \qquad\qquad -1 + 3 \overset{?}{=} \sqrt{-1 + 5}$$
$$-1 \overset{?}{=} \sqrt{1} \qquad\qquad\qquad 2 \overset{?}{=} \sqrt{4}$$
$$-1 \overset{?}{=} 1 \text{ Not true!} \qquad\qquad 2 \overset{?}{=} 2 \ ✔$$

One result, $x = -4$, doesn't check. The only solution is $x = -1$.

There are many practical functions of the form

$$y = \frac{C}{x}, \text{ where } C \text{ is a constant,}$$

for which the independent and dependent variables are said to **vary inversely** with respect to each other. As x gets larger, y gets smaller.

4. The amount of time a light stays on for a given battery varies inversely with the power rating of the light. Suppose a battery has 200 watt-hours of stored energy. How long will the battery keep a light on? The equation (function) we use is

$$t = \frac{200}{P}.$$

Lights have various power ratings (P in watts). We will find the times for a few different ratings.

Power (P watts)	25	50	60	100	150	200
Time (t hours)	8	4	3.33	2	1.33	1

Negative numbers are not in the domain or range of this function in this situation.

1. Solve each equation. Check your results.

a. $x - 5 = \dfrac{36}{x}$ **b.** $\sqrt{5x} = 10$ **c.** $\sqrt{x - 2} = x - 4$

2. A battery has 500 watt-hours of stored energy. How long can it keep lights rated 40, 60, 100, and 300 watts on?

1. How can you tell what the domain of a function is from its equation? from its graph?

2. What are some properties of algebra you use to solve equations that involve rational or radical expressions?

3. Why is it important to check your solution when you solve an equation?

Exercises

CORE

1. Getting Started Use these steps to solve the equation $\frac{36 - x}{2x} = 4$.
   a. Multiply both sides of the equation by $2x$.
   b. Collect like terms and solve for x.
   c. Check your solution(s) in the original equation.

Solve each equation. Check your solution.

2. $\frac{40 + x}{3x} = 3$

3. $\frac{18}{x} = x + 3$

4. $\sqrt{4x - 3} = 7$

5. $12 = \frac{4x + 15}{-2x}$

6. $x = \sqrt{x + 13} - 7$

7. $-2 = \frac{3}{x} + \frac{5}{2x}$

8. $\sqrt{5x + 3} = 8$

9. $20 = \frac{5x^2 - 12}{\frac{1}{2}x^2}$

10. $8 = \frac{4}{t} + \frac{6}{t}$

11. Consider the graph of the function $y = 2 + \sqrt{x + 4}$.
   a. Find the value(s) of x for which the function is not defined. Describe how the graph of this function reflects these undefined values.
   b. What are the domain and the range of this function?

12. The formula for the length of all rectangles of area 100 m² is $\ell = \frac{100 \text{ m}^2}{w}$. The length and width vary inversely with respect to each other.
   a. Make a table of five values for ℓ and w for the 100 m² rectangles.

Width (w)				
Length (ℓ)				

   b. Make a graph of the function $\ell = \frac{100 \text{ m}^2}{w}$.
   c. Can ℓ or w ever equal 0 or be negative?

13. The two triangles are similar. Find the value of s and the lengths of the sides of each triangle.

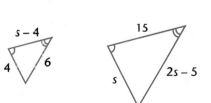

14. A battery has 100 watt-hours of stored energy. How long can it keep a light rated 250 watts (P) on? Solve the equation to find the time.

$$t = \frac{100}{P}$$

15. Head Winds A plane can travel 1000 km flying with the wind. Flying into the wind, the plane can only travel 800 km in the same amount of time. The speed of the plane in still air is 175 km/hr. Solve the equation to find the speed of the wind (w).

$$\frac{1000}{175 + w} = \frac{800}{175 - w}$$

16. The notation $f(x)$ means the value of a function at x.
Find $f(1)$ if $f(x) = x^2 + 2x + 1$.

 ## LOOK BACK

17. In 1970, 9.8% of the national budget was spent to pay the interest on the national debt. In 1980, 12.6% of the budget was spent on interest. In 1993, 20.7% of the budget was spent on interest. [1-2]
   a. Is there a positive association, negative association, or no association among the data?
   b. What are some effective ways you could show these data?

18. The amount of money (P) invested at an interest rate (r) will grow to an amount (A) in t years. The formula $A = P(1 + r)^t$ represents the amount A if the interest is compounded annually. What is the approximate interest rate if $2000 grows to $2184.05 in two years? [9-3]

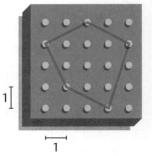

19. Find the perimeter of the pentagon. Is your answer a rational or an irrational number? [10-1]

MORE PRACTICE

Solve each equation. Check your solution.

20. $\dfrac{20 - x}{2x} = -3$

21. $2 = x - \dfrac{3}{x}$

22. $\sqrt{6x - 2} = 8$

23. $-5 = \dfrac{2x^2 - 7}{x^2}$

24. $14 - \sqrt{2x} = 4$

25. $1 = \dfrac{x^2 - 3x}{3x - x}$

26. $\sqrt{10x} + 13 = 33$

27. $64 = \dfrac{7x^2 - 5}{\frac{1}{4}x^2}$

28. $5 = \dfrac{8}{t} + \dfrac{12}{t}$

29. $9 = \dfrac{4x + 15}{x}$

30. $x = \sqrt{10 - x} - 10$

31. $\dfrac{12}{h} = \dfrac{17 + h}{5}$

32. $30 = \dfrac{8 - 5x}{-4x}$

33. $\dfrac{1}{x} = \dfrac{1}{3} + \dfrac{1}{5}$

34. $2x - \sqrt{x - 7} = 20$

35. Consider the graph of the function $y = \dfrac{1}{x+3}$.
  a. Find the value(s) of x for which the function is not defined. Describe how the graph of this function reflects these undefined values.
  b. What are the domain and the range of this function? Tell how you decided.

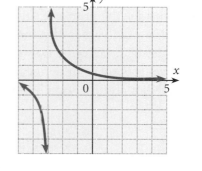

36. A battery has 12 watt-hours of stored energy. How long can it keep a light rated 8 watts (P) on? Solve the equation to find the time.

$$t = \frac{12}{P}$$

MORE MATH REASONING

37. Solve the equation $x = 8 + \sqrt{2x - 1}$. Then show that the extraneous solution of this equation is actually the solution of the equation $x = 8 - \sqrt{2x - 1}$.

38. **This Segment Is Golden** Assume that point B lies on the line segment AC between A and C. Also assume that $\dfrac{AB}{AC} = \dfrac{BC}{AB}$. Write and solve a rational equation to determine x, the length AC. Do you recognize this value?

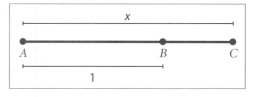

39. Can the slope of a line passing through the points $(5d^2, 2d)$ and $(5d^2, 6d)$ ever be 1? If so, find the value of d and the coordinates of both points. If not, explain why.

40. **Speedy Sputnik** The equation $v = \sqrt{\dfrac{4.0 \times 10^{14}}{R}}$ shows the relationship between the distance (R) a satellite orbits above the center of the earth in meters and the velocity (v) of the satellite in meters per second.

Sputnik I, the first satellite to orbit earth, orbited at a velocity of 7500 m/sec (about 17,000 mi/hr).

Find the approximate distance of Sputnik's orbit from the center of the earth.

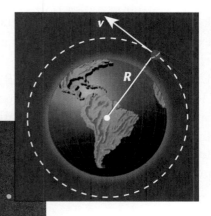

709

41. Consider the graph of the function $y = \dfrac{-5x}{x^2 + x - 6}$.

    a. Find the values of x for which the function is not defined. Describe how the graph of this function reflects these undefined values.

    b. What are the domain and the range of this function?

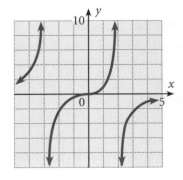

![sunflower] **10-1**
 PART C   # Making Connections

← CONNECT →   *You've reviewed the various types of numbers within the real number system. You've also explored rational and radical expressions along with functions and equations involving these expressions.*

Golden rectangles have a unique property you can use to calculate the *golden ratio*. If you draw a segment to divide a golden rectangle into a square and another rectangle, the smaller rectangle is also a golden rectangle.

Using this property to calculate the golden ratio allows you to make connections between many of the concepts you've used in this course.

EXPLORE: GOLDEN RECTANGLES

The golden rectangle *ACDF* contains the shaded, unit-square *ABEF* and the smaller golden rectangle *CDEB*.

1. Let x represent the length of rectangle *ACDF*. What expressions represent the length and width of rectangle *CDEB*?

2. Use the fact that rectangle *CDEB* is similar to rectangle *ACDF* to write a rational equation for x.

3. Solve your equation. Which solution is the golden ratio? Explain.

4. Identify various integers, rational numbers, and irrational numbers that are involved in this Explore.

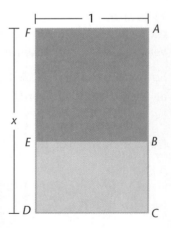

1. How are rational expressions similar to rational numbers? How are they different?
2. How are radical expressions similar to square roots of numbers? How are they different?
3. How do you find values of x where a *rational* expression is not defined? where a *radical* expression is not defined?
4. Why might the domain of a function not be all real numbers? Explain using a real-life example.

Self-Assessment

Simplify each expression.

1. $\sqrt{14} - 21 - 2\sqrt{14}$

2. $\dfrac{(x-3)^2(x-20)}{(x-20)(x-3)}$

3. $\dfrac{6y + 12}{y^2 - 4}$

4. $\dfrac{8x^3 + 2x^2}{6x^4}$

5. $\dfrac{x^3 - 4x^2}{x^2 + x}$

6. $\sqrt{5y} + 2\sqrt{5y} + \sqrt{10y}$

Find the value(s) of x for which each expression is not defined.

7. $\dfrac{x^3 + x}{x - 11}$

8. $\sqrt{3x - 6}$

9. $\dfrac{-x}{x^2 - 36}$

10. Write a rational expression that is not defined when $x = 10$.

11. Write a radical expression that is not defined when $x < -8$.

12. **ELeMentary, Watson** In Sir Arthur Conan Doyle's *The Musgrave Ritual*, the following passage had been passed down through generations of Musgraves. Sherlock Holmes determines that it is a clue to a secret.

"Whose was it? His who is gone. Who shall have it? He who will come. Where was the sun? Over the oak. Where was the shadow? Under the elm. How was it stepped? North by ten and by ten, east by five and by five, south by two and by two, west by one and by one, and so under. What shall we give for it? All that is ours. Why shall we give it? For the sake of the trust."

The 64-foot-tall elm tree had been struck by lightning and cut down to a stump. Holmes calculates where its shadow would have fallen when the sun grazed the top of the tree.

"Then I took two lengths of a fishing-rod, which came to just six feet, and I went back to where the elm had been. I marked out the direction of the shadow, and measured it. It was nine feet in length."

a. How long had the elm tree's shadow been? How did Holmes know?
b. How did Holmes find the spot where the elm's shadow reached?
c. Reginald Musgrave said he had measured that the elm was 64-feet tall by "an exercise in trigonometry. When I was a lad, I worked out every tree and building in the estate." Explain how he could have found the height of the tree.

Solve each equation. Check your solution.

13. $1 = \dfrac{x + 21}{-3x}$

14. $\sqrt{3x + 1.5} = 7.5$

15. $0 = \dfrac{x^2 - 4}{x + 2}$

16. $\sqrt{x - 4} = x - 24$

17. $20 = \dfrac{2}{2x} + \dfrac{5}{4x}$

18. $20 = \dfrac{8x^2 + 18}{0.75x^2}$

19. If you choose one of the integers from -5 to 5 at random, what is the probability that the expression $\dfrac{1}{\sqrt{x^2 - 3x + 2}}$ will not be defined for that value of x?

20. A line has a slope of $\frac{1}{2}$ and passes through the points $(3q^2, 8q)$ and $(-2q^2, -2q)$. Find the value of q and the coordinates of both points.

21. Table Design A rectangular table has an area of 5250 cm². If $L =$ the length in cm and $W =$ the width in cm, then $LW = 5250$. Solve this equation for L. Use your equation to find the value of L for each value of W.
   a. $W = 14$ **b.** $W = 35$ **c.** $W = 50$
   d. What are the values of L and W if the table is square?

22. Repelling Electrons The force, in newtons, that repels two electrons r meters apart is $F = \dfrac{2.9 \times 10^{-27}}{4\pi r^2}$.

At what distance will the force that repels two electrons be 0.01 newton?

23. Car Capers Car A drives east at 40 mi/hr. When Car A has driven 15 miles, Car B leaves from the same location driving in the same direction. Let $s =$ Car B's speed in miles per hour.
   a. If Car B eventually overtakes Car A, is s greater than or less than 40? Explain.
   b. Write an expression in terms of s for the time it takes Car B to overtake Car A.
   c. How fast would Car B have to travel to pass Car A in 1 hour?
   d. Could Car B travel fast enough to pass Car A in 10 minutes? Explain.

24. Bunny Hop In his book *Liber Abaci*, published in 1202, Leonardo Fibonacci posed this problem.

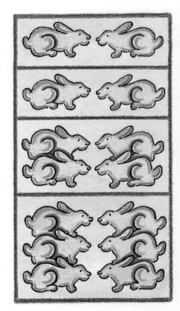

> *What is the number of pairs of rabbits at the beginning of each month if a single pair of newly born rabbits is put into an enclosure at the beginning of January, and if each pair breeds a new pair at the beginning of the second month following birth and an additional pair at the beginning of each month thereafter?*

Copy and complete this table to show the number of pairs of rabbits in the first 12 months.

J	F	M	A	M	J	J	A	S	O	N	D
1	1	2	3								

Do you recognize this sequence of numbers? Explain.

Here We Grow Again

A Persian legend speaks of a clever courtier who presented a beautiful chessboard to his king and requested that the king give him in return 1 grain of rice for the first square on the board, 2 grains for the second square, 4 grains for the third square, and so forth. The tenth square of the chessboard required 512 grains, the fifteenth square 16,384, and the twenty-first square gave the courtier more than a million grains of rice. By the fortieth square a million million grains of rice had to be brought from the store rooms. The king's entire rice supply was exhausted long before he reached the sixty-fourth square.

This exponential growth pattern is typical for populations. In 1790, the entire population of the United States was the size of the city of Chicago today! It takes only 24 hours for a single bacterium that doubles every 20 minutes to become 4.72×10^{21} bacteria. Why don't people or bacteria take over completely? There are environmental and human factors at work that control growth so that there will be space and food for all of us.

1. What are some environmental factors that could influence the growth of a population?
2. If no one moved into or out of a city, would the population remain constant? What factors must you consider?
3. What are some sociological factors that might affect world population?
4. If a city's population grew 7% one year and 7% again the next year, would it have increased by exactly 14%?

Exponential Functions

← C O N N E C T → *You have worked with various kinds of functions throughout this course. In this lesson, you will explore another kind of function associated with many real-world situations.*

If you drop a ball from a certain height, each time the ball bounces the height it rebounds decreases. In the next Explore, you will investigate this relationship.

EXPLORE: REBOUND

MATERIALS

One high-bouncing ball (ping-pong, super ball, golf ball, etc.)
Centimeter measuring tape
Graph paper

Tape the centimeter tape to a wall, or have one person hold it so that zero touches the ground. You will be measuring the heights of the first three bounces.

1. Copy and complete the table. From a height *A* of 2 meters, drop the ball onto a hard surface and record the height of the first three bounces. Repeat this five times from this height.

Height	A	B	C	D
Trial Number	Bounce 0	Bounce 1	Bounce 2	Bounce 3
1	200 cm			
2	200 cm			
3	200 cm			
4	200 cm			
5	200 cm			
Mean	200 cm			

2. Use the data from the bottom line of the table to graph the results. What are the two variables in this situation? Which is the independent variable? the dependent variable?

3. Describe the graph. Are the quantities directly or inversely related? Is the relationship linear? Explain.

4. Estimate the percent of the previous bounce height that each successive bounce height reaches.

5. Write an equation that shows the relationship between the two quantities. Show and explain your work.

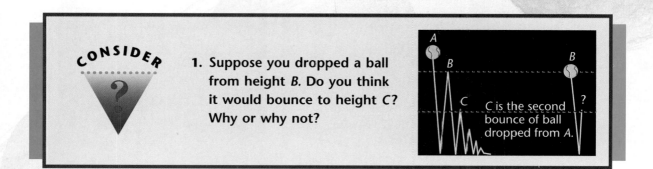

CONSIDER

?

1. Suppose you dropped a ball from height *B*. Do you think it would bounce to height *C*? Why or why not?

A

B

B

C

C is the second bounce of ball dropped from A.

?

An equation of the form $y = ab^x$ can be written to represent the functional relationship between the number of bounces (x) and the height of the bounce (y).

A function that can be represented by an equation of the form $y = ab^x$, where a and b are constants, $b > 0$, and x is any real number, is called an **exponential function.**

EXAMPLE

1. Find at least five ordered pairs of values for the exponential function $y = 2.5(2)^x$. Graph the function and describe the graph.

x	$2.5(2)^x$
1	$2.5(2)^1 = 5$
2	$2.5(2)^2 = 10$
3	$2.5(2)^3 = 20$
4	$2.5(2)^4 = 40$
5	$2.5(2)^5 = 80$

The quantities are directly related since the values increase together. The graph rises quickly. For each 1-unit change of the x-values, the y-value changes by a factor of 2; that is, it doubles.

Example 1 illustrates **exponential growth.** The Explore illustrates **exponential decay.** If the value of b in $y = b^x$ is greater than 1, the values of y will increase with increases in the values of x. But if $0 < b < 1$, the values of y will decrease as values of x increase.

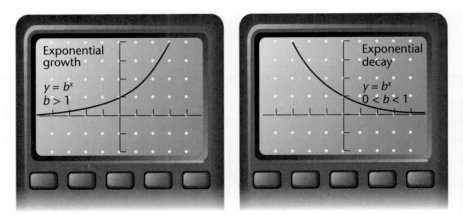

EXAMPLE

2. Since 1950, the world population has risen from 2.564 billion at a rate of 1.85% per year. The equation that represents this exponential function is $y = 2.564(1.0185)^x$, where x represents the time in years since 1950, and y represents the world population, in billions. Use the graph to estimate the world population in 1975; in 2000; in 2025.

Graph $y = 2.564(1.0185)^x$. The number of years since 1950 are 25, 50, and 75, respectively. We can trace to estimate the world population for these years.

The world population estimates are 4.055 billion for 1975, 6.412 billion for 2000, and 10.139 billion for 2025.

TRY IT

a. Graph $y = 5(0.8)^x$. Estimate the value of y when $x = 3.5$.
b. Graph $y = 0.2(3)^x$. Estimate the value of y when $x = 2.5$.

1. What is the general form of an exponential function?
2. How can you tell by examining the table of ordered pairs or the graph that a functional relationship might be exponential?
3. Is an exponential function the same as a quadratic function? Explain.
4. What does it mean for a situation to illustrate exponential growth? exponential decay? How can this be determined by examining the equation that represents the function?

Exercises

CORE

1. **Getting Started**
   a. Make a table of ordered pairs for $y = 3^x$, letting $x = 1, 2, 3, 4,$ and 5.
   b. Label the y-axis from 0 to 250 and the x-axis from 0 to 5.
   c. Plot the ordered pairs and connect them.
   d. Find $x = 2.5$ and move up to the point where it meets the graph of $y = 3^x$. Estimate the y-coordinate of that point.

2. Which is the graph of $y = 0.75^x$?

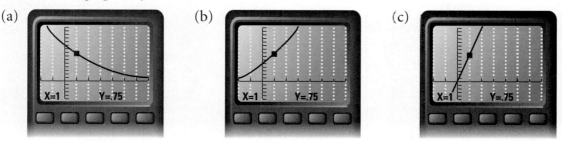

(a)   X=1   Y=.75   (b)   X=1   Y=.75   (c)   X=1   Y=.75

3. Why does the phrase *exponential function* make sense for functions that can be written in the form $y = ab^x$?

Graph each function.

4. $y = \frac{1}{2}(4)^x$

5. $y = \left(\frac{2}{3}\right)^x$

Sketch a graph for each situation.

6. A bacteria colony increases in size 10% each hour.

7. An oil spill is reduced in size by 10% per day (each day it is 90% of the previous day's size).

8. Match the function with the graph it describes.

a. $y = 0.6^x$ **b.** $y = 1.4^x$ **c.** $y = -1.4^x$

i. 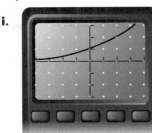   **ii.** 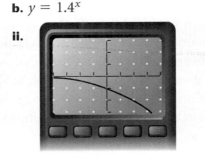   **iii.**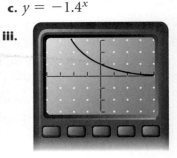

9. Use guess-and-check with a calculator to find the first whole number x such that 25^x is greater than 1,000,000. Write down each number you tried. How close was your first guess?

10. Compare the graphs of $y = 2^x$ and $y = \left(\frac{1}{2}\right)^x$. How are they related? For what value(s) of x do they have the same value?

11. Graph the quadratic function represented by $y = x^2$ and the exponential function represented by $y = 2^x$ on the same axes. Write as many statements as you can comparing these two graphs.

12. a. What was the population in Las Vegas in 1990?

    b. If the population of Las Vegas increases by 6.7% each year, what should the population have been in 1993? 1994?

    c. How many years will it be before the population of Las Vegas reaches the maximum number of people for which it can supply water? Explain your answer.

Social Science

San Francisco Chronicle   February 8, 1994

Las Vegas Tops Census List of Fastest-Growing Areas

From 1990 to 1992, the population of Las Vegas grew by 13.9 percent to 971,169. The area gets its water from the Colorado River and underground sources and has enough to support about 1.5 million people.

Experts Say Economic Outlook

13. Bounce, Bounce Suppose the equation $y = 5(0.8)^x$ shows the relationship between the number of bounces (x) and the height of the bounce (y) in feet. What is the height of the fifth bounce? What is the height of the one-hundredth bounce? Do the answers to these questions make sense? Explain.

Science

14. Water Lite The intensity of light under water decreases by 2.5% for every meter one descends. The function $y = 100(0.975)^x$ shows the relationship between the depth in meters (x) and the percent of surface light intensity that reaches that depth. Graph this function and use the graph to estimate the percent of light intensity that reaches depths of 25 meters and 75 meters.

Science

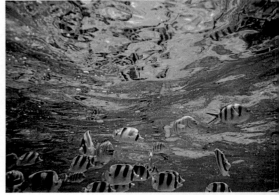

LOOK AHEAD

What exponent, if any, makes each equation true? (Hint: Graph, if necessary.)

15. $2^x = 32$

16. $10^x = 1000$

17. $5^x = \left(\frac{1}{5}\right)$

18. $7^x = 7$

19. $4^x = 0$

20. $3^x = -1$

MORE PRACTICE

21. a. Make a table of ordered pairs for $y = 0.9^x$, letting $x = 1, 2, 3, 4,$ and 5.
   b. Label the y-axis from 0 to 1 and the x-axis from 0 to 5.
   c. Plot the ordered pairs and connect them.
   d. Find $x = 3.5$ and move up to the point where it meets the graph of $y = 0.9^x$. Estimate the y-coordinate of that point.

22. Which of the following represent(s) exponential functions?
   a. $y = 4^x$ **b.** $y = 2x^4$ **c.** $y = 3(2^2)x$ **d.** $y = \left(\frac{1}{3}\right)^x$

23. Match the function with the graph it describes.

a. $y = 2\left(\frac{1}{3}\right)x$

b. $y = 2\left(\frac{1}{3}\right)^x$

c. $y = \left(\frac{1}{3}\right)2^x$

d. $y = \frac{1}{3x}$

e. $y = -\frac{1}{3x}$

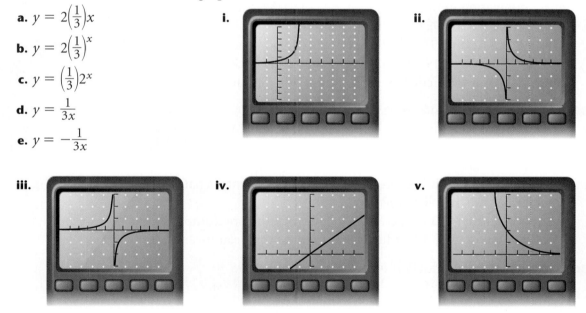

Each equation represents an exponential function. Graph each equation.

24. $y = 2^x$

25. $y = -(3)^x$

26. $y = 2(2.5)^x$

27. $y = \left(\frac{4}{5}\right)^x$

28. Graph the function $y = 3(1.8)^x$. Use the graph to estimate the value of y when $x = 3.5$.

Sketch a graph for each situation.

29. A fine increases 15% each month, from $50.

30. A prize decreases by 50% each hour from $1000.

MORE MATH REASONING

31. Graph the exponential function $y = ab^x$ for $a = 1$ and $b = 0.5$. Trace to evaluate the function for $x = 1, 4, 9,$ and 16. What does this function represent?

Use a graphing utility to graph each function.

32. $y = 5000(1.08)^x$

33. $y = -100(1.1)^x$

34. Through the Golden Gate The San Francisco Bay area's population grew at an average rate of 1.25%per year from 1990 to 1992. Use the function $y = 6{,}253{,}311(1.0125)^{x - 1990}$ to estimate the population of San Francisco in 1994. Find an almanac and check how close your prediction is to the actual population.

35. A photocopier is set to reduce each dimension to 80% of its original size. Suppose after each copy is made, the copy is used as the new original.
   a. How does the *height* of the image in the seventh copy compare to its height in the master document? What function describes this relationship?
   b. How does the *area* of the image in the seventh copy compare to its area in the master document? What function describes this relationship?

36. Each triangle is a reduction of the previous one.

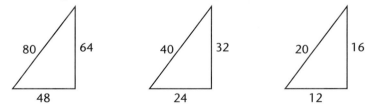

   a. What are the dimensions of the tenth triangle? Can you find it without finding the dimensions of all the other triangles?
   b. Are the triangles similar? Why or why not?
   c. Are they right triangles? Explain how you know.

37. From C to Shining C When you go up one half-tone on the piano, the frequency of vibration is multiplied by approximately 1.05946. Each arrow represents a half-tone increase in frequency.

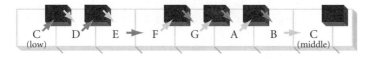

a. What is the increase in frequency when we go up one octave (from C to C)?

b. When low C is played on the piano, the string vibrates at a frequency of 264 times per second. What is the frequency of vibration of middle C?

c. What would you expect the frequency of high C to be?

38. Hurry Up and Wait *Queuing theory* is the study of waiting lines, given different rates of arrival and service. Toll booths, banks, emergency rooms, and grocery checkout stands all use *queuing systems*.

The probability that a hospital patient will be treated within n minutes at one medical center can be modeled by $1 - 5(10^{-0.1n})$.

a. What is the probability that a patient will be treated within 10 minutes?

b. What is the probability that a patient will be treated within 20 minutes?

c. For what domain of time does the model make sense? Does this seem reasonable given your answer to **38a**?

10-2
PART B Exponents and Logarithms

← **C O N N E C T** →   *You have seen that the square root function allows you to solve quadratic equations. Another function, the logarithmic function, allows you to solve exponential equations. You will study logarithms in detail in later courses.*

How long will it take for an amount of money to double? After how many trials does the probability of an event exceed one half? Solving these and many life applications requires that we find the value of an exponent. When we have an equation like $8 = 2^y$, we need some way to solve for y. This is the same as asking the question, "When I have a power of 2, what is the exponent that gives me a value of 8?"

The height of a mountain range decays exponentially over time, due to erosion. A model for the height, in kilometers, of one mountain range is given by $h = 3.65(0.96)^t$, where t is measured in millions of years.

1. What is its initial height? (Hint: let $t = 0$.)
2. How is the mountain height changing over time? Describe the rate of change.
3. Guess and check to find how long it takes for the mountain's elevation to drop to 3 kilometers; to 2 kilometers; to 1 kilometer.
4. How long does the mountain take to reach $\frac{1}{2}$ of its initial height? $\frac{1}{4}$ of its initial height?
5. Why do we need an algebraic method to find these types of answers?

We write $8 = 2^y$ as $y = \log_2 8$. In this case, we know that the value 3 is the solution.

$$8 = 2^3 \text{ means } 3 = \log_2 8$$

For $a^y = x$, the exponent is a function. We write this function as $y = \log_a x.$

It is the *inverse* of the exponential function, and it is called the **logarithmic function.**

$$\text{power} = \text{base}^{\text{exponent}} \rightarrow \text{exponent} = \log_{\text{base}} \text{power}$$
$$x = a^y \quad \text{means} \quad y = \log_a x$$

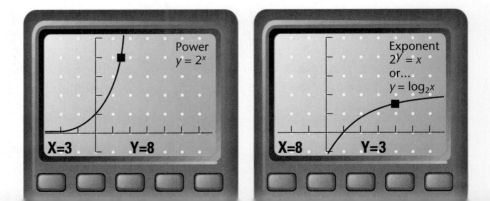

1. Evaluate the logarithm.
$\log_{10} 10{,}000$

$10^{\square} = 10{,}000$ The base of the logarithm
is the base of the exponent.

Since $10^4 = 10{,}000$, $\log_{10} 10{,}000 = 4$.

2. Rewrite the equation using logarithmic notation.
$2^x = 512$

$x = \log_2 512$ The base of the exponent
is the base of the logarithm.

3. Rewrite the equation using logarithmic notation.
$2 = (1.08)^t$ This is in the form $x = a^y$.
$t = \log_{1.08} 2$

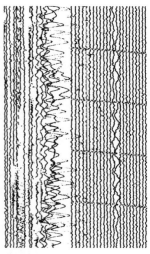

Logarithms are used to give the magnitude of an earthquake. This seismographic reading is from the Loma Prieta earthquake in 1989, which had a magnitude of 7.1.

Evaluate each logarithm.
a. $\log_{10} 0.01$ **b.** $\log_2 4$

Rewrite each equation using logarithmic notation.
c. $3^5 = 243$ **d.** $(0.25)^2 = 0.0625$ **e.** $a^x = 1$

Base 10 logarithms are available on scientific calculators. Pressing 1000 [LOG] displays 3. When we write logarithms without a base, we can assume the base is 10.

$$\log x \text{ means } \log_{10} x$$

CONSIDER

1. Since a logarithm represents the exponent of a power, what do you think log 1 is? log 0? Why?

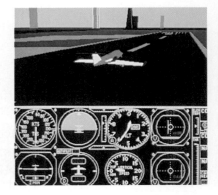

An *altimeter* measures the height of the aircraft above sea level by comparing air pressure outside the airplane to air pressure at sea level. The height of the aircraft can be modeled by

$$h = -\frac{176}{3} \log x,$$

where h = the height of the aircraft (in thousands of feet) and x is the ratio of the pressure outside the airplane to the pressure at sea level.

Suppose the outside air pressure is 14.9 inches, exactly half of the pressure at sea level, 29.8 inches. How high is the airplane?

Nicole thinks...

I'll evaluate with a calculator.

176 ÷ 3 = +/- × 0.5 LOG = 17.66042641

The airplane is 17,660 feet high.

Keisha thinks...

I'll graph the function to find out. This way, I'll also see the shape of the graph.

The airplane is 17,660 feet high.

X=.5   Y=17.660426

CONSIDER

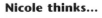

2. It is dangerous for a pilot to fly for a long time without adjusting for current sea level air pressure. Why?

We know the following from our study of exponent rules.

$$b^m \cdot b^n = b^{m + n}$$

This means that when two terms with the same base are multiplied, the exponents may be added to give the same result. What happens if we apply this idea to the logarithm of a product? Remember, logarithms are exponents.

Compare the following.

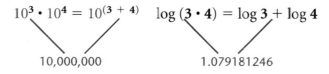

$$10^3 \cdot 10^4 = 10^{(3 + 4)} \qquad \log (3 \cdot 4) = \log 3 + \log 4$$

10,000,000   1.079181246

Another important property of logarithms follows.

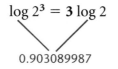

$$\log 2^3 = 3 \log 2$$

0.903089987

This property will be investigated further in later math courses.

TRY IT

Use a property of logarithms to write an equivalent expression.

f. $\log 3^7$ **g.** $\log 5 + \log 2$

REFLECT

1. Describe how powers, exponents, logarithms, and bases are related.
2. Compare and contrast logarithmic notation and scientific notation.
3. How are logarithms useful?
4. Describe how you would begin solving Step 3 of the Explore on page 722, now that you have been using logarithms.

Exercises

CORE

1. Getting Started Consider the equation $81 = 3^4$.
    a. What is the exponent? What is the base?
    b. Rewrite the equation to solve for the exponent. Use the form $\square = \log_\square \square$.

Rewrite each equation using logarithmic notation.

2. $3^2 = 9$

3. $625 = 5^4$

4. $0.01 = 10^{-2}$

5. $a^3 = b$

6. $512 = 2^n$

7. $e^x = k$

Evaluate each logarithm.

8. $\log_5 25$

9. $\log_{10} 0.1$

10. $\log_3 3$

Rewrite each equation without logarithmic notation.

11. $2 = \log_6 36$

12. $\log_2 x = 4$

13. $\log_b 20 = 2$

14. Which of these is equal to log 42?

(a) $\log 7 \cdot \log 6$ (b) $\log 21 + \log 21$ (c) $\log 14 + \log 3$ (d) $3 \log 14$

15. Which of these is *not* equal to log 64?

(a) $4 \log 3$ (b) $\log 16 + \log 4$ (c) $\log (32 \cdot 2)$ (d) not here

16. Consider the table.

Decibel Scale	Intensity	Decibels
Minimum audible sound	I	0
Grass rustling	10I	10
Soft whisper, 5 m	10^3I	30
Urban home interior	10^5I	50
Heavy traffic at 15 m, conversation at 1 m	10^6I	60
Subway train, rock concert	10^{10}I	100
Jet taking off at 60 m	10^{12}I	120
Eardrum pain	10^{13}I	130
Permanent ear damage, jet taking off at 30 m	10^{14}I	140

a. Relate the number of decibels to the intensity of the sound.

> **Problem-Solving Tip**
>
> Look for a pattern among the higher-intensity sounds

b. What happens to the intensity of sound for an increase of 20 decibels?

c. What does a sound 1000 times as intense as a jackhammer mean in terms of decibels?

d. Are the intensity scales related by a linear function? by a quadratic function?

e. Why do you think the decibel scale was created?

17. Importance Amplified A high-end stereo amplifier is rated at 56 watts power; the midrange amplifier is rated at 32 watts power. The salesperson says the extra power will make a great deal of difference.

The increase in sound intensity, in decibels, of the high-end amplifier is given by the following.

$$I = 10 \log \left(\frac{\text{power of the high-end amplifier}}{\text{power of the midrange amplifier}} \right)$$

a. What is the increase in sound of the high-end amplifier?

b. Do you think the difference is significant?

18. Search Me A *binary search* on a computer file of records requires that the program keep splitting the file in half until the record is found. The maximum number of times it needs to split the file is given by $\frac{\log (\text{number of records})}{\log 2}$ (rounded up, if it is a noninteger).

Here's how you would do a binary search to guess a number between 1 and 512. Your friend sets a number (say, 108).

Guess	Response	Find the mean between
guess 256	(lower)	1 and 255.
guess 128	(lower)	1 and 127.
guess 64	(higher)	65 and 127.
guess 96	(higher)	97 and 127.
guess 112	(lower)	97 and 111.
guess 104	(higher)	105 and 111.
guess 108	Correct!	

Total guesses: 7

---

a. A file contains 2,000,000 records with names and addresses. What is the maximum number of times a computer would need to split the file to find a record?

b. When guessing a number between 1 and 100,000, what is the maximum number of tries it should take?

19. If a population doubles every t years, its yearly rate of increase is given by $10^x - 1$, where $x = \frac{\log 2}{t}$. What yearly increase results in the population doubling every 20 years?

Equations of the form $a^x = b$ can be solved using $x = \dfrac{\log b}{\log a}$. Solve each equation.

20. $0.95^x = 0.5$ **21.** $1.07^x = 10$

22. The number line uses a logarithmic scale. Why?

Science ◀

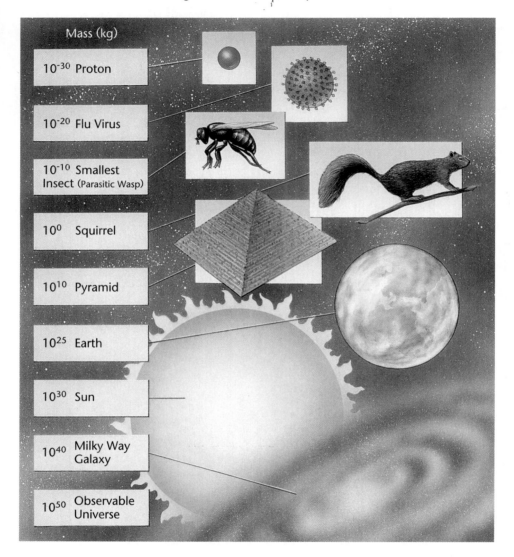

Mass (kg)

10^{-30} Proton

10^{-20} Flu Virus

10^{-10} Smallest Insect (Parasitic Wasp)

10^{0} Squirrel

10^{10} Pyramid

10^{25} Earth

10^{30} Sun

10^{40} Milky Way Galaxy

10^{50} Observable Universe

23. The Incredible Shrinking Man Suppose *The Incredible Shrinking Man*, the title character of the 1956 film, is normally 180 cm tall, but each succeeding minute he shrinks to 99% of his size of the previous minute.

Fine Arts ◀

  a. How tall is he after 1 hour? after 2 hours?

  b. How long will it take him to become 1 cm tall? 1 mm tall?

24. Iguana Be Cool When an iguana moves into hot sunlight, its body temperature adjusts as shown in the graph.

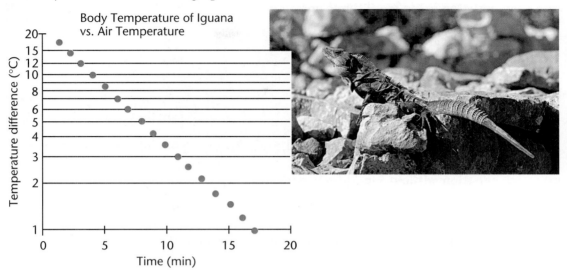

Body Temperature of Iguana vs. Air Temperature

y-axis: Temperature difference (°C)
x-axis: Time (min)

a. How much does the iguana's body temperature increase during the first minute? fifth minute? fifteenth minute?

b. Is the relationship between the change in temperature and time linear? Why?

LOOK BACK

Given *a*, *b*, and *c* for the quadratic equation $ax^2 + bx + c = 0$, use the discriminant, $b^2 - 4ac$, to determine the number of solutions. [9-3]

25. $a = 1, b = 3, c = 9$ **26.** $a = 1, b = -3, c = 9$ **27.** $a = 7, b = 6, c = 1.3$

28. As a pedestrian passes by a tree, a bicyclist rides by on the street. But they don't see each other, since the tree is always between them. $\triangle ABT \sim \triangle UVT$. [7-4]

a. If the pedestrian walks 10 feet from point *A*, how far has the bicyclist gone in that time? Why?

b. If the speed of the pedestrian is 2 mi/hr, how fast is the bicyclist traveling?

Solve. [10-1]

29. $x - 1 = \sqrt{x - 1}$ **30.** $x - 1 = \sqrt{x + 1}$

MORE PRACTICE

Rewrite each equation using logarithmic notation.

31. $2^3 = 8$ **32.** $100 = 10^2$ **33.** $0.125 = 8^{-1}$

34. $c^2 = m$ **35.** $128 = 2^x$ **36.** $y = k^t$

Evaluate each logarithm.

37. $\log_6 36$ **38.** $\log_{10} 1000$ **39.** $\log_4 4$

40. $\log_8 1$ **41.** $\log_{10} 0.001$ **42.** $\log_2 64$

Rewrite each equation without logarithmic notation.

43. $k = \log_5 10$ **44.** $\log_2 11 = x$ **45.** $\log_b 100 = 3$

Use a property of logarithms to write an equivalent expression.

46. $4 \log 2$ **47.** $\log (4 \cdot 2)$

48. a. Make a table of ordered pairs for $x = 1.5^y$.
     b. Use the ordered pairs to graph the equation.
     c. What is another way to write the equation?

MORE MATH REASONING

49. Intelligence Dr. Gorden Moore, one of the founders of Intel Corporation, made a prediction about the number of transistors that would fit on a computer microprocessor. Dr. Moore's prediction is shown by the line. The actual numbers are shown by the dots. The type of graph Dr. Moore used is called a *semi-logarithmic* plot.

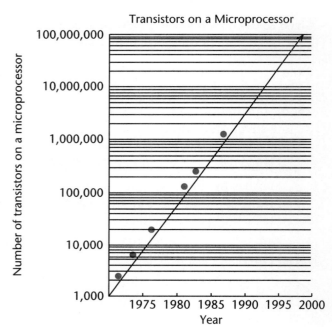

Transistors on a Microprocessor

     a. Is there a linear relationship between the variables?
     b. Describe the intervals on the y-axis.
     c. Use a graph with a y-axis interval of 100,000 and graph the six ordered pairs. Describe the graph.
     d. Could you use this graph to predict the number of chips that would fit on a microprocessor in 2000, as Moore did? Why or why not?
     e. What type of function do you think would describe your graph?

For Exercises 50–52, use a scientific calculator.

50. Begin with 1. Multiply by 10 six times. Then press $\boxed{\text{LOG}}$. What happens? Why? Press $\boxed{\text{INV}}$ $\boxed{\text{LOG}}$ (or $\boxed{10^x}$). What happens? Why do you think $\boxed{\text{LOG}}$ and 10^x usually share the same calculator button?

51. Enter 1 $\boxed{\text{EXP}}$ 25. What number is this? Press $\boxed{\text{LOG}}$. What happens? Why?

52. Use a spreadsheet.
    a. Copy and complete the following table by entering the spreadsheet formulas as shown.

	A	B	C
1	x	10^x	log (10^x)
2	–3	=10^A2	=LOG10(B2)
3	–2	=10^A3	=LOG10(B3)
4	–1	=10^A4	=LOG10(B4)
5	0	=10^A5	=LOG10(B5)
6	1	=10^A6	=LOG10(B6)
7	2	=10^A7	=LOG10(B7)
8	3	=10^A8	=LOG10(B8)
9	4	=10^A9	=LOG10(B9)

    b. How is column C related to column A?
    c. What is it about column B that makes this true?

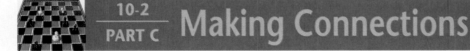

10-2
PART C Making Connections

← C O N N E C T → *You have explored exponential functions and their inverses, logarithmic functions. Now you will examine how these work together.*

Throughout this course, you have been investigating functions. Most have been polynomial, including linear and quadratic. The functions in this part are not polynomials, but you will encounter them often in future mathematics and science courses.

EXPLORE: URBAN SWELL

The data show the populations of the 10 most populated metropolitan areas in the United States in 1990.

MATERIALS

Graphing utility (optional)

Metropolitan Statistical Area	Population 1980 (1,000)	Population 1990 (1,000)	Percent Change 1980–1990	Average Annual Percent Change 1980–1990
New York–Northern New Jersey–Long Island, NY–NJ		19,342		0.331
Los Angeles–Anaheim–Riverside, CA	11,498			2.37
Chicago–Gary–Lake City, IL–IN–WI	8,114			0.153
Washington DC–MD–VA–WV		6,727	16.2	1.51
San Francisco–Oakland–San Jose, CA		6,253	16.5	1.54
Philadelphia–Wilmington–Trenton, PA–DE–NJ	5,649			0.424
Boston–Lawrence–Salem, MA–NH		5,455		0.633
Detroit–Ann Arbor, MI	5,293	5,187		−0.202
Dallas–Fort Worth, TX	3,046		32.6	2.86
Houston–Galveston–Brazoria, TX		3,731		1.81

The function $F = P(1 + r)^t$ can be used to predict the future population (F) for t years in the future when you know the present population (P) and the yearly growth rate for the population (r).

Use the model for population growth.

1. Copy and complete the table.

2. For which metropolitan area does the situation illustrate exponential decay?

3. At these growth rates, which population should be the first to double its 1980 population? In what year should this occur?

4. How many years should it be before the population of the Los Angeles area passes the population of the New York area?

5. At these growth rates, predict the top three Metropolitan Statistical Area populations for the year 2000.

1. In your own words, tell what it means for the relationship between two quantities to be exponential.
2. Give an example of a situation that shows exponential decay. What is the difference between exponential growth and exponential decay?
3. What is the meaning of a logarithm?
4. When is it useful to rewrite an equation using logarithmic notation?

Self-Assessment

Graph each function.

1. $y = 3(2)^x$

2. $y = 6\left(\frac{1}{3}\right)^x$

3. $y = 3(1.1)^x$

4. $y = -2(1.25)^x$

5. Which is the graph of $y = 1.05^x$?

   (a)   (b)   (c)

6. Graph the equation $y = 10(1.5)^x$. Use the graph to estimate the value of y when $x = 4.5$.

7. Graph the equation $y = 0.5^x$. Use the graph to estimate the value of y when $x = 2.5$.

The future value of an investment of _P_ dollars in _t_ years at an interest rate _r_ (compounded yearly) is $F = P(1 + r)^t$. Find the future value (_F_) of these values.

Industry

	F	P	r	t
8.		$800	12%	1 year
9.		$5000	8%	5 years
10.		$6000	12.5%	6.5 years
11.		$3000	10%	6 months

Rewrite each equation using logarithmic notation.

12. $30 = 5^n$ **13.** $y = -2^h$ **14.** $15 = 12^y$

Rewrite each equation without logarithmic notation.

15. $y = \log_{10} 2x$ **16.** $y = \log_e 0.5$ **17.** $y = \log_{10} 200$

18. Which of these functions is shown by the graph?

    (a) $y = 3^x$ (b) $y = \log_1 x$

    (c) $y = \log_3 x$ (d) $y = \left(\frac{1}{3}\right)^x$

X=3   Y=1

19. Growth or Decay Does the graph of $y = 0.99^x$ represent exponential growth or decay? Explain.

20. Save Now, Pay Later Suppose the cost of a college education today for one year is $10,000, increasing 5% annually. A child born today should expect to spend how much for four years of college beginning at age 18?

21. This Isn't Missouri? The population of Kansas City, KS in 1990 was 149,800 people and dropping at an average annual rate of 7%. At this rate, when would the population be about half of what it was in 1990?

Use a property of logarithms to write an equivalent expression.

22. $\log 3 + \log 3$ **23.** $\log (5 \cdot 7)$

24. Real Money A couple has $50,000 in a retirement savings account earning 5% per year. If inflation averages 3.5% per year for the next 10 years and they make no additional deposits or withdrawals from the account, how much will their money be worth in 10 years at today's dollar value?

25. Half-Life The amount of carbon-14 in dead plants and animals decreases by a factor of 0.988 every century. After n centuries, only $(0.988)^n$ as much carbon-14 remains.

    a. What percentage of carbon-14 remains in the wood of a two-century-old violin?

    b. What percentage of carbon-14 remains in an Egyptian mummy after 5000 years?

    c. Calculate powers of 0.988 to estimate how many centuries it takes for the carbon-14 in an artifact or fossil to be reduced to 50% of its original amount.

    This length of time is called the *half-life* of carbon-14 and helps archaeologists to determine the age of artifacts and fossils.

26. **Whole Lot of Shakin' Goin' On** The equation $M = \log\frac{x}{x_0}$ gives the magnitude of an earthquake (M) on the Richter scale for a seismographic reading of x. The seismographic reading for an earthquake of magnitude 0 (x_0) equals 0.001 mm.
   a. What is the magnitude of an earthquake that gives a seismographic reading of 1.5 mm?
   b. A seismographic reading of 0.01 indicates an earthquake of magnitude 1. Explain why an earthquake of magnitude 2 is 10 times more powerful than an earthquake of magnitude 1.

27. **Franklin's Mint** Benjamin Franklin's will provided for 1000 pounds to be loaned to students at 5% annual interest, compounded once each year, with all payments to be reloaned to other students. After 100 years, the amount made was to be donated to the city of Boston. He used the expression $P(1 + r)^t$ to calculate this amount, where P was the amount loaned, r the interest rate, and t the number of years. How much did he expect Boston to receive?

28. **Ease a Disease** The graph shows the number of cases of measles and polio from 1950 to 1980. The dots represent the date when immunization became available for each disease.
   a. Describe the scale of the graph.
   b. Which vaccine do you think was more effective? Why?
   c. Was the increase in the number of cases of polio in the mid-1970s significant? Why or why not?

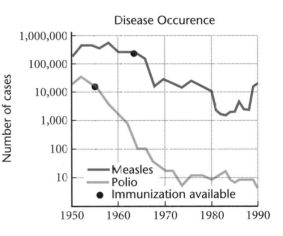

29. **They Waited for Years** In South Africa, May 1994 marked the end of 300 years of *apartheid*, a system in which black South Africans had no democratic rights. When democratic elections came, voting lines were so long, people waited *days* to cast a ballot.

   Use the equation $y = 10^{-0.05t}$ to model the probability that a person would have to wait more than t hours to vote in this election.
   a. What is the probability that a person would wait more than 8 hours to vote?
   b. What is the probability that a person would wait more than 24 hours to vote?

Chapter 10 Review

Chapter 10 completes the Focus on Algebra course by surveying the kinds of numbers and equations you have been working with throughout the year. The structure of algebra is based on the properties of the real numbers. Some new functions, exponential and logarithmic, were introduced to give you a glimpse into your future mathematics courses.

KEY TERMS

Exponential decay [10-2]   Golden ratio [10-1]

Exponential function [10-2]   Logarithmic function [10-2]

Exponential growth [10-2]   Radical expression [10-1]

Extraneous solution [10-1]   Rational expression [10-1]

Determine whether each statement is true or false. If the statement is false, change the underlined word or phrase to make it true.

1. Extraneous solutions are solutions that <u>are repeated</u>.

2. Both 0.333... and $\frac{1}{3}$ are <u>rational</u> numbers.

3. Which function is an exponential function?
   (a) $y = 2^x$ (b) $y = 2(2)$ (c) $y = ax + 2$ (d) $y = \frac{1}{x}$ (e) not here

CONCEPTS AND APPLICATIONS

For each real number, determine whether it is rational or irrational. [10-1]

4. π 5. $\frac{4}{7}$ 6. 1.464646...

7. Explain why $\sqrt{4}$ is rational while $\sqrt{5}$ is irrational. [10-1]

Simplify each expression. [10-1]

8. $2\sqrt{x} + 4 - \sqrt{x}$ 9. $\frac{1}{3}\sqrt{x} + 4 - \frac{1}{3}\sqrt{x}$ 10. $\sqrt{8y^5}$

11. $\frac{(x-7)^2(x-7)}{(x+20)}$ 12. $\frac{(x^2-1)}{x+1}$ 13. $\frac{(x+2)(x-3)}{2x^2+4x}$

Find the value(s) of x for which each expression is not defined. [10-1]

14. $\sqrt{x-5}$ 15. $\frac{x-2}{x^2-4}$ 16. $\sqrt{6-x}$

Solve each equation. Check your solution. [10-1]

17. $1 = \dfrac{x - 4}{2x}$

18. $3x = \dfrac{-4x^2 + 7}{x}$

19. $2 = \dfrac{3}{x} + \dfrac{-7}{3x}$

20. $x + 1 = \sqrt{3}$

21. $\sqrt{2x + 9} = x - 3$

22. $x = \sqrt{x + 1} + 5$

23. Consider the graph of the function $y = \dfrac{1}{x + 1}$. [10-1]
   a. Find the value(s) of x for which the function is not defined.
   b. Describe how the graph of this function reflects these undefined value(s).
   c. What are the domain and the range of this function? Tell how you decided.

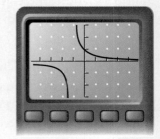

24. Can the slope of the line through $(4c^2, c)$ and $(4c^2, 3c)$ ever be 2? If so, find the value of c and the coordinates of both points. If not, explain why. [10-1]

 25. A resistor (r ohms) is connected in parallel with a 4-ohm resistor so that the total resistance is 1.5 ohms. Solve the equation to find r.
$$\frac{1}{r} + \frac{1}{4} = \frac{1}{1.5}$$

26. Explain why $y = 2^x$ is an exponential function but $y = x^2$ is not. [10-2]

Each equation represents an exponential function. Graph each equation. [10-2]

27. $y = 4^x$

28. $y = -\dfrac{1}{3}(5)^x$

29. $y = \left(\dfrac{1}{2}\right)^x$

30. The area of a 32-square-inch picture decreases 17% with each reduction. Sketch a graph of picture area vs. number of reductions. [10-2]

31. The mean SAT score in math for Alabama increased 3.5% from 1983 to 1993. The mean score in 1993 was 526. If this rate of increase remains constant,
$$\text{mean score} = 526(1.035)^x$$
can be used to predict the mean score for each successive decade. [10-2]
   a. Use the formula to predict the scores for the years 2003, 2013, and 2023. Graph the results. Include the mean score for 1993.
   b. Guess and check using your calculator to estimate when the mean score will reach 800, a perfect score. Do you think this is a reasonable estimate? Explain.

Rewrite each equation using logarithmic notation. [10-2]

32. $5^2 = 25$

33. $2^n = 32$

Rewrite each equation without logarithmic notation. [10-2]

34. $4 = \log_3 81$

35. $2 = \log_d 64$

CONCEPTS AND CONNECTIONS

36. Discrete Math To find each new number in the Fibonacci sequence you add the previous two numbers. Using the same rule, but different starting numbers, you can create other sequences called *Lucas sequences*.
   a. Write the first 15 numbers in this Lucas sequence.

$$1, 3, 4, 7, 11, \ldots$$

   b. Find the ratio of each number and the previous number. Use a calculator to approximate each ratio to six decimal places. (For example, $\frac{11}{7} \approx 1.571429$.)
   c. Compare the ratios you found to the golden ratio, $\frac{1 + \sqrt{5}}{2}$. What do you notice?

SELF-EVALUATION

Write a paragraph about the kinds of numbers, equations, and functions you've learned or reviewed in this chapter. Include any diagrams that help you organize the information. Write down which parts of the chapter were difficult for you and which sections you need to study further in order to better understand the chapter.

Chapter 10 Assessment

TEST

For each real number, determine whether it is rational or irrational.

1. 5

2. $\sqrt{5}$

3. $\frac{1}{5}$

4. Explain how a radical expression is different from a rational expression. Give an example of each.

Simplify each expression.

5. $\sqrt{x} - 3 + 4\sqrt{x}$

6. $\frac{(x + 1)(x - 5)}{x + 1}$

7. $\sqrt{18x^3}$

8. Explain what it means when an expression is not defined.

Find the value(s) of x for which each expression is not defined.

9. $\sqrt{6 + x}$

10. $\frac{(x - 1)}{(2x - 2)(6 - x)}$

Solve each equation. Check your solution.

11. $2 = \dfrac{x - 5}{3x}$

12. $\sqrt{5x - 4} = 4$

13. Consider the graph of the function $y = 1 - \sqrt{x + 2}$.
   a. Find the value(s) of x for which the function is not defined.
   b. Describe how the graph reflects these undefined values.
   c. What are the range and the domain of this function? Tell how you decided.

14. A battery has 250 watt-hours of stored energy. How long can it keep a light rated 30 watts on? Solve the equation to find t.

$$t = \frac{250}{30}$$

15. Sketch the graph of the function $y = \left(\dfrac{3}{4}\right)^x$.

16. Guess and check using your calculator to find the first whole number x such that 32^x is greater than 1,000,000. Write down each number you tried.

17. Write the letter of the second pair that best matches the first pair.
   Growth function: Decaying function as   (a) Radical: Rational
   (b) Associative Property: Distributive Property   (c) Slope: Ratio
   (d) Direct relation: Inverse relation

18. Rewrite the equation $7^2 = 49$ using logarithmic notation.

19. Rewrite the equation $4 = \log_2 x$ without logarithmic notation.

20. The interest rate on a five-year certificate of deposit is 4.25%, compounded annually. If you invest a principle (P) of $1000, what will the amount (A) be when the CD reaches maturity in five years? Use the formula $A = P(1 + r)^t$ for the amount after t years, compounded annually at an interest rate of r.

21. Return to Smallville After several years of carefully tracking the population change in Smallville, scientists adjusted their formula to reflect the current data. The population, in thousands of people, can now be represented by $3(0.925)^t$, where t is the number of years from now.
   a. What is the population today?
   b. What is the estimated population 10 years from now?
   c. Approximately what was the population last year?

PERFORMANCE TASK

Present a detailed solution of the following problem. Try to use an equation that contains a rational expression.

A person traveled 120 miles in one direction. The return trip was accomplished at twice the speed and took 3 hours less time. Find the person's original speed.

SKILLS BANK

COMPARING INTEGERS

The whole numbers and their opposites form the set of **integers.**

$$\ldots, -4, -3, -2, -1, 0, 1, 2, 3, 4, \ldots$$

An expression that compares integers is an **inequality.** When you compare two integers on a number line, the *greater* number is to the right. The *lesser* number is to the left.

We say -3 *is less than* 2.

Write the inequality: $-3 < 2$

We say *2 is greater than* -3.

Write the inequality: $2 > -3$

The inequality symbol points to the lesser number.

EXAMPLE

Write the integers 2, -4, and -1 in order from least to greatest.

Find the integers on a number line.

Use inequality symbols to write the numbers in order from left to right.

$$-4 < -1 < 2$$

TRY IT

Compare the integers using $>$ or $<$.

1. 3, 1   **2.** $-2, 0$ **3.** 1, -5 **4.** $-7, -8$

Write the integers in order from least to greatest.

5. $-5, 4, 3$ **6.** $0, -3, -6$ **7.** $-6, -1, -4$ **8.** 10, 0, 6
9. $-9, 7, -8$ **10.** $-15, 21, -21$ **11.** 33, 34, -35 **12.** $-75, -85, -74$

Write an inequality for each number line.

13.   **14.**

MODELING INTEGER ADDITION AND SUBTRACTION

We use yellow tiles to model positive integers and red tiles to model negative integers.

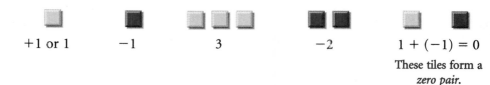

+1 or 1   −1   3   −2   1 + (−1) = 0

These tiles form a *zero pair*.

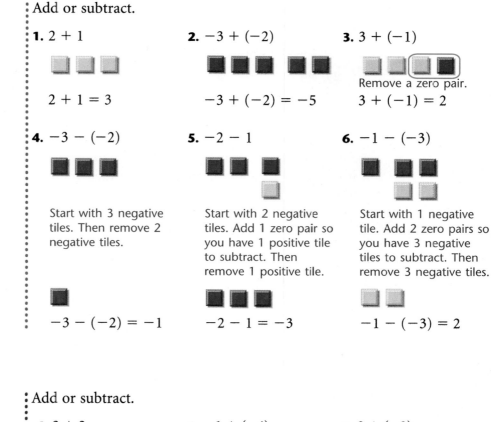

EXAMPLES

Add or subtract.

1. 2 + 1

2 + 1 = 3

2. −3 + (−2)

−3 + (−2) = −5

3. 3 + (−1)

Remove a zero pair.
3 + (−1) = 2

4. −3 − (−2)

Start with 3 negative tiles. Then remove 2 negative tiles.

−3 − (−2) = −1

5. −2 − 1

Start with 2 negative tiles. Add 1 zero pair so you have 1 positive tile to subtract. Then remove 1 positive tile.

−2 − 1 = −3

6. −1 − (−3)

Start with 1 negative tile. Add 2 zero pairs so you have 3 negative tiles to subtract. Then remove 3 negative tiles.

−1 − (−3) = 2

TRY IT

Add or subtract.

1. 3 + 2

2. −1 + (−4)

3. 2 + (−2)

4. −4 + 3

5. 1 + (−3)

6. −3 + 4

7. −1 − (−1)

8. 2 − (−4)

9. −3 − 3

10. 3 − 5

11. −3 − (−1)

12. −4 − 2

13. 2 + (−1) + 4

14. 3 + 7 − 5

15. −6 − (−2) + 1

MODELING INTEGER MULTIPLICATION AND DIVISION

We use groups of integer tiles to model integer multiplication.

EXAMPLES

Multiply or divide.

1. $2 \times (-3)$

Make 2 groups of 3 negative integer tiles.

$$2 \times (-3) = -6$$

2. $-3 \times (4)$

You can't make -3 groups. But multiplication is *commutative*, so you *can* make 4 groups of 3 negative tiles.

$$4 \times (-3) = -12$$

Notice that the product of two integers with *opposite* signs is *negative*. The *quotient* of two integers with opposite signs is also negative. If two integers have the *same* sign, then both their product and their quotient are *positive*.

3. $-8 \div 2$

Divide 8 negative tiles into 2 groups.

$$-8 \div 2 = -4$$

4. $-10 \div (-5)$

Both integers are negative, so their quotient is positive.

$$-10 \div (-5) = 2$$

Recall that when you multiply or divide 0 by any number, the result is 0. But you cannot divide by 0.

TRY IT

Multiply or divide.

1. $-2 \times (-2)$ **2.** $-12 \div 4$ **3.** 0×7 **4.** 3×3

5. $-15 \div (-3)$ **6.** $0 \div 4$ **7.** $5 \div (-1)$ **8.** $10 \div 2$

9. $4 \times (-8)$ **10.** $-16 \div 4$ **11.** -12×2 **12.** -15×0

13. $-14 \div (-7)$ **14.** $-5 \times (-4)$ **15.** $0 \div (-6)$ **16.** $-32 \div (-8)$

17. $6 \times (-7)$ **18.** $-1 \times (-7)$ **19.** $-2 \times (-2) \times 2$ **20.** $3 \times (-4) \times 2$

COMPARING FRACTIONS

To compare fractions, write them as fractions with the *least common denominator* (LCD) or write them as decimals.

EXAMPLE

Compare $\frac{7}{12}$ and $\frac{11}{18}$.

Method 1 Find the LCD by writing the prime factorizations of 12 and 18.

$$12 = 2 \cdot 2 \cdot 3$$
$$18 = 2 \cdot 3 \cdot 3$$
$$\text{LCD} = 2 \cdot 2 \cdot 3 \cdot 3 = 36$$

Rewrite both fractions with the LCD.

$$\frac{7}{12} = \frac{7 \cdot 3}{12 \cdot 3} = \frac{21}{36}$$
$$\frac{11}{18} = \frac{11 \cdot 2}{18 \cdot 2} = \frac{22}{36}$$

Compare the numerators.

$$\frac{21}{36} < \frac{22}{36}, \text{ so } \frac{7}{12} < \frac{11}{18}.$$

Method 2 Use a calculator to write the fractions as decimals.

$$\frac{7}{12} \rightarrow 7 \boxed{\div} 12 \boxed{=} 0.5833\ldots$$
$$\frac{11}{18} \rightarrow 11 \boxed{\div} 18 \boxed{=} 0.6111\ldots$$

Compare the decimals.

$$0.5833\ldots < 0.6111\ldots,$$
$$\text{so } \frac{7}{12} < \frac{11}{18}.$$

TRY IT

Compare the fractions.

1. $\frac{2}{3}, \frac{1}{2}$

2. $-\frac{3}{4}, -\frac{4}{5}$

3. $\frac{5}{7}, \frac{3}{4}$

4. $\frac{7}{8}, \frac{5}{6}$

5. $-\frac{1}{3}, \frac{5}{18}$

6. $\frac{10}{21}, \frac{3}{7}$

7. $\frac{13}{10}, \frac{4}{3}$

8. $-\frac{5}{4}, \frac{5}{6}$

9. $-\frac{7}{5}, -\frac{3}{2}$

10. $1\frac{2}{5}, \frac{21}{15}$

11. $-\frac{4}{13}, -\frac{3}{11}$

12. $-2\frac{3}{7}, -2\frac{5}{9}$

Write the fractions in order from least to greatest.

13. $\frac{2}{3}, \frac{3}{5}, \frac{5}{7}$

14. $-\frac{7}{8}, -\frac{9}{10}, -\frac{5}{6}$

15. $1\frac{2}{5}, \frac{12}{10}, 1\frac{4}{5}$

16. $\frac{7}{24}, \frac{1}{3}, -\frac{9}{24}, \frac{1}{4}$

17. $\frac{5}{9}, \frac{11}{18}, \frac{17}{36}, \frac{1}{2}$

18. $1\frac{3}{4}, 1\frac{7}{8}, 1\frac{17}{20}, 1\frac{4}{5}$

19. $-\frac{1}{3}, -\frac{9}{24}, -\frac{5}{12}, -\frac{17}{48}$

20. $1\frac{3}{10}, \frac{4}{3}, \frac{5}{2}, 1\frac{2}{7}$

21. $\frac{4}{9}, -\frac{9}{4}, -2\frac{1}{3}, 1\frac{1}{2}$

22. $-\frac{9}{24}, -\frac{5}{12}, -\frac{17}{48}$

23. $\frac{13}{10}, \frac{2}{4}, \frac{7}{2}$

24. $\frac{4}{9}, -\frac{9}{4}, 2\frac{1}{3}, 1\frac{1}{2}$

ADDING AND SUBTRACTING FRACTIONS

To add or subtract two fractions, write them as fractions with the same denominator and add or subtract the numerators.

EXAMPLES

Add or subtract.

1. $\frac{7}{12} + \frac{11}{12}$

Add the numerators.

Simplify.

$$\frac{7}{12} + \frac{11}{12} = \frac{7 + 11}{12}$$
$$= \frac{18}{12}$$
$$= \frac{3}{2} \text{ or } 1\frac{1}{2}$$

2. $\frac{3}{4} + \frac{1}{6}$

Rewrite using the LCD.

Simplify.

$$\frac{3}{4} + \frac{1}{6} = \frac{9}{12} + \frac{2}{12}$$
$$= \frac{11}{12}$$

3. $\frac{1}{2} - \frac{1}{6}$

Rewrite using the LCD.

Simplify.

$$\frac{1}{2} - \frac{1}{6} = \frac{3}{6} - \frac{1}{6}$$
$$= \frac{2}{6}$$
$$= \frac{1}{3}$$

TRY IT

Add or subtract.

1. $\frac{5}{8} + \frac{7}{8}$ **2.** $\frac{9}{14} - \frac{3}{14}$ **3.** $\frac{5}{12} - \frac{1}{3}$

4. $\frac{9}{16} + \frac{3}{8}$ **5.** $\frac{1}{3} + \frac{3}{4}$ **6.** $\frac{1}{4} - \frac{5}{20}$

7. $\frac{7}{8} - \frac{3}{10}$ **8.** $\frac{11}{12} + \frac{5}{6}$ **9.** $-\frac{3}{5} + \frac{11}{10}$

10. $-\frac{7}{8} + \left(-\frac{3}{16}\right)$ **11.** $\frac{3}{7} + \frac{1}{5}$ **12.** $-\frac{1}{15} + \frac{5}{12}$

13. $\frac{2}{21} - \frac{3}{28}$ **14.** $\frac{2}{35} + \frac{1}{7} + \frac{2}{5}$ **15.** $-\frac{2}{3} + \frac{4}{5} + \frac{7}{6}$

MULTIPLYING AND DIVIDING FRACTIONS

To multiply two fractions, multiply the numerators and multiply the denominators. To divide by a fraction, we multiply by its *reciprocal*.

EXAMPLES

Multiply or divide.

1. $\frac{3}{4} \times \frac{5}{7}$

Multiply numerators and multiply denominators.

$$\frac{3}{4} \times \frac{5}{7} = \frac{3 \times 5}{4 \times 7}$$
$$= \frac{15}{28}$$

2. $-\frac{5}{9} \times \frac{12}{25}$

Multiply numerators and multiply denominators. Then simplify.

$$-\frac{5}{9} \times \frac{12}{25} = -\frac{5 \times 12}{9 \times 25}$$
$$= -\frac{5 \times 3 \times 4}{3 \times 3 \times 5 \times 5}$$
$$= -\frac{4}{3 \times 5}$$
$$= -\frac{4}{15}$$

3. $\frac{4}{5} \div \frac{7}{3}$

Multiply by the reciprocal of $\frac{7}{3}$.

$$\frac{4}{5} \div \frac{7}{3} = \frac{4}{5} \times \frac{3}{7}$$
$$= \frac{12}{35}$$

TRY IT

Multiply or divide.

1. $\frac{3}{4} \times \frac{1}{3}$

2. $\frac{2}{5} \times \frac{6}{7}$

3. $-\frac{5}{6} \times \frac{3}{10}$

4. $\frac{1}{2} \div \frac{1}{4}$

5. $-\frac{5}{7} \div \frac{5}{6}$

6. $\frac{2}{5} \div \frac{7}{10}$

7. $15 \times \frac{1}{5}$

8. $0 \div \frac{7}{8}$

9. $-1 \times \frac{11}{12}$

10. $1 \div -\frac{3}{7}$

11. $\frac{7}{6} \times \frac{9}{14}$

12. $\frac{3}{5} \div -\frac{6}{5}$

13. $-\frac{25}{18} \div \frac{5}{3}$

14. $\frac{9}{17} \div \frac{27}{51}$

15. $\frac{2}{3} \div 8$

16. $4\frac{1}{2} \times 1\frac{2}{3}$

17. $1\frac{4}{5} \div 2\frac{1}{4}$

18. $\frac{2}{3} \times -\frac{5}{6} \times \frac{9}{10}$

RATIO

A **ratio** is a comparison of two quantities. It is interpreted as a fraction in many applications. If the ratio compares quantities with different units, such as distance and time units, then it is often called a **rate.** A **percentage** is a ratio in which the second quantity is understood to be 100.

EXAMPLES

1. A ratio can be written with words, with a colon (:), or as a fraction.

3 cars out of 15 cars   3 out of 15   3:15 $\frac{3}{15}$

2. To make a ratio equivalent to a given ratio, multiply or divide both quantities in the given ratio by the same number.

$$\frac{3}{15} = \frac{3 \cdot 8}{15 \cdot 8} = \frac{24}{120} \qquad \frac{3}{15} = \frac{3 \div 3}{15 \div 3} = \frac{1}{5}$$

3. Use fraction properties to write ratios in equivalent forms.

1 out of 5 $\frac{1}{5}$ $\frac{20}{100}$ 20%   0.2

4. Miriam earns \$60 each month. She puts \$24 of this amount into her savings account. Write this ratio in different forms and in a sentence.

- \$24 out of \$60 is $\frac{24}{60}$ or $\frac{2}{5}$ or $\frac{40}{100}$ or 0.4 or 40%.

- Miriam saves two-fifths, or 40%, of her salary.

TRY IT

Write the equivalent fraction in lowest terms for these ratios.

1. 4:6   **2.** 8:20   **3.** 10 out of 100

Write the percentage that is equivalent to each ratio.

4. 4:5   **5.** 14:200   **6.** 1:3

Write each ratio as an equivalent fraction, decimal, and percentage.

7. Bill spends \$10 of his \$25 allowance on bus fare.

8. All 24 photographs were blurred.

9. For each \$5 donation, \$1 is used for expenses.

PROPORTION

A **proportion** is an equation stating that two ratios are equivalent.

EXAMPLES

Solve the proportion to find an unknown in two equivalent ratios.

1. A recipe that serves 8 people uses 3 eggs. A cook must serve 16 people. He must find an equivalent ratio.

$$\frac{8 \text{ servings}}{3 \text{ eggs}} = \frac{16 \text{ servings}}{x \text{ eggs}}$$

To write the proportion, put corresponding quantities in the same position in each ratio.

$$\frac{8}{3} = \frac{8 \cdot 2}{3 \cdot 2} = \frac{16}{x}$$

Write equivalent fractions.

$$x = 6$$

2. $\frac{d}{48} = \frac{1}{64}$. Find the unknown value d.

$$\frac{d}{48} \cdot 48 = \frac{1}{64} \cdot 48$$

Multiply by the denominator of the ratio with the unknown term.

$$d \cdot 1 = \frac{48}{64}$$

Simplify the equation.

$$d = \frac{48 \div 16}{64 \div 16} = \frac{3}{4} = 0.75$$

Reduce the fraction.

3. $\frac{11}{20} = \frac{3}{x}$. Find the unknown value x.

$$11x = 20 \cdot 3$$

Cross multiply.

$$11x = 60$$

Multiply.

$$x = \frac{60}{11} \approx 5.45.$$

TRY IT

Solve these proportions.

1. $\frac{y}{12} = \frac{4}{3}$

2. $\frac{0.4}{0.6} = \frac{8}{k}$

3. $\frac{28}{x} = \frac{4}{5}$

4. $\frac{a}{25} = \frac{2}{5}$

5. $\frac{1.4}{8} = \frac{c}{100}$

6. $\frac{5}{0.25} = \frac{x}{5}$

7. To make green paint, Wallace uses a ratio of 4 quarts of yellow to 2 quarts of blue.
   a. How much yellow paint will he need if he uses 10 quarts of blue?
   b. How much blue paint will he need if he uses 5 quarts of yellow?
   c. How much total paint will he need if he uses 5 quarts of blue?

8. A 150 pound person has about 60 pounds of muscle. Use a proportion to determine the amount of muscle on a 200 pound person.

CONVERTING MEASUREMENTS

Measurement conversion factors allow you to change from one unit of measure to another.

EXAMPLES

Use conversion factors to change each amount to the indicated measure.

1. Convert 50 inches to feet.

Find the necessary equation in a table of measurement conversions. $12 \text{ in.} = 1 \text{ ft}$

Change to a **unit rate** by dividing by the unit you want to change. $\dfrac{12 \text{ in.}}{12 \text{ in.}} = \dfrac{1 \text{ ft}}{12 \text{ in.}}$

Since the unit rate is equal to 1, you can multiply the starting amount by the unit rate. Then simplify. $50 \text{ in.} \cdot \dfrac{1 \text{ ft}}{12 \text{ in.}} = \dfrac{50 \text{ ft}}{12 \text{ in.}} = 4\dfrac{2}{12} \text{ ft}$

$$= 4\dfrac{1}{6} \text{ ft} \approx 4.167 \text{ ft}$$

Or, write the amount in feet and inches. $4\dfrac{2}{12} \text{ ft} = 4 \text{ ft } 2 \text{ in.}$

2. Convert 4.5 kilometers to miles.

Look up the conversion factor. $1 \text{ mi} = 1.6093 \text{ km}$

Set up a proportion.
Line up corresponding units. $\dfrac{x \text{ mi}}{1 \text{ mi}} = \dfrac{4.5 \text{ km}}{1.6093 \text{ km}}$

Solve the proportion. $x \text{ mi} \approx 2.8 \text{ mi}$

TRY IT

Convert each amount to the indicated measurement.

1. 45 ft to in.
2. 8448 ft to mi
3. 40 yd to in.
4. 3.8 lb to oz
5. 7.8 m to cm
6. 28 pt to gal
7. 224 ft to yd, ft
8. 2.2 acres to ft^2
9. $3\dfrac{3}{4}$ hr to min

WRITING PERCENTAGES

A **percentage** is a ratio that compares a number with 100. *Percent* means *per hundred*.

EXAMPLES

1. Write 15% as a fraction and as a decimal.

15% means 15 percent or 15 per hundred.

Fraction $15\% = \frac{15}{100} = \frac{3}{20}$

Decimal $15\% = \frac{15}{100} = 0.15$

2. Write 0.36 as a percentage and as a fraction.

Percentage $0.36 = \frac{36}{100} = 36\%$

Fraction $0.36 = \frac{36}{100} = \frac{9}{25}$

3. Write $\frac{41}{50}$ as a decimal and as a percentage.

Decimal Use a calculator or rewrite as a fraction with denominator 100.

$41 \boxed{\div} 50 \boxed{=} 0.82 \quad \frac{41}{50} = \frac{41 \times 2}{50 \times 2} = \frac{82}{100} = 0.82$

Percentage $\frac{41}{50} = 0.82 = 82\%$

TRY IT

Write each percentage as a fraction and as a decimal.

1. 30%   **2.** 8%   **3.** 62%

4. 95%   **5.** 175%   **6.** $\frac{1}{2}$ %

Write each decimal as a percentage and as a fraction.

7. 0.77   **8.** 0.45   **9.** 0.56

10. 0.06   **11.** 0.875   **12.** 1.8

Write each fraction as a decimal and as a percentage.

13. $\frac{7}{20}$ **14.** $\frac{3}{8}$ **15.** $\frac{12}{25}$

16. $\frac{61}{100}$ **17.** $\frac{5}{6}$ **18.** $\frac{71}{50}$

FINDING A PERCENTAGE OF A NUMBER

To find a percentage of a number, write the percentage as a decimal or fraction. Then multiply by the given number. You may choose whichever method you find most convenient for the given percentage.

EXAMPLES

Find each number.

1. 56.4% of 125.
Write the percentage as a decimal and multiply by 125.
$$56.4\% = 0.564$$
$$56.4\% \text{ of } 125 = 0.564 \times 125$$
$$= 70.5$$

2. 75% of 84.
Write the percentage as a fraction and multiply by 84.
$$75\% = \frac{3}{4}$$
$$75\% \text{ of } 84 = \frac{3}{4} \times 84$$
$$= \frac{3}{4} \times \frac{84}{1}$$
$$= 3 \times 21$$
$$= 63$$

You can also use the percent key $\boxed{\%}$ on a calculator to find percentages.

3. 6.5% of 244.
$$6.5\% \text{ of } 244 \rightarrow 244 \boxed{\times} 6.5 \boxed{\%} \boxed{=} 15.86$$

(On some calculators it is not necessary to press $\boxed{=}$.)

TRY IT

Find each number.

1. 20% of 45   **2.** 13% of 140   **3.** 9.1% of 24
4. 25% of 400   **5.** 65% of 12   **6.** 125% of 8
7. 27.3% of 91   **8.** 0.7% of 2.6   **9.** $33\frac{1}{3}$ % of 333
10. 234% of 8.5   **11.** 50% of 28   **12.** 79% of 0.56
13. 1% of 763   **14.** 43.2% of 560   **15.** 200% of 15

MORE PERCENTAGE PROBLEMS

Percentage is used to solve a variety of problems.

1. 214 million people speak Arabic out of about 3,562 million people in the world. Find the percent who speak Arabic.

$$\frac{214 \text{ million}}{3562 \text{ million}} = \frac{x}{100}$$ Set up a proportion.

$$\frac{214 \text{ million}}{3562 \text{ million}} \cdot 100 = x$$ Solve.

$$x \approx 6.0\%$$ The value of x is the percent.

2. In fall 1996, tuition and registration fees for resident undergraduates at the University of California, Davis was $1411. This is 664% of the fees in fall 1975. Find the total fees for 1975.

In other words, $1411 is 664% of x.

$$\frac{\text{Fees in 1996}}{\text{Fees in 1975}} = \frac{\$1411}{x} = \frac{664}{100}$$ Write a proportion.

$$\$1411 \cdot 100 = 664x$$ Solve.

$$x = 1411 \cdot \frac{100}{664}$$

$$x = \$212.50$$

3. The population of Smallville increased about 18% in the past decade to 12,440. What was the population ten years ago?

$$100\% + 18\% = 118\%$$ Change 18% increase to the percent of the prior population.

$$1.18 \cdot x = 12,440$$ Let x = prior population. Change the percent to a decimal and write an equation.

$$x \approx 10,542$$ Solve.

Find the percentage or total as needed.

1. 62.4 out of 1560   **2.** 38.25 out of 9   **3.** 4836 out of 65.35
4. 62.5% represents 20 students.   **5.** 14 errors is 0.2% of ?

Find the starting amount.

6. The total bill, with 15% tip added, was $135.70.
7. The sales tax is 5.5%. The total charge was $25.85.

REFERENCE CENTER: Skills Bank

MAKING A BAR GRAPH

A **bar graph** displays relative sizes of data.

Jefferson High School Food Drive			
Class	Amount raised for food drive ($)	Student participation in food drive (%)	Number of families aided
Freshman	442	56	9
Sophomore	628	50	14
Junior	950	85	24
Senior	886	38	20

EXAMPLE

Draw a bar graph that displays the amounts raised for food by each class during the Jefferson High School food drive.

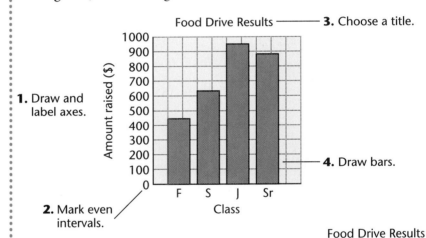

1. Draw and label axes.

2. Mark even intervals.

3. Choose a title.

4. Draw bars.

In the above bar graph, the bars are drawn vertically. You can draw bars horizontally, as shown at the right.

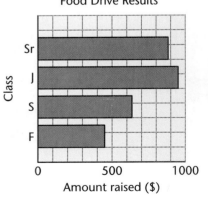

Food Drive Results

TRY IT

1. Draw a vertical bar graph that displays student participation in the food drive.
2. Draw a horizontal bar graph that displays the numbers of families aided in the food drive.

MAKING A LINE GRAPH

A **line graph** shows how data changes over time (or another variable).

Populations of Largest U.S. Cities

City	Population (millions)				
	1950	**1960**	**1970**	**1980**	**1990**
New York City	7.9	7.8	7.9	7.1	7.3
Los Angeles	2.0	2.5	2.8	3.0	3.5
Chicago	3.6	3.6	3.4	3.0	2.8
Houston	0.6	0.9	1.2	1.6	1.6

EXAMPLE

Draw a line graph that displays the population of New York from 1950 to 1990.

1. Draw and label axes.

3. Choose a title.

4. Plot data points.

5. Connect data points with line segments.

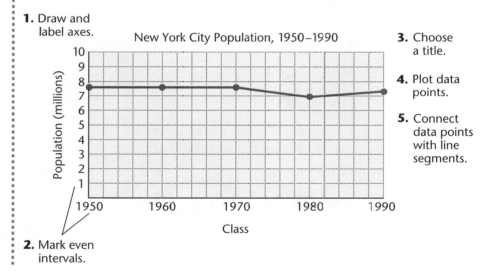

2. Mark even intervals.

TRY IT

Draw a line graph that displays each city's population from 1950 to 1990.

1. Los Angeles   **2.** Chicago   **3.** Houston

MAKING A CIRCLE GRAPH

A **circle graph** shows how *parts* relate to a *whole* and to each other.

Favorite Sport Poll Results

	Sport			
Age group	Baseball	Football	Basketball	Other
18 and under	21	40	75	18
19–50	35	58	40	21
51 and over	64	38	32	15

EXAMPLE

Draw a circle graph that displays the favorite sports for the 18-and-under age group.

Find the total number of people polled in the 18-and-under group.
$21 + 40 + 75 + 18 = 154$

Express each number as a fraction of the total and multiply by 360°.

$\frac{21}{154} \cdot 360° \approx 49.1°$ $\frac{40}{154} \cdot 360° \approx 93.5°$

$\frac{75}{154} \cdot 360° \approx 175.3°$ $\frac{18}{154} \cdot 360° \approx 42.1°$

Draw a circle. Use a protractor to draw an angle to represent each part.

Label each sector and choose a title for the graph.

Favorite Sports, Age 18 and Under

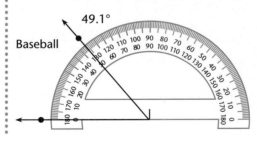

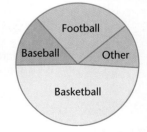

TRY IT

Draw a circle graph that displays the favorite sports for each age group.

1. 19–50   **2.** 51 and over

Two angles with measures that have a sum of 90° are **complementary angles**. Each angle is the *complement* of the other.

∠ADB and ∠BDC
are complementary.

∠M and ∠N are
complementary.

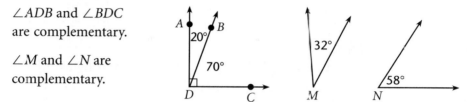

Two angles with measures that have a sum of 180° are **supplementary angles**. Each angle is the *supplement* of the other.

∠PSQ and ∠QSR are
supplementary.

∠T and ∠W are
supplementary.

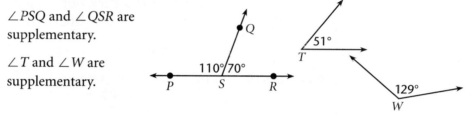

A **transversal** is a line that intersects two *coplanar* lines at different points.

Line *h* is a transversal intersecting
line *j* and line *k*.

∠3, ∠4, ∠5, and ∠6 are **interior angles**.

∠1, ∠2, ∠7, and ∠8 are **exterior angles**.

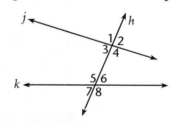

Two angles on opposite sides of a transversal are **alternate angles.**

Alternate interior angles: ∠3 and ∠6; ∠4 and ∠5

Alternate exterior angles: ∠1 and ∠8; ∠2 and ∠7

TRY IT

Find the measure of a complementary angle.

1. 30° **2.** 81° **3.** 46.7° **4.** $5\frac{1}{2}°$

Find the measure of a supplementary angle.

5. 111° **6.** 23° **7.** 88.8° **8.** $160\frac{1}{3}°$

9. Find a pair of alternate interior angles.
10. Find a pair of alternate exterior angles.

SETS

In mathematics, we study specific **sets** of things such as numbers, geometric points, probability outcomes, or functions.

EXAMPLES

1. A set is identified by description or by listing the things, or **members** (also called **elements**). Braces may enclose the description or list.

$A =$ {all positive integers less than 5} is the same as $A = \{1, 2, 3, 4\}$

2. When there are many members, an ellipsis (three dots) may be used to show that some members are left out. Enough members should be shown so the reader can tell by the pattern what set is indicated.

{all even integers} is the same as $\{ \ldots, -4, -2, 0, 2, 4, \ldots \}$

3. **Subsets** of a set may have from none to all of the members of the beginning set. The 16 subsets of $X = \{1, 2, 3, 4\}$ are

- the set with nothing in it   {}
- 4 sets with one member   {1} {2} {3} {4}
- 6 sets with two members   {1, 2} {1, 3} {1, 4} {2, 3} {2, 4} {3, 4}
- 4 sets with three members   {1, 2, 3} {1, 2, 4} {1, 3, 4} {2, 3, 4}
- the set with all four members   {1, 2, 3, 4}

Set $X = \{1, 2, 3, 4\}$, like all sets, has more subsets than members!

4. Two sets of points are $P = \{A, B, C, D\}$ and $Q = \{C, D, E, F\}$.

The set of points in

- both P **and** Q is P **intersect** Q, or $P \cap Q = \{C, D\}$.
- either P **or** Q is P **union** Q, or $P \cup Q = \{A, B, C, D, E, F\}$.

The **Venn diagram** shows the two sets together.

TRY IT

$$M = \{1, 2, 3, 5, 8\} \qquad N = \{2, 4, 8, 16, 32\}$$

1. List all the subsets of M. How many are there?

2. Draw a Venn diagram of M and N together. Is the overlapping part a subset of M?

3. Write the intersection and union of M and N as lists, with braces {}.

NUMBER THEORY

Number theory is the mathematics of integers and multiplication, and of properties of numbers that can be discovered from multiplication patterns.

One number is a **factor** of another if it divides that number with no remainder. For example, 3 is a factor of 24 because $24 \div 3 = 8$ exactly.

A **factor pair** for an integer is any whole number pair whose product is the integer. For example, 9 and 3 are a factor pair of 27.

A **prime number** has only one factor pair, 1 and itself. For example, the only factor pair for 23 is 23 and 1. A **composite number** has more than one factor pair. 6 has the factor pairs 1 and 6, and 2 and 3.

The **prime factorization** of a whole number is its expression as a product of prime numbers. Every whole number greater than 1 is a prime number or a product of prime numbers. For example, $45 = 3 \cdot 3 \cdot 5$.

A number is a **common factor** of different numbers if it is a factor of each number. For example, 2, 4, and 8 are the common factors of 16 and 40. One common factor of two numbers must be their **greatest common factor (GCF)**. 8 is the GCF of 16 and 40.

A **multiple** of a number is the product of that number and any positive integer. For example, the multiples of 2 are all the even numbers, except 0.

A **common multiple** of a pair of numbers is a multiple of both numbers. For example, 48 is a common multiple of 4 and 6 because $4 \cdot 12 = 48$ and $6 \cdot 8 = 48$. One of the common multiples of two numbers must be their **least common multiple (LCM)**. For example, 12 is the LCM of 4 and 6 because $12 = 4 \cdot 3$ and $12 = 2 \cdot 6$.

EXAMPLES

1. Write the factor pairs of 56.

Start with number 1 and write a product.	$= 1 \cdot 56$
Continue with the next number, 2.	$= 2 \cdot 28$
Try the next number, 3. There is no factor pair.	
Continue until a factor pair repeats.	$= 4 \cdot 14$
	$= 7 \cdot 8$
When the factor pair repeats, stop.	$= 8 \cdot 7$

$56 = 1 \cdot 56 = 2 \cdot 28 = 4 \cdot 14 = 7 \cdot 8$

2. Find the prime factorization of 60.
Use a factor tree.

Write 60 as a product of two factors.
Write each factor as a product of two factors.
Continue until only prime factors remains.
$60 = 2 \cdot 2 \cdot 3 \cdot 5 = 2^2 \cdot 3 \cdot 5$

60
4 • 15
2 • 2 3 • 5

3. Find the prime factorizations of 40 and 140, then find their greatest common factor.

		40	140		
These are the	2	√	√	←2	These factors
prime factors	2	√	√	← 2	are *common*
of 40 and 140.	2	√			to both numbers.
	5	√	√	← 5	
	7		√		

$40 = 2 \cdot 2 \cdot 2 \cdot 5$ and $140 = 2 \cdot 2 \cdot 5 \cdot 7$
The greatest common factor is $2 \cdot 2 \cdot 5$, or 20.

4. Find the least common multiple of 8 and 10.
List the multiples for each number.
8: 8, 16, 24, 32, **40**, 48; 10: 10, 20, 30, **40**, 50
The least common multiple is 40.

TRY IT

Find the factor pairs of each number.

1. 24 **2.** 32 **3.** 100

Find the prime factorization of each number using a factor tree.

4. 160 **5.** 186 **6.** 75

Find the greatest common factor (GCF) of each pair of numbers.

7. 16, 24 **8.** 10, 17 **9.** 39, 52

Find the least common multiple (LCM) of each pair of numbers, and the next larger common multiple of each pair.

10. 5, 6 **11.** 12, 16 **12.** 15, 25

SPIRAL REVIEW

CHAPTER 1 DATA AND RELATIONSHIPS

1-1 EXPLORING DATA

Use with or after Part 1-1A

Write each number as a percent, a fraction, and a decimal. [Page 749]

1. 0.04   **2.** 0.66   **3.** 35%   **4.** $\dfrac{3}{20}$

5. 3.28   **6.** 125%   **7.** $\dfrac{7}{2}$ **8.** 47.2%

9. $\dfrac{1}{4}$ **10.** $\dfrac{5}{6}$ **11.** 0.002   **12.** 0.14%

Find each number. [Page 750]

13. 50% of 38   **14.** 25% of 54   **15.** 150% of 70   **16.** 5.1% of 20

17. 66% of 81   **18.** 0.15% of 30   **19.** $62\frac{1}{2}$% of 36   **20.** 550% of 40

21. 0.003% of 6000   **22.** 80% of 35   **23.** 20.5% of 80   **24.** $33\frac{1}{3}$% of 162

Use with or after Part 1-1B

Round to the nearest tenth. [Previous course]

25. 53.87   **26.** 7.753   **27.** 0.0245   **28.** 1.66…

29. 67,983   **30.** 2.749   **31.** 89.318   **32.** 44.63

Evaluate. Simplify. [Page 745]

33. $\left(\dfrac{1}{3}\right)\left(\dfrac{1}{4}\right)$ **34.** $\left(\dfrac{1}{2}\right)\left(\dfrac{5}{12}\right)$ **35.** $\dfrac{1}{3} \div \dfrac{5}{6}$ **36.** $\dfrac{11}{16} \div \dfrac{3}{8}$

37. $\left(3\dfrac{5}{8}\right)\left(2\dfrac{1}{4}\right)$ **38.** $9\dfrac{5}{8} \div 3\dfrac{2}{5}$ **39.** $\left(\dfrac{7}{10}\right)\left(\dfrac{25}{14}\right)$ **40.** $\dfrac{5}{6} \div 2$

41. $\dfrac{3}{2} \div \dfrac{1}{12}$ **42.** $\left(\dfrac{11}{12}\right)\left(\dfrac{5}{6}\right)$ **43.** $5 \div \dfrac{4}{5}$ **44.** $\left(\dfrac{2}{5}\right)\left(\dfrac{5}{2}\right)$

For a circle graph representing 6000 people, find the central angle for each group. [Page 754]

45. 600 people   **46.** 1500 people   **47.** 30 people   **48.** 120 people

49. 100 people   **50.** 250 people   **51.** 180 people   **52.** 5400 people

Use with or after Part 1-1C

Evaluate. [Page 744]

53. $\dfrac{1}{6} + \dfrac{1}{5}$ **54.** $\dfrac{3}{7} + \dfrac{2}{3}$ **55.** $\dfrac{7}{6} - \dfrac{5}{9}$ **56.** $\dfrac{5}{4} + 2\dfrac{1}{2}$

57. $\dfrac{9}{16} - \dfrac{7}{16}$ **58.** $\dfrac{1}{4} + \dfrac{3}{8}$ **59.** $\dfrac{7}{8} - \dfrac{5}{16}$ **60.** $\dfrac{3}{4} - \dfrac{2}{3} + \dfrac{1}{6}$

61. $5\dfrac{7}{8} - 3\dfrac{2}{3}$ **62.** $6\dfrac{1}{6} + 2\dfrac{3}{4}$ **63.** $4\dfrac{2}{5} - 1\dfrac{4}{5}$ **64.** $8 - 6\dfrac{2}{7}$

Compare the numbers using <, or >, or =. [1-1B]

65. -5 ? -8 **66.** $\dfrac{10}{2}$? $\dfrac{10}{3}$ **67.** $-(-7)$? -9

68. $-\dfrac{2}{14}$? $-\dfrac{3}{21}$ **69.** $-(-1)$? $-(-(-1))$ **70.** $(-3 + 2)$? $(-2 + 3)$

71. -7 ? 0 **72.** 10.12 ? -20.35 **73.** $(-5 + 8)$? $(-5 + -3)$

Use with or after Part 1-1D

Find the least common multiple of each group of numbers. [Page 757]

74. 6, 8   **75.** 6, 15   **76.** 20, 8   **77.** 9, 18

78. 10, 12, 15   **79.** 9, 3, 21   **80.** 6, 15, 20   **81.** 16, 6, 20

Evaluate these matrices. [1-1C]

$$A = \begin{bmatrix} 5 & -8 & 1 \\ 0 & -2 & -3 \end{bmatrix} \quad B = \begin{bmatrix} -7 & 2 & -1 \\ -6 & 1 & -4 \end{bmatrix} \quad C = \begin{bmatrix} \frac{1}{2} & -10 & -5 \\ -\frac{1}{4} & 3 & -2 \end{bmatrix}$$

82. $A + B$ **83.** $B - A$ **84.** $\frac{1}{3}A$ **85.** $4C$

86. $A + B + C$ **87.** $A - C$ **88.** $-2B$ **89.** $-B - A$

1-2 RELATIONSHIPS IN DATA

Use with or after Part 1-2A

Write each ratio as an equivalent fraction, decimal, and percentage. [Page 746]

1. 6 out of 8   **2.** 15:25   **3.** 8:20   **4.** 8:11

5. 1:7.5   **6.** 3.5:14   **7.** 22:10   **8.** 6:3.6

Convert to the given units. [Page 748]

9. 3 ft 4 in. = _?_ in.   **10.** 12 days = _?_ hours   **11.** 1.3 m = _?_ cm

12. $1\frac{1}{3}$ hr = _?_ min   **13.** 28 in. = _?_ ft   **14.** 23.1 mm = _?_ cm

15. 2 hr 13 min = _?_ sec   **16.** 78 cm 4 mm = _?_ m

Find the mean and the median for each group of numbers. Round to the nearest tenth. [1-1D]

17. 12, 6, 12, 9   **18.** −1, 7, −5, 8, 0   **19.** 13, 2, 15, 18, 16

20. −2, 4, 10, −1, 0   **21.** −4, −10, 0, −5   **22.** −14, −18, −20, −16

23. 88, 76, 80, 85, 90   **24.** 145, 245, 175, 135   **25.** 1, 1, 1, 1, 100

Use with or after Part 1-2B

Write as a percent. Identify answers that are greater than 100%. [Page 749]

26. 0.00042   **27.** 6:3   **28.** 14.5 out of 23   **29.** 7.3:11

30. 9 out of 10   **31.** $\frac{7}{3}$ **32.** 15 out of 25   **33.** 4.5:12.3

Find each number. [Page 750]

34. 10% of ? is 34   **35.** 7.5% of ? is 11   **36.** 225% of ? is 31.68

37. 35% of ? is 31.5   **38.** 50% of ? is 23   **39.** 120% of ? is 100

40. 75% of ? is 35   **41.** 8% of ? is 10   **42.** 0.1% of ? is 0.0001

Find the next three numbers in the pattern. [Previous course]

43. 1, 2, 4, 7, 11   **44.** 1, 2, 4, 8   **45.** 100, 97, 94, 91

46. 64, 32, 16, 8   **47.** −1, 1, −1, 1, −1   **48.** 12, 6, 3, 1.5

49. 1, 1, 2, 3, 5, 8   **50.** 2, 1, 3, 4, 7, 11   **51.** 512, 1024, 2048

1-3 PROBABILITIES AND RATIOS

Use with or after Part 1-3A

Evaluate. [1-1C]

1. $4 - (-7)$ **2.** $-2.5 - 5$ **3.** $-4\frac{2}{3} + 7$

4. $5 \cdot -8$ **5.** $-15 \div -0.3$ **6.** $-8.37 + (-4.25) - 1$

7. $1\frac{3}{5} \cdot -2$ **8.** $2.1 \div -0.3$ **9.** $1.04 - (-3.4)$

Plot each set of points. Determine if they are associated. [1-2B]

10.

year	9	10	11	12	13
cost ($)	8	9	13	13	12

11.

education (yr)	10	12	14	16	18
income ($1000)	16	22	28	35	41

12. $(4, 9), (2, 6), (3, 8), (1, 4), (3, 7)$

13. $(0, 6), (-6, -8), (5, 6), (-7, -5), (2, 2)$

Use with or after Part 1-3B

Add or subtract. [Page 744]

14. $\frac{1}{5} + \left(-\frac{2}{5}\right)$ **15.** $-\frac{3}{2} + \frac{5}{2}$ **16.** $-\frac{3}{4} + -1\frac{1}{2}$ **17.** $\frac{5}{6} - \left(-\frac{2}{3}\right)$

18. $-\frac{2}{5} + \frac{3}{10}$ **19.** $-1\frac{1}{12} + \frac{1}{6}$ **20.** $2\frac{3}{4} - \left(-\frac{2}{3}\right)$ **21.** $\frac{3}{4} + \left(-\frac{2}{3}\right)$

Find the square or square root. [Page 775]

22. 3^2 **23.** $\sqrt{16}$ **24.** $(-5)^2$

25. 7^2 **26.** $-(2^2)$ **27.** $(2.5)^2$

Find the percent. [Page 751]

28. 8 out of 24   **29.** 12:9   **30.** 13:17   **31.** 2 out of 31

32. 42:26   **33.** 3:423   **34.** 0.13 out of 2.4   **35.** 22:7

CHAPTER 2 PATTERNS, CHANGE, AND EXPRESSIONS

2-1 EXPLORING CHANGE

Use with or after Part 2-1A

Find the number. [Page 750]

1. 20% of 60   **2.** 30% of 50   **3.** 4% of 25   **4.** 75% of 13

5. 2.5% of 10   **6.** 33.3% of -9 **7.** 1.25% of -5 **8.** 37.5% of 7.2

Find the mean and the median of each group of numbers. [1-1D]

9. 16, 14, 4, 14   **10.** 4.5, 3.3, 5.1, 8.3   **11.** 1.10, 1.11, 1.14, 1.11, 1.10

12. $-13.0, -14.2, -13.6, 0, -13.7$ **13.** $342, -455, 623, -501$

A spinner has 10 equal parts labeled 1 to 10. Find the probability that the spinner lands on: [1-3B]

14. 4   **15.** 1 or 2   **16.** 3, 6, or 9   **17.** 2, 4, 6, 8, or 10

18. 5 or 10   **19.** 11 or 12   **20.** 2, 5, 6, or 8   **21.** 3 or greater

Evaluate these matrices. [1-1C]

$$A = \begin{bmatrix} 1 & 2.5 & -4.3 \\ 0.7 & 3 & 0 \end{bmatrix} \quad B = \begin{bmatrix} 0.5 & 4 & -2 \\ -3 & 2.7 & -3.25 \end{bmatrix} \quad C = \begin{bmatrix} 2.5 & -3 & 0.5 \\ 1 & 0 & -1 \end{bmatrix}$$

22. $A + B$ **23.** $A - B$ **24.** $B - A$ **25.** $2C$

26. $A + 2B$ **27.** $3A + 2C$ **28.** $A + B + C$ **29.** $A + 2B + (-C)$

Plot the points on a coordinate plane. Connect the points in order. [1-2B]

30. $(2, 0), (0, -1), (-2, 0), (0, 2), (2, 0)$

31. $(1, 1), (2, 2), (3, 3), (4, 4), (5, 5)$

32. $(0, 0), (1, 1), (2, 4), (3, 9), (4, 16)$

33. $(-1, -1), (1, 1), (3, -1), (5, 1), (7, -1), (9, 1)$

Convert to the indicated unit. [Page 748]

34. 8 qt to cups   **35.** 56 oz to lb   **36.** 10 km to m

37. 2.3 m to cm   **38.** 2.5 hours to minutes   **39.** $1\frac{3}{4}$ ft to in.

40. 325 mm to m   **41.** 4.5 hours to seconds   **42.** 1.7 L to ml

43. 200 g to kg   **44.** $1\frac{1}{4}$ lb to oz   **45.** 1800 seconds to hours

Evaluate. [1-3B]

46. $6!$ **47.** $4(3)(2)(1)$ **48.** $5! \div 2!$

49. $2! \cdot 3!$ **50.** $4! \div 3!$ **51.** $3!4!$

52. $1!$ **53.** $(6)(5)(4)(3)(2)(1) \div 4!$

2-2 THE LANGUAGE OF ALGEBRA

Find the total bill, given the cost and the tax rate. [Page 751]

1. $15, 8%   **2.** $299.95, 5%   **3.** $62.50, $7\frac{1}{2}$%   **4.** $2,540.00, 8.5%

5. $43.05, 6.5%   **6.** $0.75, 7.75%   **7.** $499.95, 6.5%   **8.** $10,950.95, 7.25%

Write the equivalent ratio. [Page 746]

9. 3:5 = ?:10   **10.** 10:20 = ?:1   **11.** 12:10 = 72:?   **12.** 0.69:1 = 1030:?

13. 360:3 = ?:10   **14.** 35:12 = ?:1   **15.** 2800:5.5 = 3600:?   **16.** 14:20.5 = 30:?

Connect the points on the coordinate plane. Are the variables directly or inversely related? [2-1C]

17. $(-1, 3), (0, 1), (1, -1), (2, -3), (4, -7)$

18. $(-1, 2), (0, 0), (0.5, 1), (2, 4), (-2, 4)$

19. $(5, 2), (1, 0), (2, 1), (-4, -1), (8, 3)$

Use with or after Part 2-2B

Find the missing number. [Page 750]

20. 20% of ? is 15
21. 80% of ? is 20
22. 6% of ? is 12

23. 95% of ? is 285
24. 0.8% of ? is 1.3
25. 4.8% of ? is 1.6

26. 225% of ? is 12.4
27. 56% of ? is 3.92
28. $66\frac{2}{3}$% of ? is 150

29. 0.05% of ? is 9.2
30. 700% of ? is 210
31. 18% of ? is 12

People were surveyed on eight propositions. What is the expected number of "yes" votes out of 160,000 total votes? [1-3A]

32. 35% Yes on Prop. A
33. 22% Yes on Prop. B
34. 63% No on Prop. C

35. 11.7% Yes on Prop. D
36. 74% No on Prop. E
37. 57% Yes on Prop. F

38. 88.2% Yes on Prop. G
39. 55.1% Yes on Prop. H

Write each expression without using a • or ÷ sign. Use exponents where appropriate. [2-2A]

40. $2 \cdot x \cdot x$
41. $a \div (a + a)$
42. $p \cdot 3 + p$
43. $x \div y + z$

44. $4 \cdot m + 4 \cdot n$
45. $x \div 5 \cdot 7$
46. $(6 + x) \div x$
47. $1 \div v + 1 \div w$

2-3 THE GRAMMAR OF ALGEBRA

Use with or after Part 2-3A

Evaluate. [1-1C]

1. $-1 + \frac{1}{5}$
2. $(-3)(-1.1)$
3. $2 \cdot -20 \cdot 200$
4. $819 \div -27$

5. $\frac{9}{16} - \frac{7}{16}$
6. $\frac{1}{4} \cdot \frac{4}{9}$
7. $\frac{7}{8} \cdot 5$
8. $\frac{3}{4} \cdot \frac{2}{3} \cdot \frac{1}{6}$

9. $5.5 - 3 \div -2$
10. $\frac{36}{6} + -\left(2\frac{3}{4}\right)$
11. $\left(-4\frac{2}{5}\right) - 1\frac{4}{5}$
12. $8 \div 6\frac{2}{7}$

Evaluate the expression for $a = -4$, $b = -1$, $c = 0.25$. [2-2A]

13. $ab \div c$
14. $a^2 b^2$
15. $a^2 b^2 c^2$
16. $(a - b)(a + b)$

17. $a - 2b$
18. $b^2 - 4ac$
19. $\frac{c^2}{2ab}$
20. $\frac{c - a}{c - b}$

Use with or after Part 2-3B

Plot the ordered pairs in a scatter plot. Do they show an association? [1-2A]

21.

x	0	0	1	1	−1	−1
y	1	−1	1	−1	1	−1

22.

x	2	4	6	8	10	12
y	0.1	0.2	0.3	0.4	0.5	0.6

Evaluate each expression in the tables for the values of the given variable. [2-2B]

23.

x	1	2	3	4
3 + 2x	?	?	?	?

24.

x	−10	−1	1	10
1 − x²	?	?	?	?

25.

z	−10	−1	1	10
x² − 10x	?	?	?	?

26.

x	−10	−1	1	10
0.01x²	?	?	?	?

Use with
or after
Part 2-3C

Evaluate each expression in the tables for the values of the given variable. [2-2B]

27.

x	1	2	3	4
$2 + 5x$	?	?	?	?

28.

x	-10	-1	1	10
$3 + x^2$	?	?	?	?

Evaluate. [2-3A]

29. $3 + 4^2$ **30.** $(3 + 4)^2$ **31.** $3 \cdot 4^2$ **32.** $(3 \div 4)^2$

33. $2 + 3 \cdot 2 + 5$ **34.** $5 + 2 \cdot (1 - 8)$ **35.** $(-3 + 6) \cdot -1$ **36.** $-1^5 \cdot -1^6 + 1$

Rewrite the following expressions, leaving no grouping symbols. [2-3B]

37. $5(a - b)$ **38.** $(1 - x)x$ **39.** $x(5x - 5)$ **40.** $x - (1 - x)$

How many terms are in each expression? What are their coefficients? [2-3C]

41. $x^2 + 34$ **42.** $x^4 + x - 2$ **43.** $-2x^2 - 2x$

44. $1 - x^2$ **45.** $0.5x^2 - 1.5x - 2.2$ **46.** 12

CHAPTER 3 INTRODUCING FUNCTIONS

3-1 FUNCTIONAL RELATIONSHIPS

Use with
or after
Part 3-1A

Use the distributive property to evaluate each expression. Show your work. [2-3B]

1. $6(3 - 9)$ **2.** $\dfrac{1 + 23}{2}$ **3.** $-10(2 + 20)$ **4.** $0.1(0.2 - 0.3)$

Simplify each of the following expressions. [2-3C]

5. $(x + 5) + (x + -5)$ **6.** $(2 - 3y) - 12$

7. $3(x + 23)$ **8.** $2(x + 1) + 2(x + 2)$

9. $-2(x - 1) - 2(x - 2)$ **10.** $8(2x - 5) - 6x$

11. $5x + 5(x + 1) + 5(x + 2)$ **12.** $-6 + 6(6x - 1) - 6$

Use with
or after
Part 3-1B

Simplify each of the following expressions. [2-3C]

13. $(7 + 2x) + 8(x - 1)$ **14.** $-3(6x + 4) + 1$

15. $-2x + 8(x + 6)$ **16.** $9(x - 1) + 9(x - 2)$

17. $-3(x - 11) - 3(x - 3)$ **18.** $-9 + 9(9x - 1) - 9$

Complete each table. Write the equation of the relationship. [3-1A]

19.

x	1	2	3	4	5	6	10	x
y	-2	0	1	2	3	?	?	?

20.

x	1	2	3	4	5	6	7	x
y	1	4	9	16	?	?	?	?

Make a table of ordered pairs and graph each equation. [3-1B]

21. $y = x + 5$ **22.** $y = 2x - 1$ **23.** $y = -x - 5$ **24.** $y = 0.5x + 10$

Use with
or after
Part 3-1C

Evaluate the formulas for $r = 1.2$ cm and $h = 0.9$ cm. [2-2B]

25. sphere volume: $\frac{4}{3}\pi r^3$

26. cylinder volume: $\pi r^2 h$

27. right cone volume: $\frac{1}{3}\pi r^2 h$

28. cylinder lateral area: $2\pi rh$

Replace each Δ with an operation symbol to make the equation true. [2-3A]

29. $15 \Delta 0.2 \Delta 3 = 78$ **30.** $30 \Delta 50 \Delta 4 = -170$ **31.** $3 \Delta 1 \Delta 3 + 1 = 7$

32. $54 \Delta 9 \Delta 3 = 18$ **33.** $3 \Delta -4 \Delta -5 = -7$ **34.** $16 \Delta 4 \Delta 16 \Delta 4 = 60$

Complete each table. Replace a with a number to show the equation. [3-1A]

35.

x	2	4	6	10
$y = ax$	-4	-8	-12	?

36.

x	1	2	3	10
$y = ax + 3$	6	9	12	?

3-2 LINEAR FUNCTIONS

Use with
or after
Part 3-2A

Solve each proportion. [Page 747]

1. $x:6 = 11:4$ **2.** $8:x = 2:9$ **3.** $5:8 = 3:x$ **4.** $10:13 = 16:x$

5. $5:1.5 = 30:x$ **6.** $110:0.4 = x:8$ **7.** $9:x = 0.3:1.3$ **8.** $19:2 = x:5$

Write an equivalent expression without grouping symbols. [2-3B]

9. $-(7 + y)$ **10.** $\frac{(6x + 2)}{3}$ **11.** $(100 - x)35x$ **12.** $\frac{(18 - 6a + b)}{6}$

Make a table of values and graph. [3-1B]

13. $y = 0.15x + 20$ **14.** $y = \frac{3}{4}(x - 8)$ **15.** $y = 400x - 150$ **16.** $y = -2x^2$

Decide if y is a function of x. Why or why not? [3-1C]

17.

x	1	2	3	4
y	4	3	2	1

18.

x	1	2	2	1
y	4	5	1	2

Use with
or after
Part 3-2B

Determine whether they are always true. If sometimes true, give examples of true and untrue values. [2-3B]

19. $a + b - c = -c + a + b$ **20.** $a - b = -(b - a)$

21. $x + y - z = x - y + z$ **22.** $mx - my = (x - y)m$

23. $z + (x + y) = (z + x) + (z + y)$ **24.** $\frac{(m + 6)}{6} = m + 1$

Simplify. [2-3C]

25. $7 - 6(7 - x)$ **26.** $3x(2 + 11) - 22$ **27.** $-2(1 - 2x) - 3x$

28. $x(y + x) + xy$ **29.** $12(x^2 - 3x) + 3x$ **30.** $3x^2 - 4x^3 + 5$

Determine whether each function is linear and whether y is proportional to x. [3-2A]

31. $y = 1 + x$ **32.** $y = 3x$ **33.** $y = \frac{7}{x}$ **34.** $y = x - 2x$

CHAPTER 4 SOLVING LINEAR EQUATIONS AND INEQUALITIES

4-1 SOLVING LINEAR EQUATIONS

Use with
or after
Part 4-1A

Evaluate. [2-3A]

1. $5 + 8 \cdot 4^2$

2. $\frac{1}{4} + \frac{1}{2} \cdot \frac{1}{8}$

3. $\left(-1\right)^3 \left(2 - \frac{2}{3}\right)$

4. $\frac{3}{4} \cdot \frac{20}{27} - \frac{1}{9}$

5. $(81 \div 3) \div 3$

6. $81 \div (3 \div 3)$

7. $\frac{10 - 2}{10 + 2} \div 10$

8. $\frac{2^3}{3^2} \cdot \frac{3^4}{4^3}$

9. $\frac{1}{6} \div \frac{1}{18}$

10. $\frac{1}{18} \div \frac{1}{6}$

11. $\frac{1}{6} \cdot \frac{1}{18}$

12. $\frac{1}{6} - \frac{1}{18}$

Solve each equation using mental math or guess and check. [4-1A]

13. $9y = -27$

14. $n - 8 = 20$

15. $60 + r = 240$

16. $\frac{k}{3} = -10$

Use with
or after
Part 4-1B

Evaluate the formulas $A = L \cdot W + 2$, $B = \frac{1}{2}(L - W^2)$, **and** $C = (2L - W)^2$ **for the given values. [2-2B]**

17. $L = -1$, $W = 2$ **18.** $L = 0$, $W = -1$ **19.** $L = 1$, $W = 10$ **20.** $L = 10$, $W = 1$

Simplify. [2-3C]

21. $1 - 3(2 + x)$

22. $3 + 2(x - 3)$

23. $3x + 3(x + 1)$

24. $-(x - (x - 1))$

25. $(4x - 1) - 3$

26. $(x - 1) - (x + 1)$

27. $\frac{10x - 1}{3} - \frac{x}{3}$

28. $1.1x - 2.2x + 3.3x - 4.4x$

Solve each equation using mental math or guess and check. [4-1A]

29. $2n + 1 = 9$

30. $7m + 2 = 51$

31. $\frac{x}{4} - 8 = 12$

32. $9 - y = 15$

33. $3(g - 6) = 12$

34. $3b + 8 = 32$

4-2 OTHER TECHNIQUES FOR SOLVING LINEAR EQUATIONS

Use with
or after
Part 4-2A

For each table, write the equation of the pattern. Find y **when** $x = 100$. **[3-1A]**

1.

x	1	2	3	4	5
y	0	2	6	12	20

2.

x	1	2	3	4	5
y	-1	2	-3	4	-9

Identify the linear functions. Determine whether y **is proportional to** x. **[3-2A]**

3.

x	-10	-1	0	1	10
y	-20	-2	0	2	20

4.

x	-10	-1	0	1	10
y	100	1	0	1	100

Use a graph of $y = -2y + 3$ **or** $y = \frac{1}{2}x + 6$ **to solve each equation. [4-1B]**

5. $-2 = -2x + 3$ **6.** $5 = \frac{1}{2}x + 6$ **7.** $-3 = \frac{1}{2}x + 6$ **8.** $7 = -2x + 3$

Use with
or after
Part 4-2B

Use mental math or guess and check to solve the equations. [4-1A]

9. $4x - 9 = 15$
10. $2 + \dfrac{y}{5} = -10$
11. $0.25m + 6 = 5$

12. $40(y + 1) = -360$
13. $3(g + 3) = -15$
14. $4(x + 2) - 11 = -3$

15. $4 + 3(w - 2) = -5$
16. $\dfrac{f}{2} - 7 = -3$
17. $\dfrac{(3y - 1)}{2} = 7$

Use the graph of y = 5 – 4(x + 1) to find y for each point on the line. [4-1B]
18. $(1, ?)$
19. $(-3, ?)$
20. $(0, ?)$
21. $(-1.5, ?)$
22. $(-1, ?)$

Write the additive inverse and the reciprocal of each expression. [4-2A]

23. 7
24. $-\dfrac{3}{2}$
25. $-\dfrac{1}{8}$

26. -1000
27. $2x$
28. $5\dfrac{1}{4}$

Use with
or after
Part 4-2C

Simplify. [2-3C]

29. $(4x + 2) + (x - 1)$
30. $12\left(\dfrac{1}{3}x - \dfrac{5}{6}y\right)$

31. $-4\left(\dfrac{1}{4}m + \dfrac{3}{4}n\right) - \left(m + n\right)$
32. $w - [(w - 2) - (3 - w)]$

33. $-\dfrac{2}{3}(6c - 9d) + \dfrac{1}{8}(4d - 8c)$
34. $-\dfrac{1}{2}\left(6x - 2y\right) + 12\left(\dfrac{1}{3}x - \dfrac{5}{6}y\right)$

Solve and check each equation. [4-2C]

35. $\dfrac{1}{2}x + 90 = 180$
36. $3 + 2y = 11$
37. $\dfrac{m}{3} - 1 = -7$

38. $2315 = 3x - 8851$
39. $-0.2m - 22 = 0$
40. $-12 - 3y = -4$

41. $-93.8 - x = 28.1$
42. $0.8 - 0.3c = 2$
43. $\dfrac{1}{2} - \dfrac{d}{15} = 1$

Use the distance formula, D = rt, to find the missing amount. [4-2C]

44. $r = 90$ km/hr, $t = \dfrac{3}{4}$ hr
45. $D = 450$ mi, $t = 13.5$ hr

46. $t = 1$ hr 15 min, $r = 30$ mi/hr
47. $r = 70$ mi/hr, $D = 42$ mi

Use with
or after
Part 4-2D

Solve each literal equation for the variable indicated. [4-2C]

48. $V = Lwh$ for h
49. $m = \dfrac{d}{2}$ for d
50. $Q = \dfrac{S}{t}$ for t

51. $x = z + y$ for z
52. $d = -2a + b$ for a
53. $M = \dfrac{a}{3} - b$ for a

54. $W = \dfrac{1}{2}x - 3y$ for x
55. $S = a - b$ for b

Solve and check each equation. [4-2C]

56. $x + 4.2 = 8.1$
57. $\dfrac{3}{5} = m - 2\dfrac{1}{5}$
58. $-\dfrac{4}{9} = \dfrac{g}{15}$

59. $2.2x = -0.66$
60. $-0.8n = 16$
61. $x - (-8) = 13$

62. $3g - 9 = -21$
63. $\dfrac{c}{10} = \dfrac{2}{3}$
64. $1.7x - 1.32 = 4.12$

4-3 RELATING EQUATIONS AND INEQUALITIES

Use with or after Part 4-3A

Insert parentheses to make the equation true. [2-3A]

1. $3 \cdot 3 + 3 + 3 = 21$

2. $-1 + 2 \cdot -7 - 6 = -27$

3. $-60 \div 8 - 3 \cdot -4 = -3$

4. $22 + -2 \div -4 + 10 = 5$

5. $3 \cdot -10 \div 5 + 6 = 12$

6. $-9 \cdot 3 + 7 - 16 = -106$

7. $2 \cdot 7 - 4 \div 3 \cdot 4 - 5 = -2$

8. $4 \div 2 \cdot 7 - 5 = 1$

Solve and check each equation. [4-2D]

9. $7 - 2x + x = 11$

10. $y - 185 - 4y = -215$

11. $2.4x - 0.6x = 27$

12. $7 - 3(2x + 1) = -2$

13. $-\frac{4}{5}(10x - 5) = \frac{3}{2}$

14. $13 + 4(b + 1) = -3$

15. $5(z - 3) - (5 - z) = 0$

16. $3(y + 2) = 15$

17. $x + \frac{1}{2}x + 90 = 180$

Use with or after Part 4-3B

Use the formulas $A = Lw$ and $V = Lwh$ to find all possible missing values. [4-2C]

18. $L = 5$ cm, $w = 0.2$ cm

19. $A = 54$ in.^{2}, $w = 6$ in.

20. $L = 6$ mm, $h = 3.5$ mm, $w = 2$ mm

21. $V = 360$ m^3, $L = 9$ m, $h = 4$ m

22. $A = 6$ ft^2, $h = 0.5$ ft

23. $V = 0.12$ in.^{3}, $A = 0.3$ in.^{2}, $w = 0.6$ in.

Solve and check. [4-3A]

24. $8y = 12 + 5y$

25. $11x - 42 = 5x$

26. $5b - 10 = 6b + 8$

27. $\frac{1}{2}m + 8 = m - 3$

28. $9\left(\frac{1}{3}c - \frac{2}{3}\right) = 9 - 2c$

29. $4d - 7d = 9 - 11$

Solve and graph on a number line. [4-3B]

30. $y - 8 > -9$

31. $\frac{m}{3} \leq 6$

32. $5 - h > 6$

33. $-3\frac{1}{2} > d + 1\frac{1}{2}$

Use with or after Part 4-3C

Evaluate. [1-1C]

34. $\dfrac{(0 - -6)}{(8 - 4)}$

35. $\dfrac{(-2 - 9)}{(2 - 16)}$

36. $(-3 - 2)(5 - 8)$

37. $(-1 + -7)\dfrac{2}{(-4)^3}$

38. $\dfrac{-2(3 - 7)}{5(-1 - 3)}$

39. $-\left(6 - -4\right)\left(\frac{1}{2} - \frac{3}{4}\right)$

Identify the proportional linear functions. [3-2A]

40. $y = -x$

41. $y = -x + 6$

42. $y = -\frac{5}{3}x$

43. $y = 2x + 3$

44. $y = -2x^2$

45. $y = \frac{3}{4}x - 3$

46. $y = x^2 - x$

47. $y = -3x + 4$

Solve these inequalities. [4-3B]

48. $-2x + 7 < x - 3.5$

49. $-0.6b > 36$

50. $-3(d + 2) \leq 12$

51. $5 + 3c \leq -7$

52. $-2(y - 3) < 6y - 7(y - 4)$

53. $5d \geq 10 + 2(3d - 4)$

54. $4m + 7 < 8m - (5m + 2)$

CHAPTER 5 ANALYZING LINEAR FUNCTIONS AND THEIR GRAPHS

5-1 EXPLORING APPLICATIONS OF SLOPE

Use with or after Part 5-1A

Solve the proportions. [Page 747]

1. $\dfrac{2}{5} = \dfrac{x}{9}$ **2.** $\dfrac{6}{y} = \dfrac{15}{8}$ **3.** $\dfrac{x+1}{x} = \dfrac{2}{5}$ **4.** $\dfrac{a}{a+10} = \dfrac{2}{3}$

Evaluate the trapezoid-area formula $A = \frac{1}{2}h(b_1 + b_2)$ for the given values. [2-2B]

5. $h = 1,\ b_1 = 1,\ b_2 = 2$ **6.** $h = 1,\ b_1 = 0.001,\ b_2 = 2$

7. $h = 1,\ b_1 = 1.001,\ b_2 = 1$

Graph the linear functions. Where does the line cross the y-axis? [3-2A]

8. $y = x + 1$ **9.** $x + y = 1$ **10.** $x = y + 1$ **11.** $x + y + 1 = 0$

Use with or after Part 5-1B

Two sides of a triangle are given. What lengths are possible for the third side? [4-3C]

12. 1 cm, 1 cm **13.** 1 cm, 2 cm **14.** 10 cm, 20 cm **15.** 10 cm, 30 cm

Find the equivalent ratio. [Page 748]

16. $\dfrac{12\ \text{mi}}{5\ \text{hr}} = \dfrac{?\ \text{mi}}{1\ \text{hr}}$ **17.** $\dfrac{98\ \text{ft}}{30\ \text{sec}} = \dfrac{?\ \text{ft}}{1\ \text{sec}}$ **18.** $\dfrac{45\ \text{lb}}{25\ \text{in.}^2} = \dfrac{?\ \text{lb}}{1\ \text{in.}^2}$

19. $\dfrac{900\ \text{yd}}{60\ \text{min}} = \dfrac{?\ \text{yd}}{1\ \text{min}}$ **20.** $\dfrac{50\ \text{mi}}{75\ \text{min}} = \dfrac{?\ \text{mi}}{1\ \text{min}}$ **21.** $\dfrac{642\ \text{acres}}{6\ \text{yr}} = \dfrac{?\ \text{acres}}{1\ \text{yr}}$

Use the distance formula $D = rt$ to find the missing amount. [4-2C]

22. 55 mi/hr, 140 mi **23.** 9.5 hr, 62 mi/hr

24. $2\frac{1}{4}$ min, 130 ft/min **25.** 33 in., 15 in./sec

Solve and check. [4-3A]

26. $12a = a + 10$ **27.** $4(x + 2) = 10x$ **28.** $0.1(12 - x) = 5x$

29. $0.25 = 33x - 2$ **30.** $3x \div 18 = 104$ **31.** $-5t = 2(1 - 38)$

Use with or after Part 5-1C

Plot each pair of points. Find rise, run, and slope. [5-1A]

32. $(-2, 1),\ (-1, -3)$ **33.** $\left(\dfrac{1}{2}, 0\right), \left(-\dfrac{3}{2}, -6\right)$ **34.** $(11, 2),\ (-1, 8)$

Use the graph of $y = -2x + 1$ to find each y-coordinate. [4-1B]

35. $(0, ?)$ **36.** $(10, ?)$ **37.** $(-10, ?)$ **38.** $(0.5, ?)$

Solve the literal equations for h. [4-2C]

39. $h + g = f$ **40.** $M = hy$ **41.** $2h + d = 3y$ **42.** $y + \dfrac{h}{5} = -g$

43. $Q = \dfrac{n}{h}$ **44.** $4d - 4h = 8$ **45.** $D = \dfrac{h}{x}$ **46.** $V = Lwh$

5-2 CONNECTING SLOPE AND LINEAR FUNCTIONS

Use with or after Part 5-2A

Write an equivalent ratio with integer numerator and denominator. [Page 746]

1. 3.5:1
2. $\dfrac{1.1}{1.21}$
3. 90.6 to 2
4. $\dfrac{0.7}{1}$

5. $5\dfrac{1}{4}$ to $\dfrac{1}{2}$
6. 3.5:1.55
7. $\dfrac{2}{3} : \dfrac{5}{4}$
8. 0.063 to 0.03

For each equation, find y when $x = 0$. [3-1B]

9. $2x + 3y = 8$
10. $y - 3x = 4$
11. $y = 2x - 4$
12. $2y = 5(x + 1)$

Solve and check. [4-3A]

13. $6y = 9y - 15$
14. $7 - 3x = 2x + 17$
15. $6(y - 3) = 4(y + 2)$

16. $4\left(\dfrac{1}{2}m + 7\right) = 8m$
17. $-5c + 3(2c + 1) = 2c - 1$
18. $\dfrac{(2k + 6)}{(4 - k)} = \dfrac{3}{2}$

19. $15 - 5n - 2n = 1$ **20.** $1 - 3(1 - y) = y$

Find y so that the line containing each pair of points has the given slope. [5-1C]

21. $(7, y)$, $(5, 9)$, slope $= -4$
22. $(5, -2)$, $(-7, y)$, slope $= -\dfrac{1}{2}$

23. $(3, y)$, $(-4, 9)$, slope $= -2$

Use with or after Part 5-2B

Solve the equation and evaluate the expression. [4-2C]

24. If $m + 3 = 14$, find $7m$
25. If $x - 0.2 = 0.35$, find $8x$

26. If $2.8 - g = 4.9$, find $g - 6$
27. If $-3x = \dfrac{1}{3}$, find $27 + x$

28. If $\dfrac{y}{5} = 12.6$, find $0.3 - y$
29. If $\left(-1\dfrac{1}{4}\right)d = 5\dfrac{1}{2}$, find $d - \dfrac{3}{4}$

Write the equation in the form $y = mx + b$. Then give the slope and y-intercept. [5-2A]

30. $9 - 3y = 3x$
31. $6 + 2y = 8x$
32. $4y = 5x - 12$
33. $4y - 2x + 8 = 0$

34. $6 = 8x - 2y$
35. $y - 3x = 1$
36. $2y + 8 = 6$
37. $-2y + 4x = 7$

Use with or after Part 5-2C

Find the original value given the new price and the percent increase. [Page 751]

38. new price: $16.80, 12%
39. new price: $450, 20%

40. new price: $67.50, 10.8%
41. new price: $12,500, 25%

42. new price: $54.25, 250%
43. new price: $41.30, 40%

Use the given slope m and point to determine the equation. [5-2A]

44. $m = 4$, $(1, 3)$
45. $m = -2$, $(2, 3)$
46. $m = \dfrac{1}{2}$, $(-1, 5)$

47. $m = \dfrac{2}{3}$, $(2, -4)$
48. $m = 0.4$, $(-3, 0)$
49. $m = \dfrac{3}{4}$, $(0, -1)$

50. $m = -1$, $(5, -3)$
51. $m = 0$, $(-5, -6)$

Write the equation of the line passing through each pair of points. [5-2B]

52. $(0, 0)$, $(5, 3)$
53. $(1, 3)$, $(2, 6)$
54. $(-6, -2)$, $(-6, 9)$

55. $(-5, 3)$, $(9, -4)$
56. $(2, 6)$, $(-2, -3)$
57. $(-4, 3)$, $(8, 3)$

Use with or after Part 5-2D

Solve and graph on a number line. [4-3B]

58. $m - 5 > 8$ **59.** $-4x + 3 \le 39$ **60.** $\frac{1}{2}y > -7$

61. $1 + -\dfrac{d}{3} \ge 9$ **62.** $3d - 2 < 2d + 3$ **63.** $-2(x - 3) > 5$

64. $2x - \dfrac{3}{2} \le \dfrac{1}{2}(x + 4)$ **65.** $3(3 - y) - 5 < 1 + y$

Find the equation of the line with the given slope and through the given point. [5-2B]

66. slope $= 2$; $(-1, -3)$ **67.** slope $= 0$; $(2, -3)$ **68.** slope $= \dfrac{1}{2}$; $\left(\dfrac{1}{4}, -\dfrac{1}{2}\right)$

69. slope $= -3$; $(-2, 5)$ **70.** slope $= \dfrac{7}{10}$; $(1.1, -1.4)$ **71.** slope $= -\dfrac{2}{3}$; $(0, 8)$

CHAPTER 6 SYSTEMS OF EQUATIONS AND INEQUALITIES

6-1 PATTERNS OF LINES

Use with or after Part 6-1A

Simplify expressions. [2-3C]

1. $8.2x - 0.8 + 2.8x$ **2.** $-2(3x - 5) + 2(7 - x)$ **3.** $\frac{1}{2}(6k - 2) + 5k$

4. $3(8 - 5x + y) - (y + x)$ **5.** $\frac{3}{4}(8 - k) + \dfrac{2 - 3k}{4}$ **6.** $6y - 2(8 - 3y) - 4y$

Write the negative reciprocal of the slope of each given linear function. [5-1C]

7. $y = 3x$ **8.** $x + y = -1$ **9.** $2x + y = -14$ **10.** $3x + 5y = 15$

11. $2y = 5x - 7$ **12.** $x = y$ **13.** $y = -1.2x + 6$ **14.** $2x - 8y = 3$

Find the slope and y-intercept. Use them to graph each linear function. [5-2A]

15. $y = -3x$ **16.** $y = \frac{1}{3}x + 2$ **17.** $y = 0.8x + 1$ **18.** $x = -0.5$

Use with or after Part 6-1B

Solve and check. [4-2D]

19. $3x - 4(-5x - 2) = -15$ **20.** $2b + 4 = 2 + 4b$ **21.** $-3(17 + 5v) - 4v = 6$

22. $a + 4(2a) = 24$ **23.** $4h = 3 - 3h + 11$ **24.** $\frac{1}{6}(x + 2) = \frac{1}{4}(x - 2)$

Write the equation of the line perpendicular to the given line and through the given point. [6-1A]

25. $2x + 3y = 8$; $(0, -4)$ **26.** $y = 2x - 1$; $(1, 1)$ **27.** $y = 0.75x$; $(9, 12)$

28. $9x + 6y = 9$; $(0, -2)$ **29.** $x - 2y = 4$; $(2, -1)$ **30.** $x = -7$; $(-4, 6)$

In how many points do the graphs of each pair of equations intersect? [6-1A]

31. $2x + y = 1$ and $-6x - 3y = -3$ **32.** $y = 2x + 6$ and $y = -x - 5$

33. $k - 3j = 2$ and $k + \frac{1}{3}j = -1$ **34.** $2x + 6 = 4y$ and $2y - x = 6$

35. $v = -7u - 12$ and $3.5u + 0.5v = -4$

6-2 SOLVING SYSTEMS OF EQUATIONS

Use with or after Part 6-2A

Use the multiplication property of equality. [4-2C]

1. If $3x + y = 7$, then $6x + 2y = ?$ **2.** If $-2a + 2b = 5$, then $6a - 6b = ?$

3. If $5j - 2k = 4$, then $15j - 6k = ?$ **4.** If $\frac{3}{4}f + -\frac{1}{2}g = \frac{1}{4}$, then $3f - 2g = ?$

Solve each literal equation for the indicated variable. [4-2C]

5. $U = \frac{P}{n}$ for n **6.** $A = \frac{1}{2}h\,(b_1 + b_2)$ for h

7. $F = \frac{9}{5}C + 32$ for C **8.** $r = 3.5a + 1.5b$ for b

9. $HT = 2(j - i)$ for j **10.** $A = P + Prt$ for t

Use with or after Part 6-2B

Determine the point of intersection, if any, of each system. [6-1B]

11. $x + y = 6$ **12.** $x - 3y = 5$ **13.** $x = -2$ **14.** $x - y = -3$

   $x - y = 0$ $2x + y = 3$ $y = 4$ $y = -x$

15. $y = 2x + 2$ **16.** $y = 0.5x + 2$ **17.** $y = x + 1$ **18.** $y = -2x + 3$

   $y - 2x = -3$ $y = -2x - 3$ $y = -3x + 5$ $4x + 2y = 6$

Solve and graph on a number line. [4-3B]

19. $5x > 10 + 2(3x - 4)$ **20.** $-4m + 5(m - 2) \geq 6$

21. $9k - 2(4 - k) > 3k$ **22.** $-6(-2x + 5) + 1 \leq 7$

23. $9 + 2(4 - 2y) + 3y > 14$ **24.** $4(3a + 7) \geq 27$

Write the equation of the line that goes through the given points or has the given slope. [5-2B]

25. $(0, 3)$, slope $= \frac{1}{2}$ **26.** $(0, 0)$, $(-2, 5)$ **27.** slope $= -\frac{3}{5}$, $(-6, 5)$

28. $(0, -2)$, $(1, 0)$ **29.** $(3, -1)$, $(-3, -5)$ **30.** $(4, 8)$, slope $= 1$

Use with or after Part 6-2C

Determine whether the ordered pair solves the system or either equation. [6-1B]

31. $x + y = 7$ $(3, 4)$ **32.** $x + y = 9$ $(11, 6)$

   $2x - 3y = -6$ $x - y = 5$

33. $x + 2y = -4$ $(-2, -1)$ **34.** $y - 2x = 2$ $(1, 4)$

   $-x + y = 1$ $y = 5 - x$

35. $y = -3x$ $(-6, 2)$ **36.** $2x - 3y = -6$ $(3, 4)$

   $x + 2y = -10$ $y = 7$

37. $3x - 7y = 41$ $(2, -5)$ **38.** $y = 3x - 8$ $(2, -1)$

   $x + 7y = -33$ $x + y = 3$

Assume y is proportional to x, which means that y = ax. Find the missing y-coordinate. [3-2A]

39. $(-3, -21)$, $(1, ?)$ **40.** $(4, 1)$, $(0, ?)$ **41.** $(2, -6)$, $(6, ?)$ **42.** $(9, 6)$, $(3, ?)$

43. $\left(\frac{1}{2}, 5\right)$, $\left(4, ?\right)$ **44.** $(-3, 9)$, $(2, ?)$ **45.** $(1, 2.5)$, $(-2, ?)$ **46.** $(-1, -2)$, $(5, ?)$

6-3 SOLVING SYSTEMS OF INEQUALITIES

Use with or after Part 6-3A

Solve each linear system by substitution or the linear combination method. [6-2B]

1. $x = 8y$
$x - 4y = 12$

2. $5x = y$
$x = 2y + 9$

3. $a = b + 4$
$2a + 3b = -2$

4. $y + 2x = 0$
$x + 2y = 9$

5. $3x - \dfrac{1}{2}y = 8$
$2x - \dfrac{3}{2}y = 10$

6. $3a - b = 4$
$4a - 2b = 3$

7. $x + y = 50$
$0.15x + 0.24y = 10$

8. $2x - 3y - 8 = 0$
$7x + 3y = -2$

9. $3x - 2y = 22$
$2x - 5y = 0$

10. $x = -2y$
$-5x + 6y = 4$

11. $5a - 4b = -2$
$11a - 7b = 1$

12. $x - 4y = 2$
$-5x + 4y = 6$

Use with or after Part 6-3B

Find each product matrix. [6-2C]

13. $\begin{bmatrix} 1 & 1 \\ 2 & -1 \end{bmatrix} \begin{bmatrix} 5 \\ -2 \end{bmatrix}$

14. $\begin{bmatrix} 3 & 5 \\ 1 & -1 \end{bmatrix} \begin{bmatrix} 9 \\ -3 \end{bmatrix}$

15. $\begin{bmatrix} -1 & -5 \\ 2 & -3 \end{bmatrix} \begin{bmatrix} -6 \\ 16 \end{bmatrix}$

16. $\begin{bmatrix} 0.75 & 0.5 \\ 0.25 & 0.5 \end{bmatrix} \begin{bmatrix} -4 \\ 2.5 \end{bmatrix}$

17. $\begin{bmatrix} 4 & 3 \\ 12 & -9 \end{bmatrix} \begin{bmatrix} -2 \\ -6 \end{bmatrix}$

18. $\begin{bmatrix} 1 & -4 \\ \dfrac{1}{4} & 1 \end{bmatrix} \begin{bmatrix} 0 \\ 2 \end{bmatrix}$

CHAPTER 7 LINES AND DISTANCE

7-1 DISTANCE ON A NUMBER LINE

Use with or after Part 7-1A

Evaluate each expression. [2-3A]

1. $-(-(-3 \cdot 2)) - 4$

2. $(-5)^2 - 4^2$

3. $(-6 + 9)^2 + -(5 + -6)$

4. $\left(8 - \left(-\dfrac{1}{2}\right)\right) \div \dfrac{3}{2}$

Write the additive inverse of each number. [4-2A]

5. -9

6. 0.08

7. $1\dfrac{3}{8}$

8. $-(-5)$

Solve. [4-3B]

9. $x > 7$

10. $6n \le -18$

11. $2x + 5 > 0.5x - 3$

12. $7 - f \ge 9$

13. $-2x - 3(x + 5) > 9$

14. $\dfrac{2}{3}g + \dfrac{1}{3} < 5$

15. $-0.08(m - 120) \le -0.8$

16. $0.4(60 - g) < 36 - 0.55g$

Solve and graph each system of linear inequalities. [6-3B]

17. $y > x;\ y < -5$

18. $y \le -2x + 3;\ y \ge x - 3$

19. $x + 2y > 4;\ y \le 3x + 4$

20. $x > 3;\ 3x - 2y \ge 9$

Use with or after Part 7-1B

Find the slope and *y*-intercept. [5-2A]

21. $y = 2x - 2$ **22.** $x - y + 7 = 0$ **23.** $\frac{4}{3}y + x = 8$ **24.** $y = -5$

Convert to miles per hour. Round to the nearest tenth. [5-2C]

25. 48 ft/sec   **26.** 80 km/hr   **27.** 7200 in./min   **28.** 500,000 m/day

Use the linear combination method to solve each system of linear equations. [6-2B]

29. $x + y = 7$ **30.** $2x + 3y = 4$ **31.** $0.7x + 1.2y = -0.9$ **32.** $-x + 4y = -4$

$3x - 2y = 1$ $3x - 2y = 6$ $2.1x + y = -5.3$ $\frac{1}{4}x - y = 1$

Evaluate each expression. [7-1A]

33. $-\left| -0.38 \right|$

34. $\left| 5 - 7 \right| - \left| -1 + 8 \right|$

35. $\left| -7 \right| \cdot \left| \frac{3}{7} \right|$

36. $\left| \, \left| 1.24 \right| - \left| -0.12 \right| \, \right|$

Use with or after Part 7-1C

Solve each equation. Check your solution. [4-3A]

37. $10 + 3(x - 1) = 16$ **38.** $5 = \frac{2}{3}(d - 9)$ **39.** $-12m = -3m + 45$

40. $\frac{(8 - c)}{6} = \frac{1}{3}$ **41.** $\frac{3}{4}(f - 1) + 2 = 14$ **42.** $\frac{1}{5}x - 7 = 2x + 2$

Find the slope of each line connecting the given points. Use the formula

$m = \frac{(y_2 - y_1)}{(x_2 - x_1)}$. **[5-1B]**

43. $(0, -8), (-3, 2)$ **44.** $(-1, -3), (7, 6)$
45. $(-9, 2), (-9, 5)$ **46.** $(1000, -30), (200, -70)$

Solve each system of linear equations using substitution. [6-2A]

47. $y = 2x - 1$ **48.** $y = \frac{2}{3}x$ **49.** $2x + 3y = 8$ **50.** $4x + y = 14$

$x + 2y = 3$ $3y - x = -9$ $x = -y - 2$ $2x - 3y = 0$

7-2 SQUARE ROOTS

Use with or after Part 7-2A

Write the prime factorization of each number. Write with exponents. [Page 757]

1. 32   **2.** 121   **3.** 98   **4.** 400

Complete the table. Write an equation for the relationship. [3-1A]

5.

x	1	2	3	4	5	10	20
y	4	16	36	64	?	?	?

Convert the amounts to indicated units. [5-2C]

6. 360 in.^{2} to ft^2 **7.** 5 m^2 to cm^2
8. 26,136 ft^2 to acres   **9.** 75,000 m^2 to hectares

Use with or after Part 7-2B

Make a table of values for each expression, using integer values of *x* from −2 to 4. [2-2B]

10. $x^2 + 2$ **11.** $-2x^2$ **12.** $x^2 - x$ **13.** $\dfrac{1}{x^2}$

Determine which of these can be lengths of a triangle. [4-3C]

14. 10 yd, 24 yd, 26 yd   **15.** 8 in., 2.5 in., 5.5 in.

16. 1 ft, 2 ft, 6 in.   **17.** 0.3 mm, 0.4 mm, 0.5 mm

Write the equation of a line with the given slope and a point on the line. [5-2B]

18. $m = -2$, $(0, 5)$ **19.** $m = \dfrac{4}{3}$, $(6, 6)$

20. $m = 0.5$, $(-0.5, 0)$ **21.** $m = 3$, $(-6, -21)$

Graph each absolute value function. [7-1B]

22. $y = -3|x|$ **23.** $y = 2|x| - 1$ **24.** $y = |x + 1|$ **25.** $y = -|x| + 4$

Evaluate. [7-2A]

26. $\sqrt{169}$ **27.** $\sqrt{\dfrac{49}{81}}$ **28.** $\sqrt{0.0196}$ **29.** $\sqrt{225}$

7-3 DISTANCE IN A PLANE

Use with or after Part 7-3A

Solve the literal equations for *h*. [4-2C]

1. $A = \dfrac{1}{2}h(b_1 + b_2)$ **2.** $V = \dfrac{t}{h}$ **3.** $4(h + t) = 24 - 8v$ **4.** $\dfrac{4}{h} - 2d = \dfrac{2}{h} + d$

Find the slope of the line perpendicular to the line passing through the given points. [5-1C]

5. $A(-7, 10)$ and $B(-2, 5)$ **6.** $C(-9, -1)$ and $D(8, -5)$

7. $E(0, -2)$ and $F(-7, 1)$ **8.** $G(3, -4)$ and $H(-3, -4)$

Evaluate. [7-1A]

9. $-|-7.2|$ **10.** $\dfrac{|-9|}{|10 - 7|}$ **11.** $\left|\dfrac{1}{3} - \dfrac{3}{5}\right|$

Use with or after Part 7-3B

Write each expression without • or ÷ signs. Use exponents as needed. [2-2A]

12. $2 \cdot 2 \cdot 2 \cdot t \cdot t \cdot t \cdot t$ **13.** $(x - y)(x - y) \div (x + y)$

14. $(3 \cdot 3 \cdot b \cdot b \cdot b - 5) \div 2a$ **15.** $m \cdot (-6) \cdot n + 7$

Evaluate. [2-3A]

16. $\dfrac{3 \cdot (5^2)}{6}$ **17.** $\dfrac{(-3.8 + 1.6)}{(0.08 + 0.03)}$ **18.** $\dfrac{1}{3} \div \dfrac{1}{3} + 6$ **19.** $\dfrac{3}{7}(15 - 155)$

Use the distance formula, *D = rt*, to find the missing amount. [4-2C]

20. 55 mi/hr, 6.2 hr   **21.** 730 mi, 75 mi/hr   **22.** $\dfrac{1}{3}$ hr, 28 mi

Evaluate. [7-2A]

23. $-\sqrt{6.25}$ **24.** $\pm\sqrt{81}$ **25.** $\dfrac{\sqrt{18}}{\sqrt{32}}$ **26.** $\sqrt{-9}$

Use with or after Part 7-3C

Give the rise, run, and slope of the line segment determined by each pair of points. [5-1A]

27. $(0, 3.2), (-4.6, -5)$ **28.** $\left(1\frac{2}{5}, 2\frac{3}{5}\right), (-4, 6)$ **29.** $\left(\frac{1}{2}, \frac{2}{3}\right), \left(\frac{1}{3}, \frac{3}{4}\right)$

Find the intersection point, if any, of each system of equations. [6-1B]

30. $y = 2x - 3$ **31.** $y = \frac{1}{3}x + 2$ **32.** $2y + x = -10$ **33.** $x - y = 6$

$\quad\ y = -x$ $\quad\quad\ y = x - 4$ $\quad\quad\ 2x = y$ $\quad\quad\ x + y = -2$

Between what consecutive integers is the principal square root of each given number? [7-2A]

34. $\sqrt{40}$ **35.** $\sqrt{50}$ **36.** $\sqrt{160}$ **37.** $\sqrt{600}$

7-4 INDIRECT MEASUREMENT

Use with or after Part 7-4A

Simplify each expression. [2-3C]

1. $7.8y - 0.9z + y$ **2.** $-1.2(3y - 5) + 0.4(7 - y)$

3. $\frac{(5x - 9)}{3} + \frac{2}{3}x$ **4.** $4(2m - 8) - (1 - 8m)$

Solve each equation. [4-2C]

5. $1\frac{7}{18}x = \frac{5}{9}$ **6.** $-\frac{m}{4} = 4.8$ **7.** $\frac{8.1}{1.8} = \frac{x}{10}$ **8.** $\frac{9}{f} = \frac{2}{5}$

Write an equation of a line that is parallel to the given line and passes through the origin. [6-1A]

9. $y = \frac{2}{3}x - 9$ **10.** $5y - 2x = 10$ **11.** $y - x = 7$ **12.** $y = -6$

Determine the missing side of each right triangle. [7-3B]

13. legs: 6 cm, 8 cm   **14.** leg: 10 in., hypotenuse: 12 in.

15. $a = 12$ mm, $c = 13$ mm

Use with or after Part 7-4B

Solve the equations by clearing the fractions. [4-2D]

16. $\frac{7}{m} = \frac{3}{2}$ **17.** $\frac{62.5}{50} = \frac{x}{2}$ **18.** $\frac{0.707}{2} = \frac{3}{d}$

Write the equation of the line through (3, 1) that is perpendicular to the graph of each equation. [6-1A]

19. $y = -\frac{1}{2}x$ **20.** $2x - 3y = 9$ **21.** $x = 7$ **22.** $\frac{y}{4} + \frac{x}{2} = -1$

Solve the absolute value equations. [7-1C]

23. $|x| = 4$ **24.** $2|x - 8| = 11$

25. $|x + 3| - 7 = -6$ **26.** $-3|x + 2| - 4 = -10$

Use with or after Part 7-4C

Find the missing angle in the given triangle. [Previous course]

27. $90°, 35°$ **28.** $59°, 41°$ **29.** $4°15', 14°20'$ **30.** $22°, 68°$

For each system, find the coefficient matrix A. The inverse is A^{-1}.
Solve using matrix multiplication. [6-2C]

$$A^{-1} = \begin{bmatrix} \dfrac{5}{4} & \dfrac{3}{4} \\ -\dfrac{13}{4} & \dfrac{7}{4} \end{bmatrix}$$

31. $-7x + 3y = 16$
$13x - 5y = 6$

32. $-7x + 3y = 28$
$13x - 5y = -20$

33. $-7x + 3y + 2 = 0$
$13x - 5y - 8 = 0$

34. $-7x + 3y = -9$
$13x - 5y = 0$

CHAPTER 8 POLYNOMIALS

8-1 POLYNOMIALS AND SCIENTIFIC NOTATION

Use with or after Part 8-1A

Simplify each expression. [2-3C]

1. $-3(2x + 5)$ **2.** $2(x - y) - y$
3. $(x + 2) - (2x + 1)$ **4.** $(x - y + z) + 4(y - 3z)$

Graph the square root functions. [7-2B]

5. $y = \sqrt{x} + 2$ **6.** $y = -\sqrt{x}$ **7.** $y = \sqrt{(x + 3)}$ **8.** $y = \sqrt{(3x)}$

Use the distance formula to find the distance between the given points. [7-3C]

9. $(0, -2), (5, 5)$ **10.** $(-1, 4), (2, -2)$
11. $(2, 3), (3, 4)$ **12.** $(-1, 6), (4, -6)$

Use with or after Part 8-1B

Write each expression without • or ÷ signs. Use exponents. [2-2A]
13. $(x \cdot x \cdot x)(9 \cdot x \cdot x)$ **14.** $(-2)(-2) \div x \cdot x$
15. $x \cdot y \cdot z \div (x + y + z)$ **16.** $(7 \cdot 7)7 + 3(y \cdot y \cdot y)$

Multiply the following radicals. [7-3C]
17. $\sqrt{5} \cdot \sqrt{5}$ **18.** $\sqrt{6} \cdot \sqrt{3}$ **19.** $\sqrt{2} \cdot \sqrt{4}$ **20.** $\sqrt{5} \cdot \sqrt{10}$

Find each ratio for right $\triangle ABC$ with legs AB = 5 cm, BC = 12 cm. [7-4C]
21. $\sin A$ **22.** $\cos C$ **23.** $\tan A$ **24.** $\sin C$

Add or subtract the polynomial expressions. [8-1A]
25. $(3x^2 - x) + (1 - x^2)$ **26.** $(-5x^3 + 6 - 3x) - (2x^2 + 4 - 3x^3)$
27. $(2a^2 - 3a) - (a + a^2 + 3a^3)$

Use with or after Part 8-1C

Evaluate the matrices. **[1-1C]**

$$A = \begin{bmatrix} 1 & 5 & -2 \\ 1 & 0 & 4 \\ -3 & -6 & 2 \end{bmatrix} \qquad B = \begin{bmatrix} -3 & 5 & -2 \\ 1 & -2 & 5 \\ 4 & 1 & -8 \end{bmatrix}$$

28. $A + B$ **29.** $A - B$ **30.** $0.5A$ **31.** $3B - A$

Graph the absolute value functions. **[7-1B]**

32. $y = |2x|$ **33.** $y = |x - 3|$ **34.** $y = |x| - 5$ **35.** $y = -\frac{1}{3}|x|$

Evaluate the formulas for the given values; solve for the remaining variable. **[7-2A]**

36. $A = \pi r^2$ for $A = 29$ in.^{2}

37. $V = \sqrt{(10h)}$ for $h = 16$ ft^2/sec^2

8-2 MULTIPLYING AND FACTORING POLYNOMIALS

Use with or after Part 8-2A

Find the equation of the line passing through the given pair of points. **[5-2B]**

1. $(7, 3), (-2, 0)$ **2.** $(100, -25), (30, 65)$

3. $(1954, 0), (1996, 42)$ **4.** $(11.1, -17.2), (10.6, 19.3)$

Simplify. **[8-1C]**

5. $\dfrac{2x^2y^3}{yx}$ **6.** y^5y^5 **7.** $(4y^2x)(-2x^3y)$

8. $\dfrac{12x^4}{x}$ **9.** $9n^2m^{-4} \cdot n^3m^4$ **10.** $\dfrac{36d^4}{12d^5}$

11. $\dfrac{10^3}{10^{-4}}$ **12.** $\dfrac{(6a^3b)}{(-18a^3b^2)}$ **13.** $(a^3b^{-2})^4$

14. $\left(\dfrac{3}{2}\right)^2\left(\dfrac{cd}{9d^3}\right)$ **15.** $(2x^2y^3)^3$ **16.** $(m^0n)^2$

Use with or after Part 8-2B

Determine whether the second number is a factor of the first number. **[Page 757]**

17. $(5 \cdot 6^2);\ 6$ **18.** $3^25^2;\ 8$

19. $(3 \cdot 4 \cdot 7);\ (3 \cdot 4)$ **20.** $(52 + 1);\ 5$

Solve and check. **[4-3A]**

21. $3(2x + 1) - 2(x - 5) = 0$ **22.** $-5n = -8 + 2n - 13$

23. $1\frac{2}{3}(6 - 9g) = \frac{3}{4}(-16 + 2g)$ **24.** $1.2 + 0.2y - 8.02 = 3.52$

Evaluate. Write the answers in scientific notation. **[8-1C]**

25. $0.0024(4.1 \times 10^3)$ **26.** $\dfrac{(4 \times 10^3)}{(0.005)}$ **27.** $\dfrac{(2.8 \times 10^{-2})}{(7 \times 10^3)}$

Distribute monomials over polynomials. **[8-2A]**

28. $-3a(5a^2 - 2a + 3)$ **29.** $(y^3 - 3y)2y$

30. $6m(n^2 - 2n + 3)$ **31.** $\frac{1}{2}(x^2 - 16)$

Use with or after Part 8-2C

Evaluate the formula $h = -16t^2 + vt + s$ for the given values. [7-3B]

32. $v = 9$, $t = 6$, $s = 5$ **33.** $t = 0.5$, $s = 0$, $v = 0$

34. $t = 5$, $s = 2$, $h = 20$ **35.** $v = 0$, $s = 10$, $h = -6$

Solve each inequality. [7-1A]

36. $|x| > 3$ **37.** $|x| + 2 \leq 5$ **38.** $|x + 2| = 1$ **39.** $2|x| + 1 < 3$

Add or subtract the polynomials. [8-1A]

40. $(8w - 5x + 2y - 3z) - (4x - y + 3z + 2w)$

41. $(5a^2 - 10b^2) - (3a^2 + 4ab - 6b^2)$

42. $(-4x^3 + 6x^2 - 3x) + (-2x - 4x^2 + 2)$

Multiply the binomials. [8-2B]

43. $(2x + 5)(2x + 3)$ **44.** $(3f - 2)(2f - 7)$ **45.** $(x - 3)^2$

46. $\left(\frac{1}{2}x + 5\right)(6x + 4)$ **47.** $(a + b)(a - b)$ **48.** $\left(\frac{1}{3}m + 4\right)\left(\frac{3}{4}m - 6\right)$

Use with or after Part 8-2D

Graph each absolute value function. [7-1B]

49. $y = |2x| + 2$ **50.** $y = -|2x| - 2$ **51.** $y = \left|\frac{1}{2}x\right| - 1$ **52.** $y = |x + 2|$

Factor each polynomial (find the greatest common factor). [8-2A]

53. $6m^2 - 8m$ **54.** $-12n^2 + 20mn$ **55.** $3x^3 + 15x^2 - 6x$

56. $2b^4 - 12b^3 + 6b^2$ **57.** $ax^2 - ay^2 + a^2z$ **58.** $15y + 10y^2 - 25y^3$

Factor the trinomials. [8-2C]

59. $x^2 - 5x - 6$ **60.** $x^2 - 5x + 6$ **61.** $y^2 - 3y - 10$

62. $p^2 - 14p + 24$ **63.** $g^2 - 4g - 12$ **64.** $a^2 - 8a - 9$

65. $m^2 + 10m + 21$ **66.** $f^2 + 5f + 4$ **67.** $x^2 - 13x + 12$

68. $x^2 - 14x + 49$ **69.** $x^2 + 2x + 1$ **70.** $v^2 + 2v - 15$

CHAPTER 9 QUADRATIC FUNCTIONS AND EQUATIONS

9-1 EXPLORING QUADRATIC FUNCTIONS AND THEIR GRAPHS

Use with or after Part 9-1A

Convert to the given unit. [5-2C]

1. 90 in. to yd   **2.** 55,000 mm to m   **3.** 60 mi/hr to km/hr

4. 488 oz/in.^{2} to lb/in.^{2} **5.** 1,000,000 sec to hr   **6.** 0.00045 kg to g

7. 6.3 L/hr to L/min   **8.** 98 cm/sec to km/hr

Solve the absolute value equations. [7-1C]

9. $|b + 3| = 2$ **10.** $|-3x| = 6$ **11.** $|5 - x| = 15$

12. $-2|d| - 8 = -176$ **13.** $|3y + 6| = 4$ **14.** $|2x| + 11 = 9$

15. $3 = |x + 2| - 4$ **16.** $|0.25m + 6| - 4 = 1$

Use with or after Part 9-1B

Graph the functions. [7-1B, 7-2B]

17. $y = \sqrt{x} + 1$ **18.** $y = |x| + 1$ **19.** $y = x - 1$ **20.** $y = |x - 1|$

Simplify each radical expression. [7-3C]

21. $\sqrt{8} \cdot \sqrt{8}$ **22.** $\sqrt{9} \cdot \sqrt{81}$ **23.** $\sqrt{72} = \underline{\ ?\ }\sqrt{2}$ **24.** $\sqrt{147} = 7\sqrt{\underline{\ ?\ }}$

25. $\pm\sqrt{6 \cdot 24}$ **26.** $-\sqrt{3 \cdot 75}$ **27.** $\dfrac{\sqrt{18}}{\sqrt{50}}$ **28.** $-\sqrt{0.0121}$

Factor (find the greatest common factor). [8-2B]

29. $5t^3 - 15t^2 + 25t$ **30.** $4a^2b - 6abc - 2ab$ **31.** $18x^2 + 30x - 42$

32. $6y^4 - 9y^3 + 12y^2$ **33.** $-12g^4 + 54g - 18g^3$ **34.** $x^2y^2 - x^3y^2 + x^5y^3$

9-2 SOLVING QUADRATIC EQUATIONS

Use with or after Part 9-2A

Solve each system of linear equations. [6-2A, B, and C]

1. $2x + y = 7$
$2x - y = 13$

2. $-5g - 3h = -8$
$7g + 3h = 10$

3. $d - c = 1$
$4c - 3d = -1$

4. $x - 4 = 2(y - 2)$
$x + 7 = \dfrac{1}{2}(y + 8) + 9$

Use the Pythagorean Theorem to find the missing triangle side. [7-3C]

5. $a = 10$ in., $b = 24$ in., $c = ?$ **6.** $a = 2$ ft, $c = \sqrt{10}$ ft, $b = ?$

7. hypotenuse $= 5$ m, leg $= 1$ m

Add or subtract each polynomial. [8-1A]

8. $(4x + 2) + (3x + 1)$ **9.** $(x - 2) - (2x + 3)$

10. $(y^2 - 6 + 7y) + (-y^2 - 4y + 3)$ **11.** $3b^2 - (b + 2b^2)$

Factor each polynomial. [8-2D]

12. $3f^2 - 12$ **13.** $4 + 4x + x^2$ **14.** $x^2y^2 - 4x^4y^4$ **15.** $x^2 - x - 20$

16. $z^2 + 3z - 10$ **17.** $m^2 - 2m - 24$ **18.** $64 + 16y + y^2$ **19.** $c^2 + 7c + 12$

Use with or after Part 9-2B

Solve the absolute value equations. [7-1C]

20. $-|5y| = -10$ **21.** $|m + 1| = 9$ **22.** $|3x - 6| = 4$

23. $|x| - 8 = 15$ **24.** $2|x| - 9 = 21$ **25.** $-3|2k + 4| = -12$

Find the taxi distance and the coordinate distance between each pair of points. [7-3A, 7-3C]

26. $(5, 4), (-1, 4)$ **27.** $(14, 6), (-2, -4)$ **28.** $(-2, 5), (-7, -5)$

29. $(3, 2), (-2, -3)$ **30.** $(-2, -2), (4, -1)$ **31.** $(0, -3), (12, 0)$

Multiply. [8-2A]

32. $2x + y(8xy - 4y^2)$ **33.** $9 + y - 6(2y + 8)$ **34.** $(3x^2 - 2x - 9)(-x)$

Find the values of *a*, *b*, and *c* for each function of the form $y = ax^2 + bx + c$. [9-1A]

35. $y = 2x^2 + 3x + 8$ **36.** $y - 2 = x^2$ **37.** $y + 1 = x^2 - 3$

9-3 OTHER TECHNIQUES FOR SOLVING QUADRATIC EQUATIONS

Use with or after Part 9-3A

Solve the inequalities. [4-3B]

1. $-3n - 2(n - 1) > 0$

2. $76 + 4(2y) \leq 7y - 71$

3. $0 > 29y + 4(1 - 7y)$

4. $-3(3x + 4) \leq -2(4x - 8)$

5. $1 + 2(m + 1) \leq -3m$

6. $-7 \leq x + 3 < -2$

7. $2x \geq -8$ and $-3x > 9$

8. $7 - 3x > \frac{3}{2}(4 - x)$

Multiply the binomials. [8-2B]

9. $(x - 3)^2$

10. $(2x - y)(8x + 5y)$

11. $(x + 5)(x + 7)$

12. $(a + b)(x - y)$

13. $(a^2 + b^2)(a^3 + 3)$

14. $(2x^2 - 3y^2)^2$

Solve each equation by factoring. [9-2B]

15. $m^2 + 4m + 4 = 0$

16. $x^2 - 16 = 0$

17. $x^2 + 6x = -9$

18. $x^2 = 5x$

19. $3d^2 - 15d + 18 = 0$

20. $n - n^2 = 5n^2 + n$

21. $x^2 - \frac{9}{4} = 0$

22. $2b^2 + 6b = 20$

Use with or after Part 9-3B

Simplify. [8-1B and C]

23. $\left(\dfrac{a^2}{b}\right)^4$

24. $2^3 \cdot 2^5 \cdot 2^{-4}$

25. $\dfrac{(-3b)^2}{b^8}$

26. $\dfrac{4ab(7a^2b^3)}{(-21a^3b^2)}$

27. $\dfrac{(8 \cdot 10^{11})}{(2 \cdot 10)}$

28. $(-p)^5 \cdot \dfrac{(2^2 p^0)}{p^{-2}}$

Factor these quadratic expressions. [8-2D]

29. $5b^2 + 20b - 60$

30. $4y^2 - 36$

31. $x^2 + 6x + 9$

32. $x^2 + \frac{2}{3}x + \frac{1}{9}$

33. $8 - 9b + b^2$

34. $x^2 + 25$

Solve each quadratic equation with the square root method. [9-3A]

35. $4x^2 = 24$

36. $-3b^2 = -27$

37. $2n^2 - 50 = 288$

38. $280 = 70(1 + x)^2$

39. $-9y^2 = 90$

40. $-5(r - 1)^2 = -25$

CHAPTER 10 FUNCTIONS AND THE STRUCTURE OF ALGEBRA

10-1 REAL NUMBERS, EXPRESSIONS, AND EQUATIONS

Use with or after Part 10-1A

Simplify radicals. [7-2A]

1. $\sqrt{28} = \underline{\ ?\ } \cdot \sqrt{7}$

2. $3\sqrt{20} = \underline{\ ?\ } \cdot \sqrt{5}$

3. $\sqrt{800} = 20 \cdot \underline{\ ?\ }$

4. $\sqrt{24} = \underline{\ ?\ } \cdot \sqrt{\underline{\ ?\ }}$

Factor completely. [8-2C]

5. $5d^2 + 60d - 140$

6. $3f^3 - 33f^2 + 84f$

7. $2n^3 + 10n^2 + 14n$

8. $y^3 - y$

Use with or after Part 10-1B

Solve the linear equations. (Hint: clear fractions.) [4-2D]

9. $\dfrac{5}{6x} + 34 = 9$ **10.** $\dfrac{-3}{4y} + 12 = 84$

11. $40 = \dfrac{-3}{5x} + 7$ **12.** $2.1 = 4.3 - 1.1m$

Solve each absolute value equation. [7-1C]

13. $\left|3w\right| - 4 = 10$ **14.** $\left|6x + 2\right| + 5 = 8$

15. $\left|1 - 2k\right| - 12 = 17$ **16.** $\left|y - 2\right| + 1 = 6$

Solve the equations using the quadratic formula. [9-3B]

17. $3x^2 - 2x - 2$ **18.** $2a^2 - 5a = 1$ **19.** $3m^2 = -5m - 1$

20. $x^2 - 4x - 21 = 0$ **21.** $b^2 + 4b = 5$ **22.** $y^2 + 6y + 3 = 0$

For what value(s) are the expressions undefined? [10-1A]

23. $\dfrac{(x^2 - 3x + 2)}{(x + 2)}$ **24.** $\dfrac{-6x^3}{x^2}$ **25.** $\sqrt{9 - x}$ **26.** $\dfrac{1}{\sqrt{x - 4}}$

10-2 EXPLORING EXPONENTIAL AND LOGARITHMIC FUNCTIONS

Use with or after Part 10-2A

Multiply. [8-2D]

1. $(b + 7)(b - 3)$ **2.** $(2a + 9)(a + 5)$ **3.** $(x - 3)(x + 5)$

4. $(d + 2)(d + 3)$ **5.** $(2m - 5)(3m + 2)$ **6.** $(a^2 - b^2)(a^2 - b^2)$

7. $(4x^2 + x)(7x^2 - 2x)$ **8.** $\left(\dfrac{1}{3}x - 5\right)\left(\dfrac{1}{3}x + 6\right)$

Solve the radical equations. [10-1B]

9. $\sqrt{y} = \dfrac{3}{4}$ **10.** $\sqrt{\dfrac{m}{5}} = 2$ **11.** $8 = \sqrt{5y - 1}$ **12.** $8 - 2\sqrt{y} = 0$

Solve the rational equations. [10-1B]

13. $\dfrac{2}{x} + \dfrac{3}{x} = 5$ **14.** $\dfrac{3}{2y} - \dfrac{1}{3} = \dfrac{5}{6y}$ **15.** $\dfrac{x - 7}{x + 2} = \dfrac{1}{4}$

Use with or after Part 10-2B

Solve each equation. [7-4B and C, Optional for Core Courses]

16. $\sin 30° = \dfrac{x}{2}$ **17.** $\sin 55° = \dfrac{9}{y}$ **18.** $\tan 68° = \dfrac{m}{10}$ **19.** $\tan 41° = 6d$

20. $\cos 10° = \dfrac{x}{x - 1}$ **21.** $\cos 75° = x^2$ **22.** $20 \sin 40° = x$ **23.** $\dfrac{1}{x} = \dfrac{1}{\tan 35°}$

What exponent, if any, makes each equation true? [10-2A]

24. $2^x = 32$ **25.** $3^x = \dfrac{1}{9}$ **26.** $5^x = 625$

27. $10^x = 10,000,000$ **28.** $\left(\dfrac{1}{2}\right)^x = \dfrac{1}{8}$ **29.** $6^x = 216$

Graph each function. [10-2A]

30. $y = 3(2)^x$ **31.** $y = -(2)^x$ **32.** $y = 4\left(\dfrac{1}{2}\right)^x$ **33.** $y = 10^x$

GEOMETRIC FORMULAS

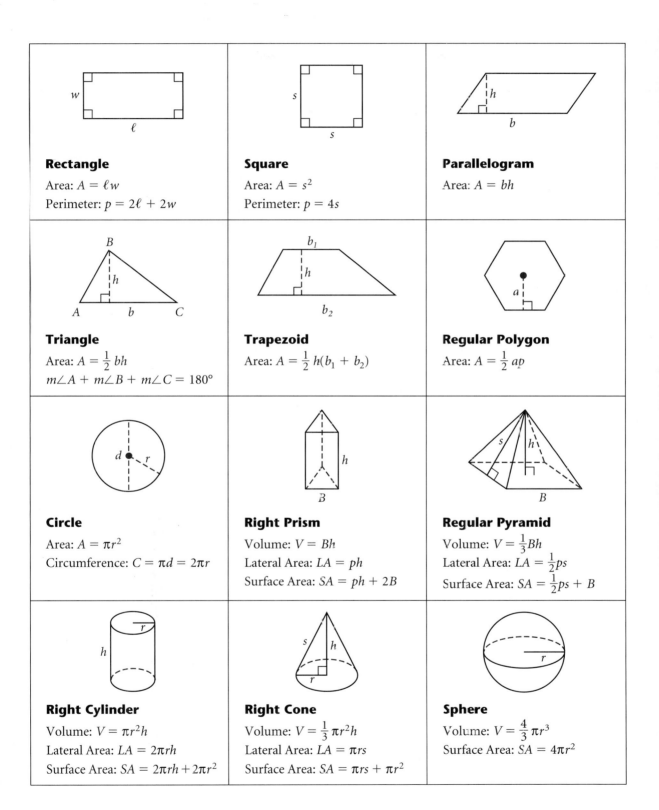

Rectangle

Area: $A = \ell w$

Perimeter: $p = 2\ell + 2w$

Square

Area: $A = s^2$

Perimeter: $p = 4s$

Parallelogram

Area: $A = bh$

Triangle

Area: $A = \frac{1}{2}bh$

$m\angle A + m\angle B + m\angle C = 180°$

Trapezoid

Area: $A = \frac{1}{2}h(b_1 + b_2)$

Regular Polygon

Area: $A = \frac{1}{2}ap$

Circle

Area: $A = \pi r^2$

Circumference: $C = \pi d = 2\pi r$

Right Prism

Volume: $V = Bh$

Lateral Area: $LA = ph$

Surface Area: $SA = ph + 2B$

Regular Pyramid

Volume: $V = \frac{1}{3}Bh$

Lateral Area: $LA = \frac{1}{2}ps$

Surface Area: $SA = \frac{1}{2}ps + B$

Right Cylinder

Volume: $V = \pi r^2 h$

Lateral Area: $LA = 2\pi rh$

Surface Area: $SA = 2\pi rh + 2\pi r^2$

Right Cone

Volume: $V = \frac{1}{3}\pi r^2 h$

Lateral Area: $LA = \pi rs$

Surface Area: $SA = \pi rs + \pi r^2$

Sphere

Volume: $V = \frac{4}{3}\pi r^3$

Surface Area: $SA = 4\pi r^2$

MEASUREMENT CONVERSION FACTORS

Metric Measures Length

1000 meters (m) = 1 kilometer (km)
100 centimeter (cm) = 1 m
10 decimeter (dm) = 1 m
1000 millimeters (mm) = 1 m
10 cm = 1 decimeter (dm)
10 mm = 1 cm

Area

100 square millimeters = 1 square centimeter
(mm^2)   (cm^2)
10,000 cm^2 = 1 square meter (m^2)
10,000 m^2 = 1 hectare (ha)

Volume

1000 cubic millimeters = 1 cubic centimeter
(mm^3)   (cm^3)
100 cm^3 = 1 cubic decimeter (dm^3)
1,000,000 cm^3 = 1 cubic meter (m^3)

Capacity

1000 milliliters (mL) = 1 liter (L)
1000 L = 1 kiloliter (kL)

Mass

1000 kilograms (kg) = 1 metric ton (t)
1000 grams (g) = 1 kg
1000 milligrams (mg) = 1 g

Temperature Degrees Celsius (°C)

0°C = freezing point of water
37°C = normal body temperature
100°C = boiling point of water

Time

60 seconds (sec) = 1 minute (min)
60 min = 1 hour (hr)
24 hr = 1 day

Customary Measures Length

12 inches (in.) = 1 foot (ft)
3 ft = 1 yard (yd)
36 in. = 1 yd
5280 ft = 1 mile (mi)
1760 yd = 1 mi
6076 feet = 1 nautical mile

Area

144 square inches = 1 square foot
(sq in.)   (sq ft)
9 sq ft = 1 square yard (sq yd)
43,560 sq ft = 1 acre (A)

Volume

1728 cubic inches = 1 cubic foot
(cu in.)   (cu ft)
27 cu ft = 1 cubic yard (cu yard)

Capacity

8 fluid ounces (fl oz) = 1 cup (c)
2 c = 1 pint (pt)
2 p = 1 quart (qt)
4 qt = 1 gallon (gal)

Weight

16 ounces (oz) = 1 pound (lb)
2000 lb = 1 ton (T)

Temperature Degrees Fahrenheit (°F)

32°F = freezing point of water
98.6°F = normal body temperature
212°F = boiling point of water

SYMBOLS

$+$	plus or positive	AB	length of $\overline{AB}$; distance between A and B
$-$	minus or negative	$\triangle ABC$	triangle with vertices A, B, and C
$\cdot$	times	$\angle ABC$	angle with sides $\overrightarrow{AB}$ and $\overrightarrow{BC}$
$\times$	times	$\angle B$	angle with vertex B
$\div$	divided by	$m\angle ABC$	measure of $\angle ABC$
$\pm$	positive or negative	$\leftrightarrow$	corresponds to
$=$	is equal to	$p \rightarrow q$	p implies q
$\neq$	is not equal to	$\log_a b$	the logarithm, base a, of b
$<$	is less than	a^n	the nth power of a
$>$	is greater than	$|x|$	absolute value of x
$\leq$	is less than or equal to	$\sqrt{x}$	principal square root of x
$\geq$	is greater than or equal to	$\bar{x}$	the mean of data values of x
$\approx$	is approximately equal to	x_1, x_2, etc.	specific values of the variable x
$\%$	percent	y_1, y_2, etc.	specific values of the variable y
$\{\}$	set braces	$f(x)$	f of x, the value of the function f at x
$a{:}b$	the ratio of a to b, or $\frac{a}{b}$	π	pi (approximately 3.1416)
$\cong$	is congruent to	(a, b)	ordered pair with x-coordinate a and y-coordinate b
$\perp$	is perpendicular to	$P(A)$	the probability of event A
$\parallel$	is parallel to	$\sin A$	sine of $\angle A$
$\sim$	is similar to	$\cos A$	cosine of $\angle A$
$^\circ$	degree(s)	$\tan A$	tangent of $\angle A$
$\overleftrightarrow{AB}$	line containing points A and B		
$\overline{AB}$	line segment with endpoints A and B		
$\overrightarrow{AB}$	ray with endpoint A and containing B		

SQUARES AND SQUARE ROOTS

N	N²	√N	N	N²	√N
1	1	1	51	2,601	7.141
2	4	1.414	52	2,704	7.211
3	9	1.732	53	2,809	7.280
4	16	2	54	2,916	7.348
5	25	2.236	55	3,025	7.416
6	36	2.449	56	3,136	7.483
7	49	2.646	57	3,249	7.550
8	64	2.828	58	3,364	7.616
9	81	3	59	3,481	7.681
10	100	3.162	60	3,600	7.746
11	121	3.317	61	3,721	7.810
12	144	3.464	62	3,844	7.874
13	169	3.606	63	3,969	7.937
14	196	3.742	64	4,096	8
15	225	3.873	65	4,225	8.062
16	256	4	66	4,356	8.124
17	289	4.123	67	4,489	8.185
18	324	4.243	68	4,624	8.246
19	361	4.359	69	4,761	8.307
20	400	4.472	70	4,900	8.367
21	441	4.583	71	5,041	8.426
22	484	4.690	72	5,184	8.485
23	529	4.796	73	5,329	8.544
24	576	4.899	74	5,476	8.602
25	625	5	75	5,625	8.660
26	676	5.099	76	5,776	8.718
27	729	5.196	77	5,929	8.775
28	784	5.292	78	6,084	8.832
29	841	5.385	79	6,241	8.888
30	900	5.477	80	6,400	8.944
31	961	5.568	81	6,561	9
32	1,024	5.657	82	6,724	9.055
33	1,089	5.745	83	6,889	9.110
34	1,156	5.831	84	7,056	9.165
35	1,225	5.916	85	7,225	9.220
36	1,296	6	86	7,396	9.274
37	1,369	6.083	87	7,569	9.327
38	1,444	6.164	88	7,744	9.381
39	1,521	6.245	89	7,921	9.434
40	1,600	6.325	90	8,100	9.487
41	1,681	6.403	91	8,281	9.539
42	1,764	6.481	92	8,464	9.592
43	1,849	6.557	93	8,649	9.644
44	1,936	6.633	94	8,836	9.695
45	2,025	6.708	95	9,025	9.747
46	2,116	6.782	96	9,216	9.798
47	2,209	6.856	97	9,409	9.849
48	2,304	6.928	98	9,604	9.899
49	2,401	7	99	9,801	9.950
50	2,500	7.071	100	10,000	10

TRIGONOMETRIC RATIOS

Degrees	Sin	Cos	Tan
0°	0.0000	1.0000	0.0000
1°	0.0175	0.9998	0.0175
2°	0.0349	0.9994	0.0349
3°	0.0523	0.9986	0.0524
4°	0.0698	0.9976	0.0699
5°	0.0872	0.9962	0.0875
6°	0.1045	0.9945	0.1051
7°	0.1219	0.9925	0.1228
8°	0.1392	0.9903	0.1405
9°	0.1564	0.9877	0.1584
10°	0.1736	0.9848	0.1763
11°	0.1908	0.9816	0.1944
12°	0.2079	0.9781	0.2126
13°	0.2250	0.9744	0.2309
14°	0.2419	0.9703	0.2493
15°	0.2588	0.9659	0.2679
16°	0.2756	0.9613	0.2867
17°	0.2924	0.9563	0.3057
18°	0.3090	0.9511	0.3249
19°	0.3256	0.9455	0.3443
20°	0.3420	0.9397	0.3640
21°	0.3584	0.9336	0.3839
22°	0.3746	0.9272	0.4040
23°	0.3907	0.9205	0.4245
24°	0.4067	0.9135	0.4452
25°	0.4226	0.9063	0.4663
26°	0.4384	0.8988	0.4877
27°	0.4540	0.8910	0.5095
28°	0.4695	0.8829	0.5317
29°	0.4848	0.8746	0.5543
30°	0.5000	0.8660	0.5774
31°	0.5150	0.8572	0.6009
32°	0.5299	0.8480	0.6249
33°	0.5446	0.8387	0.6494
34°	0.5592	0.8290	0.6745
35°	0.5736	0.8192	0.7002
36°	0.5878	0.8090	0.7265
37°	0.6018	0.7986	0.7536
38°	0.6157	0.7880	0.7813
39°	0.6293	0.7771	0.8098
40°	0.6428	0.7660	0.8391
41°	0.6561	0.7547	0.8693
42°	0.6691	0.7431	0.9004
43°	0.6820	0.7314	0.9325
44°	0.6947	0.7193	0.9657
45°	0.7071	0.7071	1.0000

Degrees	Sin	Cos	Tan
46°	0.7193	0.6947	1.0355
47°	0.7314	0.6820	1.0724
48°	0.7431	0.6691	1.1106
49°	0.7547	0.6561	1.1504
50°	0.7660	0.6428	1.1918
51°	0.7771	0.6293	1.2349
52°	0.7880	0.6157	1.2799
53°	0.7986	0.6018	1.3270
54°	0.8090	0.5878	1.3764
55°	0.8192	0.5736	1.4281
56°	0.8290	0.5592	1.4826
57°	0.8387	0.5446	1.5399
58°	0.8480	0.5299	1.6003
59°	0.8572	0.5150	1.6643
60°	0.8660	0.5000	1.7321
61°	0.8746	0.4848	1.8040
62°	0.8829	0.4695	1.8807
63°	0.8910	0.4540	1.9626
64°	0.8988	0.4384	2.0503
65°	0.9063	0.4226	2.1445
66°	0.9135	0.4067	2.2460
67°	0.9205	0.3907	2.3559
68°	0.9272	0.3746	2.4751
69°	0.9336	0.3584	2.6051
70°	0.9397	0.3420	2.7475
71°	0.9455	0.3256	2.9042
72°	0.9511	0.3090	3.0777
73°	0.9563	0.2924	3.2709
74°	0.9613	0.2756	3.4874
75°	0.9659	0.2588	3.7321
76°	0.9703	0.2419	4.0108
77°	0.9744	0.2250	4.3315
78°	0.9781	0.2079	4.7046
79°	0.9816	0.1908	5.1446
80°	0.9848	0.1736	5.6713
81°	0.9877	0.1564	6.3138
82°	0.9903	0.1392	7.1154
83°	0.9925	0.1219	8.1443
84°	0.9945	0.1045	9.5144
85°	0.9962	0.0872	11.4301
86°	0.9976	0.0698	14.3007
87°	0.9986	0.0523	19.0811
88°	0.9994	0.0349	28.6363
89°	0.9998	0.0175	57.2900
90°	1.0000	0.0000	———

GLOSSARY

absolute value

The absolute value of a number n, written $|n|$, is its distance from zero on the number line. [p. 448]

absolute value function

The function $y = |x|$, where x is any real number. [p. 456]

acute angle

An angle whose measure is less than 90°.

acute triangle

A triangle with three acute angles. [p. 502]

addition property of equality

If you add the same number to both sides of an equation, the two sides will remain equal. For any real numbers a, b, and c, if $a = b$, then $a + c = b + c$. [p. 247]

addition property of inequalities

For any real numbers a, b, and c: If $a < b$, then $a + c < b + c$. If $a > b$, then $a + c > b + c$. [p. 273]

additive inverses

A pair of numbers or expressions whose sum is 0. (See *opposites*.) [p. 234]

adjacent

Next to or attached to. [p. 535]

algebra tiles

Manipulatives for modeling algebraic expressions visually. Each tile is a geometric model of a term. [p. 143]

algebraic expression

A mathematical phrase involving letters, numbers, and operation symbols. [p. 107]

altitude

In a polygon, the perpendicular segment from a vertex to the line containing the opposite side.

angle

Two rays (that are not collinear) with a common endpoint.

angle of depression

The angle formed by a horizontal line and a line of sight downward from horizontal. The vertex is the eye of the viewer. [p. 545]

area

The number of square units contained in a plane region.

associative properties

For all real numbers a, b, and c, $a + (b + c) = (a + b) + c$ and $a \cdot (b \cdot c) = (a \cdot b) \cdot c$. [p. 130]

axes

The two perpendicular lines of a coordinate plane that intersect at the origin. [p. 48]

axis of symmetry

The line over which the parts of a symmetric figure are reflections of each other. [p. 629]

bar graph

A graph with parallel bars, each representing the value of a quantity. [p. 6]

base of a power

In n^x, n is the base. [p. 108]

base of a logarithm

In $\log_a b$, the base is a. [p. 723]

binomial

A polynomial with exactly two terms. [p. 563]

boundary line

The points where the two sides of a two-variable inequality are equal. [p. 423]

boundary point

A point where the two sides of a one-variable inequality are equal. [p. 272]

Cartesian coordinate system

A system with a coordinate plane and perpendicular axes used in mathematics for graphing number pairs. [p. 48]

center of a circle

The point equidistant from all points of the circle.

central tendency

A single, central value that summarizes a set of numerical data. [p. 26]

circle

All points in a plane that are equidistant from a given point.

circle graph

A graph representing parts of a whole as sectors of a circle. [p. 9]

circumference

The perimeter of a circle. [p. 501]

coefficient matrix

The matrix of coefficients of the variables in a system of equations written in standard form. [p. 412]

coefficient

The numerical factor of a term containing variables. [p. 142]

column

A vertical line of entries in a matrix. [p. 13]

combine like terms

Use the distributive property to express a sum or difference of like terms as a single term. [p. 145]

common monomial factor

A monomial that is a factor of every term of a polynomial. [p. 591]

commutative properties

For all real numbers a and b, $a + b = b + a$ and $a \cdot b = b \cdot a$. [p. 130]

complementary angles

A pair of angles whose measures add up to 90°.

compound interest

Interest paid on previously earned interest as well as on principal. [p. 670]

conditional statement

A statement that can be written in if-then form.

congruent

Having the same shape and size.

constant

A quantity whose value does not change. [p. 85]

converse

The converse of a statement in *if-then* form is the same statement with the clauses following *if* and *then* interchanged. [p. 503]

conversion factor

A ratio of two equal quantities used to convert a quantity in one unit of measure to its equivalent in another unit of measure. [p. 344]

coordinate geometry

A study of geometry in which a coordinate plane is imposed on geometric figures to allow the use of algebraic tools to demonstrate or prove facts about those figures.

coordinate plane

The plane determined by two axes, typically the x-axis and the y-axis. [p. 48]

coordinates

The ordered pair of numbers specifying the location of a point on a coordinate plane. [p. 48]

corresponding parts

Parts of two geometric figures that match up. [p. 525]

cosine (cos A)

For acute $\angle A$ in a right triangle, the ratio of the length of the adjacent leg to the length of the hypotenuse. [p. 541]

counterexample

An example that shows a statement to be false. [p. 25]

counting principle

If each outcome has independent parts, the total number of possible outcomes can be found by multiplying the number of choices for each part. [p. 65]

cube

A solid whose faces are congruent squares. [p. 121]

cubic function

A polynomial function of degree 3, usually written in the form $y = ax^3 + bx^2 + cx + d$. [p. 564]

789

data table

A listing of pairs of data in columns or rows. [p. 47]

data

Information. [p. 6]

deductive reasoning

A process where conclusions are drawn from given information by using rules of logic.

defining a variable

Stating in words what a variable will represent in a given situation. [p. 108]

degree of a polynomial expression

The value of the largest exponent of the variable that appears in any term. [p. 564]

degree

A unit (°) used to measure the size of an angle. There are 360° in a full circle. [p. 52]

dependent system

A system of equations with an infinite number of solutions. [p. 404]

dependent variable

When the value of y depends on the value of x, y is called the dependent variable, and is graphed as the quantity on the vertical axis. [p. 165]

descending order

Ordered from greatest to least. [p. 565]

diameter of a circle

A segment, or the length of a segment, that contains the center of the circle and has endpoints on the circle.

difference of two squares

An expression of the form $a^2 - b^2$. [p. 611]

difference

The result of subtracting one number from another. [p. 16]

dilation

A function that changes all the dimensions of a geometric figure by a factor k, the scale factor. [p. 531]

dimension of a matrix

The number of rows and columns in a matrix, listed in that order. [p. 13]

dimensional analysis

A technique in which the units of measurement accompany each quantity in a solution process, so that the solution will have the correct units. [p. 344]

directly related

If one quantity increases (decreases) as another quantity increases (decreases), then the two quantities are directly related. [p. 90]

discriminant

For a quadratic equation $ax^2 + bx + c = 0$, the expression $b^2 - 4ac$. [p. 677]

distance formulas

The distance between two points on a number line with coordinates a and b is the absolute value of the difference of their coordinates; $d = |a - b|$. [p. 449]

The distance between two points on a coordinate plane whose coordinates are (x_1, y_1) and (x_2, y_2) is $d = \sqrt{(x_2 - x_1)^2 + (y_2 - y_1)^2}$. [p. 512]

distance

The length of the line segment connecting two points. [p. 448]

distributive properties

For all real numbers a, b, and c, $a(b + c) = ab + ac$ and $a(b - c) = ab - ac$. For all real numbers a, b, and c, where $a \neq 0$, $\frac{b + c}{a} = \frac{b}{a} + \frac{c}{a}$ and $\frac{b - c}{a} = \frac{b}{a} - \frac{c}{a}$. [p. 135]

domain

The set of all possible values of the independent variable of a function. [p. 181]

enlargement

A dilation by a scale factor k, where $k > 1$.

entries

The numbers in a matrix. [p. 13]

equally likely

Expected to occur as frequently, as for two events. [p. 63]

equation

A mathematical sentence stating that two quantities are equal, written as two expressions separated by an equal sign. [p. 165]

equation box

A box used to model equations with algebra tiles. [p. 234]

equivalent expressions

Expressions that have the same value whenever the same numbers are substituted for the variables. [p. 134]

evaluate an expression

Substitute values into the variables in an algebraic expression to find the value of the expression. [p. 115]

event

A set of outcomes. [p. 63]

experimental probability

Probability found by collecting data or running an experiment. [p. 59]

exponent

In exponential notation, n^x, x is the exponent. It tells how many times the base n is used as a factor. [p. 108]

exponential decay

The pattern of decreasing values of an exponential function $y = b^x$ for which $0 < b < 1$. For each unit increase in x, y is multiplied by b. [p. 716]

exponential function

A function that can be represented by an equation of the form $y = ab^x$, where a and b are constants, $b > 0$, and x is any real number. [p. 715]

exponential growth

The pattern of increasing values of an exponential function $y = b^x$ for which $b > 1$. For each unit increase in x, y is multiplied by b. [p. 716]

expression

See *algebraic expression*.

expression tree

A special kind of graph that indicates the order in which the operations of an expression are to be done. [p. 128]

extraneous solution

When an equation is transformed, for example by squaring both sides, the transformed equation may have solutions that do not satisfy the original equation. These values are extraneous solutions. [p. 705]

face of a cube

Square region that is part of the surface of a cube. [p. 121]

factor

When two or more numbers (or expressions) are multiplied, each is a factor of the product. [p. 590]

factorial

For any natural number n, the product of the first n natural numbers ($n!$). $0!$ is defined to be 1. [p. 66]

factoring

Writing a number or expression as a product of two or more numbers or expressions. [p. 590]

Fibonacci sequence

A famous pattern of numbers (1, 1, 2, 3, 5, 8, 13, 21, . . .) named for the 13th century mathematician Leonardo Fibonacci. [p. 696]

formula

A general rule stated as an equation. [p. 248]

fractal

A pattern that is self-similar.

function

A relationship between two quantities where the value of one quantity is uniquely determined by the value of the other quantity. [p. 181]

geometric probability

The probability of an event as determined by comparing the areas (or perimeters, angle measures, etc.) of the successful regions to the total area of the figure.

golden ratio
The ratio $\left(\frac{1+\sqrt{5}}{2} \approx 1.618034\right)$ of the length to the width of a golden rectangle. [p. 696]

golden rectangle
A rectangle commonly occurring in art and architecture, with dimensions in the golden ratio. [p. 695]

graph of an ordered pair
The point on a coordinate plane that corresponds to the ordered pair. [p. 48]

graph of an inequality
The graph of an inequality consists of all ordered pairs that are solutions of the inequality. [p. 422]

graph of a function
A graph of all the ordered pairs described by a function. [p. 173]

greatest common factor
A monomial with all the integer and variable factors common to every term of a polynomial. [p. 592]

height of a polygon
The length of an altitude.

horizontal line
In a coordinate plane, a line parallel to the x-axis. [p. 312]

hypotenuse
The side of a right triangle that is opposite the right angle. [p. 502]

inconsistent system
A system of equations with no solutions. [p. 404]

independent
Unrelated, as two quantities that do not have positive or negative association. [p. 41]

independent variable
When the value of y depends on the value of x, x is called the independent variable, and is graphed as the quantity on the horizontal axis. [p. 165]

indirect measurement
Calculation of a measure by means other than measuring it directly, such as by using trigonometric ratios. [p. 532]

inductive reasoning
Making a conjecture by looking at examples and recognizing a pattern.

inequality
Two expressions separated by an *inequality sign* ($\neq, <, \leq, >, \geq$). [p. 272]

integers
The whole numbers and their opposites: $\ldots, -3, -2, -1, 0, 1, 2, 3, \ldots$ [p. 15]

interest
Money earned on an investment, such as a savings account, or paid in excess of the principal on a loan. [p. 670]

intersection
The points common to two or more lines, figures, regions, or sets.

inverse operations
Operations that undo each other: addition and subtraction or multiplication and division. [p. 247]

inverse variation
y varies inversely with x if $y = \frac{k}{x}$ for some constant k. [p. 703]

inversely related
If one quantity decreases (increases) whenever another quantity increases (decreases), then the two quantities are inversely related. [p. 90]

irrational number
A real number that cannot be expressed as the ratio of two integers, and so cannot be expressed as a repeating or terminating decimal. [p. 477]

isosceles triangle
A triangle with at least two sides of the same length. [p. 508]

latitude
A measure of the angle north or south of the equator. [p. 52]

legs of a right triangle
The two shorter sides that form a right angle in a right triangle. [p. 502]

like terms

Terms in an expression with the same variable factors. [p. 145]

line graph

A graph of ordered pairs, where the points are connected, in order, by line segments.

line of best fit

A mathematically derived trend line.

line segment

A part of a line consisting of two endpoints and all the points between these points. [p. 318]

linear combination method

A method for solving a system of linear equations by adding or subtracting the equations to eliminate a variable. It is sometimes necessary to multiply one or both of the equations by constants before adding or subtracting. [p. 402]

linear function

A function whose graph is a straight line. It can be written in the form $y = mx + b$. A polynomial function of degree 1. [pp. 192, 564]

literal equations

Equations and formulas involving several variables. [p. 248]

logarithm (log ab)

log ab is the exponent to which a number, a, must be raised so that the result is a given number, b. [p. 722]

logarithmic function

A function that can be written in the form $y = \log_a x$, where $a > 0$ and $x > 0$. [p. 722]

longitude

A measure of the angle east or west of Greenwich, England. [p. 52]

mathematical model

A representation of something in the real world using geometry, algebra, or other mathematical tools.

matrix

A rectangular arrangement of numbers written between brackets. [p. 13]

matrix multiplication

An operation on two matrices whose result is a third matrix, the product matrix, which has the same number of rows as the original left matrix and the same number of columns as the original right matrix. [p. 410]

maximum

The greatest value. For a function, the greatest value the function assumes. [p. 637]

mean

The sum of a set of data divided by the number of data. [p. 26]

measure of central tendency

A single, central value that summarizes a set of numerical data, such as mean, median, or mode. [p. 26]

median of a triangle

A segment whose endpoints are a vertex and the midpoint of the opposite side. [p. 522]

median

When a set of data are arranged in numerical order, the middle value or the mean of the middle two values. [p. 26]

midpoint

A point that divides a segment into two segments of equal length. [p. 519]

minimum

The least value. For a function, the least value the function assumes. [p. 637]

mode

The most frequently occurring value in a set of data. [p. 26]

model

See *mathematical model.*

monomial

An algebraic expression with one term. [p. 563]

multiplication property of equality

If you multiply both sides of an equation by the same number, the two sides will remain equal. For any real numbers a, b, and c, if $a = b$, then $ac = bc$. [p. 247]

multiplication property of inequalities

For any real numbers a, b, and $c \neq 0$: If $a < b$, then $ac < bc$, if c is positive; $ac > bc$, if c is negative. If $a > b$, then $ac > bc$, if c is positive; $ac < bc$, if c is negative. [p. 274]

negative association

The property that one quantity tends to decrease as the other increases. [p. 40]

negative exponent

For any nonzero real number a and any integer n, $a^{-n} = \frac{1}{a^n}$. [p. 579]

negative integers

The integers that are less than zero: -1, -2, $-3, \ldots$ [pp. 14, 21]

no association

Independent, as two quantities that do not have positive or negative association. [p. 41]

number line

A line on which points representing real numbers are labeled. [p. 15]

obtuse angle

An angle whose measure is greater than 90° and less than 180°.

obtuse triangle

A triangle with one obtuse angle. [p. 502]

opposites

A pair of real numbers that are the same distance from 0, but on opposite sides of 0 on the number line, such as 5 and -5. (See *additive inverses*.) [p. 15]

order of operations

Agreed-upon rules for the order in which to do operations when evaluating an expression. The order of operations is (1) evaluate what is inside parentheses or above or below fractions bars; (2) evaluate powers; (3) multiply and divide in order from left to right; and (4) add and subtract in order from left to right. [p. 127]

ordered pair

A pair of numbers denoting the location of a point on a coordinate plane. [p. 48]

origin

The point of intersection of the two axes of a coordinate plane. [p. 48]

outcome

Any possible result of an experiment or activity. [p. 63]

parabola

The U-shaped graph of a quadratic function. [p. 629]

parallel lines

Two lines in the same plane that do not intersect. [p. 374]

perimeter

The distance around a figure.

perpendicular lines

Lines that intersect at right angles. [p. 48]

pi (π)

The ratio of the circumference of a circle to its diameter. $\pi \approx 3.14$.

pie chart

A circle graph. [p. 6]

plot

Locate and mark a point on a coordinate plane corresponding to an ordered pair. [p. 38]

point-slope equation

The equation of a line in the form $y - y_1 = m(x - x_1)$ where m is the slope and (x_1, y_1) is a specific point on the line. [p. 340]

polygon

A closed plane figure formed by line segments that only intersect at their endpoints.

polynomial

A polynomial expression. [p. 565]

polynomial expression

A monomial or a sum of monomials. [p. 563]

polynomial function

A relationship between quantities that can be described by an equation for which y equals a polynomial expression of x. [p. 564]

positive association

The property that two quantities tend to increase or decrease together. [p. 40]

positive integers

The integers that are greater than zero: 1, 2, 3, . . . [pp. 14, 21]

power

A number that can be written as a product of equal factors. [p. 108]

principal

Initial amount of an investment or loan. [p. 670]

principal square root

Written $\sqrt{a}$, the nonnegative number c such that $c^2 = a$. [p. 477]

probability

The portion of time an event is expected to occur. (See *theoretical probability*). [p. 59]

product

The result when two values or expressions are multiplied. [p. 590]

proportion

An equation stating that two ratios are equal. [p. 525]

proportional

y is proportional to x if they are related by $y = ax$, for some $a \neq 0$. [p. 193]

Pythagorean Theorem

In a right triangle, the square of the length of the hypotenuse is equal to the sum of the squares of the lengths of the legs. [p. 503]

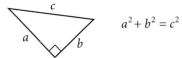

$$a^2 + b^2 = c^2$$

Pythagorean triple

Any set of three integers a, b, and c that satisfy $a^2 + b^2 = c^2$.

quadrant

One of the four regions bounded by the axes of a coordinate plane. [p. 48]

quadratic equation

An equation that can be written in the form $d = ax^2 + bx + c$, where a, b, c and d are real numbers and $a \neq 0$. [p. 650]

quadratic equation in standard form

An equation of the form $0 = ax^2 + bx + c$, where a, b, and c are real numbers and $a \neq 0$. [p. 650]

quadratic formula

If $ax^2 + bx + c = 0$, $a \neq 0$, then $x = \dfrac{-b \pm \sqrt{b^2 - 4ac}}{2a}$. [p. 676]

quadratic function

A polynomial function of degree 2, of the form $y = ax^2 + bx + c$. [p. 564]

quadrilateral

A polygon with four sides. [p. 531]

quantity

Anything that can be measured or counted. [p. 84]

radical expression

An expression that includes a radical symbol and an expression or a real number under it. [p. 698]

radical symbol

The symbol, $\sqrt{}$, used to denote the nonnegative or principal square root of a number. [p. 477]

range

The set of all values of the dependent variable of a function. [p. 181]

rate

A ratio that compares one quantity to another. [p. 308]

rate of change

The ratio of the change in one quantity to a corresponding change in another quantity. [p. 310]

ratio

A comparison by division.

rational expression

A quotient of polynomials. [p. 698]

rational number

A number that can be expressed as a ratio of two integers. A repeating decimal. [p. 477]

real numbers

The real numbers consist of the rational numbers and the irrational numbers. [p. 477]

reciprocal

For any nonzero real number a, the reciprocal of a is $\frac{1}{a}$.

rectangle

A quadrilateral with four right angles. [p. 346]

reflection

One figure is a reflection of another if they are mirror images over a line.

related

Two quantities are *related* if a change in the value of one corresponds to a predictable change in the value of the other. [p. 89]

right angle

An angle that measures 90°.

right triangle

A triangle with one right angle. [p. 502]

rise

The change in y-values as you move on a line from one point to another. [p. 302]

row

A horizontal line of entries in a matrix. [p. 13]

run

The change in x-values as you move on a line from one point to another. [p. 302]

sample space

The set of all possible outcomes of an experiment or activity. [p. 63]

scalar multiplication

Multiplication of each entry of a matrix by a single number. [p. 21]

scalar product

A matrix resulting from scalar multiplication. [p. 21]

scale factor

A factor by which a figure is enlarged or reduced. [p. 531]

scales (of a graph)

The marked intervals on the axes of a coordinate plane. [p. 344]

scatter plot

A graph showing a set of points based on paired data. [p. 39]

scientific notation

A number written as a power of 10 multiplied by a number at least 1 but less than 10. [p. 571]

sector

A region between two radii inside a circle.

set

A well-defined collection of objects. [p. 15]

SI units

Système International or International System of units of measure; metric units. [p. 638]

similar figures

Figures having the same shape, but not necessarily the same size, so that corresponding angles have the same measure and corresponding side lengths have the same ratio. [p. 525]

similar triangles

See *similar figures*. [p. 525]

simple interest

Interest paid on principal alone, not on previously earned interest as well. [p. 670]

simplifying an expression

The process of finding the simplest form of an expression. When combining like terms, simplifying means creating an equivalent expression with fewer terms. [p. 145]

sine (sin A)

For acute $\angle A$ in a right triangle, the ratio of the length of the opposite leg to the length of the hypotenuse. [p. 541]

slope

The ratio of rise to run for a line in a coordinate plane. [p. 300]

slope-intercept form

The equation of a line written in the form $y = mx + b$, where m is the slope, and b is the y-intercept. [p. 329]

solution of a linear inequality

Any ordered pair that makes the inequality true. The set of all points that are solutions is a region of a coordinate plane bounded by a line. Depending on the inequality, the points on the boundary line may or may not be solutions. [p. 423]

solution of a system

For a system of two equations, an ordered pair that makes *both* equations true. Each intersection point of the graphs of the two equations represents a solution of the system. [p. 384]

solution matrix

The matrix whose entries are the solutions for the variables of a system of equations. [p. 411]

solution of a system of linear inequalities

Any ordered pair that makes all of the inequalities true. The set of all points that are solutions is a region of a coordinate plane. [p. 429]

solutions

The values of the variables of an equation or inequality that make it a true statement. [p. 218]

sphere

The set of all points in space that are a given distance from a point, the center of the sphere.

spreadsheet

A table used in computer programs that contains numbers, text, or formulas. [p. 6]

square

A four-sided plane figure with four right angles and four congruent sides.

square root method

A method to solve equations of the form $ax^2 + b = c$ by using the properties of equality to get x^2 alone on one side of the equation, and then finding the square roots of both sides. [p. 670]

square root

The number c is a square root of a if $c^2 = a$. [p. 476]

square trinomial

A trinomial that results from squaring a binomial. [p. 611]

standard form

The equation of a line written in the form $Ax + By = C$, where A, B, and C are constants. [p. 380]

standard notation

Writing of a number in expanded, unabbreviated form, such as writing 142 million as 142,000,000. [p. 571]

statistics

The branch of mathematics that deals with the collection, organization, display, and interpretation of data.

substitution method

A method for solving a system of equations in which one equation is solved for one of the variables and the result is substituted into the other equation. [p. 394]

substitution

Replacing a quantity in an algebraic expression with an equal quantity. [p. 115]

supplementary angles

A pair of angles whose measures add up to 180°.

symmetric

A figure is symmetric if its parts on either side of a line are reflections of each other. [p. 629]

system of linear equations

Two or more linear equations considered together. [p. 383]

system of linear inequalities

Two or more linear inequalities considered together. [p. 429]

tangent (tan *A*)

For acute $\angle A$ in a right triangle, the ratio of the length of the opposite leg to the length of the adjacent leg. [p. 533]

taxi distance

The taxi distance from (x_1, y_1) to (x_2, y_2) is $|x_2 - x_1| + |y_2 - y_1|$. [p. 497]

terms

The parts of an expression that are added. [p. 142]

theoretical probability

The theoretical probability of an event, P(event), is the ratio of the number of outcomes in the event to the number of outcomes in the sample space, if all outcomes are equally likely. [p. 63]

tree diagram

A graphic representation, similar to the branches of a tree, of all the possible outcomes of an event. [p. 65]

trend line

The line that approximates the relationship between the two quantities of a scatter plot. [p. 43]

triangle

A polygon with three sides.

Triangle Inequality Theorem

The sum of the lengths of any two sides of a triangle is greater than the length of the third side. [p. 281]

trigonometry

The branch of mathematics that initially dealt with the ratios of the sides of right triangles, and now applies to all applications of trigonometric functions. [p. 532]

trinomial

A polynomial with exactly three terms. [p. 563]

unlike terms

Terms in an expression with different variable factors. [p. 151]

value

The measurement, including a unit, of a measured quantity, or the number of a counted quantity. [p. 84]

variable

A quantity whose value may change or vary, or any letter, such as $L, n, x, P, a, y,$ or others, that represents possible values of such a quantity. [p. 85]

Venn diagram

A graphic means of showing intersection and union of sets by representing them as bounded regions. [p. 697]

vertex of a cube

A point at which three edges of a cube intersect. [p. 121]

vertex of a parabola

The point where the parabola intersects its axis of symmetry. [p. 629]

vertical line

In a coordinate plane, a line parallel to the y-axis. [p. 312]

volume

The number of cubic units contained in a solid.

whole numbers

The numbers 0, 1, 2, 3, . . . [p. 15]

x-axis

Typically the horizontal axis on a coordinate plane. [p. 48]

x-coordinate

Typically the first number of the ordered pair of coordinates of a point, denoting the distance left or right from the vertical axis. [p. 48]

x-intercept

The x-coordinate of a point where a graph crosses the x-axis. [p. 651]

y-axis

Typically the vertical axis on a coordinate plane. [p. 48]

y-coordinate

Typically the second number of the ordered pair of coordinates of a point, denoting the distance up or down from the horizontal axis. [p. 48]

y-intercept

The y-coordinate of a point where a line crosses the y-axis. [p. 328]

SELECTED ANSWERS

CHAPTER 1

1-1 Part A Try It
a. 193 votes **b.** 408,000 people

1-1 Part A Exercises
1. a. A **b.** $\frac{1}{3}$ **c.** A + B + C **d.** 500 **e.** 270 **2.** 46.75 **3.** 75% **4.** 2000 **5.** (a) **6.** 412,424 mi^2 **7.** Wallace Memorial ≈ 125, Maybell Prep ≈ 325, Malcolm High ≈ 800, Lincoln Memorial ≈ 75, Chavez ≈ 425, Total ≈ 2302; To estimate enrollments, divide 552 by the length of the first bar, then multiply the result by each of the other bar lengths in turn. **11.** The differences between the cereals look greater. **13.** The percentages are often rounded from their true value to the nearest whole number. **15.** $\frac{7}{24}$ **17.** 11.46 **19.** $2\frac{1}{4}$ **21.** 1 **23.** $\frac{17}{18}$ **25.** $1\frac{1}{7}$ **27.** $\frac{8}{17}$ **29.** 54 **51.** 45 kittens **53.** 5100 bicycles **55.** J = M = 10%; K = 20%; L = N = 30% **37.** A = Fulani; B = Hausa or Yoruba; C = Ibibio; D = Other; E = Kanuri; F = Ibo; G = Yoruba or Hausa

1-1 Part B Try It
a. 3×3 **b.** 2×1 **c.** 1×4 **d.** 5×3 **e.** 4 **f.** 10 **g.** 16 **h.** -20

i. $\begin{bmatrix} 7 & -2 & 0 \\ -3 & 3 & 1 \end{bmatrix}$

j. $\begin{bmatrix} -7 & 2 & 0 \\ 3 & -3 & -1 \end{bmatrix}$

1-1 Part B Exercises
1. a. 5, 6 **b.** $-1, -2, -3, -4$ **c.** 0, 1, 2, 3 **2.** $6 - 9 = -3$ **3.** $9 - 6 = 3$ **4.** The sums of (b) and (c) are positive because the positive number is further from zero on the number line than the negative number. **5. a.** iv **b.** iii **c.** ii **d.** i **6.** 2×5

7. a. $\begin{bmatrix} 52 & 21 & 17 & 2 \\ 37 & 45 & 12 & 5 \\ 0 & 1 & 14 & 35 \end{bmatrix}$

b. 3×4

9. $\begin{bmatrix} 0 & 0 & 0 \\ 0 & 0 & 0 \end{bmatrix}$

11. $\begin{bmatrix} 2 & -3 & 4 \\ 5 & -5 & -10 \\ 0 & -4 & 5 \end{bmatrix}$

13. The matrix has the same number of rows and columns. **15.** 0.375, 37.5% **17.** 0.77, 77% **19.** 2 **21.** -11 **23.** -10 **25.** -3 **27.** $-\frac{1}{8}$ **29.** $-\frac{1}{12}$

31. $\begin{bmatrix} 0 & 0 & 4 & 3 \\ 1 & 2 & 3 & 5 \\ 5 & 1 & 1 & 1 \end{bmatrix}$

33. $\begin{bmatrix} -4 & 6 & 2 & -5 \\ 1 & 0 & 1 & 1 \\ -5 & 3 & -3 & 1 \end{bmatrix}$

35. $\begin{bmatrix} 1 & -2 & -4 & 1 \\ -1 & -2 & -1 & 1 \\ 1 & -2 & 3 & 0 \end{bmatrix}$

37. $\begin{bmatrix} 3 & -5 & -3 & 5 \\ -1 & -1 & 0 & 3 \\ 6 & -3 & 5 & 0 \end{bmatrix}$

39. $\begin{bmatrix} 10 & 0 \\ -2 & -9 \end{bmatrix}$

1-1 Part C Try It
a. 15 **b.** 1.6 **c.** -6

d. $\begin{bmatrix} -15 & 20 & -25 & 0 \\ 10 & -5 & 0 & 5 \\ -40 & 10 & 35 & -15 \end{bmatrix}$

e. $\begin{bmatrix} 6 & -8 & 10 & 0 \\ -4 & 2 & 0 & -2 \\ 16 & -4 & -14 & 6 \end{bmatrix}$

f. $\begin{bmatrix} -\frac{3}{2} & 2 & -\frac{5}{2} & 0 \\ 1 & -\frac{1}{2} & 0 & \frac{1}{2} \\ -4 & 1 & \frac{7}{2} & -\frac{3}{2} \end{bmatrix}$

g. $\begin{bmatrix} -1.5 & 2 & -2.5 & 0 \\ 1 & -0.5 & 0 & 0.5 \\ -4 & 1 & 3.5 & -1.5 \end{bmatrix}$

1-1 Part C Exercises
1. a. $-4, -8$ **b.** 2, 4, 6 **3.** 294 **5.** -3927 **7.** $4\frac{1}{2}$ **9.** -27 **11.** -1.5

13. $\begin{bmatrix} 21 & -14 \\ 14 & 7 \end{bmatrix}$

15. $\begin{bmatrix} 1 & -1 \\ -2 & -10 \end{bmatrix}$

17. $\begin{bmatrix} -10 & 7 \\ -4 & 7 \end{bmatrix}$

19. No **23. a.** 2×3

b. $\begin{bmatrix} 39.45 & 46.05 & 53.75 \\ 62.15 & 72.60 & 84.70 \end{bmatrix}$

25. $-6, -3, -2, -1, 0, 2, 4$ **27.** -6 **29.** -100 **31.** 72 **33.** $1\frac{7}{9}$ **35.** -7 **37.** -0.499849 **39.** $-\frac{1}{3}$ **41.** 0 **43.** 16

47. $\begin{bmatrix} -10 & -5 & 3 \\ 2 & -4 & 0 \end{bmatrix}$

49. $\begin{bmatrix} -12 & 0 \\ 21 & -18 \end{bmatrix}$

51. No; Zero entries stay the same.

1-1 Part D Try It
a. Data in increasing order: $-20, -16, -14, -13, -2, -1, 14, 19, 31, 33, 38, 39$; Mean = 9; Median = 6.5; Mode = no value occurs more than once

1-1 Part D Exercises
1. Sorted data: $-14, -7, -6, -5, -4, 0, 3, 8, 11, 20$ **a.** 42 **b.** -36 **c.** 6

d. 10; 0.6 **e.** Even **f.** -4 and 0; -2; -2 **2. a.** ii **b.** iii **c.** i **3.** 5.5 **4.** 5.5 **5.** Mean **7.** Mode **9. a.** The middle value, or third value, will be the median. **b.** In general no, unless the middle values are equal. **c.** The median of an even set of data points is the average of the middle two. **11.** Students may conclude that the median is 78, but more information is needed to find the median. **13.** -14 **15.** -158 **17.** 12 **19.** Mean = 6; Median = 6 **21.** Mean = -7.25; Median = -3 **23.** Count the number of values. Since odd, put the values in increasing order and choose the middle value: 41 **25.** Mean = 4.5 cm; Median = 4.7cm **27.** 40.5 **29.** The median will be negative. No prediction can be made about the mean. **33.** The mean is zero.

1-1 Part E Self-Assessment

1. $\begin{bmatrix} -7 & -3 & 7 \\ 0 & 0 & 1 \end{bmatrix}$

2. $\begin{bmatrix} -3 & 11 & 13 \\ 2 & -2 & -3 \end{bmatrix}$

3. $\begin{bmatrix} 3 & -11 & -13 \\ -2 & 2 & 3 \end{bmatrix}$

4. $\begin{bmatrix} -8 & 15 & 23 \\ 3 & -3 & -4 \end{bmatrix}$

5. $\begin{bmatrix} -1 & 18 & 16 \\ 3 & -3 & -5 \end{bmatrix}$

6. $\begin{bmatrix} -5 & 4 & 10 \\ 1 & -1 & -1 \end{bmatrix}$

7. $\begin{bmatrix} -1 & -25 & -19 \\ -4 & 4 & 7 \end{bmatrix}$

8. $\begin{bmatrix} -4 & -14 & -6 \\ -2 & 2 & 4 \end{bmatrix}$

9. b. 5×6 **c.** $2J$ **10.** (d) **11.** 1, 2, 3, 4, 6, 9, 12, 18, 36

799

12. 1, 2, 3, 4, 6, 9, 12, 18, or 36 **14.** (d) **16. b.** Yes; The entire country **c.** $\frac{41}{50} = 0.82$

17. Possible answer: Total number may not be known.

18. a.

$$\begin{bmatrix} 80 & 85 & 100 & 88 & 75 & 65 \\ 80 & 95 & 88 & 95 & 88 & 80 \\ 85 & 92 & 92 & 85 & 92 & 75 \\ 78 & 75 & 90 & 80 & 75 & 80 \\ 92 & 80 & 95 & 75 & 85 & 88 \end{bmatrix}$$

$$\begin{bmatrix} 80 & 80 & 85 & 78 & 92 \\ 85 & 95 & 92 & 75 & 80 \\ 100 & 88 & 92 & 90 & 95 \\ 88 & 95 & 85 & 80 & 75 \\ 75 & 88 & 92 & 75 & 85 \\ 65 & 80 & 75 & 80 & 88 \end{bmatrix}$$

b. Possible answer: The two are equally good. They both sort by subject and by order taken. **c.** English: 83, History: 85.4, Mathematics: 93, Spanish: 84.6, Computer Science: 83, Biology: 77.6 **19.** Half earned more than that wage and half earned less. **20.** Women: $8.40; Men: $10.95 **23. c.** Arrange the values in matrix *H* in increasing order. The median high temperature is the middle, or 11th, value.

1-2 Part A Try It

a. Positive **b.** Negative **c.** Positive

1-2 Part A Exercises

1. a. It decreases **b.** Negative **c.** The one at about (4.5, 78) **3.** Negative **5.** Positive **7.** Positive **9.** None **11.** Positive association **13. a.** 4; 8; 2 **b.** 85 **c.** Possible answer: It would pass through the middle of the points with a negative slope. **d.** Possible answer: No; There is no apparent trend.

15. a.

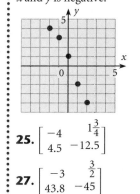

b. Possible answer: As the weight increases, the price increases proportionately. **c.** Possible answer: Lower the price of the 30-lb weight to $17. **17.** 45% **19.** 70% **21.** 0.5% **23.** Negative **25.** Negative **27.** Negative **29.** None **33.** Possible answer: Gather data relating length of feet to distance around a fist.

1-2 Part B Try It

a. (1.5, 1), I **b.** (−4, 2), II **c.** (−5, −2), III **d.** (2, −3.5), IV **e.** (−2, 0), None **f.** (0, 0), None

1-2 Part B Exercises

1.

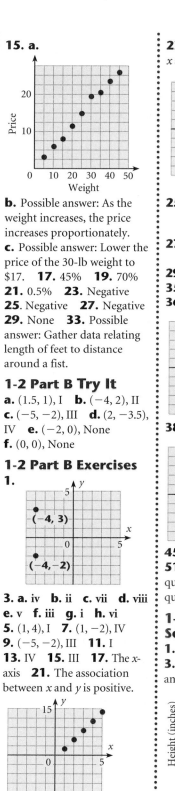

3. a. iv **b.** ii **c.** vii **d.** viii **e.** v **f.** iii **g.** i **h.** vi **5.** (1, 4), I **7.** (1, −2), IV **9.** (−5, −2), III **11.** I **13.** IV **15.** III **17.** The *x*-axis **21.** The association between *x* and *y* is positive.

23. The association between *x* and *y* is negative.

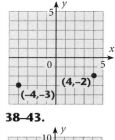

25. $\begin{bmatrix} -4 & 1\frac{3}{4} \\ 4.5 & -12.5 \end{bmatrix}$

27. $\begin{bmatrix} -3 & \frac{3}{2} \\ 43.8 & -45 \end{bmatrix}$

29. 35 km **31.** −3 **33.** *B* **35.** *D*

36–37.

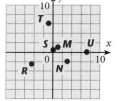

38–43.

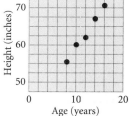

45. IV **47.** II **49.** II **51.** Sometimes: (−1, 1) is in quadrant II; (1, −1) is in quadrant IV. **53.** Positive.

1-2 Part C Self-Assessment

1. None **2.** Positive **3.** Positive **4.** Possible answer:

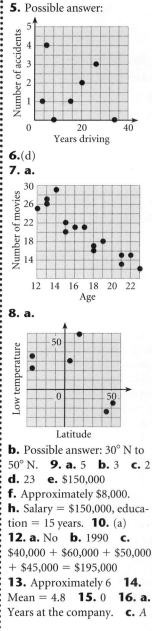

5. Possible answer:

6. (d)
7. a.

b. Possible answer: 30° N to 50° N. **9. a.** 5 **b.** 3 **c.** 2 **d.** 23 **e.** $150,000 **f.** Approximately $8,000. **h.** Salary = $150,000, education = 15 years. **10.** (a) **12. a.** No **b.** 1990 **c.** $40,000 + $60,000 + $50,000 + $45,000 = $195,000 **13.** Approximately 6 **14.** Mean = 4.8 **15.** 0 **16. a.** Years at the company. **c.** *A*

1-3 Part A Try It

a. $\frac{5}{300} = \frac{1}{60} \approx 0.0167 = 1.67\%$

1-3 Part A Exercises

1. All but (c) because it is negative, (e) and (j) because they are greater than 1, and (k) because it is greater than 100%.

2. 0, 0.95%, $\frac{2}{3}$, 0.68, 70%, $\frac{9}{12}$, $\frac{7}{7}$ **3.** Heads up = $\frac{31}{50}$ = 0.62; Tails up = $\frac{19}{50}$ = 0.38; Either = 1.00 **4.** $\frac{4}{12} = \frac{1}{3} \approx$ 0.33 **5.** Choose yellow = $\frac{13}{25}$ = 0.52; Not choose yellow = 0.48 **7.** 0 **9. a.** ii **b.** iii **c.** ii **d.** i **e.** i **f.** ii **g.** iii **11.** $\frac{1}{2}$; The number of black squares equals the number of red squares. **13.** (b), (c), (e) **15.** 70.59% = 0.7059 **17.** Heads up = $\frac{76}{100}$ = 0.76; Tails up = $1 - 0.76$ = 0.24; Either = $0.76 + 0.24$ = 1.00. **19.** 0; 1

1-3 Part B Try It
a. $\frac{1}{5}$ = 0.2 **b.** $\frac{1}{16}$ = 0.0625 **c.** (2)(3)(4) = 24 **d.** (Number of students)!

1-3 Part B Exercises
1. (2)(5)(3) = 30 **3. a.** 5040 **b.** 479,001,600 **c.** Possible answer: 69! **4.** $\frac{5}{13} \approx 0.3846$ **5.** 10! = $10 \cdot 9!$ = (10)(362,880) = 3,628,800 **6.** 5! = 120 **7. a.** Outcomes: gray, green; Sample space: {gray, green} **b.** $\frac{1}{3} \approx$ 0.33 **c.** $\frac{2}{3} \approx 0.67$ **d.** 0 **8.** 24 **9. a.** $\frac{100}{365} \approx 0.274$ **b.** 0 **10. a.** $\frac{1}{4}$ = 0.25 **b.** 10 **c.** Possible answer: It is possible but very unlikely. **13. a.** 2300; 89 **b.** 0.039 **c.** Yes **d.** No **17.** F **19.** C **21.** $\frac{1}{3} \approx 33\%$ **23.** 120 **25.** HH, HT, TH, TT **27.** 30 **29.** $\frac{3}{12}$ = 0.25

1-3 Part C Self-Assessment
1. $\frac{0}{1}$, 0.21%, 9%, $\frac{7}{39}$, $\frac{2}{11}$, $\frac{3}{16}$, 0.1895, 1.0 **2.** (d) **3. a.** 5; $\frac{5}{26} \approx 0.1923$ **b.** 8; $\frac{8}{26} \approx$ 0.3077 **c.** 4; $\frac{4}{26} \approx 0.1538$ **4.** $5 + 4 + 3 + 2 + 1$ = 15; $4! = 4 \cdot 3 \cdot 2 \cdot 1$ = 24; 4! is greater **5.** (c) **6. a.** $\frac{1}{2}$ = 0.5 **b.** $\frac{1}{6} \approx 0.167$ **c.** $\frac{5}{6} \approx$ 0.833 **d.** $\frac{2}{3} \approx 0.667$ **e.** 0 **7. a.** Left, right, forward, backward **b.** $\frac{1}{4}$ = 0.25 **c.** $\frac{3}{4}$ = 0.75 **8. a.** 25% **b.** Probability not happening $= 1 -$ probability happening

11. 8 **12. a.** $\frac{1}{48} \approx 0.021$ **b.** $\frac{1}{48} \approx 0.021$ **c.** $\frac{4}{48} \approx$ 0.083 **d.** $\frac{24}{48}$ = 0.50 **e.** $\frac{12}{48}$ = 0.25 **f.** 0 **g.** $\frac{12}{48}$ = 0.25 **h.** $\frac{12}{48}$ = 0.25 **13.** Incorrect **14.** Correct **15.** Incorrect; There are more combinations of dice that add up to 7 than any other number. **16.** Correct **17. a.** Blue = 62; Pink = 42; Yellow = 100; Green = 26 **b.** Blue = $\frac{62}{230} \approx 0.2696$; Pink = $\frac{42}{230} \approx$ 0.1826; Yellow = $\frac{100}{230} \approx$ 0.4348; Green = $\frac{26}{230} \approx$ 0.1130 **c.** Blue = 135; Pink = 91; Yellow = 217; Green = 57 **d.** None **e.** No

Chapter 1 Review
1. T **2.** T **3.** F **4.** (c) **5.** (a) **6.** (a) **7.** (a) **8.** 45 million acres; The bar graph gives the acreage. **9.** $\begin{bmatrix} 11 & -1 & 10 \\ -11 & 0 & 4 \\ -4 & -10 & -22 \end{bmatrix}$ **10.** $\begin{bmatrix} 7 & 13 & -20 \\ -3 & -12 & -20 \\ -36 & 30 & -4 \end{bmatrix}$ **11.** $\begin{bmatrix} -18 & -12 & 10 \\ 14 & 12 & 16 \\ 40 & -20 & 26 \end{bmatrix}$ **12.** Mean = 47.75°; Median = 47.5°; Mode = 55° **13.** Positive **14.** Possible answer: approximately $120. **15.** $A = (-3, 4)$; $B = (2, 5)$; $C = (5, 3)$; $D = (4, -3)$; $E = (2, -5)$; $F = (-3, -2)$ **16.** F **17.** A **18.** III **19.** IV; A positive first coordinate moves right and a negative second coordinate moves down. **20.** (b) **21. a.** Blue: $\frac{8}{32}$ = 0.25; Yellow: $\frac{9}{32}$ = 0.28125; Red: $\frac{15}{32}$ = 0.46875 **b.** Possible answer: Multiply each of the above probabilities by 100. **22. a.** The distance between the two places is growing. **b.** Japan **c.** Possible answer: Yes. If the distance between two places shrank by

3 cm one year and 4 cm the next year, the total distance moved would be 3 cm + 4 cm = 7 cm.

CHAPTER 2

2-1 Part A Try It
a. Constant **b.** Constant **c.** Variable **d.** Possible answer: 180 to 330 pounds **e.** Possible answer: 15 to 35 students

2-1 Part A Exercises
1. Constant **3.** Variable **5.** T **7. a.** No **b.** Constant **c.** Yes **d.** Variable **e.** Yes **9.** Possible answers: feet, meters **11.** Possible answer: 0 to 1 gallon **13.** Possible answer: 2 to 8 lanes **15.** No **19.** 5, 8; Increasing **21.** Constant **23.** Constant **25.** Variable **31. a.** 6,215 miles **b.** $\approx$ 69.1 miles **c.** Multiply the latitude by 69.1 miles/degree. **d.** Constant

2-1 Part B Try It
a. Number of tickets sold, amount of money raised; Directly related; As more tickets are sold, more money is raised **b.** Number of people sharing the frittata, size of one slice; Inversely related; As the number of people increases, the size of one slice decreases

2-1 Part B Exercises
1. a. Decreases **b.** Increases **c.** Increases **3.** Directly **5.** Number of people ahead of you, how long you'll have to wait; Directly related; As the number of people increases, the length of time increases. **7.** Age of a used car, price the owner can get for it; Inversely related; As the age increases, the price decreases **8.** Area of the face of a cube, volume of the cube; Directly related; As the area increases, the volume increases

2-1 Part C Try It
a. Container A corresponds to graph F; Container B corresponds to graph D; Container C corresponds to graph E. **b.** All graphs

9. a. Multiply the number of mailboxes she passes by $\frac{1}{5}$ of a mile per mailbox. **b.** Number of mailboxes, how far she has jogged; They are directly related, because the more she jogs, the more mailboxes she passes. **11. a.** The volume increases. **b.** The volume increases. **c.** The volume increases. **d.** The volume may increase, decrease, or stay the same. **13.** As the value of x increases, the value of y increases.

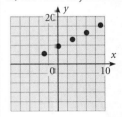

15. 24 ants **17.** Possible answer: The number of pages read in one hour **19.** Possible answer: The number of days before Thanksgiving **21.** Age of car, insurance premium; Inversely related; Possible answer: As the age increases, the premium decreases. **23.** Cost of life insurance, age of the insured person; Directly related; As the age increases, the cost increases. **25.** Average per-capita income of a country, infant mortality rate; Inversely related; As the average income increases, the infant mortality rate decreases. **27.** Container A has twice the capacity of container B. **29. a.** Ivonne rides a bike **b.** Nicole rides a bike **c.** Daniel rides a bike

2-1 Part C Exercises

1. a. Each dot represents the height of the plant at a certain time. **b.** It would be between the dots for day 3 and day 4. **c.** The relationship is direct.
2. a. Container A **b.**

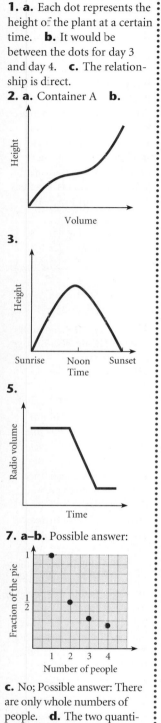

3.

5.

7. a–b. Possible answer:

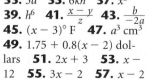

c. No; Possible answer: There are only whole numbers of people. **d.** The two quantities are inversely related because there is a negative association. **11.** Inversely related **13.** Neither; y stays constant as x varies **15.** No association **17.** 0.6 **19.** Neither **21.** Inversely related

2-1 Part D Self-Assessment

1. Variable **2.** Constant
3. Constant **4.** Variable
5. The width of the refrigerator is constant **6.** The earth is farthest from the sun in June, gets closer in September, farther in December, closer in March, and back to farthest in June. **7. a.** How many hours Erin worked in the week **b.** Directly **c.** The amount she got paid also increased by a factor of $2\frac{1}{2}$. **8.** (b) **9.** $\frac{5}{6}$
10. a. i. From time A to time B **ii.** From time C to time D **iii.** From time B to time C **b.** The top faucet
11. a. Fairbanks, U.S.A.; Quito, Ecuador; Fairbanks, U.S.A.; Quito, Ecuador
b. Rome, Italy **12. a.** The area increases. **b.** Directly related. **c.** The area may increase, decrease, or stay the same. **13.** (c) **14. a.** 6:00 a.m. Texas time **b.** 2:30 p.m. Swiss time **15. a.** Her speed is increasing. **b.** Her speed is constant. **c.** Her speed is decreasing and then she stops. **d.** From 40 to 60 minutes

2-2 Part A Try It
a. $3ppp$ **b.** $0.5y^5$ **c.** $\frac{2}{m}$

2-2 Part A Exercises
1. a. $\cdot\,2$ **b.** 88, 3 **c.** 88, n
3. $7a$ **5.** $\frac{x}{3}$ **7.** $\frac{5}{2b}$ **9.** $\frac{3y}{2}$
11. $\frac{a+b}{c}$ **13.** $2www$
15. (c) **17.** (e) **19.** (a)
21. (f) **23.** $10a+b$
25. $30-d$ m **27.** $500-3x$ sheets
29.

31.

33. $5d$ **35.** $6kn$ **37.** x^2
39. h^6 **41.** $\frac{x-y}{z}$ **43.** $\frac{b}{-2a}$
45. $(x-3)°$ F **47.** a^3 cm^3
49. $1.75+0.8(x-2)$ dollars **51.** $2x+3$ **53.** $x-12$ **55.** $3x-2$ **57.** $x-2$

59. $\frac{7x}{2}$ **61.** $540t$ mi
63. $42m+30f+7c$ lb
65. a. The number of words Evan has typed t minutes after he started typing. **b.** The number of words Gina has typed t minutes after she started typing. **c.** The number of words Gina has typed t minutes after Evan started typing. **d.** The difference in the number of words Evan and Gina have typed in t minutes. **e.** Yes; $29\frac{3}{8}$ min
f–g.

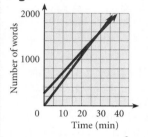

h. Yes; When time is $29\frac{3}{8}$ minutes.
67. a. Let h, q, d, n, and p represent the number of half dollars, quarters, dimes, nickels, and pennies, respectively. $50h+25q+10d+5n+p$ gives the total value in cents.
b. $\frac{50h+25q+10d+5n+p}{100}$

2-2 Part B Try It
a. $42.85 **b.** $\frac{7}{3}$, 2, $\frac{5}{3}$, $1.2\overline{3}$

2-2 Part B Exercises
1. a. 8 **b.** 9 **6.** 100 **7.** 6.9 **8.** $\frac{5}{2}$ or 2.5
10. Value of the expression
12. $\frac{k}{t}$ **13.** $0.15x$; $1.15x$
15. 10, 7, 4, -0.5, -2
17. -2, 1, 2, 1, -2
19. a. $80c$ dollars **b.** $1.6c$ dollars **c.** $64c$ dollars
d. 50 bottles **e.** $0.8c$ dollars
21. (b); The shaded portion is one-fifth of the circle graph. **23.** 18; -24
25. -18; -18 **27.** 38.35
29. 80 **31.** $28-st$ mi; There are 22 miles left.
33. 5, -4, -3.91, 0, 5
35. 512, 343, 216, 125, 64
37. -2, -1, 1, 2, 3
39. 19.5 m^2

41. 180 pounds of meat
43. Depends on n **45. a.** Let w represent the weight of gold leaves in ounces and let t represent the thickness of the gold leaves in inches. $t=\frac{w}{150}$
b. 80 books; $\frac{1}{150}$ of an inch

2-2 Part C Self-Assessment
1. $2a+7b$ lb **2.** (e)
3. $4(x-y)$ **4.** $\frac{z}{y-z}$
5. $13n^2$ **6.** b^3 **7.** $\frac{3}{2y}$
8. $\frac{x+y}{z}$ **9.** $(p-q)(r+s)$
10. $(x+y)^3$ **11.** $1000x$ m
12. $1000x+y$ m **13.** $x+\frac{y}{1000}$ km **14.** $x+\frac{y}{60}$ hr
15. $60a+b$ sec **16.** $36p+q$ in.**17.** $m+\frac{n}{1000}$ kg
18. $\frac{z}{5}$ **19.** $3y$ **20.** $a+3$
21. $n-7$ **22.** $1.2p$
23. w^2 **24.** $\frac{a}{b}$ **25.** $\frac{bh}{2}$
26. x^2 **27.** $(x+y)^3$
28. $\frac{72}{x}$ cm **29.** $\frac{17.5}{d}$ yd
30. a. $y-7$ cm **b.** $r-17$ m
31. -2, -5, -7, -9, -12
32. 2, 5, 7, 9, 12 **33.** 75, 12, 0, 12, 75 **34. a.** 148.8 beats per minute **b.** Over
35. a. $\frac{100s}{3}$ g **b.** $\frac{3w}{100}$ cm
c. 1500 g **d.** 30 cm
e.

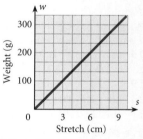

36. a. 720; 1080 **b.** Multiply the number of sides minus 2 by 180. **c.** $180(n-2)°$
d. Yes

2-3 Part A Try It
a. 55 **b.** 21
c.

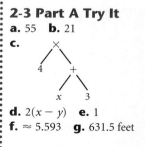

d. $2(x-y)$ **e.** 1
f. ≈ 5.593 **g.** 631.5 feet

2-3 Part A Exercises
1. a. 20 **b.** 23 **c.** −7
3. a. 12 **b.** $\frac{2}{3}$ **c.** 6
5. $-\frac{7}{3}$ **7.** −4 **9.** (d)
11. $9 + 6 \div (3 - 1) = 12$
13. $10 - (2 + 4 \div 2) = 6$
15. $6 - 2x$ **17.** 20
19. 626.5 feet; It is higher.
21. 9 **23.** 12 **27.** $5x + 3y$
29. $(a + b)^2$ **31.** $(3 + z)x$
33.

35.

37. a. 30 **b.** 30 **c.** −30 **d.** −30 **e.** (a) and (b) have the same value; (c) and (d) have the same value. **39.** 1
41. 144 **43.** 21 **45.** 43
47. −3 **49.** 11 **51.** $8 \times (6 - 3) + 1 \times 4 = 28$
53. $(10 \div 2 - 1) \times (3 + 4) = 28$ **55. a.** $\frac{7}{5}$ **b.** $\frac{1}{5}$ **c.** 0.64
57. $\frac{a+7}{b}$ **59.** $\frac{y}{3} \cdot x$
61. $17 - xy$ **63. a.** $350 - 32x$ dollars **b.** $62 **c.** $300 - 21(x - 2)$ dollars; $153
d. $(350 - 32x) - [300 - 21(x - 2)]$ dollars; Sue has $69 more than Jeff. **e.** Jeff
65. a. 16, assuming all blanks are allowed **b.** 32 (or 33 if **a** was 15)

2-3 Part B Try It
a. $-5a - 10b$ **b.** $-6y + 3z - 3$ **c.** $x + \frac{6}{5}$

2-3 Part B Exercises
1. a. $7(10 + 6)$ **b.** $(7 \cdot 10) + (7 \cdot 6)$ **3.** −26 **5.** $-2m + 3$ **7.** $2 + 6x$ **9.** $-10a + 15b - 20c$ **11. a.** 7.5 and 7.5 **b.** −5 and −5 **c.** Yes **d.** $\frac{1}{2}$ **e.** $-\frac{1}{5}$ **f.** Multiplying by 1 divided by the given number. **13.** $21 + 1.26a$; 67.62 in. **15.** Possible answer: $45 \times 98 = 45 \times (100 - 2) = 45 \times 100 - 45 \times 2 = 4500 - 90 = 4410$
17. $\frac{1}{5}(20 - 5s + 100)$; $24 - s$
19. Possible answer: $\frac{h}{2}(b_1 + 2b_2 + 2b_3 + 2b_4 + b_5)$; Yes

21. No; Positive; Negative; Yes **23.** 360; 248; No
25. 2 **27.** −1 **31.** −48
33. −5.4 **35.** $-\frac{2}{3}$
37. $3a + 3b$ **39.** $5n^2 - 3n$
41. $21 + 2w$ **43.** $\frac{x}{5} + 1$
45. $3F - \frac{3}{4}$ **47.** Possible answer: Sum up the price of 4 burgers and 4 sodas, or add the price of one burger and one soda and then multiply by 4; Distributive property of multiplication over addition
49. Not equivalent
51. Equivalent **53.** Not equivalent **55.** Equivalent
59.

2-3 Part C Try It
a. 2; 4 **b.** 4; 2, −3, 1 **c.** $2(x^2 - x + 2)$ **d.** 21 **e.** $3z^2 + 3z$

2-3 Part C Exercises
1. a. $-2x^2$ and $3x^2$ **b.** x^2 **c.** Yes
3. a.

b.

c.

5. $-x^2 + 4$ **7.** Not equivalent **9.** Not equivalent
11. Equivalent **13.** 2; 2
15. 1; There are no coefficients **17.** $3x + y + 11$
19. Not equivalent

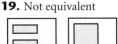

21. Sometimes positive
25. $4 + x$ **27.** $-2.9y + 3.1$ **29.** $-\frac{11}{3}k - 4$
31.

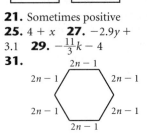

33. Possible answer:

35. Sector A represents about 5.3% of the circle. Sector B represents about 52% of the circle. Sector C represents about 3.7% of the circle. Sector D represents about 39% of the circle.
37. $\begin{bmatrix} -1 & 0 \\ 1 & 0 \\ 0 & 0 \end{bmatrix}$
39. Directly related;

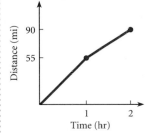

43. Not equivalent
45. Equivalent
47. Equivalent **49.** Not equivalent **51.** Not equivalent **53.** $0.87; $3.00
55. 2; 4, 1 **57.** 1; 4 **59.** 2; −1 **61.** $x + 2y + 12$ **63.** 0
65. $7y + 3$ **67. a.** 3 **b.** No
69. a. Possible answer: $x^2(4 + 5)$ **b.** $9x^2$; Fewest terms
71. a. Possible answer: $a(-1 + 6 - 11)$ **b.** $-6a$; Fewest terms

2-3 Part D Self-Assessment
1. $7q$ **2.** Simplified
3. $2r + s$ **4.** $3q + 5k$ **5.** q
6. $2a - c$ **7.** $2t$ **8.** $9y - z$
9. $2x$ **10.** Always
11. Sometimes **12.** Always
13. Always **14.** Sometimes
15. Sometimes **16.** $-6x - 6$ **17.** $27x - 27$ **18.** −1
19. 0 **20.** $16x + 14$
21. $x^2 + 2xy + 3y$
22. $1.08x + 0.02$ **23.** $3x^2$
24. (a) **26.** $180° - \frac{4}{3}m\angle B$
27. a. If x represents the time on her first lap, her average time is $\frac{3x + 2.3}{3}$ seconds.
b. ≈ 2.76 minutes per lap.
29. (d)

30. a. Let x represent the number of women getting a haircut on a given day. Then $\frac{85}{3}x$ dollars is the total amount collected. **b.** $23x$ and $16\left(\frac{x}{3}\right)$ **31. a.** $12x$
b. $15(x - 8)$ **c.** $27x - 120$
d. $120 - 3x$; The difference in the number of pounds of apples that Jena and Mark have each picked x minutes into the contest **e.** 60 lb
f. $31.2x$; $39(x - 8)$
g. $70.2x - 312$ **h.** Mark

Chapter 2 Review
1. (d) **2.** (b) **3.** (c)
4. (a) **5.** (f) **6.** (e) **7.** (c)
8. (b) **9.** Constant; Possible answer: The distance does not change. **10.** Variable; Possible answer: It depends on how fast I walk.
11. Variable; Possible answer: It depends along what latitude you measure.
12. $3x + 4$ **13.** $3(x + 4)$
14. −4, −8, −10, −14
15. 4, 8, 10, 14 **16.** 75, 3, 3, 75 **17.** Inversely; The more minutes a cake has been baking, the less time left before it can be served.
18. Directly; The more questions on a quiz, the more time you will need to take the quiz. **19.** (d) **20.** $12 + (6 \div 3) - 8 = 6$ **21.** $10 - (5 + 1) \div 2 = 7$ **22.** $4x - 3$ **23.** $x - 4$ **24.** $-x + 2$
25. 3 **26.** $4x - 29$ **27.** 1
28. Possible answer: For one thing, the fact that it is the 66th Academy Awards is being treated as if it meant that there were a total of 66 nominations. **29. a.** $\frac{1}{2}b^2$ **b.** $2(x - 5)$ **c.** $21 + 7n - n^2$ **30.** $C = 1000c$

CHAPTER 3

3-1 Part A Try It
a. Let n represent the number of triangles. $p = 6 + 4n$; 86 **b.** $y = 9x$; 900 **c.** $y = -10x$; −1000 **d.** $y = 3x + 1$; 301 **e.** $y = -x^2$; −10,000

3-1 Part A Exercises

1. a. y is 6 times x **b.** $y = 6x$ **3.** 2.5, 5, 25, $\frac{x}{2}$; $y = \frac{x}{2}$
5. a. 14, 17, 32 **b.** $y = 3x + 2$ **7.** $y = x^2 + 5$; 10,005 **9.** y is 2 more than 4 times x **11. a.** Let g represent the total number of grocery bags and t represent the number of trees, then $g = 700t$. **b.** 70,000 bags
13. $3x^2 - 3x + 1$; 271
15. $-\frac{12}{5}$ **19.** 3, 8, 18, $x - 2$; $y = x - 2$ **21.** $-25, -50, -100, -5x$; $y = -5x$ **23.** 15, 24, 99, $x^2 - 1$; $y = x^2 - 1$
25. $A = 5B$ **27.** y is 6 more than -3 times x **29. a.** $\frac{16}{3}$, $\frac{25}{3}$, $\frac{100}{3}$ **b.** y is one third the square of x **c.** $y = \frac{x^2}{3}$
33. 731, 1002, $n^3 + 2$

3-1 Part B Try It

a.

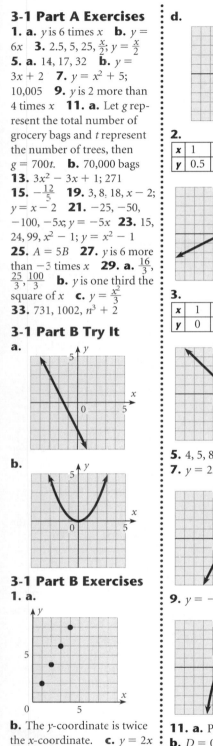

b.

3-1 Part B Exercises

1. a.

b. The y-coordinate is twice the x-coordinate. **c.** $y = 2x$

d.

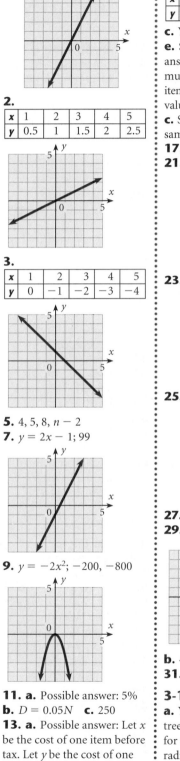

2.

x	1	2	3	4	5
y	0.5	1	1.5	2	2.5

3.

x	1	2	3	4	5
y	0	−1	−2	−3	−4

5. 4, 5, 8, $n - 2$
7. $y = 2x - 1$; 99

9. $y = -2x^2$; $-200, -800$

11. a. Possible answer: 5%
b. $D = 0.05N$ **c.** 250
13. a. Possible answer: Let x be the cost of one item before tax. Let y be the cost of one item sent immediately.

b. Possible answer:

x	10	20	30	40
y	25.80	36.60	47.40	58.20

c. Yes **d.** $y = 1.08x + 15$
e. \$79.75 **f.** Possible answer: For each order; You must pay \$15 more for each item you order. **15. a.** Same value **b.** Not the same value **c.** Same value **d.** Not the same value **e.** Same value
17. 88 **19.** 1
21.

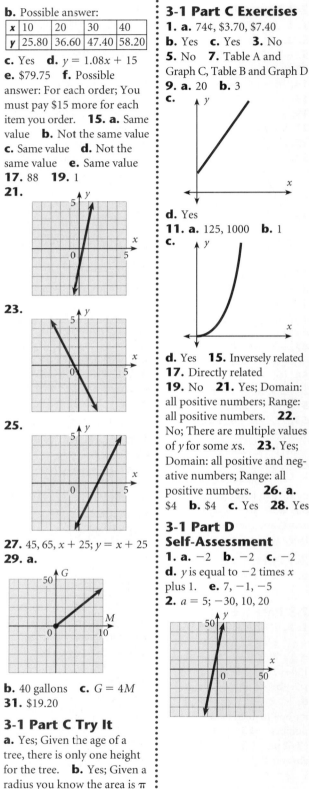

23.

25.

27. 45, 65, $x + 25$; $y = x + 25$
29. a.

b. 40 gallons **c.** $G = 4M$
31. \$19.20

3-1 Part C Try It

a. Yes; Given the age of a tree, there is only one height for the tree. **b.** Yes; Given a radius you know the area is π times the radius squared.

3-1 Part C Exercises

1. a. 74¢, \$3.70, \$7.40
b. Yes **c.** Yes **3.** No
5. No **7.** Table A and Graph C, Table B and Graph D
9. a. 20 **b.** 3
c.

d. Yes
11. a. 125, 1000 **b.** 1
c.

d. Yes **15.** Inversely related
17. Directly related
19. No **21.** Yes; Domain: all positive numbers; Range: all positive numbers. **22.** No; There are multiple values of y for some xs. **23.** Yes; Domain: all positive and negative numbers; Range: all positive numbers. **26. a.** \$4 **b.** \$4 **c.** Yes **28.** Yes

3-1 Part D Self-Assessment

1. a. -2 **b.** -2 **c.** -2
d. y is equal to -2 times x plus 1. **e.** 7, -1, -5
2. $a = 5$; $-30, 10, 20$

3. $a = 5$; 500, 0

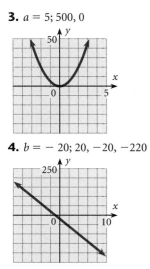

4. $b = -20$; 20, -20, -220

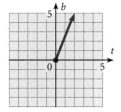

5. (a) **6.** 7, 10, 13, $3x - 2$; $y = 3x - 2$; 28 **7.** 36 people **8.** $3x + 10$ **9.** $3a + b + 6$ **10.** Let b represent the millions of bottles discarded and t represent the number of hours. Then $b = 2.5t$.

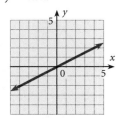

11. Let x represent the normal amount of water and y represent the amount you use with a low-flow aerator. Then $y = 0.5x$.

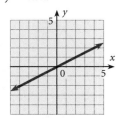

12. "...multiplying x by 6."
13. "...multiplying x by -5."
14. "...multiplying x by 3 and then adding 8."
15. "...multiplying x by 25 and then adding 50."

16.

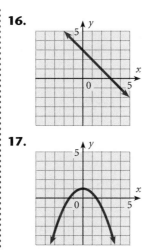

17.

18. a. Negative **b.** Inversely related **c.** No **19.** Yes; There is only one value of y for each given value of x.
20. a. Let x represent the number of households that have one phone and y represent the number of households that have five or more phones.
b. Possible answer:

x	4	20	100	200	400
y	1	5	25	50	100

c. $y = \frac{x}{4}$ **d.** 62,500
21. $S = h(22 - h)$; $S = 22h - h^2$ **22. a.** 800D
b. 1800; 2600 **c.** Let n represent the number of days and b represent the number of buns to be ordered, then $b = 800n + 1000$. **d.** 12,200 buns **23. a.** Yes **b.** Yes

3-2 Part A Try It
a. This is the equation of a linear function because it is in the form $y = ax + b$ where $a = 35$ and $b = 0$. **b.** This does not represent a linear function because it has a term with x^2 in it. **c.** This represents a linear function because it can be written as $y = -22x + (-20)$ which is in the form $y = ax + b$ where $a = -22$ and $b = -20$.
d. This does not represent a linear function because it has x in a denominator.

e. Yes; When diameter changes in equal amounts, price changes in equal amounts.

3-2 Part A Exercises
1. a. Yes; $a = 7, b = 1$ **b.** No
c. Yes; $a = -12, b = -9$
d. No **e.** Yes; $a = -1, b = 0$
3. a. Yes **b.** Yes **c.** Yes
5. a. Yes **b.** $y = 4x$; y is proportional to x.
c.

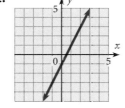

6. a. No **b.** No answer
7. a. Yes **b.** $y = 2x - 1$; y is not proportional to x.
c.

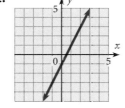

9. Linear; Not proportional
11. Not linear; Not proportional **17. a.** 3 **b.** Let x represent the number of times the larger gear has turned around and y represent the number of times the smaller gear has turned around, then $y = 3x$.
19. Possible answer:

x	0	1	2	3	4
y	0	23	46	69	92

$y = 23x$, x = weight (oz.), y = weight (gm);

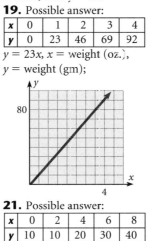

21. Possible answer:

x	0	2	4	6	8
y	10	10	20	30	40

The value of y is 5 times the value of x; $y = 5x$

23. $-35, -5, 25, 55, 85$; 25
25. 25, 27.5, 30, 32.5, 35; 280
26. c.

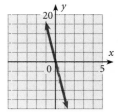

27. a. No **b.** No answer
c. No graph **29. a.** No
b. No answer **c.** No graph
31. It is a linear function and y is proportional to x because it is in the form $y = ax + b$ where $a = -9$ and $b = 0$.
33. It does not represent a linear function because x^3 is in a term. **35.** Let x represent the number of videos rented and y represent the number of laser disks rented, then $y = \frac{2}{5}x$; Yes; Yes
37. Marla; $y = 5$ is a linear function of the form $y = ax + b$, where $a = 0$ and $b = 5$.

3-2 Part B Try It
a. 1, 3, and 5 show the same function. Possible answer: The ordered pairs $(-1, -2)$ and $(1, 4)$ are in table **3**, are points of graph **5**, and satisfy equation **1**. Similar reasoning tells us that **2**, **4**, and **6** show the same function.

3-2 Part B Exercises
1. a. No **b.** No **c.** Yes
3.

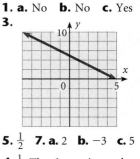

5. $\frac{1}{2}$ **7. a.** 2 **b.** -3 **c.** 5

d. $\frac{1}{2}$ The change in y-value corresponds to the value that multiplies x. **9.** $y = 3x^2 + 4x$; It does not represent a linear function.

11. $y = 12 + 0.2x$;

x	1	10	20	40
y	12.20	14.00	16.00	20.00

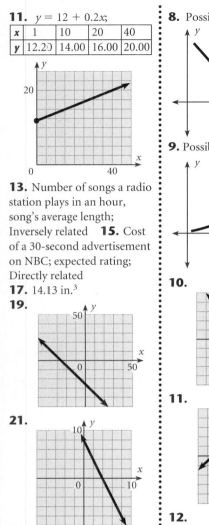

13. Number of songs a radio station plays in an hour, song's average length; Inversely related **15.** Cost of a 30-second advertisement on NBC; expected rating; Directly related

17. 14.13 in.^{3}

19.

21.

23. 1, 4, and 5 show the same function. 2, 3, and 6 show the same function. **25.** Yes **27.** $y = 2x + 1$

3-2 Part C
Self-Assessment

1. The relationship is not linear. **2.** The relationship is linear; $y = -\frac{1}{2}x + 85$
3. $\frac{1}{2}$ **4.** Let x represent the amount you get after taxes, and y represent the amount the taxman gets, then $y = 19x$
5. (b) **6.** 1, 4, and 5 show the same linear function. 2, 3, and 6 show the same linear function. **7.** Possible answer: If the equation can be written in the form $y = ax + b$

8. Possible answer:

9. Possible answer:

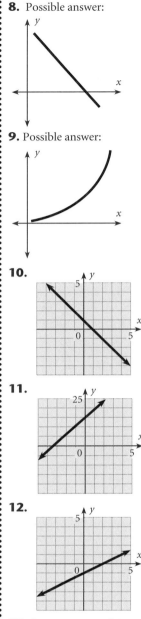

10.

11.

12.

13. Let x represent the number of copies and y represent the total cost; Then $y = 0.05x + 1$; y is dependent on x. **14.** Let x represent the number of measures in a musical piece in 4/4 time and let y represent the total number of beats in the musical piece; Then $y = 4x$; y is dependent on x. **15.** Let x represent the number of seniors and y represent the number of freshmen; Then $y = \frac{1}{2}x$; y is dependent on x.

16. Let x represent the number of teachers and y represent the number of students; Then $y = 25x$; y is dependent on x. **17.** Let x represent the number of skateboards sold and y represent the number of in-line skates sold; Then $y = 2x$; y is dependent on x. **18.** Let x represent the number of Americans and y represent the number of Americans who have appeared on television; Then $y = \frac{1}{4}x$; y is dependent on x.
19. a. Let x represent the number of bottles sold and y represent the amount in dollars they got from the bottles they sold. **b.** $y = 0.5x - 20$
c. 40 bottles **d.** 90 bottles
20. a. Let n represent the number of hours, and m represent the number of polyester suits that could be made from the discarded bottles.
b. $m = \frac{1,250,000}{13}n$
c.

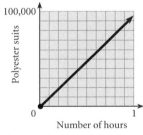

21. a. The domain and range include all numbers from 0 to 1. **b.** Yes
c.

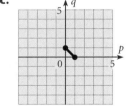

22. No

Chapter 3 Review
1. (b)
2. Possible answer:

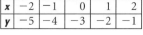

x	-2	-1	0	1	2
y	-5	-4	-3	-2	-1

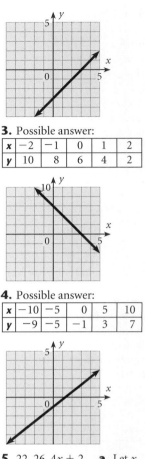

3. Possible answer:

x	-2	-1	0	1	2
y	10	8	6	4	2

4. Possible answer:

x	-10	-5	0	5	10
y	-9	-5	-1	3	7

5. 22, 26, $4x + 2$ **a.** Let x represent the figure number and y represent the perimeter. y is the dependent variable and x is the independent variable. **b.** $y = 4x + 2$
c.

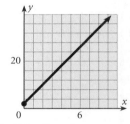

d. 402 **6. a.** Let x represent the number of black and white copies and y represent the total cost of black and white copies; Then $y = 0.035x$.
b. Let m represent the number of color copies and n represent the total cost of color copies; Then $n = 0.99m + 0.51$. **c.** Yes; It is linear.

7. Yes; When x changes by equal amounts, y changes by equal amounts.   **8.** No; When x changes by equal amounts, y does not change by equal amounts.   **9. a.** Let x represent the number of hours and y represent the cost of parking.
b.

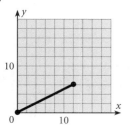

c. $y = 0.5x$ **d.** Yes; The two variables are related by $y = ax$ where $a = 0.5$.   **10.** 1, 3, and 6 represent the same function. Possible answer: The ordered pairs $(-1, 2)$ and $(1, -2)$ are in table **3,** are points in graph **6,** and satisfy equation **1.** Similar reasoning shows that **2, 4,** and **5** represent the same function.
11. Let c represent the cost (in $) and t the time (in minutes).   From home: $c = 0.20t + 0.20$ From hotel: $c = 0.95t + 1.50$ It is always cheaper to call from home.

CHAPTER 4

4-1 Part A Try It
a. $x = -3$ **b.** $r = 20$
c. $k = -6$ **d.** $y = 7$
e. $x = 64$ **f.** $c = 1$

4-1 Part A Exercises
1. a. 13   **b.** $x = 7$
3. Solutions   **5.** $m = 75$
7. $c = 3$ **9.** $x = 15$
11. a. The total cost
b. $d + 4 = 27$ **c.** $d = 23$
d. $m = 9$; For $m = 9$, $3m = 27$ **13.** $m = 10$
14. $d = 12$ **15.** $k = 2$
17. $x = 15$ **19.** (c)
21. (c)   **23.** 1   **25.** -3

27. $y = 300$; Possible answer: Choose 300 because 5 times 200 is 1000.   **29.** $c = -9$ **31.** $z = 5$ **33.** $f = 2$
35. Possible answer: It would not be a good guess since -10 times 10 is negative and a positive number is desired.   **37.** Possible answer: It would be a good guess because mental math shows that it is a solution of the equation.   **39. a.** $6\frac{1}{2}$ hours   **b.** $\approx 6.7\%$
41. a. Yes; 20% of 44% is 8.8%, which is nearly 9%.
b. Yes.   **c.** Yes

4-1 Part B Try It
a. $x = 2$ **b.** $x = 2.4$

4-1 Part B Exercises
1. a. $x = 6$ **b.** $x = -6$
3. $x = 1$ **5.** $x = 2$
7. $x = -2$

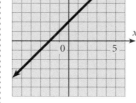

9. a.

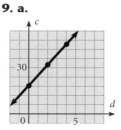

b. $46 = 7d + 18$ **c.** $d = 4$
11. $d = 13$ **13.** Let C represent the circumference and d represent the diameter. $C = \pi d$. By measuring the diameter, Betina will be able to calculate the circumference of the pot.   **15. a.** No   **b.** Yes; the ratio of the new frame is $\frac{4}{5}$ which is the same ratio as the picture.   **17.** (a)
19. Possible answer:

x	-2	-1	0	1	2
y	5	4	3	2	1

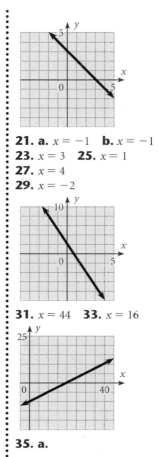

21. a. $x = -1$ **b.** $x = -1$
23. $x = 3$ **25.** $x = 1$
27. $x = 4$
29. $x = -2$

31. $x = 44$ **33.** $x = 16$

35. a.

Number of peppers (p)	Tablespoons of oil (t)
3	2
6	4
9	6
15	10
24	16

b. $t = \frac{2}{3}p$ **c.** $18 = \frac{2}{3}p$; $p = 27$

4-1 Part C Self-Assessment
1. a. $-\frac{1}{2}$ **b.** He should try a larger number because $\frac{1}{2}(x - 1)$ is an increasing expression, that is, as x increases, so does $\frac{1}{2}(x - 1)$.
c. 10   **d.** He should try a larger number because the value of $\frac{1}{2}(x - 1)$ is less than 17 when x is 21.   **e.** $x = 35$
2. $c = -9$ **3.** $f = 6$
4. $w = 10$ **5.** $x = 0$
6. $x = 6$ **7.** $x = 1$

7–10.

8. $x = -1$ **9.** $x = -4$
10. $x = 0$ **11.** (d)
12. Calvin probably covered up the $x - 3$ and thought: 10 divided by 2 is 5, so $x - 3$ must be 5. He should have asked: "What divided by 2 is 10?" He would then get $x - 3$ must be 20.   **13. a.** The amount that goes to the Special Olympics; The amount that goes to the American Cancer Society; The proceeds that will go to the two charities.   **b.** $p = \frac{3}{2}a$
c. $24,906 = \frac{3}{2}a$ **d.** The Special Olympics will receive $16,604 and the American Cancer Society will receive $8,302.   **14.** Possible answer: (d)   **15.** Possible answer: Using guess-and-check, you find that the answer seems to be between 0 and -1 and will involve fractions.   **16.** There are 12 possible combinations.   **17.**
a. $c = 120f$ **b.** $2400 = 120f$
c. $20   **18. a.** $9g$
b. $\frac{9g}{T} \times 100\%$ **c.** If Mary knows the grams of fat, g, then she can find the number of fat-derived calories from the expression $9g$. If she also knows the total calories T, then she can find the percent of fat-derived calories from the expression $\frac{9g}{T} \times 100\%$.

4-2 Part A Try It
a. $x = -4$ **b.** $-2x = 1 + x$

4-2 Part A Exercises
1. a. Add five positive unit tiles   **b.** Add two positive x-tiles   **c.** Add nothing
3. $4 + 2x = -1 - 2x$
4. $-1 = 2 + x$ **5.** $x = 0$

7. a. Let x represent the length of an iguana and y represent the length of its tail, then $y = \frac{2}{3}x$. **b.** 3 feet **9.** $\frac{8}{33}$ **11.** $2(-2x + 3)$ **13.** Possible answer: Add a positive x-tile to each side or add two positive unit tiles to each side. **19. a.** 24, 35 **b.** $y = x^2 - 1$ **c.** $y = 80$ **21. a.** Add three positive x-tiles. **b.** Add six negative unit tiles. **c.** Add two positive x-tiles and three negative unit tiles. **23.** $2x + 3 = -3x - 2$; $x = -1$ **25.** $2x + 3 = -5$; $x = -4$ **27.** $2(2x - 3)$ **29. a.**

Weight of ostrich (lbs)	Weight of egg (lbs)
160	3.2
180	3.6
150	3.0

b. She noticed that the weight of the mother is 50 times the weight of the egg. **c.** 3.44 pounds; If $y = 172$, then $172 = 50x$. $3.44 \cdot 50 = 172$. **31. a.** 10,350 pounds **b.** The amount of grown bamboo per year plus the amount of purchased bamboo per year is 10,950 pounds. **c.** No

4-2 Part B Try It
a. $2x - 4 = 8$; $2x = 12$; $2 \cdot x = 2 \cdot 6$; $x = 6$

4-2 Part B Exercises
1. (b); This is the first step towards getting only x-tiles on the left side: getting rid of the 3 unit tiles by adding 3 red unit tiles. **3.** $1 + 2x = -3$ **5.** $x = 4$ **7.** Whenever you want to remove a tile from one side of the equation box, you can add the additive inverse tile to both sides, and by the additive inverse property you remove both tiles from the one side.

9. Multiply the number of representatives by 520,000. **11. a.** 16 oz; 32 oz; 48 oz; $8n$ oz **b.** Let x represent the number of monkeys and y represent the amount of vegetables in ounces needed to feed them, then $y = 8x$. **c.** Each animal eats 3 oz. of monkey chow in one day. Therefore, each animal eats 21 oz. of monkey chow in one week. There are 16 oz. in one pound, so each animal eats $\frac{21}{16}$ lb of monkey chow in one week. **13.** Let x represent the birthweight and y represent the amount of food consumed in 56 days; Then $y = 86{,}000x$. **15.** 3 **17.** -0.8 **19.** 1.3 **21.** 3 **23.** $\frac{5}{6}$ **25.** $3 + 2x = -3$; Add three negative unit tiles to each side. **27.** $3x = 9$; Divide each side into three equal parts. **29.** $x = 9$ **31.** $x = 1$ **33.** Let x represent the head zookeeper's pay and y represent a zookeeper's pay, then $y = \frac{x}{3}$. **35. a.** $4x$, $2x$, 0, $-2x$, $-4x$ **b.** 0

4-2 Part C Try It
a. $x = -\frac{19}{2}$ **b.** $x = 36$ **c.** 1020 mi/hr

4-2 Part C Exercises
1. a. $6x = 24$ **b.** $x = 4$ **c.** $x = 4$ **3.** $x = -15$ **5.** $s = 5$ **7.** 4 **9.** $x = 1$ **11.** $x = 36$ **13.** $b = 24$ **15.** $w = -4.25$ **17. a.** $\approx 15{,}000{,}000$ **b.** $\dfrac{\text{population of N. Y. City today}}{\text{population of Tokyo today}}$ **c.** $\dfrac{\text{population of Tokyo}}{\text{population of your city}}$ **18.** Let x represent the number of apples and y represent the number of bananas, then $y = \frac{x}{3}$. **19.** Let x represent the number of reproductive years and y represent the

possible number of times the elephant could give birth, then $y = \frac{x}{6}$. **21.** Subtract eight from each side in order to get the variable alone on the left-hand side. **23.** Add 10 to each side in order to get the variable alone on the right-hand side. **25.** $n = -12$ **27.** $c = 2.8$ **29.** $p = 58$ **34. a.** $\frac{1}{5}$ mile per second **b.** $D = \frac{t}{5}$ **c.** $\frac{4}{5}$ mile away **37.** $w = \frac{P - 2l}{2}$ **38.** $\pi \approx 3.1496$ **39. a.** ≈ 431.76 miles per hour **b.** 2:49 p.m. **41.** $5x + 14$ **43.** $-2x - 8$ **45.** Subtract seven from both sides. **47.** Add four to both sides. **49.** $z = 7.2$ **51.** $t = \frac{11}{14}$ **53.** $m = 0.1$ **55.** $b = 32$ **57.** $h = 32.8$ **59.** $x = -120$ **61.** She forgot the sign on the left side. She should have gotten $-3x = 4$. **63.** $t = \frac{I}{pr}$ **65. a.** $g = 15 - \frac{m}{30}$ **b.** $11\frac{2}{3}$ gallons; $8\frac{1}{3}$ gallons; 5 gallons; After driving 450 miles **c.** Domain: any number from 0 to 15; Range: any number from 0 to 450. **67. a.** \$1500 for third place, \$3000 for second place, \$4500 for first place

4-2 Part D Try It
a. $x = 8$ **b.** $m = 0.18$ **c.** $b = -\frac{4}{9}$

4-2 Part D Exercises
1. a. $3(x - 4) + 6 = 15$ $3x - 12 + 6 = 15$; $3x - 6 = 15$ **b.** $3x = 21$; $x = 7$ **c.** Check: $x = 7$; $3(7 - 4) + 6 \stackrel{?}{=} 15$; $3 \cdot 3 + 6 \stackrel{?}{=} 15$; $9 + 6 \stackrel{?}{=} 15$; $15 = 15$; It checks. **3.** $d = -\frac{28}{3}$ **5.** $f = 9$ **7.** Use the distributive property to simplify the equation. Then combine like terms. **9.** Yes **11.** $v = -4$ **13.** $b = -3$ **15.** $x = \frac{15}{8}$ **17.** (d) **19.** $\frac{2}{5}$

21. a. $c = 2b - 50$ **b.** $465 = 2b - 50$ **c.** $465 = 2b - 50$ $515 = 2b$; Add 50 to both sides and simplify. $257.5 = b$; Divide both sides by 2 and simplify. It costs \$257.50. **23. a.** Total cost of granola bars in cents **b.** Total cost of apples in cents **c.** $45x + 32(x + 10) = 859$; 7 granola bars and 17 apples **25.** $t = -5.5$ **27.** $t = -5.3$ **29.** $y = 3$ **31.** $x = \frac{27}{2}$ **33.** $j = 1.615625$ **35.** $y = 1$ **37.** Length = 7; Width = 3 **39.** $h = \frac{13}{6}$ **41.** $c = -\frac{80}{9}$ **43.** $v = -5$ **45. a.** No **b.** They might multiply one dimension by 3. **c.** $\frac{91}{225}$ hectare **47. a.** The number of people she sent postcards **b.** $518 = 29x + 19(22 - x)$ **c.** $x = 10$ **d.** 10 letters and 12 postcards **e.** Yes; No

4-2 Part E Self-Assessment
1. a. $4 - 2x = -1 + 3x$ **b.** Possible answer: Add a positive unit tile to each side or add two positive x-tiles to each side. **c.** $x = 1$ **2. a.** $39 = 13x$ **b.** $3 = x$ **3.** Adding -1.5 to each side is equivalent to subtracting 1.5 from each side. **4.** $n = 9$ **5.** $a = \frac{9}{4}$ **6.** $x = -3.2$ **7.** $c = 10$ **8.** $b = 3$ **9.** $y = \frac{1}{5}$ **10.** (b) **11.** 15; Tuna salad and soda, tuna salad and milk, tuna salad and apple juice, ham and cheese and soda, ham and cheese and milk, ham and cheese and apple juice, avocado and bean sprouts and soda, avocado and bean sprouts and milk, avocado and bean sprouts and apple juice, smoked turkey and soda, smoked turkey and milk, smoked turkey and apple juice, roast beef and soda, roast beef and milk, roast beef and apple juice.

12. (d) **13.** Let x represent the number of crocodiles and y represent the total number of eggs that can be laid; Then $y = 100x$. **14.** Let x represent the number of tortoises and y represent the number of water turtles; Then $y = 24 + x$. **15. a.** x represents the number of posters she sells; $2.50x$ represents the amount she makes from selling the posters; 12.50 represents the amount she pays the zoo; y represents the amount she collects each day.
b. $100 = 2.50x - 12.50$
c. 45 posters **d.** $125
16. $x = 0$ **17. a.** $l = 400w$
b. 0.0075 ounce **c.** 2400 tons **d.** 4,800,000 pounds
e. 3000 pounds

4-3 Part A Try It
a. $g = -5$ **b.** $x = 6$
c. $b = 3$

4-3 Part A Exercises
1. a. $5w + 4 = 14$ **b.** $5w = 10$ **c.** $w = 2$ **3.** She subtracted $6m$ from the right-hand side instead of adding $6m$. **5.** Add $2t$ to both sides or subtract 6.3 from both sides. **7.** Let x represent the total number of businesses and y represent the number of small businesses, then $y = \frac{1}{4}x$. **9.** $x = 12$ **11.** $v = 1$ **13.** $y = 6$ **15.** $x = -28$ **17.** $x = -35$ **19. a.** Yes **b.** Red
c. $\begin{bmatrix} 75 & 135 & 63 & 36 & 30 \\ 30 & 36 & 15 & 48 & 36 \\ 15 & 48 & 24 & 12 & 6 \end{bmatrix}$
21. $x = 1$ **23.** Possible answer: $6c = 6$ and $5 = 7 - 2c$ **25.** ≈ 29 ounces **27.** On the sixth day they will have the same amount of money. $125 **29.** -51.84 **31.** Linear because it can be written in the form $y = ax + b$ **33.** Not linear because it has the term x^2 **35.** $-2x + 2 = 2x - 3$; $x = \frac{5}{4}$

37. Possible answer: Use the distributive property or subtract 10 from both sides.
39. $d = \frac{5}{3}$ **41.** $m = 5$
43. $a = 7.5$ **45.** $r = 14.5$
47. $b = -\frac{1}{2}$ **49. a.** $73 - 1.7h$; $57 + 2.7h$ **b.** $73 - 1.7h = 57 + 2.7h$ **c.** After $\frac{40}{11}$ hours **d.** $\approx 66.8°$ F
51. (b)

4-3 Part B Try It
a. $x + 3 < 5$; $x < 2$

[number line, -4 to 4]

b. Let x represent air temperatures best for pandas. Then $x \le 70$.

[number line, 20 to 100]

c. $3x + 4 \le 18$; $x \le \frac{14}{3}$

[number line, 4 to 6]

d. $4\ell \le 20$; $\ell \le 5$

[number line, 3 to 11]

4-3 Part B Exercises
1. a. (ii) **b.** (i) **c.** (iv) **d.** (iii) **3.** No **5.** $x < -2$

[number line, -6 to 2]

7. $c < -3$

[number line, -6 to 2]

9. F; Boundary point **11.** $d > 4$

[number line, 0 to 8]

13. $x > -1$

[number line, -6 to 2]

15. $n - 4 > 5$; $n > 9$

[number line, 6 to 14]

17. a. $25x + 20 \le 80$ **b.** 2.4 hours **c.** Yes **21.** $x < -2$

[number line, -6 to 2]

23. $d \ge -\frac{7}{12}$

[number line, d, -1 to 0]

25. (b),(c),(d),(e) **27.** $a \ge 30$ **28. a.** The distance Magnolia has hiked **b.** $2.5t \ge 15$ **c.** 6 hours **d.** Yes **29.** The width can be 6 feet or less. **31.** No **33.** No; Possible answer: If a triangle has a 2-in. side and a 1-in. side, then the third side must be smaller than 3 in. **35.** $w \le 740$ **37. a.** (iv) **b.** (ii) **c.** (iii) **d.** (i) **39.** $x > \frac{1}{2}$

[number line, -1 to 3]

41. $n \ge 6$

[number line, 3 to 11]

43. $g < -2.25$

[number line, -2.28 to -2.24]

45. $m > 6$

[number line, 3 to 11]

47. She will need at least 94. **49.** $-3x < -63$; $x > 21$

[number line, 19 to 22]

51. a. Yes; The dimensions determine the area. **b.** Possible answer: 50 ft $\times$ 60 ft **c.** Possible answer: 100 ft $\times$ 20 ft **d.** Possible answer: 40 ft $\times$ 80 ft **53.** The inequality $x + 3 < x + 2$ has no solutions because it implies $3 < 2$, which is never true. The inequality $x + 3 > x + 2$ is always true because $3 > 2$.

4-3 Part C Try It
a. No; $6 + 8 < 15$. **b.** $2 < x \le 5$ **c.** $y \ge -2$ and $y < 0$ **d.** Any length less than 14 ft and greater than 8 ft

4-3 Part C Exercises
1. e **2.** d **3.** d, e **4. a.** $14 > x$, $x + 8 > 6$, $x + 6 > 8$ **b.** $x < 14$, $x > -2$, $x > 2$ **c.** 14 **d.** 2 **5.** Yes **6.** No **7.** Yes **9.** Less than 11 in. and greater than 7 in.

11. $b \ge 4$

[number line, 0 to 8]

13. $s < -\frac{1}{2}$

[number line, -1 to 1]

15. a. The total length (in inches) of the six pieces **b.** 40.5 inches **c.** $6n \le 40.5$ **d.** $n \le 6.75$; 6 **17.** $\frac{1}{3}$; There are three remaining sticks. The 1-in. stick cannot form a triangle with the 2-in. and 3-in. sticks because $1 + 2 = 3$, so a condition of the Triangle Inequality is not met. Only the 4-in. stick, together with the 2-in. and 3-in. sticks, satisfies the conditions of the Triangle Inequality. **19.** $x \ge 2$, $x < 5$ **21.** "15 less than x" can be interpreted as $x - 15$, or in some cases as $15 < x$, but not as $x < 15$. **23.** $x = y$ **25.** $-8 + 3m$ **27.** $43 - 12d$ **29.** $x = 100$ **31.** b **33.** No **35.** Yes **37.** Less than 22 cm and greater than 2 cm **39.** $d > 24$

[number line, 20 to 28]

41. $k \le 8$

[number line, 4 to 12]

43. $p \ge -2$

[number line, -6 to 2]

45. 9.7 **47.** $4 < x < 122$ **49.** 28 **51.** Possible answer: $5 + 17 > 3(x + 3)$ $5 + 3(x + 3) > 17$ $17 + 3(x + 3) > 5$ **53.** (a) or (b)

4-3 Part D Self-Assessment
1. a. $x = 12$ **b.** $x > 12$ **c.** $x \le \frac{5}{6}$ **d.** $x \le \frac{5}{6}$ **2.** They are solving the same basic equation. **3.** (b) and (d) **4.** $x \ge 2.1$

5. $x < \frac{17}{30}$

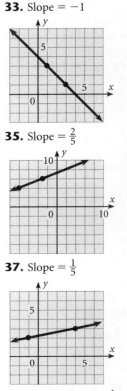

6. $x < \frac{43}{30}$

7. (c) 8. a. Amount spent on compact discs b. Number of tapes he bought c. Total amount spent on compact discs and tapes d. $7(d + 5) + 13.5d < 94$; $d < 2\frac{36}{41}$. He could have purchased 2 discs at most. 9. By the Triangle Inequality, this is not possible because $1 + 4 < 9$, and the sum of the lengths of two sides must be greater than the third. 10. 4 11. 1 cm, 6 cm, 6 cm; 2 cm, 5 cm, 6 cm; 3 cm, 4 cm, 6 cm; 3 cm, 5 cm, 5 cm; 4 cm, 4 cm, 5 cm 12. Let x represent the age of a person, then $x \geq 25$. 13. a. $3b + 75$; $3.5b$ b. $3b + 75 = 3.5b$ c. 150 books; $525

14. Always 15. Never
16. Sometimes
17. Sometimes
18. a. $x < 524 + 325$; $325 < x + 524$; $524 < x + 325$ b. $x < 849$; $-199 < x$; $199 < x$ c. No 19. 516
20. a. 140 km/hr is faster because $1.6 \times 85 < 140$. b. 140 km/hr > 85 mi/hr c. 88 21. a. $14.95b \geq 3.5b + 2565$ b. 225 books c. 272 books
22. a. Florence; Florence b. Nuremberg; Nuremberg

Chapter 4 Review
1. (c) 2. (c)
3. Boundary point 4. (c)
5. $x = 2$; Possible answer: Use mental math because it requires one step. 6. $x = 8$; Possible answer: Use inverse operations because it seems easiest. 7. $x = 4.5$; Possible answer: Use mental math because it requires only two steps. 8. $x = 1$; Possible answer: Use mental math because $4 \cdot 1 = 4$ is obvious.

9. $x = 12$; Possible answer: Use inverse operations because it requires one step.
10. $p = -5.5$; Possible answer: Use mental math
11. (d) 12. $x = -5$
13. $x = 5$ 14. $x = 0$
15. a. $4c$ b. $520 c. $4c = 520$ d. 130 cars e. Possible answer: Yes 16. a. $2x - 3 = -x$ b. $2x - 3 + 3 = -x + 3$; Three positive unit tiles were added to both sides.
c. $2x = -x + 3$; The additive inverses on the left cancel.
d. $3x = -x + x + 3$; Add one positive x-tile to each side. e. $3x = 3$; The additive inverses on the right cancel. f. $3 \cdot x = 3 \cdot 1$; Divide each side into three equal parts.
17. $r = \frac{l}{pt}$ 18. $x = \frac{1}{15}$ or 0.67 19. $x = 12$
20. $x = 3$ 21. $x = 3$
22. $x = -17$ 23. $x = \frac{11}{6}$
24. a. $3x$ b. $2x + 20$ c. $3x = 2x + 20$; $x = 20$ d. 60; 60 25. (e) 26. $x \leq 19$

27. $n > 3$

28. a. $3 + x > 12$, $12 + x > 3$, $x < 12 + 3$ b. $x > 9$, $x > -9$, $x < 15$ c. 15 d. 9
29. Let x represent a score, then $4x + 7 = 87$; $x = 20$
30. a.

b. $1200 c. No

CHAPTER 5

5-1 Part A Try It
a. 2; 4; $\frac{1}{2}$ b. -2; 6

5-1 Part A Exercises
1. a. Negative b. Positive c. Positive d. Negative
2. a. (3, 7) b. (4, 3) c. -4 d. 1 e. -4 3. $\frac{4}{7}$
5. Slope of line $r = -2$; Slope of line s is $\frac{1}{4}$; Slope of line $t = -\frac{5}{8}$; Slope of line $v = \frac{7}{8}$; Slope of line $w = 2$.
7. Slope $= \frac{5}{2}$

9. Slope $= -1$

10. Run 11. Slope of line $a = 3$; Slope of line $b = -4$; Slope of line $c = \frac{2}{3}$; Slope of line $d = -1$. 13. Slope of line $d = 1$; Slope of line $e = \frac{5}{6}$; Slope of line $f = \frac{1}{3}$; Slope of line $g = 2$; Slope of line $h = \frac{1}{5}$; Slope of line $i = \frac{1}{2}$. 15. a. The slope of a side is steeper. b. Possible answer: To make it easier for someone to climb up
17. Once they accept an invalid statement, the slide down a series of incorrect conclusions is inevitable.
19. Possible answer: $\frac{1}{2}$
21. Possible answer: 1
23. b. Yes c. A pie chart or histogram could convey the information well. A line graph would not be as easy to read. 25. Let x represent the number of species of bread mold and y represent the number of species of sac fungi, then $y = 500x$.
27. 0.7 29. $\frac{2A}{b_1 + b_2}$
31. Slope of line $a = -\frac{5}{3}$; Slope of line $b = -\frac{1}{3}$

33. Slope $= -1$

35. Slope $= \frac{2}{5}$

37. Slope $= \frac{1}{5}$

39. Slope of line $c = \frac{1}{3}$; Slope of line $d = \frac{1}{3}$; Slope of line $e = -3$; Slope of line $f = -3$. Lines c and d have the same slope. Lines e and f have the same slope. 41. Possible answer: 8 43. Possible answer: $\frac{2}{3}$ 45. Let x represent the length of one side of the square base, h represent the height of the pyramid, and V represent the volume, then $V = \frac{1}{3}hx^2$. 47. Take the reciprocal of the wrong answer to get the true slope.

5-1 Part B Try It
a. $\frac{9}{4}$ degrees per hour
b. $49\frac{1}{6}$ miles per hour
c. 6 miles per hour d. 0
e. 0 f. Undefined g. -1

5-1 Part B Exercises
1. a. -8 b. -10 c. $\frac{4}{5}$
2. a. -10 b. 5 c. -2
3. $4\frac{3}{4}$ inches per month
5. Undefined 7. 0
9. a. $6.50 per hour b. $266.50
11. a. 10; 20; 25; 30; 35; 40

b.

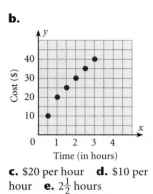

c. $20 per hour **d.** $10 per hour **e.** $2\frac{1}{2}$ hours

15. a. Airline B **b.** Airline A **c.** Airline C **d.** Airline B **e.** Airline C **17.** Slope of line $a = -\frac{1}{2}$; Line a crosses the y-axis at $(0, 3)$. Slope of line $b = -\frac{1}{2}$; Line b crosses the y-axis at $(0, 1)$. Slope of line $c = -\frac{1}{2}$; Line c crosses the y-axis at $(0, -1)$. Slope of line $d = -\frac{1}{2}$; Line d crosses the y-axis at $(0, -2)$.

19. a. $y = -\frac{3}{4}x + 5$
b. $y = \frac{1}{4}x + \frac{1}{3}$ **c.** $y = 2x - 1$
21. a. $-\frac{25}{7}$ **b.** 6
c. $-\frac{25}{42}$ **23.** $\frac{1}{9}$ **25.** $\frac{1}{7}$
27. $2\frac{1}{2}$ mi/hr **29.** Undefined **31.** 0 **33. a.** $(2, 5)$
b. $(10, 9)$ **c.** 400 ft, 8 sec
d. $\frac{400\ \text{ft}}{8\ \text{sec}}$ **e.** 50 ft/sec **f.** $\frac{1}{2}$
35. a. $11.67 **b.** $700
37. ≈ 10.84 **39.** Positive
41. Negative **43.** Negative
45. a. They are going at the same speed. **b.** 40 kilometers per hour **c.** Possible answer: In miles per hour

5-1 Part C Try It
a. $-\frac{1}{5}$

5-1 Part C Exercises
1. a. Any three of these:
$\triangle BCK$, $\triangle CDF$, $\triangle EKG$,
$\triangle KFH$, $\triangle GHJ$, $\triangle HGK$,
$\triangle FKC$, $\triangle KEB$

b. $\triangle ACG$, $\triangle ADJ$, $\triangle EFJ$,
$\triangle BDH$ **c.** $\frac{2}{3}$ **d.** $\frac{2}{3}$ **e.** $\frac{2}{3}$
f. They are the same. **3.** T
5. Slope $= 2$

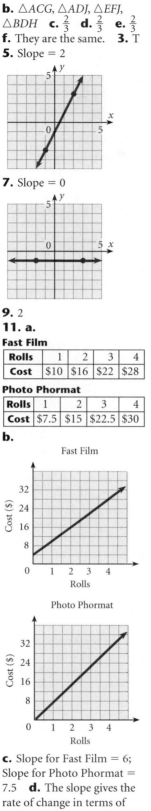

7. Slope $= 0$

9. 2
11. a.

Fast Film

Rolls	1	2	3	4
Cost	$10	$16	$22	$28

Photo Phormat

Rolls	1	2	3	4
Cost	$7.5	$15	$22.5	$30

b.

Fast Film

Photo Phormat

c. Slope for Fast Film $= 6$;
Slope for Photo Phormat $= 7.5$ **d.** The slope gives the rate of change in terms of dollars per roll. **e.** Fast Film **13.** $\frac{1}{2}$; $\frac{1}{2}$ **15.** $x = 6$

17. $n = 6$ **19.** $x = \frac{13}{2}$
21. $x = 9$ **23.** $x = 2$
25. Slope $= 2$

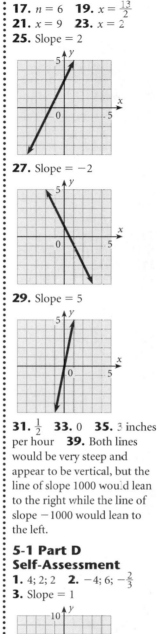

27. Slope $= -2$

29. Slope $= 5$

31. $\frac{1}{2}$ **33.** 0 **35.** 3 inches per hour **39.** Both lines would be very steep and appear to be vertical, but the line of slope 1000 would lean to the right while the line of slope -1000 would lean to the left.

5-1 Part D Self-Assessment
1. 4; 2; 2 **2.** -4; 6; $-\frac{2}{3}$
3. Slope $= 1$

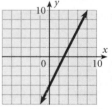

4. Slope $= \frac{7}{6}$

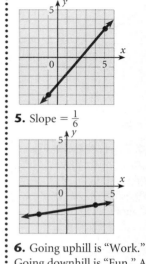

5. Slope $= \frac{1}{6}$

6. Going uphill is "Work." Going downhill is "Fun." A zero slope is "Boring." An undefined slope is "Oops."
7. -1 **8.** $\frac{1}{4}$ **9.** $\frac{1}{4}$
10. Undefined
11. $-\frac{1}{3}$ gram per minute
12. $\frac{25}{14}$ degrees per second
13. a. Sylvia **c.** No
d. 60% **14.** $x = 15$
15. $y = 27$ **16.** $d = 9$

5-2 Part A Try It
a. $m = -5$, $b = 7$ **b.** $m = -1$, $b = -3$ **c.** $m = \frac{1}{4}$, $b = 0$ **d.** Note that $m = 2$ or $\frac{2}{1}$ and $b = -6$. The point $(0, -6)$ is on the line. Plot $(0, -6)$. Then move 1 unit to the right and then 2 units up. Plot that point. Connect the points and extend the line.

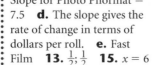

e. Note that $m = -\frac{2}{3}$ or $\frac{-2}{3}$ and $b = 1$. The point $(0, 1)$ is on the line. Plot $(0, 1)$. Then move 3 units to the right and then 2 units down. Plot that point. Connect the points and extend the line.

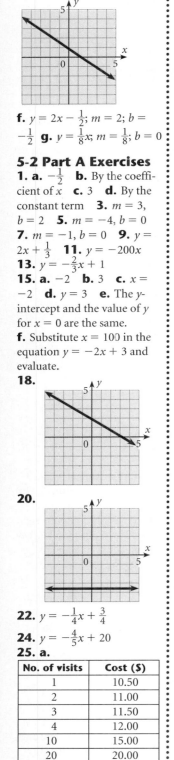

f. $y = 2x - \frac{1}{2}$; $m = 2$; $b = -\frac{1}{2}$ **g.** $y = \frac{1}{8}x$, $m = \frac{1}{8}$; $b = 0$

5-2 Part A Exercises

1. a. $-\frac{1}{2}$ **b.** By the coefficient of x **c.** 3 **d.** By the constant term **3.** $m = 3$, $b = 2$ **5.** $m = -4$, $b = 0$ **7.** $m = -1$, $b = 0$ **9.** $y = 2x + \frac{1}{3}$ **11.** $y = -200x$ **13.** $y = -\frac{2}{3}x + 1$ **15. a.** -2 **b.** 3 **c.** $x = -2$ **d.** $y = 3$ **e.** The y-intercept and the value of y for $x = 0$ are the same. **f.** Substitute $x = 100$ in the equation $y = -2x + 3$ and evaluate.

18.

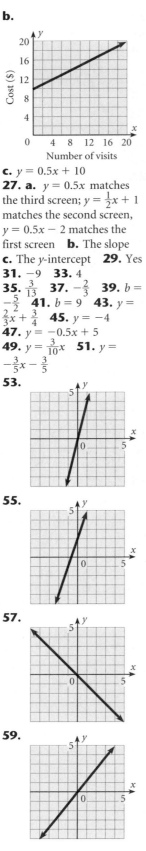

20.

22. $y = -\frac{1}{4}x + \frac{3}{4}$

24. $y = -\frac{4}{5}x + 20$

25. a.

No. of visits	Cost ($)
1	10.50
2	11.00
3	11.50
4	12.00
10	15.00
20	20.00
40	30.00

b.

c. $y = 0.5x + 10$

27. a. $y = 0.5x$ matches the third screen; $y = \frac{1}{2}x + 1$ matches the second screen, $y = 0.5x - 2$ matches the first screen **b.** The slope **c.** The y-intercept **29.** Yes **31.** -9 **33.** 4 **35.** $\frac{3}{13}$ **37.** $-\frac{2}{3}$ **39.** $b = -\frac{5}{2}$ **41.** $b = 9$ **43.** $y = \frac{2}{3}x + \frac{3}{4}$ **45.** $y = -4$ **47.** $y = -0.5x + 5$ **49.** $y = \frac{3}{10}x$ **51.** $y = -\frac{3}{5}x - \frac{3}{5}$

53.

55.

57.

59.

61. $x = \frac{y - b}{m}$; $x = \frac{11}{3}$

63. The area is $\frac{45}{4}$.

5-2 Part B Try It

a. $y = -5x + 6$
b. $y = \frac{1}{2}x + 7$

5-2 Part B Exercises

1. a. $m = -1$ **b.** $y = -x + b$ **c.** $b = 7$ **d.** $y = -x + 7$ **3.** $y = -\frac{4}{3}x - 4$ **5.** $y = -9$ **7.** $y = 0$ **9.** $1.27 per gallon. **11. a.** 29 points; 41 points **b.**

c. $y = 12x + 17$ **d.** The slope is the number of games Bruce has played plus 1. The y-intercept is Bruce's current average. **15.** $y = 4x - 14$ **17.** Distance you drive, amount of money, directly related. **19. a.** $40x$ represents the amount Ken earns from his hourly wage in one 40-hour work week; $40x + 20$ represents the amount Ken earns from his hourly wage in one 40-hour work week plus the $20 bonus for working the evening shift; y represents his weekly salary. **b.** $209.20 = 40x + 20$; $4.73 **c.** $0.25 per hour **21.** $y = 2x + 3$ **23.** $y = x + 5$ **25.** $y = -2x + 6$ **29. a.** (9, 1.25), (12, 1.60) **b.** $y = \frac{7}{60}x + \frac{1}{5}$ **c.** $2.07

d. $0.78 **31. a.** (2, 720), (8, 480) **b.** $y = -40x + 800$ **c.** 480 minutes **d.** 800 minutes **e.** 12.5 weeks **f.** -40 **g.** 800; At the beginning of her training. **h.** No; She cannot run a mile in 0 minutes.

5-2 Part C Try It

a. $2\frac{1}{2}$ pounds per week
b. $3\frac{1}{2}$ pounds per week
c. $\frac{5}{13}$ pounds per week
d. $3\frac{1}{2}$ pounds per week
e. $76\frac{12}{13}$ pounds per week
f. $\frac{1}{8}$ pounds per week

5-2 Part C Exercises

1. a. 4 people per table **b.** $99 per week **c.** 11 modems per hour **d.** $\frac{2}{3}$ million per month **e.** 1300 crates per day **f.** $15,000 per year **3.** 0.32 ounces **5.** 59% **7.** 26 pounds per month **9.** 8 miles per quart **11. a.** Graph **i**, Graph **iii**, and Graph **iv** **b.** -5 **c.** $-\frac{5}{4}$ **13. a.** The line would appear steeper. **b.** The line would appear steeper. **c.** The line would appear to be the same. **15.** 55 feet per second = 37.5 miles per hour **17. a.** $\approx 1,892$ moles **b.** 452 grams **c.** 55.6 moles; 2.2 moles **19.** $\frac{1}{2}$ **21. a.** Reduce the value of each increment on the y-axis. **b.** Increase the value of each increment on the y-axis. **c.** To make the cereal seem more popular, increase the value of each increment on the x-axis. To make the cereal seem less popular, decrease the value of each increment on the x-axis. **23.** 160 calories per cup **25.** 640 calories per pound **27.** 1568 quarts per week

5-2 Part D Try It

a. Possible answer: Use (50, 135) to get $y = 1.46x + 62$; 173 seconds.

5-2 Part D Exercises

1. a–b.

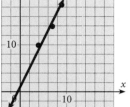

c. Yes; The line is quite close to the data points. **3.** $y = \frac{3}{2}x + \frac{1}{2}$ **5.** $y = -\frac{2}{3}x - 3$ **7. a.** $\frac{3}{25}$ **b.** $\frac{11}{25}$ **9.** $y = \frac{1}{150}x + \frac{50}{3}$; 17th Street; 98th Street **11. a.** The slopes would suggest a warming trend in Minneapolis and stable temperatures in Singapore. **b.** No, because Singapore is closer to the equator than Minneapolis. **c.** Yes; The units for the scales of the temperatures are missing.

d.

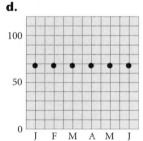

e. The rate of temperature change in Minneapolis from January to June is about 11°F per month, while the rate of temperature change in Singapore is 0° per month. **13.** Inversely related; As one quantity increases, the other decreases. **15.** Directly related; As one quantity increases the other increases. **17.** 55 mi/hr; $\frac{465 - 135}{6} = \frac{\text{change in miles}}{\text{change in hours}}$ **19. a.** 6 in. **b.** 4 pounds **c.** 1 in./lb **d.** 3 inches **e.** $y = x + 3$ **f.** 19 inches

21. a.

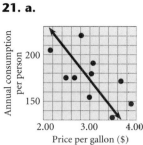

b. Weak, negative **c.** Possible answer: $y = -62.5x + 362.5$ **d.** Possible answer: 303 gallons per person. This is much less than 484 gallons per person. **e.** No **f.** No **23. a.** J and M Jewelry had the greatest increase in 1984. Its stock went up from $5 to $15. **b.** $10 per year **c.** Overland Oil had the greatest decrease in 1985. Its stock went down from $20 to $10. **d.** $10 per year **e.** $5 per year

5-2 Part E Self-Assessment

1. a. $y = \frac{3}{5}x + \frac{4}{5}$ **b.** $y = 8$ **c.** $x = 7$ **d.** Yes; $\frac{3}{5}(32) + \frac{4}{5} = 20$ **2. a.** 3 **b.** 4 **c.** $y = 3x + 4$ **3. a.**

b.

c.

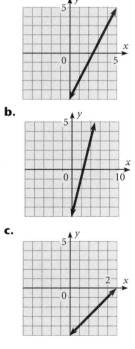

5. a.

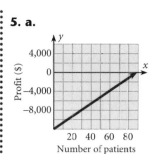

b. The y-intercept is $-\$12,000$, which represents the money spent on the machine. The slope is $135 per patient which represents the money made from each patient. **c.** The x-intercept gives the number of patients needed to break even. **d.** 89 patients **6. a.** 20 **b.** 30 **c.** About 650 calories **d.** Possible answer: The slopes might be steeper. **e.** Possible answer: The slopes might be flatter. **7.** Possible answer: She could solve for the equation of the line passing through A and B. Then she would substitute 6 for x to solve for y. **8.** $h = -\frac{5}{2}$ **9.** $x = 4$ **10. a.** $1400 + 300h$ **b.** $1700 + 50h$ **c.** 2 hours; 6 hours **11. a.** Let x represent your age and y represent your target heart rate. **b.** Possible answer:

x	15	20	25	30	40
y	164	160	156	152	144

c. $y = 0.8(220 - x)$ **e.** 136 **f.** 124 **12. a.** Let y = the number of calories used in one day. **b.** $y = 3000 + 30x$ **c.** About $-12°C$ **13. a.** Possible answer:

s	1	5	10	20	30	50
h	8	40	80	160	240	400

b. $h = 8s$ **c.** 480 ft **d.** 5.45 miles per hour **e.** No **14. b.** $y = 2x - 2$ **16. a.** There are only positive integer numbers of defective bolts, and each grid on the y-axis is an integer value. **b.** $y = \frac{3}{2000}x - 1$ **c.** No, when the machine is not running there should be 0 defective bolts, so the line should pass through the origin.

17. a. 5 seconds **b.** The car travels at a constant speed. **c.** 44 feet per second **d.** 44 feet **e.** 44 feet per second; It is the same. **18.** The advantage of the design in Orchestra Hall is that the balcony is steep so that everyone in the balcony has a direct view of the entire stage, while in Crown Theater the gradual rise makes it difficult for people in the upper rows to see the entire stage. The steeper design of Orchestra Hall puts more people closer to the stage. A disadvantage of Orchestra Hall is that the steep steps may be dangerous, and the steepness may make people uncomfortable.

Chapter 5 Review

1. F; $(0, b)$ **2.** T **3.** F; Run **4.** $-\frac{1}{2}$ **5.** $\frac{3}{2}$ **6.** $\frac{1}{2}$ **7.** 0 **8.** Slope = $-\frac{2}{3}$

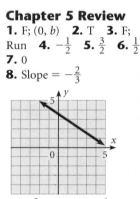

9. $14\frac{2}{3}$ ft/sec **10.** $\frac{1}{2}$ ft/hr **11.** $\overline{AB}, \overline{AD}, \overline{BE}$ lie on the same line that has a slope of $\frac{1}{2}$. **12.** $\triangle ABF, \triangle ACG \triangle ADH, \triangle AEI$. **13.** Yes, the slopes of the line segments connecting one point to the next are the same. **14.** A line with a slope of 0 is horizontal and a line with an undefined slope is vertical

15.

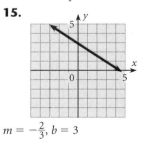

$m = -\frac{2}{3}, b = 3$

16.

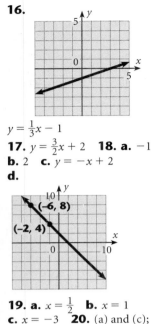

$y = \frac{1}{3}x - 1$

17. $y = \frac{3}{2}x + 2$ **18. a.** -1
b. 2 **c.** $y = -x + 2$
d.

19. a. $x = \frac{1}{2}$ **b.** $x = 1$
c. $x = -3$ **20.** (a) and (c);
Calculate the ratios of rise to
run in both graphs to see if
they are the same. The slope
is 1 for both (a) and (c).
21. Percentage of population
in towns of over 10,000; Year
22. The graphs would be lower
and flatter. **23.** Prussia;
Russia **24.** They show
trends. **25.** The slopes
would decrease over time.
26. Possible answer:

Life Expectancy
Since 1900

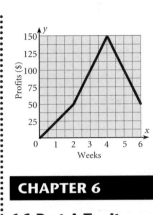

Possible answers: 47 years; 75
years. **27.** Possible answer:
$\frac{1}{4}$; -425; $y = \frac{1}{4}x - 425$
28. During the first two
weeks, the business profited
$25 per week. During the
next two weeks, the business
profited $50 per week. But
during the last two weeks, the
business lost $50 per week.
The rate of change was different during each two-week
period.

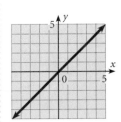

CHAPTER 6

6-1 Part A Try It
a. Intersect; Not perpendicular **b.** Intersect;
Perpendicular **c.** Parallel
d. Intersect; Not perpendicular **e.** Intersect; Perpendicular **f.** $y = x + 3$
g. $y = -\frac{1}{4}x + \frac{7}{4}$

6-1 Part A Exercises
1. a. $-\frac{1}{2}$; $-\frac{1}{2}$ **b.** The
graphs are parallel. **c.** 2;
$-\frac{1}{2}$; -1 **d.** The graphs are
perpendicular **e.** The
graphs are perpendicular
3. One point **5.** Parallel
7. Intersect; Perpendicular
9. Intersect; Not perpendicular **11.** The slope of a parallel line is 2.5. The slope of a
perpendicular line is -0.4.

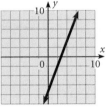

13. The slope of a parallel
line is 0. The slope of a perpendicular line is undefined.

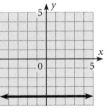

15. The slope of a parallel
line is 1. The slope of a
perpendicular line is -1.

19. A and C **21.** Parallel
23. Parallel **25.** Intersect;
Perpendicular **27.** Possible
answers: Train tracks. Intersecting: Spokes of a wheel.
Perpendicular: Edges of a
window. **28.** Infinite number; The two equations are
the same. **29.** One
30. None **31. a.** 3
b. $b = 1$ **c.** $y = 3x + 1$
33. $y = 2x + 5$ **35.** $y =$
$2x + 5$ **37.** $y = -2x + 3$
39. a. $x = -2.5$ and $x = 3$
are parallel lines with undefined slopes. They are vertical lines passing through
$(-2.5, 0)$ and $(3, 0)$, respectively. **b.** $x = -2.5$
and $y = 4.5$ are perpendicular lines with an undefined
slope and a slope of zero,
respectively. They are vertical
and horizontal lines intersecting at $(-2.5, 4.5)$. $x = 3$ and
$y = 4.5$ are also perpendicular lines with an undefined
slope and a slope of zero,
respectively. They are vertical
and horizontal lines intersecting at $(3, 4.5)$. **c.** The slopes
are either zero or undefined.
41. Possible answer: Parallel
sentences have the same basic
structure, much like parallel
lines having the same slope.
The words are different as are
the y-intercepts of parallel
lines. **43.** $y = -\frac{1}{2}x + \frac{5}{4}$
45. Parallel **47.** Intersect;
Perpendicular **49.** Intersect; Perpendicular
51. a. $-\frac{2}{3}$ **b.** $\frac{3}{2}$
53. a. Undefined **b.** 0
55. $y = -\frac{2}{3}x - 1$ **57.** $y =$
$x - 8$ **59.** $y = -\frac{2}{3}x + 2$
61. $y = -0.4x + 0.4$
63. B and D are the same.

65. B (therefore D) and C
are perpendicular to E.
67. One **69.** The slope of
the second fold is $-\frac{1}{2}$.
71. The long hand goes from
0 to 12 at the same rate every
hour. The rate, 12, is the
slope of each line. Therefore
the lines are parallel. **73.** 5

6-1 Part B Try It
a. 4 months from now
b. $(2, 3)$

6-1 Part B Exercises
1. a. $x - 3y = -9$
b. $2x + y = -4$ **c.** $(-3, 2)$
d. $(-3, 2)$ **e.** Substitute
$x = -3$ and $y = 2$ into both
equations.

$$x - 3y \stackrel{?}{=} -9$$
$$(-3) - 3(2) \stackrel{?}{=} -9$$
$$-9 = -9 \checkmark$$

$$2x + y \stackrel{?}{=} -4$$
$$2(-3) + 2 \stackrel{?}{=} -4$$
$$-4 = -4 \checkmark$$

Both equations are true. The
solution checks. **3.** F;
Ordered pair **5. a.** 1990
b. The company broke even
in 1992. This is not "good"
news because income was
decreasing while expenses
were increasing.
7.

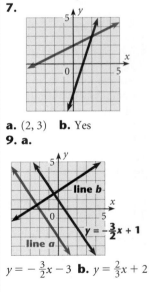

a. $(2, 3)$ **b.** Yes
9. a.

$y = -\frac{3}{2}x - 3$ **b.** $y = \frac{2}{3}x + 2$

11.

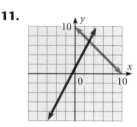

The solution is (3, 7).

13.

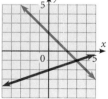

The solution is (3, −1).

19. a. $\overline{AB}$ and $\overline{BC}$ are perpendicular. **b.** $\overline{AB}$ and $\overline{DC}$ are parallel. **21. a. ii
b. iii c. i 23. a.** $3x - y = 7$ **b.** $x + 3y = -1$
c. (2, −1) **d.** (2, −1)
e. Substitute $x = 2$ and $y = -1$ into both equations to check the solution.

25.

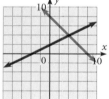

The solution is (4, 4).

27.

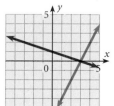

The solution is (3, 0).

29.

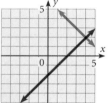

The solution is (4, 2).

31. He will catch up with the hikers in about 37 minutes.

33. a. $-\frac{7}{3}$ **b.** 0 **c.** −7
35. a. Company B
b. Company A; Company A will show a profit in the future because income is increasing and expenses are decreasing, while Company B will show a loss in the future because income is decreasing and expenses are increasing.

6-1 Part C Self-Assessment
1. a. −3 **b.** $\frac{1}{3}$ **c.** 0; This line is perpendicular to line b because line c is perpendicular to line b. **2.** (d);
Substitute $x = -1$ and $y = -\frac{2}{3}$ into both equations.
$$2x + 3y \overset{?}{=} -4$$
$$2(-1) + 3(-\frac{2}{3}) \overset{?}{=} -4$$
$$-4 = -4 \checkmark$$

$$4x - 3y \overset{?}{=} -2$$
$$4(-1) - 3(-\frac{2}{3}) \overset{?}{=} -2$$
$$-2 = -2 \checkmark$$

Both equations are true. The solution checks.

3. $y = \frac{2}{3}x + \frac{5}{3}$ **4.** $y = -\frac{3}{2}x + 6$ **5.** (d); $3x + y = 1$ and $6x + 2y = 2$ represent the same equation because the second equation is the first equation with both sides multiplied by 2. $3y = -3x + 2$ and $y = -x + \frac{2}{3}$ represent the same equation because the first equation is the second equation with both sides multiplied by 3. **6.** Kit should substitute $x = -2.4$ and $y = -2.2$ into the equations $y = 3x + 5$ and $y = -2x - 7$.

7.

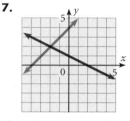

The solution is (−2, 2); The lines intersect at one point.

8.

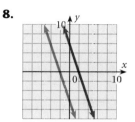

There is no solution; The lines are parallel.

9.

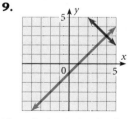

The solution is (4, 3); The lines are perpendicular.

10. a. $y = x + 1$ **b.** $y = -x - 4$ **c.** Solve the system of two equations to find the coordinates of the buffalo.
11. Since the two DF stations give the equation of the same line, a third DF is needed to locate the strike.
12. (2, 0) **13. a.** Answers should be between 0 km and 700 km. **b.** More DF stations would be required to cover the same area.
c. Possible answer:

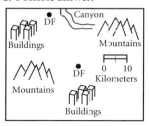

14. a. Possible answer: In both cases, sightings from two positions are used to triangulate and locate an object.
b. Use a coordinate plane containing the points A, B, C, and D, with A as the origin and B on the x-axis.

6-2 Part A Try It
a. (−3, 1) **b.** (−25, −9)
c. $(\frac{1}{3}, -\frac{4}{3})$ **d.** $s = 52, m = 7$

6-2 Part A Exercises
1. a. The second equation tells us y is equal to $-5x + 9$ for any solution to the system. **b.** $x = 2$ **c.** $y = -1$
d. Check $x = 2$ and $y = -1$ in both equations.
$$3x + 6y \overset{?}{=} 0$$
$$3(2) + 6(-1) \overset{?}{=} 0$$
$$0 = 0 \checkmark$$

$$y \overset{?}{=} -5x + 9$$
$$-1 \overset{?}{=} -5(2) + 9$$
$$-1 = -1 \checkmark$$

3. (39, 11) **5.** (−2, −6)
7. (6, 3) **9. a.** Isolate x in the first equation.
$$x - 7y = -6$$
$$x = 7y - 6$$

Substitute $x = 7y - 6$ into the second equation and solve.
$$x + y = 3$$
$$(7y - 6) + y = 3$$
$$8y - 6 = 3$$
$$y = \frac{9}{8}$$

Substitute the value of y into the first equation and solve for x.
$$x - 7y = -6$$
$$x - 7(\frac{9}{8}) = -6$$
$$x = \frac{15}{8}$$
The solution is $(\frac{15}{8}, \frac{9}{8})$.

b. Isolate y in the second equation.
$$x + y = 3$$
$$y = 3 - x$$

Substitute $y = 3 - x$ into the first equation and solve for x.
$$x - 7y = -6$$
$$x - 7(3 - x) = -6$$
$$8x - 21 = -6$$
$$x = \frac{15}{8}$$

Substitute the value of x into the second equation and solve for y.
$$x + y = 3$$
$$\frac{15}{8} + y = 3$$
$$y = \frac{9}{8}$$
The solution is $(\frac{15}{8}, \frac{9}{8})$.

c. Yes **11. a.** $x + y = 70$
b. $x - y = 24$ **c.** (47, 23)
d. 47 and 23 **13. a.** $c = 5 + 2.5n$ $c = 8 + 0.8n$

b.

Cost (thousands of dollars) vs Time (years) graph

c. 1.8 years; No   **15.** 6, 7, 8, 9   **17. a.** Mack Ave. and E. Vernor Hwy   **b.** Grand River   **c.** No, since they aren't straight and don't intersect.   **d.** Part of Canada is south of Detroit.
e. Intersecting straight lines
f. Main streets appear to radiate from a central point like spokes of a wheel.
19. Linear   **21.** Not linear
23. $y = \frac{1}{2}x - \frac{3}{2}$ **25.** $x = \frac{17}{2}, y = \frac{1}{2}$ **27.** $x = 2, y = 0$
29. $x = 8, y = -2$
31. $x = 3, y = \frac{1}{2}$ **33.** $p = 2, q = 0$ **35.** $x = -9, y = -17$ **37.** $c = 6 + 0.25r$
$c = 4 + 0.50r$ $r = 8, c = 8$;
At 8 rides the cost is the same.

graph

39. Yes; Yes   **41.** Let x represent the amount in ml of 3% solution and y represent the amount in ml of 10% solution. $0.03x$ represents the amount in ml of acid in x ml of 3% solution, $0.10y$ represents the amount in ml of acid in y ml of 10% solution, and $0.06(10) = 0.6$ represents the amount in ml of acid in 10 ml of 6% solution. Therefore, there is a system of equations: $x + y = 10$ and $0.03x + 0.10y = 0.6$.
Solve the system to calculate the amounts of solution

6-2 Part B Try It
a. $\left(-3, -\frac{1}{2}\right)$ **b.** $(3, 1)$
c. $\left(\frac{10}{3}, \frac{1}{15}\right)$ **d.** No solution
e. Every point on the line $2x - 5y = 10$

6-2 Part B Exercises
1. a. y **b.** $x = 6$ **c.** $y = 1$
d. $(6, 1)$ **3.** $(-3, -5)$
5. No   **7.** Dependent; Equations are the same since the second equation is twice the first.   **9. a.** Possible answer: Subtract the first equation from the second equation to eliminate the variable n.   **b.** Possible answer: Multiply the first equation by 5 so that the terms with the variable a match.   **11.** $c = 4, d = -1$
13. $x = 2, y = 2$ **15.** $a = 3, b = 1$ **17. a.** $y = 100 - 3x$ **b.** $y = 20 + 5x$ **c.** 10 days; Solve the system of equations to find the value of x.   **19.** $\ell = \frac{11}{3}$ cm, $w = \frac{7}{3}$ cm   **21. a.** There are 20 routes without any unnecessary backtracking.   **b.** Yes
c. It reduces the number of routes from 20 to 4.

23. $\begin{bmatrix} 49 & 74 & -42 \\ 22 & 8.3 & -27 \\ -69 & 62 & 83 \end{bmatrix}$

25. $\begin{bmatrix} -82 & 10.2 & -73 \\ 21 & 3 & 9 \\ 11 & -23 & 8.6 \end{bmatrix}$

27. $(2, -5)$ **29.** $\left(3, -\frac{1}{3}\right)$
31. Possible answer: Multiply the first equation by 2 so that the terms with the variable x match.
33. Inconsistent
35. Dependent   **37.** $a = \frac{2}{3}$, $b = -1$ **39.** $x = 3, y = -2$
41. $x = -4, y = 0$ **43.** No solutions   **45.** The number of chirps and temperature in degrees Fahrenheit are equal at $53\frac{1}{3}$.   **47.** $x = 0, y = 2$, $z = 3$ **49.** $3\frac{1}{3}$ ml of 5% solution and $6\frac{2}{3}$ ml of 2% solution

6-2 Part C Try It
a. $\begin{bmatrix} 19 \\ 47 \end{bmatrix}$ **b.** $\begin{bmatrix} 11 \\ -6 \end{bmatrix}$
c. Constant matrix $B = \begin{bmatrix} -9 \\ -14 \end{bmatrix}$. $A^{-1}B = \begin{bmatrix} 2 \\ 3 \end{bmatrix}$.
The solution to the system is $(2, 3)$.   **d.** Constant matrix $B = \begin{bmatrix} 10 \\ 17 \end{bmatrix}$. $A^{-1}B = \begin{bmatrix} 5 \\ 1 \end{bmatrix}$.
The solution to the system is $(5, 1)$.

6-2 Part C Exercises
1. $\begin{bmatrix} -3 \cdot 2 + 4 \cdot 7 \\ 5 \cdot 2 + 6 \cdot 7 \end{bmatrix} = \begin{bmatrix} 22 \\ 52 \end{bmatrix}$
3. a. v   **b.** iv   **c.** ii   **d.** i   **e.** iii
5. $\begin{bmatrix} -15 \\ 20 \end{bmatrix}$
7. $(2, 10)$ **9.** $(4, -8)$
11. $x = 3, y = 1.5$
13. $x = \frac{13}{3}, y = \frac{19}{9}$
15. a. $x + y = 1000$
b. $0.10x$ represents the number of milliliters of alcohol in x milliliters of the 10% solution; $0.25y$ represents the number of milliliters of alcohol in y milliliters of the 25% solution; $0.20(1000)$ represents the number of milliliters of alcohol in 1000 milliliters of a 20% solution.
c. $0.10x + 0.25y = 0.20(1000)$ **d.** $333\frac{1}{3}$ milliliters of the 10% solution and $666\frac{2}{3}$ milliliters of the 25% solution   **17. a.** 4.2 million
d. 4   **19. a.** 800 feet per second   **b.** 8900 feet
c. 250 feet per second
21. $\begin{bmatrix} -58 \\ -110 \end{bmatrix}$
23. $\begin{bmatrix} -13 \\ -72 \end{bmatrix}$
25. $(-2, 6)$ **27.** $(-3, 5)$
29. $(2, 1)$ **31.** $(1, -3)$
33. Possible answer: Three lines in space can be parallel to each other. They can be perpendicular to each other. Two can be parallel and one may be perpendicular to them.

They may not intersect and not be parallel. They can intersect at one point. There are many possibilities.
35. $x = 2, y = -1, z = 3$
37. There are 3 juniors.

6-2 Part D Self-Assessment
1. The solution is $(2, -2)$.
2. $(4, 8)$ **3.** $(9, -3)$
4. $(-6, 16)$ **5.** All points on the line $5x - 3y = 10$
6. $\left(-\frac{13}{14}, -\frac{51}{14}\right)$ **7.** No solutions   **8.** (e); None of the ordered pairs satisfies the system $x - 2y = 6$ and $2x - 3y = 5$.   **9.** 160 cars and 90 trucks.   **10.** (d); In System I, the second equation is twice the first equation. In System II, the first equation is three times the second equation. In System III, the two equations have different slopes.   **11. a.** $\ell = 8 + w$ and $2\ell + 2w = 46$ **b.** $\ell = 15\frac{1}{2}$ meters and $w = 7\frac{1}{2}$ meters   **c.** $116\frac{1}{4}$ square meters   **12.** Let x represent the number of students who want a corn dog and y represent the number of students who want a hot dog. Then $x + y = 30$ and $1.50x + 1.75y = 50.25$. Solving this system of linear equations gives $x = 9$ and $y = 21$. Therefore, he had to get 9 corn dogs and 21 hot dogs.
13. $(2, -2)$; Check the solution by substituting $x = 2$ and $y = -2$ into $2x - y = 6$ and $x - y = 4$.   **14. a.** The graph is the same as the graph of $x - y = 4$.   **b.** The graph is the same as the graph of $x - y = 4$.   **c.** The graph is the same as the graph of $x - y = 4$.   **15.** Let x represent the number of adults and y represent the number of children. Suppose the safety relationship can be written as a linear equation. Then $(60, 0)$ and $(0, 120)$ are solutions.

The y-intercept is 120 and the slope is $-\frac{120}{60} = -2$. Then the equation is $y = -2x + 120$. If Linda wants to load pairs, then $x = y$. Solving this system of equations gives $x = 40$ and $y = 40$. She can safely load 40 pairs. **16. a.** No intersection; No solution **b.** Every point on the course is a solution. The planes travel along the same line. **c.** There is one solution. The planes will crash at the intersection point if they both reach it at the same time. **17. a.** Yes; When each was 13 years old, each was 5 ft 3 in. tall. **b.** Their age difference **18.**

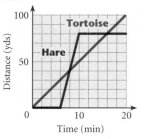

a. 2 minutes **b.** 16 minutes **c.** 20 minutes **19.** 0.75; 0.24 **20. a.** '91 **b.** '95 **c.** For a particular year, find the value of income and subtract from it the value of expenses.

6-3 Part A Try It
a. $y < 2x + 1$
b. $y \leq -0.5x + 1$
c.

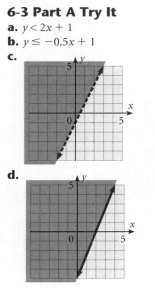

d.

6-3 Part A Exercises
1. a.

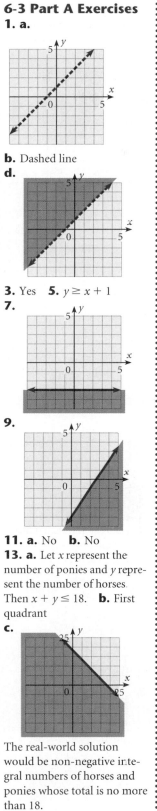

b. Dashed line
d.

3. Yes **5.** $y \geq x + 1$
7.

9.

11. a. No **b.** No
13. a. Let x represent the number of ponies and y represent the number of horses. Then $x + y \leq 18$. **b.** First quadrant
c.

The real-world solution would be non-negative integral numbers of horses and ponies whose total is no more than 18.

15. a. Let x represent the number of yearbooks bought in advance and y represent the number of yearbooks bought after publication. Then $4x + 2y > 2500$.
17. $x > -4$ **19.** 15
21. $x > 9$

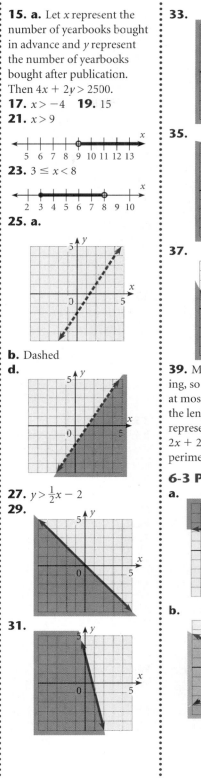

23. $3 \leq x < 8$

25. a.

b. Dashed
d.

27. $y > \frac{1}{2}x - 2$
29.

31.

33.

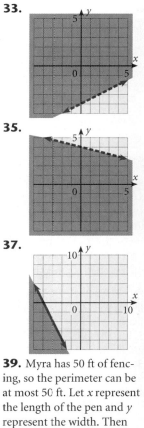

35.

37.

39. Myra has 50 ft of fencing, so the perimeter can be at most 50 ft. Let x represent the length of the pen and y represent the width. Then $2x + 2y \leq 50$. Some possible perimeters are 50, 40 or 30.

6-3 Part B Try It
a.

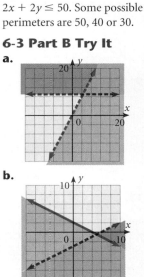

b.

6-3 Part B Exercises

1. a–b. Dotted;

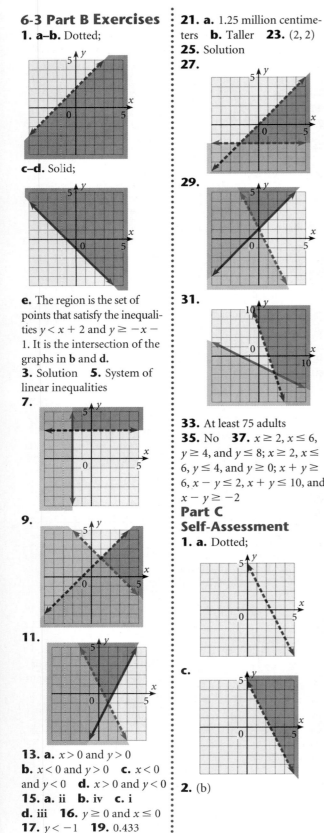

c–d. Solid;

e. The region is the set of points that satisfy the inequalities $y < x + 2$ and $y \geq -x - 1$. It is the intersection of the graphs in **b** and **d**.
3. Solution   **5.** System of linear inequalities
7.

9.

11.

13. a. $x > 0$ and $y > 0$
b. $x < 0$ and $y > 0$ **c.** $x < 0$ and $y < 0$ **d.** $x > 0$ and $y < 0$
15. a. ii   **b.** iv   **c.** i
d. iii   **16.** $y \geq 0$ and $x \leq 0$
17. $y < -1$ **19.** 0.433

21. a. 1.25 million centimeters   **b.** Taller   **23.** $(2, 2)$
25. Solution
27.

29.

31.

33. At least 75 adults
35. No   **37.** $x \geq 2$, $x \leq 6$, $y \geq 4$, and $y \leq 8$; $x \geq 2$, $x \leq 6$, $y \leq 4$, and $y \geq 0$; $x + y \geq 6$, $x - y \geq 2$, $x + y \leq 10$, and $x - y \geq -2$

Part C
Self-Assessment

1. a. Dotted;

c.

2. (b)

3. a. Possible answer: Shade the region that contains $(0, 2)$ because it is a solution of $y \geq -2x + 1.5$.

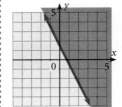

b. Possible answer: Shade the region that contains $(0, 2)$ because it is a solution of $y \geq x$.

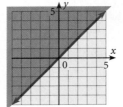

c. Possible answer: Shade the region that contains $(0, 2)$ because it is a solution of $y \leq 3$.

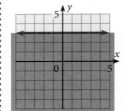

d. The region is the intersection of the three shaded regions in **a**, **b**, and **c**.
4.

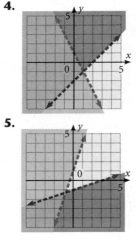

5.

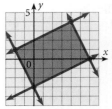

6.

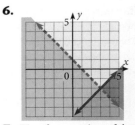

7. Give the equation of the line passing through Florida and Bermuda, and set the inequality such that the origin is a solution. Give the equation of the line through Florida and Puerto Rico, and set the inequality such that the coordinates for Bermuda is a solution. Graph the inequality $x < 0$. Then this system of inequalities describes the region.

8.

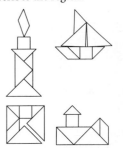

9. $(0, 12)$ and $(9, 3)$; $(0, 0)$ and $(12, 12)$; $(6, 0)$ and $(12, 6)$; $(3, 3)$ and $(3, 9)$; $(9, 9)$ and $(12, 6)$
10.

a. Rectangle   **b.** 30
c. $(-2, 1)$, $(0, -3)$, $(6, 0)$, $(4, 4)$ **11. a.** W $\leq 45°$ N, W $\geq 41°$ N, W $\leq 111°$ W, W $\geq 104°$ W   **b.** C $\leq 41°$ N, C $\geq 37°$ N, C $\leq 109°$ W, C $\geq 102°$ W   **c.** One region is U $\leq 42°$ N, U $\geq 37°$ N, U $\leq 114°$ W, U $\geq 111°$ W; another region is U $\leq 41°$ N, U $\geq 37°$ N, U $\leq 111°$ W, U $\geq 109°$ W.
d. The longitude in degrees west is measured from east to west, so it seems reversed.

12. $y \geq 1$, $x \leq 2$, $x \geq 0$, $y \leq -x + 5$ **a.** Trapezoid
b. 6 **c.** (0, 1), (2, 1), (2, 3), (0, 5)
d. Yes;

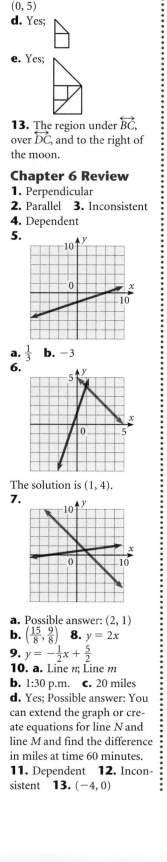

e. Yes;

13. The region under $\overleftrightarrow{BC}$, over $\overleftrightarrow{DC}$, and to the right of the moon.

Chapter 6 Review
1. Perpendicular
2. Parallel **3.** Inconsistent
4. Dependent
5.

a. $\frac{1}{3}$ **b.** -3
6.

The solution is (1, 4).
7.

a. Possible answer: (2, 1)
b. $\left(\frac{15}{8}, \frac{9}{8}\right)$ **8.** $y = 2x$
9. $y = -\frac{1}{2}x + \frac{5}{2}$
10. a. Line n; Line m
b. 1:30 p.m. **c.** 20 miles
d. Yes; Possible answer: You can extend the graph or create equations for line N and line M and find the difference in miles at time 60 minutes.
11. Dependent **12.** Inconsistent **13.** $(-4, 0)$

14. $\begin{bmatrix} -15 \\ 1 \end{bmatrix}$
15. 7 pigs and 9 ducks
16. (b)
17.

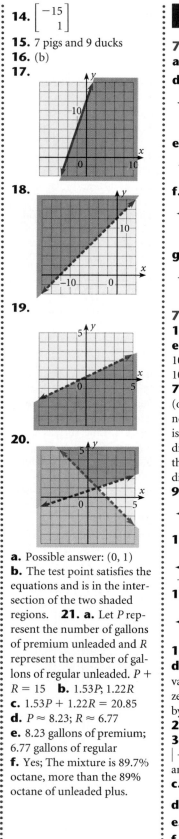

18.

19.

20.

a. Possible answer: (0, 1)
b. The test point satisfies the equations and is in the intersection of the two shaded regions. **21. a.** Let P represent the number of gallons of premium unleaded and R represent the number of gallons of regular unleaded. $P + R = 15$ **b.** $1.53P$; $1.22R$
c. $1.53P + 1.22R = 20.85$
d. $P \approx 8.23$; $R \approx 6.77$
e. 8.23 gallons of premium; 6.77 gallons of regular
f. Yes; The mixture is 89.7% octane, more than the 89% octane of unleaded plus.

CHAPTER 7

7-1 Part A Try It
a. 2.7 **b.** 0.5 **c.** 0
d. $x = 2.5$

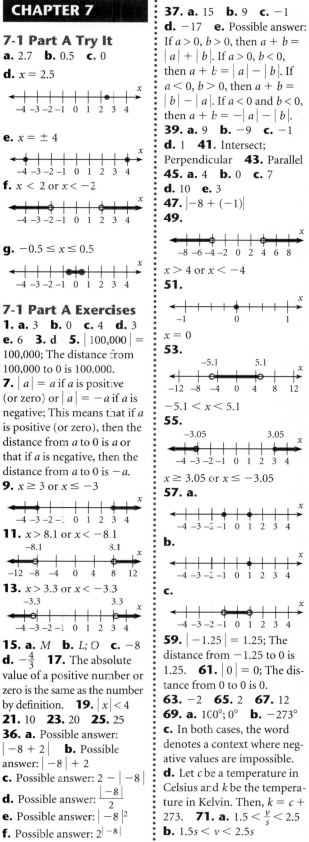

e. $x = \pm 4$

f. $x < 2$ or $x < -2$

g. $-0.5 \leq x \leq 0.5$

7-1 Part A Exercises
1. a. 3 **b.** 0 **c.** 4 **d.** 3
e. 6 **3. d** **5.** $|100{,}000| = 100{,}000$; The distance from 100,000 to 0 is 100,000.
7. $|a| = a$ if a is positive (or zero) or $|a| = -a$ if a is negative; This means that if a is positive (or zero), then the distance from a to 0 is a or that if a is negative, then the distance from a to 0 is $-a$.
9. $x \geq 3$ or $x \leq -3$

11. $x > 8.1$ or $x < -8.1$

13. $x > 3.3$ or $x < -3.3$

15. a. M **b.** L; O **c.** -8
d. $-\frac{4}{3}$ **17.** The absolute value of a positive number or zero is the same as the number by definition. **19.** $|x| < 4$
21. 10 **23.** 20 **25.** 25
36. a. Possible answer: $|-8 + 2|$ **b.** Possible answer: $|-8| + 2$
c. Possible answer: $2 - |-8|$
d. Possible answer: $\frac{|-8|}{2}$
e. Possible answer: $|-8|^2$
f. Possible answer: $2^{|-8|}$

37. a. 15 **b.** 9 **c.** -1
d. -17 **e.** Possible answer: If $a > 0$, $b > 0$, then $a + b = |a| + |b|$. If $a > 0$, $b < 0$, then $a + b = |a| - |b|$. If $a < 0$, $b > 0$, then $a + b = |b| - |a|$. If $a < 0$ and $b < 0$, then $a + b = -|a| - |b|$.
39. a. 9 **b.** -9 **c.** -1
d. 1 **41.** Intersect; Perpendicular **43.** Parallel
45. a. 4 **b.** 0 **c.** 7
d. 10 **e.** 3
47. $|-8 + (-1)|$
49.

$x > 4$ or $x < -4$
51.

$x = 0$
53.

$-5.1 < x < 5.1$
55.

$x \geq 3.05$ or $x \leq -3.05$
57. a.

b.

c.

59. $|-1.25| = 1.25$; The distance from -1.25 to 0 is 1.25. **61.** $|0| = 0$; The distance from 0 to 0 is 0.
63. -2 **65.** 2 **67.** 12
69. a. $100°$; $0°$ **b.** $-273°$
c. In both cases, the word denotes a context where negative values are impossible.
d. Let c be a temperature in Celsius and k be the temperature in Kelvin. Then, $k = c + 273$. **71. a.** $1.5 < \frac{v}{s} < 2.5$
b. $1.5s < v < 2.5s$

c. $v \leq 1.5s$ or $v \geq 2.5s$; If the aircraft cannot operate below Mach 1.5, then how will it land?

7-1 Part B Try It
a. ii **b.** iii **c.** i

7-1 Part B Exercises
1. a.

x	x + 1	x + 1
−3	−2	2
−2	−1	1
−1	0	0
0	1	1
1	2	2
2	3	3

b.

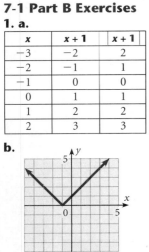

c. It is moved one unit to the left. **3.** The y-values are the same for $x \geq 0$, but the y-values are opposite for $x < 0$. **5.** The graphs are the same for $x \geq 0$, but for $x < 0$ the graph of $y = |x| + 2$ is the graph of $y = x + 2$ flipped about the line $y = 2$. **7.** $y = |x + 3|$; This is the graph of $y = |x|$ moved 3 units to the left. **9.**

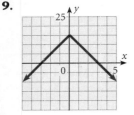

11. No **13.** (b) **15.** 25 **17.** 0.0169 **19. a.** i **b.** iii **c.** ii **21. a.** iii **b.** i **c.** ii **23. a.** $|5 - 3| = |2| = 2$ and $|5| - |3| = 5 - 3 = 2$, so $|5 - 3| = |5| - |3|$. **b.** $|-5 - (-3)| = |-2| = 2$ and $|-5| - |-3| = 5 - 3 = 2$, so $|-5 - (-3)| = |-5| - |-3|$. **c.** Yes; For example, when $x < 0$ and $y > 0$

25. a. $\left|\frac{-8}{+4}\right| = |-2| = 2$ and $\frac{|-8|}{|+4|} = \frac{8}{4} = 2$, so $\left|\frac{-8}{+4}\right| = \frac{|-8|}{|+4|}$ **b.** $\left|\frac{-16}{-2}\right| = |8| = 8$ and $\frac{|-16|}{|-2|} = \frac{16}{2} = 8$ so $\left|\frac{-16}{-2}\right| = \frac{|-16|}{|-2|}$ **c.** No

27.

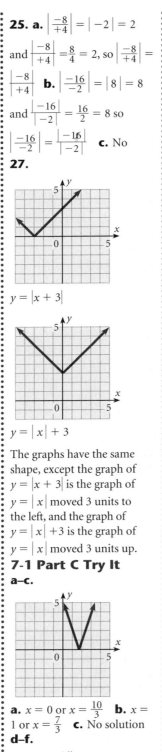

$y = |x + 3|$

$y = |x| + 3$

The graphs have the same shape, except the graph of $y = |x + 3|$ is the graph of $y = |x|$ moved 3 units to the left, and the graph of $y = |x| + 3$ is the graph of $y = |x|$ moved 3 units up.

7-1 Part C Try It
a–c.

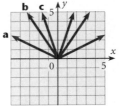

a. $x = 0$ or $x = \frac{10}{3}$ **b.** $x = 1$ or $x = \frac{7}{3}$ **c.** No solution
d–f.

y

d. $x = 0$ or $x = -3$
e. $x = -\frac{3}{2}$ **f.** $x = 2$ or $x = -5$ **g.** $x = -13$ or $x = 5$ **h.** $x = 5$ or $x = 1$

7-1 Part C Exercises
1. a. 7 or -7 **b.** $x - 4 = 7$ or $x - 4 = -7$ **c–d.** $x = 11$ or $x = -3$ **3.** $x = -5$ or $x = 9$ **5.** $x = 11$ or $x = -1$ **7.** $|c - 1.10| \leq 0.05$, Anywhere from \$1.05 to \$1.15. **11. a.** 79% and 73% **b.** $|x - 76| \leq 3$ **c.** No **13.** $a = 7$ or $a = -1$; Divide both sides by 3.
15. a–c.

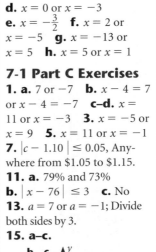

d. The steepness of the "arms" increases. **19.** No; Possible answer: There are other factors that would affect the time, such as the number of lines, style of type on the page, and the reading level. **21. a.** 7, -7 **b.** $x + 5 = 7$ or $x + 5 = -7$ **c–d.** $x = 2$ or $x = -12$ **23.** $x = -3$ or $x = 13$ **25.** $x = 5$ or $x = 11$ **27.** $x = 5$ or $x = 9$ **29.** $x = 2$ or $x = 16$ **31.** $m = 8$ or $m = -2$ **33.** $n = 10$ or $n = 2$ **35.** $c = 7$ or $c = -11$
37. a.

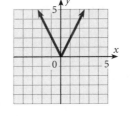

b.

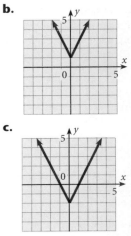

c.

y

d. For part a, the steepness of the "arms" of $y = |x|$ is increased by a factor of 2. Part b is the graph of part a shifted up one unit. Part c is the graph of part a shifted down 2 units.
39. a. $y = \frac{4}{3}|x| - 4$ **b.** Find the points where $y = 4$ and look at the corresponding x-values.

7-1 Part D Self-Assessment
1. a. i **b.** iv **c.** v **d.** ii **e.** iii **2.** $-\frac{1}{3}, -\frac{11}{3}$;

x

3. $x = 25$ or $x = -15$
4. $v = 3$ or $v = -5$
5. a. 0.011 or -0.011
b. $d - 1 \leq 0.011$ and $d - 1 \geq -0.011$
c. $0.989 \leq d \leq 1.011$
6. Let p be the amount of precipitation in cm, then $|350 - p| < 150$. **7.** Let p be the amount of precipitation, then $|10 - p| \leq 10$.
8. Let x be the yard line of the foul, then $|x - 19| = 10$.
9. (e) **10. a.** $y = \frac{3}{4}x$
b. $y = -\frac{3}{4}x$
c. $y = \frac{3}{4}|x|$ **d.** $y = -\frac{3}{4}|x|$
11. a. ii **b.** iv **c.** vi **d.** v **e.** i **f.** iii
12. Graph the equations $y = |4x + 1|$ and $y = -3$ to show that they do not intersect.

13. Let x be the pH of a solution. Then a solution that is strongly acidic or basic would satisfy the inequality $|x - 7.5| \geq 4.5$.

7-2 Part A Try It

a. 10   **b.** -13 **c.** ± 25
d. No   **e.** No   **f.** Yes
g. No   **h.** Yes   **i.** ≈ 7.3

7-2 Part A Exercises

1. a.

n	9	10	11	12	13
n^2	81	100	121	144	169

b. $(11)^2$ and $(12)^2$ **c.** 11 and 12; 11   **d.** 11.4; $(11.4)^2$ $= 129.96$ **8.** 7   **10.** $\frac{3}{4}$
12. 1.2   **14.** 10 in.; Rational   **16. a.** 144 ft^2; 16 yd^2 **b.** $\frac{3}{1}$ **c.** 9 to 1
d. Yes   **19.** $r = \frac{1}{2}\sqrt{\frac{A}{\pi}}$
21. Possible answer: 3.5
23. Possible answer: 3.5
25. Possible answer: 28.3
27. $(\sqrt{50})^2 = 50$. $(25\sqrt{2})^2 = 1250$. Therefore $\sqrt{50} \neq 25\sqrt{2}$. If they were equal, then their squares would also be equal.
29. ≈ 1235 ft   **31.** Trace and cut two small squares to get four right triangles.

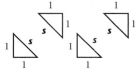

Place the four triangles on the large square.

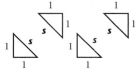

Since the area of one small square is one square unit and two small squares are used to cover one large square, the area of the large square is two square units. $s \cdot s = 2$, so $s = \sqrt{2}$.   **33.** $p \approx 0.71$
35. $\sqrt{0} = 0, \sqrt{1} = 1, \sqrt{2}$ $\approx 1.41, \sqrt{3} \approx 1.73, \sqrt{4} = 2,$ $\sqrt{5} \approx 2.24, \sqrt{6} \approx 2.45, \sqrt{8}$ $\approx 2.83, \sqrt{9} = 3$

37. 30   **39.** 0.03   **41.** $\frac{4}{5}$
43. Possible answer: 9.5
45. Possible answer: 7.35
47. Possible answer: 0.56
49. Possible answer: 8.7
51. Possible answer: 4.9
53. 22.4 ft.   **55.** 10 and 11
57. 23.8; 23.83; $\sqrt{568}$ is irrational.   **59. a.** The principle square root of a number greater than one is less than the number and greater than one. As you continue to take the square root, the result gets smaller than the previous number and gets closer to one.   **b.** The principal square root of a number between zero and one is greater than the number and less than one. As you continue to take the square root, the result gets greater than the previous number and gets closer to one.   **c.** When the number is between zero and one.

7-2 Part B Try It

a. iii   **b.** ii   **c.** i   **d.** 1.8 seconds   **e.** 19.2 seconds; 7.9 seconds

7-2 Part B Exercises

1. a.

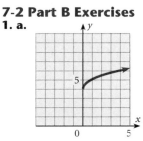

b. It moves the graph of $y = \sqrt{x}$ four units up.

2.

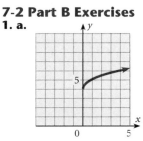

It moves the graph of $y = \sqrt{x}$ four units to the left.
3. The graphs in Exercises **1** and **2** have the same shape as the graph of $y = \sqrt{x}$, but the graph in Exercise **1** is moved

four units up while the graph in Exercise **2** is moved four units left. The difference is in whether the $+4$ is inside the radical sign or outside.
4. $y = 2$ **5.** 6.1 seconds
7. T; $y = \sqrt{2}x$ is in the form of a linear equation $y = ax + b$ where $a = \sqrt{2}$ and $b = 0$.
9. (b)   **11.** They are both right.   **13.** ≈ 21.2 miles
15. ≈ 1.81 feet
17. Glenda argues that since $a \cdot a = b$, she can divide by a on both sides of the equation to get $a = \frac{b}{a}$.   **21.** Let h be the height of the rider in feet, then $h \geq 3$.   **23.** $m = \frac{23}{14}$ and $n = \frac{40}{7}$
25.

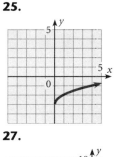

27.

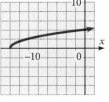

29. a. 196 ft   **b.** 44 ft deep
c. 64 ft   **d.** $t \approx 3.87$ sec

7-2 Part C
Self-Assessment

1. 36   **2.** 30.25   **3.** 16
4. 256   **5.** 0   **6.** 4   **7.** $2\sqrt{5}$
8. 0.03   **9.** 100, 121, 144, 169, 196, 225, 256, 289
10. a. $\sqrt{25}$ is rational
b. $\sqrt{35}$ is not rational   **c.** $\frac{3}{5}$ is rational   **d.** $\frac{\sqrt{32}}{\sqrt{8}}$ is rational
11. a. 121   **b.** 12,321
c. 1,234,321   **d.** 123,454,321
e. If there are n ones, then the square is written from left to right counting up from 1 to n then back down to 1.
12. a. 9 cm   **b.** 6561 mm^2
13. 20 and 21   **14.** $\sqrt{\frac{1}{7}}$

15. 0.4 ft   **16. a.** Two; The graphs of $y = \sqrt{x}$ and $y = |x - 4|$ intersect at two points.
b. Zero; The graphs of $y = |x|$ and $y = \sqrt{x - 2}$ do not intersect.
17.

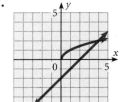

There is one value of x.
18. a. $t = \sqrt{\frac{2d}{g}}$
b. $t \approx 0.45$ sec   **c.** $\sqrt{\frac{2d}{g}}$ is in meters because d is in meters and g is in meters per second^2.
19. No; $\sqrt{150}$ is not rational.   **20. a.** v is in meters per second, so v^2 is in meters^2 per second^2. r is in meters, so $\frac{v^2}{r}$ is in meters per second^2. m is in grams, so $F = \frac{mv^2}{r}$ is in grams $\cdot$ meters per second^2.
b. $v = \sqrt{\frac{rF}{m}}$ **21.** The graph of $y = -\sqrt{2x}$ is the reflection of the graph of $y = \sqrt{2x}$ about the x-axis.

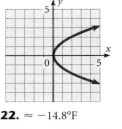

22. $\approx -14.8°F$

7-3 Part A Try It

a. 8   **b.** 4   **c.** 13

7-3 Part A Exercises

1. a. 6; 3   **b.** (2, 4) and (8, 1)   **c.** x-coordinates; y-coordinates   **3.** 6   **5.** 1   **7.** All points on the line $y = -x + 7$.   **9.** 3   **11.** 6   **13.** 8
15. a. 24 miles   **b.** 26 miles
c. 60 cents   **17.** $x = 10$ or $x = -2$ **19.** $n = -2$ or $n = -8$; $n = 0$ or $n = -10$
21. $\frac{-2}{7}$ **23.** $\frac{10}{11}$

25.

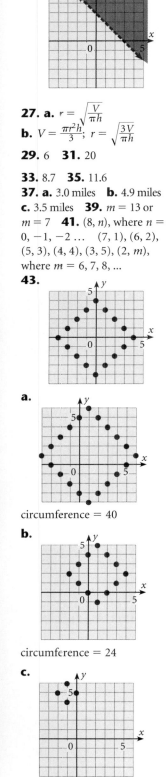

27. a. $r = \sqrt{\dfrac{V}{\pi h}}$
b. $V = \dfrac{\pi r^2 h}{3}$; $r = \sqrt{\dfrac{3V}{\pi h}}$

29. 6 **31.** 20

33. 8.7 **35.** 11.6

37. a. 3.0 miles **b.** 4.9 miles
c. 3.5 miles **39.** $m = 13$ or $m = 7$ **41.** $(8, n)$, where $n = 0, -1, -2 \ldots$ $(7, 1), (6, 2), (5, 3), (4, 4), (3, 5), (2, m)$, where $m = 6, 7, 8, \ldots$

43.

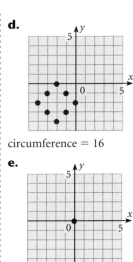

a.

circumference = 40

b.

circumference = 24

c.

circumference = 8

d.

circumference = 16

e.

7-3 Part B Try It

a. $c = 15$ **b.** $c = 13$ **c.** $c \approx 22.36$ **d.** $a = 0.5$ ft **e.** Yes; $(40)^2 + (9)^2 = (41)^2$, so by the Converse of the Pythagorean Theorem it is a right triangle.

7-3 Part B Exercises

1. a. $\overline{RT}$ **b.** $\overline{SR}, \overline{ST}$ **c.** 26 in. **3.** $a = \sqrt{3}$ **5.** $b = 120$ in. **7.** $b = 0.8$ m
9. "If you can sign this petition, then you are a registered voter." This is false.
11. Yes **13.** 22.4 in.
15. Both are right, since $90\sqrt{2} \approx 127.28$ and 0.28 ft $\approx 3\frac{3}{8}$ in. **17. a.** 3 sheets
b. Possible answer: Yes; Measure directly with a tape measure. **c.** 15 ft
19. a. 15 inches **b.** 4 times
21. Yes

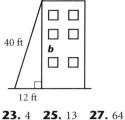

23. 4 **25.** 13 **27.** 64
29. $b = 12$ **31.** $a = 7$
33. $a = 72$ **35.** $c = 50$ m
37. $c = 17$ cm **39.** $c = 5\sqrt{2}$ yd **41.** Yes **43.** $\left(\frac{3}{4}\right)^2 + (1)^2 = (1.25)^2$, so it is a right triangle.

45. Possible answer: **a.** Express a, b, c as ordered triples (a, b, c). $(1, 3, 8)$, $(1, 4, 7)$, $(1, 5, 6)$, $(2, 2, 8)$, $(2, 3, 7)$, $(2, 4, 6)$, $(2, 5, 5)$, $(3, 3, 6)$, $(3, 4, 5)$, $(4, 4, 4)$
b. $\frac{3}{10}$ because only $(2, 5, 5)$, $(3, 4, 5)$, and $(4, 4, 4)$ satisfy the Triangle Inequality.
c. $\frac{1}{10}$ because only $(3, 4, 5)$ satisfies the Pythagorean Theorem.

7-3 Part C Try It

a. 10 **b.** 5 **c.** $\sqrt{72} = \sqrt{36 \cdot 2} = \sqrt{36} \cdot \sqrt{2} = 6\sqrt{2}$ **d.** $\sqrt{500} = \sqrt{100 \cdot 5} = \sqrt{100} \cdot \sqrt{5} = 10\sqrt{5}$
e. $2\sqrt{5}$ **f.** 5

7-3 Part C Exercises

1. a. 3; 4 **b.** 8; −8 **c.** 13
5. $8\frac{1}{2}$ **7. a.** 8 miles
b. $\sqrt{34} \approx 5.83$ miles **9.** 25; 25; 5 **11.** $\sqrt{6}$ **13.** 11
15. $(-3000, 600)$; ≈ 3059 miles **17.** These points suggest a circle.

19. Yes
21.

23. $\frac{5}{216} \dfrac{\text{calories}}{\text{second}}$ **25.** 25
27. ≈ 9.9 **29.** ≈ 13.9
31. 9; 9; 3 **33.** 64; 64; 8
35. $5\sqrt{3}$ **37.** 3 **39.** 7
41. a. 9 **b.** $3\sqrt{5}$
43. When both points lie on the same vertical or horizontal line.

7-3 Part D Self-Assessment

1. a. Using the graph, the distance is $14 - 2 = 12$.

b. Using the distance formula, the distance is $\sqrt{(8 - 2)^2 + (10 - 2)^2} = 10$
c. $\triangle ABC$ is an isosceles triangle because BC is $\sqrt{(14 - 8)^2 + (2 - 10)^2} = 10$ **2. a.** 8 blocks **b.** $4\sqrt{2}$ blocks **c.** $(1, 7), (1, 8), (1, 9), (1, 10), (1, 11), (2, 7), (2, 8), (2, 9), (2, 10), (2, 11), (3, 7), (3, 8), (3, 9), (3, 10), (3, 11), (4, 6), (5, 5), (6, 4), (7, 3), (8, 1), (8, 2), (9, 1), (9, 2), (10, 1), (10, 2), (11, 1), (11, 2)$ **3.** $b = 18$ **4.** $a = 36$ **5.** $c = 8\sqrt{2}$ **6.** (d)
7.

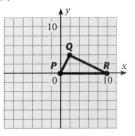

$\triangle PQR$ is a right triangle.
$PQ = \sqrt{(4 - 0)^2 + (2 - 0)^2} = \sqrt{16 + 4} = \sqrt{20}$. $QR = \sqrt{(10 - 2)^2 + (0 - 4)^2} = \sqrt{64 + 16} = \sqrt{80}$. $PR = \sqrt{(0 - 0)^2 + (10 - 0)^2} = \sqrt{100} = 10$. $PQ^2 + QR^2 = (\sqrt{20})^2 + (\sqrt{80})^2 = 20 + 80 = 100 = 10^2 = PR^2$.
8. a. Adam lives at 153rd Street and 11th Avenue.
b. $(150, 15), (151, 16), (155, 16), (156, 15), (157, 14), (158, 13), (159, 12), (160, 11), (159, 10), (158, 9), (157, 8), (156, 7), (150, 7)$ **9.** Possible answer: Not exactly; He means that the square of the length of the hypotenuse of a right triangle is equal to the sum of the squares of the lengths of the two adjacent sides. There is no such thing as the square of a side.
10. a. Possible answer: Using the map, Piura, Chiclayo, and Chimbote lie on the same line and Chiclayo is at midpoint between Piura and Chimbote.

b. Possible answer: About 220 miles between cities.
c. Possible answer: Piura, Trujillo, and Callao lie on the same line. There are about 300 miles between Piura and Trujillo and 350 miles between Trujillo and Callao.
11. a. $\frac{\triangle y}{\triangle x}$
b. $\sqrt{(\triangle x)^2 + (\triangle y)^2}$
12. a. $\left(\frac{9}{2}, 0\right)$
b.

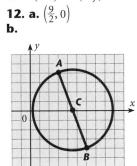

13. $2\sqrt{5}$
14.

$ABCD$ is not a square because
$AB =$
$\sqrt{(5-0)^2 + (0-0)^2} =$
$\sqrt{(5)^2} = 5$ and $AD =$
$\sqrt{(0-0)^2 + (4-0)^2} =$
$\sqrt{(4)^2} = 4$. The two sides do not have the same length.
15. a. $\sqrt{26}$; $\sqrt{26}$ **b.** N is the midpoint of $\overline{LM}$ **c.** $\overline{KN}$
16. 125 mi/hr **17.** Let c be the distance from one side on the bottom to the opposite side on top. Then $(3)^2 +$ $(7.5)^2 = c^2$ or $c^2 = 9 +$ $56.25 = 65.25$. So $c =$ $\sqrt{65.25} \approx 8.08$ inches. Therefore, an 8-inch straw will not stick out. Let c be the distance from one side on the bottom to the center on top, then $(1.5)^2 + (7.5)^2 = c^2$ or $c^2 = 2.25 + 56.25 = 58.5$. So $c = \sqrt{58.5} \approx 7.65$ inches. Therefore, an 8-inch straw will stick out.

7-4 Part A Try It
a. $AC = 24$ **b.** $DE = 20$
c. No; Possible answer: $\frac{GH}{AB} = \frac{10}{30} = \frac{1}{3}$ and $\frac{GI}{AC} =$ $\frac{5}{24}$; $\frac{5}{24} \neq \frac{1}{3}$, so the triangles are not similar.

7-4 Part A Exercises
1. a. $\frac{8}{x}$ **b.** $x = 4$ **c.** Yes
3. $x = \frac{25}{3}$ **5.** $x = 0.5$
7. Corresponding
9. Corresponding angles; Corresponding side lengths
11. Yes **15. a.** 15 ft by 9 ft
b. 30 ft by 15 ft **c.** $\frac{13}{3}$ in. by 5 in. **17.** Possible answer: $AB = \sqrt{(3)^2 + (5)^2} = \sqrt{34}$; $BC = \sqrt{(3)^2 + (1)^2} = \sqrt{10}$; $AC = 4$; $DE = \sqrt{(6)^2 + (8)^2} =$ 10; $EF = \sqrt{(6)^2 + (2)^2} =$ $2\sqrt{10}$; $DF = 6$. $\triangle ABC \not\sim$ $\triangle DEF$ because the ratios of corresponding side lengths are not all equal.
19. Possible answer: About $\frac{1.5 \text{ cm}}{700} \approx 0.02$ mm across. The actual radiolarian is similar to its picture. **21.** No; 9 cm + 5 cm < 16 cm, which contradicts the Triangle Inequality Theorem.
23. $(7, 2)$
25. Possible answer: Alligators: $|x - 31.5| < 6.5$; Lizards: $|x - 30.25| < 17.75$; Snakes: $|x - 24.5| < 13.5$; Turtles: $|x - 22.5| < 15$
27. $a = 20$; $b = \frac{24}{5}$
29. $x = 3$ **31.** $x = \frac{10}{3}$
33. $x = 2$ **37. a.** Less than 1
b.

7-4 Part B Try It
a. $\frac{12}{5}$ **b.** $\frac{5}{12}$
c. $\frac{40}{9}$ **d.** $\frac{9}{40}$
e. Possible answer:

7-4 Part B Exercises
1. a. $\overline{BC}$ **b.** $\overline{AC}$ **c.** $\overline{AC}$
d. $\overline{BC}$ **e.** $\angle B$ **3.** Adjacent to **5.** $\frac{4 \text{ m}}{4 \text{ m}}$ **7.** $\frac{5 \text{ mm}}{12 \text{ mm}}$

9. a. $\overline{RS}$ **b.** $\overline{ST}$ **c.** ST
d. 2.4 **11.** $\tan K \approx 0.5$
13. a. Possible answer: Direct; Use a tape measure
b. Possible answer: Indirect; Use shadows and similar triangles **c.** Possible answer: Indirect; Use shadows and similar triangles **d.** Possible answer: Direct; Use a tape measure **e.** Possible answer: Indirect; Use similar triangles **f.** Possible answer: Direct; Use a tape measure
g. Possible answer: Direct; Use the odometer
h. Possible answer: Indirect; Use a map and multiply by the scale factor **15. a.** 5 ft
b. 32 ft **17.** c **19. a.** $\overline{ST}$
b. $\overline{RT}$ **c.** $\overline{RT}$ **d.** $\overline{ST}$
e. $\angle T$ **21.** 0.7 **23.** 1.3
25. $\triangle AFG \sim \triangle ABC$; $\tan A = \frac{FG}{AF} = \frac{BC}{AB}$
27. a. $\tan B = 2$
b. $m\angle A = m\angle B = 45°$
c. $\tan A \cdot \tan B = \left(\frac{BC}{AC}\right)\left(\frac{AC}{BC}\right) = 1$
29. 25 ft to 40 ft

7-4 Part C Try It
a. $AC \approx 7.31$ **b.** $AC \approx 7.31$

7-4 Part C Exercises
1. a. $\overline{AB}$ **b.** $\overline{BC}$ **c.** $\overline{AC}$
3. a. $RS = 10$ ft **b.** $\frac{3}{5}, \frac{4}{5}, \frac{3}{4}$
c. $\frac{4}{5}, \frac{3}{5}, \frac{4}{3}$ **d.** $\sin S = \cos R$ and $\cos S = \sin R$; Yes
5. a. $\frac{3}{4}$ **b.** $\frac{4}{5}$ **c.** $\frac{4}{5}$ **d.** $\frac{3}{5}$
7. a. ≈ 0.0698 **b.** 0.5
c. ≈ 0.6428 **d.** ≈ 0.8660
e. ≈ 0.9998 **f.** The value of the sine increases. **9. a.** $\approx$ 0.0699 **b.** ≈ 0.5774
c. ≈ 0.8391 **d.** ≈ 1.7321
e. ≈ 57.2810 **f.** The value of the tangent of an angle increases **11.** ≈ 57.06 ft
13. $\approx 172,763$ ft; ≈ 32.72 mi
15. ≈ 76 ft; Possible answer: The school is in the city because it is tall. **17.** $\tan 8° = \frac{250 \text{ ft}}{d}$, so $d = \frac{250 \text{ ft}}{\tan 8°} \approx$ 1779 ft
19. a. 3.654 billion
b. ≈ 11.89 million per day
21. e **23.** ≈ 0.9848
25. ≈ 0.9848 **27. a.** $\overline{AB}$
b. $\overline{BC}$ **c.** $\overline{AC}$ **29. a.** $\frac{12}{5}$

b. $\frac{5}{13}$ **c.** $\frac{5}{13}$ **d.** $\frac{12}{13}$
31. a. $\frac{3}{4}$ **b.** $\frac{4}{5}$ **c.** $\frac{4}{5}$
d. $\frac{3}{5}$ **33. a.** Greater
b. Smaller **c.** Greater
d.

When $\frac{BC}{AC} = 1$, $AC = BC$
35. $m\angle A = m\angle B = 45°$
37. a. ≈ 0.3142 yd **b.** $\approx$ 0.8727 yd **c.** The beam will not strike the surface.

7-4 Part D Self-Assessment
1. a. $\angle 2$; $\angle B$ **b.** 14
2. 2.4 in. **3.** $x = \frac{3}{5}$
4. $y = 18$ **5. a.** $\overline{RS}$
b. $\overline{ST}$; $\overline{RT}$ **6. a.** $\frac{8}{17}$ **b.** $\frac{15}{17}$
c. $\frac{8}{15}$ **7.** $\frac{3}{5}, \frac{4}{5}, \frac{3}{4}, \frac{4}{5}, \frac{3}{5}, \frac{4}{3}$
8. $\frac{11}{61}, \frac{60}{61}, \frac{11}{60}, \frac{60}{61}, \frac{11}{61}, \frac{60}{11}$
9. a. ≈ 289 km away
b. 1.325 hr **c.** Possible answer: No direct roads; Favorite restaurant on the route they took **10.** 21.6 in. by 16.2 in. **11.** (e)
12. a. 1732 ft **b.** 60°
c. 13 inches **13.** Yes; In either case, one gets $45 = 7x$; $x = \frac{45}{7}$ **14.** $\frac{4.25 \text{ ft}}{\tan 3°} - \frac{4.25 \text{ ft}}{\tan 4°}$ ≈ 20 ft **15.** 0 **16.** 22.5 ft tall; Possible answer: She could have used shadows and similar triangles. **17.** $\approx$ 15.636 ft; ≈ 2.96 miles; No
18. a. ≈ 52 miles **b.** ≈ 41 miles **c.** ≈ 27 miles

Chapter 7 Review
1. Hypotenuse **2.** Rational
3. Principal square root
4. Absolute Value **5.** $x = 5$
6. $x = 3$ **7.** $x = 0.41$
8. $x = -3$ or $x = -5$
9. a. ii **b.** i
c. iii **10.** Two **11.** Two
12. Zero **13.** 9
14. $\frac{5}{10} = \frac{1}{2}$ **15.** 0.04
16. 5 and 6 **17.** 1 and 2
18. $r = \sqrt{\frac{V}{\pi h}}$

19.

$y = x^2$

$y = \sqrt{x}$

20. a. 22 blocks **b.** $11\sqrt{2}$ blocks **21.** $y = 12$ **22.** $x \approx 21.2$ **23.** No; It does not satisfy the Pythagorean Theorem, since $(14)^2 + (20)^2 \neq (24)^2$ **24.** 10
25. a. Yes; By the Distance Formula, all sides have length $\sqrt{17}$. **b.** 17; Plot the vertices to see that the quadrilateral is a square. The area of a square is the length of its side squared. **c.** 16.49 **26.** 3
27. 4 **28.** 9; 2
29.

It suggests a circle
30. Let x be the number of feet she is from her truck, then $(40)^2 + (90)^2 = x^2$ or $x^2 = 1600 + 8100 = 9700$ so $x = \sqrt{9700} \approx 98.5$. She will be able to receive calls.
31. Show that the ratios of the corresponding side lengths are the same. **32.** 0.5 **33.** 0.5 **34.** ≈ 0.58 **35.** ≈ 0.87 **36.** ≈ 15.51 in. **37.** ≈ 8.75 in. **38.** Solve for the height of the building above her eye level by multiplying 35 ft by $\tan 52°$, then add her eye level to get the height. **39.** $\tan A = \frac{3}{4}$ **40.** Possible answer: One way is to use similar triangles, so $\frac{AB}{ED} = \frac{AC}{EC}$ or $\frac{x}{6} = \frac{10}{8}$. Another way is to use right triangle trigonometry, so $\frac{x}{10} = \tan 37°$. Solving for x, $x = 7.5$. **41. a.** ≈ 321 ft **b.** A: \$24,700; B: $\approx$ \$3,860

CHAPTER 8

8-1 Part A Try It
a. 3rd degree, binomial
b. 2nd degree, monomial
c. 5th degree, trinomial
d. Quadratic **e.** Cubic
f. Linear **g.** 1
h. $5x^2 + 7x - 6$

8-1 Part A Exercises
1. a. $(6 - 10) + (4x^2 - x^2) + (8x - 5x)$ **b.** $-4 + 3x + 3x^2$ **c.** $3x^2 + 3x - 4$
3. $2; x^2 + 2x + 6$ **5. a.** iii **b.** i **c.** ii **7.** Expression
9. Function **11.** $2x^2 + x = 3x^2 + x - x^2$ **13.** $x^2 + x + 1$
15. $-4a^3 + 7a^2 - 4a + 16$
17. $-3d^3 + 4d^2 + 7d - 2$
19. $-x^3 - 5x^2 + 16x$
21.

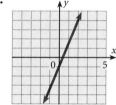

23. a. \$28 **b.** Yes **c.** 465
d. Yes, he would get \$465.
25. Yes **27.** Always
29. a. 98%, 90%, 37%
b. $n \approx 69$ tests; $(0.99)^{69} \approx 0.5$ **31.** Let A = amount Amy has; Then $2A - 52.50 = 740$ **33. a.** 2 **b.** 8 **c.** 4
d. 0 **e.** 2 **35.** $x \approx 14.14$
37. 2nd; $-x^2 + 5x + 1$
39. $5x^2 + x + 9$
41. $-8x^3 + 10x^2 - 6$
43. $-x^2 - x + 10$
45. $x^2 + 10$ **47.** $8a^3 - 4a + 4$
49. 6.62×10^9 km³
51. Yes **53. a.** No
b. (c) **55.** $x^2 + 2x$

8-1 Part B Try It
a. 3.21×10^8 km **b.** p^{35}
c. $8x^6$ **d.** $12y^6$ **e.** $20y^6$

8-1 Part B Exercises
1. a. 36,000,000 **b.** 10^7
c. 7 **3. a.** 778,300,000
b. 7.783 **c.** 7.783×10^8
5. 9.0×10^8 **7.** 2,670,000,000
9. $-8y^{10}$ **11.** $16y^{12}$
13. 8 **15.** $-c^6$ **17.** $9w^6$
19. $-10f^2g^{10}$ **21.** $-48m^{10}n^{11}$

23. $18x; 17x^2$ **25.** $49.2y^5$; No; Distance cannot be negative. **27.** -2.35×10^4; 1.23×10^3; 1.75×10^3; 1.03×10^4; 11.4×10^3
29. 2.285206×10^8 km
31. 2^6 **33. a.** 1.6×10^{10} mi; 6.8×10^8 mi; 1.9×10^5 mi
b. 4.5473×10^8 **35.** 1.00001; Possible answer: $10^{-5} < 10^{-3}$
37. $\frac{1}{1,000,000}$ **43.** y^4
45. $8b^9$ **47.** $108x^6$ **49.** -1
51. $18a^5b^3$ **53.** m^8n^{20}
55. -1.51×10^4; 1.04×10^3; 1.07×10^3; 1.01×10^4
57. a. 3.42×10^{11} **b.** 1.04×10^6 **c.** 1.28×10^5 **59.** No **61.** No; $3^2 \neq 2^3$, which disproves Pete's theory.
63. a. ●●●
b. ●● **c.** ●●●
d. ●●●● **e.** —
f. ● **g.** ●●
h. ●●●● **i.** —
j. ● **k.** ●●
l. ●●● **m.** ●●●●

8-1 Part C Try It
a. m^{-3} **b.** $\frac{y^2}{2x^3}$ **c.** 10^{-4}
d. $\frac{81}{256}$ **e.** The plant cell, by 10^5

8-1 Part C Exercises
1. a. -4 **b.** x^2 **c.** $\frac{1}{y}$
d. $-\frac{4x^2}{y}$ **3.** 4 **5.** a^2
7. d^{-3} **9.** 1 **11.** b
13. $\frac{1}{125}$ **15.** $\frac{z}{-4x^2}$
17. 2.5×10^{22} **19.** (c)
21. $(-2)^6$
23. 4,320,000,000,000,000
25. a. 2.5 **b.** 1.3 **c.** 1.1
27. $1; n^0 \neq n^4$ **29.** It will be taller, since $2^{22}x = 319.6$ m, where $x = 0.003$ in. $= 0.0000762$ m **31.** 700
33. Possible answer: Estimate length of a decimal point to be 0.6 mm; Length of a polio virus is 2^{-7} m $= 0.2$ micron $= 200$ nm **35.** $d \geq 11,000 \times 0.2$ **37.** $x = 13$; $x = 5$ **39.** $x = 88$; $x = 16$

41. 1 **43.** $\frac{1}{3j}$ **45.** $-5y$
47. $-15ce^4$ **49.** $\frac{27}{125}$
51. 32 **53.** $\frac{-27}{125}$ **55.** 1
57. 6,630,000 **59.** 100
61. $-1; 1; -1; 1; -1$ **a.** 1
b. -1 **63.** $\left(\frac{3}{5}\right)^{-3}$
65. a. 4×10^{-6} in
b. 1.016×10^{-5} cm
c. 1,000,000

8-1 Part D Self-Assessment
1. 4 **2.** 0 **3.** -5 **4.** 6
5. 7 **6.** 0 **7.** 3 **8.** 8
9. a. ii **b.** ii **c.** $3x^2 - 2x + 1$ **d.** $x^2 + 4x + 1$
10. m^8 **11.** $2m^4$ **12.** Not possible **13. a.** ii, v **b.** i. $3x^2$; iii. $2x^3$; iv. $2x^5$ **c.** Possible answer: Students make addition errors. **14.** 1
15. $\frac{3}{x^2}$ **16.** $5x^2 - 4x + 1$
17. 1 **18.** $\frac{2}{2}$ **19.** $\frac{16x^4}{81}$
20. $-8y$ **21.** $25g^8$ **22.** 6
23. Possible answer: About 7.5 microns, or 7500 nm
24. a. 3000 **b.** 1796
c. 3324 **25. c.** 2×10^7 dollars **26.** (c) **27.** 3×10^{20} miles **28. a.** 2 cm
b. 0.0098 in.; 9.8 in.
29. Possible answer: Saturn is farther away from earth than Mars and it would therefore take a longer voyage to get there. The length of the trip would depend upon where Saturn is (relative to the Sun).
30. a. 0.0000000000000001
b. 1.1×10^{-22} tons
c. 161.7 tons

8-2 Part A Try It
a. $2x^3 + 3x$ **b.** $3x^3 - 2x^2$
c. $3x^3 - 15x^2 + 9x$
d. $2(x + 5)$ **e.** $y(y + 6)$
f. $2x(9x^2 + 2x - 1)$
g. $5x^2(x^2 - 4x - 4)$

8-2 Part A Exercises
1. a. $3x; -7$ **b.** $6x^3 - 14x^2$ **3.** $48x^3 - 18x^2$
5. $x^2 + 2x$ **7.** 1, 48; 2, 24; 4, 12; 3, 16; 6, 8 **9.** 1, 64; 2, 32; 4, 16; 8, 8 **11.** (c)
13. $5x(x^2 - 4x^3 - 7)$
15. (a) **17. a.** $2x^2 - 9$
b. 119 ft² **19. a.** $V = 10\pi r^2$ **b.** $V = 10\pi(r + 3)^2$

c. 390π m³ **21. a.** 3, 7
b. 1, 2 **c.** 4, −1 **d.** 3, −3
e. −7, 2 **23. a.** x, x^5; x^2
x^4; x^3, x^3; 1, x^6 **b.** $4x$, x^4; $2x$,
$2x^4$; x, $4x^4$; $4x^2$, x^3; $2x^2$, $2x^3$;
x^2, $4x^3$; 4, x^5; 2, $2x^5$; 1, $4x^5$
c. $−x$, x^2; x, $−x^2$; −1, x^3;
1, $−x^3$ **25.** 1, 300; 2, 150; 3,
100; 4, 75; 5, 60; 6, 50; 10, 30;
15, 20; 12, 25 **27. a.** x
b. $x(x − 5)$ **c.** $x(x − 5) =$
$x^2 − 5x$ **29. a.** $14y^3$: 1, 2,
7, 14, y, $2y$, $7y$, $14y$, y^2, $2y^2$,
$7y^2$, $14y^2$, y^3, $2y^3$, $7y^3$, $14y^3$,
and their opposites.
$−21y$: −1, 1, −3, 3, −7,
7, −21, 21, $−y$, y, $−3y$,
$3y$, $−7y$, $7y$, $−21y$, $21y$
$−7y^2$: −1, 1, −7, 7, $−y$,
y, $−7y$, $7y$, $−y^2$, y^2, $−7y^2$, $7y^2$
b. 1, 7, y, $7y$, and their opposites. **c.** $7y$ or $−7y$
31. (b) **35.** $5x(x − 2)$
44. $6x^2(3 − 5x^2 − 2x)$
50. $x(4x + 8)$; $4x(x + 2)$;
$2(2x^2 + 4x)$; $2x(2x + 4)$;
$1(4x^2 + 8x)$; $4(x^2 + 2x)$
53. a. $x(0.05x + 1)$
b. 40 ft **c.** Yes

8-2 Part B Try It
a. $x^2 + 11x + 30$ **b.** $y^2 +$
$2y − 3$ **c.** $r^2 − 104r + 400$

8-2 Part B Exercises
1. a. $2x^2 − 3x$ **b.** $8x − 12$
c. $2x^2 + 5x − 12$
3. a.

	d	3
d	d^2	$3d$
−2	$−2d$	−6

$d^2 + d − 6$
4. $9x^2 − 24x + 16$ **6.** $p^2 −$
$p − 20$ **8.** $25s^2 + 20s + 4$
14. a. $(x − 2)(x + 3)$
b. $x^2 + x − 6$ **c.** 150 ft²
17. $8x^2 + 22x + 5$; $8x^2 +$
$22x + 5$; The products are
identical. Illustrates Commutative Property of Multiplication **19. a.** No; Cannot
subtract the two terms since
they have different expo-
nents. **b.** 0 ft **c.** 164 ft²
d. 0 ft; The rocket cannot be
underground.
21. $y = \frac{x}{2} − 2$

23. a. 147,100,000 km;
149,490,000 km; 152,080,000
km; 149,770,000 km **b.** 4.98
$× 10^6$ km
25.

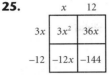

	x	12
$3x$	$3x^2$	$36x$
−12	$−12x$	−144

$3x^2 + 24x − 144$
27. a. Distributive
b. Distributive **29.** $x^2 −$
100 **31.** $s^2 − 29s + 100$
33. $9y^2 + 6y + 1$
35. $36n^2 − 60n + 25$
39. $(x + y)^2$ is greater
because $(x + y)^2 = x^2 +$
$2xy + y^2$ and $2xy$ is positive.
41. No; when the values of p
and q have opposite signs.
43. No; $7.0 × 10^2$

8-2 Part C Try It
a. $(x + 6)(x + 5)$
b. $(m − 9)(m + 5)$
c. $−3(y + 2)(y − 10)$

8-2 Part C Exercises
1. a. $x^2 + 7x + 10$ **b.** $x +$
$2, x + 5$ **c.** $(x + 2)(x + 5)$
3. 1, 100; 2, 50; 4, 25; 5, 20;
10, 10 **5.** + 2; + 5 **7.** 3; 5
9. −; + **11.** $(x + 2)(x +$
$4) = x^2 + 6x + 8$ **13.** $(e +$
$1)(e − 25) = e^2 − 24e − 25$
15. $(x − 3)(x + 2) = x^2 −$
$x − 6$ **17.** $(b + 8)(b −$
$5) = b^2 + 3b − 40$
19. $(d + 12)(d + 1) = d^2 +$
$13d + 12$ **21.** Not factorable **23. a.** $0.25R^2 +$
$0.5RW + 0.25W^2$ **b.** Red:
25%; Pink: 50%; White: 25%
27. $x^2 + 2x + 1$ **29.** $x^2 −$
1 **31.** 1, 400; 2, 200; 4, 100;
5, 80; 8, 50; 10, 40; 16, 25; 20,
20 **33. a.** $x^2 + 9x + 20$
b. $(x + 4)$ and $(x + 5)$
c. $(x + 4)(x + 5)$
35. + 6; + 3 **37.** −; +
39. $3(t + 3) = 3t + 9$
41. $(a + 3)(a + 4) = a^2 +$
$7a + 12$ **43.** $(t + 12)(t − 4)$
$= t^2 + 8t − 48$
45. $(h + 7)(h + 6) = h^2 +$
$13h + 42$ **47.** $(x − 0.4)^2 =$
$x^2 − 0.8x + 0.16$
49. $(g − 8)^2 = g^2 − 16g + 64$

51. $\frac{(x + 1)(x + 3)}{4}$; The
length and width of each
smaller rectangle is $\frac{x + 1}{2}$ and
$\frac{x + 3}{2}$. **53.** Area square $= x^2$;
Area triangle $= \frac{1}{2}(2)(x) = x$;
Total area $= x^2 + x$
55. a. The numbers form
triangles
b.

c.

d	n
4	10
5	15
6	21
10	55

d.

```
            1
          1   1
         1  2  1
        1  3  3  1
       1  4  6  4  1
      1 5 10 10 5 1
     1 6 15 20 15 6 1
```

e. 5050 dots **f.** A square
number.

8-2 Part D Try It
a. $x^2 + 20x + 100$ **b.** $y^2 −$
$16y + 64$ **c.** $(x + 6)(x + 6)$
d. $(x − 7)(x + 7)$
e. $(y − 11)(y − 11)$

8-2 Part D Exercises
1. a. $d^2 − 20d + 100$
b. The last term is the square
of the constant term.
c. The middle term is twice
the constant term of the
binomial. **3.** $y^2 − 24y +$
144 **5.** $(s + 9)(s + 9)$;
Square **7.** $(h − 13)(h +$
$13) = h^2 − 169$ **9.** No;
Constant term would have to
be −144 **11.** $x + 2$
13. $(c + 4)(c − 4)$
15. $(y − 9)(y + 8)$
17. $11(p − 3)(p − 3)$
19. a. $16t(6 − t)$ **b.** 144 ft
21. a. 4 **b.** 2 **c.** 4
d. (a) and (c) **23.** (b)
25. First expression is
greater if $y > 0$. The second
expression is greater if $y < 0$.
27. $x = 5$; $y = 9$

29. a. $\sqrt{13}$ **b.** 5
c. $(5, 3.5)$ **d.** $\frac{3}{2}$ **31.** $x^2 +$
$30x + 225$ **33.** $s^2 + s + \frac{1}{4}$
35. $(x − 9)(x − 9)$
37. Not square **39.** No
41. No **43.** $(d + 4)(d − 4)$
45. $(z − 7)(z + 6)$
47. $3(m − 5)(m + 5)$
49. $(t − 3)(t + 2)$
51. $3(d + 5)(d + 5)$
53. $2(t + 1)(t + 1)$
55. $(x + 2)(x − 2)(x^2 + 1)$
57. (c) **59. a.** Yes; 5 =
$2^2 + 1^2$; 25 = $3^2 + 4^2$
b. 13; Yes; $2^2 + 3^2 = 13$; Yes;
$12^2 + 5^2 = 169$
61. a. $x^3 + 1$ **b.** $x^4 − 1$
c. $x^5 + 1$ **d.** $x^6 − 1$
e. All of the middle terms
cancel; Possible answer:
$(x + 1)(x^6 − x^5 + x^4 −$
$x^3 + x^2 − x + 1)$

8-2 Part E Self-Assessment
1. Multiply $3x^2$ by $4x$
2. Multiply x by $5x$
3. a. $x(2x + 3) = 2x^2 + 3x$
b. $6x(3x + 4) = 18x^2 + 24x$
c. $16x^2 + 21x$ **4.** 3 terms,
$x^2 + 4x + 4$ **5.** 2 terms,
$x^2 − 4$ **6.** 3 terms, $x^2 −$
$8x + 16$ **7.** (c)
8. $(x + 7)(x − 1)$
9. Cannot be factored
10. $2x(x^2 − 3x + 1)$
11. $(5x)(x − 5)(x + 5)$
12. (d); Cannot be factored
13. $(x + 3)(x − 3)$
14. a. 0 **b.** 0 **c.** 0
15. (c); $−14 + 3 = −11$;
$(−14)(3) = −42$
16. a. $2\pi r(r + h)$
b. 747.7 cm² **17. a.** iv
b. i **c.** iii **d.** i and iii
18. a. 1 **b.** 2 **c.** 4, 8
d. Yes; 64 **e.** 11
19. a. $(25 − 2x) × (20 −$
$2x) × x$ **b.** 672 cm³
c. No; Width would then be
0 cm **20. a.** 32.3%
21. 19; 45 **22. a.** $t(8 − 5t)$
b. 0 m **c.** 3 m **d.** A negative result would mean the
ball hit the ground again;
$h = −4$ at $t = 2$ etc. You do
not have much time to hit the
ball.

23. Farmer must take the goat, then the cabbage, bring the goat back, take the wolf, leave the wolf on the other side with the cabbage, and then come back for the goat.

Chapter 8 Review

1. F; Trinomial **2.** T
3. a. iii; $x + 1$ has degree 1.
b. ii; $-6x^2 - x$ has degree 2.
c. i; $x^3 + 1$ has degree 3.
4. a. ii **b.** i **c.** iii
5. 3.6×10^{-10} joules
6. $2x^3 + 5x^2 - 8$
7. $-x^2 - 5x$ **8.** x^2
9. $-x^3$ **10.** x^6 **11.** $2x^2$
12. $\frac{2y}{x}$ **13.** $2x^3 + 4x^2 + 6x - 3$ **14.** (d) **15.** $125 = 5^3, 25 = 5^2$; Therefore, $(125)(25)(5) = 5^3(5^2)(5^1) = 5^6$ **16.** $7x^2$; 175
17. 0.0000000000000000000 0000016605 **18.** 6.0221 $\times 10^{23}$ **19.** 394.737
20. $36x + 27$ **21.** $6x^3 - 30x^2 + 2x$ **22.** $x^2 + 10x + 21$ **23.** $x^2 + 2x + 1$
24. $x^2 - 1$ **25.** $12x^2 - 11x - 5$ **26.** No; $(x + 3)^2$ has a middle term equal to $6x$. **27.** $3(x^2 - 2)$ **28.** $5x$ $(x - 8)(x - 2)$ **29.** $(x + 3)$ $(x - 3)$ **30.** $(x + 8)(x + 8)$
31. (b) **32. a** $-0.1x^2 - 0.6x + 3.0$ **b.** $2.30; $1.40

CHAPTER 9

9-1 Part A Try It
a–c.

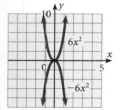

a. y-axis; y-axis **b.** (0, 0); (0, 0) **c.** Possible answer: (1, 6) and (−1, 6); (1, −6) and (1, −6)

9-1 Part A Exercises
1. a. $(-2, 3)$; $(2, 3)$
b. $(4, -4)$; $(-4, -4)$
c. $(-4, 1)$; $(4, 1)$ **3.** Vertex
5. Reflection **6.** T and U, S and V, R and W
7.

9. $a = -1, b = 3, c = 2$
11. $a = 1, b = 0, c = -2$
13.

x	$2x$	x^2	$2x^2$
0	0	0	0
1	2	1	2
2	4	4	8
3	6	9	18
4	8	16	32
5	10	25	50

a. The value of $2x$ increases from 0 to 10 **b.** The value of x^2 increases from 0 to 25 **c.** The value of $2x^2$ increases from 0 to 50 **d.** 20; 100; 200 **15. a.** i, iii, iv, v, vi **b.** i, iii, iv, v **c.** ii **17.** A
19. E **21.** B **23.** 1.6 horse power **25.** It is a parabola that opens down, has a vertex at (0, 7), and is wider than $y = -x^2$. **27.** 5
29. $\frac{C}{B} - \frac{A}{B}x$
31. a. $(3, 4)$; $(-3, 4)$
b. $(-2, 1)$; $(2, 1)$
c. $(-3, -4)$; $(3, -4)$
33. $a = -5, b = 0, c = 0$
35. $a = \frac{1}{2}, b = 0, c = -3$
37. $a = \frac{2}{5}, b = -6, c = 0$
39. C **41.** A **43.** B
45. a. y-axis **b.** (0, 0)
c. Possible answers: (1, 0.8), and (−1, 0.8), (2, 3.2) and (−2, 3.2), (3, 7.2) and (−3, 7.2)
47. a. ii **b.** All
49.

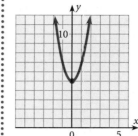

51. a. $x = 1$ **b.** $(1, -1)$
c. Possible answers: (0, 0) and (2, 0), (−1, 3) and (3, 3), (−2, 8) and (4, 8)

9-1 Part B Try It
a–c.

a. y-axis **b.** (0, 5) **c.** $y = 5$
d. $h = -4.9t^2 + 10t + 1.5$; The ball goes about 6.6 m up; The ball takes about 2.2 seconds to hit the ground.

9-1 Part B Exercises
1. a. y-axis **b.** (0, 4) **c.** 4
2. a. y-axis **b.** (0, 1) **c.** 1
3. a. y-axis **b.** (0, 8) **c.** 8
5. a. $h = -4.9t^2 + 28t + 1$
b.

t	h
1	24.1
2	37.4
3	40.9
4	34.6

c.

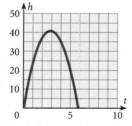

The ball has a maximum height of about 41 m; It will hit the ground in about 5.7 seconds. **7.** F **9.** B
11. C **13.** $c = 0$
15. a. 31.4 m; 31.9 m
b. 2.55 sec **c.** $\approx$ 5.14 sec
17. She could solve the equation $0 = \frac{1}{2}(-32)t^2 + 600$ for t. **19.** $3x^3 + 2x^2 - 4x - 1$ **21.** ≈ 55.74 m²; The depth of the base.
23. a. y-axis **b.** (0, 6)
c. 6 **25. a.** y-axis
b. (0, −6) **c.** −6 **27.** A
29. E **31.** B
33. a. Both graphs are parabolas that open up and pass through (0, 0). The

graph of $y = 2x^2 + 5x$ is a translation of $y = 2x^2$. The axes of symmetry and vertices are different. **b.** b rotates the original parabola. **c.** The vertex position is raised by 6 units. **d.** The y-value of the vertex changes.

35. a.

x (sec)	y (m)
1	2
2	8
3	18
4	32
5	50

b. 10 m; 18 m; The rate of change increases, reflecting an increase in velocity. The rate of change for a linear function is constant.

9-1 Part C Self-Assessment
1. a. y-axis **b.** (0, 0)
c. Possible answers: $(1, -0.25)$ and $(-1, -0.25)$; $(2, -1)$ and $(-2, -1)$; $(3, -2.25)$ and $(-3, -2.25)$
2. (d) **3.** The lines of symmetry are the six lines passing through opposite vertices of the inner star. Across these lines, halves of the basket are reflections of each other.
4. a. Upward; a is positive
b. Yes; The function is in the form $y = ax^2 + c$ **c.** No; $c \neq 0$ **d.** A minimum value since a is positive. **5. a.** ii
b. iii **c.** i **6. a.** When r is doubled, the area is 4 times larger. When r is tripled, the area is 9 times larger. When r is 5 times larger, the area is 25 times larger. When r is $\frac{1}{3}$ smaller, the area is $\frac{1}{9}$ the size of the original. **b.** When the radius is doubled the circumference is doubled. When the radius is tripled the circumference is tripled. When the radius is halved, the circumference is halved.

When the radius is 5 times larger, the circumference is 5 times larger. When the radius is $\frac{1}{3}$ smaller, the circumference is $\frac{1}{3}$ smaller. **c.** Linear; Quadratic **7.** Linear **8.** Quadratic **9.** Linear **10. a.** Directly **b.** No **c.** 4.9 sec **11.** Any equation of the form $y = ax^2 + b$, with $a < 0$ and $b < 0$. **12.** Four; $3x^2 + 4x - 5$, $3x^2 + 4x$, $3x^2 - 5$, $3x^2$

9-2 Part A Try It
a–c.

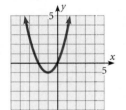

a. $x = -4$ and $x = 2$
b. $x = -1$ **c.** $x = 1$, and $x = -3$ **d.** 20 sec

9-2 Part A Exercises
1. a. $(0, -8)$ **b.** 2 **c.** No solutions **d.** $y = -8$
3. $x^2 - 4x = 0$ **5.** $x = 0$ and $x = -6$ **7.** $x = -3$
9. Rewrite the equation as $0 = x^2 - 4$. Graph $y = x^2 - 4$ and find the x-intercepts.
11. a. $h = -16t^2 + 5280$ **b.** 4880 ft **c.** 18.166 sec **d.** Earth's moon **13.** A
15. a. $3125 **b.** $3.50 **17.** $-5t(t^2 + 15)$ **19.** 9 **21.** 8 **23.** Not factorable **25.** $x = 2$ and $x = 3$ **27.** No solutions **29.** $x^2 - 3x = 0$ **31. a.** None **b.** Two **c.** Any value of y such that $y > -12.25$ **35.** (a) **37.** $x = -3$ and $x = 5$ **39.** $x = -3$ and $x = -4$ **41. a.** $h = -4.9t^2 + 1000$

b. $t \approx 4.5$ sec; Find the positive value of t such that the graph intersects the graph of $h = 900$. **c.** $t \approx 9$ sec **d.** No **43.** 76.5%; $\frac{90}{100} \cdot \frac{85}{100} = 0.765$

9-2 Part B Try It
a. $m = 9$ or $m = -3$
b. $g = -1$ or $g = 5$
c. $z = 6$ or $z = 4$

9-2 Part B Exercises
1. a. $x^2 - 7x + 12 = 0$ **b.** $(x - 3)(x - 4)$ **c.** $x = 3$ or $x = 4$ **4.** $x = -3$ or $x = -4$ **8.** $x = 0$ or $x = 1$
9. $x = -5$ or $x = 2$
11. Possible answers: 1 m $\times$ 110 m, 2 m $\times$ 55 m, 5 m $\times$ 22 m, 10 m $\times$ 11 m; 1 m $\times$ 110 m; 10 m $\times$ 11 m; 10 m $\times$ 11 m because it is the least restrictive.
13. a. $x = 6$ **b.** There is a place where the right-hand values change from positive to negative, so the graph must cross the x-axis. **c.** $x = -2$ and $x = -1$ **d.** It will be closer to $x = -1$ since the y-value at that point is closer to 0. Interpolate between the two values to estimate the solution. **e.** $x = -1.2$ **f.** $x < -1.2$ and $x > 6$ **g.** $-1.2 < x < 6$ **15.** $x = 6$ **17.** $x = 4$ and $x = 8$ **19.** F; Quadratic equation **21.** 2 **23.** 1 **25. a.** 4.08 seconds **b.** Yes **27. a.** Wide change **b.** 2.9% to 3.28% **c.** The graph would be moved up on the vertical axis and its variations would appear smaller. **29.** $f^4 - 16$ **31.** $g^2 + 4g + 4$ **33. a.** $x^2 - 9x + 18 = 0$ **b.** $(x - 3)(x - 6) = 0$ **c.** $x = 3$ or $x = 6$ **35.** $-10x^2 + 3x - 14 = 0$ **37.** $x = -3$ or $x = -6$ **39.** $x = 0$ or $x = 9$ **41.** $x = 3$ or $x = -3$ **43.** $x = 2$ or $x = -16$ **45.** No solution **47.** 2 **49.** None **51.** 8 and 9 or 8 and 9 **53.** ... 63, 127, 255

55. Bill could plot the data and look for a relationship between the points. He could try to approximate a curve (or line) through the points. From his approximate curve he could develop an equation to describe the curve.

9-2 Part C Self-Assessment
1. a. $(0, -4)$ **b.** Two **c.** None **d.** -4; The graph of $y = -4$ intersects the graph only once. **2.** $x = 0$, or $x = -4$ **3.** No solutions **4.** $x = -2$ **5. a.** 0 seconds
b.

t	h
0	0
0.5	16
1	24
1.5	24
2	16
2.5	0

c. At 0.5 seconds and at 2 seconds **d.** Between 1 and 1.5 seconds **e.** 25 ft **6.** (c)
7.

x	$x^2 + 3x$
-5	10
-4	4
-3	0
-2	-2
-1	-2
0	0
1	4
2	10

a. $x = -3$ or $x = 0$
b. $x = -4$ or $x = 1$
8. Possible answer: $x + 2 = 0$
9. Possible answer: $x^2 + 4x + 4 = 0$ **10.** $x = 0$ or $x = 2$ **11.** $x = -1$
12. $x = -7$, or $x = -2$
13. a. $0.5 + 0.1x$
b. $50{,}000 - 5000x$ **c.** $I = (0.5 + 0.1x)(50{,}000 - 5000x)$
d. 10 cents, 20 cents, 30 cents, 40 cents **e.** Between a 20 cent and 30 cent price increase **f.** 75 cents

9-3 Part A Try It
a. $g = \pm 2$ **b.** $y = \pm\sqrt{3}$
c. $m = \pm\sqrt{6}$ **d.** 5%

9-3 Part A Exercises
1. a. $5x^2 = 17$ **b.** $x^2 = \frac{17}{5}$
c. $x = \pm\sqrt{\frac{17}{5}}$ **3.** Factoring; Possible answer: The equation can be factored.
5. $x = 2\sqrt{2}$ or $x = -2\sqrt{2}$
7. $x = \pm 12$; Square root method **9.** $w = \pm 4$; Square root method **11.** $y = \pm\frac{2}{3}$; Square root method
13. a. $919.60 = 880(1 + r)^2$
b. $1.045 = (1 + r)^2$ **c.** $\pm\sqrt{1.045} = (1 + r)$; $r = -1 \pm 1.022$ **d.** $r = 2.2\%$
15. $x = \pm 4$ **16. a.** 11.1%
b. $358.91 **17.** 3.1%
19. Julita **21.** T **23. a.** $x = \pm 4$ **b.** $x = \pm 4$; The solutions are the same as the x-intercepts. **c.** $x = \pm 4$; $x < -4$ and $x > 4$; $-4 < x < 4$ **d.** $(0, -16)$ **25.** 49 **27.** $x^2 - 24 = 0$; $a = 1$; $b = 0$; $c = -24$ **33.** $r = \pm\sqrt{85}$ **35.** $y = \pm\sqrt{2}$ **37.** $x = -1$ or $x = 4$ **39.** $k = \pm 3\sqrt{10}$ **41.** $c = \pm 3$ **43.** $n = \pm 10$ **45.** $g = -3$ or $g = 14$ **47. a.** $A = 4000(1 + 0.05)^2$ **b.** $A = 4000(1.1025)$ **c.** $4,410 **49.** The solution to the equation $x^2 = a$ for $a \geq 0$ is either the positive or negative square root of a. **51.** $m = 3$ or $m = 11$ **53. a.** $+ 9$; $(x - 3)^2$ **b.** $+ 16$; $(c + 4)^2$ **c.** $+ \frac{49}{4}$; $\left(d + \frac{7}{2}\right)^2$ **55.** $A = P(1 + r)^3$; $A = P(1 + r)^t$; Each year adds another factor of $(1 + r)$.

9-3 Part B Try It
a. $x = -1 \pm \sqrt{6}$
b. $s = \frac{3 \pm \sqrt{5}}{2}$

9-3 Part B Exercises
1. a. $2x^2 + 5x - 3 = 0$
b. $x = \dfrac{-5 \pm \sqrt{25 - 4(2)(-3)}}{2(2)}$
c. There are two solutions. **d.** $x = -3$ and $x = \frac{1}{2}$ **3.** $a = 1, b = -49, c = 0$ **5. a.** $x = 2$ or $x = -8$

b. $(x + 8)(x - 2) = 0$; $x = 2$ or $x = -8$ **c.** Factoring **d.** Graphing   **7.** $x = -\frac{3}{2}$ or $x = \frac{5}{3}$ **15.** No solutions **17.** $x = -5$ or $x = -\frac{3}{2}$ **19.** Two solutions   **15.** Two solutions   **23.** The value is negative, since the graph does not cross the x-axis, meaning that the equation has no solutions.   **25. a.** 2 and 18 seconds   **b.** Quadratic formula **c.** 1028 ft   **d.** 1050 ft **27.** (b)   **31.** Six   **33.** $a = 1, b = 0, c = -5$ **35.** $a = 2, b = -3, c = 1$ **37.** $c = 4$ or $c = -7$ **39.** $v = -\frac{1}{3} \pm \frac{\sqrt{31}}{3}$ **41.** No solutions **43.** $k = \frac{3}{2}$ or $k = -\frac{4}{3}$ **45.** Two solutions   **47.** No solutions   **49.** $x^2 + 2x + 3 = 0$; No solutions $2x^2 + x + 3 = 0$; No solutions $3x^2 + x + 2 = 0$; No solutions $x^2 + 3x + 2 = 0$; $x = -2, -1$ $3x^2 + 2x + 1 = 0$; No solutions $2x^2 + 3x + 1 = 0$; $x = -1, -\frac{1}{2}$ The probability is $\frac{1}{6}$.   **51.** $k = 16$ **53.** 21 people were there. **55.** $x = \dfrac{-p - \sqrt{p^2 + 4q}}{2}$

9-3 Part C Self Assessment

1. $a = 1, b = 2, c = 0$ **2.** $a = 3, b = -2, c = -1$ **3.** $a = 1, b = 0, c = -4$ **4.** No solutions   **5.** Two solutions   **6.** No solutions **7.** $\approx 4.76\%$ **8.** $x = \pm 3$ **9.** $c = \pm\sqrt{15}$ **10.** $w = -2 \pm 2\sqrt{3}$ **11.** $d = -2$ or $d = -3$ **12.** $k = -4$ or $k = \frac{1}{3}$ **13.** $n = 2$ or $n = 3$ **14.** $y = -3$ or $y = 15$ **15.** $e = \pm\sqrt{21}$ **16.** $z = \pm 9$ **17.** $f = -1$ or $f = -9$ **18.** $\ell = -\frac{7}{3}$ or $\ell = \frac{1}{2}$ **19.** $h = 6$ or $h = 7$ **20.** 42.19 m   **21. a.** 1 and 3 seconds   **c.** At 4 seconds **d.** No   **22.** The two equations match when $a = -32$, $v = 64$, and $s = 0$, only if $\sin A = 1$.

23. (a)   **24. a.** If the graph crosses the x-axis at two points, then there are two solutions.

b. If the discriminant is greater than zero, then there are two solutions.   **c.** Sylvia substituted $a = 3$, $b = 11$, and $c = -4$ into the quadratic formula to find the two solutions.   **25. a.** Married **b.** No   **c.** Possible answer: 70% employment of married women with children under 6 and 60% employment in each of the other two groups.

Chapter 9 Review

1. T   **2.** F; Quadratic **3. a.** y-axis   **b.** $(0, 0)$ **c.** Possible answer: $(1, 3)$ and $(-1, 3)$; $(2, 12)(-2, 12)$; $(3, 27)$ and $(-3, 27)$ **4.** a **5.** c   **6.** b   **7.** Linear **8.** Quadratic   **9.** Linear **10.** 2300 ft   **11.** $3x^2 - 8x + 5 = 0$ **12.** $x^2 + 2x - 8 = 0$ **13. a.** $(-2, -9)$ **b.** $x = -2$ **c.** -9 **d.** Two **e.** One   **f.** None **14. a.** 245.482 pounds **b.** The force would double. **c.** The force would quadruple.   **15.** $x = 0$ or $x = 1$; Possible answer: Factoring **16.** $x = -2$ or $x = -4$; Possible answer: Factoring **17.** $x = -3$ or $x = -5$; Possible answer: Factoring **18.** $x = 1$; Possible answer: Factoring   **19.** $x = -12$; Possible answer: Factoring **20.** $x = 3$ or $x = -5$; Possible answer: Factoring **21.** No solution; Using the table, the vertex of the graph for the function $y = x(x + 3)$ is at $x = -1.5$ for which $y = -2.25$. The graph opens up, so the minimum y-value is -2.25.   **22. a.** 20.4° **b.** $-0.6°$ **c.** $-44.4°$ **23.** \$8,197.40   **24.** $n = \pm\sqrt{\dfrac{2933F}{Wr}}$ **25.** Discriminant $= 0$; One solution   **26.** Discriminant $= 25$; Two solutions

27. Discriminant $= -4$; No solutions   **28.** (d) **29.** $x = \pm 8$ **30.** $x = \pm 2\sqrt{3}$ **31.** $x = \frac{7}{4}$ or $x = -1$ **32.** $x = 2$ or $x = 3$ **33.** No solutions   **34.** $x = 0$ or $x = -2$ **35. a.** 6.125 m/s **b.** 4.9 m   **c.** ≈ 1.37 sec

CHAPTER 10

10-1 Part A Try It
a. $-5\sqrt{2x} + 6$ **b.** $\frac{3}{2} + \frac{5}{2x}$ **c.** $7x\sqrt{x}$ **d.** $x + 2$ **e.** $4, -4$ **f.** $x < -17$

10-1 Part A Exercises
1. a. Irrational   **b.** Rational **c.** Rational   **d.** Irrational **e.** Rational   **f.** Rational **2. a.** ii   **b.** iii   **c.** i **3.** $4\sqrt{3}$; Irrational $\frac{3}{4}$; Rational $2 + 2\sqrt{3}$; Irrational $\frac{4}{3}$; Rational **5.** $2x + 4\sqrt{x}$ **7.** $11y\sqrt{y}$ **9.** $8 + 9\sqrt{x}$ **11. a.** 1.0594; 1.0594; 1.0594   **b.** 1108.7 **13.** $x < -1$ **15.** $x > 8$ **17.** $x < -18$ **19.** Possible answer: $\sqrt{x - 6}$ **21.** No **23. a.** Triangle with legs 1,1, hypotenuse $\sqrt{2}$.   **b.** Triangle with legs 1, 2, hypotenuse $\sqrt{5}$.   **c.** Triangle with legs 3, 2, hypotenuse $\sqrt{13}$. **25.** $9x(x - 2)$ **27.** $(x + 18)(x - 2)$ **29.** $(x + 6)(x + 6)$ **31.** $7p$ **33.** $13\sqrt{3} - 3\sqrt{2}$ **35.** $-7x\sqrt{x}$ **37.** $\frac{8}{3}x^2 - \frac{4}{3}x$ **39.** $x - 5$ **41.** $\frac{x + 6}{x}$ **43.** $0, -5$ **45.** 2 **47.** $8, -8$ **49.** $5, -4$ **51.** $\sqrt{5} + 4\sqrt{2} + 3$; Irrational   **53.** Possible answer: $\dfrac{1}{(x + 3)(x - 2)}$

55. a. $A^2 = \begin{bmatrix} 2 & 1 \\ 1 & 1 \end{bmatrix}$

$A^3 = \begin{bmatrix} 3 & 2 \\ 2 & 1 \end{bmatrix}$ $A^4 = \begin{bmatrix} 5 & 3 \\ 3 & 2 \end{bmatrix}$

$A^5 = \begin{bmatrix} 8 & 5 \\ 5 & 3 \end{bmatrix}$ $A^6 = \begin{bmatrix} 13 & 8 \\ 8 & 5 \end{bmatrix}$

b. Each entry in the matrix A^n is a number in the Fibonacci sequence.   **57.** $\frac{125}{999}$

10-1 Part B Try It
1. a. $x = -4, x = 9$ **b.** $x = 20$ **c.** $x = 6$

10-1 Part B Exercises
1. a. $36 - x = 8x$ **b.** $x = 4$ **c.** $\dfrac{36 - 4}{2(4)} = \dfrac{32}{8} = 4$ **3.** $x = -6, x = 3$ **5.** $x = -\frac{15}{28}$ **7.** $x = -\frac{11}{4}$ **9.** No solutions   **11. a.** $x < -4$. The graph does not exist for $x < -4$.   **b.** Domain: $\{x: x \geq -4\}$; Range: $\{y: y \geq 2\}$.   **13.** $s = 10$; $s - 4 = 6$; $2s - 5 = 15$ **15.** $w = \frac{175}{9}$ **17. a.** Positive   **b.** Possible answer: Plot the data on a graph, make a table. **19.** $4\sqrt{5} + \sqrt{10}$; Irrational **21.** $x = -1, x = 3$ **23.** $x = 1, x = -1$ **25.** $x = 5$ **27.** No solutions   **29.** $x = 3$ **31.** $h = -20, h = 3$ **33.** $x = \frac{15}{8}$ **35. a.** $x = -3$; The graph has an asymptote at $x = -3$.   **b.** Domain: $\{x: x \neq -3\}$; Range: $\{y: y \neq 0\}$.   **37.** $x = 13$. The extraneous solution is $x = 5$.   Since $5 = 8 - \sqrt{2(5) - 1} = 8 - \sqrt{9} = 8 - 3 = 5$, $x = 5$ is the solution to the equation $x = 8 - \sqrt{2x - 1}$.   **39.** No; The slope of the line passing through these two points is always undefined. **41. a.** $-3, 2$; There are asymptotes at these x-values.   **b.** Domain: $\{x: x \neq -3, 2\}$; Range: $\{y : \text{all real numbers}\}$

10-1 Part C Self-Assessment
1. $-\sqrt{14} - 21$ **2.** $x - 3$ **3.** $\dfrac{6}{y - 2}$ **4.** $\dfrac{1 + 4x}{3x^2}$ **5.** $\dfrac{x(x - 4)}{x + 1}$ **6.** $3\sqrt{5y} + \sqrt{10y}$ **7.** 11   **8.** $x < 2$ **9.** $6, -6$ **10.** Possible answer: $\dfrac{1}{x - 10}$ **11.** Possible answer: $\sqrt{x + 8}$

12. a. Using similar triangles, Holmes knew that $\frac{x}{9} = \frac{64}{6}$, where x is length of the elm's shadow. Solve for x to get $x = 96$ ft. **b.** Holmes walked 96 ft. in the direction of the rod's shadow.
c. Possible answer: Reginald Musgrave could have found the height by using similar triangles. He would measure the tree's shadow to find its height. **13.** $x = -\frac{21}{4}$
14. $x = 18.25$ **15.** $x = 2$
16. $x = 29$ **17.** $x = \frac{9}{80}$
18. $x \approx 1.60$, $x \approx -1.60$
19. $\frac{2}{11}$ **20.** $q = 4$. The points are (48, 32) and $(-32, -8)$. **21. a.** 375 cm
b. 150 cm **c.** 105 cm
d. $5\sqrt{210}$ cm **22.** $\approx 1.5 \times 10^{-13}$ m **23. a.** Greater. Car B must be going faster than Car A to overtake it.
b. $t = -\frac{15}{40 - s}$ **c.** 55 mph
d. No. **24.** 5, 8, 13, 21, 34, 55, 89, 144; The sequence is the Fibonacci sequence. It occurs because the number of pairs is "additive" in that each pair, once it starts producing rabbits, continues to breed.

10-2 Part A Try It
a.

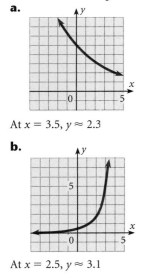

At $x = 3.5$, $y \approx 2.3$
b.

At $x = 2.5$, $y \approx 3.1$

10-2 Part A Exercises
1. a.

x	3^x
1	3
2	9
3	27
4	81
5	243

b–c.

d. 15.6 **3.** Graphs of this form represent the product of a constant (a), and another constant (b), that is raised to an exponent (x).
5.

7. Possible answer:

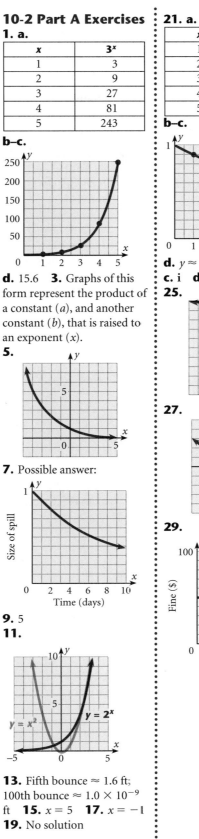

9. 5
11.

13. Fifth bounce ≈ 1.6 ft; 100th bounce $\approx 1.0 \times 10^{-9}$ ft **15.** $x = 5$ **17.** $x = -1$
19. No solution

21. a.

x	0.9x
1	0.9
2	0.81
3	0.729
4	0.6561
5	0.59049

b–c.

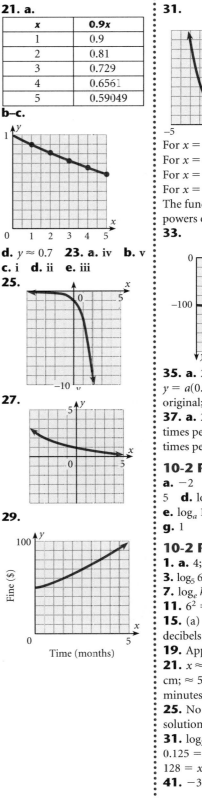

d. $y \approx 0.7$ **23. a.** iv **b.** v
c. i **d.** ii **e.** iii
25.

27.

29.

31.

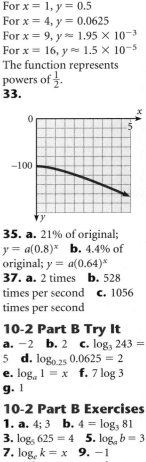

For $x = 1$, $y = 0.5$
For $x = 4$, $y = 0.0625$
For $x = 9$, $y \approx 1.95 \times 10^{-3}$
For $x = 16$, $y \approx 1.5 \times 10^{-5}$
The function represents powers of $\frac{1}{2}$.
33.

35. a. 21% of original; $y = a(0.8)^x$ **b.** 4.4% of original; $y = a(0.64)^x$
37. a. 2 times **b.** 528 times per second **c.** 1056 times per second

10-2 Part B Try It
a. -2 **b.** 2 **c.** $\log_3 243 = 5$ **d.** $\log_{0.25} 0.0625 = 2$
e. $\log_a 1 = x$ **f.** $7 \log 3$
g. 1

10-2 Part B Exercises
1. a. 4; 3 **b.** $4 = \log_3 81$
3. $\log_5 625 = 4$ **5.** $\log_a b = 3$
7. $\log_e k = x$ **9.** -1
11. $6^2 = 36$ **13.** $b^2 = 20$
15. (a) **17. a.** ≈ 2.43 decibels **b.** No
19. Approximately 3.5%
21. $x \approx 34$ **23. a.** ≈ 98.5 cm; ≈ 53.9 cm **b.** ≈ 517 minutes; ≈ 746 minutes
25. No solutions **27.** No solutions **29.** $x = 1$ or 2
31. $\log_2 8 = 3$ **33.** $\log_8 0.125 = -1$ **35.** $\log_2 128 = x$ **37.** 2 **39.** 1
41. -3 **43.** $5^k = 10$

45. $b^3 = 100$ **47.** log 4 + log 2 **49. a.** No. **b.** The intervals are marked in successive powers of 10.

c.

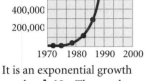

It is an exponential growth graph. **d.** No; The graph would require 1,000 intervals on the y-axis.

e. Exponential function **51.** 1×10^{25}; You get 25 because log $10^{25} = 25$.

10-2 Part C
Self-Assessment

1.

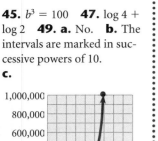

2.

3.

4.

---

5. (a)
6.

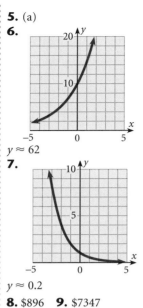

$y \approx 62$
7.

$y \approx 0.2$

8. \$896 **9.** \$7347
10. \$12,902 **11.** \$3146
12. $n = \log_5 30$ **13.** $h = \log_2(-y)$ **14.** $y = \log_{12} 15$
15. $2x = 10^y$ **16.** $0.5 = e^y$
17. $200 = 10^y$ **18.** (c)
19. Exponential decay
20. About \$103,729 **21.** In 1999 **22.** log 9 **23.** log 5 + log 7 **24.** \$57,034
25. a. $\approx 97.6\%$ **b.** $\approx 54.7\%$ **c.** ≈ 57 centuries
26. a. ≈ 3.2 **b.** An earthquake of magnitude 2 has a seismographic reading of 0.1 mm. This is 10 times greater than 0.01 mm, which indicated an earthquake of magnitude 1. **27.** 131,501 pounds
28. a. The vertical axis uses a logarithmic scale. **b.** The polio vaccine was more effective since the percent incidence of polio cases decreased more. **c.** No; There were very few cases.
29. a. $\approx 40\%$ **b.** $\approx 6\%$

Chapter 10 Review
1. F; Are not actual solutions. **2.** T **3.** (a)
4. Irrational **5.** Rational
6. Rational **7.** $\sqrt{4} = 2$ which is rational. $\sqrt{5}$, in its decimal form, does not terminate or repeat and therefore cannot be written as an integer over an integer.

---

8. $\sqrt{x} + 4$ **9.** 4
10. $2y^2\sqrt{2y}$ **11.** $\frac{(x-7)^3}{x+20}$
12. $x - 1$ **13.** $\frac{x-3}{2x}$
14. $x < 5$ **15.** $x = \pm 2$
16. $x > 6$ **17.** $x = -4$
18. $x = \pm 1$ **19.** $x = \frac{1}{3}$
20. $x = \sqrt{3} - 1$ **21.** $x = 8$ **22.** $x = 8$ **23. a.** $x = -1$ **b.** There is an asymptote at $x = -1$ **c.** The domain is all real numbers except -1 because the function is not defined at -1. The range is all real numbers except 0, because there is no solution to $\frac{1}{x+1} = 0$.
24. No; The line through $(4c^2, c)$ and $(4c^2, 3c)$ will always be vertical since both points have the same x-coordinate. **25.** $r = 2.4$ ohms
26. $y = 2^x$ is expressed in the form of an exponential equation, $y = ab^x$ where $a = 1$ and $b = 2$, while $y = x^2$ is not. It is a quadratic.
27.

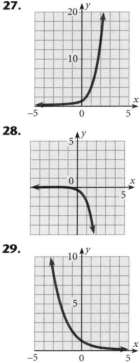

28.

29.

30.

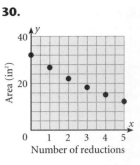

31. a. For 2003, $x = 1$, so Mean Score ≈ 544; For 2013, $x = 2$, so Mean Score ≈ 563; For 2022, $x = 3$, so Mean Score ≈ 583;

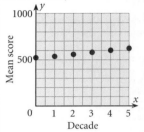

b. Mean score would reach 800 around 2113. It is not reasonable to expect that everyone will get a perfect score. **32.** $2 = \log_5 25$
33. $n = \log_2 32$ **34.** $3^4 = 81$ **35.** $d^2 = 64$ **36. a.** 1, 3, 4, 7, 11, 18, 29, 47, 76, 123, 199, 322, 521, 843, 1364
b. $\frac{3}{1} = 3$, $\frac{4}{3} \approx 1.333333$, $\frac{11}{7} \approx 1.571429$, $\frac{18}{11} \approx 1.636363$, $\frac{29}{18} \approx 1.611111$, $\frac{47}{29} \approx 1.620690$, $\frac{76}{47} \approx 1.6170213$, $\frac{123}{76} \approx 1.618421$, $\frac{199}{123} \approx 1.617886$, $\frac{322}{199} \approx 1.618090$, $\frac{521}{322} \approx 1.618012$, $\frac{843}{521} \approx 1.618042$, $\frac{1364}{843} \approx 1.618031$.

c. The ratios approach the golden ratio.

CREDITS

PHOTOGRAPHS

Front Cover   **Left** Jerry Jacka Photography   **Right** Jon Feingersh/Tom Stack & Associates

Spine   **Left** Jerry Jacka Photography   **Right** Jon Feingersh/Tom Stack & Associates

Back Cover   **TL** Thomas Kitchin/Tom Stack & Associates **TCL** Giraudon/Art Resource, NY   **TCR** Jerry Jacka Photography **TR** Jon Feingersh/Tom Stack & Associates   **BL** Art Resource **BCL** Jerry Jacka Photography/Courtesy: Museum of Northern Arizona, Flagstaff   **BCR** Cheryl Fenton*   **BR** Antonio M. Rosario/The Image Bank

Front Matter   **FM4–5** Telegraph Colour Library 199/FPG International   **FM5** Cathlyn Melloan/Tony Stone Images **FM6B** The Bettmann Archive   **FM6T** Geoffrey Nilsen Photography*   **FM7B** R. Dahlquist/Superstock, Inc.   **FM7T** Shahn Kermani/The Gamma Liaison Network   **FM8B** Bob Taylor/FPG International   **FM8T** Connie Coleman/AllStock   **FM9B** Reuters/ Bettmann   **FM9T** Robert Graham/FPG International **FM10BL** Motion Picture & TV Archive/Superstock, Inc. **FM10BR** Jerry Jacka Photography   **FM10T** G. Outerbridge/ Superstock, Inc.   **FM11B** Deborah Denker/Liaison International **FM11C** Universal/The Kobal Collection   **FM11T** Masahiro Sano/The Stock Market   **FM12** Henneghien/Bruce Coleman Inc.

Getting Started   **i** Ken Karp*   **ii** Dennis Hallinan/FPG International   **vi** Ken Karp*

Chapter 1   **2B** Courtesy of Geochron Enterprises, Inc. **2T** Stanley King Collection   **3**(background) Stephen Frisch* **9** Cathlyn Melloan/Tony Stone Images   **12** M. Bertinetti/Photo Researchers   **14** Richard Hamilton Smith/AllStock   **18** Lawrence Migdale/Tony Stone Images   **21** Kyodo News   **23** Stephen Frisch* **24** Ralph Fasanella   **29** Jack Mitchell, 1993   **30** Reproduced from THE MAN WHO COUNTED by Malba Tahan, illustrated by Patricia Reid Baquero, with permission of W. W. Norton & Company, Inc. Illustration © 1993 by W. W. Norton & Company, Inc.   **31** Gail Shumway/FPG International   **32** Richard Lord/ The Image Works   **36** Stephen Frisch*   **37** Geoffrey Nilsen Photography*   **39** Stephen Frisch*   **45** Mike Powell/Allsport **47** Tom Walker/Stock, Boston   **48** The Bettmann Archive **53** Geoffrey Nilsen Photography*   **54** Russell B. Phillips, 1984 **57B** Zig Leszczynski/Animals, Animals   **57T** Linda Svendsen **61** Art Wolfe/AllStock   **64** Dave Bartruff   **66** Supreme Court Historical Society   **67** Ulf Andersen/Gamma Liaison   **73** Rick Friedman/Black Star

Chapter 2   **80BL** Bob Daemmrich/The Image Works **80CR** Stephen Frisch*   **80TL** James Prince/Photo Researchers **80TR** Willie Hill/FPG International   **81**(background) Richard Megna/Fundamental Photographs   **81**(frame) Cheryl Fenton* **85B** Tom Keck/Gamma Liaison   **85C** Olivier Suzereau/Gamma Liaison   **85T** Olivier Suzereau/Gamma Liaison   **86** Robert Landau/Westlight   **88** Tom Van Sant/Geosphere Project, Santa Monica/SPL/Photo Researchers   **89** Stephen Frisch*   **90** Susan Vogel*   **94** Geoffrey Nilsen Photography*   **100** David Madison **103L** Owen Franken/Stock, Boston   **103R** Dan Guravich/Photo Researchers   **106** Uniphoto Picture Agency   **110** Courtesy of the Estate of Romare Bearden   **113** The Bettmann Archive **115** Geoffrey Nilsen Photography*   **118** Tom Van Sant/Geosphere Project, Santa Monica/SPL/Photo Researchers   **123** Geoffrey Nilsen Photography*   **125** Michael Tamborrino/FPG International   **126** Susan Vogel*   **127** Stephen Frisch*   **129** E. Gebhardt/

FPG International   **133** Stephen Frisch*   **136** Ken Karp* **138** Stephen Frisch*   **139** Steve Bly/AllStock   **141** Rob Boudreau/ Tony Stone Images   **154** Giraudon/Art Resource, NY/© 1994 C. Herscovici, Brussels/Artist Rights Society (ARS), New York **157** West/FPG International   **159** R. Dahlquist/Superstock, Inc.

Chapter 3   **160** Cesar Rubio*   **161**(background) Stephen Frisch*   **161**(frame) Cheryl Fenton*   **163BR** Leen Van Der Slik/ Earth Scenes   **163L** Ron Thomas/FPG International **163TR** Telegraph Colour Library 199/FPG International **164** Cesar Rubio*   **165** Stephen Frisch*   **172** Geoffrey Nilsen Photography*   **174** Ken Karp*   **175** Ken Karp*   **177** Spencer Grant/Liaison International   **178** Ralph Mercer/Tony Stone Images   **179** Stephen Frisch*   **181T** Kitagawa II/Superstock, Inc. **183** Jean Kugler/FPG International   **185R** Bob Daemmrich/The Image Works   **187B** Ken Friedman   **187T** H. P. Merten/The Stock Market   **190** Van Bucher/Photo Researchers/Collection Vincent van Gogh Foundation/Van Gogh Museum, Amsterdam **191C** The Bettmann Archive   **191L** B. & C. Alexander/Black Star **192** Geoffrey Nilsen Photography*   **201** Ken Karp*   **202** NASA **207** E. Nagele/FPG International   **208** John Launois/Black Star **209** Geoffrey Nilsen Photography*

Chapter 4   **214L** Cesar Rubio*   **214R** Stephen Frisch* **215**(background) Stephen Frisch*   **215**(frame) Cheryl Fenton* **217**(background) E. Masterson/AllStock   **217C** Geoffrey Nilsen Photography*   **217L** Geoffrey Nilsen Photography* **217R** Geoffrey Nilsen Photography*   **219** Stephen Frisch* **221** Geoffrey Nilsen Photography*   **227** Geoffrey Nilsen Photography*   **228** Nelson Morris/Photo Researchers/© 1994 Artist Rights Society (ARS), New York/SPADEM, Paris.   **229L** Peter Menzel/Stock, Boston   **229R** Archive Photos   **232** B. Daemmrich/ The Image Works   **233C** Kevin Schafer & Martha Hill/AllStock **233L** Stephen Krasemann/AllStock   **233R** A. H. Rider/Photo Researchers   **237** Shahn Kermani/The Gamma Liaison Network **238** Stephen Frisch*   **240** Art Wolfe/AllStock   **243** Gail Shumway/FPG International   **244T** Mary Clay/Tom Stack & Associates   **245** Robert A. Tyrrell   **246** Geoffrey Nilsen Photography*   **248** Geoffrey Nilsen Photography*   **250** Tony Stone Images   **254** Stephen Frisch*   **255** Ken Karp*   **260** Ted Wood/ AllStock   **263** Courtesy of Catco Inc.   **264** Geoffrey Nilsen Photography*   **265** Ken Karp*   **279** Stephen Frisch* **286** Stephen Frisch*

Chapter 5   **296B** Cindy Lewis   **296TL** Cesar Rubio* **296TR** The Dickmans/Westlight   **297**(background) Stephen Frisch*   **299** Dallas & John Heaton/The Stock Shop   **300** Joe Sohm/AllStock   **303** Phil Schofield/AllStock   **305** S. Vidler/ Superstock, Inc.   **306B** Don & Pat Valenti/DRK Photo **306T** Nicholas DeVore/Tony Stone Images   **309** T. Tracy/FPG International   **311** Archive Photos   **312** Ken Karp*   **317** Ronald William May/Liaison International   **319** Ken Karp*   **321** Stephen Frisch*   **325** Cesar Rubio*   **326** Maxwell Mackenzie/Tony Stone Images   **327** David Madison   **332** Connie Coleman/AllStock **336** Masahiro Sano/The Stock Market   **338B** David R. Frazier/ Photo Researchers   **338T** Bob Daemmrich/The Image Works **340** R. Dahlquist/Superstock, Inc.   **342** Cesar Rubio*   **348** The Bettmann Archive—from *20,000 Leagues Under the Sea* by Jules Verne   **350** Cesar Rubio*   **351** Cesar Rubio*   **352** David Muench   **359** C. Ursillo/AllStock   **360** Dimaggio/Kalish/The Stock Market   **363** Stephen Frisch*

Chapter 6   **370L** Jim Corwin/Photo Researchers   **370R** Stephen Frisch*   **371**(background) Stephen Frisch*   **375L** Steve

Gottlieb/FPG International **375R** Photoworld/FPG International **377B** Renato Rotolo/The Gamma Liaison Network **377** Ken Karp* **379** The Bettmann Archive **380** Richard Mackson/FPG International **382** Ken Friedman **387** Chris Johns/AllStock **390** Bob Taylor/FPG International **393B** UPI/Bettmann Newsphoto **393T** The Bettmann Archive **394** Courtesy of Dollywood, Pigeon Forge, TN **396** H. P. Merten/The Stock Market **398** Bill Bachmann/Stock, Boston **399** National Museum of American Art, Washington, DC/Art Resource **401** Steve Hansen/Stock, Boston **403** J. T. Miller/The Stock Market **414** Asian Art Museum of San Francisco, The Avery Brundage Collection **416** Geoffrey Nilsen Photography* **417** J. Warden/Superstock, Inc. **419** Charles Palek/Tom Stack & Associates **422** Howard Sochurek/The Stock Market **424** Jamey Stillings/Tony Stone Images **427** Meri Simon/Contra Costa Times **428** Lawrence Migdale/Stock, Boston **430** Courtesy of the Ford Archives, Dearborn, Michigan **431** Keith Gunnar/FPG International **433** R. Glandes/Superstock, Inc. **434** P. Jones Griffiths/Magnum Photos

Chapter 7 **444B** J. F. Causse/Tony Stone Images **444TR** Bob Daemmrich/Stock, Boston **445**(background) Stephen Frisch* **447**(background) Stephen Frisch* **451** Ellis Herwig/Stock, Boston **454T** Lisa Quinones/Black Star **456** Robert Graham/FPG International **458** Stephen Frisch* **461** K. Schotz/Superstock, Inc. **465** Stephen Frisch* **468** The Bettmann Archives **469R** Lawrence Barns/Black Star **473L** Darrell Gulin/AllStock **473R** Rod Planck/Tony Stone Images **478** Ken Karp* **479** Randy Wells/AllStock **481** Stephen Frisch* **482** Stephen Frisch* **483** Tim Thompson/AllStock **486B** NASA **486T** Geoffrey Nilsen Photography* **487** Stephen Frisch* **489R** Charles Kennard/Stock, Boston **491** Charles Moore **492** Cesar Rubio* **494** Cesar Rubio* **497** S. Vidler/Superstock, Inc. **498** P. Amranand/Superstock, Inc. **502** Greig Cranna/Stock, Boston **505** Stephen Frisch* **507** Gabor Demjen/Stock, Boston **508** Kobal Collection/Superstock, Inc. **513** Ken Karp* **514** Reuters/Bettmann **516** Adrienne Gibson/Earth Scenes **519** Steve Bisson/Savannah News **523**(background) Stephen Frisch* **523R** Ben Glass/Orion Pictures Corp. **527** Fritz Henle/Photo Researchers/© 1994 Artist Rights Society (ARS), New York/ADAGP, Paris **528** Courtesy of Claes Oldenburg/Coosje van Bruggen **529** E. R. Degginger/Animals, Animals **530R** Joe McDonald/Animals, Animals **532** Pam Taylor/Bruce Coleman Inc. **535** Alan Hicks/AllStock **537** © American International Television Inc./The Kobal Collection **539** Dale E. Boyer/AllStock **542** Ken Karp*

Chapter 8 **558** Stephen Frisch* **559**(background) Stephen Frisch* **561** NASA/Tom Stack & Associates **563B** Rob Goldman/FPG International **563C** Lori Adamski Peek/Tony Stone Images **563T** Stephen Frisch* **565** R. Dahlquist/Superstock, Inc. **566** Stocktrek Photo Agency/Tom Stack & Associates **567** USGS/Tom Stack & Associates **568** The Bettmann Archive **569** NASA/Superstock, Inc. **570** Culver Pictures Inc. **571** NASA **572** Geoffrey Nilsen Photography* **573** Archive/Superstock, Inc. **574** Telegraph Colour Library 199/FPG International **575** Paul Barton/The Stock Market **576B** Ong & Assoc./Superstock, Inc. **577B** Cash LTD/Superstock, Inc. **577T** USGS/Tom Stack & Associates **580** Stephen Frisch* **582** Ken Eward/Science Source/Photo Researchers **583** G. Outerbridge/Superstock, Inc. **584R** A. B. Dowsett/SPL/Photo Researchers **587** Rutherford/Superstock, Inc. **588** Pete Saloutos/The Stock Market **594** Ulrike Welsch/Photo Researchers **598** Ken Karp* **600** Jeff Zaruba/AllStock **602** Stephen Frisch* **603** Katrine Naleid* **609** The Bettmann Archive **612** Stephen Frisch* **613** David Madison/Bruce Coleman Inc. **616** Asian Art Museum of San Francisco, The

Avery Brundage Collection **618** Charles Gupton/Tony Stone Images **619B** Cesar Rubio* **619T** Jack W. Dykinga/Bruce Coleman Inc.

Chapter 9 **624B** Cindy Lewis **624C** Stephen Frisch* **624T** Stephen Frisch* **625**(background) SPL/Photo Researchers **627** J. Carini/The Image Works **628** Lester Lefkowitz/Tony Stone Images **631** Gary Retherford/Photo Researchers **633** David Barnes/The Stock Market **636** C. Bradley Simmons/Bruce Coleman Inc. **637** TPS Catalog/Superstock, Inc. **640** Richard Megna/Fundamental Photographs **643R** Fred Hirschmann/AllStock **645** Willinger/FPG International **647** Jerry Jacka Photography **648** Motion Picture & TV Archive/Superstock, Inc. **651** Masahiro Sano/The Stock Market **652** K. Iwasaki/The Stock Market **654R** Kerwin B. Roche/FPG International **656** Jack W. Dykinga/Bruce Coleman Inc. **660** NASA **663T** Schuster/Superstock, Inc. **666** The Kobal Collection/Superstock, Inc. **667** Peter Fox/Klutz Press, Palo Alto, CA **669**(background) NASA **669**(inset) Courtesy of Evelyn Granville **670** Wendy T. Kaiser/Uniphoto, Inc. **672** H & L Wright Photo Studio, Columbia, CA **676** Boltin Picture Library **678** Ken Karp* **679** Ken Karp* **683** Henneghien/Bruce Coleman Inc. **684** NASA **685** Mauritius/Superstock, Inc. **686** NASA **686T** A. Devaney/Superstock, Inc.

Chapter 10 **692B** Courtesy of Steinway & Sons **692TL** Stephen Frisch* **692TR** Kevin Schafer/Tom Stack & Associates **693**(background) Stephen Frisch* **695L** S. Vidler/Superstock, Inc. **695R** L. Kolvoord/The Image Works **696** Deborah Denker/Liaison International **698** P. Van Rhijn/Superstock, Inc. **699** Gregory Sams/SPL/Photo Researchers **700** Bob Daemmrich/The Image Works **704** Geoffrey Nilsen Photography* **705** Digital Art/Westlight **709** AP/Wide World Photos **711** Cesar Rubio* **713** Cesar Rubio* **716B** R. A. Lee/Superstock, Inc. **716T** Courtesy of Ralph Rambo **718** R. Dahlquist/Superstock, Inc. **720** Joe Sohm/The Image Works **721** B. Roberts/Superstock, Inc. **722** P. & R. Manley/Superstock, Inc. **723** Courtesy of the University of California Seismographic Station at Berkeley **724B** Ken Karp* **724C** Ken Karp* **724T** Gamma-Liaison **726B** R. Heinzen/Superstock, Inc. **726T** Joseph Schuyler/Stock, Boston **727** Courtesy of Maxell Corporation of America **728** Universal/The Kobal Collection **729** S. Vidler/Superstock, Inc. **734** Bob Daemmrich/Stock, Boston **735B** Denis Farrell/Associated Press/Wide World Photos **735T** Corinne Dufka/(Reuter)/Bettmann Archive

Look Ahead/Look Back icons photographed by Ken Karp*

*Photographed expressly for Addison-Wesley Publishing Company, Inc.

TEXT AND ART

Chapter 1 1-1 Part D: p. 30, Exercise 12: text excerpt from *The Man Who Counted: A Collection of Mathematical Adventures* by Malba Tahan, translated by Leslie Clark and Alastair Reid. Copyright © 1979 by Helio Marcial de Faria Pereira. Translation © 1993 by Leslie Clark and Alastair Reid. Reprinted by permission of W. W. Norton & Company, Inc.

Chapter 2 p. 159, text excerpt from Ira Flatow, *Rainbows, Curve Balls and Other Wonders of the Natural World Explained,* NY: Harper & Row, 1989, p. 28. © 1988 by Ira Flatow.

Chapter 3 Opener 3-1: p. 163, text excerpt from PG&E and The Earth Works Group, *30 Simple Energy Things You Can Do To Save The Earth,* Berkeley, CA: The Earth Works Group, 1990. © 1990 by John Javna.

Chapter 5 p. 362, graph for Exercise 6 adapted with permission of the University of California at Berkeley Wellness Letter. © 1992 Health Letter Associates.

Chapter 6 p. 380, poem excerpt from Maya Angelou, *On The Pulse of Morning.* NY: Random House, 1993. © 1993 by Maya Angelou. Reprinted by permission of Random House, Inc. Opener 6-1: p. 373, paraphrased text from Bill Crosby, "War In Our Forests," *Sunset,* July 1993.

Chapter 7 p. 495, maps adapted from Edmund N. Bacon, *Design of Cities* (UK: Viking Penguin, 1967.) © 1967 by Edmund N. Bacon. Adapted with permission of the publisher.

Chapter 8 p. 588, graph adapted from *BART: History in the Making,* with permission of BART (Bay Area Rapid Transit).

ILLUSTRATIONS

Christine Benjamin 420a, 701a, 712a

Bryce Bowles 649b

Warren Budd & Associates 57b, 238a, 266a, 356c, 369a, 392c, 409a, 438d, 580a, 580b, 586a, 607a

Julie Downing 577c, 578a, 611a, 631c, 663c

Don Dudley 262c, 268b, 342a, 389a

Len Epstein 15b, 92a, 122a, 170a, 180a, 212a, 224a, 230a, 289a, 346a, 396a

Eureka Cartography 43a, 249a, 284a, 315a, 341a, 356a, 400a, 438a, 516c

Steve Gray 160e

Terry Guyer 214b, 558a

Linda Harris 615a

Joe Heiner 5a, 37a, 57a, 83a, 105a, 125a, 163a, 191a, 217a, 233a, 263a, 299a, 327a, 373a, 393a, 421a, 447a, 475a, 495a, 523a, 561a, 589a, 627a, 649a, 669a, 695a, 713a

John Hersey 22a, 305c, 308a, 318b, 323c, 323d, 334b

Donna Ingemanson 109b, 149a, 275a, 419a, 617a, 665b

Eric Joyner 421c

Marilyn Kreiger 589b

Laszlo Kubinyi 521b

Loose Cannons 78b, 103a, 108a, 169b, 206b, 384a, 407b, 489d, 522d, 547d, 714–715, 728a

Chuck McKenna 370a

Karen Minot 134a, 277a, 282a, 289b, 386b, 390b, 436a, 505a, 510b, 643b

Joy Monte 65

Helene Moore 199b, 324, 697a, 721a

Tony Morse 83b, 84a, 101b, 102a, 122b, 287g, 393b

Andrew Muonio 87a, 128d, 129b, 153c, 188a, 253a, 290b, 321a, 358a, 379a, 392a, 408a, 448a, 471b, 496a, 538d, 540b

Ron Peterson 96d, 97b, 181c, 299b, 511a, 519b

Mike Reagan 5a, 6a, 52a, 495b

William Rieser 93a, 98c, 479a, 481b, 508b, 509a, 528b, 531a, 535a, 535b, 542a, 545a, 545d, 545e, 546a, 547d, 550b, 551a, 551b, 551c, 554a, 554e, 555a, 557c, 601a, 613b, 638a, 639a, 639b, 657a, 659a, 688b, 729c

Rob Schuster 10a, 14b, 20a, 46a, 47b, 252a, 441a, 455a, 521c, 524a, 529a, 530a, 548a, 549b, 575d, 629a, 646a, 663b, 709c, 718d

Joe VanDerBoes vb, 421b, 447b

Carol Verbeeck 97a, 106a, 174b, 245e, 280a, 330a, 336c, 356b, 383a, 384a, 423a, 435a, 450, 469a, 503a

Richard Waldrep 257a, 262a

Cameron Wasson va, 139c, 146a, 189b, 200a, 270b, 311a, 325c, 374a, 457a, 484b, 492b, 510c, 590b

Jeffrey West 373c

Sarah Woodward 561b

Qin-Zhong Yu 124a, 539c

▼ INDEX